D1613881

Adobe® Illustrator® 10: The Complete Reference

Sandra E. Eddy

McGraw-Hill/Osborne

New York Chicago San Francisco
Lisbon London Madrid Mexico City
Milan New Delhi San Juan
Seoul Singapore Sydney Toronto

McGraw-Hill/Osborne
2600 Tenth Street
Berkeley, California 94710
U.S.A.

To arrange bulk purchase discounts for sales promotions, premiums, or fund-raisers, please contact **McGraw-Hill/**Osborne at the above address. For information on translations or book distributors outside the U.S.A., please see the International Contact Information page immediately following the index of this book.

Adobe® Illustrator® 10: The Complete Reference

1234567890 CUS CUS 0198765432

ISBN 0-07-219362-x

Publisher
  Brandon A. Nordin

Vice President & Associate Publisher
  Scott Rogers

Acquisitions Editor
  Megg Bonar

Senior Project Editor
  Pamela Woolf

Acquisitions Coordinator
  Tana Diminyatz

Technical Editor
  Carrie Gatlin

Copy Editor
  Rachel Lopez

Indexer
  David Heiret

Computer Designers
  Tabitha M. Cagan, Tara A. Davis

Illustrators
  Michael Mueller, Lyssa Wald

Series Design
  Peter F. Hancik

This book was composed with Corel VENTURA™ Publisher.

About the Author

Sandra E. Eddy is a prolific author and freelance writer specializing in how-to and reference books on topics ranging from graphics to Web design and technologies to business applications and related computer and Internet skills. Before she became a full-time computer book author, she was a documentation manager and technical writer for a major software company. Her recent books include *XML in Plain English, Second Edition* (Hungry Minds); *HTML in Plain English* (Hungry Minds); *XHTML in Plain English* (Hungry Minds); *Teach Yourself Active Server Pages* (Hungry Minds); *Teach Yourself XML* (Hungry Minds); and *Mastering Lotus SmartSuite* (Sybex). This is her first book for Osborne/McGraw-Hill.

About the Artists

Brenda Bennett offers creative solutions for print and Web design projects—helping businesses grow and succeed, whether it's to enhance an existing design or create a new look from the beginning. Specialties include logos, stationery packages, brochures, web site design and development, print advertisements, postcards, newsletters (print and online), banner ads and more. She holds a bachelor of fine arts degree in graphic design from the College of Saint Rose in Albany, NY (Brenda Bennett Design, Creative Design Solutions, http://www.brendagraphics.com, design@brendagraphics.com)

Valeri Darling is the talent behind Missing Masterpiece Graphx based in Vancouver, Washington. A graduate of the Art Institute of Seattle, she is an experienced graphic artist and a respected instructor for graphics and web design courses at Washington State University Vancouver and Clark College. Valeri has a phenomenal range of styles and media. The images on her web site illustrate her versatility. Whether hand-drawn or entirely computer generated, her productions shimmer with a luxurious depth not often encountered in the world of electronic media. (Valeri Darling, Missing Masterpiece Graphx, http://www.missingmasterpiece.com, valeri@missingmasterpiece.com)

Janet McLeod is a Toronto-based illustrator in the medium of computers. Working predominantly in Adobe Illustrator, her work is bold and graphic often with a strong sense of line. Her clients include magazines, children's magazines, print, and advertising. Born in London, Ontario, Canada, Janet studied visual arts at the University of Western Ontario. Currently Janet is represented in the United States by Liz Sanders and in Canada and all other countries by herself. (Janet McLeod, www.portfolios.com/illust/mcleod.janet, www.lizsanders.com, looner@idirect.com)

DraSan' Nitti, principal of Silver Dragon Studio, was formally trained in graphic and fine art at the American Academy of Art in Chicago. Silver Dragon Studio is a full-service design studio specializing in web design, graphics, and animation. Silver Dragon Studio is based in Skokie, a North Shore suburb of Chicago, IL, and provides services worldwide. (DraSan' Nitti, Silver Dragon Studio, http://www.SilverDragonStudio.com, DraSan@SilverDragonStudio.com)

For Jay Shankin

Contents at a Glance

Contents

Part I

Presenting Illustrator

Part II

Illustrator Essentials

Part III

Illustrator FX

Part IV

Outside Illustrator

Part V

Appendixes

Acknowledgments

Writing a computer book is a team effort. Although the author may work alone in a home office, the support from editors, family, and friends is always important.

At the top of my list of thanks are the editors at Osborne/McGraw Hill. Special thanks go to two acquisitions editors, Gretchen Ganser Campbell—who started the project—and Megg Bonar—who brought it to a very successful conclusion. My enthusiastic thanks to the acquisitions coordinator, Tana Diminyatz—who coordinated chapter deliveries, to the senior project editor, Pamela Woolf—who oversaw the production of the book, Lyssa Wald—who is responsible for producing the art for this book, the painstaking copy editor, Rachel Lopez, and the meticulous indexer, David Heiret.

For accuracy and good humor in reviewing every word and figure, a very special thank you to the technical editor, Carrie F. Gatlin.

Thanks also to the four artists whose outstanding work graces the color insert. Special thanks for the talent and enthusiastic cooperation of Valeri Darling, Brenda Bennett, Janet McLeod, and DraSan' Nitti.

As always, thanks to my patient and diligent agent, Matt Wagner of Waterside Productions.

I would be negligent if I forgot to thank Mordy Golding and the other very helpful people at Adobe.

For their continued encouragement, my family and friends.

For their special and continuing contributions—Eli and Grace.

In loving memory of Toni, Bart, and Indy.

Introduction

Welcome to *Adobe Illustrator 10: The Complete Reference*. This illustrated how-to/reference combination comprehensively covers Illustrator features and tools from the basics to the most complex topics.

Adobe Illustrator is a vector graphics application that has been around since 1987. Since its first release with fundamental drawing tools and not much more, Illustrator has grown to include all types of sophisticated tools and features.

You can use Illustrator's large set of tools, palettes, and other features to create and edit images for business or home—for printed illustrations, pamphlets, and books. You can group selected objects, change colors, change dimensions, and perform other transformations and apply filters and effects. You can work on the tiniest details of your artworks by zooming in, placing and editing individual pieces on layers, and merging those layers into finished works of art.

Using Illustrator, you can make graphic images from scratch, import images from other applications, export images to other applications, and save and optimize images for the web.

Who Should Use This Book

This book is designed for those who are familiar with computing within the Windows or Macintosh environments but may or may not be new to Illustrator. If you are an Illustrator novice, be sure to read the first few chapters to learn about Illustrator's user interface. If you already know certain aspects of Illustrator or are new to Illustrator 10, you can fill in the blanks by browsing through chapters that cover new or unfamiliar features and topics.

How This Book Is Organized

Adobe Illustrator 10: The Complete Reference is designed to be easy to use, regardless of your level of experience. The first chapters are for Illustrator novices; the book builds from the early chapters to more complicated subjects. This book is both a tutorial and reference. Throughout the book, you will find useful illustrations, tables, and sets of procedures to teach you how to use many Illustrator features.

The book is organized into five parts that progressively move you from novice to knowledgeable. Part I, comprised of Chapter 1 through 4, introduces you to Illustrator basics and the user interface. Part II contains Chapters 5 through 14 and covers Illustrator essentials, its features, tools, and palettes, and how to use them to create and edit artworks. Part III is comprised of Chapters 15 through 18 and concentrates on features with which you can change the appearance of your artworks and work more efficiently. Part IV, with Chapters 19 through 22, describes how Illustrator works with other applications and how you can prepare artwork for export and printing—on your own printers or at a commercial printer. Part V includes six appendixes, which cover a variety of topics ranging from installation to setting to shortcut keys and key combinations and much more, and a glossary.

In the center of the book, you will find 16-page color insert of artworks created by four artists. On some of the facing pages, you will see "deconstructed" versions of the art that demonstrate how these wonderful artworks were created.

- Chapter 1 covers basics such as launching and exiting Illustrator and starting a new document. You also will tour the illustration window, toolbox tools, and the palettes.

- Chapter 2 compares Illustrator's vector graphics compare with raster graphics, introduces you to Illustrator color models, and teaches you how to create and manipulate basic shapes. In this chapter, you'll learn how to use Illustrator's help system and manage Illustrator and "foreign" documents.

- Chapter 3 shows you how to navigate documents, change views, and select objects. Then, you'll learn how to manipulate selected objects and groups and selected parts of objects and groups.

- Chapter 4 covers the nine Illustrator graph types—how to create and edit them.

- Chapter 5 discusses using the grid, guides, and Smart Guides to align objects in the illustration window and to resize the Artboard to fit your artwork.

- Chapter 6 informs you about the ins and outs of paths and points and the Pencil, Pen, and other tools; palettes; and commands used to add, modify, and delete paths and points.

- Chapter 7 emphasizes the selection and use of colors, three color-related palettes, and the Color Picker.

- Chapter 8 shows you how to customize strokes and fills and use the Eyedropper tool and Paint Bucket tool.

- Chapter 9 covers gradients and mesh objects with which you can decorate the fills of your artwork.

- Chapter 10 demonstrates the ways in which you can transform selected objects—moving, rotating, reflecting, scaling, and shearing—using a variety of tools, palettes, and dialog boxes.

- Chapter 11 introduces you to the basics of type and teaches you how to add type to your artworks in three ways: extending type from a point in the illustration window, inserting type within objects, and placing type along paths.

- Chapter 12 shows how to enhance type in your artwork by selecting it and applying various character and paragraph formats. You'll also learn how to convert type to graphical objects.

- Chapter 13 teaches the methods of painting strokes with the Paintbrush tool and the Brushes palette.

- Chapter 14 covers layers and the Layers palette with which you can organize complicated artworks.

- Chapter 15 introduces you to transparency, shows you how to set opacity and transparency levels, and apply transparency and blending effects.

- Chapter 16 shows you how to use filters and effects to change the appearance of objects and illustrates each filter and effect in Illustrator's inventory.

- Chapter 17 covers predefined and user-defined actions and action sets with which Illustrator procedures are recorded and played to ease your work.

- Chapter 18 instructs you about appearance attributes and styles, with which you change an object's appearance; symbols, which are multiple identical and editable objects; and envelopes, with which you can enclose and distort objects.

- Chapter 19 shows you how to save and optimize your artwork as raster graphics for use on the web.

- Chapter 20 covers Illustrator's special features with which you can create images and image maps for the Web and divide Web graphics to be able to apply event-driven effects to individual slices.

- Chapter 21 discusses the interaction between Illustrator and other applications: opening and placing documents from other applications and saving and exporting Illustrator documents to other applications.

- Chapter 22 describes printing artwork on your own printers and preparing artwork to be printed commercially.

- Appendix A discusses minimum system requirements for installing Illustrator on Windows and Macintosh computers and covers the installation procedures for both types of computers.

- Appendix B provides information about customizing your Illustrator working environment.

- Appendix C contains a variety of Illustrator resources on the web.

- Appendix D consists of the Adobe Web siteinformation that discusses how you can become an Adobe Certified Expert.

- Appendix E provides information about the artists who created the images in the color pages in the center of the book and how they produced the images.

- Appendix F shows you how to define your own sets of shortcut keys and lists shortcuts for Illustrator commands, tools, palettes, and other features.

- The glossary provides a list of descriptions of Illustrator, color, printing, and graphics terms.

Conventions Used in This Book

As you read through this book, you'll find these special features:

Note *A note emphasizes important information about a topic.*

Tip *A tip provides a shortcut or easy-to-use method for performing an action.*

Caution *A caution warns you about potential problems and hazards that might be ahead.*

This book provides the following keyboard and text conventions:

- Shortcut keys (one key on your computer keyboard) and key combinations (two or three keys on the keyboard) are shortcuts for executing commands or performing actions. For example, rather than choosing a menu and then a command to open a dialog box or activate a tool, you'll press a shortcut key or key combination. To execute an action with a key combination, press and hold down the first key (and optionally the second key) in the combination and then press the last key.

- Shortcut keys and key combinations are presented for both Windows and Macintosh computers, in that order. For example, to print a document in Windows, press CTRL-P; to print a document on a Macintosh computer, press ⌘-P. In this book, the syntax for the Print command is CTRL-P/⌘-P.

- If one shortcut serves both Windows PCs and Macs, you'll see a single instance. For example, the shortcut for the Selection tool is the letter v, so in the book the syntax is Selection tool (V).

In this book, *italicized* text represents variables and terms introduced to you for the first time.

The Complete Reference

Adobe Illustrator 10

Part I

Presenting Illustrator

The Complete Reference

Chapter 1

Getting Acquainted with Illustrator

T his chapter covers Illustrator basics for both the PC and the Macintosh. You will learn how to launch and exit the program and start a new document. You also will find out about Illustrator's unique application and illustration windows, including its toolbox tools and palettes.

Starting Illustrator

You can start Illustrator as you start most other Windows or Macintosh programs. The first time you start Illustrator, the program prompts you to register Illustrator either online or by fax. (Appendix A steps you through the installation process for both Windows and Macintosh computers.)

In Windows you can start Illustrator in a variety of ways: from the Start menu in the taskbar, as an icon on the Desktop, or as an icon on the taskbar. The launch procedure you choose depends on how often you plan to use the program. Starting from the Start menu requires three steps (but leaves your Desktop and taskbar uncluttered with extra icons), starting from the Desktop requires double-clicking an icon, and launching from the taskbar calls for single-clicking an icon. So, if you plan to use Illustrator often, it makes sense to add a shortcut icon to the taskbar or to the Desktop. On a Macintosh you can start Illustrator by double-clicking the Illustrator icon or double-clicking an Illustrator document—if it happens to be on the Desktop.

Starting a New Document

Once you start Illustrator, create a new document by following these steps:

1. Choose File | New or press CTRL-N/⌘-N. Illustrator opens the New Document dialog box (you'll learn about the options in this dialog box in "Setting Up the Artboard" in Chapter 5):

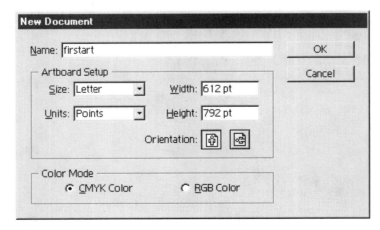

2. Fill in the filename in the Name text box; then click OK.

Using the Keyboard

You can activate certain Illustrator commands by pressing *shortcut keys,* which are single keys or key combinations that are implemented by pressing two or three keys at the same time. Throughout this book, key combinations are shown as series of keys, each separated by a hyphen (-). For example, the key combination used to print an Illustrator file is CTRL-P/⌘-P, where the / separates the Windows key combination from the Macintosh key combination. This is the convention for shortcuts and keyboard combinations shown in this book. Appendix F lists the most common Illustrator shortcut keys and key combinations.

For some actions in Illustrator, using the mouse is the general rule; however, using the keyboard for some tasks can be faster. For example, saving an existing file using the mouse takes two separate clicks: clicking the File menu in the menu bar and clicking the Save command from the open File menu. However, you can save one step by pressing CTRL-S/⌘-S to quickly save the file without opening the File menu. Getting help is another example of faster keyboard action. To get help using the mouse, choose Help | Illustrator Help. However, to get help using the keyboard, simply press F1. Many shortcut keys are displayed next to their related commands on Illustrator menus. To learn about menus, read "Using Illustrator Menus" later in this chapter.

Viewing the Illustrator Workspace

The Illustrator workspace (see Figure 1-1) consists of the application window and many components. If you're familiar with other Windows- or Macintosh-based programs, you'll recognize many of the features in the Illustrator workspace; however, some are unique to Illustrator and other programs used to create artwork.

Using Illustrator Menus

Menus offer lists of commands with which you construct and modify your artwork, set preferences, and get help in using Illustrator, among many other things. When you choose a command from a menu, an action takes place, a submenu opens to the side of the menu, or a dialog box appears.

Illustrator provides two types of menus: Standard menus open from the menu bar, and context-sensitive menus list a few commonly used commands and some commands related to the currently selected object (hence, they are context-sensitive). Choose a menu command in one of the following four ways:

- Click a name on the menu bar to open a standard menu of commands from which you can select.

- Press ALT /OPTION to activate the menu bar, press the underlined character in the menu name, and then press the underlined letter in the command name.

■ Right-click an object to open a context-sensitive menu of commands from which you can select.

■ Press a shortcut key or key combination to implement a command.

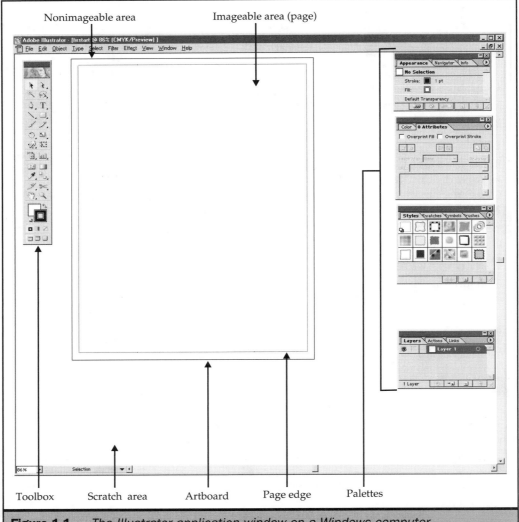

Figure 1-1. *The Illustrator application window on a Windows computer*

Both standard and context-sensitive menus share certain common characteristics:

- When an *ellipsis*, three dots, follows a menu command, choosing the command opens a dialog box.
- When a right-pointing arrow appears to the right of a menu command, selecting the command opens a submenu related to the selected command.
- When a check mark precedes a command, that command is currently active.
- When a menu command is dimmed, it is not currently available for use. You may have to select an object or perform another action before it becomes available.
- Horizontal lines separate related groups of menu commands.
- When a shortcut key or key combination appears to the right of a menu command, press the key or key combination to execute the command. For a detailed list of Illustrator shortcut keys and key combinations, see Appendix F.

Inspecting an Illustrator Dialog Box

A dialog box (refer to Figure 1-1) is a small window that contains a title bar with a Close button and sometimes even a control icon. Some dialog boxes display a message and a couple of command buttons that you click to accept or reject the message. At the other extreme are complex dialog boxes made up of multiple sections, which contain many varied components that are unique to dialog boxes. Table 1-1 briefly describes each component in a dialog box.

Component	Description
Title bar	A horizontal bar in which appears the name of the dialog box and the Close button.
Close button	A button you click to close the dialog box without taking any action. You also can press the ESC key to close the dialog box.
Text box	An area into which you can type text.
Option box	A box in which you can type a number or scroll through values from which you can choose.
Radio buttons	Sets of buttons from which you can choose only one. When you select a radio button, it is filled in and another button is cleared.

Table 1-1.   *The Components of a Dialog Box*

Component	Description
Check box	A box that you can check (to activate the option associated with the check box) or clear (to inactivate the option). You can choose one or more check boxes at a time.
Pop-up menu/ drop-down menu	A small menu that opens when you click its arrow. To choose an option in the menu, click it.
Command button	A rectangular button that when clicked performs an action. For example, click OK to save your changes and close the dialog box, or click Cancel to close the dialog box without saving your changes.

Table 1-1.   *The Components of a Dialog Box* (continued)

The Illustration Window

The Illustration window—the largest element on your Desktop when Illustrator is active—is the area in which you create and modify your artworks. Within the working area of the illustration window are several components: the artboard, the page, the imageable area, the nonimageable area, and the scratch area, as discussed in the following.

■ The *artboard* is a virtual board on which sits the page that holds your printable artwork. Think of the board to which you tape your pastel or watercolor paper or the table on which you create your paper illustrations. You can adjust the size and orientation of the artboard to hold illustrations of different dimensions (see "Setting Up a Document" in Chapter 5), and you can show or hide the artboard, which is shown by default. To hide the shown artboard, choose View | Hide Artboard; to show the hidden artboard, choose View | Show Artboard.

Note   *The Hide Artboard and Show Artboard commands are in the same place on the View menu, depending on whether the artboard is visible. If the artboard appears in the illustration window, the Hide Artboard command is on display; if the artboard is hidden, the Show Artboard command appears. This situation occurs in other cases, too: If the words Show or Hide precede a command name, chances are good that the command name changes to reflect the appearance (or nonappearance) of a component.*

- The *page* is the only area of the illustration window that contains the artwork you can print—although you can create artwork almost anywhere on the window.

- The *imageable area* is the part of the page that can be printed—depending on the default printer. Some printers allow very small margins; others require that the margins be larger. For example, a Hewlett-Packard LaserJet might enable you to set margins as small as 0.25 inch, but an Epson Stylus printer might allow margins of only 0.5 inch. On the page, the imageable area falls within the dotted lines.

- The *nonimageable area* represents the margins of the page; you cannot print from this area.

- The *scratch area* is every part of the illustration window outside the artboard. Use the scratch area to experiment; for example, create or copy objects from the artboard and edit them, and then drag all the winners back to the artboard. You also can use the scratch area to hold extra objects before you place them on the artboard.

Introducing the Toolbox

The toolbox contains more than 70 tools, which you can click to perform many Illustrator actions. Using Illustrator tools, you can create and edit a variety of objects and make selections to edit your work. You can drag the toolbox by its title bar to a more convenient place on the computer Desktop, show or hide it, or pop up and optionally "tear off" *toolslots,* which are hidden sets of related tools. Figure 1-2 shows every tool in the toolbox and on its toolslots.

If the toolbox is onscreen, you can hide it by choosing Window | Tools or pressing TAB; to show a hidden toolbox, choose Window | Tools or press TAB again.

Selecting a Tool

To select a tool, either click it or press its shortcut key or key combination—that is, if the tool has a shortcut. To see if a tool on the toolbox (or a palette) has an associated shortcut key, move the mouse pointer over the tool until a *tooltip* (a rectangular box with the tool name) appears. The letter or key combination within parentheses is the shortcut. A complete list of shortcut keys for toolbox tools appears Appendix F.

Selecting a Toolslot Tool

If a tool has a toolslot, it has a tiny arrow in its lower-right corner. Note that the first tool in a toolslot is the tool that normally appears on the toolbox.

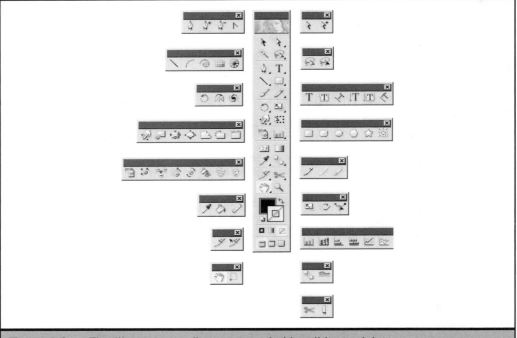

Figure 1-2.   *The Illustrator toolbox surrounded by all its toolslots*

| Tip | *To cycle through a set of toolslot tools, press and hold down* CTRL-ALT/⌘-OPTION *and repeatedly click the tool.* |

To select a toolslot tool, follow these steps:

1. With the mouse, press and hold down the parent tool associated with the desired pop-up tool. Illustrator opens a toolslot.

2. Drag the mouse pointer over the desired tool. Illustrator highlights the tool.

3. Release the mouse button. Illustrator activates the tool and replaces the parent on the toolbox.

PRESENTING ILLUSTRATOR

To replace the new tool with another, repeat the prior steps.

Tearing Off Toolslots

When you use particular toolslot tools often, you can tear off their toolslots so that the tools are always on display. To do so, follow these steps:

1. With the mouse, press and hold down the parent tool associated with the desired toolslot tool. Illustrator opens a toolslot.

2. Move the mouse pointer to the Tearoff section on the right side of the toolslot and click. Illustrator adds a title bar to the toolbar.

3. Drag the toolslot away from the toolbox.

To close the toolslot, click its Close button. Although the toolslot is closed, it remains on the toolbox, ready to be opened again.

Presenting the Illustrator Toolbox Tools

This section includes brief descriptions and illustrations of all toolbox tools, either individually (such as the Selection Tool and the Magic Wand, which are not on a toolslot) or as components of a toolslot (almost every tool on the toolbox). Every tool is covered more thoroughly later in the book.

Many tools have associated shortcut keys and key combinations, which you can find by moving the mouse pointer over the tool and looking at the tooltip. To select a tool using a shortcut, simply press its key or key combination. In this section, shortcuts are placed within parentheses immediately after the tool name. For a complete list of Illustrator shortcut keys and key combinations, see Appendix F.

The Selection Tool

Selection (V), which is the active tool when you start Illustrator the first time, selects an object, complete *path* (a set of straight and curved lines that form the outline of an object in an artwork), or complete group or identifies object parts. Note that the Select menu contains commands related to the Selection tool.

The Magic Wand

The Magic Wand (Y) selects objects based on fill and stroke color, the stroke weight, opacity or transparency, or the blending mode.

The Pen Toolslot

The tools on this toolslot with which you can draw and edit paths are Pen, Add Anchor Point, Delete Anchor Point, and Convert Anchor Point.

- Pen (P) draws a freeform path composed of straight line and curved line segments.
- Add Anchor Point (+) inserts an anchor point in a path.
- Delete Anchor Point (-) deletes a selected anchor point from a path.
- Convert Anchor Point (SHIFT-C) changes a smooth point to a corner point or a corner point to a smooth point.

The Line Segment Toolslot

The tools on this toolslot with which you can create open or closed paths are Line Segment, Arc, Spiral, Rectangular Grid, and Polar Grid.

- Line Segment (\) draws a straight line.
- Arc draws a curved line.
- Spiral draws a spiral in a clockwise or counterclockwise direction.
- Rectangular Grid draws a rectangle separated by horizontal and vertical dividers.
- Polar Grid draws a circle separated by concentric and radial dividers.

The Paintbrush Tool

Use the Paintbrush (B) to draw lines and add brushstrokes to paths.

The Rotate Toolslot

The tools on this toolslot with which you can transform objects are Rotate, Reflect, and Twist:

- Rotate (R) turns a selected object around an axis.

- Reflect (O) flips a selected object across an axis.
- Twist converts a selected object into a hurricane-like object with trailing tails.

The Warp Toolslot

The tools on this toolslot with which you can apply effects to objects are Warp, Twirl, Pucker, Bloat, Scallop, Crystallize, and Wrinkle:

- Warp (SHIFT-R) applies a warp effect to a selected object.
- Twirl turns a selected object around an axis.
- Pucker curves the edges of the selected object toward the center of the object.
- Bloat curves the edges of the selected object away from the center of the object.
- Scallop adds scallop-like shapes to the edges of the selected object.
- Crystallize adds thin rays to the edges of the selected object.
- Wrinkle adds wrinkles to the top and bottom edges of the selected object.

The Symbolism Toolslot

The tools on the Symbolism toolslot are Symbol Sprayer, Symbol Shifter, Symbol Scruncher, Symbol Sizer, Symbol Spinner, Symbol Stainer, Symbol Screener, and Symbol Styler.

- Symbol Sprayer (SHIFT-S) "sprays" a selected symbol onto an artwork.
- Symbol Shifter moves one or more selected symbols on the page.
- Symbol Scruncher moves one or more selected symbols toward or away from the center of the symbol group.
- Symbol Sizer increases the size of one or more selected symbols within the symbol group.
- Symbol Spinner rotates one or more selected symbols.
- Symbol Stainer mixes the current fill color with the colors of one or more selected symbols.
- Symbol Screener "fades" the colors of one or more selected symbols.
- Symbol Styler applies an Illustrator style to a group of symbols.

The Mesh Tool

The Mesh tool (U) adds a mesh to an object to add or change degrees of colors.

The Eyedropper Toolslot

The tools on this toolslot with which you can sample or apply a color or pattern or measure are Eyedropper, Paint Bucket, and Measure.

- Eyedropper (I) copies paint or type characteristics from an object.
- Paint Bucket (K) pastes paint or type characteristics into an object's fill.
- Measure calculates the distance between two points.

The Slice Toolslot

The tools on this toolslot are Slice and Slice Selection.

- Slice (SHIFT-K) cuts a Web graphic into small sections so that you can work with the sections separately.
- Slice Selection selects a slice for editing.

The Hand Toolslot

The tools on this toolslot are Hand and Page.

- Hand (H) moves the artboard around the illustration window.
- Page changes the dimensions of the imageable area of the page to control how much of the artwork is printed.

The Direct Selection Toolslot

The tools on this toolslot (the top toolslot on the right side of the toolbox) with which you can select paths and objects are Direct Selection and Group Selection.

- Direct Selection (A) selects paths and points in an object within a bounding box.
- Group Selection selects a single path, all the paths in a *group* (a collection of objects), single objects within groups, and entire groups.

The Direct Select Lasso Toolslot

Direct Select Lasso and Lasso are the tools on this toolslot with which you can select paths and objects within a selection bounding box.

- Direct Select Lasso (Q) selects paths and points in an object that you have drawn.
- Lasso selects one or more objects within a selection path you have drawn.

The Type Toolslot

The tools on this toolslot, which is devoted to entering and editing type, are Type, Area Type, Path Type, Vertical Type, Vertical Area Type, and Vertical Path Type.

- Type (T) enters or edits type horizontally in your artwork.
- Area Type enters or edits type horizontally within a path.
- Path Type enters or edits type on a path.
- Vertical Type enters or edits type vertically in your artwork.
- Vertical Area Type enters or edits type vertically within a path.
- Vertical Path Type enters or edits vertical type on a path.

The Rectangle Toolslot

The tools on this toolslot, most of which are devoted to drawing closed paths (without beginning and end points) are Rectangle, Rounded Rectangle, Ellipse, Polygon, Star, and Flare.

- Rectangle (M) draws rectangles and squares with straight corners.
- Rounded Rectangle draws rectangles and squares with rounded corners.

- Ellipse (L) draws ellipses and circles.
- Polygon draws objects with multiple sides.
- Star draws stars with varying numbers of points.
- Flare adds a lens flare to an artwork.

The Pencil Toolslot

Pencil, Smooth, and Eraser are the tools on this toolslot with which you can draw, smooth, or erase paths.

- Pencil (N) draws a freeform line composed of a single path.
- Smooth smoothes a path by removing extra anchor points.
- Erase erases part of a path and the anchor points within the erased area and adds new end points to the resulting new ends.

The Scale Toolslot

The tools on this toolslot with which you can change the size or look of an object are Scale, Shear, and Reshape.

- Scale (S) changes one or more dimensions of a selected object either in proportion or not.
- Shear slants (or skews) a selected object.
- Reshape smoothes a path by dragging an anchor point or line segment.

The Free Transform Tool

The Free Transform tool (E) combines the functions of the Scale, Rotate, and Shear tools to scale, rotate, or slant a selected object.

The Graph Toolslot

The tools on this toolslot with which you can construct or convert from the current graph type are Column Graph, Stacked Column Graph, Bar Graph, Stacked Bar Graph, Line Graph, Area Graph, Scatter Graph, Pie Graph, and Radar Graph.

PRESENTING
ILLUSTRATOR

- Column Graph (J), the default graph tool, creates a graph with vertical bars or changes the current graph to that graph type.

- Stacked Column Graph creates a graph with stacked vertical bars or changes the current graph to that graph type.

- Bar Graph creates a graph with horizontal bars or changes the current graph to that graph type.

- Stacked Bar Graph creates a graph with stacked horizontal bars or changes the current graph to that graph type.

- Line Graph creates a graph that shows one or more series of data points over time, thereby showing trends, or changes the current graph to that graph type.

- Area Graph creates a line graph that shows one or more series of data points over time; the filled area emphasizes totals or changes the current graph to that graph type.

- Scatter Graph creates a graph that shows points of data drawn from two axes or changes the current graph to that graph type.

- Pie Graph creates a graph that shows the parts of one data range compared with the entire range or changes the current graph to that graph type.

- Radar Graph creates a graph that shows values plotted around a central point or changes the current graph to that graph type.

The Gradient Tool

The Gradient tool (G) fills the selected object with the current gradient colors from the Gradient palette or edits a gradient.

The Blend Toolslot

The tools on this toolslot with which you can edit an entire object are Blend and Auto Trace.

- Blend (W) transforms the color, shape, and/or size of a path from one end of the path to another.

- Auto Trace automatically traces the outline of all or part of the selected object.

The Scissors Toolslot

The tools on this cutting toolslot are Scissors and Knife.

- Scissors (C) cuts a path at an anchor point, forming two paths.
- Knife cuts a path area.

The Zoom Tool

The Zoom tool (Z) changes the level of magnification of the illustration window.

Exploring Other Toolbox Components

At the bottom of the toolbox are elements with which you can set the color of the *fill* and *stroke* of an object. A fill of an object is one or more colors or patterns enclosed within a path. A stroke of an object is one or more colors on a path. So, for a rectangle the fill is the color or pattern inside the borders; the stroke is the border itself.

Other elements at the foot of the toolbox enable you to change the appearance of the fill or stroke and the application window. Figure 1-3 focuses on the components at the bottom of the toolbox.

The Fill and Stroke (X) show the current fill and stroke values. Click the Fill to activate it; click the Stroke to make that active. Then, depending on whether Fill or Stroke is active, you can either fill the selected object with the value of the Fill or apply the Stroke value to the path that outlines the object.

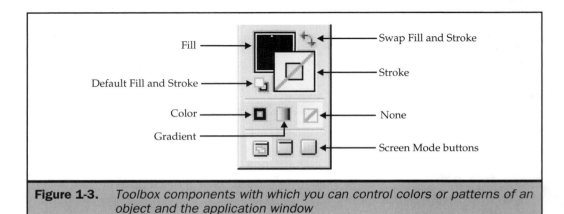

Figure 1-3.   *Toolbox components with which you can control colors or patterns of an object and the application window*

You can set the values of the Fill and Stroke with the Default Fill and Stroke and Swap Fill and Stroke buttons. To return the fill and stroke to the defaults of white for the fill and black for the stroke, click the Default Fill and Stroke button. To reverse the colors of the fill and stroke (that is, apply the fill color to the stroke and the stroke color to the fill), click the Swap Fill and Stroke button.

The Color, Gradient, and None buttons control the appearance of the fill or stroke, depending on which is active, as explained here:

- Click Color (<) to set the fill or stroke to its most recent color.

- Click Gradient (>) to set the fill or stroke to its most recent gradient.

- Click None (/) to set the fill or stroke to no color or gradient.

With the Standard Screen Mode, Full Screen Mode with Menu Bar, and Full Screen Mode buttons, you can manage the appearance of the application window. All three modes display all active palettes and the toolbox—if you have not hidden them.

- Click Standard Screen Mode (F), the default, to display the application window, illustration window, menu bar, and status bar. (To learn about the Illustrator status bar, read "The Status Bar," later in this chapter.)

- Click Full Screen Mode with Menu Bar (F) to maximize the application and illustration windows, show the menu bar, and hide the status bar.

- Click Full Screen Mode (F) to maximize the application and illustration windows and hide the menu and the status bars.

Note   *Press* F *to cycle through the three screen modes.*

Introducing Illustrator Palettes

Illustrator provides a set of 27 palettes (or small windows) that you can use to check the status of your artwork or enhance it in various ways. Because the palettes are small and you can move them around the Desktop (even from the Illustrator application window), you can create and edit your artwork without them getting in your way. In fact, you can reduce the size of many palettes—even to a title bar. All palettes have title bars—with Minimize, Restore, and Close buttons—and pop-up menus. Figure 1-4 shows a typical palette.

To move a palette, drag it by its title bar. The natural place for a palette is on an edge of the illustration window. When you drag a palette to an edge, the palette snaps into position. Move another palette under this palette, and you'll notice the "snap" effect again.

Resizing a Palette

To minimize a palette, simply click the Minimize button. The palette is minimized in place; in other words, the palette does not move to the bottom of the window or anywhere else.

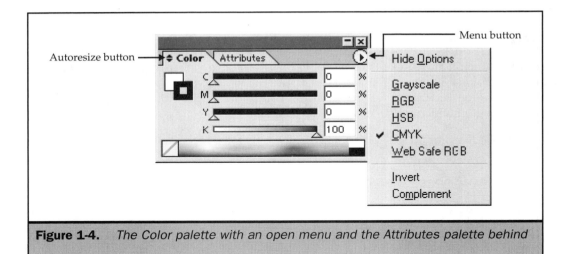

Figure 1-4. *The Color palette with an open menu and the Attributes palette behind*

To save room on the desktop, you can resize any palette that has an Autoresize button. To toggle through a palette's resize settings, click the Autoresize button. Figure 1-5 shows the Color palette in its three resized states.

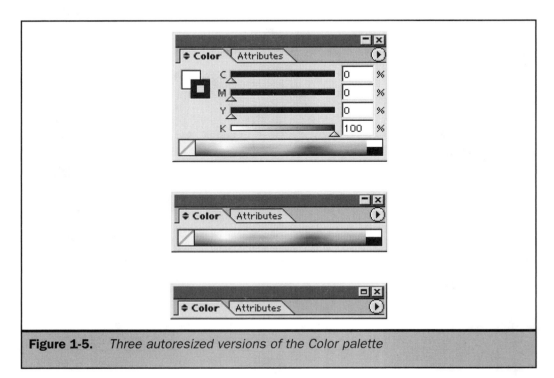

Figure 1-5. *Three autoresized versions of the Color palette*

You can resize some palettes by dragging them by their borders. If you see three diagonal lines in the lower-right corner of a palette, you can resize it.

Showing a Palette

To open a palette, open the Window menu and select the command name that matches the palette name. For example, to open the Navigator palette, choose Window | Navigator. When a palette is onscreen, its command on the Windows menu is checked.

If a palette shares its window with another (as the Color and Attributes palette in the preceding figures), you can display the other palette by clicking its title tab right below the title bar.

Hiding One or More Palettes

To close a palette, click its Close button or choose its name from the Windows menu. To close all palettes and the toolbox, press TAB. To close all palettes but leave the toolbox onscreen, press SHIFT-TAB.

Tabbing a Palette

You can add one or more palettes to another palette. This enables you to organize palettes in a way that is logical to you. To tab a palette into another palette, follow these steps:

1. Drag the palette by its tab onto the palette of which it will become a part. You'll see an image of the palette as you drag it. When the dragged palette is in the proper position, the receiving palette displays a rectangular-shaped box with a dark border.

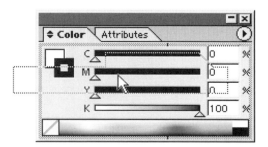

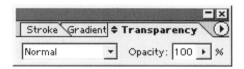

2. Release the mouse button. The palette is added to the receiving palette, and other sections of that palette remain separate.

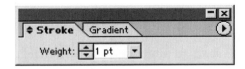

To "untab" a palette from another, drag the palette you want to move to another area of the illustration window.

Docking a Palette

You can attach two or more palettes to another palette. This means you can open and close the docked palettes simultaneously. Each docked palette keeps its own attributes. To dock a palette, follow these steps:

1. Drag the palette to be docked by its tab to the bottom of the palette to which it will be docked. You'll see an image of the palette as you drag it. When the dragged palette is in the proper position, the bottom of the receiving palette shows a dark horizontal bar.

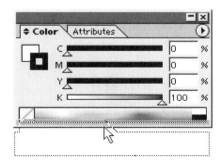

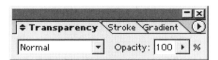

2. Release the mouse button. Illustrator docks one palette to the other.

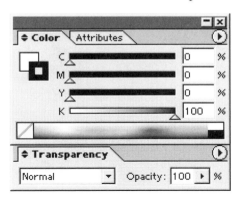

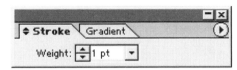

To undock docked palettes, move the mouse pointer to the bottom palette and drag it far away from the top palette. (If you don't drag far enough, the palettes will remain docked.)

Presenting the Illustrator Palettes

This section includes descriptions and illustrations of all Illustrator palettes. Every palette and all its components are covered in detail later in the book.

The Actions Palette

The Actions palette enables you to define *actions* (sets of recorded commands used to automate commonly used events) and also contains predefined actions.

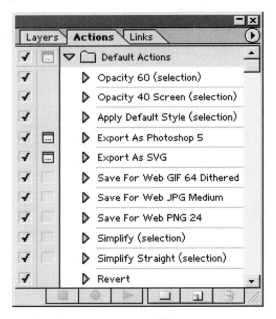

To toggle between showing and hiding the Actions palette, choose Window | Actions.

The Align Palette

The Align palette enables you to align and evenly distribute objects, both horizontally and vertically.

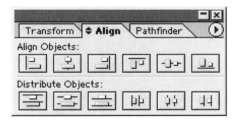

To toggle between showing and hiding the Align palette, choose Window | Align or press SHIFT-F7.

The Appearance Palette

The Appearance palette lists all the options and functions you have applied to the current object.

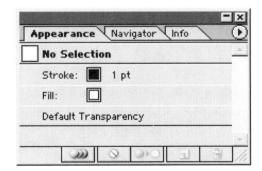

To toggle between showing and hiding the Appearance palette, choose Window | Appearance or press SHIFT-F6.

The Attributes Palette

The Attributes palette enables you to set certain characteristics and make notes about the selected object.

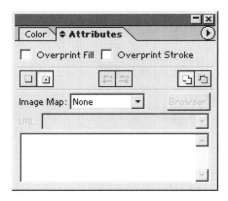

To toggle between showing and hiding the Attributes palette, choose Window | Attributes or press F11.

The Brushes Palette

The Brushes palette enables you to display predefined and user-defined art, calligraphic, pattern, and scatter brushes for the Paintbrush tool.

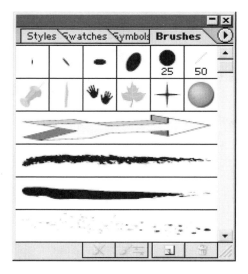

To toggle between showing and hiding the Brushes palette, choose Window | Brushes or press F5.

The Color Palette

The Color palette, which shows the current fill and stroke colors, enables you to "mix" new colors and define color attributes.

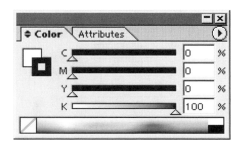

To toggle between showing and hiding the Color palette, choose Window | Color or press F6.

The Document Info Palette

The Document Info palette provides a detailed list of characteristics about the current document.

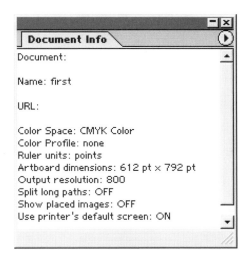

To toggle between showing and hiding the Document Info palette, choose Window | Document Info.

The Gradient Palette

The Gradient palette enables the creation and color editing of gradients.

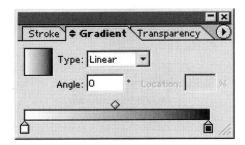

To toggle between showing and hiding the Gradient palette, choose Window | Gradient or press F9.

The Info Palette

The Info palette provides information about color and coordinates of the point under the mouse pointer, and height and width of an object being created or edited.

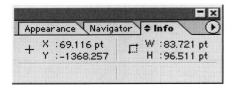

To toggle between showing and hiding the Info palette, choose Window | Info or press F8.

The Layers Palette

The Layers palette enables management of the layers making up an artwork.

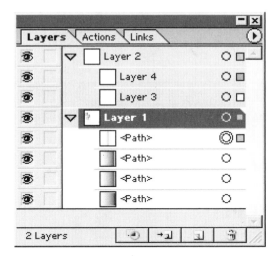

To toggle between showing and hiding the Layers palette, choose Window | Layers or press F7.

The Links Palette

The Links palette lists all the linked and embedded images in the current document: a thumbnail picture, the filename, and an icon indicating the type of image.

To toggle between showing and hiding the Links palette, choose Window | Links.

The Magic Wand Palette

The Magic Wand palette sets the tolerances used to select like objects using the Magic Wand tool.

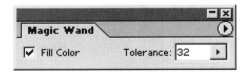

   To toggle between showing and hiding the Magic Wand palette, choose Window | Magic Wand.

The Navigator Palette

The Navigator palette enables zooming in and out of the current artwork.

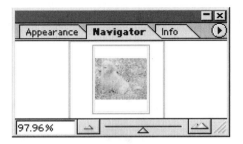

   To toggle between showing and hiding the Navigator palette, choose Window | Navigator.

The Pathfinder Palette

The Pathfinder palette combines or splits two or more objects.

PRESENTING
ILLUSTRATOR

To toggle between showing and hiding the Pathfinder palette, choose Window |
Pathfinder or press SHIFT-F9.

The Stroke Palette

The Stroke palette controls noncolor characteristics of the stroke.

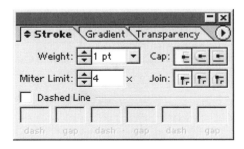

To toggle between showing and hiding the Stroke palette, choose Window | Stroke
or press F10.

The Styles Palette

The Styles palette stores and displays groups of appearance settings.

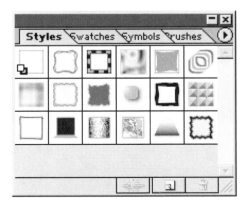

To toggle between showing and hiding the Styles palette, choose Window | Styles
or press SHIFT-F5.

The SVG Interactivity Palette

The SVG Interactivity palette enables dynamic behavior of an artwork that will be exported to a Web page.

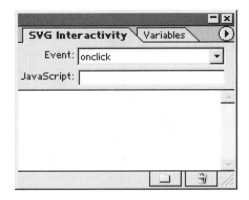

To toggle between showing and hiding the SVG Interactivity palette, choose Window | SVG Interactivity.

The Swatches Palette

The Swatches palette stores and displays predefined and user-defined *swatches* (samples of colors, patterns, and gradients).

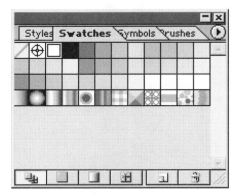

To toggle between showing and hiding the Swatches palette, choose Window | Swatches.

The Symbols Palette

The Symbols palette enables the use and creation of symbols for Illustrator artwork.

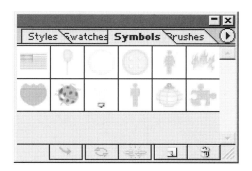

To toggle between showing and hiding the Symbols palette, choose Window |
Symbols or press SHIFT-F11.

The Transform Palette

The Transform palette enables detailed transformation (moving, rotating, scaling,
and skewing) of objects using specific measurements.

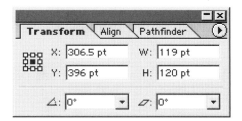

To toggle between showing and hiding the Transform palette, choose Window |
Transform or press SHIFT-F8.

The Transparency Palette

The Transparency palette controls the level of transparency and applies transparency
effects to the current object.

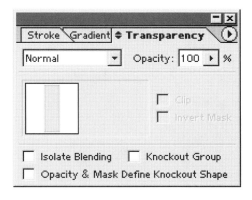

To toggle between showing and hiding the Transparency palette, choose Window |
Transparency or press SHIFT-F10.

The Character Palette

The Character palette controls the formats of selected characters in an artwork.

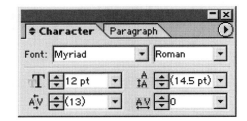

To toggle between showing and hiding the Character palette, choose Window |
Type | Character or press CTRL-T/⌘-T.

The MM (Multiple Master) Design Palette

The MM (Multiple Master) Design palette controls many characteristics of
Multiple Master fonts.

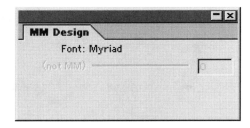

To toggle between showing and hiding the MM Design palette, choose Window |
Type | MM Design.

The Paragraph Palette

The Paragraph palette controls the formats of selected paragraphs in an artwork.

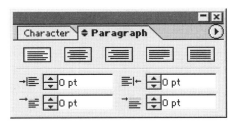

To toggle between showing and hiding the Paragraph palette, choose Window |
Type | Paragraph or press CTRL-M/⌘-M.

The Tab Ruler Palette

The Tab Ruler palette enables the use of several types of tabs for both horizontal and
vertical types.

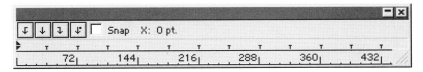

To toggle between showing and hiding the Tab Ruler palette, choose Window |
Type | Tab Ruler or press CTRL-SHIFT-T/⌘-SHIFT-T.

The Variables Palette

The Variables palette defines an object in an artwork as a variable that will be linked to a database field.

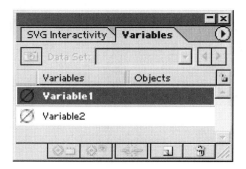

To toggle between showing and hiding the Variables palette, choose Window | Variables.

The Status Bar

At the very bottom of the application window is the status bar, which contains two pop-up menus and a scroll bar.

Using the first pop-up menu, you can either select or type a zoom level. To select a zoom level, click the small arrow on the right side of the menu and click a zoom value. To type a zoom level, just overtype the contents of the text box and press Enter. To learn about zooming and how to zoom, refer to "Zooming a Document," in Chapter 3.

The second pop-up menu in the status bar contains information options. To select an option, click the large arrow on the right side of the menu and click one of the following:

- Current Tool displays the current active tool on the toolbox.

- Date and Time shows the current date and time for your computer system.

- Free Memory shows the percentage and amount of memory that is currently available for use.

- Number of Undoes displays the number of undoes and redoes you have done. The number of undoes available depends on your computer's memory and the number of undoes that you have set. The default is 5. To learn how to change the number of undoes, refer to "Setting Preferences" in Appendix B.

- Document Color Profile displays the current color profile for the current document. To learn more about color in Illustrator, refer to Chapter 7, "Illustrator Color Basics."

Exiting Illustrator

To exit Illustrator, choose File | Exit, click the Close button at the top-right corner of the application window, or press CTRL-Q/⌘-Q or ALT+F4 (Windows only). If you have not saved your current artwork, Illustrator prompts you to save it before exiting. Click Yes to save and exit Illustrator; click No to exit Illustrator but not save; or click Cancel to return to Illustrator without exiting.

The
Complete
Reference

Adobe
Illustrator

Chapter 2

Getting Started
with Illustrator

Now that you have learned about Adobe Illustrator basics—how to launch, exit, and explore the Illustrator workspace—you are ready to discover what Illustrator actually does and how it works. At the beginning of this chapter you'll learn Illustrator's role in computer life, discover how Illustrator's vector graphics compare with raster graphics, and explore Illustrator color models. You'll also get a chance to try out particular Illustrator tools when you learn how to create and manipulate basic shapes.

Additionally, although this book looks at Illustrator comprehensively, in this chapter you'll become familiar with the features of Illustrator's help system, which will help you consider issues from different perspectives. Finally, you'll learn about basic file management in Illustrator—the file types Illustrator supports, how to manage Illustrator, and "foreign" files from within Illustrator. (You can place files from other programs into your Illustrator artwork so that you can enrich and enhance your work.)

What Is Illustrator?

Illustrator is a drawing program that uses vector graphics to produce illustrations for books, magazines, and advertising; and increasingly to create art for Web pages and other multimedia. As one application in a family of programs developed by Adobe, Illustrator works with other relatives, including Adobe Photoshop, Adobe Acrobat, Adobe InDesign, Adobe GoLive, Adobe AlterCast, Adobe LiveMotion, and several others. Illustrator also cooperates with other programs such as Macromedia Flash, Microsoft Visual Basic, and Corel Draw; technologies such as JavaScript, Visual Basic, XML, XHTML, HTML, ODBC, and CSS (Cascading Style Sheets); and standards such as CGM, EPS, GIF, JPEG, PNG, SVG, and SWF.

Vector Graphics Versus Raster Graphics

Illustrator uses *vector graphics* to produce its images. Vector graphics are created by using mathematical calculations to determine the location, span, and course of straight or curved lines. Such lines are the basis of each element of a vector-based image. A filled circle drawn in Illustrator—even when zoomed in—is smooth:

In contrast, the foundation of *raster graphics* (bitmapped graphics) are *pixels*, which are rectangular dots. Raster graphics are composed of sets of pixels arranged in grids of rows and columns; where a row and column intersects is one pixel. A strictly horizontal or vertical arrangement of pixels looks smooth. However, arcs and diagonal and circular arrangements of pixels are jagged. For example, look at this zoomed-in filled circle created in Adobe Photoshop, a raster graphics program:

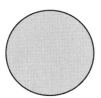

 Any slight "jagginess" of vector-based images is because computer monitors display both text and images in pixels. So, vector graphics programs such as Illustrator must convert their vector images to rasterized images for display on monitors.

Introducing Illustrator Color Models

A *color model* is a system for designating colors for process printing, graphic arts, and computer graphics. Illustrator supports the following color models: CMYK, RGB, Web-safe RGB, HSB, and grayscale.

CMYK

CMYK is an acronym that represents cyan-magenta-yellow-black, the *process colors* (subtractive primary colors) used for printing four-color separations. To the human eye, CMYK colors are produced by absorbing (that is, subtracting) light and then adding black. CMYK is the default Illustrator color model.

A closely related color model is CMY, which mixes cyan, magenta, and yellow to produce all colors, including black. In contrast, CMYK combines cyan, magenta, and yellow but uses a separate component for black.

To create a CMYK (or CMY) color, mix percentages of cyan, magenta, and yellow, which are the subtractive complements of red, green, and blue (see "RGB," which follows), respectively. Subtractive complements are produced as follows:

- 100% magenta + 100% yellow = red (the R in RGB)
- 100% cyan + 100% yellow = green (the G)
- 100% cyan + 100% magenta = blue (the B)

White and black are produced as follows:

- 100% cyan + 100% magenta + 100% yellow = black (for CMY only)
- 0% cyan + 0% magenta + 0% yellow = white

RGB

RGB, an acronym that represents red-green-blue (the additive primary colors), is the primary color model for Web graphics—especially those viewed on a monitor. To the human eye, RGB colors are produced by emitting (that is, adding) light. To create an RGB color, mix percentages of red, green, and blue, which are the additive complements of cyan, magenta, and yellow, respectively. Additive complements are produced as follows:

- 100% green + 100% blue = cyan (the C in CMYK)
- 100% red + 100% blue = magenta (the M)
- 100% red + 100% green = yellow (the Y)

White and black are produced as follows:

- 100% red + 100% green + 100% blue = white
- 0% red + 0% green + 0% blue = black (the K in CMYK)

Web-Safe RGB

Web-safe RGB is a version of RGB created to recognize the lack of unified RGB standards in the three main operating systems: Windows, Macintosh, and UNIX. For example, GIF, a common Web graphical file type, supports 256 RGB colors, but the Windows, Macintosh, and UNIX operating systems support 216 RGB colors in common.

HSB

HSB is an acronym that represents hue-saturation-brightness. *Hue* is the name of the mixed color; that is, the dominant color. *Saturation* is the amount of hue in a mixed color. The closer the gray value of a color is to white, the greater the saturation; the closer the gray value of a color is to black, the less saturation. *Brightness* (or value) is the intensity of light reflected by a mixed color.

HSB is based on a 360-degree rainbow-color wheel, with about 6–10 colors on display. Red usually is the first color followed by orange, yellow, green, cyan, blue, and magenta.

Grayscale

Grayscale ranges from white to black and all the grays between. White is at 0%; black is at 100%. During the printing process, grayscale is a strip on the side of the page that serves as a printing reference. Illustrator uses grayscale to present a monochrome graphic image.

For more information about using color in Illustrator, refer to Chapter 7. In addition, be aware that most chapters from here forward include information about how various Illustrator features and functions work with Illustrator's color models.

Creating Simple Shapes

Illustrator has tools that enable you to make and adapt simple shapes to your needs. This section introduces you to those tools, shows you the creation process step by step, and teaches you how to make simple changes to the objects that you create. As you continue working through this book, you'll learn much more about modifying both simple and complex objects.

 Note   *When you create any object in Illustrator, you actually create paths, which are the foundation of vector art. Remember that paths, which form the outline of an object, enable you to edit your artworks in the greatest detail. To learn more about paths, refer to Chapter 6.*

Drawing a Line

Illustrator has a set of tools with which you can create straight and curved lines (that is, open paths with two ends): the Line Segment tool, Arc tool, Paintbrush, Pencil, Pen, and Spiral tool. In this section you'll learn how to draw a straight line using the Line Segment tool and a curved line using the Arc tool.

To find out how to use the Paintbrush, refer to Chapter 13. Learn about the Pencil in the "Using Paths and Points" section in Chapter 6. To learn how to use the Pen tool, refer to "Drawing with the Pen Tool" in Chapter 6. You'll learn about using the Spiral tool in "Making a Spiral" later in this chapter.

Drawing a Straight Line

 Although Illustrator tools may serve the same purpose, each tool behaves differently. For example, when you use the Line Segment tool to draw a straight line, Line Segment produces a straight path with two end points, which is known as a *line segment*. So when you use Line Segment to construct more than one line, each line created is a separate straight path. Note that when you use the Pen to draw a line, you can continue to add other straight and curved lines to form an open or closed path. To learn how to use the Pen tool, refer to "Drawing with the Pen Tool" in Chapter 6.

To use the Line Segment tool to draw a straight line, follow these steps:

1. Click the Line Segment tool (or press \) to select it. Illustrator activates the tool and changes the mouse pointer to a crosshatch.

2. Move the mouse pointer to the desired starting point of the line and press and hold down the mouse button.

3. To draw a line at any angle, drag the mouse pointer to the end point and release the mouse button.

4. To draw a vertical line (90° and 270°), a horizontal line (0°, 180°, and 360°), or diagonal lines (45°, 135°, 225°, and 315°), press and hold down SHIFT while you are dragging the line to its end point; then release the mouse button.

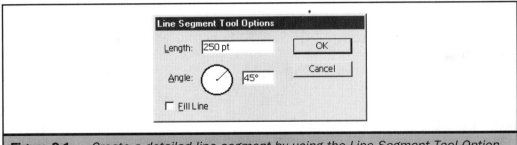

Figure 2-1.   *Create a detailed line segment by using the Line Segment Tool Option dialog box.*

You also can use the Line Segment tool to open the Line Segment Tool Options dialog box (see Figure 2-1) with which you can set the length and angle of a straight line. If you have used this installed version of Illustrator to create a line segment before either with the Line Segment tool or the Line Segment Tool dialog box, those values remain in the dialog box; otherwise Illustrator's default values appear.

To create a line segment using a dialog box, follow these steps:

1. Click the Line Segment tool to select it. Illustrator activates the tool and changes the mouse pointer to a cross-hairs mouse pointer.

2. Move the mouse pointer to the desired starting point of the line and click. Illustrator opens the Line Segment Tool Options dialog box.

3. In the Length text box, type the length, in points, of the line segment.

4. In the Angle text box, type the degree of the angle.

    Click outside the Angle text box in the dialog box to preview a line representing the current angle of the line segment.

5. Click OK. Illustrator closes the dialog box and places the line segment on the page.

Drawing a Curved Line

The Arc tool produces a curved line segment with two end points. As is the case with the Line Segment tool, each segment the Arc tool creates is a separate curved path. The Arc tool is on the Line Segment tool's Toolslot, so to select it, drag open the Toolslot, drag the mouse pointer to the Arc tool, and then release the mouse button.

To use the Arc tool to draw a curved line segment, select the Arc tool. Move the mouse pointer to the desired starting point of the line, drag to the end point, and release the mouse button. Illustrator creates the line and adds an end point to either end of the line.

You also can use the Arc tool to open the Arc Segment Tool Options dialog box (see Figure 2-2), with which you can set the length and angle of a straight line. If you have

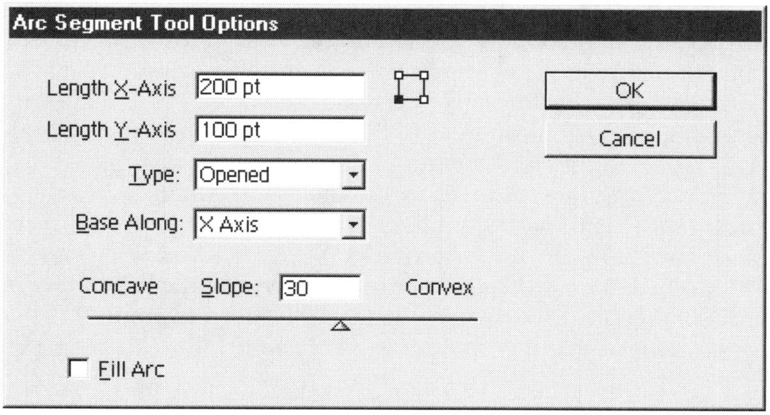

Arc Segment Tool Options

Length X-Axis [200 pt]
Length Y-Axis [100 pt]
Type: [Opened ▼]
Base Along: [X Axis ▼]

Concave   Slope: [30]   Convex

☐ Fill Arc

[OK]
[Cancel]

Figure 2-2.   Use the Arc Segment Tool Options dialog box to create an arc with specific measurements

used this installed version of Illustrator to create an arc before—either with the Arc tool or the Arc Segment Tool dialog box—those values remain in the dialog box; otherwise, Illustrator's default values appear.

To create an arc using a dialog box, follow these steps:

1. Select the Arc tool.

2. Move the mouse pointer to the desired starting point of the line and click. Illustrator opens the Arc Segment Tool Options dialog box.

3. In the Length X-Axis text box, type the length, in points, of the *x-axis* (the horizontal part of the arc).

4. In the Length Y-Axis text box, type the length, in points, of the *y-axis* (the vertical part of the arc).

5. From the Type drop-down menu, select the type of arc. For an open path, select Opened; for a closed path, select Closed.

6. From the Base Along drop-down menu, select the axis on which the arc is based: X Axis or Y Axis.

7. To slope the arc in a concave or convex shape, slide the slider between Concave and Convex or type the slope in the Slope text box.

8. Click OK. Illustrator closes the dialog box and places the line segment on the page.

Adding Arrowheads to a Line

Filters and effects alter the look of a selected object—but in different ways. *Filters* change the object permanently; the only way to reverse the alteration is to choose Edit | Undo (or press CTRL-Z/⌘-Z). Although *effects* also change an object's appearance, the original shape remains, so you can modify the effect or even delete it. So, although the Illustrator Filter and Effect menus contain many of the same commands, the end result is completely different: Filters are permanent; effects are editable.

You can add arrowheads as either filters or effects using the Add Arrowheads dialog box (see Figure 2-3). Illustrator provides 27 arrowheads, which are shown in Figure 2-4. The size of the arrowhead depends on the size of the line. If the line is wide, the arrowhead is large; if the line is narrow, the arrowhead is small.

To add an arrowhead to either or both ends of a line, follow these steps:

1. Click the line to be changed. A selected object is blue and displays its points.

2. To apply the arrowhead filter, which is a permanent addition to the line, choose Filter | Stylize | Add Arrowheads. Illustrator opens the Add Arrowheads dialog box.

3. To apply the arrowhead effect, which does not permanently affect the underlying line, choose Effect | Stylize | Add Arrowheads. Illustrator opens the Add Arrowheads dialog box again.

4. In the dialog box, click through the arrows in the Start area to be applied to the line end that you first drew: Click the left-facing arrow button to move back

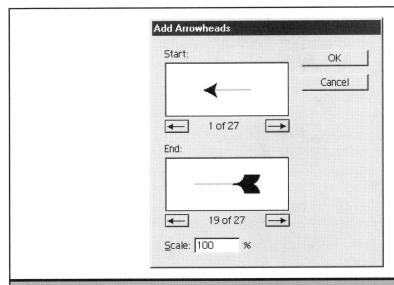

Figure 2-3.   *Choose a beginning and ending arrowhead style from the Add Arrowhead dialog box*

PRESENTING
ILLUSTRATOR

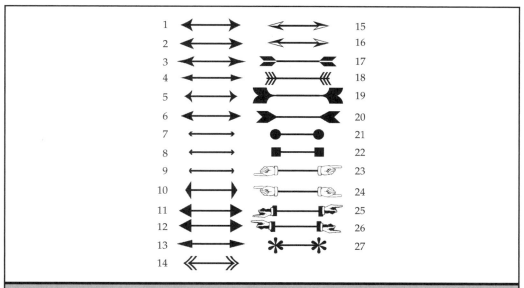

Figure 2-4.   *Illustrator's 27 different arrowhead filters on 6-point lines with the arrowheads scaled to 80%*

through the prior choices, and click the right-facing arrow button to move through the following choices. Select None to leave that end of the line without an arrowhead.

5. Click through the arrows in the End area to be applied to the line end that you last drew. Select None to leave that end of the line without an arrowhead.

6. In the Scale text box, type the size of the arrow, by percent. The default value is 100%.

7. When you have finished selecting options, click OK. Illustrator closes the dialog box and applies the arrowheads you have selected.

Tip   *One of Illustrator's great shortcut features is four special commands that make the last filter or effect available. Choose Filter | Apply Last Filter (CTRL-E/⌘-E) or Effect | Apply Last Effect (CTRL-SHIFT-E/⌘-SHIFT-E) to automatically apply the last filter or effect without changing any options. Choose Filter | Last Filter (CTRL-ALT-E/⌘-OPTION-E) or Effect | Last Effect (CTRL-SHIFT-ALT-E/⌘-SHIFT-OPTION-E) to open a dialog box (if one is available) with which you can select options for the last effect or filter to be applied to a selected object. If a dialog box is not available for a particular command, Illustrator automatically issues the menu command. The Apply command takes the name of the filter or effect that was most recently applied. So, for example, if you just added used the arrowheads filter to a line, the menu commands would be Filter | Apply Add Arrowheads (CTRL-E/⌘-E) and Filter | Add Arrowheads (CTRL-ALT-E/⌘-OPTION-E).*

You can learn much more about other filters on the Filter menu and other effects on the Effect menu (refer to Chapter 16).

Creating Rectangles and Squares

To create either a rectangle or a square, which are both closed paths without end points, use Illustrator's Rectangle tool by dragging the mouse pointer from one corner diagonally to another corner.

Drawing a Rectangle or a Square

To draw a rectangle or square, follow these steps:

1. Click the Rectangle tool, or press M.

2. Move the mouse pointer to the desired starting point of the rectangle and drag.

3. To draw a rectangle, move the mouse pointer to the desired starting point and drag the mouse pointer diagonally to the opposite corner of the rectangle. Release the mouse button to complete the rectangle.

4. To draw a square, move the mouse pointer to the desired starting point and drag the mouse pointer diagonally to the opposite corner of the square. While you drag, press and hold down SHIFT. Illustrator forces the creation of a square rather than a rectangle. Release both the button and SHIFT to complete the square.

You also can use the Rectangle tool to open the Rectangle dialog box (see Figure 2-5) with which you can set the width and height of a rectangle or square. If you have used this installed version of Illustrator to create a rectangle or square before, either with the Rectangle tool or the Rectangle dialog box, those values remain in the dialog box; otherwise, Illustrator's default values appear.

To create a rectangle or square using a dialog box, follow these steps:

1. Click the Rectangle tool.

2. Move the mouse pointer to the desired starting point of the rectangle and click. Illustrator opens the Rectangle dialog box.

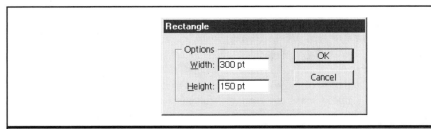

Figure 2-5.   *Specify an exact width and height of a rectangle or square using the Rectangle dialog box*

3. In the Width text box, type the width, in points, of the rectangle.

4. In the Height text box, type the height, in points, of the rectangle. (If the width and height match, a square is the result.)

5. Click OK. Illustrator closes the dialog box and draws the rectangle or square.

Rounding a Rectangle's Corners

One way to round a rectangle's corners is to draw it as a rounded rectangle. Simply select the Rounded Rectangle tool from the toolslot on which the Rectangle tool is located. However, once you have drawn a standard rectangle with the Rectangle tool, you still have the opportunity to change to rounded corners by applying an effect. (Remember that effects incorporate the change into the object, but the object's original shape remains.)

The Shape Options dialog box (see Figure 2-6) enables you to convert a rectangle to a rounded rectangle or ellipse, a rounded rectangle to a rectangle or ellipse, or an ellipse to a rectangle or rounded rectangle. If you used this installed version of Illustrator to round a rectangle, the values that you selected fill the dialog box; otherwise, Illustrator's default values appear.

To convert a rectangle's corners to rounded corners using a dialog box, follow these steps:

1. Select the rectangle to be changed.

2. Choose Effect | Convert To Shape | Rounded Rectangle. Illustrator opens the Shape Options dialog box.

3. To see the rectangle change to a rounded rectangle as you type values in the dialog box, check the Preview check box. As you type values and move the mouse to other text boxes, you get a preview of the changing rectangle.

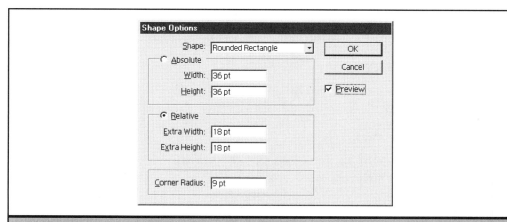

Figure 2-6. *The Shape Options dialog box enables converting the shape of rectangles, rounded rectangles, and ellipses*

4. The Absolute section of the dialog box enables you to set absolute values, in points, for the width and height of the rectangle. Type the new width in the Width text box, and type the new height in the Height text box. Typing causes the automatic selection of the Absolute radio button.

5. The Relative section of the dialog box enables adding extra width and height to the rectangle. Type the extra width in the Extra Width text box, and type the extra height in the Extra Height text box. Typing automatically fills in the Relative radio button.

6. To affect the amount of rounding of the corners, type values in the Corner Radius text box. A value of 0 points indicates unrounded corners. As you type higher numbers, the corners become rounder and eventually result in an ellipse.

7. When the selected rectangle looks as desired, click OK. Illustrator closes the dialog box and fixes the look of the newly rounded rectangle with its underlying shape on display. Figure 2-7 shows the rectangle in its original condition and after it has changed.

You can set corner rounding of a rectangle or rounded rectangle in another way: Choose Filter | Stylize | Round Corners. Then, in the Round Corners dialog box, type a rounding value in the Radius text box and click OK.

Creating Ellipses and Circles

Ellipses and circles are both closed paths—just like rectangles and squares; none of those objects have end points. To create an ellipse or a circle, use the Ellipse tool, which is on the same Toolslot as the Rectangle tool. Then, drag the mouse pointer until the ellipse or circle is the appropriate diameter.

To draw an ellipse or a circle, follow these steps:

1. Click the Ellipse tool or press L.

2. To draw an ellipse, move the mouse pointer to an edge of the new ellipse and drag away from the starting point. Release the mouse button when the ellipse is the desired size.

3. To draw a circle, move the mouse pointer to an edge of the new circle and drag away from the starting point. As you drag, press and hold down SHIFT. Illustrator compels the creation of a circle. Release the mouse button and SHIFT to complete the circle.

You also can use the Ellipse tool to open the Ellipse dialog box (see Figure 2-8) to set specific dimensions for an ellipse or a circle. If you have previously created an ellipse or a circle using the installed version of Illustrator, those values remain in the dialog box; otherwise, Illustrator's default values appear.

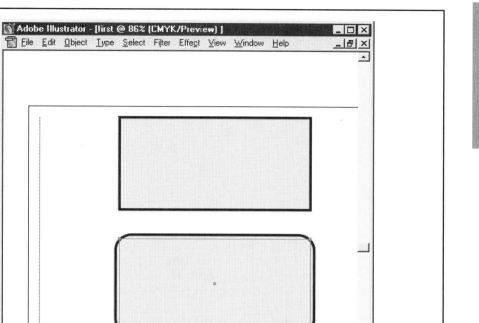

Figure 2-7. *The original rectangle changed to a rounded rectangle*

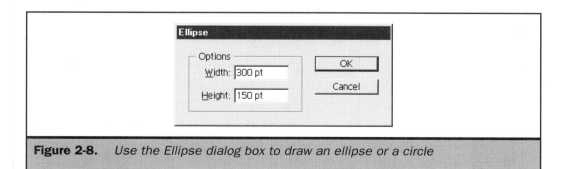

Figure 2-8. *Use the Ellipse dialog box to draw an ellipse or a circle*

To create an ellipse or circle using a dialog box, follow these steps:

1. Click the Ellipse tool.

2. Move the mouse pointer to an edge of the new ellipse and click. Illustrator opens the Ellipse Tool Options dialog box.

3. In the Width text box, type the width, in points, of the ellipse.

4. In the Height text box, type the height, in points, of the ellipse. (If the width and height match, you will create a circle.)

5. Click OK.

Drawing a Star

A star is also a closed path with no beginning and end, just like rectangles, squares, ellipses, and circles. To create a star, which can have 3 to 1,000 points, activate the Star tool, which is on the Rectangle Toolslot. Then drag the mouse pointer until the star is the appropriate diameter. When you start using Illustrator, a dragged star has 5 points. However, after you have created your first star with a certain number of points, your future stars have the same number of points—until you construct a star that has a different number of points.

To draw a star, select the Star tool from the Rectangle Toolslot, drag the mouse pointer from a starting point, and release the mouse button when the star is the desired size. As you drag a star during its creation, you can rotate it to a certain position. You also can use the following keys while you drag:

■ To create a star whose bottom points rest on an invisible horizontal line, press and hold down SHIFT while dragging.

■ To add points to a star being created, press and hold down ↑ while dragging. Illustrator continues to add points to the star until you release the key or reach the upper limit of 1,000 points.

■ To remove points from a star being created, press and hold down ↓ while dragging. Illustrator continues to remove points from the star until you release the key or reach the lower limit of 3 points.

■ To make the points grow longer while the body of the star remains the same size, press CTRL/⌘ while dragging.

■ To create a star whose points and body are completely in proportion with each other, press ALT/OPTION while dragging.

■ To create several stars simultaneously, press and hold down ` (back-tick or left single quote on the left side of the keyboard) while dragging. The result is a set of identical stars, each a separate object. To place them around the illustration window, select the Selection tool (V); then drag each star off the pile to another area of the window.

Tip	*Whenever creating several objects at once, restraint should be the rule. Consider making multiple objects in the scratch area; then drag the desired number of objects to the page and delete the rest.*

■ To move a star as you are creating it, press SPACEBAR and drag the star.

Figure 2-9 shows a variety of stars created with the help of shortcuts. You can also use the Star tool to open the Star dialog box (see Figure 2-10), which sets specific dimensions for a star. As with other Illustrator object creation dialog boxes, the Star dialog box contains the values that you have given to the prior star that you created.

To create a star using a dialog box, follow these steps:

1. Select the Star tool.

2. Move the mouse pointer to the center point of the future star and click. Illustrator opens the Star dialog box.

3. In the Radius 1 text box, type the length, in points, of the star points from the center point.

4. In the Radius 2 text box, type the distance, in points, from the center point to the outer edge of the body of the star.

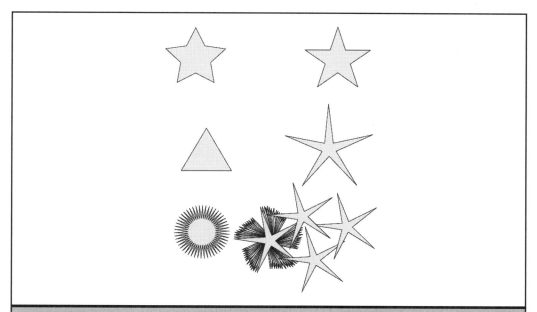

Figure 2-9.   *The left column, from top to bottom, shows a star created without the help of any key, a star with deleted points, and a star with added points; the right column contains a proportional, horizontally aligned star; a star with longer points; and a pile of stars.*

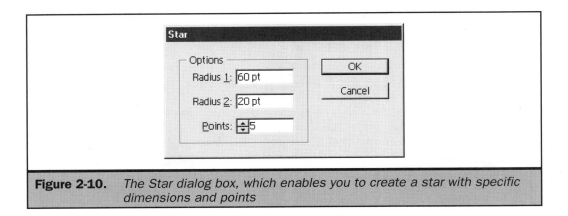

Figure 2-10. *The Star dialog box, which enables you to create a star with specific dimensions and points*

5. Either type or select the number of points in the star from the Points option/text box.

6. Click OK. Illustrator closes the dialog box and creates the star.

Making a Spiral

A spiral is a curved line that kind of goes overboard. It's an open path that is wound tightly like a watchspring or relaxed into an arc. To create a spiral, use the Spiral tool, which is in the same Toolslot as the Line Segment and Arc tools. Then, drag the mouse pointer until the spiral is the appropriate size.

To draw a spiral, select the Spiral tool, drag the mouse pointer away from the starting point, and release the mouse button when the spiral is the desired size. As you drag a spiral during its creation, you can rotate it to its desired position. You also can use the following keys while you drag:

■ To create a spiral whose trailing line is aligned to a 0°, 45°, 90°, or 135° angle, hold down SHIFT while dragging.

■ To add or delete the number of turns in a spiral, press ALT/OPTION while dragging the spiral. Drag away from the starting point to add more turns, and drag toward the starting point to delete turns.

■ To wind the spiral tighter or looser, press CTRL/⌘ while dragging.

■ To create multiple copies of a spiral, press and hold down ` while dragging. The result is a pile of identical spirals, each a separate object. To place them around the illustration window, create them in the scratch area and select them; then drag the ones that you want onto the Artboard.

■ To move a spiral as you are creating it, press SPACEBAR and drag the spiral.

Figure 2-11 shows several versions of spirals.

Figure 2-11.   *A variety of spirals, including loose and tight ones, an arc-like spiral, and a bunch of spirals*

You also can use the Spiral tool to open the Spiral dialog box (see Figure 2-12), with which you can create a spiral with attributes that you specify. If you have used the currently installed version of Illustrator to create a spiral before, those values remain in the dialog box; otherwise, Illustrator's default values appear.

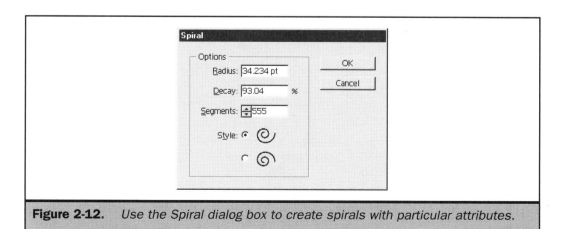

Figure 2-12.   *Use the Spiral dialog box to create spirals with particular attributes.*

To create a spiral using a dialog box, follow these steps:

1. Click the Spiral tool.

2. Move the mouse pointer to the center point of the future spiral and click. Illustrator opens the Spiral dialog box.

3. In the Radius text box, type the radius, in points, of the spiral.

4. In the Decay text box, type the tightness or looseness of the spiral, ranging from 5% to 150%. The lowest values result in an arc; the highest values result in a circle.

5. Either type or select the number of segments in the spiral from the Segments option/text box. Note that a tightly wound spiral is made up of arc segments that are one-quarter of a circle from point to point.

6. The Style radio buttons enable you to wind the spiral counterclockwise or clockwise. Click the top radio button to create a counterclockwise spiral (the default), or click the bottom radio button to coil the spiral in a clockwise direction.

7. Click OK. Illustrator closes the dialog box and creates the spiral.

Constructing a Polygon

A polygon is a multisided object with no beginning and end; therefore, it is a closed path. To create a polygon, which can range from having three (a triangle) and four (a rectangle) sides to 1,000 sides, use the Polygon tool, which is on the Rectangle Toolslot. Move the mouse pointer to the illustration window and drag the polygon until it is the desired size. Your very first polygon will have six sides unless you set a different number. However, after you have drawn a polygon with a different number of sides, Illustrator will use that value as the default until you specify a different number of sides.

To draw a polygon, click the Polygon tool, drag the mouse pointer away from the starting point on the illustration window, and release the mouse button when the polygon is the desired size. While you drag a polygon, you can rotate it to its desired position. You also can use the following keys while you drag:

- To create a polygon whose bottom points rest on an invisible horizontal line, press and hold down SHIFT while dragging.

- To add sides to a polygon, press and hold down ↑ while dragging. Illustrator adds sides to the polygon either until you release the key or reach the upper limit of 1,000 sides.

- To remove sides from a polygon, press and hold down ↓ while dragging. Illustrator removes sides from the polygon until you release the key or reach the lower limit of 3 sides.

- To create many copies of a polygon simultaneously, press and hold down ` while dragging. The result is a bunch of identical polygons, each a separate object.

- To move a completed polygon, press SPACEBAR and drag the polygon.

Figure 2-13 illustrates several versions of polygons created with and without using shortcut keys.

You also can use the Polygon tool to open the Polygon dialog box (see Figure 2-14) to set specific dimensions for the polygon. As with other Illustrator object creation tools, the dialog box contains the values that you have given to the previously created polygon using the currently installed version of Illustrator.

To use a dialog box to create a polygon, follow these steps:

1. Click the Polygon tool.

2. Move the mouse pointer to the center point of the future polygon and click. Illustrator opens the Polygon dialog box.

3. In the Radius text box type the length, in points, of a polygon side.

4. Either type or select the number of sides in the polygon from the Sides option/text box.

5. Click OK. Illustrator closes the dialog box and creates the polygon.

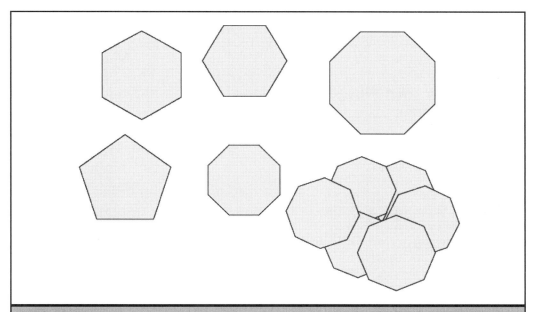

Figure 2-13.   *In the top row, a polygon constructed without pressing a shortcut, a polygon with a horizontal bottom line, and a polygon with one more side; in the bottom row, polygons with five and six sides and a bunch of polygons*

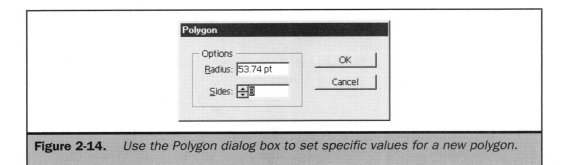

Figure 2-14. *Use the Polygon dialog box to set specific values for a new polygon.*

Managing Illustrator Files

The File menu of almost any Windows- or Macintosh-based program looks just about the same as Illustrator's File menu. You'll see several familiar commands (such as New, Open, Close, Save, Save As, and so on), which behave just about the way they do in other programs. On the other hand, some unfamiliar commands (such as Revert, Place, Document Color Mode, and others) enter the picture. This section touches some commands with which Windows and Mac users should be familiar from an Illustrator prospective and covers file management operations that are completely unique to Illustrator.

Opening Files and Placing Images

When you choose File | Open (CTRL-O/⌘-O) to open a file in Illustrator, the actual file appears in the illustration window. During the opening process, Illustrator probably performs some work on the file to enable you to edit the file. However, if you choose File | Place, you don't open a file; you insert an image of an image created in a program other than Illustrator in the Illustrator window.

A *placed image* is a representation of that foreign image. Placing an image rather than opening that same image as a file saves storage space. If you were to paste an actual image from another program into an Illustrator document, the resulting document might be very large and slow down both Illustrator and your computer. However, because a placed image is not an actual image, documents with placed images do not drastically grow in size. You'll learn more about placed images in Chapter 21.

Using a unique menu command, you can easily open any of the Illustrator documents on which you most recently worked. To do so, choose File | Open Recent Files; then select from the list of documents in the submenu.

Saving and Exporting Files

Illustrator provides four commands with which you can save your artwork and one command that enables you to export files. Choose File | Save (CTRL-S/⌘-S) to save a file that has already been given a filename. The Save command saves a file under its current name using Illustrator's .AI file type and keeps the file in the location in which you last saved it. The Save command also saves files with the PDF, EPS, SVG, and SVGZ file types.

Choose File | Save As (CTRL-SHIFT-S/⌘-SHIFT-S) to give a new file a name and location, or to provide a new name or new location for an existing file. Using the Save As command also enables you to select a non-Illustrator file type for a file that you created in Illustrator. This allows you to distribute your work to those who might create their art with another program or an earlier version of Illustrator. If you choose File | Save to save an unsaved file, Illustrator opens the Save As dialog box so that you can name the file as you save it, assign a new file type, and explicitly place the file in a particular location.

If you choose File | Save a Copy (CTRL-ALT-S/⌘-OPTION-S), Illustrator makes a copy of the file; then you can work on the copy rather than change the original. You also can make copies for specific purposes: for sending to your commercial printer or for development as a Web page.

The File | Save for Web (CTRL-SHIFT-ALT-S/⌘-SHIFT-OPTION-S) command is no surprise: It saves a file for use on the Web. Save for Web gives you the option of saving in the three most common Web graphics file types: JPEG, GIF, and PNG. When you save in a Web format, the Save for Web dialog box previews the artwork in the file type that you have chosen. When you use the Save for Web command, you can also save files with the SVG and SWF formats.

Whenever you save a file in a format that is not Illustrator's AI file type, you actually create a file for another program to use. Choosing File | Export offers you some file types that may not be available with the Save As, Save a Copy, and Save for Web commands.

Illustrator-Supported File Types

To be compatible with many other vector-based drawing programs, other programs with which Illustrator is a partner, and certain raster-based programs used for Web page development, Illustrator supports many file types for opening, placing, saving, and exporting. Illustrator does not necessarily support every single file type for every operation. Table 2-1 lists all the file types supported by Illustrator for opening, placing, saving, and exporting files. An X in a cell indicates support for opening, placing, saving, or exporting.

File Type	Extension(s)	Open	Place	Save As, Save a Copy	Save for Web	Export
Adobe Illustrator	ai	X		X		
Adobe Illustrator Encapsulated PostScript	eps, epsf, ps	X		X		
Adobe PDF	pdf	X	X	X		
Adobe Photoshop	pdd	X	X			
Adobe Photoshop	psd	X	X			X
AutoCAD Drawing	dwg	X	X			X
AutoCAD Interchange File	dxf	X	X			X
Bitmap raster graphics	bmp, rle	X	X			X
CompuServe GIF89a	gif	X	X		X	
Computer Graphics Metafile	cgm	X	X			X
CorelDRAW 5-10	cdr	X	X			
Encapsulated PostScript	eps, epsf, ps	X	X			
Enhanced Metafile	emf	X	X			X
Filmstrip	flm	X	X			
Freehand 4, 5, 7, 8, 9	fh4, fh5, fh7, fh8	X	X			
JPEG	jpg	X	X			X
Kodak PhotoCD	pcd	X	X			
Macintosh PICT	pic, pct	X	X			X
Macromedia Flash	swf					X
Microsoft RTF	rtf	X	X			
Microsoft Word	doc	X	X			

Table 2-1.   *Files Types Supported by Illustrator*

File Type	Extension(s)	Open	Place	Save As, Save a Copy	Save for Web	Export
PCX	pcx	X	X			X
Pixar	pxr	X	X			X
PNG	png	X	X		X	
SVG	svg	X	X	X	X	
SVG Compressed	svgz	X	X	X		
SWF					X	
Targa	tga, vda, icb, vst	X	X			X
Text	txt	X	X			X
TIFF	tif	X	X			X
Windows Metafile	wmf	X	X			X

Table 2-1.   *Files Types Supported by Illustrator* (continued)

Reverting to the Previously Saved File

Illustrator offers the File | Revert (F12) command, which is very similar to the Edit | Undo (CTRL-Z/⌘-Z) command. The Undo command undoes one action at a time, up to the number of undoes that you have specified (see Appendix B) or that your computer's memory will allow. Choosing the Revert command enables you to undo everything that you have done since you last saved the file; however, once you save a file you cannot undo or revert until you start working on the file again.

Getting Help

Illustrator provides help for users who know how to ask for it. To get help, open the Help menu and choose one of several commands. For example, choose Help | Illustrator Help or press F1 to open the help window, with which you can search Illustrator help topics in several ways.

If you choose Help | About Illustrator, Illustrator displays its "splash screen," featuring the *Birth of Venus* by Botticelli. The screen includes license information for your copy of the program and a list of all those people who have developed and refined the current version of Illustrator. If you wait for a few seconds, you'll see a scrolling list of developers and their jobs as well as the history of Illustrator. (You also can open the splash screen by launching Illustrator or by clicking the small Venus illustration at the top of the toolbox.)

Choosing Help | About Plug-ins opens a window with a list of Illustrator *plug-ins* (small programs that enhance one or more functions of an application in some way). Select a plug-in and click the About button to show copyright and developer information for that plug-in.

Choose Help | System Info to get information about your particular version of Illustrator, including the operating system under which Illustrator runs, the Illustrator version, the built-in memory available for Illustrator, your user name, and your Illustrator serial number.

The remaining commands on the Help menu enable you to view certain pages at the Adobe Web site. For more information about these commands, refer to "Using Online Help" later in this chapter.

Touring the Illustrator Help System

When you choose Help | Illustrator Help or press F1, Illustrator opens its help system in a browser window (see Figure 2-15) using either your default browser or whatever browser is open at the time.

With the help system in a browser window, you can take full advantage of hypertext links: Click a link to quickly display a topic or click Previous, Next, or Top to navigate the help system from the current topic.

Note
It is best to ignore most of the buttons at the top of your browser window while getting help. For example, clicking Home in your default browser results in an attempt to connect to the Web to display your default home page. Use the links in the Illustrator help window itself to move around. However, to print a topic, click your browser's Print button.

The Illustrator help window is divided into two panes: hyperlinks listed in the left pane and the currently selected topic or the introductory screen displayed on the right. Click a hyperlink in the left pane to display a topic in the right pane. Many topic pages contain links to related topics. Click a link on the topic page to replace that topic with the requested topic.

In the upper-left corner of the left pane you'll find five different ways of getting help:

- Using Help shows you how to use the help system (Using Help). Click one of the Using Help links to display related information.

- Contents enables you to click through a table of contents, the default. Click a link in the table of contents to show the associated topic.

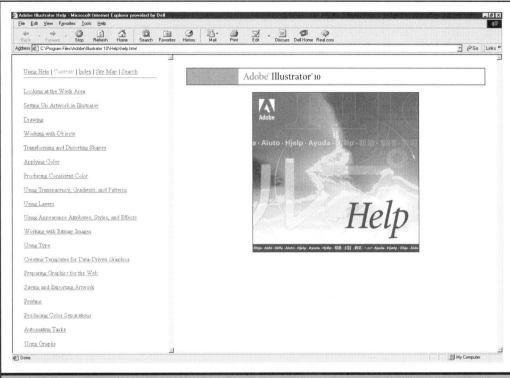

Figure 2-15. *The Illustrator help window enables you to view or search for specific topics*

- Index enables you to browse through the index. To use the index, click a letter (A, B, C, and so forth) to go to a list of topics arranged alphabetically under that letter in the left pane. Then click a link to display that topic in the right pane.

- Site Map enables you to view a site map, which lists all the Using Help, Contents, and Index topics. Once again, click a link in the left pane to reveal a topic in the right pane.

- Search enables you to look for occurrences of a particular term among all the topic pages. In the Find Pages Containing text box, type keywords or key phrases. After you click Search, Illustrator displays a related list of help topics from which you can select.

Using Online Help

Most of the commands in the Help menu bring you to pages at the Adobe Web site. Table 2-2 lists those commands and briefly describes those Web pages.

Menu Command	Connects To
Help	Top Issues	The Adobe customer support page, which enables you to access the Adobe knowledge base, training materials, forums, support personnel, and so on.
Help	Downloadables	A dialog box from which you can download updated Illustrator and other files.
Help	Corporate News	The Adobe press room from which you can read press releases and other press materials.
Help	Registration	The Adobe Registration – Registration Choice dialog box, which you can use to register your copy of Illustrator online, by fax, or by mail.
Help	Adobe Links	Home Page	The Adobe home page, which quickly or eventually leads you to any page at the Adobe Web site.
Help	Adobe Links	Store Specials	The Adobe store from which you can order Adobe products.
Help	Adobe Links	Online Services	The Adobe online services page from which you can get professional help from Adobe and its partners.
Help	Adobe Links	Free Tryouts	The Adobe product tryouts page from which you can download tryout versions (generally, you cannot save your test files).
Help	Adobe Links	Type Library	The home page of the Adobe type library from which you can buy Adobe fonts.

Table 2-2. *Illustrator Help Pages on the Web*

Menu Command	Connects To
Help | Adobe Links | ePortfolio	An Adobe careers page with links to resumés, freelance work, and design portfolios.
Help | Adobe Online	The Adobe Online dialog box that leads you to pages from which you can download updates and additional programs and plug-ins for Illustrator and your other Adobe programs.

Table 2-2.   *Illustrator Help Pages on the Web* (continued)

The Complete Reference

Chapter 3

Editing 101

With just about every Windows- and Macintosh-based application you can move around documents, alter the way you see them, and select objects to edit them in some way. Illustrator has all these capabilities, too, but some menu commands and shortcuts are unique to Illustrator.

In this chapter you will learn how to navigate, change views, and select objects. Once you know how to select objects in Illustrator, you'll learn how to manipulate them in many ways—as entire and partial paths, as groups, and even as groups of groups.

Viewing, Zooming, and Moving

Learning about the various ways you can view an Illustrator document can save you a great deal of frustration. For example, while working on a complex piece of art, you'd occasionally like to get a simplified view of the objects making up the art. Or, if you are working on a tiny detail of an artwork, being able to magnify the area could help you see the smallest changes as you make them. In contrast, if a large artwork extends beyond the visible part of the illustration window, you'd probably like to know how to view the work as a whole.

Viewing in Preview and Outline Modes

By default, Illustrator displays your artwork with all its colors and patterns; its paths are hidden within each object. This is known as Preview mode and looks like a standard piece of art (see Figure 3-1).

The counterpart to Preview mode is Outline mode, which displays the underlying structure of an Illustrator artwork—all the paths and points, center points (the axis on which it will turn if you rotate, skew, or flip it), and its type (in black rather than its original color) of each object making up the whole (see Figure 3-2).

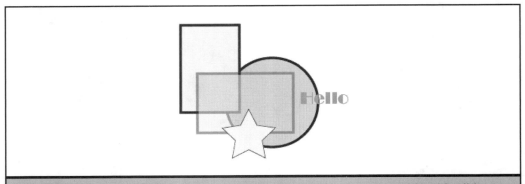

Figure 3-1.   *An Illustrator graphic in Preview mode shows the graphic with all its colors as it would print.*

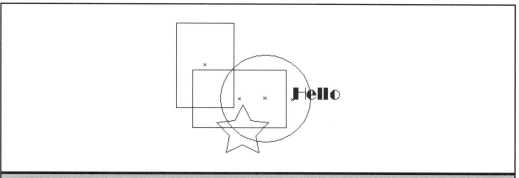

Figure 3-2.   *The same Illustrator graphic in Outline mode shows the paths, center points, and black type*

To toggle from Preview mode to Outline mode, choose View | Outline (CTRL-Y/⌘-Y). To switch from Outline mode to Preview mode, choose View | Preview (CTRL-Y/⌘-Y).

Zooming a Document

Illustrator provides many ways to *zoom,* which means to change the magnification level of the illustration window and any artwork therein. Zooming does not change the actual size of your artworks; it puts a virtual telescope into use: Look through one end to see a bigger view of the artwork and look through the other end to see a much smaller version. Zooming helps you to work more efficiently: You can examine and change the details or inspect the entire work to shift objects into better locations.

You can zoom using a variety of tools. For example, you can use the Zoom tool (and other tools), the zoom commands on the View menu or a context-sensitive menu, or the pop-up menu on the status bar.

Choosing a Preset View Size

The View menu and status bar pop-up menus enable you to adjust the illustration window to a preset size.

- Choose View | Fit in Window (CTRL-0/⌘-0) to center the artboard in the illustration window. You also can open the pop-up menu and click Fit in Window or double-click the Hand tool (H).

- Choose View | Actual Size (CTRL-1/⌘-1 on the Mac) to zoom to a 100% zoom level. Another way of zooming to 100% is to open the pop-up menu on the status bar and select 100%, or double-click the Zoom tool (Z).

Selecting the View from a List

The pop-up menu in the status bar provides a long list of zoom values ranging from a miniscule 3.13% to 6,400%, which is more than enough to see the extreme details of your work.

```
6400%
4800%
3200%
2400%
1600%
1200%
800%
600%
400%
300%
200%
150%
100%
66.67%
50%
33.33%
25%
16.67%
12.5%
8.33%
6.25%
4.17%
3.13%

Fit On Screen
```

When you select a value from the menu, Illustrator automatically zooms the illustration window to that value.

Zooming Your View

Zooming in and out with the View menu or the context-sensitive menu enables you to zoom the illustration window a large chunk at a time. For example, if you choose View | Zoom In (CTRL-+/⌘-+) when your view is at 100%, the illustration window increases to 150%, 200%, and 300% as you repeatedly choose the command. Or, if you choose View | Zoom Out (CTRL--/⌘--) at 100%, the illustration window decreases to 66.67% and then 50%.

The Zoom In and Zoom Out values match those listed on the pop-up menu, so to reach a particular zoom level without repeatedly choosing View | Zoom In or View | Zoom Out, select from the pop-up menu.

Zooming with the Zoom Tool

The Zoom tool offers a choice of zooming actions: You can use the tool with or without accompanying keystrokes. To start zooming, click the Zoom tool (Z); the mouse pointer changes to a magnifying glass with a plus sign within.

- To zoom in, move the magnifying glass pointer to a place in your artwork that will be the center of the magnified area and click. Illustrator magnifies the illustration window to the next higher level (remember the list of values in the pop-up menu).

- To zoom in on a particular area, move the magnifying glass pointer to one corner of the area to be magnified. Then drag diagonally from that corner to the opposite corner, creating a bounding box. When you release the mouse button, the desired area is increased to fit the entire illustration window.

- To zoom to the actual size (that is, 100%), double-click the Zoom tool.

 To move the bounding box while you are creating it and before you release the mouse button, press and hold down the spacebar and drag the box.

- To zoom out, press and hold down ALT/OPTION. Illustrator changes the plus sign in the zoom pointer to a minus sign. Then, move the zoom mouse pointer to a place in your artwork that will be the center of the reduced area and click.

Figure 3-3 shows a photograph zoomed in to 300%, and Figure 3-4 illustrates the same photograph zoomed out to 66.67%.

Zooming with Other Toolbox Tools

While you are using another Illustrator tool, you can temporarily replace that tool to zoom the contents of the illustration window. To zoom in, press and hold down CTRL-SPACEBAR/ ⌘-SPACEBAR. Illustrator changes the current tool to the plus-sign (+) zoom pointer. To zoom out, press and hold down CTRL-ALT-SPACEBAR/⌘-OPTION-SPACEBAR. Illustrator changes the current tool to the minus sign (–) zoom pointer. When you release CTRL-SPACEBAR/ ⌘-SPACEBAR or CTRL-ALT-SPACEBAR/⌘-OPTION-SPACEBAR, Illustrator returns to the tool that you originally selected.

Figure 3-3. *A photograph zoomed in to show the details*

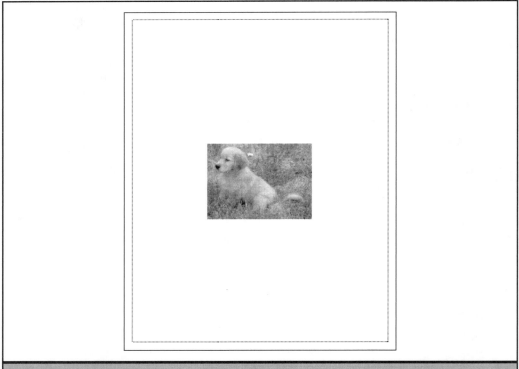

Figure 3-4.   *The same photograph zoomed out to show the layout on the page*

Exploring the Navigation Palette

Two main purposes of the Navigator palette (see Figure 3-5) are zooming and showing a thumbnail illustration of all or part of the objects in the illustration window. To toggle between showing and hiding the palette, choose Window | Navigator.

In the center of the Navigator palette is a window containing a rectangle on top of the current artwork. The rectangle indicates the portion of the artwork that is currently on view. (If you don't see the rectangle, it is larger than the window. To reveal the rectangle, zoom in.)

 You can change the dimensions of the rectangle to zoom and move the artwork at the same time. Press and hold down CTRL/⌘ *and drag the borders of the rectangle.*

You can resize the Navigator palette to make its display artwork larger or smaller. Just drag a border or corner of the palette until it and your work are the desired size.

PRESENTING ILLUSTRATOR

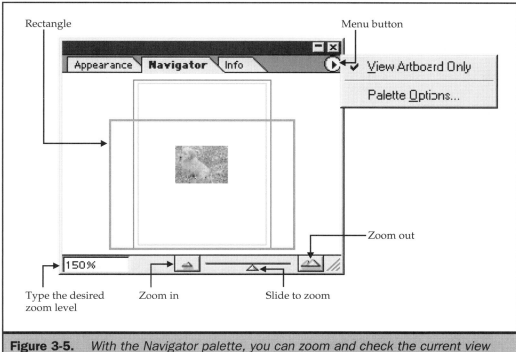

Rectangle

Menu button

Zoom out

150%

Type the desired zoom level

Zoom in

Slide to zoom

Figure 3-5.   *With the Navigator palette, you can zoom and check the current view of your art.*

To open the palette's menu, click the menu button.

■ The View Artboard Only command sets the display within the rectangle. If the command is active, the rectangle shows only the contents of the artboard; otherwise, the rectangle can include objects outside the artboard.

■ The Palette Options command opens the Palette Options dialog box with which you can change the color of the rectangle and set other display options. To learn how to customize Illustrator palettes, read "Customizing a Palette" in Appendix B.

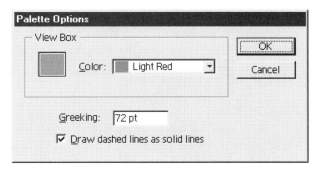

Zooming with the Navigator Palette

The bottom bar on the Navigator palette contains elements with which you can control zooming. From left to right:

- To set a specific zoom level, type a value in the zoom level text box. Then press ENTER/RETURN to apply the value.

- To zoom out to the next lower Illustrator-defined zoom percentage, click the Zoom Out button.

- To zoom in or out to levels that fall on or between the Illustrator-defined percentages, slide the Zoom slider.

- To zoom in to the next higher Illustrator-defined zoom percentage, click the Zoom In button.

Creating and Saving Custom Views

When you spend a great deal of time specifying a complex view of an artwork, you can save that view (and up to 24 more) for later use when you work on that document only. Once you have saved a custom view, Illustrator adds it to the bottom of the View menu. However, the custom view is not available for any other document. Custom views can include information about zooming and the view mode (Preview or Outline).

Creating a Custom View

To create a custom view of the current artwork, follow these steps:

1. Zoom the artwork to the desired level, and select the view mode.

2. When the artwork looks exactly the way you want it, choose View | New View. Illustrator opens the New View dialog box.

3. Type the name of the new view in the dialog box, and click OK. Illustrator adds the name of the custom view to the bottom of the View menu.

Choosing an Existing Custom View

To choose an existing custom view, select its name from the bottom of the View menu. If you plan to use this document for a long time, consider associating a shortcut key or key combination with its custom views. To learn about defining shortcuts, refer to "Defining Shortcut Keys" in Appendix B.

Editing a Custom View

Editing a custom view consists of two activities: renaming and deleting. To edit a custom view, follow these steps:

1. Choose View | Edit Views. Illustrator opens the Edit Views dialog box, which lists all the custom views created for the current document.

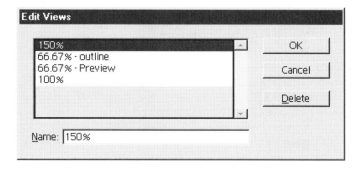

2. To rename a custom view, select it, type its new name in the Name text box, and click OK. Illustrator replaces the old name with the new name at the bottom of the View menu.

3. To delete a custom view, select it, click the Delete button, and then click OK. Illustrator removes the view name from the Edit Views dialog box and the View menu.

Moving Around a Document

When you work with a large document—especially one that is larger than the illustration window—you need to be able to move around the document from top to bottom and from left to right. Illustrator provides the following ways to navigate a document: the horizontal and vertical scrollbars, which you already know about, and the Navigator palette. To display another part of the artwork using the Navigator palette, move the mouse pointer to the rectangle and drag until the desired part of the artwork is inside the Navigator palette window.

Selecting Objects

If you could not select objects, you couldn't edit and refine them. You would be able to create things like rectangles, ellipses, and stars; but without selecting them you couldn't change their color, shape, and size, among many other things. Luckily, Illustrator provides many selection tools so you can produce the best artwork you are capable of. Illustrator enables you to select with several toolbox tools, the keyboard, and an entire menu.

Grouping and Ungrouping Objects

A *group* is a set of objects that becomes a single object for future selecting. So, once you group selected objects, you can move the group in its entirety to a new location in the illustration window or edit it as a whole. For example, you might want to create an image of a television set by creating the screen, controls, and cabinet individually. Then you'll drag each component into its proper place, select all the objects, make them into one group, and then drag the television set group, which now is a single object, into an illustration of a family room. At this point you might want to add the television set group into a home theater group, merge the home theater group with a bookcase group, and so on.

Illustrator is programmed to remember the components of each group and the hierarchy of groups within groups, so if you wish to ungroup several nested groups, you can—in the reverse order in which they were grouped. For example, you might want to ungroup the bookcase group, then the home theater group, and finally the television set group to design a new set of knobs for the television set image. After you change the knobs, you could regroup each group again.

To group a set of selected objects, choose Object | Group (CTRL-G/⌘-G). To ungroup one group, choose Object | Ungroup (CTRL-SHIFT-G/⌘-SHIFT-G). So, if an artwork is made up of nested groups, you will have to ungroup them one group at a time.

To test whether an object is part of a group, click it with the Selection tool or the Group Selection tool (V). You'll learn about using these tools later in this chapter.

The Anatomy of a Selection

In Illustrator it's important to be able to select the item that you actually want to select and to know what that selection should look like. For example, to apply an effect or a filter to a single line segment, you don't want to choose the entire object; you want to select only the line segment you want to modify. Illustrator provides a set of features with which you can select part or all of a path, an entire path, a group of paths, and groups of groups. This section shows you what certain selections look like.

 Beware that although you select a particular part of a path, Illustrator does not always allow you to edit just that portion. As you go through the book, you will learn more about what you can and cannot do with selections.

Viewing the Selection of One Point or Segment

In Illustrator you can select one or more points or one or more segments within a path. It's easy to spot selected and unselected anchor points: Selected anchor points are filled-in rectangles; unselected points are not filled in. Figure 3-6 shows you a polygon with one point chosen (on the left side of the figure) and the same polygon with two points, which equals one line segment, chosen (on the right).

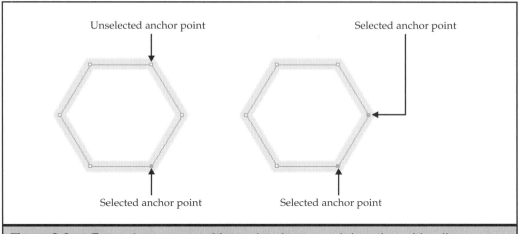

Figure 3-6.   *Two polygons, one with a point chosen and the other with a line segment chosen*

Viewing the Selection of a Path

When you select one or more paths, every anchor point in those paths is filled in. Figure 3-7 illustrates a single selected polygon on the left and one selected polygon among several polygons on the right.

Viewing the Selection of a Group

When you group paths, the result is a single object. Figure 3-8 demonstrates that you can select a group as a whole. Note that every anchor point is filled in the selected group. You will learn how to group paths later in this chapter.

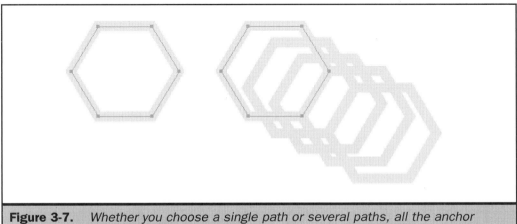

Figure 3-7.   *Whether you choose a single path or several paths, all the anchor points are filled in.*

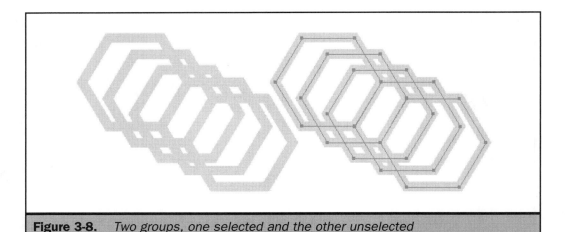

Figure 3-8.   *Two groups, one selected and the other unselected*

Viewing the Selection of Groups and Paths

With Illustrator, you can perform miracles of selecting: You can select entire groups
and paths within groups. Figure 3-9 shows three groups, the leftmost group completely
unselected, the rightmost group entirely selected, and the middle group with two
objects selected.

Selecting with Toolbox Tools

Illustrator provides six selection tools on the toolbox: Selection (V), Direct Selection (A),
Group Selection, Direct Select Lasso (Q), Lasso, and Magic Wand (Y). Each tool has its
own specific purpose, although some of those purposes overlap. This section covers
each tool and discusses how each works.

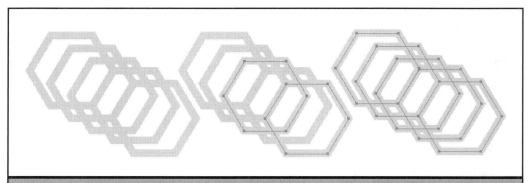

Figure 3-9.   *Three groups, one not selected, one with two selected objects, and one
selected in its entirety*

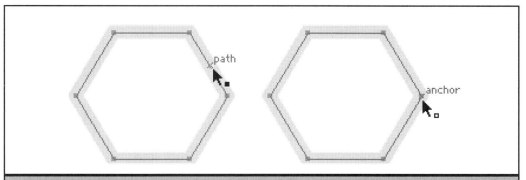

Figure 3-10. *The polygon on the left shows a pointed-to path; the one on the left illustrates a pointed-to anchor point.*

As you move the mouse pointer around an object, Illustrator can indicate with Smart Guides the pointed-to paths and points (see Figure 3-10 above) with small labels. Note that when you point to a path, Illustrator adds a small filled-in rectangle to the end of the mouse pointer and when you point to an anchor point, Illustrator adds a small unfilled-in rectangle. When you see the desired label, click to select the labeled object. As you learn more about editing, you'll find out about other labels that Illustrator displays on or near a selected object. (For more information on Smart Guides refer to Chapter 5.)

Selecting with the Selection Tool

The Selection tool (V), which is always active when you launch Illustrator, works in three ways: You can click to select an object (that is, a path or group), drag a *marquee* or *bounding box* (a dotted line that you draw to enclose a selection), or drag an object. You cannot use the Selection tool to select part of an object.

To use the Selection tool to enclose an object with a marquee, move the mouse pointer outside the object to be selected. Then drag the marquee in the same way that you would create a rectangle (move to the opposite corner of the marquee), as shown in the following illustration.

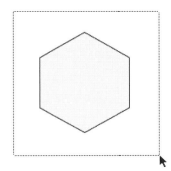

When the dotted line encloses all or part of all the objects that you want to select, release the mouse button. Illustrator selects all the objects completely or even partly within the marquee. To use the Selection tool to drag an object, move the mouse pointer within the path or group or on its border. Then drag the object to a new location in the illustration window.

You also can use the Selection tool in conjunction with keys:

- To toggle between the Selection tool and the Direct Selection tool (if the Direct Selection tool is on the toolbox), press CTRL-TAB/⌘-TAB.

- To toggle between the Selection tool and the Group Selection tool (if the Group Selection tool is on the toolbox), press CTRL-TAB/⌘-TAB.

- To temporarily select the selection tool (Selection, Direct Selection, or Group Selection only) that you used most recently when you are using any tool but a selection tool, press and hold down CTRL/⌘.

- To add one path to or remove one selected path from a selection, move the mouse pointer to the desired path. Then press SHIFT and click the path while the Selection tool is active.

- To create a copy of an object, drag while pressing and holding down ALT. Illustrator leaves the original object in its original location and places the copy when you stop dragging and pressing ALT.

- To delete a selected object, press DEL. (To undo a deletion, press CTRL-Z/⌘-Z.)

Selecting with the Direct Selection Tool

The Direct Selection tool (A), which is the default tool in its toolslot, enables you to select individual points and segments of paths by clicking or dragging a marquee. You also can use the Direct Selection tool to select objects that are not paths: placed images and type (text) objects.

To use the Direct Selection tool to select a point or path, click the point or path. One or two rectangles indicate the selection fill. (Other unselected points have unfilled rectangles.) If all points fill, click outside the object and try again. Figure 3-11 shows two objects: an unselected rectangle and a rectangle with one point selected and dragged to make an irregularly shaped polygon.

To use the Direct Selection tool to select using a marquee, drag the marquee. When you release the mouse button, Illustrator selects all points, paths, placed images, and text objects within the marquee. To use the Direct Selection tool to drag an object, move the mouse pointer within the object—away from any points or paths—and move the object to its new location.

You also can use the Direct Selection tool with keys:

- To toggle between the Direct Selection tool and the Selection tool, press CTRL-TAB/⌘-TAB.

- To cycle between the Direct Selection tool and the Group Selection tool, press and hold down CTRL-ALT/⌘-OPTION, and repeatedly click the active tool.

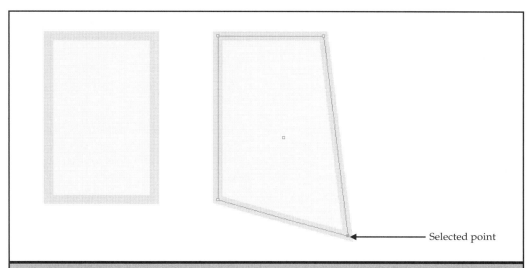

Figure 3-11. *An odd-looking polygon results when you select one point at the lower-right corner of the rectangle and drag.*

- To temporarily select the selection tool (Selection, Direct Selection, or Group Selection only) you used most recently when you are using any tool but a selection tool, press and hold down CTRL/⌘.

- To add one path or point to or delete one selected path or point from the selection, press and hold down SHIFT and click the path or point while the Direct Selection tool is active.

- To create a copy of an object, drag while pressing and holding down ALT. Illustrator leaves the original object in its original location and places the copy when you stop dragging and pressing down ALT.

- To delete the paths running from a selected point to unselected points, press DEL. For example, if you select one point on a rectangle and press DEL, the rectangle becomes a triangle. The three unselected points remain as do the paths that run between those points.

Selecting with the Group Selection Tool

The Group Selection tool, which shares a toolslot with the Direct Selection tool, accumulates selections each time you click starting with an entire path, then an entire group, a group of groups, groups that encompass groups of groups, and so on. Figure 3-12 illustrates the results of the first, second, and third clicks.

To use the Group Selection tool to select using a marquee, drag the marquee. When you release the mouse button, Illustrator selects all points, paths, placed images, and text objects within the marquee.

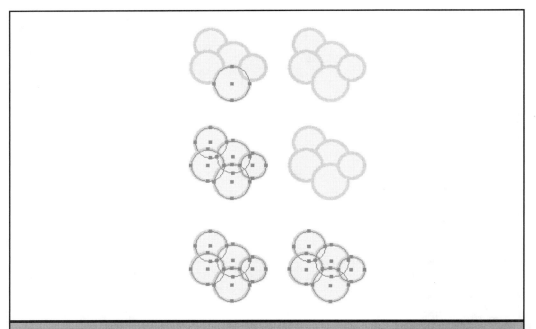

Figure 3-12. *From the top, selecting a path, a group, and a group of two groups*

You also can use the Group Selection tool with keys:

■ To toggle between the Group Selection tool and the Selection tool, press CTRL-TAB/⌘-TAB.

■ To temporarily select the selection tool (Selection, Direct Selection, or Group Selection only) you used most recently when you are using any tool but a selection tool, press and hold down CTRL/⌘.

■ To cycle between the Group Selection tool and the Direct Selection tool, press and hold down CTRL-ALT/⌘-OPTION and repeatedly click the active tool.

■ To add one path or point to or delete one selected path or point from the selection, press and hold down SHIFT and click the path or point while the Group Selection tool is active. However, with SHIFT pressed down, the Group Select tool acts as if it were the Selection tool or Direct Selection tool: It no longer continues selecting from path to group to a group of groups.

■ To create a copy of an object, drag while pressing and holding down ALT. Illustrator leaves the original object in its original location and places the copy when you stop dragging and pressing down ALT.

■ To delete the selected path or group, press DEL.

Selecting with the Direct Select Lasso Tool

The Direct Select Lasso tool (Q), which is the default tool in its toolslot, is a close relative of the Direct Selection tool (A): You use the tool to select single points and path segments by creating a marquee. The primary difference is in the marquee: Rather than a rectangular marquee, you draw an irregular marquee. You also can use the Direct Select Lasso tool to select placed images and type objects.

To select with the Direct Select Lasso tool, draw a marquee to include the area you want to select. When you release the mouse button, Illustrator selects all points, paths, placed images, and text objects within the marquee. So, you can drag a small marquee around a single point or a very large marquee around the entire contents of the illustration window.

You can also use the Direct Select Lasso tool with keys:

- To add one path or point to the selection, press and hold down SHIFT and click the path or point while the Direct Select Lasso tool is active. While this version of the tool is active, Illustrator adds a small plus sign icon to the mouse pointer.

- To delete one selected path or point from the selection, press and hold down ALT and drag the path or point while the Direct Select Lasso tool is active. While this version of the tool is active, Illustrator adds a small minus sign icon to the mouse pointer.

- To delete the paths running from a selected point to unselected points, press DEL.

Selecting with the Lasso Tool

The Lasso tool, which shares a toolslot with the Direct Select Lasso tool and behaves in much the same way, also is a close relative of the Selection tool (V). To use the Lasso tool, draw a marquee around the area that you want to select. Illustrator selects any object partly or completely within the marquee.

You also can use the Lasso tool in conjunction with keys:

- To add one path to or remove one selected path from a selection, move the mouse pointer to the desired path. Then press SHIFT and click the path while the Lasso tool is active.

- To cycle between the Direct Select Lasso tool and the Lasso tool, press and hold down CTRL-ALT/⌘-OPTION and repeatedly click the active tool.

- To delete a selected object, press DEL.

Selecting with the Magic Wand Tool

The Magic Wand tool (Y) selects objects based on one or more of the following attributes: the fill color, the stroke color and weight, the level of opacity or transparency, and the blending mode (see Figure 3-13). For example, if you want to reduce the stroke weight of every object having a stroke weight of 15 points or above, you can select all these objects after selecting options on the Magic Wand palette and clicking your Magic

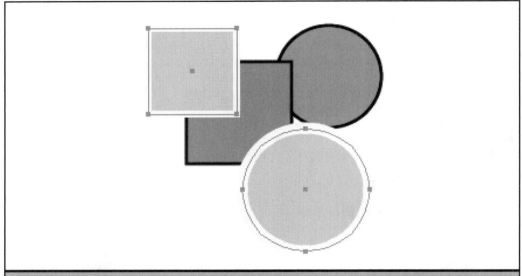

Figure 3-13.   *The Magic Wand selected two objects with the same light fill and stroke colors, but ignored two other objects.*

Wand. Or, if you want to change all objects filled with green to light blue, adjust the Magic Wand palette settings and click the Magic Wand.

Use the Magic Wand palette to select attributes and levels of tolerance. The more attributes you select and tolerances you set, the more precise is the level of selection.

Exploring the Magic Wand Palette

The Magic Wand palette (see Figure 3-14) and Magic Wand (Y) tool work together, as you might guess from their names. Use the Magic Wand tool to select objects whose similar characteristics you set with the Magic Wand palette. To toggle between showing and hiding the palette, choose Window | Magic Wand.

Four of five components in the Magic Wand palette work in the same way: Check a box to select a particular attribute and then either click the right-pointing arrow on the right side of the Tolerance slider/text box to open and slide the Tolerance slider or type a value in the Tolerance check box. Of course, when you check more boxes, the Magic Wand tool is more discerning in choosing related objects. You can set tolerances for the following characteristics of objects in your artwork:

The fill color of an object is the color inside the path. Fill color tolerances range between 0 and 100, where 0 is the most sensitive to fill color differences (that is, fewer like objects are chosen) and 100 is the least sensitive (that is, most like objects are selected). The default tolerance is 20. This section of the palette is always available.

The stroke color of an object is the color of the path itself. Stroke color tolerances range between 0 and 100, where 0 is the most sensitive to stroke color differences and

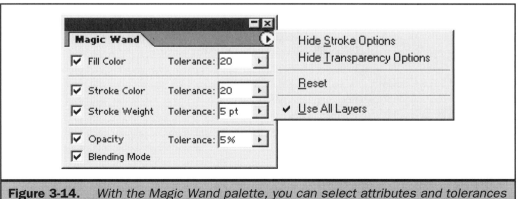

Figure 3-14.   *With the Magic Wand palette, you can select attributes and tolerances for the Magic Wand tool.*

100 is the least sensitive. The default tolerance is 20. For this option to be available, you must have chosen Show Stroke Options from the palette's menu.

The stroke weight of an object is the width of the path. Stroke weight tolerances range between 0 pt and 1,000 pt, where 0 pt is the most sensitive to stroke weight differences and 1,000 pt is the least sensitive. The default tolerance is 5 pt. The default tolerance is 20. For this option to be available, you must have chosen Show Stroke Options from the palette's menu.

The opacity of an object is the percentage of transparency. Opacity tolerances range between 0% and 100%, where 0% is the most sensitive and 100% is the least sensitive. The default opacity is 5%. For this option to be available, you must have chosen Show Transparency Options from the palette's menu.

The *blending mode* of an object is the mix of the color of the original object and the color of the final object in a blend. To include the blending mode in the Magic Wand tool selection, check the Blending Mode box. For this option to be available, you also must have chosen Show Transparency Options from the palette's menu.

To open the palette's menu, click the menu button.

■ The Show/Hide Stroke Options command displays or hides the stroke section of the palette.

■ The Show/Hide Transparency Options command displays or hides the transparency section of the palette.

■ If you choose the Reset command, all the tolerance values return to the Illustrator defaults.

■ The Use All Layers command enables the Magic Wand tool to evaluate and possibly select objects from every layer in the artwork. If the command is not checked (that is, inactive), the Magic Wand tool works on the current layer only. To learn more about layers, refer to Chapter 14, "Working with Layers."

Selecting with Menu Commands

Illustrator dedicates an entire menu to selecting. With commands on the Select menu, you can select all the objects in the illustration window, deselect or reselect a selection, inverse a selection, or select objects based on their positions in an artwork or certain attributes. You also can save and edit selection criteria.

Selecting All Objects at Once

You can select every object in the illustration window—regardless of whether they are on the artboard or in the scratch area. To do so, choose Select | All (CTRL-A/⌘-A).

Deselecting a Selection

Regardless of whether you have selected objects with toolbox tools, shortcut keys, or commands from the Select menu, you can quickly reverse all current selections by choosing Select | Deselect (CTRL-SHIFT-A/⌘-SHIFT-A). If nothing in the illustration window is selected, the Deselect command is dim.

If you change your mind about selecting or deselecting, choose Select | Reselect (CTRL-6/⌘-6), which is like an undo operation for selecting. The Reselect command reverts to the most recent selection. Note that in previous versions of Illustrator, the Reselect command was Edit | Select | Select Again.

Inversing a Selection

What if you want to deselect a selection and select any unselected objects or groups? You can do this in one operation by choosing Select | Inverse. If you have selected every object in the illustration window, the Inverse command deselects every object. If you have selected some objects, those objects are no longer selected and every object that was previously unselected is now selected.

Selecting Objects by Position

When you add an object to the illustration window, Illustrator places it above other objects previously added. The first object added is considered to be below the rest. However, if you rearrange objects so that newly added objects are above or below others, you change the position. The objects that you have placed below the others are at the bottom, and those that you have moved forward are above most or all the others.

You can deselect a selected object and select another object depending on their current positional relationship to each other. To select the next higher object in the total order of objects, choose Select | Next Object Above (CTRL-ALT-]/⌘-OPTION-]). If there is no higher-level object, the current selection remains. To select the next lower object, choose Select | Next Object Below (CTRL-ALT-[/⌘-OPTION-[). If there is no lower-level object, the current selection remains. You'll learn about rearranging the order of objects in the "Arranging Objects and Groups" section later in this chapter.

Command	Selects Based On
Select | Same | Blending Mode	Almost the same blending mode
Select | Same | Fill & Stroke	Almost the same fill and stroke characteristics
Select | Same | Fill Color	Almost the same fill color
Select | Same | Opacity	Almost the same level of opacity
Select | Same | Stroke Color	Almost the same stroke color
Select | Same | Stroke Weight	Almost the same stroke weight
Select | Same | Style	Almost the same defined style with a specific fill color, stroke color, and stroke weight
Select | Same | Symbol Instances	Almost the same symbol occurrences

Table 3-1.   *The Same Submenu Commands*

Selecting Similar Objects

Before the Magic Wand tool and palette, Illustrator provided a set of commands to
select similar objects. On the Select submenu of the Edit menu, the Same... commands
enabled users to select several objects at a time based on their similarities in style, fill
and stroke, fill and stroke colors, stroke weight, blending mode, and opacity. Now
these commands are on the Same submenu of the Select menu. Table 3-1 above briefly
describes each of these commands.

Illustrator's magic wand commands are new and improved along with the new
capabilities provided by the Magic Wand tool and palette.

Hiding and Showing Objects

If the illustration window holds a great number of objects, you might want to temporarily
remove some large objects from view to edit others that might be beneath. You can
conceal selected objects by choosing Object | Hide | Selection (CTRL-3/⌘-3). This command
completely hides selected objects; the mouse pointer doesn't change when you move it
over hidden objects, you cannot select them, and you can't print them. Obviously, if an
object is hidden you can't work on it in any way. Hiding objects is in effect only during
the current work session. When you close Illustrator and then relaunch it, all hidden
objects are unhidden.

Once you hide one or more objects, you cannot hide others: Illustrator dims the commands on the Hide submenu. The only way to hide additional objects is to reveal all hidden objects, select all the objects you want to hide, and then choose Object | Hide | Selection (CTRL-3/⌘-3) again. To simultaneously unhide all hidden objects and select them, choose Object | Show All (CTRL-ALT-3/⌘-OPTION-3).

Illustrator provides two other commands on the Hide submenu: All Artwork Above and Other Layers. If you want to hide all the objects above a particular object, select that object and choose Object | Hide | All Artwork Above.

When you become more proficient in Illustrator, you'll work with *layers*. A layer is a single level of an artwork. Every piece of Illustrator art starts on one layer. However, as your artwork becomes more complex, you can either remain with one layer or overlay the work with another layer. One layer might contain the background, one or two might include an intricate illustration, and another might include a paragraph or two of type.

Layers are like the plastic sheets in some anatomy books: Each of the bottom layers might contain certain inner organs and the skeleton and the top layers might show the skin, arms, legs, and facial features. The major advantage of layers is that you can work on one layer without disrupting any other. To hide all layers but the one you are working on, choose Object | Hide | Other Layers. If your artwork consists of one layer, Illustrator ignores the Other Layers command. To learn more about layers, refer to Chapter 14.

Locking and Unlocking Objects

When you lock an object, you can still see it in the illustration window but you cannot select, edit, or move it. However, you can print it. So when a piece of art is complete, consider locking it to prevent inadvertent modification, moving, or resizing within an area that must conform to specific dimensions. Because locking prevents selection, you can lock an object to choose paths in the object underneath. To lock selected objects, choose Object | Lock | Selection (CTRL-2/⌘-2). When you close Illustrator and then relaunch it, all locked objects remain locked. To unlock locked objects, choose Object | Unlock All (CTRL-ALT-2/⌘-OPTION-2). If no objects are locked, the Unlock All command is dimmed and not available.

Illustrator provides two other commands on the Lock submenu: All Artwork Above and Other Layers. If you want to lock all the objects above a particular object, select that object and choose Object | Lock | All Artwork Above. To lock all layers but the one you are working on, choose Object | Lock | Other Layers. If your artwork consists of one layer, Illustrator ignores the Other Layers command.

Aligning and Distributing Objects

You can use the Align palette to align and distribute objects from a point that is determined either by the location of all the objects in the illustration window or by the dimensions of the page. To align and distribute objects, select one or more objects; then click a button in the Align palette.

The Align palette is just one of several ways to align objects in Illustrator. You'll learn how to align with the grid in the "Snapping to the Grid" section in Chapter 5, with guides in "Using Guides to Set Up Your Art" in Chapter 5, with Smart Guides in "Using Smart Guides" in Chapter 5, and how to align paragraphs in "Modifying Paragraph Attributes" in Chapter 12.

Exploring the Align Palette

The Align palette (see Figure 3-15) contains a grand total of 12 buttons and one option/drop-down list box. This all looks complicated but is much easier once you find out what all these elements do. To toggle between showing and hiding the palette, choose Window | Align (SHIFT-F7).

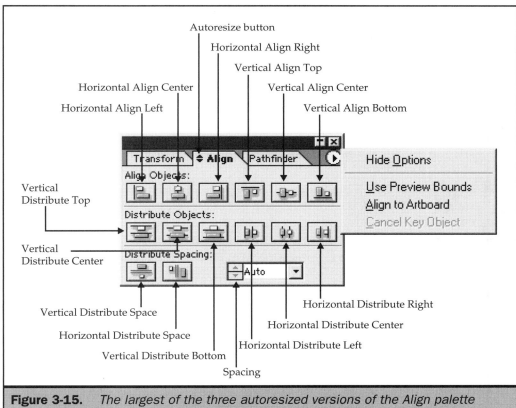

Figure 3-15.   *The largest of the three autoresized versions of the Align palette*

The top row of buttons on the Align palette align one or more selected objects either horizontally or vertically.

- Click Horizontal Align Left to align the selected objects either with the leftmost point in those objects or with the left edge of the artboard.
- Click Horizontal Align Center to center the selected objects with the horizontal center point in those objects or centered horizontally in the artboard.
- Click Horizontal Align Right to align the selected objects either with the rightmost point in those objects or with the right edge of the artboard.
- Click Vertical Align Top to align the selected objects either with the topmost point in those objects or with the top edge of the artboard.
- Click Vertical Align Center to center the selected objects with the vertical center point in those objects or centered vertically in the artboard.
- Click Vertical Align Bottom to align the selected objects either with the bottommost point in those objects or with the bottom edge of the artboard.

The second row of buttons distribute selected objects vertically (from top to bottom) or horizontally (from left to right). When Illustrator *distributes* objects, it places them equally distant from one another.

- Click Vertical Distribute Top to distribute the selected objects vertically starting from either the topmost point in the selected objects or from the top edge of the artboard.
- Click Vertical Distribute Center to distribute the selected objects vertically starting from either the vertical center point in the selected objects or the center of the artboard.
- Click Vertical Distribute Bottom to distribute the selected objects vertically starting from either the bottommost point in the selected objects or the bottom edge of the artboard.
- Click Horizontal Distribute Right to distribute the selected objects horizontally starting from either the rightmost point in the selected objects or the right edge of the artboard.
- Click Horizontal Distribute Center to distribute the selected objects horizontally starting from either the horizontal center point in the selected objects or the center of the artboard.
- Click Horizontal Distribute Left to distribute the selected objects horizontally starting from either the leftmost point in the selected objects or the left edge of the artboard.

The third row of buttons sets spacing between selected, distributed objects. Use the drop-down option/text box to set or type the spacing, or select Auto to have Illustrator automatically set the spacing. The default spacing is Auto.

- Click Vertical Distribute Space to set spacing between vertically distributed objects.
- Click Horizontal Distribute Space to set spacing between horizontally distributed objects.

To open the palette's menu, click the menu button.

- The Show/Hide Options command either shows or hides the Distribute Spacing section of the palette.
- The checked Use Preview Bounds command aligns paths and factors in the stroke weights, too. If this command is unchecked, Illustrator aligns based only on the paths.
- The active Align to Artboard command sets alignment within the artboard. If the command is inactive, the selected objects are aligned or centered between the leftmost and rightmost sides of all the selected objects.
- The Cancel by Key Object command enables you to select a key object out of a selection of several objects and then base alignments and distributions on the key object.

Aligning Objects

Now that you have learned about the Align palette, it's time to see how it aligns objects. To align objects with the Align palette, follow these steps:

1. Select the objects to be aligned.
2. Choose Window | Align (SHIFT-F7) to open the Align palette.
3. To align the selected objects within their selection's outer dimensions, open the palette menu and make sure Align with Artboard is not selected.
4. To align the selected objects with the artboard, ensure that Align with Artboard is selected.
5. Click one or more of the buttons in the top row of the Align palette.

Note   *To reverse an alignment, choose Edit | Undo (CTRL-Z/⌘-Z).*

Figure 3-16 shows a succession of alignments. The artboard on the left shows several selected rectangles. The largest was created first, so it is at the bottom of the order. The smallest was created last, so it is at the top. The center artboard shows what

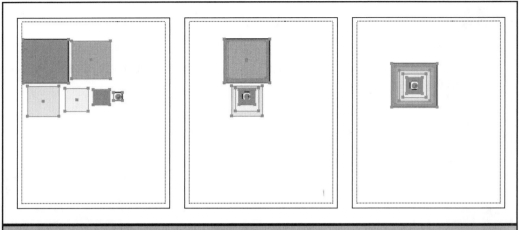

Figure 3-16. *The progression of rectangles horizontally aligned and then vertically aligned*

happens when you click the Horizontal Align Center button: The rectangles are centered between the leftmost and rightmost sides of all the selected objects. The artboard on the right illustrates the result of clicking Vertical Align Center: All the rectangles are centered from top to bottom. They are piled on each other, and all the center points are in the same location.

Distributing Objects

Distribution works much differently from alignment. The distribution buttons on the Align palette control the placement of selected objects along a horizontal or vertical plane. To distribute objects with the Align palette, follow these steps:

1. Select the objects to be distributed.
2. Choose Window | Align (SHIFT-F7) to open the Align palette.
3. To distribute the selected objects within their selection's outer dimensions, open the palette menu and make sure Align with Artboard is not selected.
4. To distribute the selected objects with the artboard, ensure that Align with Artboard is selected.
5. Click one or more of the buttons in the second row of the Align palette.

Note *To reverse a distribution, choose Edit | Undo (CTRL-Z/⌘-Z).*

Figure 3-17 shows a horizontal distribution aligned to the artboard. The artboard on the left shows several small, undistributed rectangles soon after they were created. The artboard on the right illustrates the result of clicking Horizontal Distribute Center: All the

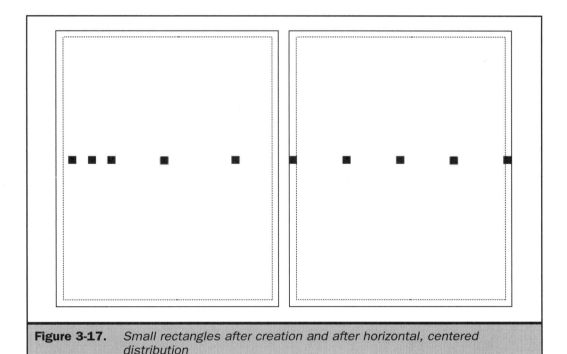

Figure 3-17.   *Small rectangles after creation and after horizontal, centered distribution*

rectangles are centered from left to right. The leftmost and rightmost rectangles are aligned with the artboard edges, and the center rectangle is in the center of the artboard.

Arranging Objects and Groups

In "Selecting Objects by Position," earlier in this chapter, you learned how the order in which objects are created or arranged in an artwork affects selecting and grouping objects. What if you create an object that will replace an earlier one? Or what if you want to determine the order of objects that you have added in a different order? Illustrator provides four commands with which you can rearrange objects and groups:

- Object | Arrange | Bring to Front (CTRL-SHIFT-]/⌘-SHIFT-]) moves the selected object in front of all other objects in the illustration window.
- Object | Arrange | Bring Forward (CTRL-]/⌘-]) shifts the selected object ahead one position, but not necessarily to the front of all the other objects.
- Object | Arrange | Send Backward (CTRL-[/⌘-[) repositions the selected object back one position, but not necessarily behind all the other objects.
- Object | Arrange | Send to Back (CTRL-SHIFT-]/⌘-SHIFT-]) moves the selected object all the way to the back of all the other objects.

Figure 3-18 contains four artboards containing objects that are 75% opaque. The upper-left artboard shows the original image with four objects: the largest, a square, is in the back; the object that is just forward of the square is a circle; the next higher object is a polygon; and the top object is a star. The upper-right artboard shows the star sent to the back (Object | Arrange | Send to Back). Now the polygon is in the front with the circle underneath and the square between the polygon and the star. The lower-left artboard illustrates the circle in the front (Object | Arrange | Bring Forward); it moves forward one place. The remaining artboard shows the star back in front (Object | Arrange | Bring to Front) with the polygon and circle below and the square in the back. In Chapter 14 you'll learn how to rearrange objects using layers.

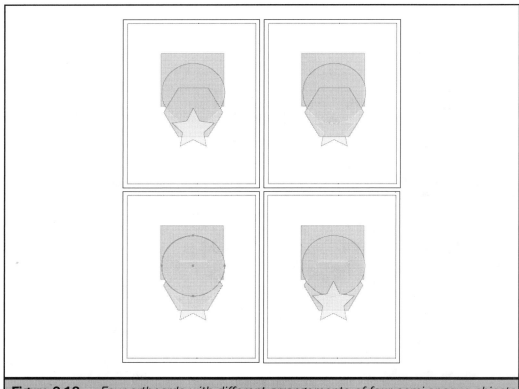

Figure 3-18.   *Four artboards with different arrangements of four semi-opaque objects*

The
Complete
Reference

Chapter 4

Building Graphs

A *graph* is a pictorial representation of related data. It presents text and numbers in a format that is easy to read and to understand. In fact, a graph might enable you to spot a trend over time or a relationship between the data being presented. Graphs are important enough to the Illustrator development team that one toolslot contains nine graphing tools. Illustrator's graphing feature also includes commands on the Object menu. In this chapter you will learn all about creating and editing graphs in Illustrator.

Note that as you read through future chapters, you will find out how to enhance all your artwork, including graphs, with the vast variety of other Illustrator features. At the end of this chapter you will see examples of graphs that have been embellished using Illustrator features.

Learning about Types of Illustrator Graphs and Tools

Illustrator tools enable you to create nine popular graph types. This section discusses the Graph Type dialog box with which you can change from one type of graph to another as well as set options, which change depending on the selected graph type. This section also summarizes Illustrator graph types and discusses the options that you can select for each type.

Exploring the Graph Type Dialog Box

Illustrator provides distinctive versions of Graph Type dialog boxes for either changing to or editing most graph types. Each dialog box has a row of buttons and a Value Axis drop-down list box in the Type section, which enables you to choose the location of the value axis: on one side or on both sides. (If you choose On Both Sides, Illustrator creates two value axes, each with a different scale of values.) Each also has the same four check boxes in the Style section. However, the options in the Options section vary for most graph types. Figure 4-1 illustrates the Graph Type dialog box for a column graph.

Note   *Graphs have two or three axes. The x-axis is the horizontal axis, usually used for time or area data. The y-axis is the vertical axis, usually used for units of measure (for example, years, weights, and currency). In Illustrator, the y-axis is commonly known as the value axis, and the x-axis is generally the category axis.*

PRESENTING
ILLUSTRATOR

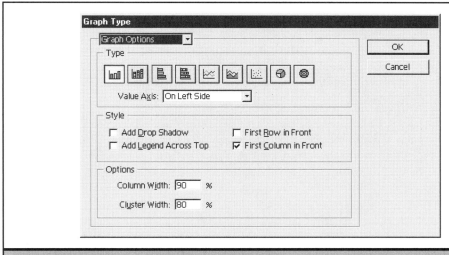

Figure 4-1.   *The Graph Type dialog box for a column graph*

The common options in the Graph Type dialog box are as follows:

- In the Type section, click one of the nine graph-type buttons to change the current graph type. When you click, the dialog box changes to reflect the options for the new graph type.

- In the Type section, accept Illustrator's choice of the value axis location or select from the drop-down list. The *value axis* is the side on which values (rather than time periods) are graphed. Note that pie graphs do not include a value axis, and radar graphs have value axes on all sides.

- If you check the Add Drop Shadow box, Illustrator adds a drop shadow to the graph.

- If you check Add Legend Across Top, Illustrator places the *legend* at the top of the graph. The legend, which is the key to the graph, shows each data series and its associated color or pattern.

- If you check First Row in Front or First Column in Front (the default), Illustrator overlaps rows or columns, respectively, whenever the opportunity to overlap presents itself.

Column Graphs

A vertical column graph, Illustrator's default, shows individual values in a series of columns over a specific time period. The columns in this type of graph enable you to visually compare values very easily. Enter positive or negative numbers column by column. Use the Column Graph tool (J) to create a graph with vertical columns.

In the Graph Type dialog box, column graph options are as follows:

- Use Column Width to specify the width of each column. If the column width is 100%, each column touches both the preceding and following columns. Percentages less than 100% decrease the column width. A value of more than 100% overlaps the columns. Valid values for Column Width range from 1% to 1,000%; the default is 90%.

- Use Cluster Width to specify the width of each cluster of columns. If the cluster width is 100%, each cluster touches both the prior and following clusters. Percentages less than 100% decrease the cluster width. Percentages greater than 100% overlap the clusters. Valid values for Cluster Width range from 1% to 1,000%; the default is 80%.

Stacked Column Graphs

A vertical stacked column graph shows the relationship of each value in a column to the whole rather than as a set of individual columns as in column graphs. Use the Stacked Column Graph tool to create a graph with stacked vertical bars. Enter positive or negative numbers column by column. In the Graph Type dialog box, the options for stacked column graphs are the same as those for column graphs.

Bar Graphs

The horizontal bar graph shows individual values in a series of horizontal columns. This type of graph emphasizes the progress of time. Enter positive or negative numbers row by row. Use the Bar Graph tool to create a bar graph with horizontal bars.

In the Graph Type dialog box for bar graphs, bar-graph options are as follows:

- Use Bar Width to specify the height of each bar. If the bar height is 100%, each bar touches both the prior and following bars. Percentages less than 100% decrease the bar height. A value of over 100% overlaps the bars. Valid values for Bar Width range from 1% to 1,000%; the default is 90%.

- Use Cluster Width to specify the height of each cluster of bars. If the cluster height is 100%, each cluster touches both the prior and following clusters. Percentages less than 100% decrease the cluster height. Percentages greater than 100% overlap the clusters. Valid values for Cluster Width range from 1% to 1,000%; the default is 80%.

Stacked Bar Graphs

A horizontal stacked bar graph also shows the relationship of each value in a column to the whole. Enter positive or negative numbers row by row. Use the Stacked Bar Graph tool to create a graph with stacked horizontal bars. In the Graph Type dialog box, the options for stacked bar graphs are the same as those for bar graphs.

Line Graphs

A line graph shows one or more series of individual data points over time. Each set of related data points is joined by a line, and every line is a different color. Enter positive or negative numbers that signify quantities column by column and time periods row by row. Line graphs illustrate subtle trends and changes better than column graphs. Use the Line Graph tool to create a line graph.

In the Graph Type dialog box for line graphs, line-graph options are as follows:

- Check Mark Data Points to place small squares at each data point. A cleared check box allows Illustrator to mark data points merely by changing direction of the line that attached one point to another in the graph.

- Check Edge-to-Edge Lines to extend the lines on the left and right of the graph beyond the first and last data points, respectively.

- Check Connect Data Points to draw lines between each data point and the next. Without this box checked (the default), the resulting graph wouldn't look like a line graph.

- Check Draw Filled Lines to fill the line with the legend color for that set of data points and to emphasize the line by making it heavier and black.

Area Graphs

Like the line graph, an area graph shows one or more series of data points over a period of time. However, the filled part (the area) of the graph emphasizes the total more than a line graph, which accentuates the data series. Enter all positive or all negative numbers that signify quantities column by column and time periods row by row. Use the Area Graph tool to create a graph that shows both individual data and the totals of that data. The Graph Type dialog box does not provide options for area graphs. You must always select either First Row in Front or First Column in Front for an area graph; otherwise, Illustrator might not display all areas.

Scatter Graphs

Scatter or XY graphs show data points drawn from the horizontal (x) and vertical (y) axes. If the data points form a line, the two sets of values correlate. If the data points are scattered around the chart, the two sets of values do not correlate. Enter numbers in both the columns and rows; labels are ignored. Use the Scatter Graph tool to create a scatter graph.

In the Graph Type dialog box for scatter graphs, line graph options are as follows:

- Check Mark Data Points to place small squares at each data point. A cleared check box allows Illustrator to mark data points by changing direction of the line that attached one point to another in the graph.

- Check Connect Data Points to draw lines between each data point and the next. Without this box checked (the default), the resulting graph wouldn't look like a line graph.

- Check Draw Filled Lines to fill the line with the legend color for that set of data points and to emphasize the line by making it heavier and black.

Pie Graphs

Pie graphs show one row of all positive or all negative data as a slice of a pie. The entire graph represents the total of all the slices. Use the Pie Graph tool to create a pie graph.

In the Graph Type dialog box for pie graphs, line graph options are as follows:

- From the Legend drop-down list box, select Standard Legend (which is like a legend for any other graph), Legends in Wedges (a legend on each wedge), or No Legend at all. Standard Legend is the default.

- From the Position drop-down list box, select Ratio (the default), Even, or Stacked. Ratio sizes each graph proportionally, Even makes all graphs the same size, and Stacked stacks multiple pie graphs on top of each other and sizes them proportionally.

- From the Sort drop-down list box select All, First, or None (the default). All sorts the pie wedges from the highest to the lowest value, First sorts wedges so that the highest value is in the first wedge and the lowest value is in the last wedge, and None places values in the order you entered them.

Radar Graphs

Radar charts, which are also known as web graphs (from spider webs—not the World Wide Web) are related to both line and area graphs. However, values are clustered in a circle around the center of the graph. Enter labels in the first column and numbers in the remaining rows. Use the Radar Graph tool to create a radar graph. In the Graph Type dialog box, the options for radar graphs are the same as those for line graphs.

Planning a Graph

When you plan a graph, consider the purpose of the graph, the data to be presented, and the type of graph that would best illustrate the data. Perhaps the two most important questions to ask are "What do I want to prove to my audience?" and "What data do I want to show them?" Only you can answer those questions.

When choosing the data to be included in a graph, keep everything parallel. For example, do not treat details and totals as equals. Choose the appropriate totals or suitable details. Omit data that is not important for this particular graph.

As a final point, make sure you match the data with the proper graph type. Do you want to emphasize the data, the totals, or both? Do you want to prove that the data is closely correlated? Once you have selected the graph type, be aware that you don't have to stay with it. Illustrator enables you to switch graph types quite easily.

Viewing the Graph Data Dialog Box

Each graph needs data to make it viable. To enter data for an Illustrator graph, use the Graph Data dialog box (see Figure 4-2), which actually is a small *spreadsheet* window with an entry line and buttons across the top. A spreadsheet is made up of *rows, columns,* and *cells.* Rows run horizontally, and columns run vertically; rows and columns meet to form cells. Each cell holds one piece of data. Although Illustrator does not require it, you should label your data. So, the top row of a spreadsheet labels each column, and the leftmost column labels each row. Illustrator column labels are known as *legend labels*; row labels are known as *category labels.*

Tip *If you want to use a number as a label, enclose it within quotation marks or single quote marks; otherwise, Illustrator will think you are entering data.*

Illustrator enables you to create a spreadsheet up to 32,767 rows and 32,767 columns—depending on your computer's memory. However, if you plan to fill a vast number of cells, you should use a standard spreadsheet program and import the data into an Illustrator graph. In fact, it's not a good idea to create any graph based on a large number of data. The graph would be much too big to be easy to view and understand.

Whether you enter a label or data in a cell, select the cell and type the label or data information in the entry line in the Graph Data dialog box. Once you have completed typing a label or data for one cell, press ENTER, TAB, or an arrow key to move to another cell. Pressing ENTER enters the label or data in the cell and selects the cell below the cell you just filled. Pressing TAB enters the information and selects the cell to the right of the cell that you filled. The up, down, left, and right arrow keys enter the information and then select the cell above, below, to the left, and to the right, respectively. You also can click a particular cell to select it.

 Caution *Do not add separators, such as commas, or decimal points to numbers. Illustrator converts numbers only into graph elements; it is not programmed to understand non-numbers (such as separators and decimal points).*

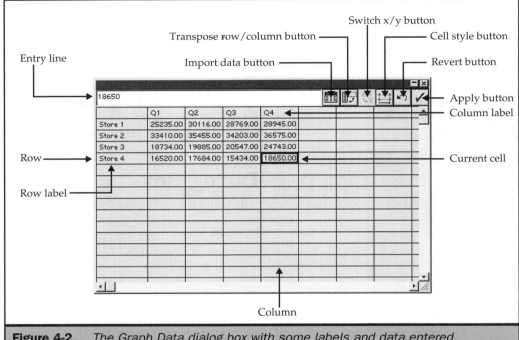

Figure 4-2. The Graph Data dialog box with some labels and data entered

The buttons in the Graph Data dialog box behave as follows:

■ To import a data file, open the Import Graph Data dialog box by clicking the Import Data button. You'll learn more about importing in "Importing a Spreadsheet," later in this chapter.

■ Click the Transpose Row/Column button to switch the columns to rows and the rows to columns. All the data moves with the rows and columns.

■ Click the Switch x/y button to switch the x-axis to the y-axis and the y-axis to the x-axis. This button is available only for scatter graphs.

■ Click the Cell Style button to open the Cell Style dialog box to set the number and width of the column, in digits. Valid values for Number of Decimals range from 0 to 10, and valid values for Column Width range from 0 to 20.

Note | *You also can change the width of a column by moving the mouse pointer to the border between the column to be adjusted and the column adjacent on its right. Once the mouse pointer changes to a double-arrow, drag the current column until it is the desired width. You cannot change the height of rows.*

■ Click the Revert button to return the Graph Data dialog box to its starting condition, with 1.00 in the top corner cell, or revert to the last data that you applied to a graph. Note that you can undo the entry of information one cell at a time.

■ Click the Apply button to signal that you have finished entering data and to instruct Illustrator to create the graph. The Graph Data dialog box remains onscreen.

■ Click the Close button in the upper-right corner of the dialog box to signal that you have finished entering data, and to instruct Illustrator to create the graph and close the dialog box.

Creating a Graph

You can create a graph in three ways:

■ Drawing the outline of a graph and then selecting the options
■ Selecting options and then drawing the graph
■ Entering graph dimensions in the dialog box

Whichever way you create the graph, you must open a new or existing document first.

Creating a Graph by Drawing It First

When you draw a graph before filling it in, you actually drag its shape in the same way that you would create a rectangle or ellipse. Then you use dialog boxes to fill in the data and select options specific to the type of graph.

To create a graph by drawing it first, follow these steps:

1. Click one of the nine graph tools to select the initial graph type. A cross-hairs mouse pointer appears in the illustration window.

2. To draw the graph as you would a rectangle, drag diagonally from the starting point to the opposite corner. When you release the mouse button, Illustrator opens the Graph Data dialog box.

3. To draw the graph as you would an ellipse, press and hold down ALT/OPTION while dragging; the center point is clearly in the middle of the graph. When you release ALT/OPTION and the mouse button, Illustrator opens the Graph Data dialog box.

4. Fill in the row labels, column labels, and the data. Then click the Apply button.

5. If you like the look of the graph in the illustration window, click the Close button to close the Graph Data dialog box.

6. Optionally, open the Graph Type dialog box and modify the graph.

7. Save the graph document and then continue to edit the graph using other Illustrator features.

Creating a Graph by Selecting Options First

When you construct a graph in a spreadsheet, you provide the labels and data before commanding the program to create the graph itself. Then you can modify the graph by resizing it, editing and adding components, and changing the way it looks. When you select Illustrator graph options first, you are following that traditional graph creation route.

To create a graph by selecting options first, follow these steps:

1. Double-click a graph tool or choose Object | Graph | Type. Illustrator opens the Graph Type dialog box.

2. If the button for the graph type that you want to create does not look as if it is pressed down, click the appropriate button. Illustrator might change the contents of the Graph Type dialog box.

3. Select other graph options and click OK. A cross-hairs mouse pointer appears in the illustration window.

4. To draw the graph in the illustration window as you would a rectangle, drag diagonally from one corner to the opposite corner. When you release the mouse button, Illustrator opens the Graph Data dialog box.

5. To draw the graph in the illustration window from the center of the graph, press and hold down ALT/OPTION while dragging. When you release ALT/OPTION and the mouse button, Illustrator opens the Graph Data dialog box.

6. Fill in the row labels, column labels, and the data. Then click the Apply button.

7. If you like the results in the illustration window, click the Close button. Illustrator closes the Graph Data dialog box.

8. Save the graph document and then continue to edit the graph using other Illustrator features.

Creating a Graph with a Dialog Box

As you learned in Chapter 2, the toolbox tools with which you create rectangles, ellipses, and so on have associated dialog boxes you can use to produce an object with exact dimensions. Each graphing tool also is accompanied by a dialog box. As with the other dialog boxes you learned about, Illustrator fills in the width and height of the

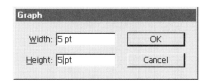

graph that you most recently created. It's up to you to either accept the starting dimensions or change to a new width, height, or both.

To create a graph by using a dialog box, follow these steps:

1. Click a graph tool. A cross-hairs mouse pointer appears in the illustration window.
2. Click the illustration window. Illustrator opens the Graph dialog box.

3. Fill in the width and height in the dialog box, and click OK.

 Be sure you specify width and height dimensions that are large enough to result in a graph of proper size. Remember that 72 points equal an inch, so a graph that is 5 inches wide and 4 inches high would be 360 points wide by 288 points high.

4. In the Graph Data dialog box, fill in the row labels, column labels, and the data. Then click the Apply button.
5. If you like the look of the graph in the illustration window, click the Close button to close the Graph Data dialog box.
6. Optionally, open the Graph Type dialog box and modify the graph.
7. Save the graph document and continue to edit the graph using other Illustrator features.

Looking at an Illustrator Graph

Depending on the graph type, most graphs—regardless of whether you create them in Illustrator—start with almost the same components (see Figure 4-3). The most important difference between most graphs and Illustrator graphs is that in Illustrator, each component is a path. So, you can select all or some paths of a graph in order to make modifications.

 Earlier in this chapter you learned about three graph components: the x-axis, y-axis, and legend. Other graph elements include the plot and tick marks. The plot *is the core of the graph; the columns, bars, lines, areas, or slices of pie that present the data. Each column, bar, line, area, point, or entire pie chart is based on one row or column of data. A* tick mark *is a little horizontal or vertical line that identifies a value on one of the axes.*

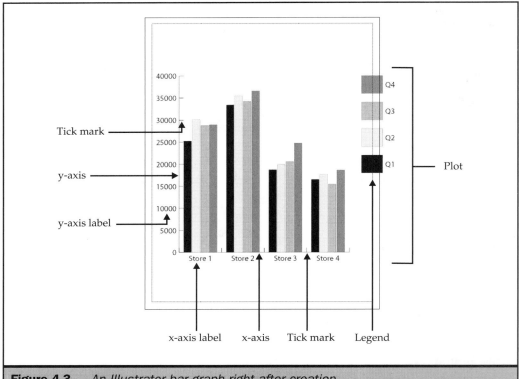

Figure 4-3.   *An Illustrator bar graph right after creation*

Selecting All or Part of a Graph

Because an Illustrator graph is made up of paths, you must make selections as you would other Illustrator paths with various toolbox tools. You can select an entire graph, a data series (a set of data from one column or one row, depending on the graph type), or a single component.

After you select a data series or entire graph, consider grouping it (choose Object | Group or press CTRL-G/⌘-G) before you start editing. This is a safeguard to prevent Illustrator from formatting or changing one value rather than a set of values. Remember that you can ungroup a group by choosing Object | Ungroup (CTRL-SHIFT-G/⌘-SHIFT-G).

To select an entire graph, choose the Selection tool (V) and then click any component within the graph.

To select one component and add more and more selections from a graph, choose the Group Selection tool. Click a column, bar, or line once to select it. Click the same column, bar, or line again to select the entire data series (all related columns, bars, or lines). To extend the selection to all columns, bars, or lines, click again. Continue to click to add to the selection.

To select an entire data series with the Group Selection tool, click the legend related to that data set twice (more slowly than a double-click).

To select type in a graph, choose the Group Selection tool. Click once to select the baseline under the type; click again to select the baseline and the type as well.

To deselect a path, choose the Direct Selection tool (A). Press and hold down SHIFT and click the selection to be deselected.

Modifying a Graph

After you have created a graph you can modify it using menu commands; for example, you can change the graph type for the entire graph or for a particular data series. You also can edit a graph's data.

Changing the Graph Type

Changing the type for an entire graph might involve more than just selecting a command. For example, switching from a column graph to a stacked column graph or changing a bar graph to a stacked bar graph is simple: You do not have to trade the x-axis for the y-axis and the y-axis for the x-axis. Illustrator is intelligent enough to know that it has to change axes when you switch from a column graph to a bar graph. However, you have to use your knowledge of graphs to choose an appropriate graph type. For example, a line graph, which demonstrates trends, might not be as good as a bar graph or column graph at showing individual values.

Sometimes you might improve on a graph by changing a particular data series to another graph type. Once again, it's your call.

To change a graph type, follow these steps:

1. Select the entire graph or a data series.

2. Choose Object | Graph | Type, right-click and select Type, or double-click a graphing tool on the toolbox. Illustrator opens the Graph Type dialog box (refer to see Figure 4-1).

3. Click a graph-type button in the Type section.

4. Select any options that you want to apply; then click OK. Illustrator closes the dialog box and changes the type for the graph or data series.

Editing Graph Data

What if one of your colleagues (or even you) has furnished incorrect data for a graph? It's easy to edit the data in a graph. Just follow these steps:

1. Select the entire graph.

2. Choose Object | Graph | Data, or right-click and select Data. Illustrator opens the Graph Data dialog box (refer to Figure 4-2).

3. Select the cell that contains a value to be changed.

4. Type the replacement value in the entry line.

5. Repeat steps 3 and 4 as needed.

6. After you have completed your modifications, click either the Apply button to apply the data and keep the dialog box open or the Close button to apply the data and close the dialog box.

Figures 4-4 and 4-5 show graphs that have been created and enhanced using Illustrator. Figure 4-4 starts with the column graph shown in Figure 4-3. Then, perform the following actions on the graph:

1. Select the Type tool (T) and add a comma and dollar sign to each value in the y-axis.

2. With the Direct Selection tool (A), select the rectangle preceding the Q1 label, press and hold down SHIFT, and select Q1. Then, drag to the left edge of the page above the graph. Repeat these steps to rearrange each of the legend items.

3. With the Group Selection tool, click one bar three times to select the first data series and its legend item. Choose Window | Swatches. Then click a swatch to apply its color to the data series and legend item. Repeat for the other three data series.

4. Select the Type tool (T) again to add a title to the graph. Click the upper-left corner of the graph and type the title.

5. With the Select tool (V), select the title.

6. While the title is selected, choose Window | Type | Character (CTRL-T/⌘-T) to open the Character palette. Select a font such as Lucida Sans and 24 pt to slightly increase the size of the title. Then, drag the title to a better location within the artboard.

7. The *pièce de résistance* is adding a drop shadow. First, activate the Group Selection tool. Click a column three times to select all the columns and the boxes in the

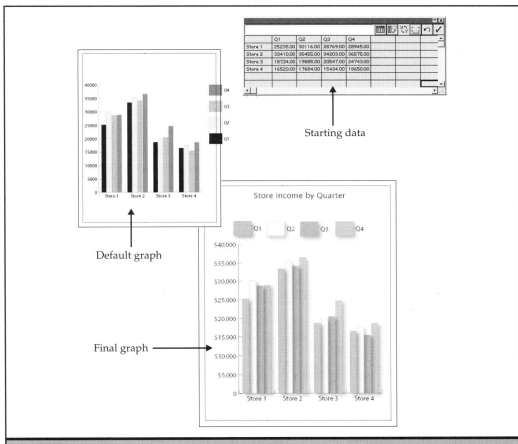

Figure 4-4. *The sequence of starting data, a default column graph, and the enhanced graph*

legend. Then, choose Effect | Stylize | Drop Shadow. When the Drop Shadow dialog box opens, click OK to apply the default drop shadow to the columns and legend boxes.

Figure 4-5 shows a pie graph created within Illustrator and enhanced using the following actions:

1. With the Group Selection tool, click three times to select the graph without also selecting the labels. Then use the Scale tool (S) to flatten the pie graphs and to pull them from the center of the artboard toward the edges.

2. Use the Rectangle tool to create a rectangle that is much narrower than pie graphs and centered under one of the pie graphs.

3. Use the Direct Selection tool (A) to select the top-left anchor point. Drag the anchor point toward the left until it reaches the left edge of the chosen pie graph. Then use the Direct Selection tool to select the top-right anchor point. Drag that anchor point toward the right until it reaches the right edge of the graph.

4. Use the Direct Selection tool to select the rectangle-turned-polygon.

5. Choose Window | Swatches. Then click a pie-crust color (yellow, tan, or yellow-orange) to fill the polygon. Keep the Swatches palette open.

6. Use the Direct Selection tool to select the polygon, if it is not already selected. Choose Edit | Copy (CTRL-C/⌘-C) to copy the polygon. Choose Edit | Paste (CTRL-V/⌘-V) to paste the polygon into the illustration window. Move the polygon onto one of the pie graphs. Repeat the paste operation. Move the polygon onto the remaining pie graph.

7. Use the Direct Selection tool while pressing and holding down SHIFT to select all three polygons. Choose Object | Arrange | Send to Back (CTRL-SHIFT-[/⌘-SHIFT-[) to send the polygons behind the pie graph.

8. Click the Group Selection tool and click a wedge twice to select all three wedges. Click a swatch to change the color of the wedge. Repeat this for the other sets of wedges.

9. With the Direct Selection tool (A), drag the labels under the graphs apart and over each pie.

10. Using the Direct Selection tool (A) and pressing and holding down SHIFT, select all the labels on the wedges and increase their point size to 12 pt.

11. Make two rectangles—one around the pies and one touching and underneath the first rectangle. Select the top rectangle and click a gray swatch to fill the rectangle. Select the bottom rectangle and click a lighter gray swatch to fill that rectangle.

12. Draw a rectangle around the longest label above the pie graphs. Choose Window | Stroke (F10) and make the stroke 2 pt. Choose Object | Arrange | Send to Back (CTRL-SHIFT-[/⌘-SHIFT-[) to send the rectangle behind the label.

13. Use the Direct Selection tool (A) to select the rectangle. Choose Edit | Copy (CTRL-C/⌘-C) to copy the rectangle.

14. Choose Edit | Paste (CTRL-V/⌘-V) to paste the rectangle into the illustration window. Center the rectangle over another label above a pie graph. Choose Object | Arrange | Send to Back (CTRL-SHIFT-[/⌘-SHIFT-[) to send the rectangle behind the label. Repeat this step for the remaining label.

PRESENTING
ILLUSTRATOR

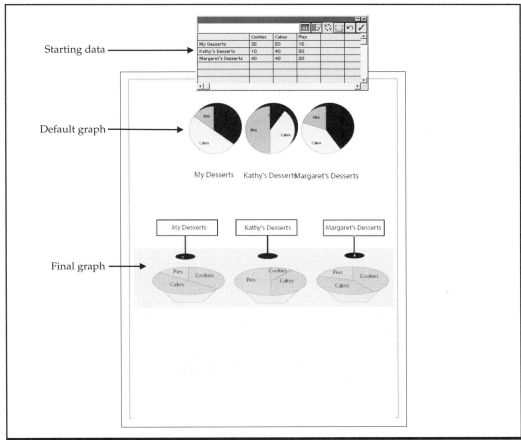

Starting data

Default graph

Final graph

Figure 4-5. *The progression of the data with which a basic pie graph is created, the graph itself, and the enhanced graph*

15. With the Ellipse tool (L), draw a filled ellipse immediately above a pie graph. Select the ellipse and choose Edit | Copy (CTRL-C/⌘-C) to copy the ellipse.

16. Choose Edit | Paste (CTRL-V/⌘-V) to paste the ellipse into the illustration window. Center the ellipse above another pie graph. Repeat this step for the remaining ellipse.

17. With the Line Segment tool (\), draw a line between the label and the ellipse. Repeat for the other two labels.

Editing an Axis

You can use the Graph Type dialog box to modify the value and category axes. Remember that the value axis usually shows values such as years and currency, and the category axis usually illustrates time or area data. Illustrator enables you to change the value and category axes for most graphs, with the following exceptions: Radar graphs have a value axis but no category axis; scatter graphs have a bottom axis, which has the same options as those for the value axis, and no category axis; and pie graphs have no axes at all.

Modifying the Value Axis

To modify the value axis (or the bottom axis for a scatter graph), follow these steps:

1. Select the graph to be modified.

2. Choose Object | Graph | Type or right-click and select Type. Illustrator opens the Graph Type dialog box.

3. From the drop-down menu at the top of the dialog box, select Value Axis (or Bottom Axis for a scatter graph). Illustrator opens the Value Axis section of the Graph Type dialog box, as shown in Figure 4-6.

4. To explicitly set minimum and maximum values, and sections between tick marks, check the Override Calculated Values check box and then type values in the Min, Max, or Divisions text box. Do not add commas or decimal points.

5. To set the length of tick marks, open the Length drop-down menu and select None (no tick marks), Short (short tick marks), or Full Width (tick marks that are the width of the graph). Short is the default.

6. To insert extra tick marks between the default tick marks at the division indicator, type a number in the Draw text box.

7. To insert a prefix (such as a currency symbol) before a label, type it in the Prefix text box.

8. To insert a suffix (even a space), type it in the Suffix text box.

9. When you have completed selecting or typing, click OK to close the dialog box and apply the changes.

Modifying the Category Axis

To modify the category axis, follow these steps:

1. Select the graph to be modified.

PRESENTING
ILLUSTRATOR

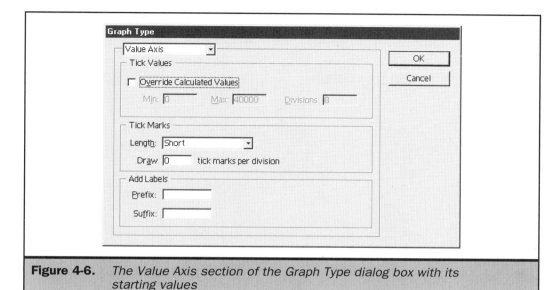

Figure 4-6.   *The Value Axis section of the Graph Type dialog box with its starting values*

2. Choose Object | Graph | Type or right-click and select Type. Illustrator opens the Graph Type dialog box.

3. From the drop-down menu at the top of the dialog box, select Category Axis. Illustrator opens the Value Axis section of the Graph Type dialog box, as shown in Figure 4-7.

4. From the Length drop-down menu, select the length of tick marks: None (no tick marks), Short (short tick marks), or Full Width (tick marks that are the width of the graph). Short is the default.

5. To insert extra tick marks between the default tick marks at the division indicator, type a number in the Draw text box. In addition, check the Draw Between Tick Marks check box.

6. When you have completed selecting or typing, click OK to close the dialog box and apply the changes.

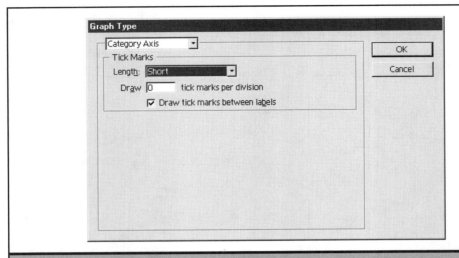

Figure 4-7.   *The Category Axis section of the Graph Type dialog box showing its default options*

Importing a Spreadsheet

To this point in the chapter, you have gotten an all-around education in most of the Illustrator graphing features, including a tour of both of the important graphing dialog boxes: the Graph Type dialog box and the Graph Data dialog box. When you already have a spreadsheet created in a spreadsheet program, why reenter it into Illustrator's Graph Data dialog box? Instead, you can import the information into the Illustrator Graph Data dialog box.

To import information into an Illustrator graph, follow these steps:

1. Create a spreadsheet and enter both labels and data.
2. Launch Illustrator and open a new or existing document.
3. Draw a graph using one of the Illustrator graphing tools.
4. Select the graph if it is not already selected.
5. Choose Object | Graph | Data. Illustrator opens the Graph Data dialog box.
6. Click the top-left cell in the Graph Data dialog box. This cell represents the starting point of the imported information.
7. Click the Import Data button. Illustrator opens the Import Graph Data dialog box.
8. Find the document to be imported and double-click it. Illustrator imports the information into the Graph Data dialog box.

9. Click the Apply button. Illustrator places the labels and data into the graph.

10. Click the Close button to close the dialog box.

11. Save the graph and modify it as needed using Illustrator features.

Figure 4-8 shows an Excel spreadsheet, its information imported into the Graph Data dialog box, and the graph just created in the illustration window.

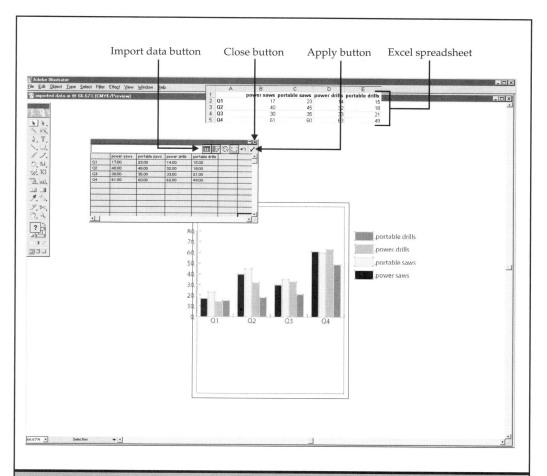

Figure 4-8. *The progression of an Excel spreadsheet, the Graph Data dialog box with the spreadsheet imported, and the Illustrator graph featuring the imported information*

Pasting Information into a Graph

Copying and pasting data into an Illustrator graph follows many of the steps in the preceding section: Create a spreadsheet, usually in a non-spreadsheet program such as a word processor or even a text file; create an empty graph in Illustrator; and open the Graph Data dialog box into which you will paste the information.

However, when you create this type of spreadsheet, you should imagine the way in which a spreadsheet is formatted: Each row is made up of cells, which are enclosed within borders. When you enter labels and data in the document, signal the end of each cell by pressing TAB, which inserts a tab character. To indicate the end of each row, press ENTER, which inserts a carriage return character and starts a new row. Each row should contain the same number of cells, and each cell should contain a value. In other words, this type of spreadsheet should be completely symmetrical.

To paste information into an Illustrator graph, follow these steps:

1. Create a data file and enter both labels and data. Press TAB after each label or piece of data, and press ENTER at the end of each row.
2. Choose Edit | Copy (CTRL-C/⌘-C) to make a copy of the information that you want to paste.
3. Launch Illustrator and open a new or existing document.
4. Draw a graph using one of the Illustrator graphing tools.
5. Select the graph if it is not already selected.
6. Choose Object | Graph | Data. Illustrator opens the Graph Data dialog box.
7. Click the top-left cell in the Graph Data dialog box.
8. Choose Edit | Paste (CTRL-V/⌘-V). Illustrator pastes the information into the Graph Data dialog box.
9. Click the Apply button. Illustrator places the labels and data into the graph.
10. Click the Close button to close the dialog box.
11. Save the graph and modify it as needed using Illustrator features.

Using Illustrator Objects in Your Graphs

You can represent data in standard and stacked columns and bars, and data markers in line and scatter graphs with Illustrator objects. These are known as *graph designs*. For example, you can apply a person, a clock tower, a mill building, or other vertical objects onto a column. Or you can draw a swimmer, bicycle, boat, or other horizontal object to replace a bar. Create a small insect, logo, or clock face to represent a data point. Your imagination (and the amount of time that you can devote to creating this type of artwork) is your only limit.

PRESENTING
ILLUSTRATOR

When you create a graph design, you scale it to fit within a column, bar, or data marker and, ideally, you should plan a design that is related in some way to the data that it represents. Types of graph designs include the following:

- A *vertically scaled design* should be taller than it is wide. Scaling should lengthen or shorten the entire object vertically. In general, use vertically scaled designs for standard columns.

- A *sliding design* is related to a vertically scaled design—with one exception: You choose an area of the object to scale and leave the remaining area unscaled.

- A *horizontally scaled design* should be wider than it is tall. Scaling should increase or decrease the entire object horizontally. In general, use horizontally scaled designs for standard bars.

- A *uniformly scaled design* can be scaled both vertically and horizontally. In general, use uniformly scaled designs for data markers.

- A *repeating design* piles repeated versions of an object to fill a column. You can use one instance of the design to represent one value. So, you might stack four objects to indicate four inches or nine books and nine objects to indicate nine inches or nine books.

Creating a Graph Design

Creating a graph design is just the same as creating another artwork in Illustrator. However, you should make sure that the object's shape roughly conforms to the shape of the column, bar, or data marker. Note that you should create the graph design in the document in which you will use it. (Remember that objects not on the page in the illustration window do not print, so you can work in the scratch area.)

To create a graph design, follow these steps:

1. Create an image that is roughly the same shape as the column, bar, or data marker.

2. Draw a rectangle as close to the border of the image as you can make it. Illustrator uses the rectangle border rather than the image border as the replacement column, bar, or data marker.

3. If the graph design will stretch, draw a horizontal line at a place at which the design will stretch up and down. Then choose View | Make Guide to convert the line into a *guide* (a path that is used to align artwork).

4. Select the image, rectangle, and guide.

5. Choose Edit | Group (CTRL-G/⌘-G) to group the selection into one object.

6. To make copies of the grouped object so that you can create a graphic design for each data series in the graph, select the object and choose Edit | Copy (CTRL-C/⌘-C).

7. To paste the object into the illustration window, choose Edit | Paste (CTRL-V/⌘-V). Then move the pasted object off the page. Repeat this step as many times as you need. Change the object (for example, select a different fill color) to make it unique for a particular data set.

8. Select one of the objects.

9. Choose Object | Graph | Design. Illustrator opens the Graph Design dialog box.

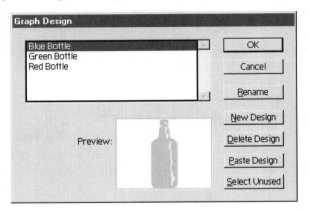

10. Click New Design. Illustrator shows a preview image of the object, dims the New Design button, and undims the Rename button.

11. Click Rename. The Rename dialog box appears.

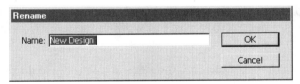

12. Type the name of the graph design in the text box, and click OK.

13. Click OK again. Illustrator closes the Graph Design dialog box.

14. To make another object a graph design, repeat steps 8–13.

Note *If you want to use a graph design in another graph, either create an Illustrator document to hold the design or copy the object and paste it into the new graph document.*

Applying a Graph Design

Once you have created graph designs for a graph, you can apply them to the graph in place of the current columns and bars using the Graph Column dialog box. To do so, follow these steps:

1. With the Group Selection tool, click the legend box twice. This action selects every column, bar, or data marker of the data series.

2. Choose Object | Graph | Column. The Graph Column dialog box appears.

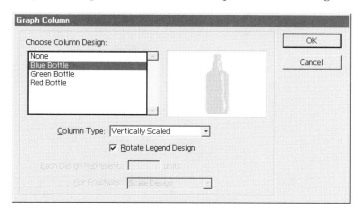

3. From the Choose Column Design list, select the name of the graph design that you want to apply to the selected data series.

4. From the Column Type drop-down list box, select a type: Vertically Scaled, Uniformly Scaled, Repeating, or Sliding.

5. To change the alignment of the legend graphic, check or clear the Rotate Legend Design check box. The alignment depends on the type selected from the Column Type drop-down list box.

6. If you have selected Repeating from the Column type drop-down list box, you can type the number of units that each graph design represents and choose whether fractional values are chopped or scaled.

7. When you have completed filling in the dialog box, click OK. Illustrator closes the dialog box and applies the chosen options to the graph (see Figure 4-9).

To apply graph designs to data markers, choose Object | Graph | Marker. Then select options from the Graph Marker dialog box.

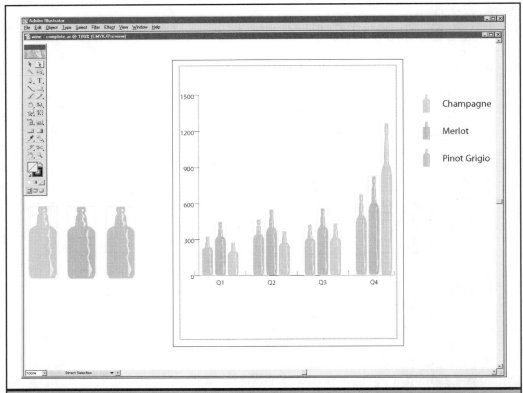

Figure 4-9. *A graph with graph designs replacing columns and the original objects used for those designs*

You can export graph designs to other files by creating a startup file, which then is added to the list of designs in the Graph Design dialog box. To learn how to make a startup file, refer to "Creating a Startup File" in Appendix B.

Note. *You can use Illustrator to create charts such as organization charts and flow charts. To create one of these charts, you'll have to create shapes such as rectangles, diamonds, and circles using the Rectangle tool (M), Polygon tool, and Ellipse tool (L). Because all shapes in an organization chart and some in a flow chart contain text, consider creating dummy shapes with text already included. Once you have grouped the shapes and text, you can copy and paste to construct your charts; then overtype the text with the real names or instructions. After you have moved all the shapes to specific locations on the artboard, join all the shapes with lines created by using the Line Segment tool (\).*

The Complete Reference

Adobe Illustrator 10

Part II

Illustrator Essentials

The
Complete
Reference

Adobe
Illustrator
10

Chapter 5

Setting Up Your Workspace

Until now you have used Illustrator defaults when creating simple objects such as rectangles, ellipses, stars, spirals, and so on. That is fine as far as it goes, but having real control over your working environment provides for better control over your artwork.

In this chapter you will learn how to use the grid and guides of all types to fine-tune the alignment of objects that you create in Illustrator. The *grid* consists of horizontal and vertical lines that enable you to align multiple objects by eye or by *snapping,* automatic movement to the closest grid line. *Guides* are paths used to align artwork in various ways. In Chapter 3 you learned about aligning and distributing objects using the Align palette. In this chapter you will discover how to align objects to the grid, ruler guides, guide objects, and Smart Guides.

In this chapter you also will learn how to resize the artboard to fit artworks of different dimensions and orientations. If you are familiar with a certain unit of measure, Illustrator enables you to choose from several of the most commonly used.

Setting Grid Options

As you gain experience in Illustrator, you'll find that the grid is one of your most useful helpers. For example, when you need to align several objects by one or two edges, turn on the grid and its snap feature. These actions automate alignment as you drag each object. Even without the snap feature turned on, you can use the grid to align objects by eye. In this section you'll learn how to show and hide the grid, turn on the snap feature, rotate the grid to align in nonhorizontal and nonvertical ways, and use the grid to check objects for their levels of transparency. To learn how to set grid preferences, refer to "Setting Preferences" in Appendix B.

Showing and Hiding the Grid

By default, the grid is hidden from view. To display it, choose View | Show Grid (CTRL-"/⌘-"). To hide it, choose View | Hide Grid (CTRL-"/⌘-"). Note that when you print a document while the grid is onscreen, the grid does not print. Figure 5-1 shows several unaligned objects on the grid.

Snapping to the Grid

Whether the grid is hidden or visible, you can use the snap-to-grid feature. To turn on this feature, choose View | Snap to Grid (CTRL-SHIFT-"/⌘-SHIFT-"); a check mark precedes the command. To turn off snap-to-grid, choose View | Snap to Grid (CTRL-SHIFT-"/⌘-SHIFT-") again.

When you turn on the snap-to-grid feature, you might imagine all the objects in the illustration window wildly jumping to lines on the grid—but this does not happen. Instead, when you have turned on snap-to-grid, you must drag an object near a vertical

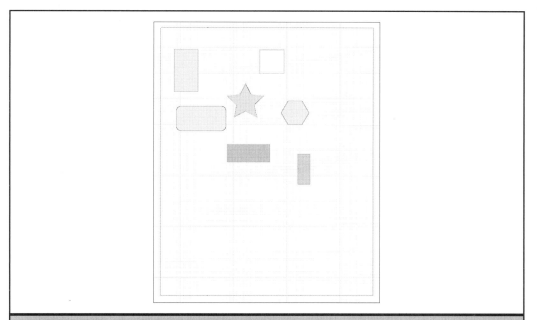

Figure 5-1.   *Unaligned objects in the illustration window with the grid on display*

or horizontal line on the grid. When you drag close enough to a line, the object seems to stick to the line. You can keep dragging the object, but you will encounter a little resistance to the drag when the object reaches another vertical or horizontal line. And when you create an object, it will automatically align with the nearest vertical and horizontal lines. Once again, you can drag the object, but it will be attracted to the nearest vertical and horizontal gridlines every time you move it.

Sometimes the snap feature gets in the way by forcing an object to align. When that happens, turn snap off and just "eyeball" alignments against the grid. Figure 5-2 shows objects from Figure 5-1 aligned on their left and top edges on the visible grid.

 To move a selected object in extremely fine increments, press an arrow key instead of dragging with the Selection tool (V). For example, to gradually shift the object to the left, repeatedly press ←.

Rotating the Grid

Illustrator's grid has a unique capability: You can rotate it so that you can align objects on a plane other than the horizontal or vertical. To rotate the grid, choose Edit | Preferences | General (CTRL-K/⌘-K). In the General section of the Preferences dialog

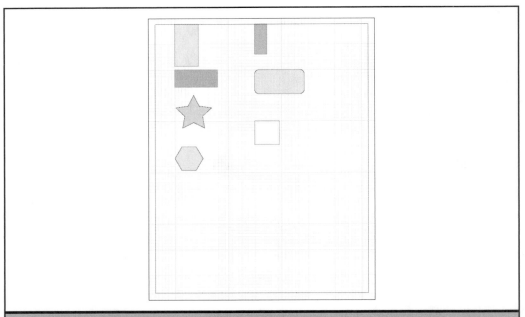

Figure 5-2.   *Geometric objects snapped to the grid on their left edges*

box, type the desired angle in the Constrain Angle text box and click OK. Figure 5-3 illustrates a constrain angle of 45°. Notice that the objects created before this change remain in the same alignment, regardless of the new constrain angle. However, new objects such as the newly created rectangle snap to the modified grid—assuming that snap-to-grid is still active. Note that the grid's constrain angle remains the same for all future documents until you select a new angle.

Checking for Transparency with the Grid

The grid has one more benefit: It can test objects with white fill for transparency. As you probably noticed in Figures 5-1, 5-2, and 5-3, you cannot see the grid behind objects that are filled with any color when the objects are mostly or totally opaque. When an object is transparent you can see the grid to a certain extent, depending on how transparent the object is. When the fill is white (as is the illustration window, including the artboard) you might find it difficult to detect whether an object is transparent or opaque.

ILLUSTRATOR
ESSENTIALS

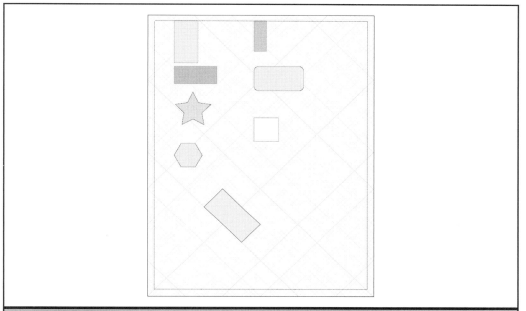

Figure 5-3.   *The grid set to a new constrain angle of 45° with the preexisting objects "unsnapped" and the new rectangle snapped*

So that you can see for yourself, Figure 5-4 shows opaque and transparent objects on the grid. The stars are filled with yellow; the spiral with white. The leftmost star and spiral are 100% opaque, the middle objects are 60% opaque (40% transparent), and the rightmost objects are 30% opaque (70% transparent). Of course, there are other ways of checking whether a selected object is opaque: You can choose Window | Transparency (SHIFT-F10) and look at the opacity level displayed in the Transparency palette, or you can see whether the Color or None button is selected at the bottom of the toolbox. When the None button is active, an object has no fill; therefore, transparency and opacity of the fill don't matter.

Note   *When you find out about transparency, you'll discover that Illustrator features a transparency grid, which is not to be confused with the grid. The transparency grid is a checkerboard of light and dark colors that presents an ideal background for semitransparent objects. You'll learn much more about transparency and the transparency grid in Chapter 15.*

Figure 5-4.   *A combination of opaque and transparent objects with fills of different colors*

Using Guides to Set Up Your Art

Like grids, guides help you align your artwork. However, instead of a gridwork of multiple lines, a guide is a single line with which you can align one or more objects anywhere on the illustration window. You can add multiple guides to the illustration window one at a time. Note that when you print artwork aligned by using guides, the guides do not print. Illustrator provides three types of guides: *ruler guides*, *guide objects*, and *Smart Guides*.

- *Ruler guides*, which are based on the rulers, are vertical and horizontal lines that extend from one edge of the illustration window to the other.

- *Guide objects* start out as any object except type; so a guide object can be an open or closed path—a line, a rectangle, an ellipse, a group of objects, and so on.

- *Smart Guides* flash onscreen when you create or *transform* (move, rotate, flip, scale, or skew) an object if an anchor point on that object is in alignment in some way with a nearby object in the illustration window. By default, Smart Guides are turned on.

Setting Up and Using Guides

Both ruler guides and guide objects require a brief setup period. After that, both ruler guides and guide objects are ready to go. Ruler guides and guide objects work in much the same way: You align objects by dragging them to the guides. When you drag an object close to a guide, the object snaps to the guide. You can maintain ruler guides and guide objects in various ways: You can move them, show and hide them, lock and unlock them, and release and clear them.

Setting Up Ruler Guides

Before you create a ruler guide, the rulers must appear in the illustration window. To reveal the horizontal and vertical rulers, choose View | Show Rulers (CTRL-R/⌘-R). Once the rulers are onscreen, you can hide them by choosing View | Hide Rulers (CTRL-R/⌘-R).

To create a vertical ruler guide, move the mouse pointer to the ruler and drag the guide across the illustration window from any location on the vertical ruler. To create a horizontal ruler guide, drag it down from the horizontal ruler. Notice that dotted lines on both rulers show you the current position of the cursor. Use those lines to move the ruler guides to the desired locations.

 You can switch ruler guides from vertical to horizontal or horizontal to vertical as you create them. As you drag the guide, press and hold down ALT/OPTION *to change the orientation.*

Setting Up Guide Objects

Before you create a guide object, you must make an object using a toolbox tool. You can draw a path as simple as a line or an arc or as complex as a star or group. Once the object or group is complete, you select it and then convert it to a guide object. To convert a selected object or group, choose View | Guides | Make Guides (CTRL-5/⌘-5). You can create several guide objects at a time. Using the Selection tool (V) and pressing and holding down SHIFT, make multiple selections. Then choose View | Guides | Make Guides (CTRL-5/⌘-5).

Using Ruler Guides and Guide Objects

Both ruler guides and guide objects work in the same way: Drag an object toward the guide or an intersection of two guides to align it. When the object is close to the guide or guides, it snaps to them. If one guide is a horizontal line and another is a vertical line, snapping works the same as it would if you were using the grid and the snap-to-grid feature. Figure 5-5 shows a rectangle aligned with both a horizontal and vertical line.

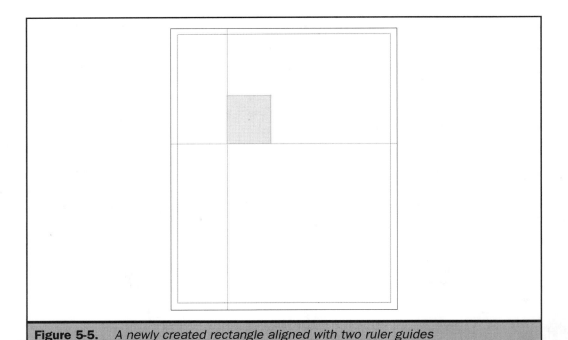

Figure 5-5.   *A newly created rectangle aligned with two ruler guides*

Using guide objects to align multiple objects enables you to create effective images. For example, you could make a logo using a square object guide and four small rectangles. To create the logo, follow these steps:

1. With the Rectangle tool (M), make a square.

2. Choose View | Guides | Make Guides (CTRL-5/⌘-5) to convert the square to an object guide.

3. With the Rectangle tool (M), create a small, black-filled rectangle the same length as the top side of the object guide.

4. With the Direct Selection tool (A), pull one corner of the rectangle to create a point.

5. Using the Selection tool (V), select the newly changed object and choose Edit | Copy (CTRL-C/⌘-C) to copy it.

6. Paste the object onto the illustration window three times.

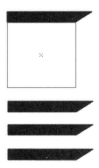

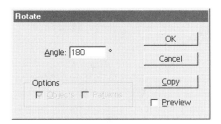

7. Select one copy, and choose Object | Transform | Rotate. Illustrator opens the Rotate dialog box.

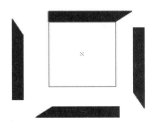

8. In the Angle text box, type **180**; then click OK.

9. Repeat steps 7 and 8 for the two remaining copies. For one copy, the value in the Angle text box is 90, and for the other copy the value is 270.

ILLUSTRATOR ESSENTIALS

10. Drag each object to one side of the object guide.

11. Clear the object guide by choosing View | Guides | Clear Guides.

12. Choose Select | All (CTRL-A/⌘-A) to select all four objects.

13. Choose Object | Group (CTRL-G/⌘-G) to group the objects.

14. Choose Object | Transform | Rotate. Illustrator opens the Rotate dialog box.

15. In the Angle text box, type **45**; then click OK.

16. Save the document.

Showing and Hiding Guides

Although guides do not print under any circumstances, at times you'll want to view your artwork without guides displayed onscreen. For example, if you create a complicated and exact image with the help of many guides, the presence of both guides and objects might make the work seem more intricate than it really is. So, to hide all the ruler guides and guide objects, choose View | Guides | Hide Guides (CTRL-;/⌘-;). Hidden guides do exist; they are not released or cleared.

Once you have hidden guides, you'll have to explicitly show them—even if you have exited Illustrator and launched it again. To show all the ruler guides and guide objects, choose View | Guides | Show Guides (CTRL-;/⌘-;).

Locking and Unlocking Guides

By default, both ruler guides and guide objects are locked in place after you have created them. After all, guides are onscreen to help you set up your artwork. If you can move guides as you are creating or modifying your artwork, you might have to align objects again; so once you have moved guides to appropriate locations in the illustration window, you should lock them. To check the locked status of guides, try to move a guide; if you can't move it, guides are locked. When guides are locked, the Lock Guides command is preceded by a check mark.

To unlock all ruler guides and guide objects, thereby enabling you to move or select them, choose View | Guides | Lock Guides (CTRL-ALT-;/⌘-OPTION-;). To lock all guides, choose View | Guides | Lock Guides (CTRL-ALT-;/⌘-OPTION-;) again. To lock a single guide, select it and press CTRL-2/⌘-2.

Releasing Guides

Releasing guide objects converts them to paths, their original condition. You can release individual guide objects or all guide objects simultaneously. Any guide objects to be released must be unlocked and selected. Select individual guide objects with the Selection tool (V); press and hold down SHIFT if you want to add other guide objects to the selection. To select all guide objects, choose Edit | Select All (CTRL-A/⌘-A). To release all selected guide objects, choose View | Guides | Release Guides (CTRL-ALT-5/⌘-OPTION-5).

Clearing Guides

When you have finished aligning all the objects in the illustration window, clearing the guides removes extraneous guidelines and other guide objects, tidying up the window and showing a clear view of your artwork. Clearing guides permanently deletes them—whether they are locked or unlocked, selected or unselected. To clear both ruler guides and guide objects, choose View | Guides | Clear Guides.

Introducing Smart Guides

If activated, Smart Guide guidelines appear in the illustration window when you construct or transform an object; they will show up as you move the mouse pointer to a location related to parts of a neighboring object. Smart Guides flash onscreen when the mouse pointer is at a point related to a border, center, or corner of the nearby object. By default, guidelines appear when the mouse pointer passes over anchor points that are at angles of 0°, 45°, 90°, and 135° from the object. You can select new combinations of degrees and other options in the Smart Guides section of the Preferences dialog box.

By default, Smart Guide guidelines provide text labels, too. For example, the Align label shows the angle at which the mouse pointer is related to the targeted anchor point of the nearby object. Where two guidelines intersect, you'll see the Intersect label. When you move the mouse pointer over the center of an object, a path, or an anchor point, text labels stating Center, Path, or Anchor appear.

Turning On Smart Guides

To activate Smart Guides, choose View | Smart Guides (CTRL-U/⌘-U). If Smart Guides are turned on, a check mark precedes the Smart Guides command. To turn off Smart Guides, choose View | Smart Guides (CTRL-U/⌘-U) again; Illustrator removes the check mark. You don't have to set up Smart Guides; after you activate them, guidelines appear whenever you move the mouse pointer to a position that is related to an anchor point.

Using Smart Guides

To use Smart Guides, just move the mouse pointer around the illustration window. As you create, move, or otherwise transform an object, guidelines appear and disappear as you move the pointer. Note that at least one object must be in the illustration window for Smart Guides to work. Figure 5-6 illustrates four instances of Smart Guides at work.

Setting Smart Guide Preferences

You can customize Smart Guides in various ways. For example, you can select a different set of angles, show or hide text labels, and specify the features for which Smart Guides are active. To set Smart Guide preferences, choose Edit | Preferences | Smart Guides & Slices. The Smart Guides & Slices section of the Preferences dialog box (see Figure 5-7) enables your changing Smart Guide Preferences.

The Display Options section includes four check boxes that turn on features when you move the mouse pointer over an object:

- If you check Text Label Hints, text labels appear.
- If you check Construction Guides, guidelines show.
- If you check Transform Tools, Smart Guides appear.
- Object Highlighting highlights the object.

In the Angles section you can select sets of angles or define a custom set consisting of angles from 0° to 360° degrees. Either open the Angles drop-down menu and choose a set or type as many as six angles in the text boxes. The preview box illustrates the chosen angles.

As you might predict, the value in the Snapping Tolerance text box controls the snapping area around objects. If the value is low, you have to move one object very close (for example, the default four points) from another object before they snap together. If the value is too high, an object might inadvertently snap to a third object as you move it around the illustration window. To learn how to set other preferences, including those for grid and guide colors and line styles, refer to Appendix B.

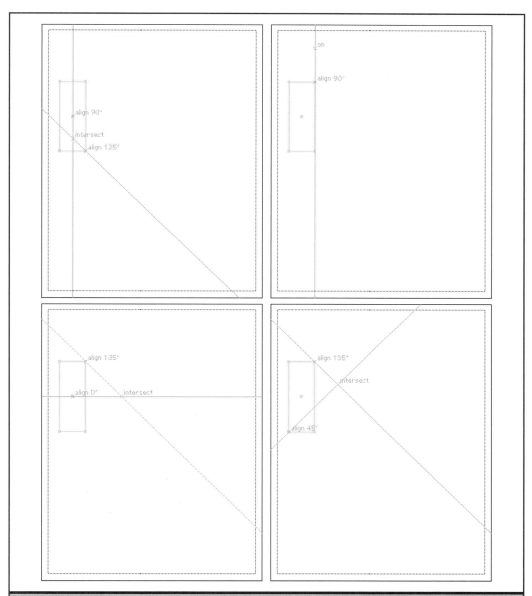

Figure 5-6.   *Four artboards showing several Smart Guide guidelines and labels*

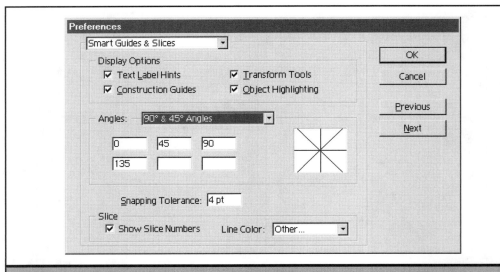

Figure 5-7.   *The Smart Guides & Slices section of the Preferences dialog box showing the default settings for Smart Guides*

Setting Up the Artboard

Until now we have accepted Illustrator's default artboard size and orientation for all our artwork. You can change the artboard dimensions in two ways:

- When you start a new document, choose File | New (CTRL-N/⌘-N) to open the New Document dialog box (see Figure 5-8) in which you can select artboard options.

- As you edit an existing document, you can modify the dimensions and orientation of the artboard, set a default unit of measure, and control some aspects of the view by choosing File | Document Setup (CTRL-ALT-P/⌘-OPTION-P) to open the Document Setup dialog box (see Figure 5-9).

Because the Document Setup dialog box provides additional artboard options, we will concentrate on that.

Setting the Artboard Size

By default, the artboard is 612 points wide and 792 points high. With the Document Setup dialog box you can select from a list of artboard sizes or set a custom size.

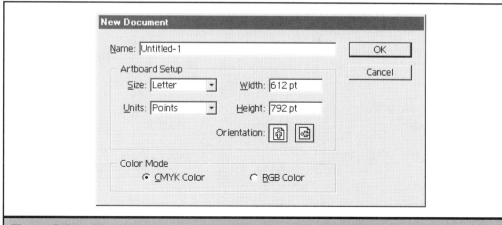

Figure 5-8. *The New Document dialog box enables you to name the document and set the artboard size and color mode*

From the Size drop-down menu, you can select one of the following predefined artboard sizes:

- Custom, any width and height entered in the Width and Height text boxes
- 640×480 (640 by 480 pixels), the size of a low-resolution monitor screen
- 800×600 (800 by 600 pixels), the size of a high-resolution monitor screen
- 468×60 (468 by 60 pixels), the size of a title frame on a typical Web page
- Letter (8.5 by 11 inches/612 by 792 points), the standard dimensions of letter paper
- Legal (8.5 by 14 inches/612 by 1008 points), the standard dimensions of legal papers and forms
- Tabloid (11 by 17 inches/792 by 1224 points), the size of some posters and newspapers
- A4 (8.27 by 11.69 inches/595.28 by 841.89 points), a standard European paper size
- A3 (11.69 by 16.54 inches/841.89 by 1190.55 points), a standard European paper size
- B5 (7.17 by 10.12 inches/515.91 by 728.5 points), a standard European paper size
- B4 (10.12 by 14.33 inches/728.5 by 1031.81 points), a standard European paper size

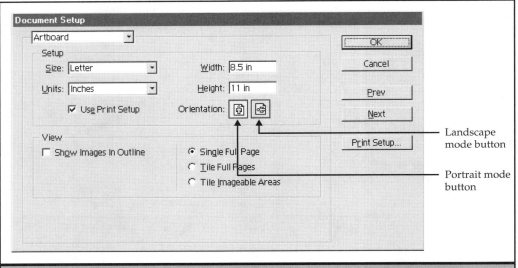

Figure 5-9. *The Document Setup dialog box controls the artboard, the units of measure, and some aspects of the view*

In both the New Document and Document Setup dialog boxes you can specify a custom width and height for the artboard. The default width is 8.5 inches; the default height is 11 inches or the Letter size in the Size drop-down menu. Valid values for both the width and height are 0.02 (the most miniature of miniatures) to 227.54 inches (a billboard almost 19 feet square).

Setting the Unit of Measure

You can select a unit of measure for the current document or all future documents. Valid units of measure are points, picas, inches, centimeters, or millimeters. The Illustrator development team decided to make points the default because that unit of measure is the standard for the printing and graphics industries.

- *Points* are units of measure in the printing industry. A point is approximately 1/72 inch.
- *Picas* are units of measure used by typographers. A pica is equal to 12 points or about 1/6 inch.
- *Inches* are standard units of measure for those not using the metric system. An inch is 2.54 centimeters.
- *Centimeters* (one hundredth of a meter) are standard units of measure for the metric system. A centimeter is .3937 inch.

- *Millimeters* (one thousandth of a meter) are standard units of measure for the metric system. A millimeter is 0.03937 inch.

- *Pixels* are standard units of measure for computer graphics, the smallest measurable unit of a bitmap. The size of a pixel depends on the graphic resolution of the image or computer monitor.

To select a unit of measure for the current document, follow these steps:

1. Choose File | Document Setup (CTRL-ALT-P/⌘-OPTION-P).

2. In the Document Setup dialog box open the Units drop-down menu and select a unit of measure.

3. Click OK.

To select a unit of measure for the current document and all future Illustrator documents (until you select a new unit of measure), follow these steps:

1. Choose Edit | Preferences | Units & Undo.

2. In the Units section open the General drop-down menu and select a unit of measure.

3. Click OK.

 To specify the unit of measure for the object's strokes, choose from the Stroke drop-down menu. To set the unit of measure for the type, choose from the Type drop-down menu.

Orienting the Artboard

Because the artboard's starting height is greater than its width, its default orientation is in *portrait* mode. Examples of documents usually in portrait mode are business letters, reports, and proposals. The other orientation mode, *landscape,* has a width that is greater than its height. The primary example of landscape mode is a spreadsheet. Click the portrait mode button to orient the artboard to portrait mode; click the landscape mode button to shift to landscape mode.

In the Document Setup dialog box you can check the Use Print Setup/Use Page Setup box to have the artboard assume the page size and orientation shown in the Print Setup dialog box (in Windows) or Page Setup dialog box (on the Mac). To view either dialog box, choose File | Print Setup (CTRL-SHIFT-P) or File | Page Setup (⌘-SHIFT-P).

Setting View Options for Pages

In the lower half of the Document Setup dialog box is the View section, which enables you to control your view of images or the page within the artboard. A page can have certain dimensions and orientation, which can be completely different from the dimensions and orientation of the artboard. Illustrator gets the page size and orientation from the settings in the Print Setup dialog box or the Page Setup dialog box, and the artboard size and orientation from the settings in the Document Setup dialog box.

The check box and radio buttons in the View section work as follows:

- Check Show Images in Outline to display Encapsulated PostScript (EPS) placed images. When the check box is cleared, an X in a box is a placeholder for EPS placed images.

- Click Single Full Page (the default) to display an outline of one page within the artboard. Figure 5-10 illustrates a landscape mode artboard in Tabloid size (17 inches wide and 11 inches high) and one portrait Letter size (8.5 inches wide and 11 inches high) page.

- Click Tile Full Pages to tile one or more page outlines within the artboard, depending on the dimensions and orientation of the page. Figure 5-11 illustrates the landscape mode, Tabloid artboard with side-by-side portrait, Letter pages. *Tiling* aligns multiple pages on all four sides within the artboard. You can tile several pages to print very large images that extend beyond a single page. The tiled pages print one by one, and you join the printed pages to form one gigantic page. Note also the page numbers in the lower-left side of each page.

- Click Tile Imageable Areas to tile page outlines (see Figure 5-12) in the imageable area.

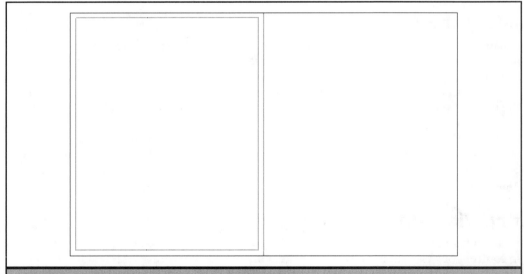

Figure 5-10. *A landscape mode artboard with one portrait mode page*

Figure 5-11.   *A landscape mode artboard containing side-by-side pages in portrait mode*

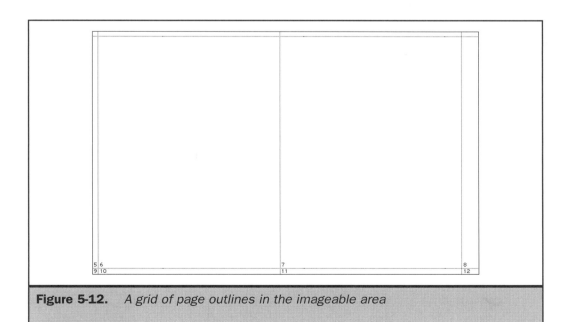

Figure 5-12.   *A grid of page outlines in the imageable area*

ILLUSTRATOR ESSENTIALS

You can use the Page tool to drag a page outline by its bottom-left corner within the artboard or the imageable area, depending on the selected radio button in the View section. Do this to be able to place different areas of the page in the printable area.

Measuring Objects

Illustrator provides several measuring features: the Measure tool, the horizontal and vertical Rulers, and the Info palette. You also can be your own measuring tool by placing an unmeasured object next to an object you have already measured and, of course, using your eyes to gauge the difference between the two objects. To get back to the Illustrator measurement tools… the Measure tool is a small ruler that you drag around the illustration window, the Rulers appear on the top and left edges of the illustration window, and the Info palette provides the X- and Y- coordinates and the width and height of the mouse pointer location.

Exploring the Info Palette

As its name implies, the Info palette (see Figure 5-13) provides information about an object or the current mouse pointer location as well as the current fill and stroke colors. To toggle between showing and hiding the palette, choose Window | Info (F8).

At its largest, the Info palette is composed of three sections: The top section displays X- and Y-coordinates and width and height. The middle section shows distance and angle. In both sections the measurements are expressed in the current unit of measure. The bottom section presents the percentages of primary colors for the current color mode. You can measure both objects and the entire illustration window.

- X (the X-coordinate) is the current position of the mouse pointer on a horizontal plane. When X reads 0 in the Info palette, the mouse pointer is located on the left side of the artboard.

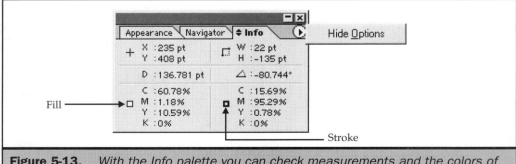

Figure 5-13. *With the Info palette you can check measurements and the colors of the fill and stroke*

- Y (the Y-coordinate) is the current position of the mouse pointer on a vertical plane. When Y reads 0, the mouse pointer is located at the bottom of the artboard.

- W (width) is the width measured from the starting click to the ending click or from the starting click to the end of a drag.

- H (height) is the height measured from the starting click to the ending click or from the starting click to the end of a drag.

- Distance (D) measures the distance drawn with the Measure tool between the current location of the pointer and another location to which you drag.

- Angle (<) measures the angle of a line drawn with the Measure tool to a location to which you drag.

You can resize the Info palette to show the title bar, the top two sections, or all three sections. To change the palette size, click the Autoresize button. To show the full palette, click the menu button and select Show Options. To hide the third section, select Hide Options.

 In addition to its standard duties of transforming selected objects, the Transform palette also displays measurements. Choose Window | Transform (SHIFT-F8) to show the Transform palette. Before you transform an object, the measurements in the W and H boxes echo those in the Info palette. However, because the Transform palette serves a different purpose (of moving, rotating, scaling, and skewing), it is best to use the Info palette to get X, Y, D, and < values. To learn about the Transform palette and its real purpose in life, refer to "Using the Transform Palette" in Chapter 10.

Measuring with the Measure Tool

 The Measure tool, which is on the Eyedropper toolslot, enables you to measure from one clicked point to another clicked point or from a clicked point to the end of a drag. Clicking the Measure tool the first time opens the Info palette, if it is hidden. Double-clicking the Measure tool opens the Guides and Grid section of the Preferences dialog box.

To use the Measure tool, move the mouse pointer to a starting point, click, and then move the mouse pointer to an ending point and click. At this point you'll see the measurements in the Info palette. An alternative method is to click a starting point and drag to an ending point. When you release the mouse button the measurements appear in the Info palette. In either case, if the mouse pointer is at the bottom-left corner of the artboard, both X and Y are 0. Both X and Y don't become negative until they move beyond the 0 point; that is, X must move to the left of the left edge of the artboard, and Y must move below the bottom of the artboard.

- If you measure from the bottom to the top of the illustration window vertically, you'll see a change in the values of Y and D in the Info palette. Both values will be positive. In addition, the angle will be approximately 90 (degrees).

- If you move from the left to right horizontally, the values of X and D change; again, the values will be positive. Additionally, the angle will be about 0.

- If you move from right to left horizontally, the values of X and D will be negative. The angle will be approximately 0.

- If you move from top to bottom vertically, the Y and D values again will be negative. The angle will be about 90.

- When you measure diagonally from a bottom point to a point closer to the top of the illustration window, all values register a change. Note that X, Y, and D will be positive.

- When you measure diagonally from top to bottom, X, Y, and D change to negative values.

 You also can use the Selection tool (V) to measure the illustration window. However, if you move the mouse pointer to an object, you'll drag it rather than measure it. It's better to stick with the Measure tool.

Measuring with the Rulers

When you learned about ruler guides you got your first exposure to Illustrator's vertical and horizontal rulers. In fact, remember that you use ruler guides, guide objects, and Smart Guides to place an object at a precise location in the illustration window— another form of measuring. However, you can use the rulers to measure the coordinates of the current mouse pointer location in the current unit of measure. To toggle between showing and hiding the rulers, choose View | Show/Hide Rulers (CTRL-R/⌘-R). Figure 5-14 shows both rulers in the illustration window.

When the rulers appear in the illustration window, the *ruler origins* (the 0 point on each ruler) are aligned with the page. For example, when you display a single page in the artboard, the vertical ruler's ruler origin is aligned with the bottom edge of the page, and the horizontal ruler's ruler origin is aligned with the left edge of the page. Where the ruler origins intersect is the bottom-left corner of the page. If you choose a tiling option from the Document Setup dialog box (see Figure 5-9), both ruler origins appear relative to the page labeled 1.

If you plan to measure a page, the default positions of the ruler origins are fine. However, you might want to measure an object from time to time. Fortunately, you can move the ruler origin. To do so, place your mouse pointer in the small box in the upper-left corner of the illustration window at the point at which the rulers cross. Then, drag one or two dotted lines (to adjust the ruler origin for one or two rulers, respectively) to the place at which you want to place the ruler origin—probably one corner of the object to be measured. When you release the mouse button, the ruler

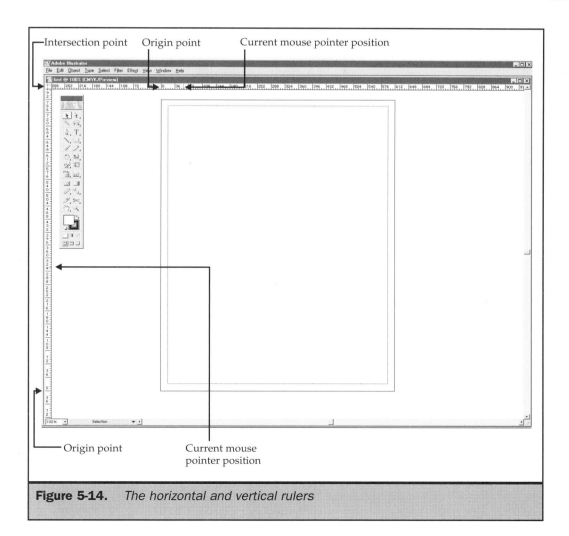

Figure 5-14. *The horizontal and vertical rulers*

origin is in its new location and the dotted lines disappear. To return the ruler origins to their original locations, double-click the small box in the upper-left corner.

To measure an object using the rulers, move the mouse pointer to a starting point, perhaps at the ruler origin on both rulers. Notice that dotted lines within the rulers show you the current position; then move the mouse pointer to the end point of the measurement and look at the dotted lines. Assuming you started at 0, the current position of the dotted lines shows you the measurement.

Chapter 6

Using Paths and Points

Although you have created and edited paths and points in every chapter before you turned to this page, now you'll get the full treatment. You'll learn much more about the minutiae of paths and points; how paths and points come together to form objects; and the tools, commands, and palettes used to create and manipulate paths and points.

In this chapter you will find out about each type of path and point and discover how to draw freeform paths using two tools. You'll learn about a variety of editing techniques: cutting and slicing and adding, joining, converting, reshaping, and deleting points. You'll also manipulate paths by uniting, intersecting, excluding, dividing, trimming, and deleting. In short, you'll find out everything you ever wanted to know about paths and points in Illustrator.

What Are Paths and Points?

As you learned in Chapter 1, a path is one or more straight and curved lines that can be combined to fashion the outline of an object, such as a single straight line; a series of curves; or a rectangle, ellipse, or polygon. Paths and points are the foundation of vector graphics on which Illustrator is based.

Now for some path and point terms:

- An *open path* is made up of one or more *line segments* (straight lines) or *arc segments* (curved lines) and two or more anchor points, including two end points. Examples of open paths are lines, arcs, and spirals.

- A *closed path* is a continuous path that does not end. A closed path has anchor points but no end points. Examples of closed paths are rectangles, ellipses, polygons, and stars.

- A *compound path* is comprised of two or more open or closed, overlapping paths. Wherever paths overlap, you can set areas of transparency.

- An *anchor point* marks a curve or corner in a path, the location at which two line segments join, and the ends of open paths. Anchor points are rectangular control handles that you can select individually and then drag to change the shape of a path. Illustrator enables you to add and remove anchor points to a path. As you add or delete anchor points, you can reshape a path in greater detail.

- An *end point* is the name of an anchor point that marks each end of an open path.

Editing Paths

In earlier chapters you learned about Illustrator's extensive selection tools and commands on the Select menu. You also found out about certain elementary aspects of editing artwork—primarily rearranging objects in the illustration window by dragging, aligning, and distributing. This type of manipulation is just a small part of all the editing features of Illustrator. For example, you can start with an easy-to-draw object—such as a rectangle—and convert it to an object with both curves and straight lines such as a bottle, an airplane wing, or a telescope. Or you can draw a curving line that is nearly what you want but not exactly. In this chapter you will learn how to modify all types of paths.

To edit any curved arc segment of a path, select it with the Direct Selection tool (A). At first, a selected arc segment looks just like any other selection. However, when you click between anchor points or on anchor points that connect curved segments, Illustrator runs lines through the adjacent anchor points (see Figure 6-1). These *direction lines* show the direction in which the curve is heading at the anchor point. According to the Illustrator User Guide, "direction lines are always tangent to (perpendicular to the radius of) the curve at the anchor points. The angle of each direction line determines the slope of the curve, and the length of each direction line determines the height, or depth, of the curve."

The points at the end of the direction lines are *direction points,* circular handles by which you can drag a direction line to a new course to change the shape of the arc segment. By dragging a couple of direction points, you can edit the line until it matches your idea of perfection.

Figure 6-1.   *Curved open and closed paths with all their direction lines and direction points*

Figure 6-2 demonstrates several changes in an arc, from the top left to right and the bottom left and right. As you continue through this chapter you'll see more examples of modifying paths using direction lines and direction points—but using objects that have been created using two Illustrator freehand drawing tools, Pencil and Pen.

Drawing with the Pencil Tool

The Pencil tool (N) enables you to draw a single freeform path. You can draw either open or closed paths using the Pencil. As you use the Pencil, Illustrator either completely smooths the path or keeps any jagged parts—depending on smoothing tolerances that you can set.

The speed with which you draw determines the number of anchor points on a path: Drag slowly to create many points; drag quickly to add fewer points to the path. When

Figure 6-2. *A standard arc segment changed to an S shape by dragging and turning direction points*

you draw with the Pencil, you actually create a stroke. If the path curves, Illustrator automatically adds the fill color between the end points.

 If you don't like the current fill color, click the Default Fill and Stroke button (D). Illustrator changes the fill to white and the stroke to black. You also can click None (/) to have no current fill color.

Penciling an Open Path

To draw a freeform open path with the Pencil, follow these steps:

1. Click the Pencil tool (N).

2. Drag a path in the illustration window using the Pencil mouse pointer. The path follows the Pencil's point.

 If you want to use a cross-hairs mouse pointer instead, press CAPS LOCK. *As you drag the path, the path originates from the center of the cross-hairs.*

3. Release the mouse button. Illustrator changes the dotted line that showed the path as it was being drawn to a selected solid line.

4. To continue the path, move the mouse pointer to the end of the path you just completed (it must be selected) and start dragging. If the Pencil mouse pointer has an X next to it, you are drawing a new path. If the mouse pointer has no X, you are adding to the old path.

Penciling a Closed Path

When you attempt to create a closed path using the Pencil alone, the two end points may never join and the path never closes. However, if you switch from the Pencil to the Smooth tool at the last stage of drawing the path, you can close the path in a sneaky way. The Smooth tool, which you will learn about later in this chapter, smooths paths and erases extra anchor points. So, using the Smooth tool as you complete the path converts the two end points into one.

1. Click the Pencil tool (N).

2. Drag a path in the illustration window.

3. When you have dragged the end of the path close to the origin of the path, press and hold down ALT/OPTION. Illustrator changes the Pencil tool to the Smooth tool. As you continue dragging, and when the beginning and end points of the paths touch, the X next to the Pencil tool becomes an O and the two end points become one anchor point.

4. Release the mouse button and ALT/OPTION. Illustrator changes the dotted line to a selected solid closed path.

Changing the Course of a Path

You also can use the Pencil to edit a path; that is, to change its curves and lines. The Pencil can modify any path, including those created with other tools. For example, you can replace one side of a rectangle with a wavy line, perhaps to convert it into an aquarium, cross-section of the ocean, or something completely different.

To change the track of a path, follow these steps:

1. Select the path to be edited.

2. Click the Pencil tool (N).

3. Drag a new segment from one place on the path to another. Illustrator replaces the old segment with the new, inserting anchor points in the new segment.

4. You can undo any changes by choosing Edit | Undo (CTRL-Z/⌘-Z).

Figure 6-3 shows a complete chocolate chip cookie (with no macadamias), with both cookie and chips created using the Ellipse tool. After moving the chips to the cookie, both cookie and its chips were selected and then grouped by choosing Object | Group (CTRL-G/⌘-G). Finally, the Pencil took a bite from the cookie.

Setting Pencil Tool Preferences

As you used the Pencil for the first time, you might have noticed that the dotted line that follows your dragging the mouse pointer is not an identical twin of the final path. In fact, the final path sometimes looks more like a fraternal twin or maybe even a more attractive sibling. The options in the Pencil Tool Preferences dialog box (see Figure 6-4)

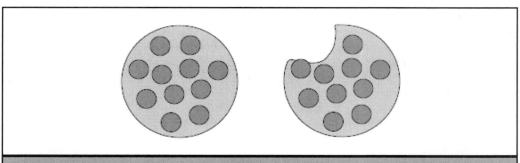

Figure 6-3.   *On the left, the original path; and on the right, the edited path*

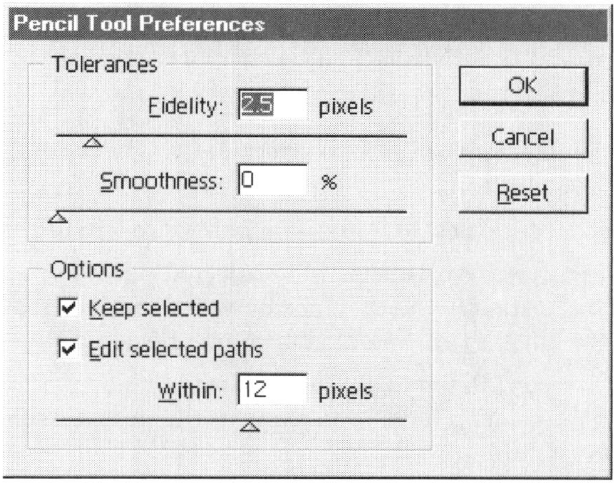

Figure 6-4.   *The Pencil Tool Preferences dialog box with its default settings*

control the final shape of the path and its changes in direction. So, you can determine whether you get a gorgeous, smooth path or a primitive, jagged path.

In the dialog box, Fidelity determines how closely the final path follows the dotted line. Valid values range from 0.5 (within 0.5 pixels of the dotted line) to 20 (within 20 pixels of the dotted line). The default Fidelity value is 2.5 pixels.

Illustrator provides two types of anchor points showing a change of direction. A *corner point* is sharp and definite. A typical corner point joins two straight paths or indicates a sharp turn (for example, in a rectangle). A *smooth point* is more curved and smooth. A smooth point indicates some sort of turn in a curved path.

In the Pencil Tool Preferences dialog box, the Smoothness option determines whether a corner is sharp or smooth. You must draw corners somewhat sharply for Smoothness to be effective. Valid values range from 0% (the least smooth and the default) to 100% (the smoothest). Figure 6-5 illustrates four Pencil paths. On the top the path on the left is set to 0.5 and the one on the right is set to 20 pixels. At the bottom of the figure are examples of 0% Smoothness (on the left) and 100% Smoothness (on the right). Notice that the points on the right side are quite sharp, which is the way they were drawn, but the inner points are smooth, also as drawn.

However, the outer points on the left side are not quite sharp and the inner points not quite rounded. Both paths have a Fidelity value of 2.5 pixels, the default. When you start working with the Pen, later in this chapter, you'll learn more about corner points and smooth points.

The Keep Selected and Edit Selected Paths check boxes work in tandem: If one check box is checked or cleared, the other option works one way or another.

- Check Keep Selected to continue to select the newly created path after you release the mouse button.
- Clear Keep Selected to "deselect" the new path once you release the mouse button.
- Check Edited Selected Paths to edit the selected path. Type a value in the Within text box to specify the distance between the selected path and a new path that might have an editing effect on the selected path.
- Clear Edited Selected Paths to enable the Pencil to keep adding paths or editing older selected paths. You have to use one of Illustrator's selection tools to explicitly select a path for editing.

Note *When both Keep Selected and Edited Selected Paths are checked and a path is selected, a new path drawn with the Pencil replaces the selected path—if it is within the distance specified in the Within text box. Checking both options prevents you from drawing paths close together.*

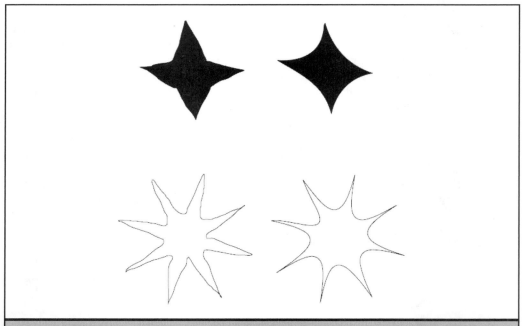

Figure 6-5. *At the top, a path that is faithful to the dotted line; on the right, a path that is much less faithful; at the bottom, the leftmost path is set to 0% Smoothness; and the one on the right is set to 100% Smoothness*

Smoothing a Path

The Smooth tool, which is on the same toolslot as the Pencil tool, removes extra anchor points from a path or a segment of a path. You could have created the path or segment using any Illustrator tool. The act of smoothing and deleting anchor points results in a path or segment that is less jagged, so it looks more finished. To smooth an area, drag the Smooth tool over it.

To use the Smooth tool, follow these steps:

1. Select the path to be smoothed.
2. Activate the Smooth tool from the Pencil toolslot.
3. Drag the Smooth tool over the path or part of the path to be smoothed. Continue dragging until the path is as smooth as you wish.

Figure 6-6 shows three objects with tops that are successively smoother. The topmost object is the original; the second is a smoothed copy of the first; and the third is a copy of the second, even smoother. Each drag of the Smooth tool along the top of the object removed more anchor points. Notice that the unsmoothed anchor points on the sides and bottom of the object remain the same.

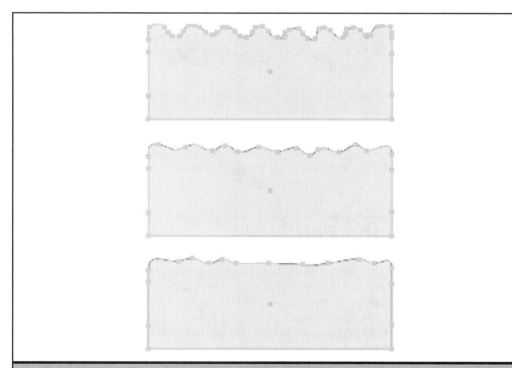

Figure 6-6. *The wavy tops of the three rectangles are smoother and have fewer anchor points.*

ILLUSTRATOR
ESSENTIALS

You can set Smooth tool preferences in much the same way you specify Pencil tool preferences. To set preferences, double-click the Smooth tool. When Illustrator opens the Smooth Tool Preferences dialog box, you can set the Fidelity and Smoothness, which work exactly as they do for the Pencil.

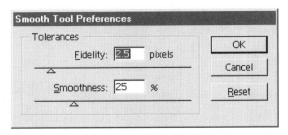

Erasing a Path

The Erase tool, the other tool on the Pencil toolslot, erases part of a path and the anchor points within the erased area and adds new end points to the new ends. You can use the Erase tool to erase an entire path, but using the Select tool (V) and pressing Delete is quicker.

Just like the Pencil and the Smooth tools, the Erase tool is programmed to edit a path that was constructed by using any Illustrator path creation tool. The Erase tool erases any paths but type (except type converted to a graphic) and meshes. You'll learn about type in Chapters 11 and 12. In the second half of Chapter 9 you'll find out about meshes.

To use the Erase tool, follow these steps:

1. Using one of Illustrator's selection tools, select the path of which you will erase part.

2. Select the Erase tool from the toolbox.

3. Drag the mouse pointer along the area to be erased. Illustrator highlights the area with a densely dotted line. When you stop dragging, Illustrator adds end points to the remaining ends.

Drawing with the Pen Tool

By all accounts, the Pen tool (P) is the most important and most difficult of all Illustrator tools. With the Pen you can draw paths composed of straight line and curved line segments. To create a straight path click either end of the path—which is very easy. To create a curved path, which is the thorny part of Pen usage, drag and move direction handles until the path turns as you wish. Once you have constructed a straight or curved path, you can add or remove anchor points using the Pen: Click a path to add an anchor point, or click an anchor point to remove it.

Learning about the Pen Mouse Pointers

Illustrator provides several Pen mouse pointers. Each variation means something different as you are working on paths created or edited with the Pen.

Click the Pen tool to reveal the standard Pen mouse pointer. Use this mouse pointer to create straight paths and to drag initial curved paths. When the Pen is away from any path in the illustration window, it looks like this.

When you move the Pen mouse pointer onto the illustration window, this is the first version you see. The small X next to the Pen indicates the origin of the path—if you click or start dragging right now.

This mouse pointer represents the Add Anchor Point tool (+). When you move the Pen mouse pointer along a path, the mouse pointer gains the plus sign, which indicates that you can click the path to add an anchor point. However, if you move the Pen mouse pointer to an anchor, Illustrator removes the plus sign altogether or replaces the mouse pointer with one of the following pointers. For more information about the Add Anchor Point tool, refer to "Adding Anchor Points," later in this chapter.

A mouse pointer with a minus sign represents the Delete Anchor Point tool (-). When you move the Pen mouse pointer to an anchor point within a path, Illustrator adds a minus sign to the mouse pointer. However, if you move the Pen mouse pointer away from the anchor, it gets a plus sign instead. For more information about the Delete Anchor Point tool, refer to "Eliminating Anchor Points," later in this chapter.

This mouse pointer is related to and behaves like the Convert Anchor Point tool (SHIFT-C). When the Pen mouse pointer is near the most recently created anchor point (which is currently selected), Illustrator adds the convert anchor point symbol to the mouse pointer, which means you can add a new segment to the current path. When you add a path, Illustrator converts the end point to a smooth or corner anchor point.

When the Pen mouse pointer has an added circle, clicking will close an open path.

When the Pen mouse pointer has an added slash, you are pointing exactly to an end point of a selected path. When the slash appears, you can click the end point to add to the path.

This mouse pointer appears when you point to an end point of a path other than the currently selected one. If you click the end point of another path using this mouse pointer, Illustrator connects end points of two distinct paths.

Creating Straight Paths

Drawing straight paths with the Pen is a matter of two clicks and you're done. To create one or more straight paths, follow these steps:

1. Select the Pen tool (P).
2. Click one end of the future line.

3. Click the other end of the line. Illustrator fills the area between the two clicked points with a line. At either end of the line is an end point.

4. To continue making straight lines, click new places in the illustration window.

Figure 6-7 shows a triangle as its development progresses. Notice the many changes in the mouse pointer during construction. In the top left the mouse pointer aims at the start of the triangle. Below that, the mouse pointer is located at the other end of the triangle's first line. Next is the Smart Guide line showing the first line; following that is the completed line. At the top right of the figure is the Smart Guide aimed at 135° and the mouse at the end point of the second line. Immediately below are the completed line and changed mouse pointer. Next is the mouse pointer aimed at the end of the third line (and the beginning of the first line). Finally, the third line is complete and you have closed the path.

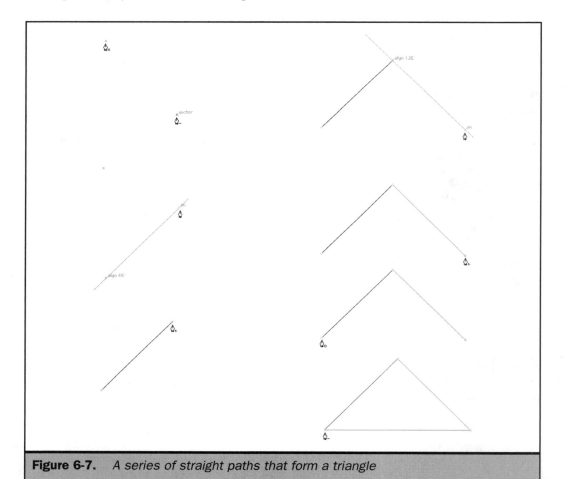

Figure 6-7. *A series of straight paths that form a triangle*

Bézier Curves

The Bézier curve and its inventor Pierre Bézier have been instrumental in the development of Illustrator and other drawing programs based on vector graphics.

A Brief Biography of Pierre Bézier

Pierre Bézier (September 1, 1910–November 25, 1999) was an engineer who worked for French automobile manufacturer Renault for 42 years. Bézier rose through the ranks of Renault as a tool setter, tool designer, and manager of tool design. Later he became the head of production engineering and then head of the machine tool division. His last position at Renault was managing staff member for technical development from 1960 to his retirement in 1975.

In 1960 Bézier researched and designed a computer-aided design/computer-aided manufacturing (CAD/CAM) system. In the 1970s, while a professor of production engineering at Conservatoire National des Arts et Metiers, Bézier invented the Bézier curve for an automobile body design.

An Overview of the Bézier Curve

The Bézier curve, which is described by mathematical formulas, is the foundation of the curved paths used in Illustrator and other vector graphics programs. In addition, Adobe PostScript is based in large part on the formulae of the Bézier curve. You'll also find Bézier curve mathematics used in animation and numerical machine control.

A Bézier curve and a curved path both have end points (an origin point and destination point) on each end of the curve or path, points (on or off the curve) that represent changes in direction, and handles (also known as direction points, tangent points, and nodes). When you move the handles you change the shape of the curve or path. For a list of online resources that discuss Bézier curves, refer to Appendix C.

Creating Curved Paths

When you first put a crayon in your hand, you probably drew nothing but curves—most of your straight lines were not particularly straight. You drew any line by picking up a crayon, putting it on the paper, and moving from one point to another. As you developed your art talent, you still put pen to paper and just drew.

Using the Pen to create curves is somewhat more problematic; instead of drawing as you would with the Pencil, you must plan ahead and answer some questions. What sort of curve do you want? How do you set up the shape of this curve? Constructing a curve involves not only a starting point and ending point, but it also necessitates dragging direction points in one direction or another to actually copy the curve that is in your imagination. Then if you visualize a winding path made up of several curves, you might compound your potential confusion. So, drawing curved paths with the Pen may be daunting at first, but you can master it with a little help.

Before You Draw Your First Curving Paths

Before you create your first curved path, get all the help you can: Choose View | Smart Guides (CTRL-U/⌘-U) to turn on Smart Guides if they aren't already activated, show the Grid by choosing View | Show Grid (CTRL-"/⌘-"), and turn on the snap-to-grid feature by choosing View | Snap to Grid (CTRL-SHIFT-"/⌘-SHIFT-"). You might not need these helpers later, but use every tool at your disposal at this point.

Drawing a Curve from the Horizontal Plane

To draw a curved path using horizontal direction lines, follow these steps:

1. Select the Pen tool (P).

2. Move the Pen mouse pointer to the center of the illustration window.

3. Drag toward the right from the origin point. Illustrator extends direction lines horizontally with direction points from both sides of the origin point.

4. Release the mouse button.

5. Drag the direction point on the right side straight down and release the mouse button. Illustrator creates the curve.

When you drag a direction point at another angle the curve and its angle change. Figure 6-8 shows the development of the curved path (at the top) and four versions caused by dragging the direction point in different directions. At the center left is a curve that results from dragging the right direction point down and to the left; in the center right is a curve created by dragging the right direction point down and to the right; in the bottom left is the consequence of dragging straight up; the last curve is the product of dragging up and to the left. The black pointers in the figure show the directions in which the direction point has been pulled.

Drawing a Curve from the Vertical Plane

To draw a curved path using vertical direction lines, follow these steps:

1. Select the Pen tool (P).

2. Move the Pen mouse pointer to the center of the illustration window.

3. Drag down from the origin point. Illustrator extends direction lines with direction points vertically from both sides of the origin point.

4. Release the mouse button.

5. Drag the direction point toward the right side and release the mouse button. Illustrator creates the curve.

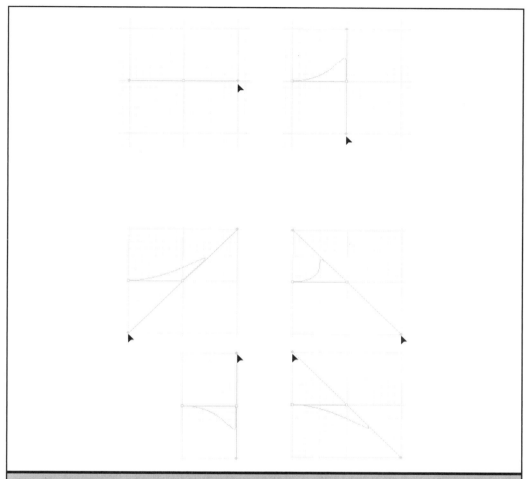

Figure 6-8.   *A curved path under construction and four curves that might result from dragging a direction point in four different directions*

Controlling the Curve

Until now, Illustrator has determined the angle of curves. Because you have dragged the direction points near the original location of the direction lines, the curves have been pretty unattractive. Now you will take one more step to create a rounded curve: Move the mouse pointer away from the original direction lines before you finish the curve. To produce better-looking curves, follow these steps:

1. Select the Pen tool (P).

2. Move the Pen mouse pointer to the center of the illustration window.

3. Drag horizontally from the origin point. Illustrator extends direction lines left and right from both sides of the origin point.

4. Release the mouse button.

5. Click below the origin point. Illustrator creates a curve between the origin point and the location of the click.

6. Drag to the left and release the mouse button. Illustrator creates a more rounded curve.

You can continue clicking and dragging to add a series of curves to the path.

If you press and hold down SHIFT during the drag, you can constrain the drag to 0°, 45°, 90°, 135°, 180°, 225°, 270°, and 315°. Keep in mind that most of these angles do not produce good-looking curves, so restrain yourself as you constrain.

Figure 6-9 shows a rounded curve step by step (from top to bottom): dragging horizontally, clicking to form the other side of the curve, and dragging the curve.

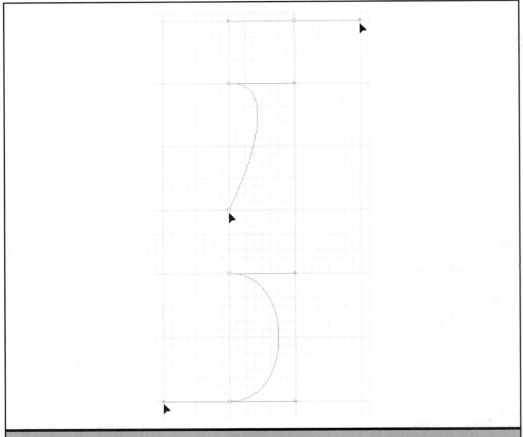

Figure 6-9.   *An improved curve path under construction*

Emulating a Circle with the Pen

As you know, it's easy to create a perfect circle in Illustrator: Select the Ellipse tool, press and hold down SHIFT, and drag a circle. Why bother to use the Pen to create a circle when the end result will not be perfect? The answer is that you will practice, practice, practice using the Pen—and you might be doing something that other Illustrator users would never do. Emulating a circle using the Pen takes four main steps and a few substeps: You'll create four quadrants, join them, and group the parts into one object. To emulate a circle, follow these steps:

1. Choose View | Show Grid (CTRL-"/⌘-") to reveal the grid, which you will use to set the size of the quadrants. However, do not turn on the snap-to-grid feature; when you assemble the circle, snap-to-grid will work against you.

2. Select the Pen tool (P).

3. Moving from left to right, drag a horizontal line across 16 cells in the grid, from one bold vertical line, across another, and ending on another.

4. Click eight cells up from the rightmost direction point. Illustrator forms the first quadrant.

5. Select the Selection tool (V) and click away from the quadrant. (If you didn't deselect the quadrant, the next click or drag of the Pen would act on the finished quadrant.)

> **Tip** *If you don't want to explicitly select the Selection tool (V), you can press and hold down* CTRL, *which temporarily converts any tool to the Selection tool.*

6. Select the Pen tool (P) again.

7. In another part of the illustration window, drag a horizontal line 16 cells across the grid from left to right.

8. Click eight cells down from the rightmost direction point. Illustrator creates another quadrant.

9. Select the Selection tool (V) and deselect the new quadrant.

10. Select the Pen tool (P).

11. Moving from right to left, drag a horizontal line across 16 cells in the grid.

12. Click eight cells above the left direction point. Illustrator creates the third quadrant.

13. Select the Selection tool (V) and deselect the new quadrant.

14. Select the Pen tool (P).

15. Moving from right to left, drag a horizontal line across 16 grid cells.

16. Click eight cells below the left direction point. Illustrator creates the last quadrant.

17. Assemble the four quadrants into a circle-shaped object.

18. Select the Selection tool (V) and drag a bounding box around the joined quadrants.

19. Choose Object | Group (CTRL-G/⌘-G) to group the quadrants.

Figure 6-10 illustrates the progress from the first line (at the top), and moving clockwise, to the final circular object (at the bottom). You can also imitate a perfect circle using vertical lines. Why not try to figure it out?

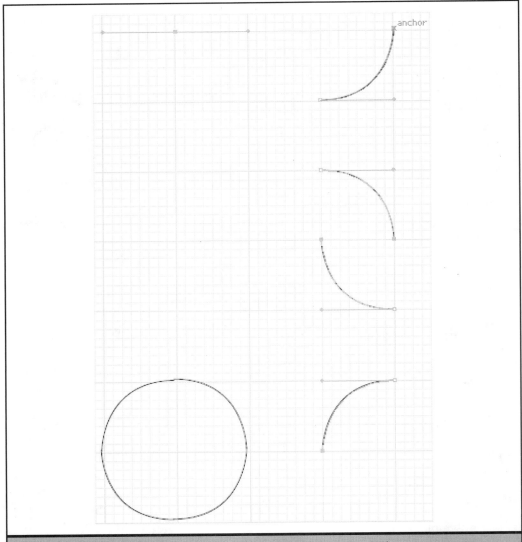

Figure 6-10.   *An emulated circle from the beginning to the end*

Learning the Rules of the Curving Path

Experienced Pen users follow these rules when working with curves:

- Dragging direction points too far or too little affects the angle of a curve, sometimes badly. For the best results, a direction line should be approximately one-third the length of a curve from end point to end point. However, there are always exceptions to this rule: Your eyes can tell you whether a curve looks good or whether a little more or less dragging will help its look.

- Use the origin point as your guide to symmetrical curves. Click a point related to the origin point (for example, at a 90° or 0° angle) to create an evenly balanced curve.

- Keep in mind that direction lines always point at the same angle as the future curve.

- The direction in which you draw from the origin point affects the direction of the resulting curve. If you draw from left to right, the curve flows to the right; if you draw from right to left, the curve flows to the left; if you draw from top to bottom, the curve flows down; if you draw from bottom to top, the curve is toward the top.

- When you construct a curved path that you know that you can never correct, don't fix it; undo it and start over. However, if the curve is just a little off, remember you can edit it. For example, you can select the Direct Selection tool (A) and drag direction points of a path.

- Drag a direction handle in the opposite direction from which you want its curve to move.

- Don't hesitate to add anchor points to curves; especially those that might need a little work later on. Every time a curve changes direction, insert an anchor point if Illustrator hasn't done it already—but don't overdo it.

An Overview of Illustrator Anchor Points

When two paths meet, they make anchor point corners. You've experienced some of these corners already. For example, when a closed path takes a distinct bend (for example, the corner of a rectangle or square or the point at which a polygon side turns into another side), an anchor point appears. Illustrator supports four types of anchor points:

- A *smooth point* marks a minor change in direction. Direction lines for a smooth point always point in opposite directions; when you drag one direction point, the other direction point adjusts so that both direction lines remain opposed. The smooth point is not a corner point.

- A *straight corner point* usually marks the clear junction of two straight line segments. A straight corner point has no direction lines.

- A *curved corner point* indicates the meeting of two curved segments. The end of each segment has a single direction line. Dragging one direction line does not have any effect on the other direction line.

- A *combination corner point* combines one curved segment and one straight segment. A combination corner point has just one direction line—for the curved path. The straight path has no direction line.

To summarize the direction line count in one sentence: Curved paths have one direction line on each end, and straight paths have no direction lines. To learn how to convert any type of anchor point to another type of anchor point, refer to "Converting Points with the Convert Anchor Point Tool," later in this chapter.

Merging Straight and Curved Segments

In a perfect, easy world you might be a specialist in creating straight paths only or just spend your time constructing curved paths. However, in the real world you'll not only create both straight and curved paths, you'll also combine each type often. Merging both types of paths into a *mixed path* means you'll use the line and curve creation methods you learned earlier in this chapter. The anchor point that links the straight and curved segments is a combination corner point.

Drawing a Line Followed by a Curve

To draw a line segment followed by a curved segment, follow these steps:

1. Select the Pen tool (P).
2. Click to start the line and click to end the line. Both clicks create corner points.
3. From the corner marking the end of the line, drag a direction line in the starting angle of the future curve.
4. Click at a location at the other end of the curve. Illustrator fills in the curve between the end point and the point you just created.

Figure 6-11 shows the development of a line segment succeeded by a curved segment from the first line to the final image. Note that one of the lines below the third image from the left is a Smart Guide.

ILLUSTRATOR
ESSENTIALS

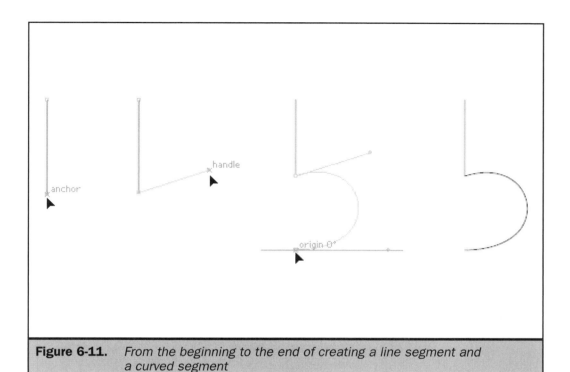

Figure 6-11.   *From the beginning to the end of creating a line segment and a curved segment*

Drawing a Curve Followed by a Line

To draw a curved segment followed by a line segment, follow these steps:

1. Select the Pen tool (P).

2. Drag from top to bottom to form the first side of a curve. When you release the mouse button, Illustrator creates one smooth point at the origin of the curve.

3. Directly across from the origin, drag toward the top of the illustration window. When the curve is symmetrical, release the mouse button. Illustrator makes another smooth point.

4. Click the smooth point on the right side of the curve. Illustrator converts the smooth point to a corner point.

5. Move the Pen mouse pointer away from the newly created corner point and click to make the straight segment.

Figure 6-12 demonstrates the steps in creating and joining a curved segment and line segment.

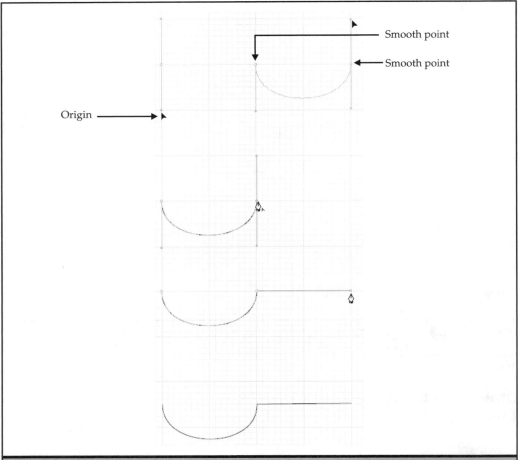

Smooth point

Smooth point

Origin

Figure 6-12.   *Creating a curved segment and line segment, from start to finish*

Drawing Two Curves Joined by a Corner

To draw two curved segments joined by a corner, follow these steps:

1. Select the Pen tool (P).

2. Drag to start the first side of the first curve. When you release the mouse button, Illustrator creates a smooth point.

3. Move the mouse pointer to the other side of the first curve and click to set the curve's distance from the first side to the second.

4. Drag a direction point to shape the curve.

5. Move the Pen mouse pointer to the start of the next curve at the end of the first curve.

6. To start the second curve, start dragging a direction point from the smooth point.

7. While dragging the direction point, press and hold down ALT, and change the direction in which you are dragging to set the track of the second curve.

8. Release the mouse pointer and ALT. Illustrator changes the curve's smooth point to a curved corner point.

9. Click the end location of the second curve and drag a direction point to shape the curve.

Figure 6-13 shows two curves as they are created and then joined by a corner point.

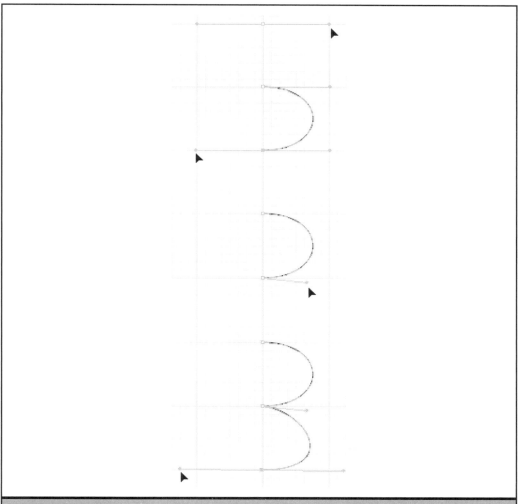

Figure 6-13.   *Constructing two curved segments connected by a corner point*

ILLUSTRATOR
ESSENTIALS

Modifying Paths and Points

For a tool as important as the Pen tool (P), you would expect plenty of editing tools and you wouldn't be wrong. Illustrator provides a number of toolbox tools as well as several menu commands that you can use to modify paths and points. Among the many things you will learn in this section are how to add, delete, convert, average, and join anchor points. You'll also find out how to reshape, offset, split, and slice (but not dice) paths. Finally, if you leave a lot of spare points and objects around the illustration window, you'll discover how to clean up a document.

Adding Anchor Points

When you learned about the Pen tool (P), you found out that sometimes the Pen mouse pointer changes so that you can add an anchor point to a path. Adding an anchor point to a path enables you to modify part of the path or make the path longer. For example, you can add an anchor point so you can use the Direct Selection tool (A) to drag the point and the path to which it is attached to a new location and change the shape of the path. After you have created a path and are finished with the Pen—for now, anyway—Illustrator provides a tool and a command for adding anchor points at any time.

Using the Add Anchor Point Tool

To add an anchor point to a path, follow these steps:

1. Select the Add Anchor Point tool (+) from the Pen toolslot.

2. Move the mouse pointer to the location of the new anchor point on a path.

3. Click to add the anchor point to the path.

If you click away from a path, Illustrator displays an error message. If you press and hold down ALT while the Add Anchor Point tool is active, you can use the Delete Anchor Point tool to delete anchor points. Holding down CTRL while using the Add Anchor Point tool temporarily shifts to the Selection tool (V).

Using the Add Anchor Points Command

When you want to add several anchor points simultaneously to a path and don't care where you place the anchor points, use the Add Anchor Points command. Every time you choose Object | Path | Add Anchor Points, Illustrator inserts anchor points between the existing anchor points on the selected path. So, every time you choose the command, the number of anchor points on a path doubles.

Eliminating Anchor Points

As you know, the Pen tool (P) anticipates your possible needs by changing its purpose as well as its appearance from time to time. For example, when you move the Pen mouse pointer over an anchor point, the mouse pointer converts into the Delete Anchor Point mouse pointer so you can remove the anchor point and change the shape of the path. After you have completed a path, you may want to return to it in order to change its shape or just clean it up a bit. For this purpose, Illustrator provides both the Delete Anchor Point tool (-) and the Simplify command.

Deleting Points

You've already seen the Pen tool convert into the Delete Anchor Point mouse pointer whenever you moved the Pen mouse pointer over an anchor point. You can select the Delete Anchor Point tool (-) on its own. To delete an anchor point from a path, follow these steps:

1. Select the Delete Anchor Point tool (-) from the Pen toolslot.
2. Move the mouse pointer to an anchor point on a selected path.
3. Click to remove the anchor point from the path. If the deleted anchor point indicated a change in the path's direction, Illustrator redraws the path using the current anchor points as a guide.

If you click away from a path or don't point to an anchor point, Illustrator displays an error message. If you press and hold down ALT while the Delete Anchor Point tool is active, you can use the Add Anchor Point tool to add anchor points. Holding down CTRL while using the Delete Anchor Point tool temporarily shifts to the Selection tool (V).

Simplifying Paths

You can delete any anchor points that do not have an effect on the direction or shape of a path, according to Illustrator's programmed point of view. When you choose Object | Path | Simplify, Illustrator opens the Simplify dialog box (see Figure 6-19) in which you can set several simplification options.

- Slide the Curve Precision slider or type a value in the text box to set the fit between the original path and the simplified path. Valid values range between 0% (no fit to the original path) and 100% (a precise fit to the original path). The default is 50%.

- Slide the Angle Threshold slider or type a value in the text box to set the sharpness of the corners. Valid values range between 0 (relatively smooth angles) and 180° (relatively sharp angles). The default is 0.

- Check Straight Lines to place straight lines between the original path's anchor points. The results vary depending on the Angle Threshold setting.

- Check Show Original to display the original path behind the simplified one.

- Check Preview to see how the changes affect the original path before you click OK to apply the changes and close the dialog box.

Figure 6-14 shows the Simplify dialog box along with the original version of a face on the left and the simplified version on the right.

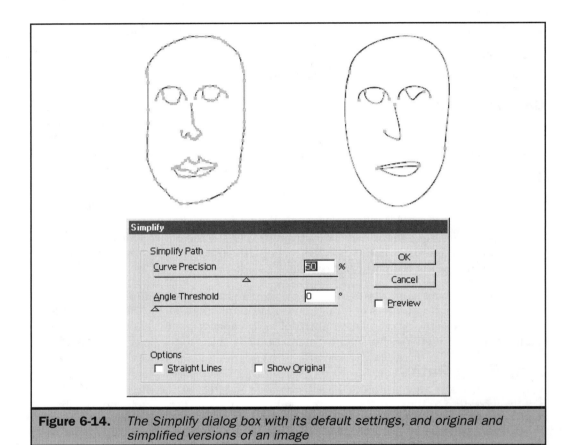

Figure 6-14. *The Simplify dialog box with its default settings, and original and simplified versions of an image*

Converting Points with the Convert Anchor Point Tool

The Convert Anchor Point tool (SHIFT-C) is another tool with which you have already had some experience because of your work with the Pen tool (P). When you worked with drawing combinations of curves and straight lines, you converted smooth points to corner points by using the convert anchor point Pen mouse pointer. The Convert Anchor Point tool works in much the same way as its temporary Pen version; however, you can convert all types of anchor points to smooth points and straight corner points using the Convert Anchor Point tool, sometimes with the help of the Direct Selection tool (A).

Converting Smooth Points to Corner Points

You can convert smooth points, which indicate a slight change in direction in a path and which have two direction points, to straight corner points, curved corner points, and combination corner points.

■ To convert a smooth point to a straight corner point, click the anchor point with the Convert Anchor Point tool. At the new corner point, the path definitely changes direction rather than flowing smoothly.

■ To convert a smooth point to a curved corner point, drag a control handle with the Convert Anchor Point tool. At this point you'll find that the two control handles associated with the smooth point move in any direction; they no longer move in tandem, but always in an opposite direction.

■ To convert a smooth point to a combination corner point, select the point with the Direct Selection tool. Then drag the visible direction point toward the anchor point.

Converting Straight Corner Points

You can convert straight corner points, which are the meeting of two straight segments and which have no direction lines, to smooth points, curved corner points, and combination corner points.

■ To convert a straight corner point to a smooth point, drag the anchor point a short distance using the Convert Anchor Point tool. As you drag, new direction lines appear, enabling you to shape the curve related to the smooth point.

■ To convert a straight corner point to a curved corner point, use the preceding instructions. Then drag one of the direction points to make it independent of the other direction point.

■ To convert a straight corner point to a combination corner point, use the Convert Anchor Point tool to drag the anchor point. When you see two direction lines, drag one direction point into the anchor point.

The top section of Figure 6-15 illustrates a starting curved point (on the left) and three corner points: from left to right, straight, curved, and combination. The bottom section of the figure shows the starting straight corner point (on the left) and, from left to right, its conversion to a smooth point, curved corner point, and combination corner point. In both rows, all the images are selected so that all the possible anchor points and direction lines are shown.

Converting Curved Corner Points

You can convert curved corner points, which are the distinct meeting of two curved segments and which have two independent direction lines, to smooth points, straight corner points, and combination corner points.

■ To convert a curved corner point to a smooth point, drag the anchor point with the Convert Anchor Point tool. Switch to the Direct Selection tool to move the direction points to set the angle of the curve.

■ To convert a curved corner point to a straight corner point, click the anchor point with the Convert Anchor Point tool.

■ To convert a curved corner point to a combination corner point, drag a direction point into the anchor point with the Direct Selection tool.

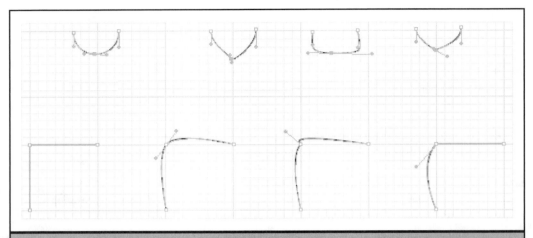

Figure 6-15.   *An original curved point and the converted straight, curved, and combination corner points; and an original straight corner point and its conversion to a smooth point, curved corner point, and combination corner point*

Converting Combination Corner Points

You can convert combination corner points, which are the meeting of one straight segment and one curved segment and which have one direction line, to smooth points, straight corner points, and curved corner points.

- To convert a combination corner point to a smooth point, drag the anchor point with the Convert Anchor Point tool. Then move the direction points to set the angle of the curve.

- To convert a combination corner point to a straight corner point, click the Convert Anchor Point tool once on the anchor point.

- To convert a combination corner point to a curved corner point, drag the anchor point using the Convert Anchor Point tool. Then drag one of the direction points to make it independent of the other direction point.

The top row of Figure 6-16 shows the starting curved corner point and its conversion to, from left to right, a smooth point, straight corner point, and combination corner point. The bottom row in the figure illustrates a combination corner point and the smooth point, straight corner point, and combination corner point that result from using the Convert Anchor Point tool. Every image is selected so that you can view all the anchor points and direction lines.

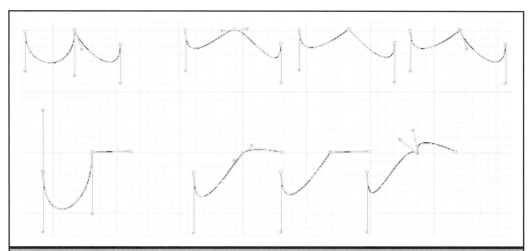

Figure 6-16. *On the top, an original curved corner point and the resulting smooth point, straight corner point, and combination corner point; on the bottom, a combination corner point and its converted points; a smooth point, straight corner point, and curved corner point*

> **Note** *Normally, pairs of direction lines work together; they always flow in opposite directions. With the Convert Anchor Point tool, you can drag a single direction point to change the shape of a path.*

Averaging Points

When Illustrator averages points, it moves the segments so the selected points are arranged horizontally, vertically, or both. Illustrator calculates the center of the selected points and averages them so that they are aligned, making it easier to join them with an additional line segment or move them together.

> **Note** *You must select two or more points before you average them. If you inadvertently select all the points in an object, the command will either align the points in a horizontal or vertical line or place all the points in one spot in the illustration window.*

To average points, follow these steps:

1. With the Direct Selection tool (A), select one point. Pressing and holding down SHIFT, select one or more additional points.

2. Choose Object | Path | Average (CTRL-ALT-J/⌘-OPTION-J). Illustrator opens the Average dialog box (see Figure 6-17).

3. Click Horizontal to average the selected points horizontally, Vertical to average the selected points vertically, or Both to average the points both horizontally and vertically.

4. Click OK. Illustrator computes the averages and changes the selected points and their lines.

In addition to showing the Average dialog box, Figure 6-17 illustrates an original open path, on the left; next, a version averaged horizontally; one averaged vertically; and the rightmost image averaged both horizontally and vertically.

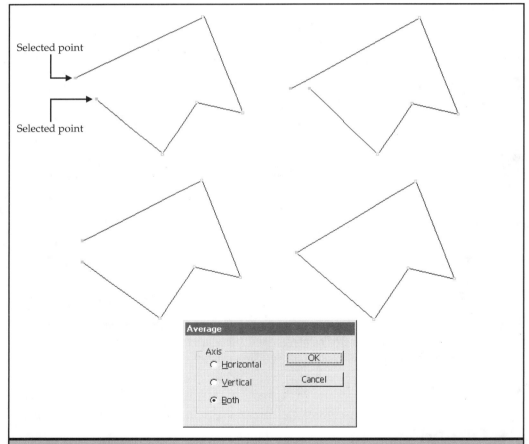

Figure 6-17. *The average dialog box and four versions of an open path: the original at the top left, the horizontally averaged path at the top right, vertically averaged path at the bottom left, and the path averaged both horizontally and vertically at the bottom right*

Joining Points

Illustrator joins open-end points in two ways: It either draws a line segment between them or merges them. The choice depends on how near the points are to each other. If the points are not exactly on top of each other, Illustrator draws a line. If one point covers the other point, Illustrator merges them into a single point. The points to be joined can be in the same path or different paths. If the points are in different paths, they cannot be the end points of text paths or in a graph. If the points are grouped, they must be in the same group.

To join end points that are separated, follow these steps:

1. With the Direct Selection tool (A), select one open end point.

2. While pressing and holding down SHIFT, select another open end point.

3. Choose Object | Path | Join (CTRL-J/⌘-J). Illustrator draws a line between the points.

To join end points that are on top of each other, follow these steps:

1. With the Direct Selection tool (A), drag a bounding box just large enough to enclose the two end points that occupy the same location.

2. Choose Object | Path | Join (CTRL-J/⌘-J). Illustrator opens the Join dialog box.

3. Select a Corner or Smooth point, and click OK. Illustrator merges the points.

In addition to illustrating the Join dialog box, Figure 6-18 shows prejoined and joined versions of two curved paths. At the top of the paths before joining, the end points are on top of each other. At the bottom of the paths before joining, two end points are separated. One path is selected and the other is not, to show that the paths are separate. Notice that the joined versions meet at the top. Because the two bottom end points were apart, a line joins them.

 Note   *The snap-to-point feature works in about the same way as the snap-to-grid feature. When snap-to-point is turned on, you can move one point on top of another. To do so, drag one end point with the Selection tool (v) or the Direct Selection tool (a). When the filled black arrowhead pointer looks as if it is unfilled, release the mouse button. The dragged point will snap to the target point. To activate the snap-to-point feature, choose View | Snap to Point (CTRL-ALT-"/⌘-OPTION-").*

Reshaping a Segment

 Use the Reshape tool to drag one or more anchor points and associated path segments into a new shape. Unselected anchor points and segments remain in their original locations. Before you use the Reshape tool, select at least one anchor point. You can press and hold down SHIFT and click to add anchor points and paths to the selection.

When the Reshape tool is active, its mouse pointer changes as you move it around the illustration window. If you point to an anchor point or move around

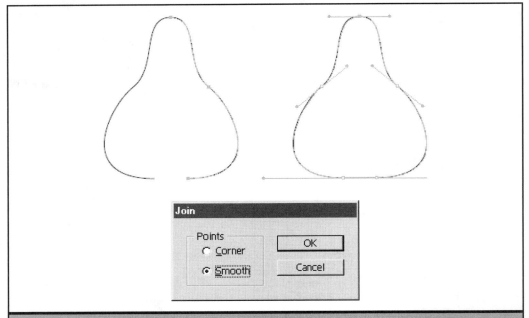

Figure 6-18.   *The Join dialog box and, on the left above it, an open path with separate end points and the path with a line between the end points; on the right, a path with two end points in the same place and the same path with one joined end point*

the illustration window away from any selected path, the gray mouse pointer has no associated icons. However, if you point to a selected path, the mouse pointer adds a small rectangle enclosing a dot. This added icon indicates that you can click to create a new anchor point.

The behavior of the Reshape tool varies depending on how many paths and points are in the selection:

- If you select one anchor point, move the mouse pointer to that anchor point. Then drag to move the anchor point and reshape the paths on either side.

- If one path is part of a selection, add an anchor point by moving the mouse pointer to a path and click. Illustrator adds an anchor point that you can drag to reshape the path.

■ If you select more than one anchor point, all points and the paths within the points move when you drag. However, the anchor point you are dragging moves more than any others.

What's the difference between dragging with the Direct Selection tool (A) and the Reshape tool? When you use the Direct Selection tool to drag a line segment, the position of the line segment changes but its shape does not. The Reshape tool also changes the location of the line segment. However, it goes beyond that to reshape, depending on the placement of the anchor point that the Reshape tool adds.

Offsetting a Path

You can use the offset feature to create a new path using an existing path as its basis. For example, if you draw a series of line segments, you can construct a snake-like closed path by offsetting an open path and specifying a round join, or you can use offsetting to create a series of ever smaller rectangles within rectangles.

To offset a path, select it and choose Object | Path | Offset Path. Illustrator opens the Offset Path dialog box (see Figure 6-19).

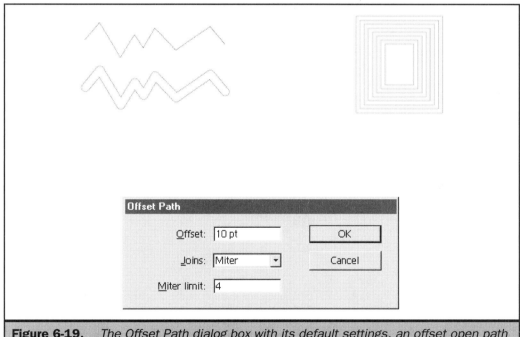

Figure 6-19.   *The Offset Path dialog box with its default settings, an offset open path on the left, and an offset closed path on the right*

Use the options in the dialog box as follows:

■ Type an offset value in the Offset text box. If you enter a positive number, the offset path is outside the path on which it is based. The snake path has been offset by a positive number, the default 10 points. The rectangle offsets are based on a negative number, -10pt. A value of 0 creates a duplicate of the path on top of the path.

■ A *join* is the shape of the turn of a corner. A *miter join* adds a sharp point to a corner, a *round join* creates a curving corner, and a *bevel join* squares a corner. From the Joins drop-down menu select Miter, Round, or Bevel.

■ If you choose a miter join, you can type a value in the Miter Limit text box. The miter limit determines when a miter join point decreases to a flat bevel join. If you accept the default Miter Limit value of 4, the current miter point is 4 times the stroke weight of 1. So, depending on the stroke weight, a lower miter limit flattens the miter join and a higher miter limit increases the angle of the point.

Note   *Illustrator also provides a command for offsetting paths as an effect. To do so, choose Effect | Path | Offset Path. The Offset dialog box resulting from this command is almost identical to the Offset dialog box that you just learned about. One exception is that the new dialog box also includes a Preview check box, so you can preview the offset path before you click OK and close the dialog box. Another difference is that you cannot drag the original path away from the offset path. For more information about using effects on your artwork, refer to Chapter 16.*

In addition to showing the Offset Path dialog box, Figure 6-19 illustrates before-and-after versions of an offset open path (on the left) and an offset closed path whose original path is the largest rectangle.

Splitting Paths with the Scissors Tool

The Scissors tool (C) enables you to split a path into two separate paths. If you cut a closed path, one click of the scissors on a path or anchor point is all you need to do. If you split a closed path, you'll have to cut in two separate places. You cannot use the Scissors tool on a type path.

To split a path with the Scissors tool, follow these steps:

1. Select the path.

2. Select the Scissors tool (C). When you move the mouse pointer onto the illustration window, it becomes a cross-hairs pointer.

3. If you want to split an open path, click anywhere on the path or an anchor point.

4. If you want to split a closed path, click one part of the path or an anchor point. Then click another location on the path or an anchor point to finish the split.

5. If you want to cut a straight line, press and hold down ALT/OPTION while dragging.

When you split an open or closed path, Illustrator creates end points at the point of the split and leaves one new path selected and the other unselected.

Cutting Path Areas with the Knife Tool

 The Knife tool slices pieces of a path in the same way that you would cut a piece from a wedge of cheese. Before you cut, you do not need to select all or part of the path. To use the Knife tool, follow these steps:

1. Select the Knife tool.
2. Drag the mouse pointer across the paths to be cut. Illustrator selects the part of the path that has been cut, including the section that has been removed by the Knife.
3. Select the section that has been taken off and drag it away.
4. Use a drawing tool to repair any missing pieces of the remaining path.

Figure 6-20 shows the before and after images of a chunk of cheese. The Knife tool has cut a couple more holes in the lower piece. Of course, using the Knife on the edges

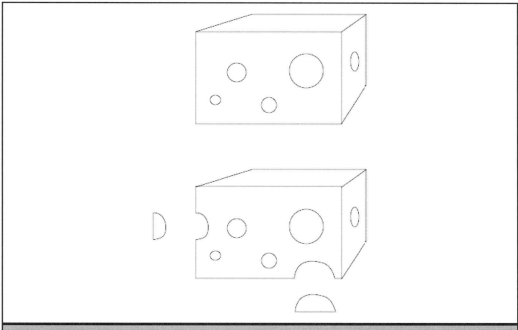

Figure 6-20. *A piece of Swiss cheese that has been enhanced by cutting with the Knife tool*

of the image is much easier than cutting from within the image. Sometimes it makes sense to use quick-and-dirty methods to edit artwork.

Cutting Path Areas with a Command

You can choose the Divide Objects Below command to cut an object using another object as the cutting instrument. To use the Divide Objects Below command, follow these steps:

1. Create two objects, one to be cut and the other to be the cutter.

2. Place the cutting object over the object to be cut in the exact location to be cut. Now the object to be cut is below the other object (hence, the name of the command).

3. Choose Object | Path | Divide Objects Below. Illustrator removes the cutting object and cuts a new path into the object below.

Figure 6-21 shows the two objects side by side (at the top), one object over the other, the cut object, and the two sections of the cut object dragged apart (at the bottom).

Cleaning Up a Document

When you have worked extensively on artwork, you may leave a clutter of odds and ends lying around the illustration window. Cleanup works on the entire document—regardless of whether all or part is selected—but does not clean locked and hidden paths, paths on locked and hidden layers, or paths converted into guides. To run the cleanup feature, choose Object | Path | Cleanup. When Illustrator opens the Cleanup dialog box (see Figure 6-22), check one or all of the options and click OK.

- Check Stray Points to eliminate any anchor points that are not associated with any of the images that you want to keep. Sometimes, stray points have characteristics such as colors that might appear as dots in a printed document.

- Check Unpainted Objects to delete paths that are invisible because they have Fill and Stroke of None.

- Check Empty Text Paths to remove any text paths without type.

It's a good idea to run cleanup whenever you finish a document; if no cleanup is necessary, Illustrator displays a message.

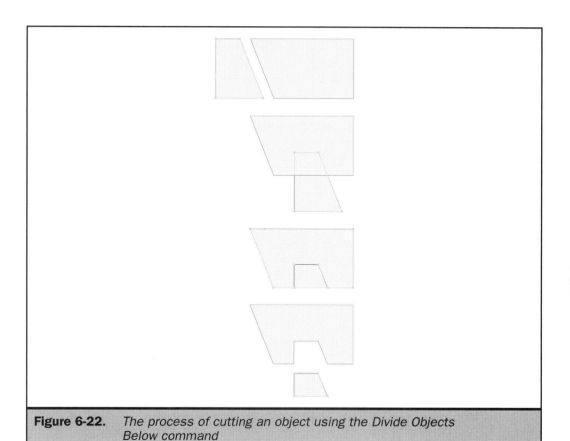

Figure 6-22.   *The process of cutting an object using the Divide Objects Below command*

Figure 6-21.   *The Clean Up dialog box with its default settings of three checked check boxes*

Editing Paths with the Pathfinder Palette

Earlier in the chapter you learned about the Join feature, which joins two anchor points on top of each other or unites two unattached anchor points with a line segment. You also found out about the Scissors and Knife tools with which you can separate paths and cut pieces off a path, respectively. With the Pathfinder palette, you can join, separate, and cut selected overlapping paths in more sophisticated ways than you can using some of the tools that you have learned about earlier in this chapter. When you use the Pathfinder palette to work on individual paths, the resulting objects are known as *compound shapes*.

Exploring the Pathfinder Palette

The Pathfinder palette (see Figure 6-23) contains a set of buttons that make it easy to perform a variety of actions on two or more paths. Rather than select a command or wield a toolbox tool, you can open the palette and click a button. To toggle between showing and hiding the palette, choose Window | Pathfinder (SHIFT-F9). Note that all actions in the Pathfinder palette also are available as effects using the Effect | Pathfinder menu. For more information about effects, refer to Chapter 16.

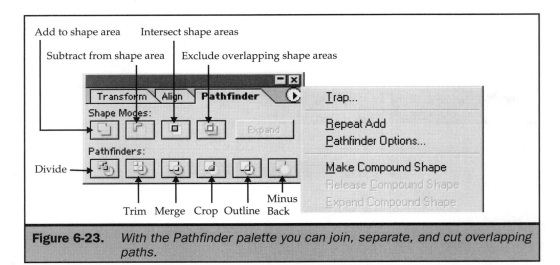

Figure 6-23.   *With the Pathfinder palette you can join, separate, and cut overlapping paths.*

To open the palette's menu, click the menu button.

- The Trap command opens the Pathfinder Trap dialog box with which you can set trapping options. *Trapping* adjusts for colors that are not properly aligned with adjacent or overlapping colors by overprinting a color.

- The Repeat command repeats the most recent action. So if you have added to the shape area, the Repeat command is called Repeat Add; if you have subtracted from the shape area, the Repeat command is known as Repeat Subtract.

- The Pathfinder Options command opens the Palette Options dialog box with which you can select the accuracy of Pathfinder results and clean up extra points and unpainted artwork. To learn how to customize Illustrator palettes, read "Customizing a Palette" in Appendix B.

- The Make Compound Shape command repeats the most recent action generated from within the Pathfinder palette.

- The Release Compound Shape command releases the top path from a selected compound shape. The path remains on the compound shape but can be removed.

- The Expand Compound Shape command combines all (that is, flattens) the paths within a compound shape into a single path.

Note *Many Pathfinder buttons act on shapes that are not only overlapping but also in certain positions: in front or in back of another selected shape. To move a shape to the front of all other selected shapes, choose Object | Arrange | Bring to Front (CTRL-SHIFT-]/⌘-SHIFT-]). To move a shape one shape forward in the pile, choose Object | Arrange | Bring Forward (CTRL-]/⌘-]). To move a shape to the back of all other selected shapes, choose Object | Arrange | Send to Back (CTRL-SHIFT-[/⌘-SHIFT-[). To move a shape one shape back of the pile, choose Object | Arrange | Bring Forward (CTRL-[/⌘-[).*

Figure 6-24 illustrates some of the changes that you can make using the Pathfinder palette. At the top of the figure are the two original star and rectangle paths that are converted by clicking various buttons on the palette. From left to right, you can see the results of clicking Add to the Shape Area, Subtract from the Shape Area, Intersect Shape Areas, Exclude Overlapping Shape Areas, and Minus Back.

Figure 6-24.   *Add to the Shape Area, Subtract from the Shape Area, Intersect Shape Areas, Exclude Overlapping Shape Areas, and Minus Back*

Adding to the Shape Area

Clicking Add to the Shape Area adds the shape of the path in front to the path in back. If the selected paths have different fill and stroke colors, the combined shape assumes the characteristics of the shape that is on top.

Subtracting from the Shape Area

Clicking Subtract from the Shape Area removes the shape of the path in front from the path in back. In previous versions of Illustrator, this button was called Minus Front.

Intersecting Shape Areas

The Intersect Shape Areas button removes everything from the selected paths except the parts that intersect. If the selected paths have different fill and stroke colors, the combined shape assumes the characteristics of the shape that is on top.

Excluding Overlapping Shape Areas

When you click Exclude Overlapping Shape Areas, the result is exactly opposite the outcome of clicking the Intersect Shape Areas button: Illustrator removes all intersecting parts of the selected paths. If the selected paths have different fill and stroke colors, the combined shape assumes the characteristics of the shape that is on top.

Minusing Shape Areas

When you click Minus Back, the outcome is exactly opposite of clicking Subtract from the Shape Area. Instead of removing the shape of the path in front from the path in back, Illustrator removes the shape of the path in back from the path in front.

Expanding Selected Shape Areas

Clicking the Expand button flattens compound shapes: It combines all selected shapes into one path. Pressing Expand is exactly the same as selecting the Expand Compound Shape command from the Pathfinder palette menu.

 When you press and hold down ALT *while clicking any of these buttons, Illustrator expands the selected shape.*

Dividing Selected Shape Areas

When you click the Divide button, Illustrator draws new paths where each selected shape intersects with other selected shapes. The shapes retain their original fills, and strokes are applied to all the new paths. Figure 6-25 shows the results of dividing selected shapes. Note that most of the divided segments have been pulled away from each other using the Direct Selection tool (A).

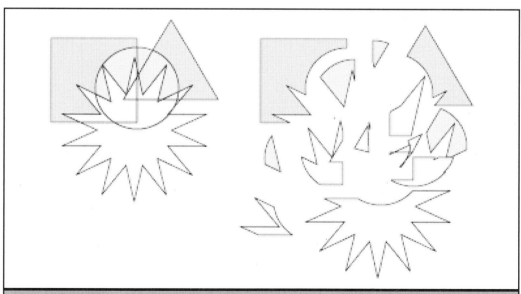

Figure 6-25. *On the left, several overlapping shapes; on the right, divided pieces of the original shapes dragged apart*

Trimming Selected Shape Areas

If you select paths that overlap other paths and click Trim, Illustrator removes all the overlapping areas in the back; the remaining parts lose their strokes: Illustrator sets stroke to None. Figure 6-26 shows the progression from the original shapes unselected and selected and the aftermath of trimming, selected, unselected, and pulled apart.

Figure 6-26.   *Five steps with the original shapes (at the top) and, moving clockwise, down to the trimmed shapes pulled apart*

Merging Selected Shape Areas

Clicking the Merge button evaluates selected objects and trims and then goes beyond that to unite overlapping shapes that have the identical fill color. Figure 6-27 illustrates the effect of clicking Merge on several objects, some with a red fill and others with a yellow fill. Before the merge, each circle is a single object; after merging, pairs of red circles are combined, yet the yellow circles remain separate. Note that all the circles have no stroke after merging.

Cropping Selected Shape Areas

When you click the Crop button, Illustrator separates overlapping shapes and then removes all the pieces that are outside the top shape. At the same time, Illustrator changes the color of the top object to that of the bottom and sets the stroke to None. The top row of Figure 6-28 illustrates the original shapes, a light-colored circle on top of a darker rectangle, and the cropped outcome, a dark-colored circle.

Outlining Selected Shape Areas

The Outline feature works in much the same way as Divide: Clicking Outline creates new paths at the intersections of all the selected shapes. Outlining selected shapes divides them, gives the stroke the fill color, and sets the fill to None. The bottom row of Figure 6-28 starts with original objects, which are black squares with a stroke set to 4 points wide. After clicking Outline, each of the squares has no fill and a black stroke. You can use

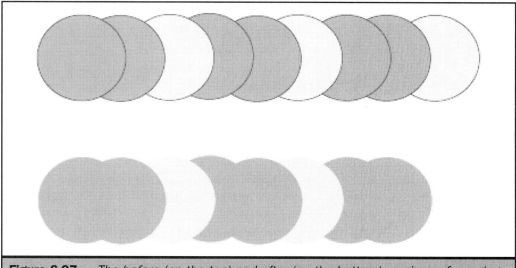

Figure 6-27. *The before (on the top) and after (on the bottom) versions of merging on several circles, some red and others yellow*

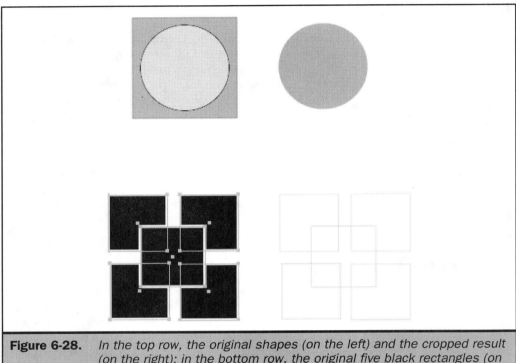

Figure 6-28.   *In the top row, the original shapes (on the left) and the cropped result (on the right); in the bottom row, the original five black rectangles (on the left) and the aftereffects of outlining (on the right)*

the Direct Selection tool (A) to pull the pieces apart. To do so, make sure all the anchor points of a chosen segment are selected (that is, filled in).

Setting Pathfinder Trap Options

When you choose the Trap command from the Pathfinder palette menu, Illustrator opens the Pathfinder Trap dialog box (see Figure 6-29). For more information about traps, see "Trapping" in Chapter 22.

Select one or more of the following options from the dialog box:

- Type the thickness of the trap, the area of color that stretches beyond the current area, in the Thickness text box. Valid values range from 0.01 to 5,000. The default thickness is 0.25 points.

- In the Height/Width text box, type the percentage by which the height of the trap varies from the width. Valid values range from 25 to 400. The default is 100%.

- In the Tint Reduction text box, type the percentage of reduction of the lighter color with which Illustrator tints the trap area. Valid values range from 0 to 100. The default is 40%.

- Check Traps with Process Color to change *spot colors* (colors in an artwork that are printed with particular inks) to the comparable *process colors* (process inks, which are printed over each other to produce a color print). You'll learn more about spot colors and process colors in Chapter 7.

- Check Reverse Traps to change traps that are dark colored to light colored.

- Click Defaults to return to the original values in the dialog box.

Setting Pathfinder Options

When you choose the Pathfinder Options command from the Pathfinder palette menu, the Pathfinder Options dialog box (see Figure 6-30) appears. Work with the following options in the dialog box:

- In the Calculate Precision text box, type a value (in points) indicating the exact tolerances that Illustrate uses to act on your button clicks in the palette. Valid values range from 0.001 to 100; the default is 0.028.

- Check Remove Redundant Points to clean up overlapping points that result from some of the actions taken from within the palette.

- Check Divide & Outline Will Remove Unpainted Artwork to clean up pieces of objects with fill and stroke values of None. These pieces usually occur when you divide selected space areas.

- Click Defaults to return to the original values in the dialog box.

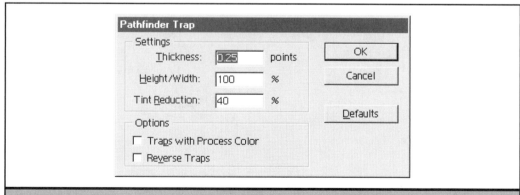

Figure 6-29.   *The Pathfinder Trap dialog box with its default settings*

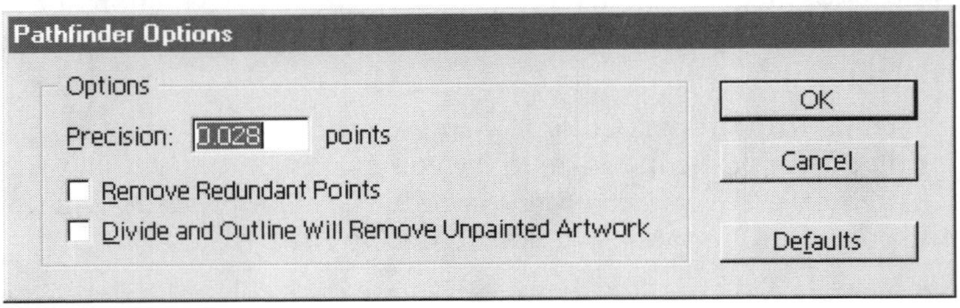

Figure 6-30. *The Pathfinder Options dialog box with its original options*

The
Complete
Reference

Chapter 7

Illustrator Color Basics

Most artworks created in Illustrator combine colors, white, grays, and black rather than using only black, white, and grays; so it follows that color is very important to every Illustrator user. In this chapter you'll learn more about the fill and stroke and other significant color features of Illustrator: the Stroke palette, the Swatches palette, and the Color palette. You'll learn how to choose and mix colors using the color spectrum and color sliders in the Color palette and how to use the Color Picker dialog box.

What Are the Fill and Stroke?

The *fill* of an object is a color, pattern, or gradient inside a closed path or between the end points of a curving open path. A *gradient* is a gradual transition from one color through intermediate colors to a final color, from one edge of an image to another or from the center to the outside.

A *stroke* is a color or pattern—but not a gradient—that always uses a path as a center point. You can set the stroke to any thickness using the Stroke palette. You'll learn about the Stroke palette and stroke attributes you can set later in this chapter.

You can set the fill or stroke to None, which means Illustrator removes the color, pattern, or gradient for a selected object. Of course, if you set both the fill and stroke to None, your artwork becomes completely invisible, which doesn't make much sense. For most of your artwork, you'll use both fill and stroke color characteristics. However, sometimes you can create an image with the stroke only—that is, if you have made the stroke wide enough or fill only.

Figure 7-1 shows assorted objects with different fill and stroke settings. On the left are two images with reversed fill and stroke colors and a stroke width of 6 points. In the middle is an image with no fill (the fill is set to None) and a Camouflage pattern stroke of 30. At the right side is an image with no stroke and a Copper gradient fill. For more information about gradients, refer to Chapter 9.

Setting Fill and Stroke from the Toolbox

As you learned in Chapter 1, you can click buttons at the bottom of the toolbox (see Figure 7-2) to toggle between the fill and stroke (X); return to the default fill of white and stroke of black; swap the fill and stroke; or set the fill or stroke (whichever is active) to the most recent Color (<), Gradient (>), or None (/)—no color at all. When you change the fill or stroke in any way, the fill or stroke also changes in the Color palette.

Applying the Current Fill or Stroke to an Object

When you complete a newly created object, Illustrator automatically applies the current fill and stroke colors because the object is selected as you create it. Using this technique, you cannot apply fill and stroke colors unless an object is selected—either routinely in the case of an object on which you are working or explicitly when you select an object in the illustration window.

ILLUSTRATOR
ESSENTIALS

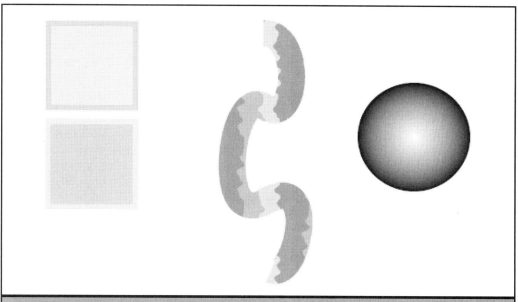

Figure 7-1.   *Several images with various fill and stroke settings*

You also can apply the fill or stroke color to an object—selected or unselected—by dragging the fill or stroke to the object. You also can apply a color to an object by dragging a swatch from the Swatches palette, the fill or stroke from the Color palette, or a gradient from the Gradient palette.

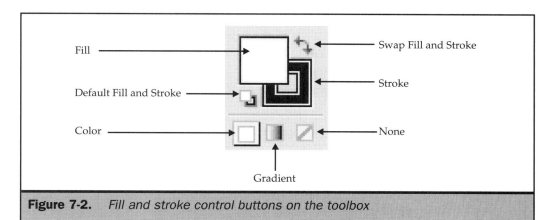

Figure 7-2.   *Fill and stroke control buttons on the toolbox*

Sometimes you'll forget to deselect an object as you get ready to make another. As you choose fill and stroke colors for the new object, Illustrator applies those new colors to the selected object. To remove the new colors, choose Edit | Undo (CTRL-Z/⌘-Z); the fill and stroke boxes revert to the prior colors. Then deselect the object that was inadvertently changed.

Swapping Fill and Stroke

You might want to color some objects with particular fill and stroke colors and then reverse the fill and stroke colors for other objects in the same artwork. For example, if you make a checkerboard with blue and yellow squares, you could apply blue fill and yellow stroke colors to half the pieces, swap colors, and then apply yellow fill and blue stroke to the other half. To swap the fill and stroke, click the Swap Fill and Stroke button (SHIFT-X). However, before you do so remember to deselect all selected objects that you don't want to affect with the color changes.

Reverting to the Default Fill and Stroke Colors

Sometimes it's better to start from scratch than to keep adjusting colors. To return to the default black stroke and white fill, just click the Default Fill and Stroke button (D). It doesn't matter if the fill is set to a gradient and the stroke is currently a pattern. When you click Default Fill and Stroke, the fill and stroke are white and black, respectively.

Specifying the Fill or Stroke Type

When you select a new fill or stroke color, you can set its type: Color for the fill and stroke, Gradient for the Fill only, or None for the fill and stroke. To set a color type, follow these steps:

1. Make the fill or stroke active.

2. To use the most recent color or pattern for the fill or stroke, click Color (<).

3. To use the most recent gradient for the fill, click Gradient (>). Illustrator opens the Gradient palette as it changes the fill to a gradient.

4. To remove all color characteristics from the fill or stroke, click None (/).

Figure 7-3 shows the results of selecting Color (on the left) for the fill and stroke, with the stroke active; Gradient (in the center) for the fill, with the fill active; and None (on the right) for the fill, with the fill active. To show the effects of the various selections, the grid is active in the illustration window. Notice that when the fill is active, the Color button looks like the fill; however, when the stroke is active the Color button looks like the stroke.

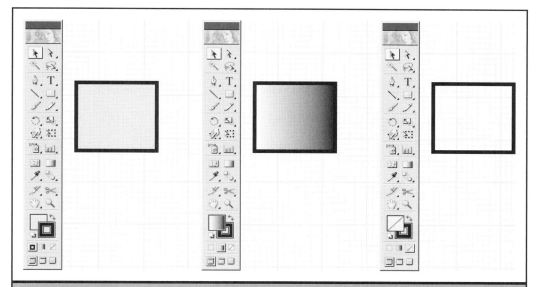

Figure 7-3. *Several versions of the toolbox and affected objects with Color, Gradient, and None selected*

Exploring the Stroke Palette

The Stroke palette (see Figure 7-4) enables you to apply characteristics to the stroke. Using the Stroke palette you can convert the stroke—which is solid by default—to a dashed line. You also can set the stroke weight, and specify the appearance of the ends and corners of lines. To toggle between showing and hiding the palette, choose Window | Stroke (F10).

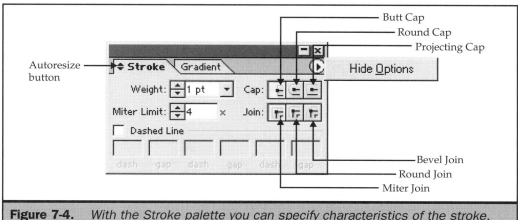

Figure 7-4. *With the Stroke palette you can specify characteristics of the stroke.*

To open the palette's menu, click the menu button. The Show Options/Hide Options command shows or hides the bottom section of the palette. Hiding is equivalent to clicking the Autoresize button until the palette is between its smallest and largest sizes. Showing is equivalent to displaying the palette at its largest.

> **Note**   *To learn how to set the unit of measure for the stroke, refer to Appendix B.*

Setting the Stroke Width

To set the stroke width for a particular object, select it, and either select or type a value in the Width text box/option box/drop-down menu. If you follow the value with a unit of measure (*in* for inches, *mm* for millimeters, *cm* for centimeters, or *pi* for picas), Illustrator converts that value to points. Valid values range from 0 (no stroke) to 1,000 points (an extremely wide stroke). The default value is 1 point.

Specifying a Miter Limit

As you learned in the "Offsetting a Path" section in Chapter 6, the value of the miter limit determines when a miter join point decreases to a flat bevel join. A low miter limit flattens the join; a high miter limit adds to the angle of the point. The miter limit is available only for miter joins. Valid miter limit values range from 1 to 500; the default value is 4.

Adding a Cap or Join

For open paths you can affect the look of the corners and ends. Remember that a join is the shape of the turn of a corner; a cap is the shape of the end of a line. To specify the form of a join or cap, click one of the buttons in the Stroke palette. For caps, you can choose from Butt (the default), Round, and Projecting. You can select from the following joins: Miter (the default), Round, and Bevel. Figure 7-5 demonstrates the variety of Illustrator caps and joins. At the top is an open path with default Butt caps and Miter joins; the center path has Round caps and joins; and the bottom path shows Projecting caps and Bevel joins.

Changing Strokes to Dashed Lines

With the Stroke palette you can change the stroke from a solid line to a dashed line. In addition, you can customize the look of the dashes and set the distance between the dashes. To make the stroke a dashed line, follow these steps:

1. Select an open or closed path.
2. Click a cap button.
3. Check the Dashed Line box.
4. Type numbers in the text boxes at the bottom of the palette. If you follow the value with a unit of measure (*in* for inches, *mm* for millimeters, *cm* for centimeters, or *pi* for picas), Illustrator converts that value to points. You don't have to fill in every text box; just type a complete pattern of values. Illustrator applies the dashes and spaces to the selected path.

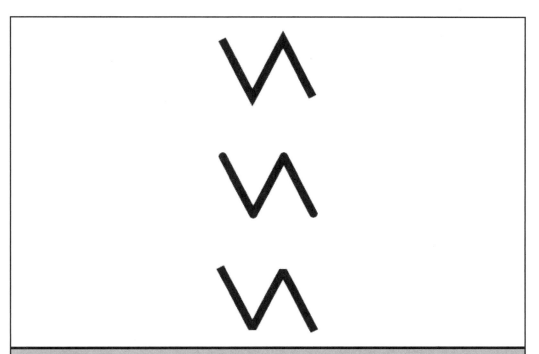

Figure 7-5.   *Three open paths with various joins and caps*

Figure 7-6 illustrates three dashed lines. On the top is a pattern of 20-point dash, 20-point gap, 1 point dash, and 20-point gap with Butt caps. In the middle is a pattern of 25-point dashes and gaps with Round caps. At the bottom is a pattern of 10-point dashes and 20-point gaps with Bevel caps.

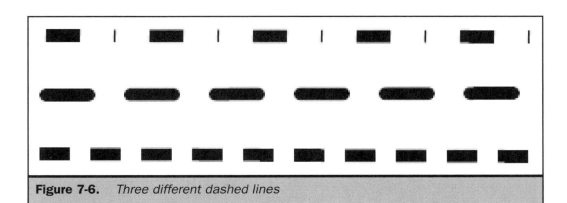

Figure 7-6.   *Three different dashed lines*

Working with Swatches

Illustrator swatches hold samples of premixed colors, patterns, and gradients as well as colors, patterns, and gradients you have blended. By default, the Swatches palette contains standard colors, a few gradients, and some patterns. You also can load swatches from several libraries into the palette. Illustrator provides libraries from Pantone, Focoltone, Toyo, Trumatch, and many more. In addition, you can create your own swatches and custom libraries of swatches.

The Swatches palette can display swatches of both spot color and process colors.

- *Spot colors* are specific colors in an artwork. Think of spot colors as individual tubes of paint, which can be stand alone or mixed to produce other colors. In printing, spot colors are used in solid or screened forms, primarily for nonphotographic uses. Certain companies develop libraries of named spot colors; essentially they set the standards for spot colors. In the United States the company that's recognized as the standard setter is Pantone. Commercial printers support certain collections of spot colors, so if your commercial printer uses Pantone colors then you should, too. In the Swatches palette, spot color swatches contain white triangle icons in their lower-right corners.

- *Process colors* combine the primary colors cyan, magenta, and yellow along with the spot color black (that is, CMYK, where *K* represents black) or red, blue, and green (that is, RGB) into a color print. During processing, an image is split into its basic colors and each of the colors is printed on a separate sheet. During processing, the paper on which the final image will be duplicated is actually printed three or four times, one for each primary color. Because of the limited number of process colors, there is no need for color standards.

Exploring the Swatches Palette

The Swatches palette (see Figure 7-7) is the collection point for color, pattern, and gradient swatches shown in any order you want: all colors, patterns, and gradients or just colors, gradients, or patterns. To toggle between showing and hiding the palette, choose Window | Swatches.

The first two swatches in the Swatches palette are labeled None and Registration. The None swatch has the same purpose as the None button near the bottom of the toolbox. Click None to remove any color, pattern, or gradient from the fill, and a color or pattern from the stroke. In process printing, *registration* is the matching of color dots printed on color separations so that all the images are aligned and all colors print as planned, without gaps or overprinting. The Registration swatch mixes all inks, producing black. However, the black is for registration marks only—definitely not for black in an artwork. You cannot modify or delete either of these swatches.

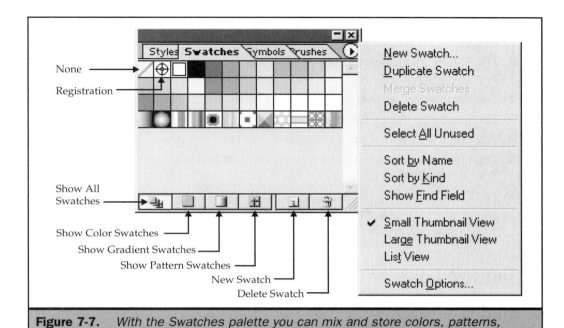

Figure 7-7.   *With the Swatches palette you can mix and store colors, patterns, and gradients to apply to your artwork.*

To open the palette's menu, click the menu button. Two commands (New Swatch and Delete Swatch) also have a corresponding button at the bottom of the palette. The commands on the palette's menu are as follows:

- The New Swatch command enables you to name a new swatch and add it to the Swatches palette. The counterpart button to this command is New Swatch.

- The Duplicate Swatch command makes a copy of a swatch in the Swatches palette.

- The Merge Swatches command merges two or more swatches under the name of the first swatch selected and its color.

- The Delete Swatch command removes a swatch from the Swatches palette. The counterpart button to this command is Delete Swatch.

- The Select All Unused command selects all swatches that are not used in the current document.

■ The Sort by Name command sorts all swatches currently in the Swatches palette by alphabetically ordered name.

■ The Sort by Kind command sorts all swatches currently in the Swatches palette by type (color, gradient, and pattern) and in ascending order.

■ The Show Find Field command enables you to find a swatch by name.

■ The Small Thumbnail View command displays small images of the swatches.

■ The Large Thumbnail View command displays large images of the swatches.

■ The List View command shows the name of each swatch preceded by a small image of the swatch.

■ The Swatch Options command opens the Swatch Options dialog box with which you can edit the current swatch. You also can double-click a swatch to open the Swatch Options dialog box. To learn how to customize Illustrator palettes, read "Customizing a Palette" in Appendix B.

Changing the Look of Swatches

You can change the arrangement and look of the swatches in the Swatches palette using commands on the palette's menu or by clicking buttons at the bottom of the palette. To change the look of the swatches in the palette, which are initially shown by color type (color, gradient, and pattern) and families of color, select one of three commands. To display small images of the swatches, choose Small Thumbnail View (the default). To show large images of the swatches, choose Large Thumbnail View. Choose List View to see a list of color names preceded by a small swatch and, for colors, followed by an icon representing None, Registration, or a color.

 The None icon marks the None swatch, which removes all color from the selected object.

 The Registration icon marks the Registration swatch.

 The Spot color icon marks all spot color swatches in List view.

 The Spot Color icon marks the lower-right corner of all spot color swatches in Small Thumbnail and Large Thumbnail views.

 The Global Color icon marks the lower-right corner of all global color swatches in Small Thumbnail and Large Thumbnail views.

A global color is a process color that is linked to a swatch in the Swatches palette, so that when you change the swatch color, Illustrator updates every image that includes the color. To specify that a process color is global, check the Global box in the New Swatch dialog box or the Swatch Options dialog box.

 The CMYK icon marks all CMYK swatches.

 The RGB icon marks all RGB swatches.

 The HSB icon marks all HSB swatches. (These are rare in Illustrator.)

Figure 7-8 shows the three views of the Swatches palette. On the left is Small Thumbnail view, in the center is a longer and wider palette in Large Thumbnail view, and on the right is a long list of swatches in List view.

 You can see the name of each swatch, regardless of the view. Obviously, List view enables you to view each swatch name as you scroll up and down the list. However, if you choose a thumbnail view, just move the mouse pointer to any swatch to see its name as a tooltip—assuming you have turned on ToolTips. To do so, choose Edit | Preferences | General (CTRL-K/⌘-K), check the Show ToolTips box, and click OK.

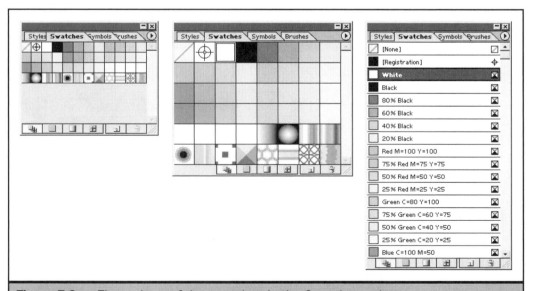

Figure 7-8. *Three views of the swatches in the Swatches palette*

Displaying Specific Swatch Types

Using buttons arranged along the bottom of the palette, you can display all swatches or particular types of swatches, as follows:

- To display all swatches (the default), click the Show All Swatches button.
- To display color swatches only, click the Show Color Swatches button.
- To display gradient swatches only, click the Show Gradient Swatches button.
- To display pattern swatches only, click the Show Pattern Swatches button.

Figure 7-9 shows each version of the default Swatches palette, from left to right: all swatches, color swatches only, gradient swatches only, and pattern swatches only. Notice that the button for each selection looks as though it is pressed down.

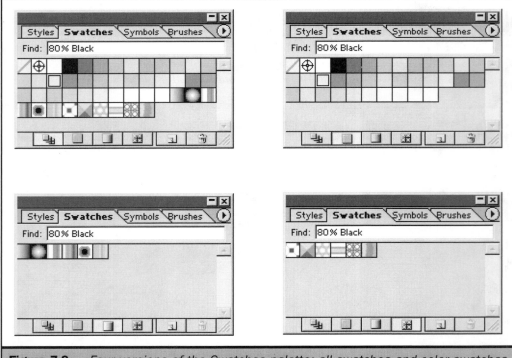

Figure 7-9.   *Four versions of the Swatches palette: all swatches and color swatches at the top left and right, respectively; and gradient swatches and pattern swatches at the bottom left and right, respectively*

Sorting Swatches by Name and Kind

You can sort swatches in the Swatches palette by name and type.

- Choose Sort by Name from the palette's menu to sort all the swatches by name, in ascending order, first numerically and then alphabetically.

- Choose Sort by Kind to sort by type. After the sort, the swatch order is colors, followed by gradients, and ending with patterns. Within those categories, Illustrator sorts swatches by name in ascending order.

Sorting Swatches Manually

If you want to spend plenty of time on what some might call busy work, you can sort swatches one at a time by dragging each to a new location in the palette. For example, if you want to arrange all colors into rainbow order, first drag all shades of reds, then oranges, yellows, greens, blues, and ending with all gradations of violets. When you drag a swatch around the palette, watch for a black vertical line that pops up when the dragged swatch is close to a new location. That line represents the new location of the dragged swatch. If you drop the swatch into place, the swatch on the right moves to make room. Figure 7-10 shows a before version of the palette (at the top), a swatch being moved (in the center), and the palette with many newly sorted color swatches. In the center palette, notice the hand mouse pointer and the black vertical line.

Finding a Swatch by Typing Its Name

You can use a command in the Swatches palette menu to find a swatch by name. This is particularly helpful when you work with a Swatches library that contains many swatches.

When you choose the Show Find Field command, Illustrator opens a small find field at the top of the palette. When you type a character or number in the find field, Illustrator completes the name in the field and with a white border highlights the first swatch it finds that starts with or contains that character or number. For example, if you type **2**, which could represent 20% Black; 25% Red M=25 Y=25; or 25% Green, C=20, Y=25, Illustrator finds the swatch that is closest to the top of the palette. Or, if you type **B**, Illustrator might find 80% Black rather than Blue.

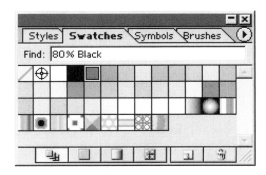

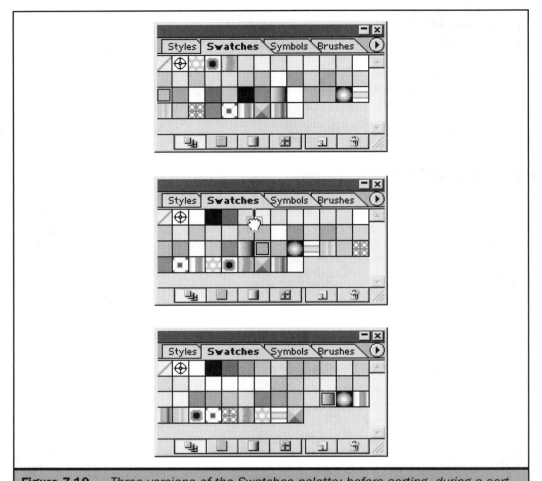

Figure 7-10. *Three versions of the Swatches palette: before sorting, during a sort, and after the sort is complete*

Another way to find a swatch by its name without opening the find field is to press CTRL-ALT/⌘-OPTION and click in the Swatches palette. Type the first character in the name of the swatch that you want to find and Illustrator highlights that swatch.

Applying a Swatch Color to a Path

It's very easy to apply a swatch color to a path's fill or stroke. Before you apply a color, you must select the fill or stroke at the bottom of the toolbox, Color palette, or Gradient palette. To apply a swatch color to a fill or stroke, follow these steps:

1. Select the path to which you want to employ the swatch color.

2. Click the Fill or Stroke (X) in the toolbox.

3. Click the swatch to be used. (Remember you cannot apply gradients to the stroke.) Illustrator changes the fill or stroke color and applies that color to the selected path's fill or stroke.

You also can apply the fill or stroke color to an object—selected or unselected—by dragging the fill or stroke to the object from the Swatches palette, the Color palette, or the Gradient palette.

Touring the Swatch Options Dialog Box

You can use the Swatch Options dialog box (see Figure 7-11) and its near duplicate New Swatch dialog box to specify the characteristics of the selected swatch or a swatch as it is created. You can rename a swatch or change its color mode, color type, and even its color. To open one of these dialog boxes, take one of the following actions:

■ Click the New Swatch button at the bottom of the Swatches palette while pressing down ALT/OPTION. Illustrator opens the New Swatch dialog box.

■ With an existing swatch selected, choose Swatch Options from the Swatches palette's menu. Illustrator opens the Swatch Options dialog box.

■ Double-click a swatch in the Swatches palette. Illustrator opens the Swatch Options dialog box.

Both the New Swatch dialog box and the Swatch Options dialog box enable you to name a swatch, select its color type and color mode, and set its color. In addition, the Swatch Options dialog box contains a Preview check box so that you can immediately see any changes in the selected swatch before you click OK to apply the changes.

■ In the Swatch Name text box, type a unique and descriptive swatch name. You can choose to name a swatch or leave a new swatch unnamed. The main advantage of naming a swatch is that you can find and edit a named swatch more easily than an unnamed one.

■ From the Color Type drop-down menu, select Process Color (the default) or Spot Color. For a current swatch, you can switch from spot color to process color to be able to process print it using CMYK or RGB.

■ Check the Global box to have Illustrator recognize the changes to the swatch and apply those changes in every document in which you used this particular swatch in the past. Obviously, you have to open a document to have Illustrator modify the color, color type, or color mode for the target swatch.

■ From the Color Mode drop-down menu, select one of Illustrator's color models: Grayscale, RGB, HSB, CMYK (the default), or Web-safe RGB.

ILLUSTRATOR ESSENTIALS

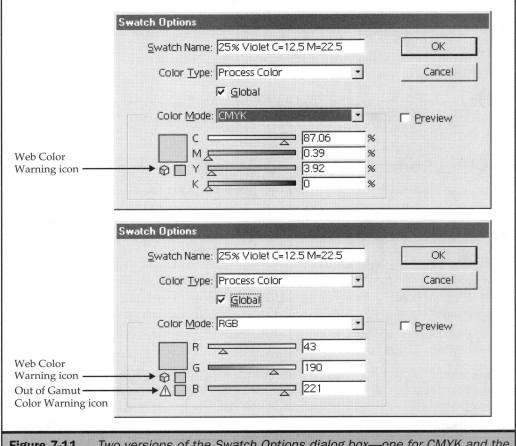

Figure 7-11. *Two versions of the Swatch Options dialog box—one for CMYK and the other for RGB—both for the same color*

- Check the Preview check box to view the selected swatch in the color you have just mixed in the dialog box; this enables you to view the color without permanently applying it. If you don't like the color, you can either adjust it or click Cancel to close the dialog box without changing the color.

- Slide the color sliders or type values in the text boxes to adjust the mix of the primary colors. As you move a slider, the value in its associated text box changes, and as you change the value in a text box, its associated slider moves. Whether or not you change a value using a slider or text box, the color in the color box changes.

- The Web Color Warning icon appears when the swatch color is not one of the 216 colors that you can safely use on Web pages. If the Web Color Warning icon appears and you want to mix a Web-safe color for Grayscale, RGB, HSB, or CMYK, click the icon or box to the right of the icon, or slide the slider a little to change the color and make the Warning icon disappear. For more information about colors that are safe for the Web, refer to "Web-Safe RGB" in Chapter 2.

- The Out of Gamut Color Warning icon indicates that the swatch color does not fall within the colors in the RGB or HSB color model. If the Out of Gamut Color Warning icon appears and you want to stay within the *gamut* or range of colors for RGB or HSB, click the icon or box to the right of the icon, or slide the slider a bit to adjust the color. When the color is within the gamut, the Out of Gamut Color Warning icon disappears.

Note *The Color Mode sections of the dialog box, Color palette, and Color Picker all contain color sliders, text boxes, and versions of the color box. In addition, you can sometimes find the Web Color Warning icon and Out of Gamut Color Warning icon. You will learn about the Color palette and the Color Picker later in this chapter.*

A Few Words About Gamut

The Out of Gamut Color Warning icon is just the tip of the iceberg when it comes to discussing the term gamut and its place in Illustrator. Each color model supported by Illustrator offers its own gamut or range of colors. For example, the RGB color model includes more colors than the CMYK model. Therefore, it follows that many RGB colors fall outside the gamut of CMYK colors.

Although the CMYK gamut has far fewer colors than RGB, many of those colors differ from any RGB color. So, RGB colors that do not match any CMYK color and CMYK colors that do not have counterparts in the RGB model are said to be "out of gamut." When you change from one color model to another for an existing Illustrator document, chances are good that at least a few colors will be out of gamut for the new color model.

Adding a Swatch to the Swatches Palette

You can create sets of swatches containing your favorite colors or colors for a particular artwork—but not for every Illustrator document you have created in the past or will create in the future. However, if you create a startup file with stored swatches, those swatches will be available to any new document. To learn about startup files, refer to "Creating a Startup File" in Appendix B.

Before you add a swatch, get the current fill or stroke color from the Fill box or Stroke box, or "mix" a color using the Color palette or a gradient using the Gradient palette. You'll learn about the Color palette later in this chapter. For information about the Gradient palette, refer to "Exploring the Gradient Palette" in Chapter 9.

You can add swatches in two ways: with or without the Swatch Options dialog box. If you don't open the Swatch Options dialog box, you won't be able to name the swatch or set it to a process color or a spot color. In this section, you'll learn both ways of adding a swatch to the Swatches palette.

Adding a Swatch Without the Swatch Options Dialog Box

To add a swatch to the Swatches palette without opening the Swatch Options dialog box, follow these steps:

1. Create a color using the Color palette or the Gradient palette. Illustrator applies the color to the fill or the stroke, depending on which is active.

2. Click the New Swatch button at the bottom of the Swatches palette. To create a new spot color swatch, press and hold down CTRL/⌘ when you click the New Swatch button. Illustrator adds a new swatch after the last swatch in the palette. If the new swatch is a spot color, Illustrator places an icon in the lower-right corner of the swatch.

 You can add a swatch by dragging a color from the fill box, the stroke box, the fill box or stroke box from the Color palette, or the gradient fill box from the Gradient palette. To make the new swatch a spot color, press and hold down CTRL/⌘ while dragging.

Adding a Swatch with the Swatch Options Dialog Box

To add a swatch to the Swatches palette using a dialog box, follow these steps:

1. Create a color using the Color palette or the Gradient palette. Illustrator applies the color to the fill or the stroke, depending on which is active.

2. Press and hold down ALT/OPTION, and click the New Swatch button at the bottom of the Swatches palette. Illustrator opens the New Swatch dialog box.

3. Select options in the dialog box. When you have finished, click OK.

4. Illustrator adds a new swatch after the last swatch in the palette. If the new swatch is a spot color, Illustrator places an icon in the lower-right corner of the swatch.

Editing Swatches

You can modify virtually anything in Illustrator, such as your documents and many of the tools with which you create paths and images. You can change swatches in order to rearrange the Swatches palette as well as create artwork as efficiently as possible.

Selecting Swatches

Before you can edit a swatch, you have to select it. Selecting a single swatch is easy—just click it. Illustrator highlights the selected swatch and changes the fill or stroke (whichever is active) to the highlighted color.

You can select several swatches by pressing keys and clicking:

- To select contiguous or noncontiguous swatches, press and hold down CTRL/⌘ and click the desired swatches. Every time you click, Illustrator adds another swatch to the selection.

- To select contiguous swatches, click one end of the range, press and hold down SHIFT, and click the other end of the range. Illustrator selects the entire range of swatches.

- To deselect a selected swatch, press CTRL/⌘ and click the swatch. To deselect all selected swatches, click away from the Swatches palette.

- To select almost all swatches whose colors, patterns, or gradients are not being used in the current document, choose the Select All Unused command from the Swatches palette's menu. Illustrator highlights the unused swatches except for None, Registration, White, and Black. Then drag the group of highlighted swatches to the Delete Swatch button at the bottom of the Swatches palette; Illustrator deletes the unused swatches. If you delete the unused swatches, you can keep a strict eye on all the colors in the document.

Exercising Your Swatch Skills

Figure 7-12 shows an image made up of circles within squares in four different colors and the Swatches palette after choosing Select All Unused. To create this image, follow these steps:

1. Make one circle. Consider turning on the grid by choosing View | Show Grid (CTRL-"/⌘-") to align the circle with the gridlines.

2. Draw a square whose sides hug the circle.

3. If you need to slightly adjust the dimensions of the square after you have created it, select two anchor points at a time using the Direct Selection tool (A). Then press the arrow keys to make any fine adjustments.

4. Place the square behind the circle by choosing Object | Arrange | Send to Back (CTRL-SHIFT-[/⌘-SHIFT-[).

5. Select the circle and click the Blue C=100 M=50 swatch.

6. Select the square and click the Red M=100 Y=100 swatch.

7. Select the circle and the square and group them by choosing Object | Group (CTRL-G/⌘-G).

8. Copy the group by choosing Edit | Copy (CTRL-C/⌘-C). Paste the group 16 times by repeatedly choosing Edit | Paste (CTRL-V/⌘-V).

9. Arrange the groups in four rows by four columns. To fine-tune the arrangement of the groups, press a combination of arrow keys to slightly move one group closer or farther away from another group.

ILLUSTRATOR
ESSENTIALS

10. Select the entire assemblage and ungroup by choosing Object | Ungroup (CTRL-SHIFT-G/⌘-SHIFT-G).

11. To every other circle, click the Yellow swatch.

12. To every square under a recolored circle, click the Green C=80 Y=100.

13. Choose Select All Unused from the Swatches palette menu. Illustrator highlights all the unused swatches. Then drag the group of highlighted swatches to the Delete Swatch button on the Swatches palette. Illustrator reduces the colors in the palette except for None, Registration, White, and Black, and the colors in the document: Blue C=100 M=50, Red M=100 Y=100, Yellow, and Green C=80 Y=100.

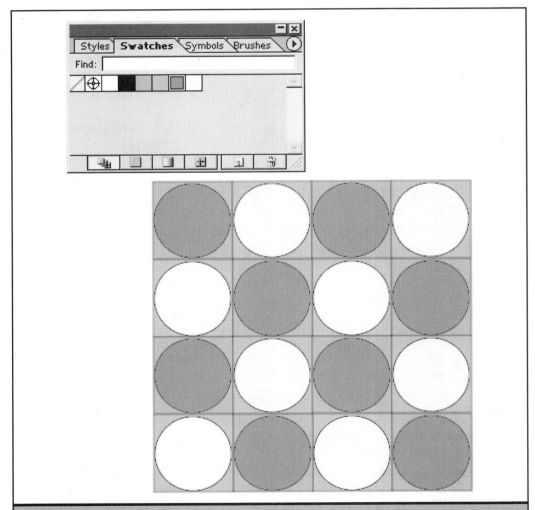

Figure 7-12. *Circles enclosed by squares and the four-color-plus Swatches palette*

Deleting a Swatch

To delete a swatch, select it and do one of the following:

■ Open the Swatches palette menu and choose the Delete Swatch command.

■ Click the Delete Swatch button at the bottom right of the Swatches palette.

■ Drag the swatch to the Delete Swatch button.

When you delete a swatch, Illustrator opens a message box that prompts you to verify the deletion. Click Yes to delete; click No to not delete.

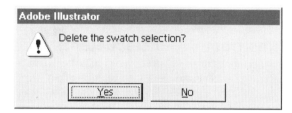

Remember that any swatches you add to or delete from the Swatches palette apply to the current document. If you delete a swatch—even one of the standard swatches—you will not universally delete the swatch from the Swatches palette for any other document.

 When you delete a spot color or a process color that is global (that is, used in several documents and defined as global in the Swatch Options dialog box), Illustrator recolors objects having that color with a corresponding nonglobal process color.

Duplicating a Swatch

You can duplicate a swatch so that a new swatch will start with that color, pattern, or gradient; then you can modify the replica swatch in any way that you wish. To duplicate a swatch, select the swatch and either choose Duplicate Swatch from the Swatches palette's menu or drag the selected swatch to the New Swatch button at the bottom of the palette.

Replacing a Swatch

You can replace one swatch with another in the Swatches palette. To do so, follow these steps:

1. Create a new color, pattern, or gradient.

2. While pressing and holding down ALT/OPTION, drag the fill or stroke box, the fill or stroke from the Color palette, or a gradient from the Gradient palette to the swatch you want to replace in the Swatches palette. When the replacement color is close to the swatch to be replaced, Illustrator highlights that swatch.

3. Drop the new color, pattern, or gradient onto the swatch to be replaced.

Think twice about replacing swatches. Instead, why not add a new swatch? If you replace swatches, Illustrator does not universally delete the swatches from the Swatches palette associated with any other document. However, the reason for this caution is that Illustrator will replace every instance of the source colors—except if they are nonglobal process colors—in any objects having the source colors with the replacement colors.

Merging Swatches Within the Current Document

You can merge two or more swatches in the Swatches palette. To do so, select the swatches and then choose Merge Swatches from the Swatches palette menu. Illustrator merges the swatches and gives the new swatch the name and color of the first swatch you selected.

Merging Swatches from Other Documents

When you paste, drag, or place an object created in another Illustrator document in the current document, Illustrator adds custom color swatches that are part of the object into the current Swatches palette. If a custom swatch has the same name as a swatch in the current Swatches palette, the Swatch Conflict dialog box opens so you can work out the naming conflict.

Selecting a Swatches Library

Illustrator provides many swatch libraries from which you can select many more colors, patterns, and gradients than you can get from the Swatches palette. You'll find several libraries containing swatches with Pantone and HKS colors, system colors for both Windows and Macintosh, families of colors such as earth tones and harmonies, and colors supported for use on the Web. You cannot edit any of these libraries, but you can drag a swatch from one of these libraries to the Swatches palette for a particular document. You can apply colors from a swatch library as you would from the Swatches palette. Table 7-1 names and briefly describes each of the custom swatch libraries. Note that no library contains the None and Registration swatches.

Name	Description
Default_CMYK	The default CMYK palette with more than 40 process color swatches and several pattern and gradient swatches
Default_RGB	The default RGB palette with more than 40 process color swatches and several pattern and gradient swatches; process colors

Table 7-1.   *Custom Swatch Libraries in Illustrator*

Name	Description
Diccolor	A Japanese standard of more than 1,200 spot color swatches
Earthtones_1	30 CMYK process color swatches in earth tone colors
FOCOLTONE	More than 750 global CMYK process color swatches
Harmonies_1	More than 40 process color swatches in a variety of muted colors
HKS E, HKS K, HKS N, HKS Z	A German standard (Hostmann-Steinberg, K+E, Schmincke); four libraries with more than 50 spot-color swatches each
PANTONE Metallic Coated	More than 200 CMYK process color swatches
PANTONE Pastel Coated, PANTONE Pastel Uncoated	More than 100 CMYK process color swatches on each palette
PANTONE Process Coated, PANTONE Process Uncoated	More than 3,000 CMYK process color swatches each
PANTONE Solid Coated, PANTONE Solid Matte, PANTONE Solid Uncoated	More than 1,100 CMYK process color swatches each
Pastels	30 CMYK process color swatches in pastel colors
System (Macintosh)	The Macintosh system color palette with 256 process color swatches
System (Windows)	The Windows system color palette with 256 process color swatches
Toyo Color Finder 1050	A Japanese standard with more than 1,000 spot color swatches
Trumatch	More than 2,000 process color swatches
VisiBone2	More than 200 process color swatches
Web	216 Web-safe process colors

ILLUSTRATOR
ESSENTIALS

Table 7-1.   *Custom Swatch Libraries in Illustrator* (continued)

Using a Custom Swatch Library

To open a swatch library, choose Window | Swatch Libraries and select a library from
the submenu. Illustrator opens a palette showing the swatches for the selected library.
To close the library, click the Close button or choose Window | Swatch Libraries and
select the library again. Figure 7-13 shows many swatches from three libraries: Pantone
Solid Matte, System (Mac), and Toyo.

Each swatch library palette looks very similar to the Swatches palette. However,
if you look closely you'll find some differences. For example, because you cannot edit
a swatch library, the buttons along the bottom of the Swatches palette are missing. In
addition, a swatch library's menu contains a few different commands from the Swatches
palette's menu:

- Choose the Add to Swatches command to add the selected swatch from
  a library palette to the Swatches palette. You also can drag the swatch
  from the library palette to the Swatches palette.

- Choose the Persistent command to have Illustrator automatically keep
  the library in the illustration window until you deactivate Persistent.

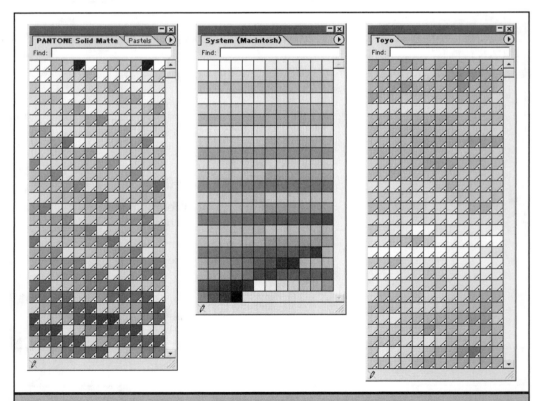

Figure 7-13. *A selection of swatches from three swatch libraries*

Creating a Swatch Library

Swatch libraries actually are Illustrator documents stored in a subfolder of the Adobe program files. To create your own swatch library, choose Window | Swatches to open the default Swatches palette. Then add swatches by following the instructions in "Adding a Swatch to the Swatches Palette," earlier in this chapter.

You can edit or delete swatches in your new library using some of the directions in the "Editing Swatches" section, also earlier in the chapter. For example, to make the library completely your own, consider deleting any default swatches you don't plan to use. When you have completed changing the Swatches palette, save the Illustrator document as you would any other document—and be sure to give the library a unique name and save it into the folder in which the other Illustrator swatches libraries are stored. The illustration window can be completely blank; the Swatches palette is the important item in the document.

In Table 7-1 you learned that System (Mac) is one of Illustrator's swatches libraries. Figure 7-14 shows the System (Mac) library as it appears in the illustration window, including a statement about the document and the Swatches palette associated with

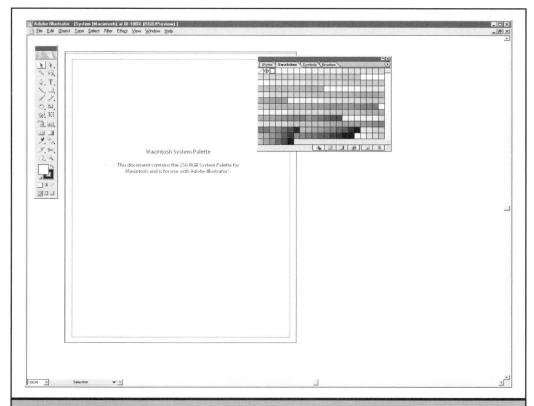

Figure 7-14.   *The System (Mac) library as it appears in the illustration window*

that document. Notice that the resized palette shows all 256 colors in the Macintosh system, plus the None and Registration swatches.

Mixing Colors

Until now you have used premixed colors for Illustrator objects. To mix your own colors, use the Color palette. In this section you will tour the Color palette and find out how to create your own colors by sliding a slider or typing color values, using one of the several versions of the palette. You'll also learn how to apply colors from the Color palette.

Exploring the Color Palette

The Color palette (see Figure 7-15) contains a set of features with which you can customize the colors of the fill, the stroke, or both. To show the palette, choose Window | Color (F6) or click the Fill box or the Stroke box in the toolbox. To hide the palette, choose Window | Color (F6) or click the Close button on the palette. Figure 7-15 shows all the versions of the Color palette, with the CMYK type on top, the next row containing RGB and Web-safe RGB palettes, and the bottom row showing the HSB and Grayscale versions.
    To open the palettes menu, click the menu button.

- The Show Options/Hide Options command automatically resizes the palette, cycling through the title bar/palette tabs only, the spectrum slider only, or the full-size palette.

- The Grayscale, RGB, HSB, CMYK, and Web-Safe RGB commands display the version of the palette for each of those color models. To quickly cycle through these commands, move the mouse pointer to the spectrum bar at the bottom of the palette, press and hold down SHIFT, and repeatedly click.

- The Invert command switches the fill color to the stroke and the stroke color to the fill.

- The Complement command chooses the complementary color for the fill or stroke—whichever is active.

Choosing a Color Model

When you open the Color palette, the sliders and text boxes for the current color model are on display. However, if you change the color model, the number of sliders and text boxes also might change. To choose a color model, choose the Grayscale, RGB, HSB, CMYK, or Web-Safe RGB command from the palette's menu.

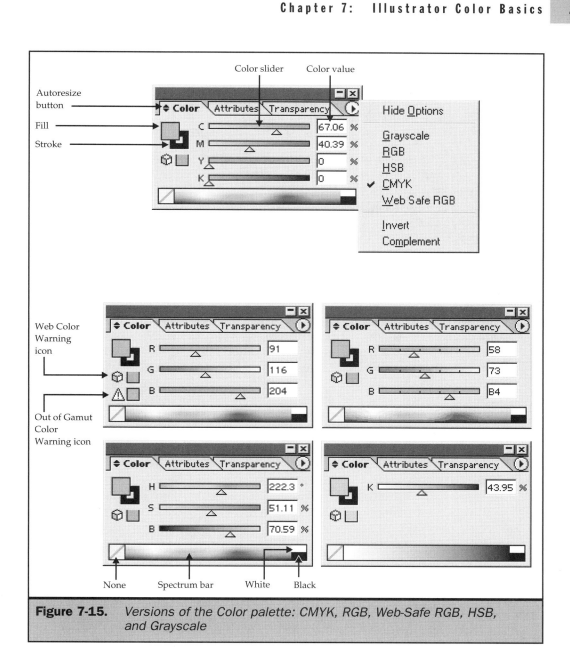

Figure 7-15.   *Versions of the Color palette: CMYK, RGB, Web-Safe RGB, HSB, and Grayscale*

Selecting Colors with Sliders and Text Boxes

Before you mix a color in the Color palette, click the Fill or Stroke box (X) in the toolbox or the Color palette to choose whether to mix a new fill or stroke color. Then slide one or more sliders, or type one or more values in text boxes.

Depending on the color model, you mix colors in different ways:

- In Grayscale, mixing involves sliding or typing a percentage value from 0 to 100. The number you select determines the level of white (0%) or black (100%), with all the grays between those two extremes.

- In RGB, valid R, G, and B values range from 0 to 255, where if all text boxes contain 0, the color is black, and 255-255-255 equals white. Red is 255-0-0, green is 0-255-0, and blue is 0-0-255. If all numbers are greater than 0 and less than 255, but equal (for example, 204-204-204), the mixed color is a shade of gray.

- The H, S, and B values in HSB indicate hue, saturation, and brightness, respectively. The H value represents the dominant color in the mixed color. If the H slider bar were made into a circle (in other words, a 360° color wheel), the two ends would meet at the color red (0 and 360). Other important H colors are orange (36), yellow (60), green (120), cyan (180), blue (240), and magenta (330). The S value is a percentage of saturation in the new color, where 0% is white (the least amount of saturation) and 100% is the total hue (the most amount of saturation). The B value is a percentage of brightness in the new color, where 0% is the least amount of brightness (that is, black) and 100% is the most amount of brightness (that is, the most intense version of the new color).

- In CMYK, valid C, M, and Y colors range from 0 to 100%. If all text boxes contain 0, the color is white and 100-100-100-100 represents black. Cyan is 100-0-0-0, magenta is 0-100-0-0, and yellow is 0-0-100-0. Black (K) is the percentage of black in the mixed color. If all numbers are greater than 0 and less than 100, but equal (for example, 10-10-10-10), the mixed color is a shade of gray.

- Web-Safe RGB is a subset of RGB with some significant differences: The values range from 0 to FF, the hexadecimal equivalents of 0 to 255, and the slider bar is tick marks (at 0, 33, 66, 99, CC, and FF) to which each slider snaps to ensure that you select colors that are in the Web-safe set of colors.

Sliding to Mix Colors

To mix a color using the slider, move the slider left or right. Slide a little to make a small adjustment; slide a lot to drastically change the color. If you press and hold down SHIFT as you slide in CMYK, RGB, or Web-Safe RGB, Illustrator slides all the sliders in proportion. As you change colors, Illustrator updates the fill and stroke boxes in the toolbox and the Color palette.

The slider is the best way to mix Web-Safe RGB colors; as you slide, the slider snaps to the Web-safe tick marks.

If the Web Color Warning icon appears, the current color is not one of the 216 Web-safe colors. If you would prefer to choose a Web-safe color, click the icon or the box to the right of the icon or slide the slider a little to change the color and make the warning icon disappear.

If the Out of Gamut Color Warning icon appears, the current color does not fall within the gamut of colors for the chosen color model. If you would rather stay within the gamut, click the icon or the box to the right of the icon or slide one or more of the sliders a bit until the warning icon disappears.

Entering Color Values in Text Boxes

If you know the set of values for a particular color, enter them in the text boxes to the right of the color sliders. If the Web Color Warning icon or Out of Gamut Color Warning icon appears, click the icon or the box to the right of the icon or slide a slider a slight amount until the warning icon disappears. As you change colors, Illustrator updates the fill and stroke boxes in the toolbox and the Color palette.

- To quickly highlight a text box, click the letter preceding its slider.

- To rehighlight the text box into which you just typed a value, press SHIFT-ENTER/SHIFT-RETURN.

 You can add, subtract, multiply, or divide within the text boxes. To do so, move the mouse pointer to the right of the current value, enter a mathematical operator, follow that by the value to be calculated, and press ENTER/RETURN.

Selecting from the Spectrum Bar

The spectrum bar (sometimes known as the *color ramp*) at the bottom of the Color palette contains a rainbow of colors—or grades of gray in the case of Grayscale—and sections for applying None (on the left), black (on the bottom right), and white (on the top right). To use the spectrum bar, follow these steps:

1. Move the mouse pointer over the spectrum bar. Illustrator changes the mouse pointer to an Eyedropper mouse pointer. (You'll learn more about the Eyedropper tool and its characteristics and options in "Using the Eyedropper Tool" in Chapter 8.)

2. Click the Eyedropper mouse pointer on the desired color. Illustrator paints the fill and stroke boxes with your selection.

3. To fine-tune your color selection, either slide the sliders or edit one or more values in the text boxes. Whenever you change the fill and/or stroke in the Color palette, Illustrator automatically applies the color to any selected objects in the illustration window. Remember you also can apply the fill or stroke color to an object—either selected or unselected—by dragging the fill or stroke box from the Color palette to the object.

Using Spectrum Bar Shortcuts

The spectrum bar features some hidden shortcuts. If you know where to find them, you can use them to save yourself extra steps.

- When you click None on the spectrum bar, Illustrator adds a small square showing the last fill or stroke color (depending on which is active). To return to that color, click either the rectangle or Color button near the bottom of the toolbox.

- When you move the mouse pointer to the spectrum bar, you can cycle through the color models by pressing and holding down SHIFT while clicking the spectrum bar.

- You can quickly apply spectrum bar colors successively to the fill and stroke: Press the fill-stroke toggle, X, to switch from the inactive to the active, and click within the spectrum bar to apply a color. Then repeat for the fill or stroke, whichever is currently inactive.

Changing Global Colors

Remember that you define a color as global in the New Swatch dialog box or the Swatch Option dialog box. When you select a global color swatch for an artwork, the Color palette changes its appearance (see Figure 7-16). Instead of three or four sliders, the palette has a single slider, labeled T (Tint). Thus, for a global color you can change the tint of the color only in the Color palette.

When you change the tint of a global color, you can save a swatch with the new color in the same way you would save another swatch. If you save the new tint, Illustrator names the swatch with the same name as the swatch you retinted and adds the tint percentage after the name, which creates a unique name automatically. Note that if you edit the original swatch or any retinted swatch, Illustrator changes all swatches related to the original.

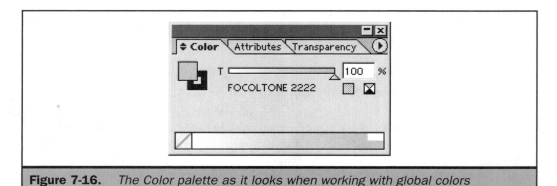

Figure 7-16. *The Color palette as it looks when working with global colors*

Using the Color Picker

The Color Picker (see Figure 7-17) incorporates all the features of the Color palette and then some. You can open the Color Picker by double-clicking the fill or stroke box on the toolbox or the Color palette. When you open the Color Picker, it contains the current fill or stroke color—whichever is active at this time—for every color model.

Although you can open the Color Picker when you are using Grayscale, you might not get much benefit—after all, grayscale blends shades of gray, black, and white only. Use the Color Picker to mix colors using a variety of tools to help you get just the right color. As you change the color using various means, Illustrator changes the look of the Color Picker, which includes most of the following: the values in the text boxes next to the radio buttons, the look of the color field and color slider, and the current hexadecimal value in the # text box.

On the left side of the Color Picker is the color field, which contains a blend of colors that have contributed to the currently selected color. The colors in the color field vary depending on the active radio button on the right side of the dialog box. One way of changing the current color is to move the mouse pointer around within the color field.

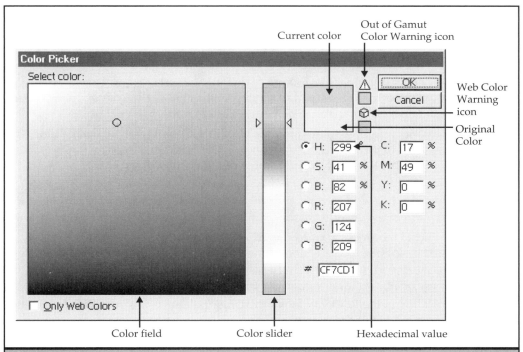

Figure 7-17. *The Color Picker enables you to select colors in a more complex way than the Color palette.*

As you change the color, Illustrator changes the values in the text boxes next to the radio buttons, modifies the look of the color slider, and places its current hexadecimal value in the # text box. The color field remains the same. The circle within the color field shows the current color in relation to the other colors in the color field.

The vertical color slider to the right of the color field displays another blend of colors, which also change as you select different radio buttons. To adjust the current color, slide one of the sliders up or down the color slider or click in the color slider to have the sliders jump to that location in the bar. As you change the color, Illustrator changes the values in the text boxes next to the radio buttons, modifies the look of the color field, and places its current hexadecimal value in the # text box. The color field looks just the same. Check Only Web Colors to restrict your color selections to Web-Safe RGB colors.

The small color box above the radio buttons indicates the current color (in the top half) and starting color (in the bottom half) as you change colors using the various parts of the Color Picker. To return to the starting color, click it.

When you select one of the radio buttons and adjust the color field or color slider in the Color Picker, Illustrator changes the values in one or more of the text boxes next to the other radio buttons, changes the appearance of the color field and color slider, and places the hexadecimal value of the current color in the # text box. The radio buttons in the Color Picker are as follows:

- *H* represents hue, the dominant color in the current color. This radio button is a counterpart to the H slider and text box in the HSB version of the Color palette. Click to be able to change the hue.

- *S* represents saturation, the amount of hue in the current color. This radio button is a counterpart to the S slider and text box in the HSB version of the Color palette. Click to be able to change the percentage of saturation.

- *B* represents brightness, the intensity of light reflected by the current color. This corresponds to the B slider and text box in the HSB version of the Color palette. Click to be able to adjust the brightness of the current color.

- *R* represents the amount of red in the current color. This is related to the R slider and text box in the RGB version of the Color palette. Click to be able to modify the redness in the current color.

- *G* represents the amount of green in the current color. This is related to the G slider and text box in the RGB version of the Color palette. Click to be able to change the amount of green in the current color.

- *B* represents the amount of blue in the current color. This is related to the B slider and text box in the RGB version of the Color palette. Click to be able to adjust the levels of blue in the current color.

- *C* represents the amount of cyan in the current color. This is related to the C slider and text box in the CMYK version of the Color palette. Click to be able to modify the amount of cyan in the current color.

- ■ *M* represents the amount of magenta in the current color. This is related to the M slider and text box in the CMYK version of the Color palette. Click to be able to modify the amount of magenta in the current color.

- ■ *Y* represents the amount of yellow in the current color. This is related to the Y slider and text box in the CMYK version of the Color palette. Click to be able to modify the amount of yellow in the current color.

- ■ *K* represents the amount of black in the current color. This is related to the K slider and text box in the CMYK version of the Color palette. Click to be able to modify the amount of black in the current color.

Depending on the current color, the Color Picker can display the Web Color Warning icon or Out of Gamut Color Warning icon. To correct the color, click the icon or the box to its right, slide the slider a little, or change the value in a text box to adjust the color and make the warning icon disappear.

ILLUSTRATOR ESSENTIALS

Chapter 8

Customizing Strokes and Fills

In Chapter 7 you learned how to blend and apply colors to the fills and strokes that make up your artwork, and modify certain characteristics of strokes. You are not finished with fills and strokes, however. In this chapter you'll learn to customize both strokes and fills; for example, you'll find out how to make strokes into images that stand on their own, and you'll learn the details of creating patterned fills. Later in the chapter you'll be introduced to two new (for you) toolbox tools: the closely related Eyedropper tool and Paint Bucket tool.

Customizing Strokes

Using the features of the Stroke palette and a menu command, you can enhance strokes. In fact, you can create artwork using one or more strokes only. For example, you can draw a stroke of any shape and then use a command to convert the stroke to a filled object. Or, you can draw a wide stroke; copy and paste several replicas in the illustration window; and then move them together to form a unified image of a segment of a country road, string of beads, a strip of film, or a rainbow. Note that a stroke, regardless of its weight, is equally dispersed on either sides of a path and you cannot vary the width of a stroke on a particular path.

Outlining a Stroke

Illustrator provides a menu command with which you can outline the selected strokes in a document and convert those strokes to filled outlines of the same size and appearance as the originals. The only way to see the difference between the before and after versions is to select it. The original object has one path with the stroke drawn on either side of the path. The converted object has an outer path and an inner path. During the transformation, Illustrator changes the stroke to a fill and sets the stroke to None. If the original stroke has a corresponding fill, the converted object contains that fill, which is a separate object.

This command enables you to change the new fill just as you would any fill. For example, you already know that if you want to apply a gradient to a stroke, you are out of luck; strokes do not accept gradients. However, if you convert that stroke to a fill, you can apply colors, patterns, and gradients.

Select the stroke and choose Object | Path | Outline Stroke to convert a stroke to a filled outline. Figure 8-1 illustrates before and after versions of converted strokes. On the left is an original circular, 30-point stroke. Next to that is the toolbox, which shows the fill and stroke values for the stroke. On the right is the converted object with a gradient fill applied along with its version of the toolbox.

Figure 8-2 illustrates a filled and stroked object turned into two filled objects with no strokes. On the left of the figure is the initial filled rectangle with a 50-point stroke and its associated toolbox. To the right of the original figure is the product of applying the Outline Stroke command. To the right are the two filled objects that actually resulted from converting the stroke to the filled outline. Next to each result is its associated toolbox. Note the values of the fill and stroke buttons.

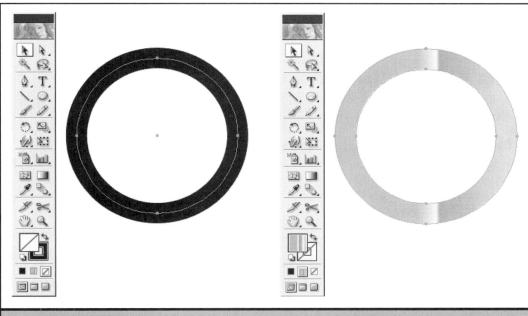

Figure 8-1.   *A before and after examples of a stroke converted to a filled object*

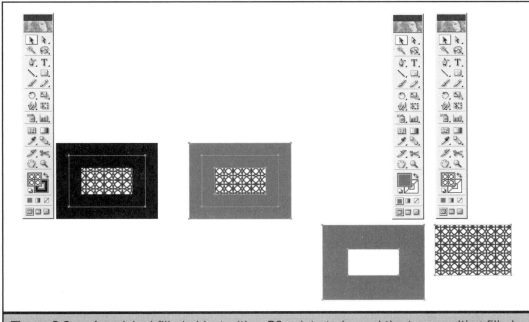

Figure 8-2.   *An original filled object with a 50-point stroke and the two resulting filled objects dragged apart*

Note   *Illustrator also provides an Outline Stroke effect. You'll learn more about effects in Chapter 16.*

Working with Multiple Strokes

One way of using strokes is to create multiple versions, change their widths, and cover each stroke with others or place them adjacent to each other.

Placing Multiple Strokes Next to Each Other

You can make several copies of a stroke and place the copies next to each other to form an artwork. To do so, choose Edit | Copy (CTRL-C/⌘-C) to copy the original stroke and then choose Edit | Paste (CTRL-V/⌘-V) to paste the copies onto the illustration window. Then drag the copies next to the original to form the artwork. In this section you will learn how to create a simple hand-like object out of a rectangle and five curved strokes with rounded caps.

To create the hand, follow these steps:

1. In the Stroke palette, select a 40-point width and click the Rounded Cap button.

2. With the Pencil tool (N), draw a curved line.

3. If needed, adjust the plane of the line by using the Rotate tool (R) and dragging one end of the line.

4. Pressing and holding down SHIFT and using the Direct Selection tool (A), select two or three of the leftmost anchor points and straighten the left side of the line.

5. Select the curved line and copy it by choosing Edit | Copy (CTRL-C/⌘-C).

6. Choose Edit | Paste (CTRL-V/⌘-V) to paste four copies onto the illustration window.

7. With the Selection tool (V), move one copy to the bottom of the illustration window.

8. Move three copies into position forming fingers next to the original stroke. (Look at your hand to see how the length of each of your fingers relates to the other fingers.)

9. Select the final curved line at the bottom of the illustration window. You will change this object into the thumb.

10. Activate the Reflect tool (O), which is on the same toolslot as the Rotate tool. Drag the thumb down slightly to flip it from top to bottom.

11. Drag the thumb just above the four fingers.

12. Use the Rotate tool (R) to rotate the thumb so that it fits better with the fingers. (Again, look at your hand to see how the thumb relates to the fingers.) Then drag the thumb into its final location to the left of the ends of all the fingers.

13. By pressing and holding down CTRL to change the current tool to the Selection tool, click away from the objects to deselect the thumb.

14. In the Stroke palette, change the stroke to black and the stroke weight to 10 points.

15. In the Swatches palette, change the fill to black.

16. Select the Rectangle tool (M).

17. Draw a rectangle whose origin point is slightly below and to the left of the end of the thumb. Drag down to slightly above the little finger and to the right to cover all the spaces between the ends of all the fingers.

18. Select all the fingers and the thumb, and group them by choosing Object | Group (CTRL-G/⌘-G).

19. Save the document.

Figure 8-3 illustrates the steps, from the top and moving clockwise direction, of creating a hand using multiple strokes.

ILLUSTRATOR
ESSENTIALS

Figure 8-3.   *The process of constructing a hand using multiple strokes*

Covering One Stroke with Others

Another way to combine strokes into an artwork is to copy the original stroke by choosing Edit | Copy (CTRL-C/⌘-C). Then choose Edit | Paste in Front (CTRL-F/⌘-F) to superimpose each copy on the original. As you assemble the artwork, you can change each stroke so that a little or a lot of the prior stroke peeks through. To illustrate pasting in front, you will learn how to make a rainbow consisting of seven strokes, each of which decreases in weight by 30 points.

To create a rainbow of overlaid objects, follow these steps:

1. With the fill active in the toolbox, click the None button.

2. Activate the stroke (X).

3. From the Stroke palette, select a 210-point width and click the Butt Cap button.

4. In the CMYK version of the Swatches palette, click the Red M=100 Y=100 swatch.

5. With the Pen tool (P), create a curved line by drawing the first line from the bottom to the top on the left, clicking the right side of the artboard and dragging down.

6. Copy the stroke by choosing Edit | Copy (CTRL-C/⌘-C).

7. Choose Edit | Paste in Front (CTRL-F/⌘-F) to superimpose the copy on the original.

8. Change the stroke weight to 180 points and click the Orange M=50 Y=100 swatch. Illustrator changes the color and width of the copied stroke.

9. Repeat steps 7 and 8 five more times to apply the following colors and stroke widths:

Swatch Color	Stroke Width
Yellow	150 points
Green C=80 Y=100	120 points
Blue C=100 M=50	90 points
50% Blue C=50 M=25	60 points
Violet C=50 M=90	30 points

10. Save the document.

Figure 8-4 illustrates the progress of the rainbow-like image from start to finish. Note that you can enhance the rainbow by creating custom color swatches rather than using the standard CMYK colors.

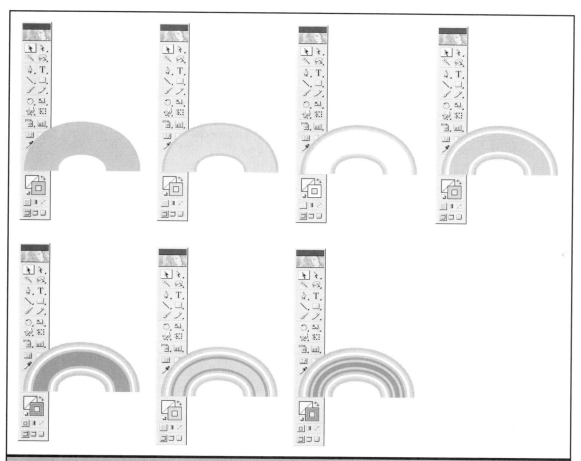

Figure 8-4. *The creation of a double rainbow, step by step*

Dotting Your Dashes

In Chapter 7 you learned about dashed lines in the Stroke palette. When you combine dashes and spaces plus other options in the Stroke palette, you can come up with some fantastic dash patterns—especially if you copy multiple strokes over each other. For example, you can create a stroke that looks like a set of rounded black beads and then copy the stroke four times to construct a pattern of black within white, and white within black circles. To do so, follow these steps:

1. Draw a 20-point black stroke with a fill of None.
2. Choose Window | Stroke (F10) to open the Stroke palette.

3. Apply a pattern of 2-point dashes and 20-point gaps. Click the Round Cap and Round Join buttons.

4. Copy the stroke by selecting it and choosing Edit | Copy (CTRL-C/⌘-C).

5. Paste the stroke four times by choosing Edit | Paste (CTRL-V/⌘-V) four times.

6. Drag the copies apart in the illustration window.

7. Select a copy and change it to a 16-point weight. (The dash and gap pattern remains the same for each of the copies.)

8. Choose Window | Swatches to open the Swatches palette.

9. Select a copy and change it to a 12-point weight, and click the Black swatch.

10. Select a copy; change it to an 8-point weight; and click a light-colored swatch, which enables you to construct the image more easily. (Then change the color to white after assembly.)

11. Select a copy, change it to a 4-point weight, and click the Black swatch.

12. Drag the 16-point copy onto the 20-point black stroke. Change its color to white after you have placed it in its centered location.

13. If needed, choose Object | Arrange | Bring to Front (CTRL-SHIFT-]/⌘-SHIFT-]) to place the copy over the original.

14. If you need to center a smaller bead over the larger bead, repeatedly press any combination of arrow keys.

15. Repeat steps 12, 13, and 14, dragging copies in the following order: 12-point, 8-point, and 4-point. Change all light-colored strokes to white after you have centered them over the larger stroke.

Figure 8-5 shows the individual strokes and the assembled version. Note that the white strokes are colored light blue (so that you can see them in the figure) and then painted white for the collated version.

Figure 8-6 shows the following assemblages:

■ The film strip is made up of three strokes: 50-point black, 40-point white (shown in light blue in the figure) with a 4-point dash and 4-point gap, and a 38-point black. All strokes have a Butt Cap and Miter Join. Create the image by dragging the smaller sizes onto larger sizes: 40-point white onto the 50-point black and the 38-point on top.

■ The squares collection is constructed from four strokes: 20-point black with a 20-point dash and 20-point gap, 16-point white (shown as light blue in the figure) with a 16-point dash and 24-point gap, 12-point black with a 12-point dash and 28-point gap, and 8-point white (shown in light blue in the figure) with a 8-point dash and 32-point gap. Note that the dash and gap total is

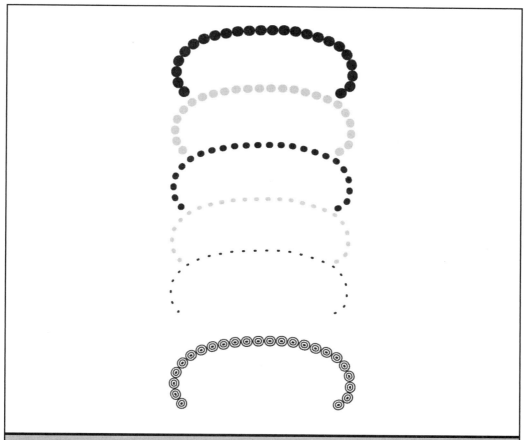

Figure 8-5.   *Single strokes (from the top down) and an assembled version of all the strokes (at the bottom)*

always equal to 40 points, and the dash size is always equal to the stroke weight. All strokes have a Butt Cap and Miter Join. Create the image by dragging small strokes onto larger strokes.

■ The roadway assembly is composed of four strokes: 50-point black, 44-point white (shown in light blue in the figure), 40-point gray, and 4-point yellow with a 10-point dash and 10-point gap. All strokes have a Butt Cap and Miter Join. The largest stroke is the roadbed, which enables you to show the white lines (that is, the next largest stroke) on either side of the road. Place the 40-point gray stroke on the white stroke to form the road, resulting in the appearance of white lines on either side of the road. Then place the dashed yellow line on top.

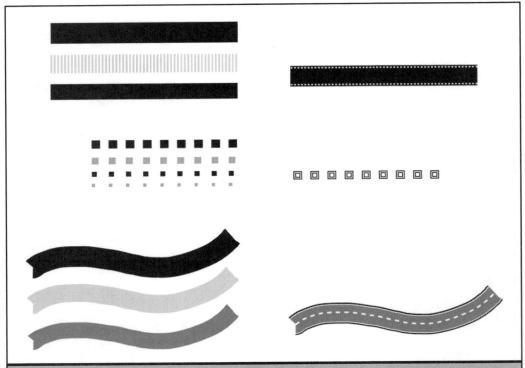

Figure 8-6. *Three or four strokes each (on the left) that comprise three assemblages (on the right)*

Customizing Fills with Patterns

As this book progresses you'll learn techniques to change the look of fills and—to a lesser extent—strokes. For example, you'll find out about gradients and gradient meshes in Chapter 9, learn about transparency and opacity in Chapter 15, and discover all of Illustrator's effects and filters in Chapter 16. In this section, you'll learn all about patterns.

Patterns are small images that are repeated throughout a fill or stroke, in much the same way wallpaper decorates the Windows desktop. As you know, Illustrator provides several predefined pattern swatches in the Swatches palette. In this section you'll learn how to apply a pattern to the fill or stroke and find out how to create your own custom patterns using another pattern as the basis or from scratch.

Note *It's always a good idea to browse through any program's installation CD-ROM as well as its folders once you have gone through the installation process. For example, many programs provide extra files and features with which you can enhance your artwork. You can be sure you'll find a variety of files, including extra filters, effects, patterns, symbols, and samples.*

Using a Pattern as a Fill or Stroke

Applying a pattern to an object's fill works in the same way as applying a swatch: Select the object, and activate the fill by clicking the fill box in the toolbox or in the Color palette or by pressing X. Then click the pattern swatch in the Swatches palette in the same way you would click a color swatch. You also can apply the pattern by dragging the pattern to the object—regardless of whether the object is selected.

When you paint a stroke with a pattern, use the same method: Select the object, activate the stroke box (X), and click the pattern swatch; or drag the pattern to the selected or unselected object. Your only concern in applying a pattern to a stroke is the width of the stroke: A narrow stroke will not show the pattern in all its glory. Figure 8-7 shows fills and strokes decorated with some of Illustrator's predefined patterns. At the top of the figure is a star whose stroke is the Honeycomb pattern. In the middle of the figure is a square filled with the Mediterranean tiles pattern. At the bottom is a stroke whose pattern is Pyramids.

ILLUSTRATOR
ESSENTIALS

Figure 8-7.   *Three objects whose fills and strokes are embellished with default patterns*

The top object in Figure 8-7 shows that fills and heavy strokes overlap. (Note the fill behind the patterned stroke.) The stroke's partial cover of the fill might not be your goal in designing the object. If you want the fill to take up the original space you assigned it, copy the path, paste it to another part of the illustration window, set its stroke value to None, and then drag the edited path over the original one.

Creating a Pattern

A pattern is made up of an image on a rectangle, which is known as a *pattern tile*. The tile enables you to place pattern images and separate them by an amount of space you control. Each tile is adjacent to another tile—above, below, to the left, and to the right—unless the tile is at the edge of the pattern. You can create a pattern using a predefined pattern as its basis, or you can plan and construct a pattern from scratch.

You save a pattern to the Swatches palette—just as you would a customized color. Like newly mixed color swatches, a saved pattern swatch is associated with the current document and does not remain on the default Swatches palette for any other document. Thus, you will want to set up a custom swatches library to contain swatches you create and want to save for future use. For more information in creating a swatches library, refer to "Creating a Swatch Library" in Chapter 7.

You also can create patterns for the Paintbrush tool. Refer to "Creating a Brush Pattern" in Chapter 13 to learn how to create and use brush patterns.

Making a Pattern from an Illustrator Pattern or Image

To create and save a pattern, follow these steps:

1. Create an image using a pattern as a template or starting with an empty illustration window.

2. To space the image from the adjacent images, draw a rectangle with both fill and stroke equal to None.

3. If the image is made up of several paths, select them all and choose Object | Group (CTRL-G/⌘-G).

4. Choose Window | Swatches to open the Swatches palette.

5. Select the artwork and drag it to the Swatches palette.

6. When a black rectangle appears around the swatches in the palette, drop the artwork into place. Illustrator adds a new swatch holding your artwork.

7. If you want to manage your swatches, it's best to give the new pattern swatch a name. To do so, double-click the new swatch in the Swatches palette, or select the swatch in the illustration window and choose Edit | Define Pattern. Illustrator opens the New Swatch dialog box or the Swatch Options dialog box, respectively.

8. Type the name of the pattern in the dialog box and click OK.

Figure 8-8 illustrates five images used as patterns. Each image is selected so that you can see whether it has a border. On the upper left is a newly drawn black spiral with a 6-point stroke weight within a very small invisible rectangle. Under that is the same spiral within a larger rectangle. Notice the difference between the patterned circles. At the bottom of the column is a group of stars converted into a pattern. A medium-sized invisible rectangle separates adjacent patterns. On the right side of the figure is a pattern based on the Pyramids pattern and a pattern made up of four columns: three wide ones and one very narrow white one. Neither pattern is enclosed within an invisible rectangle, so the patterns in the circle hug each other.

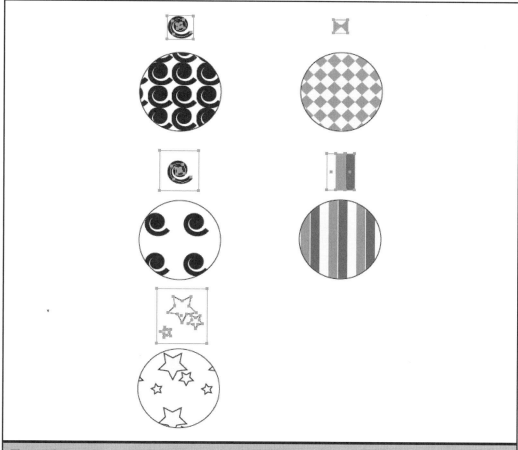

Figure 8-8. *Five patterns shown within circles*

Learning Some Fine Points of Pattern Making

When you create patterns, you can use any combination of existing paths, compound paths, text, or you can make patterns from original artwork. However, Illustrator has placed some limits on the way you produce patterns. For example, you cannot use bitmap images, blends, brushstrokes, gradients, graphs, masks, meshes, placed files, or other patterns in a pattern.

When you plan, design, and create a pattern, consider the following facts:

- Illustrator tiles patterns from left to right and from the bottom of the artwork being filled to the top.

- Your first patterns should be rectangular; otherwise, tiling might create awkward joints. If you create a circular pattern, place it within a rectangle with fill and stroke both set to None—unless you want to paint the background of the pattern with a specific color.

- You can move, resize, rotate, flip, scale, and skew the pattern in the way you would transform any other image.

- Use the Direct Selection tool (A) to select individual paths (that is, strokes) to change their color and other attributes.

- One method of tiling a pattern with straight edges without showing where the edges meet is to make the paths forming the edge half the width of the inner paths. Then, when the edges fit together, they form a path that looks like the inner paths.

- Another tiling method applies to rectangles that space one pattern from another: give the rectangle's stroke a value of None.

- When you want to construct an irregular pattern, you don't want to see any straight seams. Place objects that overlap the edge of the pattern around all four edges, and cut away other areas so that the patterns will fit together like jigsaw puzzle pieces. Experiment by copying the tile and pasting the copies around the edges of the tile. Then edit until you are satisfied with the results. Be aware that this type of pattern takes a lot of effort to complete.

- To create patterns made up of grids or lines, reveal the grid by choosing View | Show Grid (CTRL-"/⌘-"). Then draw vertical, horizontal, or even diagonal paths along the grid lines. If needed, place the resulting artwork within a rectangle. To learn more about the grid, refer to "Setting Grid Options" in Chapter 5. You also can use the Rectangular Grid or Polar Grid tools, which are covered in the following section, to create patterns made of grids.

- To create a pattern whose paths run diagonally, create a square pattern. Then double-click the Rotate tool (R) to open the Rotate dialog box. In the Angle text box, type 45 (for degrees), 135, 225, or 315.

Making Patterns Using the Grid Tools

Illustrator provides two tools to create grids, which lend themselves to interesting patterns and can be valuable components of other artwork. In this section you'll explore the Rectangular Grid and the Polar Grid tools.

 Once you set the fill color of a rectangular grid or polar grid, you cannot change it. However, you can place a filled rectangle behind a pattern with a Fill equaling None. The fill of the object seems to fill the pattern. At the same time, the rectangle also affects the overall size of the pattern.

Using the Rectangular Grid Tool

 Use the Rectangular Grid tool, which is on the Line Segment tool's toolslot, to draw a gridwork of horizontal and vertical paths enclosed within a rectangle or square. Illustrator gives lines in the grid the current stroke color and may fill the background with the current fill color, depending on the tool's options. Create a rectangular grid just as you would a standard rectangle: Move the mouse pointer to the starting point of the rectangle and drag. To draw a square grid down from an origin point, press and hold down SHIFT as you drag. To draw a square grid from a central origin point, press and hold down SHIFT-ALT/SHIFT-OPTION as you drag.

You also can use the Rectangular Grid tool to open the Rectangular Grid Tool Options dialog box (see Figure 8-9) with which you can set the width and height of a rectangular or square grid. If you have used this installed version of Illustrator to create a rectangular or square grid before, either with the Rectangular Grid tool or the Rectangular Grid Tool Options dialog box, those values remain in the dialog box; otherwise, Illustrator's default values appear. Other than creating patterns, you can use the Rectangular Grid tool to create tables in which you can place text, images, or both.

To create a rectangular or square grid using a dialog box, follow these steps:

1. Click the Rectangular Grid tool.
2. Move the mouse pointer to the desired starting point of the rectangular grid and click. Illustrator opens the Rectangular Grid Tool Options dialog box.
3. In the Width text box, type the width, in points, of the grid.
4. In the rectangle to the right of the Width text box, click the corner that will be the starting point.
5. In the Height text box, type the height, in points, of the grid. (If the width and height match, the result is a square grid.)
6. In the Number text box in the Horizontal Dividers section, type the number of dividers (horizontal lines) within the grid. Valid values range between 0 and 999. The default is 5.

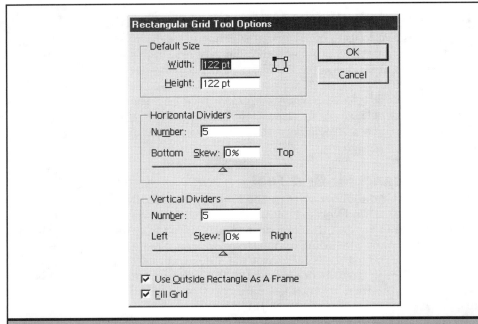

Figure 8-9.   *Specify an exact width and height of a rectangle or square using the Rectangular Grid Tool Options dialog box.*

7. In the Skew text box in the Horizontal Dividers section, either type a logarithmic skew value or slide the slider to skew the grid toward the bottom (up to –500%) or the top (up to 500%). The default is 0%, which means no skew.

8. In the Number text box in the Vertical Dividers section, type the number of dividers (vertical lines) within the grid. Valid values range between 0 and 999; the default is 5.

9. In the Skew text box in the Vertical Dividers section, either type a logarithmic skew value or slide the slider to skew the grid toward the left (up to –500%) or the right (up to 500%). The default is 0%, which means no skew.

10. Check the Use Outside Rectangle As a Frame check box to convert the border of the grid to a separate rectangle so that you can fill it with one background color.

11. Check the Fill Grid check box to fill the grid with the current fill color. If the check box is clear, the fill color is set to None.

12. Click OK. Illustrator closes the dialog box and "draws" the grid.

Because the lines making up the grid are strokes, you can vary their widths, caps, joins, and dash and gap characteristics.

As you drag a rectangular grid, you can also use the following keys:

- To add horizontal lines to a rectangular grid being created, press and hold down ↑ while dragging. Illustrator continues to add lines until you release the key or reach the upper limit of 999.

- To remove horizontal lines from a rectangular grid being created, press and hold down ↓ while dragging. Illustrator continues to remove lines until you release the key or reach the lower limit of no lines.

- To add vertical lines to a rectangular grid being created, press and hold down → while dragging. Illustrator continues to add lines until you release the key or reach the upper limit of 999.

- To remove vertical lines from a rectangular grid being created, press and hold down ← while dragging. Illustrator continues to remove lines until you release the key or reach the lower limit of no lines.

- To create a rectangular grid that expands from all sides of the origin point, press ALT/OPTION while dragging.

- To create several grids simultaneously, press and hold down ` (back-tick or left single quote on the left side of the keyboard) while dragging. The result is a set of identical grids, each a separate object. To place them around the illustration window, select the selection tool or press V; then drag each grid off the pile to another area of the window.

- To increase the skew value for horizontal lines by 10%, press V.

- To decrease the skew value for horizontal lines by 10%, press F.

- To increase the skew value for horizontal lines by 10%, press C.

- To decrease the skew value for horizontal lines by 10%, press X.

- To move a rectangular grid as you are creating it, press SPACEBAR and drag the grid.

Figure 8-10 shows two rectangular grid patterns. On the left is a pattern with a red fill and a series of 2-point blue horizontal and vertical strokes surrounded by 1-point blue strokes. On the right is a yellow-filled pattern with an assortment of characteristics: Every other line is an undashed 2-point, black stroke; the other strokes are 10-point black with a 2-point dash, 2-point gap, and 6-point dash. The entire pattern is surrounded by a 1-point stroke. Note that the outer strokes are smaller to provide a seamless look in the sample circles.

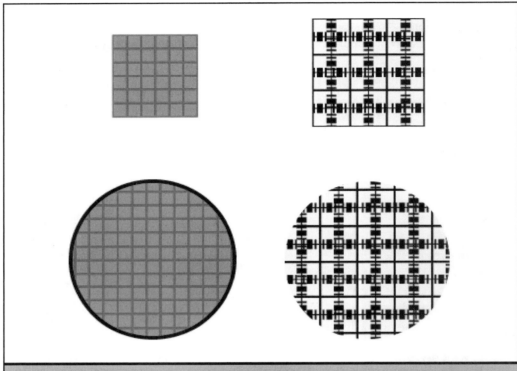

Figure 8-10.   *Two patterns created with the Rectangular Grid tool and examples of each*

Using the Polar Grid Tool

Use the Polar Grid tool, which is on the Line Segment tool's toolslot, to draw a series of strokes radiating from the center of an ellipse or circle, which is surrounded by a stroke. Illustrator gives the radiating strokes the current stroke color and fills the background with the current fill color, depending on the tool's options.

Create a polar grid just as you would an ellipse: Move the mouse pointer to the starting point of the ellipse and drag. To draw a circular grid down from an origin point, press and hold down SHIFT as you drag. To draw a circular grid from a central origin point, press and hold down SHIFT-ALT/SHIFT-OPTION as you drag. You also can use the Polar Grid tool to open the Polar Grid Tool Options dialog box (see Figure 8-11) with which you can set the dimensions and other options of a polar grid. If you have used this installed version of Illustrator to create a polar grid before, either with the Polar Grid tool or the Polar Grid Tool Options dialog box, those values remain in the dialog box; otherwise, Illustrator's default values appear.

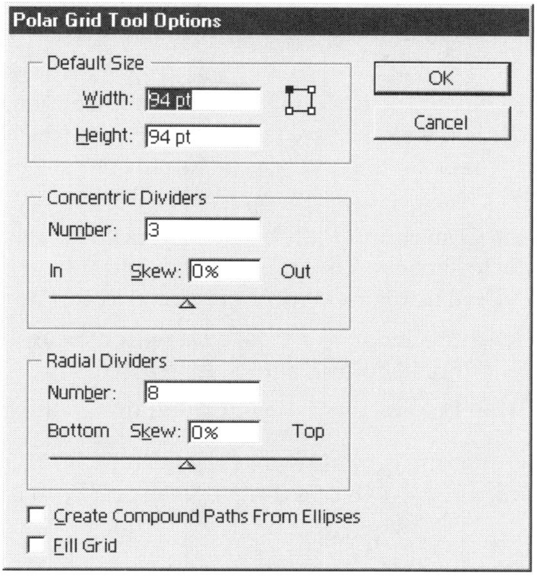

Figure 8-11. *Use the Polar Grid Tool Options dialog box to draw an elliptical or circular polar grid.*

To create an elliptical or circular grid using a dialog box, follow these steps:

1. Click the Polar Grid tool.

2. Move the mouse pointer to the desired starting point of the polar grid and click. Illustrator opens the Polar Grid Tool Options dialog box.

3. In the Width text box, type the width, in points, of the grid.

4. In the rectangle to the right of the Width text box, click the corner that will be the starting point.

5. In the Height text box, type the height, in points, of the grid. (If the width and height match, the result is a circular grid.)

6. In the Number text box in the Concentric Dividers section, type the number of dividers (concentric ellipses or circles) within the grid. Valid values range between 0 and 999. The default is 5.

7. In the Skew text box in the Concentric Dividers section, either type a logarithmic skew value or slide the slider to skew the grid toward the center (up to –500%) or the outer border (up to 500%). The default is 0%, which means no skew.

8. In the Number text box in the Radial Dividers section, type the number of radiating dividers within the grid. Valid values range between 0 and 999. The default is 5.

9. In the Skew text box in the Radial Dividers section, either type a logarithmic skew value or slide the slider to skew more dividers toward the bottom of the grid (up to – 500%) or the top of the grid (up to 500%). The default is 0%, which means no skew.

10. Check the Create Compound Path from Ellipses check box to change the concentric paths to separate compound paths and fill every other path within the grid. If the check box is cleared, the entire grid can be filled with one color.

11. Check the Fill grid check box to fill the grid with the current fill color. If the check box is clear, the fill color is set to None.

12. Click OK. Illustrator closes the dialog box and draws the grid.

Because the lines within the grid are strokes, you can vary their widths, caps, joins, and dash and gap characteristics. As you drag a polar grid, you can also use the following keys:

- To add concentric lines to a polar grid being created, press and hold down ↑ while dragging. Illustrator continues to add lines until you release the key or reach the upper limit of 999.

- To remove concentric lines from a polar grid being created, press and hold down ↓ while dragging. Illustrator continues to remove lines until you release the key or reach the lower limit of no lines.

- To add radiating lines to a polar grid being created, press and hold down → while dragging. Illustrator continues to add lines until you release the key or reach the upper limit of 999.

- To remove radiating lines from a polar grid being created, press and hold down ← while dragging. Illustrator continues to remove lines until you release the key or reach the lower limit of no lines.

- To create a polar grid that expands from all sides of the origin point, press ALT/OPTION while dragging.

- To create several grids simultaneously, press and hold down ` (back tick or left single quote on the left side of the keyboard) while dragging. The result is a set of identical grids, each a separate object. To place them around the illustration window, select the selection tool or press V; then drag each grid off the pile to another area of the window.

- To change the skew value clockwise for radiating lines by 10%, press V.

- To change the skew value counterclockwise for radiating lines by 10%, press F.

- To increase the skew value for concentric lines by 10%, press C.
- To decrease the skew value for concentric lines by 10%, press X.
- To move a polar grid as you are creating it, press SPACEBAR, and drag the grid.

Figure 8-12 shows two polar grids on the left and one polar-grid pattern and an example of its use as a fill in a rectangle. At the top left is a target with no radiating lines and alternate concentric circles filled with black. Below that is a more complex image whose concentric lines are given stroke colors of either white or yellow. The outer three concentric strokes have a 3-point weight, and the inner strokes have a 1-point weight. The orange radiating lines each have a stroke value of 30 points and a projecting cap. On the right side of the figure is a pattern with alternate red circles and radiating blue lines of 10 points and rounded caps.

Figure 8-12.   *On the left, two polar grids; on the right, one polar grid pattern*

Using the Eyedropper and the Paint Bucket Tools

When you studied the Color palette in Chapter 7, you learned about the spectrum bar at the bottom of the Color palette. Remember that when you selected from the spectrum bar, the mouse pointer changed to an Eyedropper pointer. This was your first exposure to the Eyedropper tool (I). You can use the Eyedropper and the Paint Bucket (K) in tandem to obtain many types of styling information, including color, and then place the information on a selected object.

Setting Eyedropper and Paint Bucket Preferences

You can select options in the Eyedropper/Paint Bucket Options dialog box (see Figure 8-13) to customize the information that the Eyedropper picks up and the Paint Bucket applies. To open the dialog box, double-click the Eyedropper tool (I) or the Paint Bucket tool (K), which is on the Eyedropper toolslot.

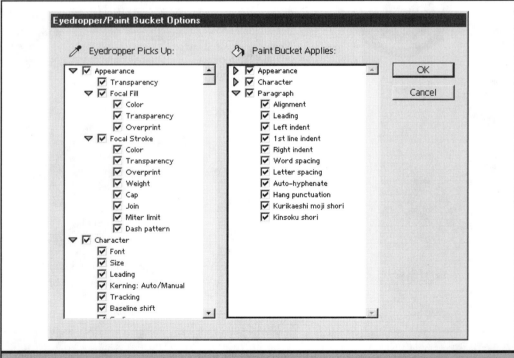

Figure 8-13.   *The Eyedropper/Paint Bucket Options dialog box showing every option*

The options on both sides of the dialog box, which are arranged under three headings, are not only exactly the same but, by default, all are selected. The options under the Appearance heading in both columns of the dialog box relate to the appearance of artworks, including color, transparency, and overprint for both fill and stroke and stroke attributes such as weight, the cap and join types, the miter limit, and the current dash pattern.

Other options in each of the columns control type and paragraph characteristics for the Eyedropper and Paint Bucket. For more information about modifying type and paragraphs with the Eyedropper and the Paint Bucket, refer to "Copying Type Attributes with the Eyedropper" and "Pasting Type Attributes with the Paint Bucket" in Chapter 12. To select an option, check its check box; to remove an option from the Eyedropper or Paint Bucket repertory, clear the check box. When you have completed selecting or deselecting options, click OK.

Using the Eyedropper

With the Eyedropper (I) and shortcut keys, you can grab different types of attributes from many kinds of objects (including the spectrum bar; stroke and fill of an object; or a clicked section of a pattern, gradient, placed image, or meshed object) on your computer screen, depending on the options set in the Eyedropper/Paint Bucket Options dialog box. If you have selected an object before using the Eyedropper, Illustrator applies the picked-up characteristics to it and updates both the fill and stroke in the toolbox and the Color palette.

- If you click the Eyedropper, Illustrator collects all appearance characteristics, including color, from an object and applies those characteristics to selected objects.

- If you click the Eyedropper while pressing and holding down SHIFT, Illustrator picks up the color only from the object and applies those characteristics to selected objects. If clicking the Eyedropper doesn't gather information from a section of a particular object, try SHIFT-clicking to obtain the color from that section.

- If you click the Eyedropper while pressing and holding down SHIFT and ALT/OPTION, Illustrator copies the object and its attributes.

- To toggle between the Eyedropper and the Paint Bucket—whichever is currently active—press ALT/OPTION.

Using the Paint Bucket

When you activate the Paint Bucket tool (K), you can repaint one or more selected objects with the contents of the Eyedropper; that is, the current fill and stroke. If you are in Outline view or the selected object has a fill that is equal to None, click the stroke of either closed or open paths.

The Complete
Reference

Chapter 9

All About Gradients
and Gradient Meshes

251

This chapter is all about gradients and gradient meshes with which you can decorate the fills of your artwork. In the first part of this chapter you will learn how to use Illustrator's Gradient palette and Gradient tool, in conjunction with other palettes and features, to apply and modify gradients. In the second half of the chapter you'll learn about *mesh objects* (or *gradient meshes*) with which you can apply gradient-like highlights or shading and edit artwork by dragging or applying color to mesh lines, which are unique types of paths; and mesh points, which are distinctive anchor points.

What Is a Gradient?

A *gradient* is a gradual transition from one color or shade of a color through intermediate colors to a final color or shade from one side of an object to another or from the center of an object to its edge. Illustrator supports gradients with CMYK and RGB process colors and any type of spot color. However, gradients that mix two or more color models change to CMYK process color when they are printed or prepared for process printing. You can apply gradients to fills but not to strokes, type (except for those converted to outlines), or patterns. However, you can change strokes and patterns so that they accept gradients. For more information, see "Working Around Gradient Limits," later in this chapter.

Note   *Illustrator also provides blends, which are gradual transitions from one color and shape of an initial object, through intermediate changes to a color and shape of a final object. So, although gradients and blends would seem to be related, they are two separate and different Illustrator features. To learn about blends, refer to "Blending on a Path" in Chapter 18. Blends are not to be confused with blending modes, which are used with transparency in Illustrator. To learn about blending modes, refer to "Using Blending Modes" in Chapter 15.*

Exploring the Gradient Palette

The purpose of the Gradient palette is to help you create and modify all the gradients you'll ever make with Illustrator. To toggle between showing and hiding the palette, choose Window | Gradient (F9). Another way of opening the palette is double-clicking the Gradient tool.

The Gradient palette contains three options:

■ Select the type of gradient from the Type drop-down menu. If you choose Linear, the gradient runs from one side of an object to another; if you choose Radial, the gradient originates at the center of the object and runs to the outer edges.

■ In the Angle text box, type the angle at which you want a linear gradient to move. (This option is not available for radial gradients.) Valid values range from –80 to 180; the default is 0.

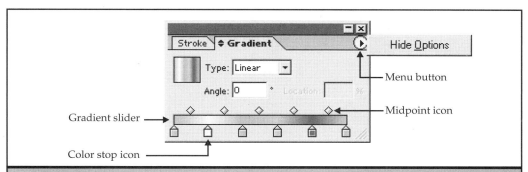

Figure 9-1. *With the Gradient palette you can create and adjust all types of gradients in your artwork.*

- The Location text box contains the percentage at which a gradient color starts or is half the current color and half the next color. Click a color stop icon or a midpoint icon, and type the percentage of the slider at which the color change will take place or the halfway point will be reached. The left edge of the slider is at 0%, and the right edge is at 100%. You also can slide the selected icon along the gradient slider to visually set the location. If you take advantage of the full length of the slider (that is, icons are at the 0% and 100% locations), the gradient adjusts gradually from the starting color to the ending color. If both the start and end points are closer to the midpoint, the gradient adjusts quickly from color to color.

- Slide the gradient slider or its icons to adjust the progression from the first color to the last. As you move the slider, the value in the Location text box changes, and the preview in the gradient fill box varies.

To open the palette's menu, click the menu button.

- The Show Options command shows the complete palette with its Type, Angle, and Location options and the gradient slider; the Hide Options command shows the slider only.

The Gradient palette works with the Swatches palette and the Color palette. So, when you open the Gradient palette you also should reveal the other two palettes. To learn more about the Color palette, see "Exploring the Color Palette" in Chapter 7. Read "Exploring the Swatches Palette," also in Chapter 7, to find out about the Swatches palette.

Using Gradient Swatches

When you browsed through Chapter 7 you discovered that the Swatches palette contains several predefined gradient swatches with which you can fill an object (but not apply to the stroke). In the "Working with Swatches" section, you learned how to create and save custom color swatches. In this section you'll learn how to apply, create, and edit custom gradient swatches. Note that gradient swatches fill an open or closed path; you cannot paint a stroke with a gradient.

Applying the Default or Last Gradient to an Object

 When you start an Illustrator session, the Gradient button (>) at the bottom of the toolbox contains the default gradient, which is labeled White, Black and ranges from white to black linearly. If you have worked with gradients in the current document, the Gradient button always shows the last gradient on which you worked. To apply the default gradient or the previously used gradient to an object, select the object and click the Gradient button.

Applying a Gradient from a Swatch

Filling an object with the contents of a gradient swatch is a matter of selecting and clicking. To apply a gradient swatch to an object's fill, follow these steps:

1. Open the Gradient palette by choosing Window | Gradient (F9).
2. Select the path to which you want to employ the gradient swatch.
3. Activate the fill (X) in the toolbox.
4. Click the swatch to be used. Illustrator applies the gradient to the fill and the selected path's fill.

You can use the Gradient palette, Swatches palette, and Color palette to apply the current gradient fill (in the case of the Gradient palette) or both the fill and stroke color or pattern (with the Swatches palette or the Color palette) to an object—selected or unselected. Just drag the gradient, color, or pattern from the palette to the object.

Creating a Two-Color Gradient

To create a two-color gradient, follow these steps:

1. Select the type of gradient—linear or radial—by choosing Linear or Radial from the Type drop-down menu.
2. Set the starting color in the gradient by clicking the leftmost color stop icon, whose top fills with black when it is active. Then mix a color in the Color palette or click a swatch in the Swatches palette. Illustrator applies the current gradient to the fill in the toolbox and in the Color palette, and also displays the color at the starting edge of a linear gradient or in the center of a radial gradient.

3. Set the ending color in the gradient by clicking the rightmost color stop icon. Then mix a color in the Color palette or click a swatch in the Swatches palette. Illustrator applies the current gradient to the fill in the toolbox and in the Color palette, and also displays the color at the ending edge of a linear gradient or in the outer edge of a radial gradient.

4. Adjust the look of the gradient by selecting options or sliding icons along the gradient slider. As you work, Illustrator applies the current gradient to the fill in the toolbox and in the Color palette.

5. Add the new swatch by clicking the New Swatch button at the bottom of the Swatches palette, dragging the gradient from the fill box in the toolbox or the Color palette, or dragging the gradient fill box from the Gradient palette.

6. To name the swatch, double-click it in the Swatches palette. Illustrator opens the Swatch Options dialog box. In the Swatch Name text box, type a descriptive, unique name; then click OK.

When you save a gradient to the Swatches palette, it applies only to the current document. So, consider adding all custom swatches—color, pattern, and gradient—to a custom library of swatches. For more information on creating a swatches library, refer to "Creating a Swatch Library" in Chapter 7.

Note
After you install Illustrator, you should browse through the contents of the installation CD-ROM as well as the Illustrator folders and subfolders on your computer. For example, many programs provide extra files and features with which you can enhance your artwork. You can be sure that you'll find a variety of files, including extra gradients and samples.

Adding Colors to a Gradient

You can add colors to a gradient by using one of two methods:

■ Drag a color from the fill box in the Color palette or from the Swatches palette to the gradient slider at the bottom of the Gradient palette.

■ Click below the gradient slider on the Gradient palette to add a color stop icon representing a color that is halfway between the two closest colors in the current version of the gradient (see Figure 9-2).

Tip
When you print objects with gradients on certain printers—particularly older ones—you might be surprised by the slowdown in processing speed. To improve printing, choose File | Document Setup (CTRL-ALT-P/⌘-OPTION-P) and select Printing & Export in the Document Setup dialog box. Clear the Compatible Gradient & Gradient Mesh Printing check box and click OK. If you see an improvement in printing speed, leave the check box cleared.

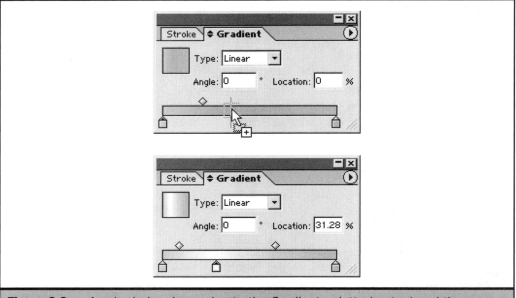

Figure 9-2.   *A color being dragged onto the Gradient palette (on top) and the new color stop icon (on the bottom)*

Adjusting the Look of a Gradient

Once you have added your last color to a gradient, you can modify the gradient by sliding icons back and forth along the gradient slider, dragging icons from one part of the gradient slider to another, dragging icons off the slider and back onto the slider in completely different positions, and typing values in the Gradient palette. For example, selecting and moving a color stop icon varies the location at which the gradient changes to the color represented by the icon. Moving a gradient midpoint changes the halfway point between two colors. Dragging a color icon to another position creates bands of alternate colors. Figure 9-3 shows the results of sliding and adding icons to various locations on the gradient slider and associated samples of linear and radial grayscale gradients and images.

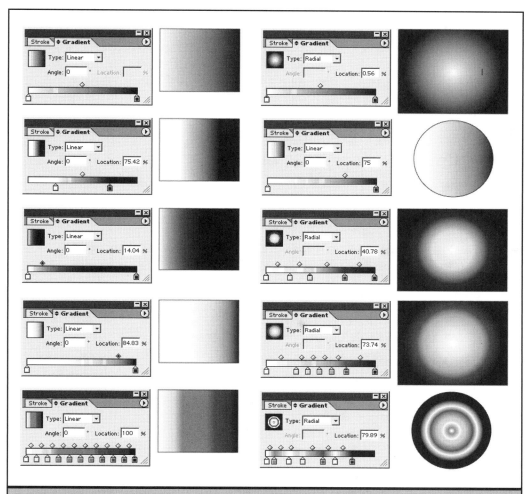

Figure 9-3.   *Several versions of grayscale linear and radial gradients, and changes to the Gradient palette for each version*

Deleting a Color from a Gradient

To delete a color from a gradient, drag its color stop icon off the gradient slider. Illustrator not only removes the icon, it deletes the color from the gradient.

Using the Gradient Tool

The Gradient tool (G) is an editing—not a creation—tool. Once you have created and modified a gradient using the Gradient palette, you can use the Gradient tool to further refine the gradient. You can use the Gradient tool to change the direction at which the gradient is angled, and you can specify the point at which the gradient starts and ends for one or more objects. Double-clicking the Gradient tool opens the Gradient palette, if it isn't already onscreen.

Changing the Look of a Gradient

To use the Gradient tool to change the gradient for one object, follow these steps:

1. Select the object.

2. Activate the Gradient tool (G).

3. To move a radial gradient's highlight or shading to a particular location, click the Gradient tool on that location.

4. To adjust the entire gradient, click the starting point and drag across the object in any direction.

5. To constrain the direction of the drag at 45°, 90°, 135°, 180°, 225°, 270°, or 315° press and hold down SHIFT as you drag.

6. Release the mouse button at the ending point. Illustrator changes the options in the Gradient palette and applies the gradient from one end of the object to the other.

Figure 9-4 shows a two-color (white on both ends and blue in the middle) gradient. At the top of the figure are objects with the original linear and radial gradients. The

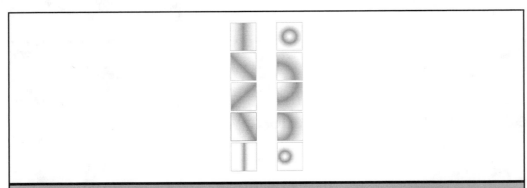

Figure 9-4.   *Examples of using the Gradient tool on single objects*

objects immediately below have a constrained 45° angle with a starting point at the bottom left and the ending point at the top right. If you drag the mouse pointer at the same angle but from a starting point at the top right and the ending point at the bottom left, the changed gradient would be identical.

The following objects start in the upper-right corner and end at the lower-left corner without constraint. The objects just above the bottom objects have starting points in the middle of the left side moving to the upper-right corner. The final objects at the bottom result from dragging the mouse pointer along horizontally for a short distance in the center of the object.

Spreading a Gradient over Several Objects

When you apply the same gradient to several objects, you can use the Gradient tool to extend that gradient over the objects. If you interrupt the gradient with a different gradient, a color, or a pattern, Illustrator ignores your efforts. To extend a gradient from one end of the selected objects to the other end, drag the mouse pointer from a starting point in one object to an ending point in another object. Illustrator applies the gradient to all selected objects; you don't even have to drag the mouse pointer through them all.

To use the Gradient tool to change the gradient over more than one object, follow these steps:

1. Apply one gradient to several objects using the Gradient palette, the Color palette, or the Swatches palette.

2. Select all the objects.

3. Activate the Gradient tool (G).

4. Click the starting point and drag across the objects in any direction.

5. To constrain the direction of the drag at 45°, 90°, 135°, 180°, 225°, 270°, or 315°, press and hold down SHIFT as you drag.

6. Release the mouse button at the ending point. Illustrator changes the options in the Gradient palette and spreads the gradient from one end of the drag to the other.

Figure 9-5 illustrates several examples of applying a gradient to a group of objects. At the top are the original objects, each with the predefined Rainbow gradient applied. The following two groups show the Gradient tool's effect when the mouse pointer is dragged left to right and then right to left. The bottom two groups show the consequence of rearranging the group in two ways and then dragging from left to right (in the next to last group) and dragging from right to left (at the bottom).

ILLUSTRATOR
ESSENTIALS

Figure 9-5. *Examples of applying the gradient to four groups of objects*

Working Around Gradient Limits

As you learned in the introduction of this chapter, Illustrator officially does not enable you to use gradients in strokes or patterns. Because Illustrator is so full of features, you can find a workaround for these limitations, as you will see in this section.

Using a Gradient in a Stroke

You might not be able to apply a gradient to a stroke; however, who says a stroke has to remain a stroke—even if it looks like one? In the "Outlining a Stroke" section in Chapter 7, you learned how to convert a stroke to a filled outline having the same size and appearance as the original. To change a stroke to a filled outline, select the stroke and then choose Object | Path | Outline Stroke. Then you can apply a gradient to the former stroke. Figure 9-6 shows a stroke (on the left) after it becomes a filled

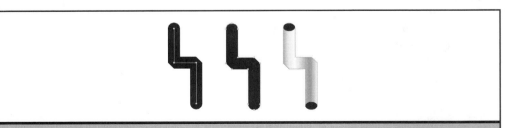

Figure 9-6. *A stroke converted to a filled outline to a stylized copper pipe*

outline (in the center) and a stylized copper pipe with the Copper gradient applied (on the right).

Using a Gradient in a Pattern

Using a gradient as the fill of a pattern is a little more difficult than converting a stroke to a fill: You'll have to take a few more steps:

1. Create an object and fill it with a gradient.

2. Select the object and choose Object | Expand.

3. In the Expand dialog box (see Figure 9-7), check the Fill check box and type **255** in the Specify Objects text box.

4. Click OK. Illustrator expands the object.

5. Open the Pathfinder palette by choosing Window | Pathfinder (SHIFT-F9), unless the palette is already open.

6. With the object selected, click the Merge button (the third button from the left in the bottom row). Illustrator trims the object to its former shape.

7. Open the Swatches palette by choosing Window | Swatches, unless the palette is already open.

8. Drag the object, which still looks like a gradient, to the Swatches palette. If you move your mouse pointer over the new swatch, you'll see it is now a pattern.

Figure 9-8 shows the progress of converting a gradient to a pattern swatch; from a gradient-fill object at the top, to the expanded and trimmed object; and the edited pattern with the gradient as the fill and new vertical and horizontal dashed strokes.

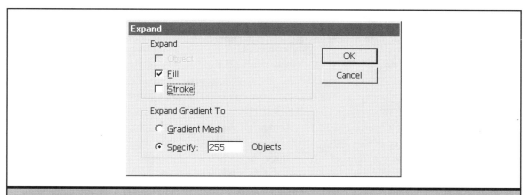

Figure 9-7. *The Expand dialog box with the Fill check box checked*

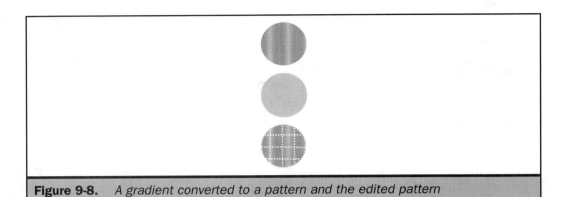

Figure 9-8. *A gradient converted to a pattern and the edited pattern*

Using Mesh Objects

A *mesh object* is a special filled path that contains one or more colors that act like spray-painted gradients with the object's original fill as a background. You can create and edit mesh objects that look as if they are highlighted, shaded, or both, so they appear to be three-dimensional.

You can convert paths and bitmap images into mesh objects. However, you cannot convert compound paths, type (unless you have changed them to outlines), or linked EPS files. To learn about compound paths, refer to "Using Compound Paths" in Chapter 16. Type is covered in both Chapters 11 and 12. You'll find out about EPS in Chapter 22.

An object to be converted to a mesh object should have a color fill. If you want to apply highlights, you should start with a medium- to dark-color fill; if you would prefer to apply shading, the fill should be a lighter color. Illustrator ignores gradient fills (unless you use the Expand command to convert them) and pattern fills and just converts them to a solid black. If the fill is set to None, Illustrator sets the mesh over the blank background.

Illustrator provides three methods of converting a filled path to a mesh object: the Mesh tool (U), the Create Gradient Mesh command dialog box, and the Expand command and dialog box. When you use the Mesh tool, you start out with a plain mesh object with a starting highlight of your choice. If you use the Create Gradient Mesh dialog box, the mesh object you create usually is further along in its development; however, it either has a highlight or no highlight; shading is not a possibility in the starting mesh object. When you convert a gradient-filled path to a mesh object with the Expand dialog box, the mesh object is similar to one created with the Mesh tool.

When Illustrator converts the path to a mesh object, it adds certain components to the mesh object:

- *Mesh lines*, which look like paths, are horizontal and vertical lines with which you can change the shape of the object.

- At the intersection of each mesh line is a *mesh point*, which is a special kind of anchor point to which you can apply color. You can edit, drag, and delete mesh points just as you do anchor points. Mesh points are marked by a diamond shape, and anchor points are small squares.

- ■ The section inside four mesh points is known as a *mesh patch*. You can apply color to mesh patches in the same way you paint a mesh point.

Note that Illustrator also incorporates anchor points into mesh objects. Most of these anchor points start in the object before it is converted. However, additional anchor points can be present. As with any other object, you can add and delete anchor points and drag them to reshape the mesh object.

Creating a Mesh Object Manually

Use the Mesh tool (U) to change a filled path—preferably a simple one—to a mesh object manually. The mesh object you create has a highlight or shading—depending on the highlight or shading color you select—and minimal grid of mesh lines and mesh points starting from the place on which you click the Mesh tool. To create and convert an object to a mesh object with the Mesh tool, follow these steps:

1. Create a path with a dark- or light-colored fill. If you want to apply a highlight, the fill color should be medium to dark colored. If you prefer to apply shading, select a lighter-colored fill.

2. Deselect the path.

3. Change to a fill color that Illustrator will use as a highlight or shade—depending on the lightness or darkness of the original color and whether you want to highlight or shade the object.

4. Select the path.

5. Select the Mesh tool (U). Illustrator changes the mouse pointer to one of the following:

6. Click the mouse pointer with the mesh tail (on the left above) within the path. (If the mouse pointer has the "no" sign (on the right above), it is not pointing to a path or inside the path.) Illustrator removes the path's stroke and converts the path to a mesh object, adds mesh lines and mesh points, and sprays a contrasting highlight or shading at the location of the click.

Figure 9-9 contains three mesh objects, all highlighted, as they are created with the Mesh tool. The left column shows the selected objects; the right column illustrates the unselected objects. In each case, the highlight surrounds the area on which the Mesh tool was clicked. In the left column, note the central location of the mesh point, which indicates the exact point of the click.

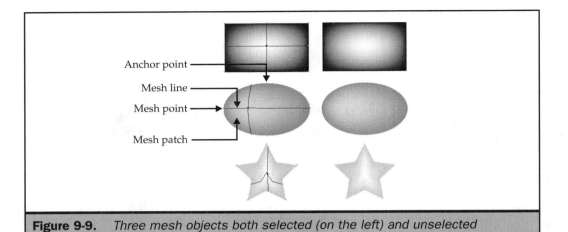

Anchor point

Mesh line

Mesh point

Mesh patch

Figure 9-9.   *Three mesh objects both selected (on the left) and unselected (on the right)*

Creating a Mesh Object Automatically

When you create a mesh object using the Create Gradient Mesh dialog box, you can select or enter options that set up the characteristics of the mesh object automatically. This method is best for converting complex objects. The resulting object has regularly spaced mesh lines and mesh points and a highlight. Shading is not an option. However, you can apply shading later, if you want. To create and convert an object to a mesh object with the Create Gradient Mesh dialog box, follow these steps:

1. Create a path with a color fill.
2. Make sure the path is selected.
3. Choose Object | Create Gradient Mesh. Illustrator opens the Create Gradient Mesh dialog box (see Figure 9-10).
4. In the Rows text box, type the number of rows of mesh lines.
5. In the Columns text box, type the number of columns of mesh lines.
6. From the Appearance drop-down menu, select the course of the highlight. The Flat option (the default) uses the fill color with no highlight, To Center applies the highlight in the center of the object, and To Edge employs the highlight at the edges.
7. In the Highlight text box, type the percentage of white in the highlight. Valid values range from 0% (no white) to 100% (all white). The default is 100%; that is, a highlight.
8. Click OK. Illustrator removes the path's stroke and converts the path to a mesh object with the specified number of horizontal and vertical mesh lines, and an optional highlight.

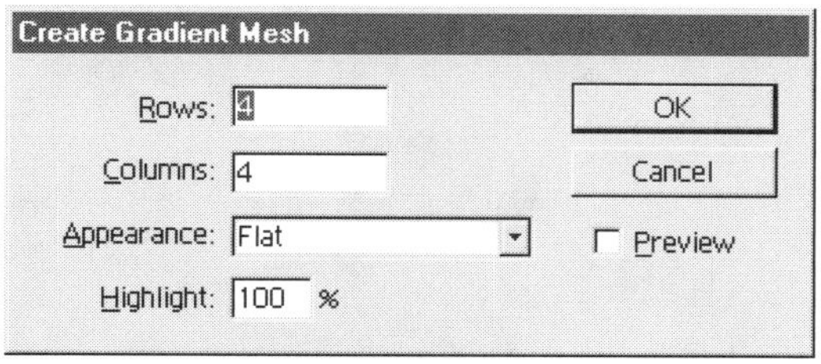

Create Gradient Mesh

Rows: 4

Columns: 4

Appearance: Flat

Highlight: 100 %

OK

Cancel

☐ Preview

Figure 9-10.   *The Create Gradient Mesh dialog box with its default options*

Figure 9-11 shows four examples of polygon mesh objects, both selected and unselected, and all highlighted. The top object has four rows and four columns of mesh lines and a Flat appearance. The following object has six rows and four columns of mesh lines and a To Center highlight at 100%. Under that is an object with four rows and six columns of mesh lines and a To Edge highlight of 100%. The bottom object has eight rows and ten columns of mesh lines and a To Edge highlight of 75%.

Converting a Gradient-Filled Object to a Mesh Object

In the section "Using a Gradient in a Pattern," you learned how to convert a gradient-filled object to a pattern using the Expand command. You also can use the Expand command

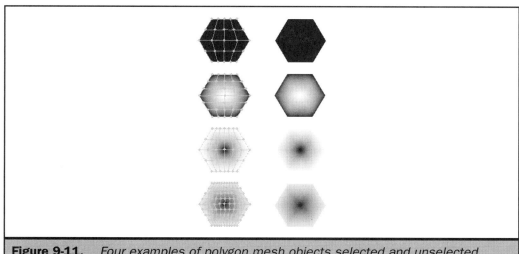

Figure 9-11.   *Four examples of polygon mesh objects selected and unselected*

Figure 9-12.   *On the top, an object filled with the Rainbow gradient from the Swatches palette; on the bottom, the resulting mesh object with its grid of mesh lines and mesh points*

to convert a gradient-filled object to a mesh object still containing the gradient. To do so, follow these steps:

1. Create an object and fill it with a gradient.

2. Select the object and choose Object | Expand.

3. In the Expand dialog box (see Figure 9-7), check the Fill box and click the Gradient Mesh radio button.

4. Click OK. Illustrator expands the object into a mesh object (see Figure 9-12) with a gridwork of mesh lines and mesh points at the intersections of the lines.

Modifying a Mesh Object

Once you have created a mesh object, you can edit it in much the same way you edit paths—sometimes using different methods and tools, including the Direct Selection tool (A), the Mesh tool (U), The Add Anchor Point tool (+), and the Delete Anchor Point tool (-). You can add, modify the direction of, and delete mesh lines, mesh points, and anchor points, thereby changing the shape of the object. In addition, you can apply highlight or shading colors to both mesh lines and mesh points.

Adding Mesh Points and Mesh Lines

When you add mesh points and mesh lines to a mesh object, the mesh object can be either selected or unselected. The angle of the new mesh lines depends on the shape of the object. To add several mesh points and two mesh lines to a mesh object, activate the Mesh tool (U) and click anywhere within the mesh object.

■ If you click a mesh patch (that is, away from a mesh line), Illustrator inserts a mesh point at the click location and two mesh lines that intersect at the new mesh point, adds mesh points wherever the mesh line intersects another mesh line, and attaches direction lines and direction points to the new mesh point. Illustrator also applies the current fill color to the new mesh point.

- If you click a mesh line, Illustrator inserts a new mesh point and one mesh line at the click, adds mesh points wherever the mesh line intersects another mesh line, and attaches direction lines and direction points to the new mesh point. Illustrator also applies the current fill color to the new mesh point.

- If you press and hold down SHIFT while clicking a mesh patch or mesh line, Illustrator adds the new mesh points and mesh lines as described in the prior two bullets but does not apply the current fill color.

Figure 9-13 shows the differences between objects (on the left) you created in "Creating a Mesh Object Manually," earlier in this chapter, and the same objects (on the right) with many mesh lines and mesh points inserted. Notice the differences in the highlighting from the left side and the right side.

Moving and Reshaping Mesh Points and Mesh Lines

To move and reshape mesh lines, use the Direct Selection tool (A) or the Mesh tool (U) to select and drag mesh points just as you would anchor points. If you want to limit a mesh line to its original dimension and size so it does not bend to adjust to the drag, press and hold down SHIFT as you drag. If you need to make a fine adjustment, set the level of zoom to 200% or greater, depending on the size of the mesh object you are editing. When you click a mesh point with the Direct Selection tool or the Mesh tool, Illustrator reveals direction lines and direction points. To straighten a mesh line, drag one of the direction points so that it is in the same plane as the line.

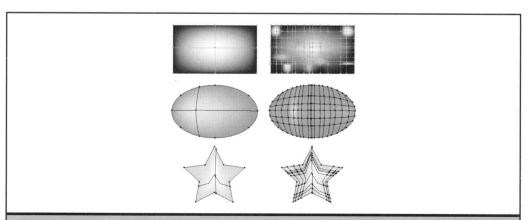

Figure 9-13. *Newly created objects (on the left) and the objects with extra mesh lines and mesh points (on the right)*

Deleting Mesh Lines and Mesh Points

To delete a mesh point and the mesh lines that are associated with it, activate the Mesh tool (U) and click the mesh point while pressing and holding down ALT/OPTION.

Adding Color to a Mesh Object

You can add color to a mesh object in the same way you would apply color to other objects. To paint part of a mesh object with color, use one of the following methods:

■ Select a mesh patch or mesh point using the Direct Selection tool (A). Mix the color in the Color palette and drag the palette's fill box to the selected area.

■ Select a mesh patch or mesh point using the Direct Selection tool (A). Click a swatch in the Swatches palette or drag it to the selected area.

■ Drag a color to the object—selected or unselected—from the fill.

■ Select a mesh patch or mesh point using the Direct Selection tool (A). Activate the Paint Bucket (K), which is on the Eyedropper (I) toolslot. Move the mouse pointer to the selected point or patch, and click.

If you have selected a mesh patch, you can adjust its size by dragging the mesh points that form its borders.

Exercising Your Gradient Mesh Skills

The only way to learn new skills is to combine practice with experimentation. Here we create a computer mouse using a rounded rectangle, a circle, and a bunch of Illustrator tools. To construct the mouse, follow these steps:

1. Draw a rounded rectangle and fill it with light gray.
2. Draw a circle with the same fill.
3. Drag the circle over the bottom part of the rectangle.
4. Choose Window | Pathfinder (SHIFT-F9) to open the Pathfinder palette.
5. Select both paths, and click the Merge button.
6. Deselect the merged path and change the fill to white.
7. Activate the Mesh tool (U) and click the lower part of the path. Illustrator converts the path to a mesh object.
8. Add horizontal and vertical lines to the mesh object.

9. With the Direct Selection tool (A), select the upper-left mesh point and apply a darker gray. Continue painting each mesh point on the left side around the bottom corner to the first mesh point on the bottom of the object.

10. With the Direct Selection tool, apply white to all the mesh points on the right side and around the corner to the first mesh point on the bottom.

11. With the Direct Selection tool, select two anchor points in the middle of the left edge and slightly narrow the mesh object. Repeat for the right side.

12. With the Pencil, draw a slightly curved horizontal line across the mouse and a vertical line from the top of the mouse to the horizontal line.

13. With the Selection tool, select the entire mouse.

14. Choose Filter | Stylize | Drop Shadow.

15. Click OK to apply the default values from the Drop Shadow dialog box to the object.

16. With the Pencil, draw a light gray mouse tail (a six-point stroke) at the top of the mouse.

17. Select the mouse tail, and repeat steps 14 and 15.

Figure 9-14 illustrates the steps starting with drawing the objects on which the mouse is based (at the top left), moving clockwise to the finished mouse (near the bottom left).

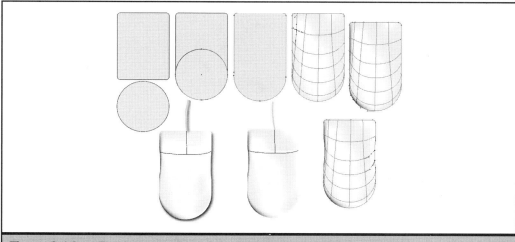

Figure 9-14.   *The construction of a mouse from beginning to end*

The Complete Reference

Chapter 10

Transforming Objects

As you have learned in prior chapters, when you transform an object, you move, rotate, reflect (flip), scale, or shear (skew) it. Transforming an object does not change the object's general appearance. For example, when you move an object, you just place it in another location in the illustration window. The object looks exactly the same in any place onscreen. When you rotate or reflect an object, you turn it on an axis or flip it from one side of an axis to another—but it looks just about the same as it did originally.

Scaling an object makes the object larger or smaller—if the object is in proportion to its original version, it looks the same; if it's out of proportion, it's distorted to the extent that its dimensions are not uniform with the original. Shearing an object slants it to one side or another, but you can still tell it's a version of the original.

In Illustrator, transforming objects is so important that you can transform objects using a collection of toolbox tools, a set of commands on the Object menu, and a palette. Table 10-1 summarizes the support for each transformation function. In the leftmost column is the name of the tool or feature. Along the top row are the types of transformation. If a tool or feature supports a particular transformation, you'll see a Yes in the row for that tool or feature. Otherwise, you'll see a No, which indicates no support from that tool or feature.

Tool/Feature	Move?	Rotate?	Reflect?	Scale?	Shear?
Transform palette	Yes	Yes	Yes	Yes	Yes
Free Transform tool	Yes	Yes	Yes	Yes	Yes
Transform Each dialog box	Yes	Yes	Yes	Yes	No
Move dialog box	Yes	No	No	No	No
Reflect tool	No	No	Yes	No	No
Reflect dialog box	No	No	Yes	No	No
Rotate tool	No	Yes	No	No	No
Rotate dialog box	No	Yes	No	No	No
Selection tool	Yes	Yes	Yes	Yes	No
Scale tool	No	No	No	Yes	No
Scale dialog box	No	No	No	Yes	No
Shear tool	No	No	No	No	Yes
Shear dialog box	No	No	No	No	Yes

Table 10-1. *Summary of Illustrator Transformation Tools and Features*

Exploring the Transform Palette

In the note at the bottom of the "Exploring the Info Palette" section in Chapter 5, you learned that the main purpose of the Transform palette (see Figure 10-1) is to move, rotate, reflect, scale, and shear objects (and sometimes patterns) from within one location. You also can use the Transform palette to show measurements of a selected object. To toggle between showing and hiding the palette, choose Window | Transform (SHIFT-F8).

The Transform palette contains seven options, which you can use to transform a selection:

■ Click one of the small squares in the reference point box to indicate the location of the origin point of the selected object from which the object is measured. The squares represent parts of the object. For example, the square in the center of the reference point box indicates the center of the object; the squares on the outer corners represent the location of the corners of a rectangle or a bounding box surrounding a nonrectangular object. The squares between the corners indicate the midpoints between the corners.

■ The number in the X text box shows the current location of the x-axis (horizontal plane) of the object or bounding box surrounding the object, in points, from the left side to the right. With the upper-left square of the reference point box selected, a value of 0 indicates that the left side of a rectangular object or bounding box around the object is aligned with the left side of the artboard. Valid values range from –16,384 points to 16,384 points.

■ The number in the Y text box shows the current location of the y-axis (vertical plane) of the object or bounding box surrounding the object, in points, from the bottom edge to the top. With the upper-left square of the reference point box selected, a value of 0 indicates that the bottom edge of a rectangular object or bounding box around the object is aligned with the bottom edge of the artboard. Valid values range from –16,384 points to 16,384 points.

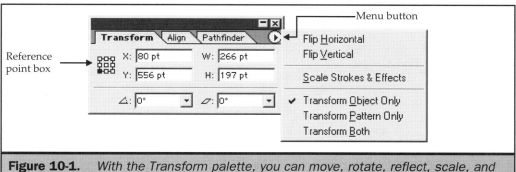

Figure 10-1. *With the Transform palette, you can move, rotate, reflect, scale, and shear objects*

- The number in the W text box shows the current width of a rectangular object or bounding box enclosing the object, in points. Before you start transforming an object, the value in the W text box is the same as those in the Info palette. Valid values range from 0 points to 16,384 points.

- The number in the H text box shows the current height of a rectangular object or bounding box enclosing the object, in points. Before you start transforming an object, the value in the H text box is identical to those in the Info palette. Valid values range from 0 points to 16,384 points.

- The Rotate drop-down menu/text box enables you to rotate the selected object by choosing or typing the number of degrees of rotation. Valid values range from –180 points to 180 degrees.

- The Shear drop-down menu/text box enables you to shear the selected object by choosing or typing the number of degrees of slant. Valid values range from –60 points to 60 degrees.

To open the palette's menu, click the menu button.

- The Flip Horizontal command flips the selected object from one side to another along the horizontal plane toward the left side of the illustration window.

- The Flip Vertical command flips the selected object from the bottom to the top along the vertical plane toward the top edge of the illustration window.

- The Scale Strokes & Effects command scales the stroke of the selected object as well as the fill. If this command is not active (with a check mark preceding the command), Illustrator scales the fill but leaves the stroke its original width.

- The Transform Object Only command transforms the selected object but not its patterned fill—if the fill is a pattern, of course.

- The Transform Pattern Only command transforms the patterned fill of the selected object but not the object itself.

- The Transform Both command transforms both the object and its patterned fill.

As you continue browsing through this chapter, you'll learn how to use each of the options in the Transform palette.

Moving Objects

In earlier chapters, you found out how to move an object a relatively long distance from one place in the illustration window to another: You select the object and then drag it by using the mouse. You also learned how to move an object a very short distance: Select the object and then repeatedly press a combination of the four arrow keys to move the object up, down, left, or right. In this section you will learn how to move an object using the Selection tool, the Transform palette, the Move dialog box, or the Transform Each dialog box. Note that however you move an object, Illustrator displays a message when you attempt to move the object off the illustration window.

Moving with the Transform Palette

To move an object using the Transform palette (refer to Figure 10-1), follow these steps:

1. Open the Transform palette by choosing Window | Transform (SHIFT-F8).

2. Select the object to be moved.

3. To move the object horizontally, type a number in the X text box and press ENTER/RETURN. A positive number moves the object to the right in the illustration window; a negative number moves the object to the left.

4. To move the object vertically, type a number in the Y text box and and press ENTER/RETURN. A positive number moves the object up the illustration window; a negative number moves the object down.

Figure 10-2 shows a series of moves. The accompanying Transform palette shows the changes to the X and Y text boxes.

Moving with the Move Dialog Box

The Move dialog box (see Figure 10-3) enables you to accurately move one or more selected objects horizontally, vertically, or both. You can move any object except for type currently being edited with a Type tool. To open the Move dialog box, select an object and then either choose Object | Transform | Move (CTRL-SHIFT-M/⌘-SHIFT-M) or double-click the Selection tool.

When you open the Move dialog box, the text boxes contain the values by which you moved any object using a selection tool, the Transform palette, the Move dialog box, or the Transform Each dialog box. To move the selected object, use the following options from the dialog box:

1. In the Horizontal text box, type the value, in points, by which you want the object to move horizontally. A positive number moves the object toward the right side of the illustration window; a negative number moves the object to the left. Illustrator changes the values in the Distance and Angle text boxes.

2. In the Vertical text box, type the value, in points, by which you want the object to move vertically. A positive number moves the object toward the top of the illustration window; a negative number moves the object down. Illustrator changes the values in the Distance and Angle text boxes.

3. In the Distance text box, type the distance of the move from the current settings.

4. In the Angle text box, type the number of degrees the object will move both horizontally and vertically. Illustrator calculates the angle from the horizontal axis. Type a positive value to move the object in a counterclockwise direction; type a negative value to move the object in a clockwise direction.

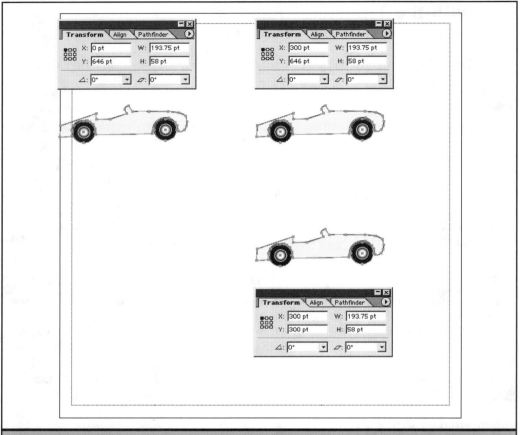

Figure 10-2.   *An object moving around the artboard, thanks to changed values in the X and Y text boxes in the Transform palette*

5. Click Copy to make a copy of the moved object in the new location. Illustrator copies and moves the object, closes the dialog box, and keeps the original object at the pre-move location.

6. Check the Preview box to see a preview of the moves you have entered in the text boxes before they become final.

7. Check the Objects box to move objects; check the Patterns box to move patterned fills. If you check both check boxes, Illustrator moves both objects and patterns. If the selected object does not have a patterned fill, both check boxes are not available.

8. Click OK to have Illustrator apply the options and close the dialog box.

Note   *To repeat the most recent transformation, regardless of how you did it, choose Object | Transform | Transform Again (CTRL-D/⌘-D).*

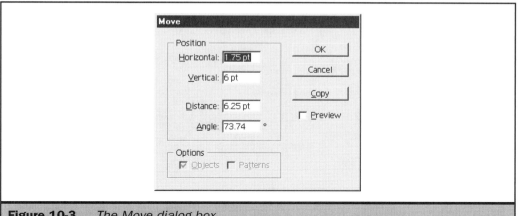

Figure 10-3. *The Move dialog box*

Learning About the Transform Each Dialog Box

The Transform Each dialog box (see Figure 10-4) is another all-purpose transformation feature of Illustrator. With this dialog box, you can scale, move, rotate, and reflect selected objects. To open the Transform Each dialog box, select an object and then choose Object | Transform | Transform Each (CTRL-SHIFT-ALT-D/⌘-SHIFT-OPTION-D). The options in the dialog box are as follows:

- In the Scale section, slide the Horizontal slider or type a value in the text box to scale the selected object horizontally, either lower or higher than its current size. Valid values range from 0 to 200%. The default value is 100%, or no scaling.

- In the Scale section, slide the Vertical slider or type a value in the text box to scale the selected object vertically, either lower or higher than its current size. Valid values range from 0 to 200%. The default value is 100%, or no scaling.

- In the Move section, slide the Horizontal slider or type a value in the text box to move the selected object to the left or right in the illustration window. Valid values range from –4,000 to 4,000 points, although the slider shows just –100 to 100 points. The default value is 100 points, or no horizontal move.

- In the Move section, slide the Vertical slider or type a value in the text box to move the selected object up or down in the illustration window. Valid values range from –100 to 100 points. The default value is 100 points, or no vertical move.

- In the Rotate section, either type the degree of rotation in the Angle text box or drag the line around the circle. Valid values range from 0 (the default) to 360 degrees.

- To copy the selected object, click the Copy button. Illustrator copies the selected object at its new location, closes the dialog box, and keeps the original object in its pre-transformation condition and location.

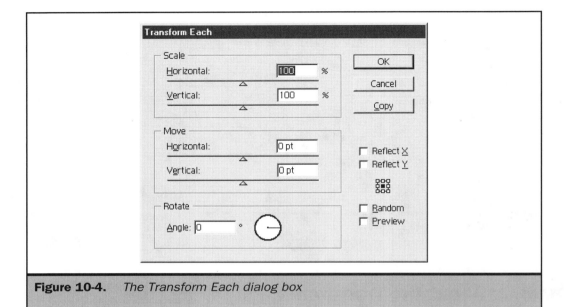

Figure 10-4. *The Transform Each dialog box*

■ Check the Reflect X box to flip the selected object from one side to another along the horizontal plane toward the left side of the illustration window.

■ Check the Reflect Y box to flip the selected object from the bottom to the top along the vertical plane toward the top edge of the illustration window.

■ Click one of the small squares in the reference point box to indicate the location of the origin point of the selected object from which the object is transformed. The squares represent parts of the object—just as they do in the Transform palette.

■ Check the Random box to transform the selected object randomly using the changed options in the dialog box as a guide.

■ Check the Preview box to see a preview of the transformations you have selected in the dialog box before they become final.

Moving with the Transform Each Dialog Box

Just like the Move dialog box, the Transform Each dialog box enables you to move an object accurately. To move an object using the Transform Each dialog box, follow these steps:

1. Select the object to be moved.

2. Choose Object | Transform | Transform Each (CTRL-SHIFT-ALT-D/ ⌘-SHIFT-OPTION-D). Illustrator opens the Transform Each dialog box.

3. To move the object to the left or right in the illustration window, slide the Horizontal slider or type a value in the text box in the Move section.

4. To move the object up or down in the illustration window, slide the Vertical slider or type a value in the text box in the Move section.

5. To make a copy of the object, click Copy. Illustrator closes the dialog box, copies the object, places it in its new location, and keeps the original in its initial location.

6. To get a preview of your actions on the object, check the Preview check box. Illustrator doesn't show the results until you click in another area of the dialog box.

7. Click OK. Illustrator closes the dialog box and moves the object.

Scaling Objects

When you scale an object, you resize it either in proportion or out of proportion to its original dimensions along the horizontal plane (the x-axis) or the vertical plane (the y-axis). If you scale proportionally, the dimensions of both the x-axis and the y-axis change and those dimensions are in the same relationship as those of the original object. If you scale disproportionally, Illustrator modifies the dimension of the axes disproportionally or changes one axis only. You can scale an object using the Selection tool, Scale tool, Transform palette, Scale dialog box, Transform Each dialog box, or Free Transform tool.

Scaling with the Selection Tool

You can scale an object using the Selection tool (V) by following these steps:

1. Activate the Selection tool. Illustrator surrounds the object with a bounding box.

2. Move the mouse pointer to one of the handles on the bounding box.

3. Drag the handle until the object is the desired size.

4. To constrain the object to its original proportions, start dragging a handle, and press and hold down SHIFT.

5. To scale from the middle of the object, start dragging a handle, and press and hold down ALT/ OPTION.

Scaling with the Transform Palette

You can scale an object proportionally or disproportionally using the Transform palette (refer to Figure 10-1); this is a good way to scale using exact measurements. If you want to keep an object proportional, change both the width and height identically. For example, you can multiply both the height and width by 2, or divide both dimensions by 1.5.

As you know, the W and H text boxes in the palette contain the current width and height of the selected object. To scale a selected object horizontally (in other words, change an object's width), overtype the value in the W text box and press ENTER/RETURN. When you do so, Illustrator changes the location of the right side of the object. To scale the selected object's height, overtype the value in the H text box and press ENTER/RETURN. Then, Illustrator moves the bottom of the object.

Scaling with the Scale Tool

The Scale tool (S) is dedicated to scaling of all types, depending on how you use the tool. To use the Scale tool on an object, select the object with a selection tool, and then click the Scale tool. Then do one of the following:

- To scale the selected object horizontally from both sides of the center point of the object, drag to the left or right of the object.

- To scale the selected object vertically from both top and bottom of the center point of the object, drag toward the top or bottom of the object.

- To set a new center point, click within the object, and then drag to scale the object from the center point.

- To scale the object in large increments, drag from a location close to the center point.

- To scale the object in fine increments, drag from a location away from the center point.

- To scale the selected object proportionally, drag diagonally while pressing and holding down SHIFT.

- To scale the selected object from the current horizontal plane while constraining movement of the current vertical plane, drag horizontally while pressing and holding down SHIFT.

- To scale the selected object from the current vertical plane while constraining movement of the current horizontal plane, drag vertically while pressing and holding down SHIFT.

- To scale a copy of the object, drag while pressing and holding down ALT. The original object stays at its initial size and in its original location.

Figure 10-5 shows an illustration scaled proportionally and disproportionally using the Scale tool. At the top of the figure is the original automobile. The group of three at the right is disproportionate to the original. The bottom two automobiles are proportional.

Scaling with the Scale Dialog Box

The Scale dialog box (see Figure 10-6) enables you to scale one selected object, pattern, or both, uniformly or ununiformly using exact percentages. To open the Scale dialog box, select an object and then choose Object | Transform | Scale or double-click the Scale tool.

When you open the Scale dialog box, the text boxes contain the values by which you scaled the previously scaled object using the Scale tool, the Free Transform tool, the Transform palette, the Scale dialog box, or the Transform Each dialog box. To scale the selected object, use the following options from the dialog box:

- Click the Uniform radio button to scale the selected object proportionally by a percentage that you type in the Scale text box. So, when Illustrator scales the figure, both the x- and y-axes are changed uniformly. Valid values range from −20,000% to 20,000%.

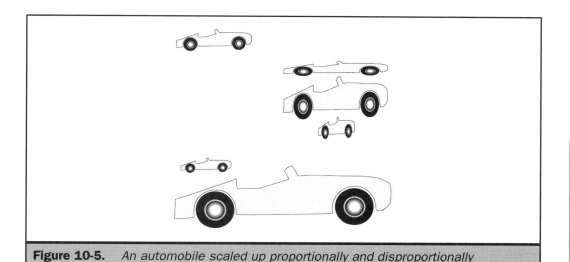

Figure 10-5.   *An automobile scaled up proportionally and disproportionally*

- Click the Non-Uniform radio button to scale the selected object disproportionally. Type the percentage by which you want to scale the x-axis in the Horizontal text box and the percentage by which you want to scale the y-axis in the Vertical text box. Valid values for both text boxes range from –20,000% to 20,000%.

- Check the Scale Strokes & Effects box to scale the stroke of the selected object as well as the fill. If the check box is cleared, Illustrator scales the fill but leaves the stroke its original size.

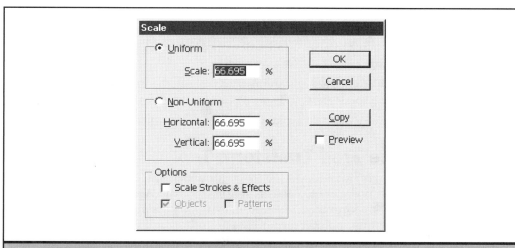

Figure 10-6.   *The Scale dialog box*

- If you have checked the Scale Strokes & Effects box and the selected object has a patterned fill, you can check the Objects check box to scale the selected object, or check the Patterns box to scale the patterned fill. If you check both boxes, Illustrator scales both objects and patterns at once. If the selected object does not have a patterned fill, both check boxes are not available.

- Click Copy to make a copy of the scaled object. Illustrator copies and scales the object, closes the dialog box, and keeps the original object at the pre-scale location.

- Check the Preview check box to see a preview of the moves that you have entered in the text boxes before they become final.

- Click OK to have Illustrator apply the options and close the dialog box.

Scaling with the Transform Each Dialog Box

To scale an object using the Transform Each dialog box (refer to Figure 10-4), follow these steps:

1. Select the object to be scaled.

2. Choose Object | Transform | Transform Each (CTRL-SHIFT-ALT-D/ ⌘-SHIFT-OPTION-D). Illustrator opens the Transform Each dialog box.

3. Select an origin point by clicking one of the small squares in the reference point box.

4. In the Scale section, slide the Horizontal slider or type a value in the text box to scale the selected object horizontally, from 0 to 200%. (Note that you can type values up to 4,000.)

5. In the Scale section, slide the Vertical slider or type a value in the text box to scale the selected object vertically, from 0 to 200%. (Note that you can type values up to 4,000.)

6. To make a copy of the object, click Copy. Illustrator closes the dialog box, copies the object and places it in its new location, and keeps the original in its initial location.

7. To get a preview of your actions on the object, check the Preview check box. Illustrator doesn't show the results until you click another area of the dialog box.

8. Click OK. Illustrator closes the dialog box and scales the object.

Learning About the Free Transform Tool

The Free Transform tool (E) is an all-in-one tool with which you can move, rotate, scale, reflect, and shear one or more selected objects simultaneously. When you select an object and activate the Free Transform tool, Illustrator surrounds the object with a bounding box. As you move the mouse pointer around the bounding box, it takes on a number of shapes, depending on the transformation Illustrator thinks you are about to do.

Curved double-pointed mouse pointers indicate that you can rotate the selected object. Straight double-pointed mouse pointers represent scaling, reflecting, and shearing. You can use a solid arrow to move an object.

You can modify a selected object by dragging one of the handles surrounding the selected object. When you use shortcut keys with the Free Transform tool, you can achieve quite a bit—as you will find out as you read through the rest of the chapter.

The Free Transform tool is a relative newcomer to Illustrator. In earlier versions of the program, the actions of the Free Transform tool were accomplished by using the Free Distort filter, which is no longer part of Illustrator.

Scaling with the Free Transform Tool

To scale one or more selected objects using the Free Transform tool (see Figure 10-7), activate the Free Transform tool. Then drag a handle to increase or decrease the size of the object in proportion or not. To force the object to remain in proportion, drag and then press and hold down SHIFT. To scale from the center of the object, drag and then press and hold down ALT/OPTION. If you don't start dragging first, Illustrator removes the bounding box.

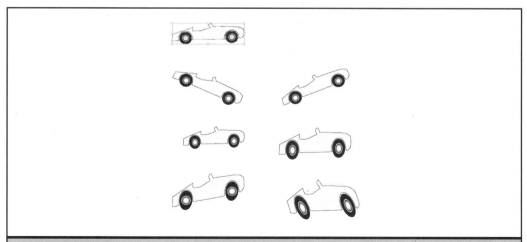

Figure 10-7.   *An object enclosed within the Free-Transform bounding box and copies that are modified using the Free Transform tool*

Rotating Objects

When you rotate an object, you turn it around the object's default center point or a center point that you specify. You can rotate an object using the Transform palette, the Rotate tool, the Rotate dialog box, the Free Transform tool, and the Transform Each dialog box.

Rotating with the Transform Palette

You can rotate an object using the Transform palette (refer to Figure 10-1). Then you can rotate the object to a specific number of degrees. To rotate an object using the Transform palette, select the object and then either type a value or select a value from the Rotate text box/drop-down menu. If you select from the menu, degrees are incremented by 15 or 30 degrees, ranging from –180 to 180. If you type a number of degrees above or below the range on the menu, and Illustrator doesn't like your choice, it might ignore you.

Rotating with the Rotate Tool

The Rotate tool (R) is the specialist in rotating objects. To use the Rotate tool on an object, select the object using the Selection tool (V) and then activate the Rotate tool. Then do one of the following:

- Drag the object around its center point.

- Click the object to set a new location for the center point. Then drag in a circular motion to rotate the object around the new center point.

- When you drag while pressing and holding down SHIFT, you can force the rotation to stick at 45°, 90°, 135°, 180°, 225°, 270°, 315°, and 360°. To continue rotating beyond one of these points, release SHIFT, and then press and hold it down again.

- To rotate the object in large increments, drag from a location close to the center point.

- To rotate the object in fine increments, drag from a location away from the center point.

- To rotate a copy of the object, drag while pressing and holding down ALT. The original object stays at its initial rotation angle and in its original location.

Figure 10-8 demonstrates the difference between an object rotated around a center point in the object (at the top) and rotated around a center point outside the object (at the bottom).

Rotating with the Rotate Dialog Box

The Rotate dialog box (see Figure 10-9) enables you to rotate one or more selected objects, patterns, or both. To open the Rotate dialog box, select one or more objects and then choose Object | Transform | Rotate or double-click the Rotate tool.

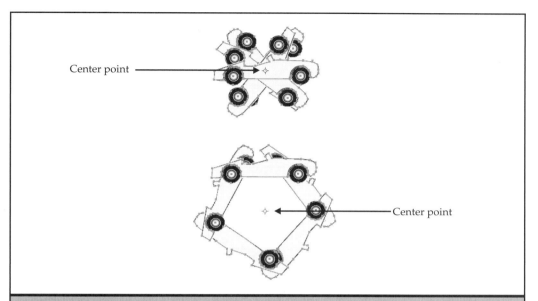

Center point

Center point

Figure 10-8. *Two groups of rotated objects rotated from a center point within the object (at the top of the figure) and from a center point below the object (at the bottom)*

When you open the Rotate dialog box, the text boxes contain the values by which you rotated the previously rotated object using the Rotate tool, the Free Transform tool, the Transform palette, the Rotate dialog box, or the Transform Each dialog box. To rotate the selected object, use the following options from the dialog box:

■ Type the angle by which you want to rotate the object in the Angle text box.

■ If the object has a patterned fill, you can check the Objects check box to rotate the selected object but not its pattern, or check the Patterns check box to rotate the patterned fill but not the object. If you check both boxes, Illustrator rotates both objects and patterns at once.

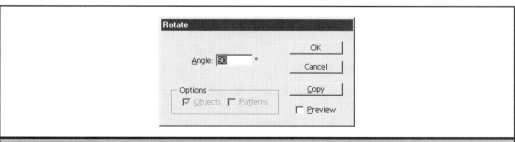

Figure 10-9. *The Rotate dialog box*

- Click Copy to make a copy of the rotated object. Illustrator copies and rotates the object, closes the dialog box, and keeps the original object at the pre-rotation location.

- Check the Preview check box to see a preview of the rotation angle that you have entered in the Angle text box before it becomes final.

- Click OK to have Illustrator apply the options and close the dialog box.

Rotating with the Free Transform Tool

To rotate one or more selected objects using the Free Transform tool, activate the Free Transform tool. Move the mouse pointer around the sides and corners of the bounding box until the mouse pointer becomes a curved, double-pointed arrow. Then drag a handle to rotate the object.

Rotating with the Transform Each Dialog Box

To rotate an object using the Transform Each dialog box (refer to Figure 10-4), follow these steps:

1. Select the object to be rotated.

2. Choose Object | Transform | Transform Each (CTRL-SHIFT-ALT-D/ ⌘-SHIFT-OPTION-D). Illustrator opens the Transform Each dialog box.

3. Select an origin point by clicking one of the small squares in the reference point box.

4. In the Rotate section, either type the degree of rotation in the Angle text box or drag the line around the circle.

5. To make a copy of the object, click Copy. Illustrator closes the dialog box, copies the object, and rotates it, keeping the original in its initial location.

6. To get a preview of your actions on the object, check the Preview check box. Illustrator doesn't show the results until you click another area of the dialog box.

7. Click OK. Illustrator closes the dialog box and rotates the object.

Reflecting Objects

When you reflect an object, you flip it from one side of a vertical axis to the other side, or from the top of a horizontal axis to the other side. You can reflect an object using the Selection tool, Transform palette, Reflect tool, Reflect dialog box, Free Transform tool, and Transform Each dialog box.

Reflecting with the Selection Tool

You can reflect an object using the Selection tool (V). To do so, follow these steps:

1. Activate the Selection tool. Illustrator surrounds the object with a bounding box.

2. Move the mouse pointer to one of the handles on the bounding box.

3. Drag the handle across and beyond the object. Illustrator appears to flip the object from one side to another.

4. To constrain the object to its original proportions, start dragging a handle, and press and hold down SHIFT.

Reflecting with the Transform Palette

You can reflect an object using the Transform palette (refer to Figure 10-1):

- To flip an object along the horizontal plane, select the object and then choose Flip Horizontal from the palette's menu. Every time you choose this command, Illustrator flips the object toward the left edge of the illustration window.

- To flip an object on the vertical plane, select the object and then choose Flip Vertical from the palette's menu. Every time you choose this command, Illustrator flips the object toward the top edge of the illustration window.

 You can change the direction of a horizontal or vertical flip by changing the position of the point marking the axis on which an object is transformed.

Figure 10-10 shows the automobile flipped horizontally (at the top) and vertically (at the bottom).

Reflecting with the Reflect Tool

 The Reflect tool (O), which is on the same toolslot as the Rotate tool, flips objects horizontally, vertically, and at an angle. To use the Reflect tool on an object, select the object using the Selection tool (V), click the Reflect tool, and then do one of the following:

- Click the object. Illustrator adds a center point and flips the object horizontally.

- Click the object again to set a new location for the center point.

- Drag the object around the center point to flip the object and rotate it to a new axis.

- Clicking the center point does not flip the object. In fact, nothing happens.

- To rotate the object in large increments to a new axis before flipping, drag from close to the center point.

- To rotate the object in fine increments to a new axis before flipping, drag from farther from the center point.

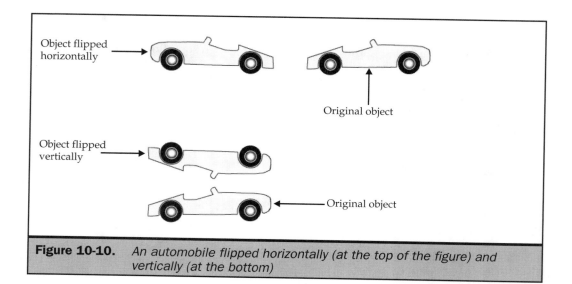

Figure 10-10. *An automobile flipped horizontally (at the top of the figure) and vertically (at the bottom)*

- If you start dragging and then press and hold down SHIFT, Illustrator constrains any new axis to 90°, 180°, 270°, and 360°. To continue rotating beyond one of these points, release SHIFT and then press and hold it down again.

- To flip a copy of the object, drag while pressing and holding down ALT. The original object stays at its initial rotation angle and in its original location.

Reflecting with the Reflect Dialog Box

The Reflect dialog box (see Figure 10-11) enables you to reflect one or more selected objects, pattern, or both. To open the Reflect dialog box, select one or more objects, and then either choose Object | Transform | Reflect or double-click the Reflect tool.

When you open the Reflect dialog box, the text boxes contain the values by which you flipped the previously flipped object using the Reflect tool, the Free Transform tool, the Transform palette, the Reflect dialog box, or the Transform Each dialog box. To flip the selected object, use the following options from the dialog box:

- To flip the object horizontally, click the Horizontal radio button.

- To flip the object vertically, click the Vertical radio button.

- To flip the object at any angle but horizontal or vertical, type the angle to reflect the object in the Angle text box. (Illustrator automatically selects the Angle radio button.)

- If the object has a patterned fill, you can check the Objects box to flip the selected object but not its pattern, or check the Patterns check box to flip the patterned fill but not the object. If you check both check boxes, Illustrator flips the object and its pattern.

- Click Copy to make a copy of the reflected object. Illustrator copies and flips the object, closes the dialog box, and keeps the original object at the pre-reflection location.
- Check the Preview check box to see a preview of the flip before you close the dialog box and the flip becomes final.
- Click OK to have Illustrator apply the options and close the dialog box.

Figure 10-11 also shows the automobile flipped at a 70° angle.

Reflecting with the Free Transform Tool

To flip one or more selected objects using the Free Transform tool, activate the Free Transform tool. Move the mouse pointer, which should be straight and double pointed, to a handle. Then drag the handle beyond the handle on the opposite side of the object. The flipped object might have different proportions and dimensions than the original. Figure 10-12 illustrates, step by step, how the Free Transform tool reflects the automobile. In each step, the mouse pointer drags the object down toward the bottom of the illustration window.

Reflecting with the Transform Each Dialog Box

To flip an object using the Transform Each dialog box (refer to Figure 10-4), follow these steps:

1. Select the object to be flipped.

2. Choose Object | Transform | Transform Each (CTRL-SHIFT-ALT-D/ ⌘-SHIFT-OPTION-D). Illustrator opens the Transform Each dialog box.

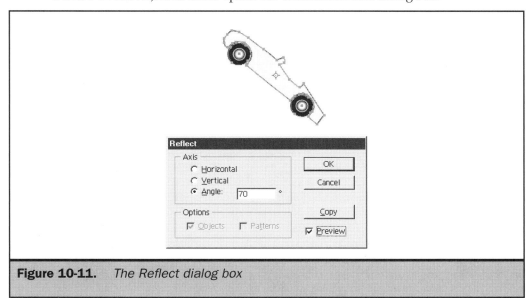

Figure 10-11. *The Reflect dialog box*

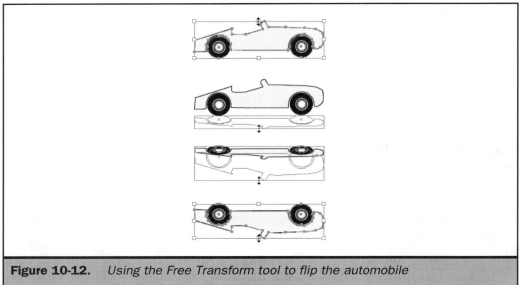

Figure 10-12. *Using the Free Transform tool to flip the automobile*

3. Select an origin point by clicking one of the small squares in the reference point box.

4. Check the Reflect X check box to flip the selected object from one side to another along the horizontal plane toward the left side of the illustration window. (Remember you can change the point from which the object is flipped.)

5. Check the Reflect Y box to flip the selected object from the bottom to the top along the vertical plane toward the top edge of the illustration window.

6. To make a copy of the object, click Copy. Illustrator closes the dialog box, copies the object, and flips it, keeping the original in its initial location.

7. To get a preview of your actions on the object, check the Preview check box. Illustrator doesn't show the results until you click another area of the dialog box.

8. Click OK. Illustrator closes the dialog box and rotates the object.

Shearing Objects

When you shear an object in Illustrator, you slant or skew it from one side of an axis to the other. Where did the term *shear* come from? It's the very last definition of shear in the *Random House Dictionary of the English Language*, "the lateral deformation produced in a body by an external force, expressed as the ratio of the lateral displacement between two points lying in parallel planes to the vertical distance between the planes." Just think of a heavy load of books placed on a metal table whose legs are not braced adequately. As the table slowly collapses to one side or the other under the pile of books, you see an example of severe shearing. In Illustrator, you can shear an object using the Transform palette, Shear tool, Shear dialog box, or Free Transform tool.

Shearing with the Transform Palette

You can use the Transform palette (refer to Figure 10-1) to shear an object by an exact certain number of degrees. To shear an object using the Transform palette, select the object and then either type a value or select a value from the Shear text box/drop-down menu. If you select from the menu, degrees are incremented by 10° or 15°, ranging from –60 to 60. If you type a number of degrees above or below the range on the menu, and Illustrator doesn't like your choice, it might ignore you. Figure 10-13 shows two objects sheared by –45° (in the center) and 45° (at the bottom). The original automobile is on the top.

Shearing with the Shear Tool

The Shear tool, which shares a toolslot with the Scale tool, enables you to slant an object in one direction or another along an axis. To use the Shear tool on an object, select the object using a selection tool, and then click the Shear tool. Then do one of the following:

- To shear the selected object horizontally from both sides of the center point of the object, drag to the left or right of the object.

- To set a new center point, click within the object. Then drag to shear the object from the center point.

- To shear the object in large increments, drag from a location close to the center point.

- To shear the object in fine increments, drag from a location away from the center point.

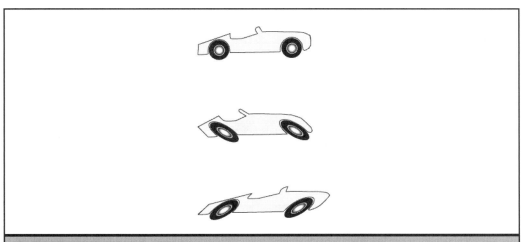

Figure 10-13. *The original object, the object sheared by –45° (heavy foot on the brake) and by 45° (pedal to the metal)*

- To constrain the shear to angles of 45°, 90°, 135°, 180°, 225°, 270°, 315°, or 360°, drag and rotate while pressing and holding down SHIFT.

- To shear a copy of the object, drag while pressing and holding down ALT. The original object stays at its initial size and in its original location.

Figure 10-14 illustrates the automobile with a distorted shadow. To do this, use a combination of the Shear tool while pressing and holding down ALT, and the Free Transform tool to distort a copy of the automobile. Then use the Selection tool and Rotate tool to join the original object and its distorted copy by the tires. Finally, fill the shadow with black.

Shearing with the Shear Dialog Box

The Shear dialog box (see Figure 10-15) enables you to shear a selected object, pattern, or both. To open the Shear dialog box, select an object and then choose Object | Transform | Shear or double-click the Shear tool.

When you open the Shear dialog box, the text boxes contain default values by which you can shear an object, regardless of its current shear condition. To shear the selected object, use the following options from the dialog box:

- In the Shear Angle text box, type the number of degrees at which Illustrator will slant the object from an axis. Valid values range from −360 to 360. Type a positive value to move the object in a clockwise direction; type a negative value to shear the object in a counterclockwise direction.

- To shear the object on a horizontal axis, click the Horizontal radio button.

- To shear the object on a vertical axis, click the Vertical radio button.

- To shear the object at an angle, type the number of degrees from the x axis in the Angle text box. (When you enter a value in the Angle text box, Illustrator automatically selects the Angle radio button.)

Figure 10-14. *An automobile with a sheared shadow*

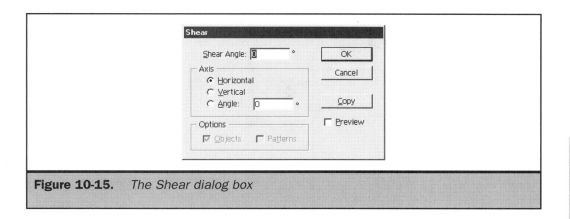

Figure 10-15.   *The Shear dialog box*

- Check the Scale Strokes & Effects check box to scale the stroke and the fill of the selected object. If the check box is cleared, Illustrator scales the fill but leaves the stroke its original size.

- If the object has a patterned fill, you can check the Objects box to shear the selected object but not its pattern, or check the Patterns box to shear the patterned fill but not the object. If you check both check boxes, Illustrator shears both objects and patterns at once.

- Click Copy to make a copy of the sheared object. Illustrator copies and shears the object, closes the dialog box, and keeps the original object at its pre-shear condition and location.

- Check the Preview check box to see a preview of the options you have selected or entered in the text boxes before they become final.

- Click OK to have Illustrator apply the options and close the dialog box.

Shearing with the Free Transform Tool

To shear one or more selected objects using the Free Transform tool, activate the Free Transform tool. Move the mouse pointer to a corner of the bounding box and start dragging—very slightly to allow yourself to use a shortcut key. (If you don't start the dragging operation before you use the shortcut key, Illustrator removes the bounding box.) Press and hold down CTRL-ALT/⌘-OPTION, and continue dragging. Illustrator shears the object.

You can drag one side of an object using the Free Transform tool. To do so, start dragging a side, top, or bottom handle; then press and hold down CTRL/⌘. To drag out one corner only, start dragging and then press and hold down CTRL/⌘. To drag out opposite corners of an object, start dragging and then press and hold down CTRL-ALT-SHIFT/⌘-OPTION-SHIFT.

The
Complete
Reference

U p to this point in the book you've worked exclusively on creating images. However, when you add type to your artworks, you can personalize it. For example, you probably can remember many company logos that incorporate one or two characters from the company name. When was the last time you saw text as the background of a piece of art? Perhaps you have seen a flag image with stripes made up of patriotic sayings or lists of standard and optional features behind an illustration of an automobile in the foreground. Adding type to your artworks opens a whole new set of design possibilities.

What Are Fonts and Point Size?

A *font* or *typeface* is a set of letters, numerals, and symbols based on one design. A font contains characters in different sizes, with their heights usually measured in points, and different enhancements such as regular or normal (nonboldface, nonitalicized), boldface, italics, and bold italics. Some fonts come in wide-ranging point sizes; others are limited to two or three sizes. In addition, fonts differ greatly in their styles, some having a number of boldface weights and others having various slants of italics.

Proportional Versus Monospace Fonts

Fonts come in two types: proportional and monospace (or nonproportional or fixed width). Characters in *proportional* fonts are of different widths. In a proportional font, the letter *I* or the number *1* is not wide at all, but the letter *W* and any number but *1* is much wider than *I*. Characters in a *monospace* font (and the spaces on either side of each character) are always the same width: The letter *I* takes the same amount of space as the letter *W*. For this reason, monospace fonts are very useful in tables where you want to align characters from one row to the next. In general, you'll want to choose a proportional font for body text because it is much easier to read.

Figure 11-1 shows the difference between a list of six-letter words in the Courier New monospace font, the Times New Roman PS MT proportional font, and the ITC Franklin Gothic proportional font. Note that all the words in Courier New start and end at the same place, but the same words in Times New Roman PS MT and ITC Franklin Gothic vary in length—both different lengths.

Serif Versus Sans Serif Fonts

Fonts also come in two other categories: serif and sans serif (that is, without serif). A serif font includes *serifs,* which are decorations at the ends of most of the strokes from which a character is constructed. (A *stroke* is one of the lines that make up a character.) Note that the Illustrator Type tools all are in serif fonts.

The three fonts in Figure 11-1 are serif (on the left and in the middle) and sans serif (on the right). Although the Courier New font is relatively simple in contrast to many other serif fonts, many of its characters have small decorations. The Times New Roman

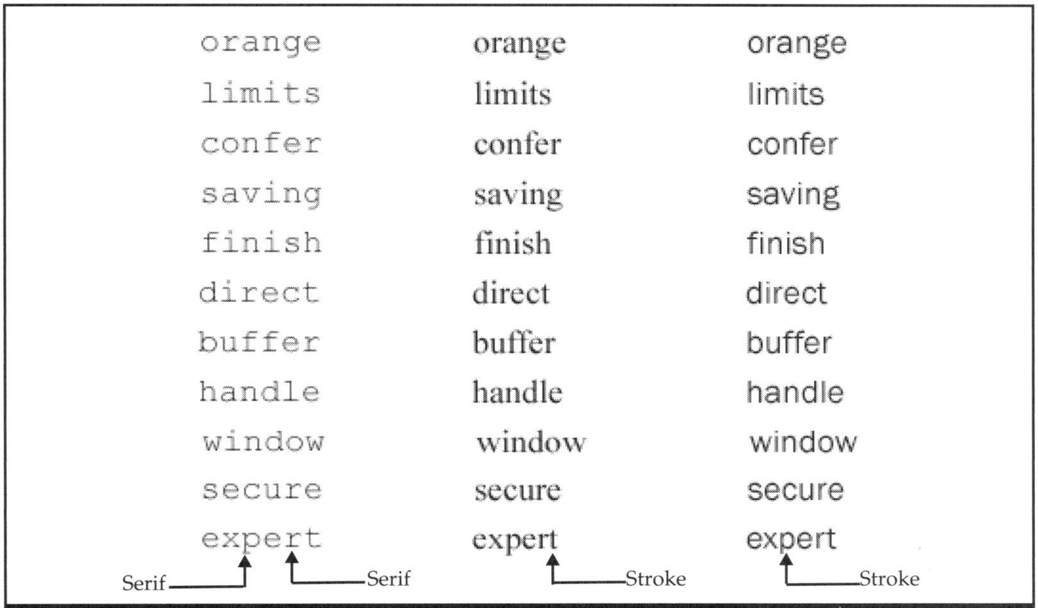

orange	orange	orange
limits	limits	limits
confer	confer	confer
saving	saving	saving
finish	finish	finish
direct	direct	direct
buffer	buffer	buffer
handle	handle	handle
window	window	window
secure	secure	secure
expert	expert	expert

Serif⎯⎯⎯┘ └⎯⎯Serif   └⎯⎯Stroke   └⎯⎯Stroke

Figure 11-1.   *Three columns of six-letter words in monospace (on the left) and proportional (in the middle and on the right) fonts*

PS MT font has even more serifs. In addition, some of the strokes in Times New Roman PS MT are wider than others. Just compare the letters *x*, *p*, and *r* in the word *expert*. Each of those letters has a decoration at the top and bottom of each stroke. In general, you'll want to use sans serif fonts for headings and headlines, and serif fonts for body text. The serifs seem to lead a reader's eyes from one word to another.

Choosing a Point Size

Point size refers to the height of a character in a font measured from the top of a character such as *b*, *l*, or *t* to the bottom of a character such as *g*, *p*, or *q*. Typically, body text is in a 10- to 12- point size, and the smallest headings start at 12 or 14 points to a very large 72 points or even greater than that. One point equals approximately 1/72 inch, depending on the font; so a character in a 10-point size is about 1/7 inch high and a 12-point character is about 1/6 inch high. Obviously, a 72-point character is roughly 1 inch high. All three fonts in Figure 11-1 are 24 points high. Notice that the type in each of the columns varies in size from font to font.

The best way of choosing a point size is to start at the lowest size; for example, 12-point body text. The lowest level of heading should be at least 2 points higher than body text, about 14 points. So, increment each higher level by approximately

2 points. Another approach is to vary the styles of headings while increasing point size. For example, the top heading could be boldface 18 points, and the next level down might be bold italics 16 points. Figure 11-2 shows an Illustrator page of headings and text. Does it look familiar?

Selecting an Appropriate Font

One method of emphasizing a certain section of type is to change its font. You'll do this for headings, headlines, notes, tables of contents, and so on. For example, most headings, which are meant to draw your attention, are shown in a large, bold, sans serif font; and body text, which can go on for pages and should be easy to read, usually is formatted in a smaller serif font. You should limit the number of fonts per page to two; otherwise, your document will begin to look like a ransom note.

Learning Character and Baseline Basics

As you learn about fonts, you'll find that characters have their own special terminology. This section contains brief descriptions of some of those terms, and Figure 11-3 illustrates them.

Choosing a Point Size

Point size refers to the height of a character in a font measured from the top of a character such as b, l, or t to the bottom of a character such as g, p, or q. Typically, body text is in a 10 to 12 point size and the smallest headings start at 12 or 14 points to a very large 72 points or even greater than that. One point equals approximately 1/72 inch, depending on the font. So a character in a 10-point size is about 1/7 inch high and a 12-point character is about 1/6 inch high. Obviously, a 72-point character is roughly one inch high. All three fonts in Figure 11-1 are 24 points high. Notice that the type in each of the columns varies in size from font to font.

The best way of choosing a point size is to start at the lowest size - for example, 12-point body text. The lowest level of heading should be at least two points higher than body text, about 14 points. So, increment each higher level by approximately two points. Another approach is to vary the styles of headings while increasing point size. For example, the top heading could be boldface 18 points, and the next level down might be bold italics 16 points. Figure 11-2 shows an Illustrator page of headings and text. Does it look familiar?

Selecting an Appropriate Font

One method of emphasizing a certain section of type is to change its font. You'll do this for headings, headlines, notes, tables of contents, and so on. For example, most headings, which are meant to draw your attention, are shown in a large, bold, sans serif font, and body text, which can go on for pages and should be easy to read, is usually formatted in a smaller serif font. You should limit the number of fonts per page to two. Otherwise, your document will begin to look like a ransom note.

Figure 11-2.   *Body text and headings in the illustration window*

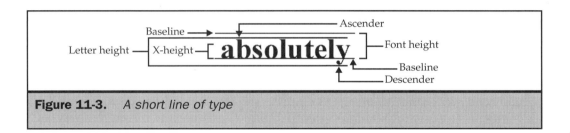

Figure 11-3.   *A short line of type*

- The *x-height* is the height of the body of a character.
- An *ascender* is the part of a character that rises above the body of a character.
- A *descender* is the part of a character that falls below the body of a character.
- The *letter height* is the elevation of the entire character, including the x-height, ascender, and descender.
- The *baseline* is the line on which the type rests.
- The *font height* is the elevation from baseline to baseline of a particular typeface.

Distinguishing Among Font Types

As with graphics, fonts come in raster and vector versions. Raster fonts are bitmaps; and vector fonts, also known as outline fonts, are sets of lines drawn between points and based on mathematical calculations. Illustrator supports the following vector fonts: TrueType, Type 1, and Multiple Master—among others.

TrueType Fonts

Illustrator and many other popular programs support TrueType fonts, which were developed by Apple Computer and extended by other companies such as Microsoft. TrueType fonts are vector fonts that have been designed to look exactly the same on the computer screen and in printed output. This makes it easy to produce artwork without having to guess at its final printed appearance. TrueType is used for both Windows and Macintosh computers.

Type 1 Fonts

According to the Adobe Font Formats page (www.adobe.com/type/topics/info9.html), "Adobe PostScript Type 1 is a worldwide standard for digital type fonts (International Standards Organization outline font standard, ISO 9541). It was first developed by Adobe Systems for use in PostScript printers." Many font creation organizations support the Type 1 standard. In fact, Adobe states that companies worldwide have designed more than 30,000 Type 1 fonts.

Multiple Master Fonts

As you have learned, most fonts are limited in a number of ways. For example, a particular font might enable you to select normal weight and one or two levels of boldface, or condense or expand the width of a specific character. Or, as you select a small or large point size, the typeface design would probably not change—even subtly. And you certainly couldn't change from serif to sans serif or from sans serif to serif.

Multiple Master fonts, which are Type 1 fonts, are unique in that both professional typographers and amateur font designers actually can edit them. With Illustrator and the Adobe Type Manager program, you can change the dimensions of a Multiple Master font:

- You can vary its weight, from light through normal to very bold.

- You can change the width from condensed (narrow) to expanded (wide).

- You can change the optical size and adjust the look of characters to take advantage of the size.

- You can apply different styles that you won't find in most fonts.

Illustrator's default font is Myriad MM, a Multiple Master font. Adobe makes other Multiple Master fonts available through the Adobe Type Library. For information about resources at Adobe's Web site, refer to Appendix C.

Exploring the MM Design Palette

The MM (Multiple Master) Design palette (see Figure 11-4) works in conjunction with the Adobe Type Manager program, enabling you to edit Multiple Master fonts. To toggle between showing and hiding the palette, choose Window | Type | MM Design. Depending on the Multiple Master font you select, the MM Design palette contains sliders with which you can adjust the font. The MM Design palette has no menu.

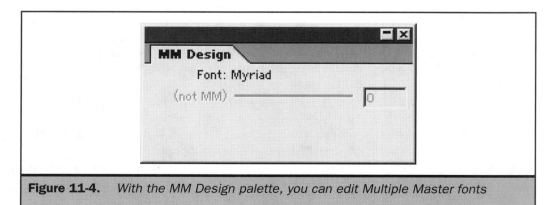

Figure 11-4. *With the MM Design palette, you can edit Multiple Master fonts*

Studying the Type Tools

In the toolbox, Illustrator provides six tools (see Figure 11-5) with which you can add type to a document. Use the first three tools in the toolslot—Type, Area Type, and Path Type—to enter horizontally aligned type; for example, for most Western languages. The last three tools—Vertical Type, Vertical Area Type, and Vertical Path Type—are for use in entering characters in many Eastern languages, as well as for some posters and brochures.

The Type Tool

The all-purpose Type tool (T) enables you to create horizontal type in almost any way: You can enter *point type* (which starts at any place in the illustration window and does not wrap unless you press ENTER/RETURN), create a *type rectangle* (or *text rectangle*) into which you enter type, enter type in an object, or enter type on a path.

The Type tool also changes its appearance and purpose, depending on its location in the illustration window and the optional use of shortcut keys.

- When you move the Type tool to an open path, Illustrator automatically changes the tool to the Path Type tool.

- When you move the Type tool to an open path, and press and hold down ALT/OPTION, Illustrator changes the tool to the Area Type tool.

- When you move the Type tool to a closed path, Illustrator automatically changes the tool to the Area Type tool.

- When you move the Type tool to a closed path, and press and hold down ALT/OPTION, Illustrator changes the tool to the Path Type tool.

- You can toggle between the Type tool and the Vertical Type tool by pressing and holding down SHIFT.

- You can press and hold down CTRL/⌘ to temporarily convert the Type tool to the Selection tool (V) or the Direct Selection tool (A), depending on which tool you last used.

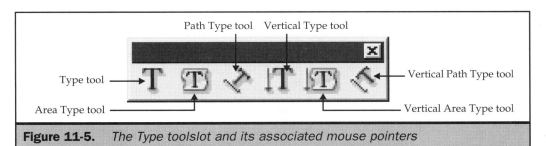

Figure 11-5. *The Type toolslot and its associated mouse pointers*

The Vertical Type Tool

The Vertical Type tool, which is the counterpart to the Type tool, produces vertical type starting at a point on the illustration window, creates a type rectangle, or enters type in an object or on a path. Just like the Type tool, the Vertical Type tool changes when you move the mouse pointer around the illustration window, and optionally press and hold down certain shortcut keys.

- When you move the Vertical Type tool to an open path, Illustrator automatically changes the tool to the Vertical Path Type tool.
- When you move the Vertical Type tool to an open path, and press and hold down ALT/OPTION, Illustrator changes the tool to the Vertical Area Type tool.
- When you move the Vertical Type tool to a closed path, Illustrator automatically changes the tool to the Vertical Area Type tool.
- When you move the Vertical Type tool to a closed path, and press and hold down ALT/OPTION, Illustrator changes the tool to the Vertical Path Type tool.
- You can toggle between the Vertical Type tool and the Type tool by pressing and holding down SHIFT.
- You can press and hold down CTRL/⌘ to temporarily convert the Vertical Type tool to the Selection tool (V) or the Direct Selection tool (A), depending on which tool you last used.

The Area Type and Vertical Area Type Tools

With the Area Type tool and the Vertical Area Type tool, you can fill open or closed paths with type. These tools support the following shortcut keys:

- With the Area Type tool active, press and hold down ALT/OPTION to convert the tool to the Path Type tool.
- With the Vertical Area Type tool active, press and hold down ALT/OPTION to convert the tool to the Vertical Path Type tool.
- You can toggle between the Area Type tool and the Vertical Area Type tool by pressing and holding down SHIFT.
- You can press and hold down CTRL/⌘ to temporarily convert the Area Type tool or the Vertical Area Type tool to the Selection tool (V); or the Direct Selection tool (A), depending on which tool you last used.

The Path Type and Vertical Path Type Tools

When you use the Path Type tool or the Vertical Path Type tool, you can enter type on a path. These two tools support the following shortcut keys:

- With the Path Type tool active, press and hold down ALT/OPTION to convert the tool to the Area Type tool.

- With the Vertical Path Type tool active, press and hold down ALT/OPTION to convert the tool to the Vertical Area Type tool.

- You can press and hold down CTRL/⌘ to temporarily convert the Path Type tool or the Vertical Path Type tool to the Selection tool (V); or the Direct Selection tool (A), depending on which tool you last used.

Specifying a Type Area

In Illustrator you can enter type at a specific point in the illustration window (that is, *point type*) within a type rectangle, object, open or closed path, or along a path. You also can modify type in various ways after you have entered it. For example, you can resize a type rectangle, convert a standard rectangle to a type rectangle, and move type to a new location on a path.

Entering Type at a Particular Point

You can enter horizontally or vertically aligned type starting from any location in the illustration window. For example, if you want to type a caption (such as a copyright or the address of your Web site under an artwork), you can insert it as horizontally aligned point type. Or, you can enter vertical type as part of an artwork that includes other type and a variety of objects.

Entering Horizontally Aligned Type

To enter horizontally aligned type at a particular location, follow these steps:

1. Activate the Type tool (T). Illustrator changes the mouse pointer to the Type-tool mouse pointer. The small horizontal line near the bottom of the I-beam marks the position of the type baseline.

2. Move the mouse pointer to the location at which you want to start typing. Make sure you do not move to an object. (If you click an object, Illustrator creates a type container or path.)

3. Click and start typing, pressing ENTER/RETURN whenever you want to start a new line immediately under the first character you typed.

4. To indicate that you have completed typing, select another toolbox tool or press CTRL/⌘ to temporarily convert the Type tool to the Selection tool.

Entering Vertically Aligned Type

To enter vertically aligned type at a particular location, follow these steps:

1. Activate the Vertical Type tool. Illustrator changes the mouse pointer to a Vertical Type tool mouse pointer.

2. Move the mouse pointer to the location at which you want to start typing. (If you click an object, Illustrator creates a type container or path.)

3. Click and start typing, pressing ENTER/RETURN whenever you want to start a new line to the left of the top character that you typed in the previous line.

4. To indicate that you have completed typing, select another toolbox tool or press CTRL/⌘ to temporarily convert the Type tool to the Selection tool.

Figure 11-6 shows the default look of horizontally and vertically aligned type in the illustration window.

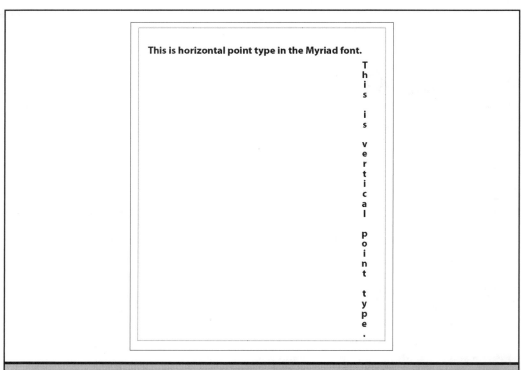

Figure 11-6.   *Horizontally aligned type across the top and vertically aligned type running down the right side*

Entering Type in a Rectangle

You can confine text within a type rectangle in the following ways:

- Use the Type tool (T) to create a type rectangle to enclose horizontally aligned type.

- Use the Vertical Type tool to create a type rectangle to enclose vertically aligned type.

- Use the Rectangle tool (M) to create a rectangle and then use one of the type tools to transform the rectangle to a type rectangle. Then use a type tool to enter type.

A newly created type rectangle does not contain a fill or stroke. You cannot see a type rectangle in Preview view unless it is selected or change its fill or stroke colors to a value other than None.

When you enter type in a type rectangle, the location of the first character depends on the text alignment you have selected. For example, if you use the default left alignment, the first character you enter appears in the upper-left corner for horizontal type or in the upper-right corner for vertical type. If you choose right or centered alignment, the first character of horizontal type appears in the upper-right corner or in the middle of the row, respectively.

Creating a Type Rectangle and Entering Type

To create a type rectangle using the Type tool or Vertical Type tool and enter type, follow these steps:

1. Activate the Type tool (T) or the Vertical Type tool. Illustrator changes the mouse pointer.

2. To create the type rectangle, drag diagonally. To create a type square, drag diagonally while you press and hold down SHIFT. When you release the mouse button, the pointer reverts to an I-beam without the dotted rectangle.

3. Enter the type without moving the mouse pointer or clicking.

   - By default, Illustrator starts horizontal type at the upper-left corner, adding characters from left to right until the last character ends at the upper-right corner, and wraps the type to the following "row" under the first character you entered. If you change the alignment using the Paragraph palette, the type starts as follows: Left-aligned type and justified type start at the upper-left corner of the type rectangle, centered type begins in the top center of the type rectangle, and right-aligned type begins at the top-right margin of the type rectangle.

■ By default, Illustrator starts vertical type at the upper-right corner, adding characters from top to bottom until the last character ends at the lower-right corner, and wraps the type to the next "column" to the left of the first character that you entered. If you change the alignment using the Paragraph palette, the type starts as follows: Left-aligned type and justified type start at the upper-right corner of the type rectangle, centered type begins on the right side between the top and bottom of the type rectangle, and right-aligned type begins at the bottom right of the type rectangle.

4. To begin a new paragraph within the type rectangle, press ENTER/RETURN.

If the type rectangle is completely full of lines of type (see Figure 11-7), Illustrator inserts a small box with a plus symbol next to the location at which the type overflowed the rectangle. You can resize the type rectangle using the bounding box or the Direct Selection tool (A).

From top to bottom, Figure 11-8 illustrates horizontal type aligned with the left margin, centered between the margins, and aligned with the right margin as well as

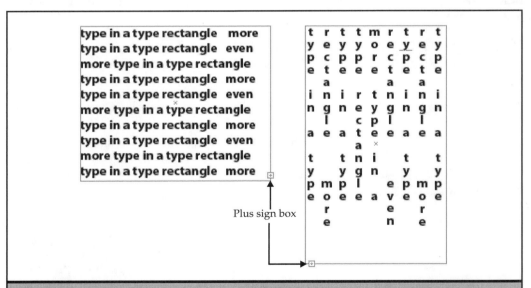

Plus sign box

Figure 11-7. *Horizontally aligned and vertically aligned type shown inside their selected type rectangles*

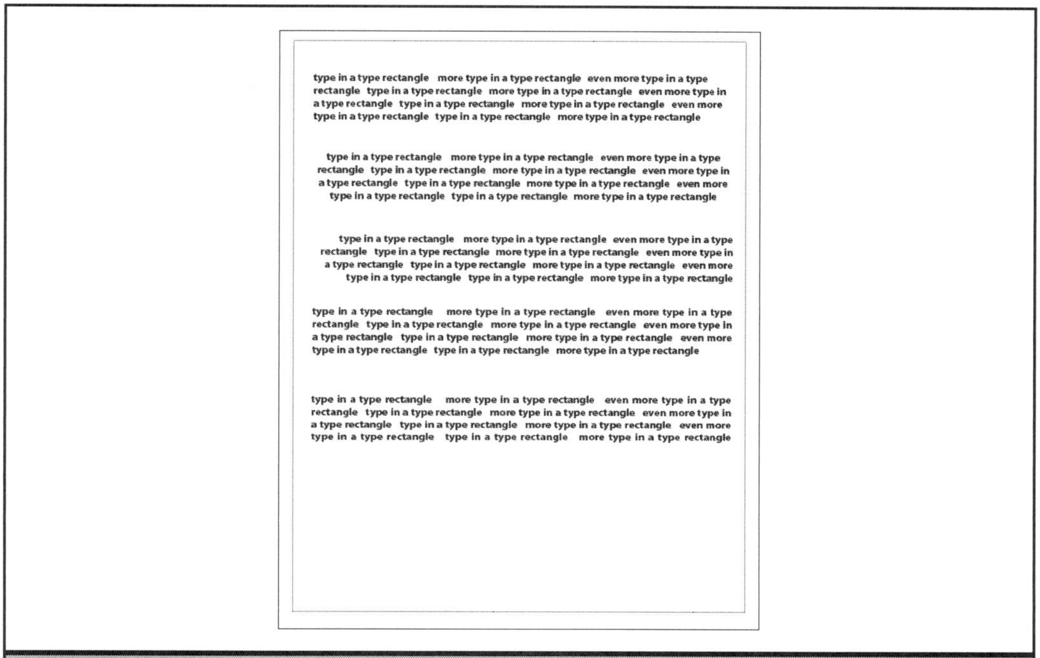

Figure 11-8.   *Five examples of horizontal type alignment: left-aligned, centered, right-aligned, and two types of justification*

full lines justification and all lines justification. For more information about alignment, refer to "Aligning and Justifying Paragraphs" in Chapter 12.

When you work with type, realize that the type itself—not the type rectangle—is filled, stroked, or both when you apply a fill or stroke. So when you use fill and stroke together, the characters might look ultra-bold and even blurry. Using combinations of fill and stroke, you can produce filled type, filled and stroked type, and outlined type (see Figure 11-9).

Converting a Standard Rectangle to a Type Rectangle

If you want to place type in a rectangle with set dimensions, create a rectangle using the Rectangle tool and convert that rectangle to a type rectangle in which you can enter type. Remember that you can create a rectangle by opening the Rectangle dialog box. Just select the Rectangle tool (M) and click the illustration window away from any object. When the Rectangle dialog box opens, type the width and height and then click OK to create the rectangle. Refer to "Creating Rectangles and Squares" in Chapter 2 to

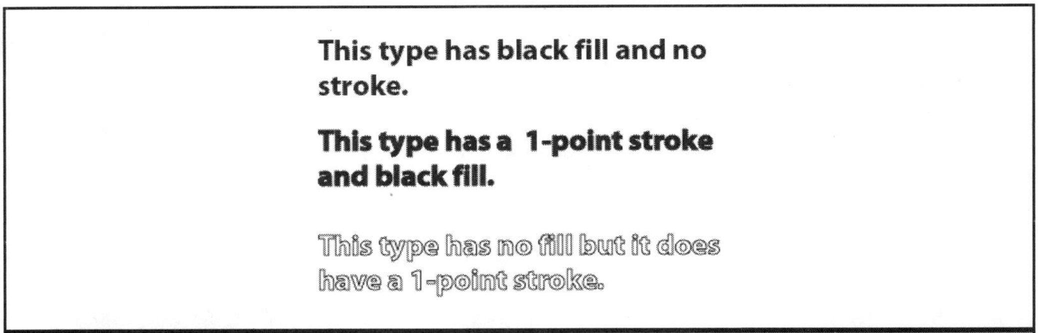

This type has black fill and no stroke.

This type has a 1-point stroke and black fill.

This type has no fill but it does have a 1-point stroke.

Figure 11-9.   *Filled type (on the top), filled and stroked type (in the middle), and outlined type (on the bottom)*

learn more about working with rectangles. To enter type in a rectangle of set dimensions, follow these steps:

1. Activate the Type tool (T), the Area Type tool, the Vertical Type tool, or the Vertical Area Type tool.
2. Click an edge of the rectangle. Illustrator permanently converts the rectangle to a type rectangle. (To undo this, choose Edit | Undo or press CTRL-Z/⌘-Z.)
3. Enter the type contents of the rectangle.
4. When you have completed entering type, select another tool or press CTRL/⌘ to convert the type tool to a selection tool and click outside the rectangle.

Tip   *You can create a type rectangle with specific dimensions without converting a standard rectangle to a type rectangle. To do this, choose Window | Info (F8) to open the Info palette. Then, activate the Type tool (T) and drag the rectangle while you observe the dimensions in the W and H text boxes. When the dimensions are on target, release the mouse button.*

Resizing a Type Rectangle

You can change the size of a type rectangle either for aesthetic reasons or to fit overflowing text (which is indicated by a small plus sign next to the type rectangle). After resizing the rectangle, Illustrator reflows the type into the altered rectangle. To change the dimensions of a type rectangle, use the bounding box or the Direct Selection tool (A). When you select type and a type rectangle along with other objects, Illustrator will resize all the selections, which may or may not be what you want to do.

To force extra type to flow into another rectangle or area, you can use the Link command. Refer to "Using the Link Command" in Chapter 12 to learn more about using this feature.

Resizing a Type Rectangle Using a Bounding Box

To use the bounding box to resize a type rectangle, follow these steps:

1. Activate the Selection tool (V).

2. Click the type rectangle to select it. Illustrator surrounds the rectangle with a bounding box.

3. To resize the type rectangle without worrying about maintaining its current proportions, drag a bounding box handle.

4. To resize the type rectangle while keeping its proportions, drag while pressing and holding down SHIFT.

5. When the type rectangle is the desired size, release the mouse button.

Resizing a Type Rectangle Using the Direct Selection Tool

To use the Direct Selection tool to resize a type rectangle, follow these steps:

1. Activate the Direct Selection tool (A).

2. Click the type rectangle to select it. (Do not select the type within the rectangle.)

Tip *One way to select the type rectangle is to move the mouse pointer around until you see a small square attached to the Direct Selection mouse pointer. That means you have moved over an anchor point. To select the rectangle, click. Another way to actually see the type rectangle is to switch to Outline view (choose View | Outline). However, you can't select in Outline view.*

3. Select an edge of the type rectangle to be able to drag a side. Select a corner of the type rectangle to drag the corner, thereby being able to create an irregular shape.

4. To resize the type rectangle without maintaining its current proportions, drag the selection.

5. To resize the type rectangle while constraining its proportions to 45°, 90°, 135°, 180°, 225°, 270°, 315°, and 360°, drag while pressing and holding down SHIFT.

Entering and Modifying Type Within an Object

You can use any object you have created in Illustrator to contain type. When you convert an object to hold type, it is known as a *type path*. If the object to be filled with type is an open path, Illustrator treats the type path just as it does any open path: The path is filled with type rather than a fill color, pattern, or gradient. If the object is a closed path, Illustrator acts toward it as it would a type rectangle: It's completely filled with type instead of a fill color, pattern, or gradient. Whether a path is open or closed, Illustrator considers it an area to be filled. Consider the following:

- Regardless of whether the object originally had a fill, stroke, or both, when you convert it to a type path Illustrator removes the fill and stroke. In addition, when you select the type path to apply color, Illustrator colors the type and leaves the type path untouched. After you enter type, you can select the type path using the Direct Selection tool and apply paint with the Color palette or the Swatches palette.

- A type area is just about the same as a type rectangle: If you overfill the area with type, Illustrator displays a plus sign box to indicate that the area is overflowing with characters. In addition, you can resize the area using the bounding box or Direct Selection tool.

- When you select an object to be a type path, consider its shape. If the path is irregular, the twists and turns should be gradual rather than abrupt. Illustrator will attempt to flow the type into the nooks and crannies of the object. If certain areas are constricted in any way (for example, like the arms of a star or extremely narrow sides of an hourglass), type might not reach every extreme. Also try to avoid paths whose edges almost meet. The constricted areas will affect the flow of characters. One way to control the pouring of type into an area with sharp turns is to decrease the point size and try different types of alignments. To learn more about type alignment, refer to "Setting Alignment and Justification" in Chapter 12.

Entering Type Within a Type Path

To convert an object to a type path and enter type into the path, follow these steps:

1. Activate the Area Type tool to insert horizontally aligned type, or click the Vertical Area Type tool to enter vertically aligned type.

2. Move the mouse pointer to the path and click. Illustrator converts the object to a type path, places an insertion point at the edge of the path (depending on the set alignment), and removes the fill and stroke.

3. Without further clicking, enter some type. Illustrator fills the path with the characters.

Figure 11-10 illustrates four objects before conversion to a type path and after type has been entered. To enable you to see how the type flows, the type paths have been selected. Notice the difference in the way that type flows; the flow depends on the shape of the path and the size of the type.

Note   *You can transform Illustrator type just as you can objects. To learn more, refer to Chapter 10. To find out how to apply effects and filters to type and other Illustrator objects, read Chapter 16.*

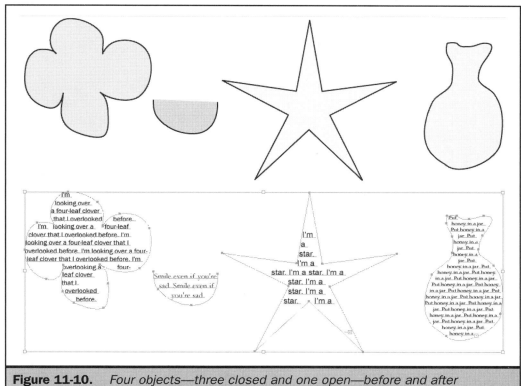

Figure 11-10. *Four objects—three closed and one open—before and after conversion to a type path*

Entering and Modifying Type on a Path

When you see arcs of type above and below a horizontal line, those arcs actually are on invisible, arced paths. You can create this and other effects by entering and modifying type on open or closed paths of any shape. To create type on any path, make the path and then use the Path Type tool or Vertical Path Type tool to enter horizontal or vertical type, respectively. Illustrator removes the fill and stroke, if you have applied either to the path. The type aligns to the path in different ways, depending on the orientation (horizontal or vertical) and the set alignment.

Path type behaves in unique ways depending on how you click or whether you use a shortcut key. For example:

- ■ When you use the Path Type tool to enter type, the characters on the path are perpendicular to the baseline.

- ■ Using the Vertical Path Type tool results in type that is parallel to the baseline.

ILLUSTRATOR
ESSENTIALS

- When you press ENTER/RETURN as you enter type, Illustrator inserts a space at the insertion point rather than moving the path type to a new line.
- When you click the I-beam insertion point with a selection tool, you can drag the type along the path.
- To flip the type, drag the I-beam insertion point to the opposite side of the path.
- While you drag type, you can press and hold down ALT/OPTION to create a copy of the type in a new location on the path. The original type remains in its original location.

For more information about manipulating path type, refer to "Shifting from the Baseline" in Chapter 12.

Entering Horizontal Type on a Path

To enter horizontal type on a path, follow these steps:

1. Activate the Type tool (T) or the Path Type tool.
2. Move the mouse pointer to the location on the path on which you want to enter type and click. Illustrator adds an I-beam insertion point to the path at the click location.
3. Enter the type. As you add type, Illustrator runs it along the path oriented perpendicularly to the baseline.

Figure 11-11 shows a circle right after it has been created (at the top left) and converted to a circular path. Then, horizontal type is moved to the top of the path and changed in point size, and a copy is dragged using a selection tool while pressing and holding down ALT/OPTION. Finally, after the type is moved to the bottom of the path, it's edited to show its new location.

Selecting a Language

Vertical type typically is based on an Eastern language in which type runs vertically on a page. If you wish to enter this kind of language vertically on a path, you'll have to open the Character palette to select the proper language. To do so, follow these steps:

1. Choose Window | Type | Character (CTRL-T/⌘-T).
2. To display the Multilingual section of the palette, choose Show Multilingual from the palette's menu.
3. From the Direction drop-down menu, select Standard.

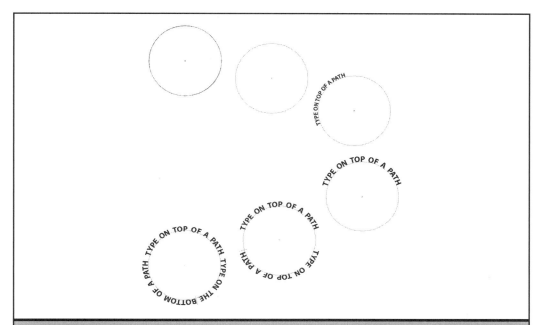

Figure 11-11.   *Stepping clockwise through creating, moving, editing, and duplicating horizontal type on the top and bottom of a circular path*

Entering Vertical Type on a Path

You can enter any language vertically on a path by following these steps:

1. Activate the Vertical Type tool or the Vertical Path Type tool.

2. Move the mouse pointer to the location on the path on which you want to enter type and click. Illustrator adds an I-beam insertion point to the path at the click location.

3. Enter the type. As you add type, Illustrator runs it along the path and orients it parallel to the baseline.

Figure 11-12 shows two forms of vertically aligned type on a winding path—one selected and one unselected.

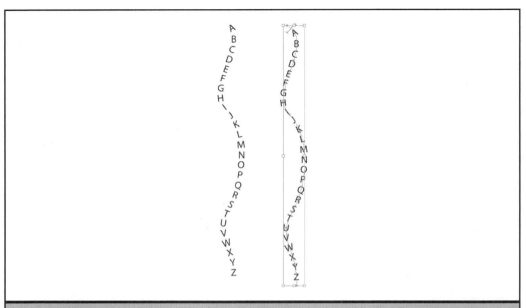

Figure 11-12. *Two versions of a vertically aligned alphabet on a curving path*

Moving Type on a Path

To move type on a path, follow these steps:

1. Select the type path using the Selection tool (V) or the Direct Selection tool (A).
2. Move the mouse pointer to the I-beam insertion point.
3. With the selection tool, drag the type to another location on the path.

 If you inadvertently drag across the path, Illustrator flips the direction of the type on the path.

Flipping Type Direction on a Path

When you enter type on a path, Illustrator adds the type in the order in which you have inserted points to the path. So, if you want to compel type to run in a particular direction, create a path and add anchor points to control the direction. Another way to set the direction of type flow is to flip the direction. (To learn more about editing type on a path, refer to "Shifting from the Baseline" in Chapter 12.)

To change the direction of the type on a path, follow these steps:

1. Activate the Selection tool (V) or the Direct Selection tool (A).

2. Move the mouse pointer to the I-beam insertion point.

3. Either drag the I-beam insertion point across the path, or double-click the insertion point.

If your work results in your having empty paths in an Illustrator document, remember that you can clean up your paths. To do so, choose Object | Path | Clean Up. Then, in the Clean Up dialog box, check Empty Text Paths, and click OK.

Opening "Foreign" Type in Illustrator

If you are used to entering type into a word processor, you might want to start there by creating a document and then opening it in Illustrator. When you do so, note that Illustrator opens both horizontal and vertical type as horizontal.

To import a document into Illustrator, choose File | Open (CTRL-O/⌘-O). In the Open dialog box, make sure the file type is either All Types or the specific type of file you are opening (for example, Microsoft Word (*.DOC)). Then select the file to be opened and click Open.

Fine-Tuning Words

As with any other word processor, Illustrator offers a slew of helpful tools. In this section you will learn how to use Illustrator's spell checker and dictionaries and the Smart Punctuation feature. You'll also learn how to change the case of selected type and how to show and hide nonprinting characters.

Checking Your Spelling

Regardless of whether you consider yourself a good speller, it's a good idea to test the type that you enter or open—especially before you add it to an artwork. Once you add type to an artwork, you cannot reverse misspellings. If you take a long time to construct a complex image, envision how you would feel if any of the words in the image were misspelled.

About the Check Spelling Dialog Box

The Check Spelling dialog box (shown in Figure 11-13) enables you to check and correct your spelling, select a language, and add words to the user dictionary from within the current document.

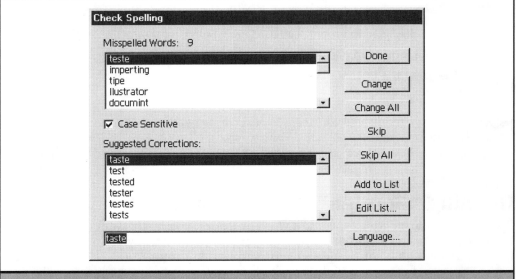

Figure 11-13.   *The Check Spelling dialog box enables you to correct spelling errors and do much more*

The options in the dialog box are as follows:

- The Misspelled Words list box displays all the words that are either misspelled or not in one of the dictionaries. If you select a word in this list, Illustrator displays possible replacement words from one of the dictionaries in the Suggested Corrections list box.

- Check the Case Sensitive check box to have the spell checker recognize the case of words. If the combination of uppercase and lowercase characters in a word does not match the words in a dictionary, the spell checker places the words in the Misspelled Words list.

- The Suggested Corrections list box shows possible replacements for the word selected in the Misspelled Words list box.

- Click Change to replace the current instance of the selected word in the Misspelled Words list with the selected word in the Suggested Corrections list.

- Click Change All to replace all instances of the selected word in the Misspelled Words list with the selected word in the Suggested Corrections list.

- Click Skip to disregard the current instance of the selected word and move on to the next word the spell checker "thinks" is misspelled.

- Click Skip All to disregard all instances of the selected word throughout the document and move on to the next misspelled word.

- Click Add to List to add a word, spelled correctly or not, to your user dictionary. (If you want to ensure that Illustrator placed the word in the user dictionary, you can click Edit List.)

- Click Edit List to open the Learned Words dialog box, which lists the words currently in your user dictionary. In the Learned Words dialog box, you can add, modify, or delete words from the user dictionary. To learn how to use the Learned Words dialog box, read "Editing the User Dictionary," later in this chapter.

- Click Language to change the dictionary for the current language to a dictionary for another language. By default, Illustrator provides several dictionaries, all of which you'll find in the Plug-In filters folder; their file extensions are .dct.

Running a Spell Check

To run a spell check on the current document, follow these steps:

1. Choose Type | Checking Spelling. Illustrator opens the Check Spelling dialog box.

2. If no words are misspelled, Illustrator displays the following message: *no spelling errors found.*

3. If some words are misspelled or not in a dictionary, Illustrator displays those words in the Misspelled Words list.

4. To enable the spell checker to recognize case, check the Case Sensitive box, if it is not already checked.

5. Highlight a word in the Misspelled Words list. Illustrator displays a list of suggested replacement words in the Suggested Corrections list box.

6. If you see a replacement word in the Suggested Corrections list box, select it.

7. To change the current instance of the word in the document, click Change.

8. To change all instances of the word in the document, click Change All.

9. If you believe the word Illustrator thinks is misspelled actually is correct, you can add it to the dictionary by clicking Add to List.

10. If you believe the "misspelled" word is correct, you can move on to the next misspelled word by clicking Skip. If you want to skip all instances of the word in the document, click Skip All.

11. Repeat steps 5–10 until you have gone through the entire list in the Misspelled Words list box.

12. Click Done to close the dialog box.

13. Save the document.

Editing the User Dictionary

Illustrator has a main dictionary, which cannot be edited, and a user dictionary, which you build by adding words from the Check Spelling dialog box. When you edit the user dictionary, you should open the Check Spelling dialog box. If every word in the document is correct, Illustrator displays a message and then opens the Check Spelling dialog box. If Illustrator finds a word that is not in a dictionary, the Check Spelling dialog box opens without a message. Adding words to the dictionary is a good idea when your documents include many company names and terms that might be unique to your industry. You can check to see if certain words are already in the dictionary by adding them. If a word exists in the dictionary, Illustrator displays a message.

To revise the dictionary from within the Check Spelling dialog box, follow these steps:

1. Click Edit List. Illustrator opens the Learned Words dialog box (see Figure 11-14).

2. To add a word to the list, type it in the text box at the bottom of the dialog box, making sure you use the correct combination of uppercase and lowercase characters. Then click Add.

3. To edit a word in the dictionary, select it from the list. Illustrator places the word in the text box at the bottom of the dialog box. Modify the word in the text box, and click Change.

4. To delete a word from the list, select it from the list. Illustrator places the word in the text box at the bottom of the dialog box. Then click Remove. Illustrator leaves the word in the text box until you select another word; so, if you want to undo the deletion, you can click Add.

5. When you have completed your work, click the Done button.

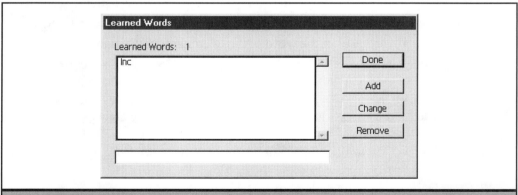

Figure 11-14. *The Learned Words dialog box with one word*

Note *Some programs allow you to add entries to their user dictionaries by using a word processor. However, in Illustrator the only way to add words is to follow the prior steps. In addition, if you inadvertently create a new dictionary by reinstalling Illustrator or move the dictionary from its default location in the Plug-Ins folder and discover the error later, you cannot combine two versions of the user dictionary.*

Using Smart Punctuation

The Smart Punctuation feature enables you to replace certain punctuation and some other characters with others that match those that editors and printers prefer to use. Illustrator replaces selected characters after you have entered type in the current document; not as you type it. To use the Smart Punctuation dialog box (see Figure 11-15), select type with one of the selection tools or a type tool and then choose Type | Smart Punctuation.

The options in the Smart Punctuation dialog box work as follows:

- Check the ff, fi, ffi Ligatures check box to replace instances of ff, fi, or ffi characters with *ligatures,* which combine the individual characters into one single character.

- Check ff, fl, ffl Ligatures to replace instances of ff, fi, or ffi characters with ligatures.

- Check Smart Quotes to convert straight single quote marks (' ') and quotation marks (" ") with smart quotes (' ' and " ").

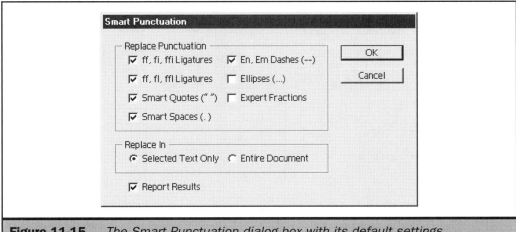

Figure 11-15. *The Smart Punctuation dialog box with its default settings*

- Check Smart Spaces to search the document for sentence-ending periods followed by two spaces and replace the two spaces with one space. Editors and printers prefer single spaces after periods.

- Check En, Em Dashes to replace hyphens (-) and double hyphens (--) with en dashes (–) and em dashes (—), respectively.

- Check Ellipses to replace three periods (...) with an ellipsis (…).

- Check Expert Fractions to substitute hand-typed fractions (such as 1/2 or 3/4) with smaller versions (such as ¼ or ¾). If you are using an Adobe font that does not include Expert Fractions or a font that is not from Adobe, Illustrator will not replace your fractions.

- Click the Selected Text Only radio button to replace characters in the selection only; click Entire Document to replace characters throughout the document.

- Check Report Results to produce a report of the changes.

Figure 11-16 shows the Smart Punctuation dialog box along with two samples of before (on the left) and after (on the right) type.

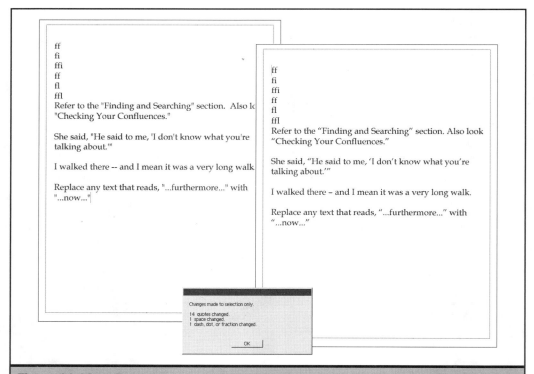

Figure 11-16. *Two samples of text before (on the left) and after (on the right) using the Smart Punctuation dialog box*

Changing Case

The barebones Change Case dialog box (see Figure 11-17) enables you to transform the case of selected letters to all uppercase, all lowercase, or mixed case. To use the Change Case feature, select type to be changed using a type tool (not a selection tool), and then choose Type | Change Case. When Illustrator opens the Change Case dialog box, select an option and click OK to apply the changes and close the dialog box.

The options in the Change Case dialog box are as follows:

- Click the Upper Case (ABC) radio button to transform all selected letters from any combination of uppercase and lowercase characters to uppercase only.

- Click Lower Case (abc) to change all selected letters in any combination of uppercase and lowercase characters to lowercase only.

- Click Mixed Case (Abc) to convert each selected word, regardless of case, into a word having an initial uppercase letter followed by all lowercase letters.

Showing and Hiding Nonprinting Characters

When you enter type in an Illustrator document (as well as in almost any word processor), you cannot view nonprinting characters such as paragraph marks, spaces, and tab marks. However, for editing purposes, sometimes it's a good idea to be able to view every character and space, regardless of whether it will appear in printed output. To show all characters, including nonprinting characters, choose Type | Show Hidden Characters.

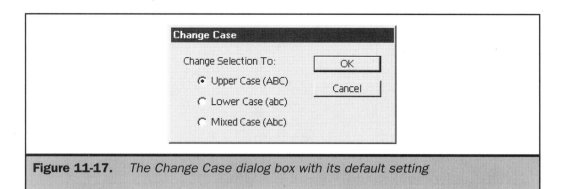

Figure 11-17.   *The Change Case dialog box with its default setting*

Splitting Objects into Rows and Columns

When you use the Rows & Columns dialog box (see Figure 11-18), you can partition objects, type rectangles, type paths, or chunks of text into blocks made up of rows and columns. If the object is not rectangular, Illustrator uses the object's overall height and width for the division. You can specify exact dimensions for the width and height of the blocks, and set the width of the gutters between the blocks.

You also can change the direction in which horizontally aligned and vertically aligned text runs—from left to right or from right to left. If you just think of the layout of a birthday card or a small brochure, you'll get the idea of how important this feature could be for you. Additionally, you can use the dialog box to create rectangles out of an object, lay out objects within rectangles, and create guides for aligning objects.

Learning about the Rows & Columns Dialog Box

Use the options in the Rows section of the dialog box as follows:

- In the Number list box/text box, select or type the number of rows into which you want to divide the selected object.
- In the Height list box/text box, select or type the height, in points, of each new row.
- In the Gutter list box/text box, select or type the height, in points, of the gutter between the rows. Note that when you change the Gutter value, Illustrator adjusts the Height value to maintain the original height of the object.
- In the Total list box/text box, select or type the height, in points, of the overall object.

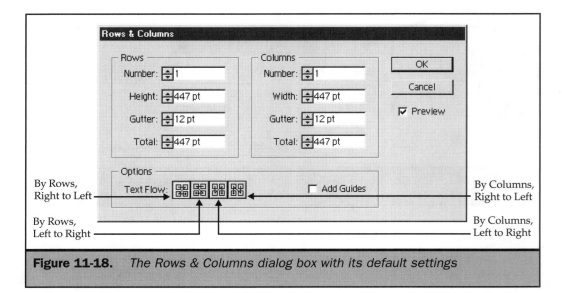

Figure 11-18. *The Rows & Columns dialog box with its default settings*

Use the options in the Columns section of the dialog box as follows:

- In the Number list box/text box, select or type the number of columns into which you want to divide the selected object.
- In the Width list box/text box, select or type the width, in points, of each new column.
- In the Gutter list box/text box, select or type the width, in points, of the gutter between the columns. Note that when you change the Gutter value, Illustrator adjusts the Width value to maintain the original width of the object.
- In the Total list box/text box, select or type the width, in points, of the entire object.

Use the options in the Options section of the dialog box as follows:

- Click the By Rows, Left to Right button to run text horizontally, from the top-left rectangle to the right and wrapping from left to right to the bottom-right rectangle.
- Click the By Rows, Right to Left button to run text horizontally, from the top-right rectangle to the left and wrapping from right to left to the bottom-left rectangle.
- Click the By Columns, Left to Right button to run text vertically, from the top-left rectangle to the bottom and wrapping from top to the bottom, ending at the bottom-right rectangle.
- Click the By Columns, Right to Left button to run text vertically, from the top-right rectangle to the bottom and wrapping from top to the bottom, ending at the bottom-left rectangle.
- Check the Add Guides check box to create guides along the edges of the rows and columns.

To preview the changes you make before you apply them, check the Preview box.

Breaking Up Objects

To break an object, type rectangle, or type path into rows and columns follow these steps:

1. With the Selection tool (V) or Direct Selection tool (A), select the object, type rectangle, or type path.
2. Choose Type | Rows & Columns. Illustrator opens the Rows & Columns dialog box.
3. To see the changes that will be made, check the Preview check box, if it isn't already checked.

4. Type or select row options in the Rows section of the dialog box. As you type or select values, watch and adjust the changes in the illustration window.

5. Type or select column options in the Columns section. Again, modify the options based on the look of the selected objects in the illustration window.

6. To set the direction in which type will flow, click one of the four type flow buttons.

7. To add guides at the edges of the rows and columns, check the Add Guides check box.

8. When you have selected all the options, and the rows and columns are as you desire, click OK. Illustrator creates a set of rectangles that can be converted to type rectangles.

9. To enter type, use a type tool to click the edge of one of the rectangles to convert it to a type rectangle. Then enter type as you learned in previous sections.

The two following figures demonstrate two different conversions into rows and columns. Figure 11-19 shows the simple change from a large rectangle to nine small rectangles. Figure 11-20 illustrates the alteration of a type rectangle and the type within to a set of smaller type rectangles, each containing type controlled by selecting the By Rows, Left to Right button.

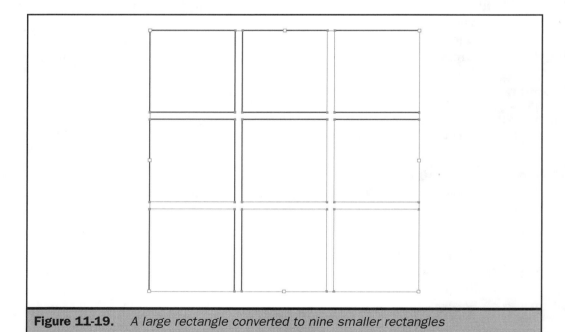

Figure 11-19.   *A large rectangle converted to nine smaller rectangles*

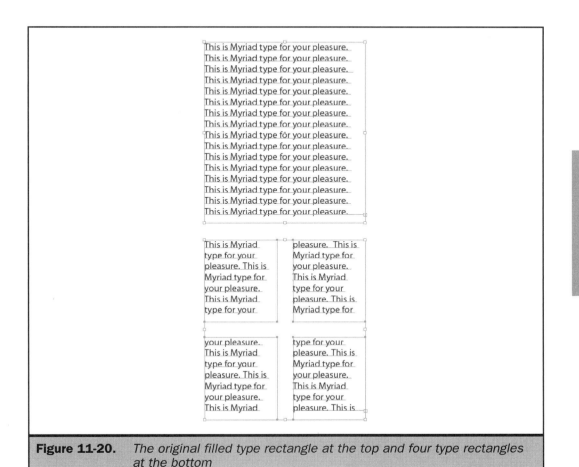

ILLUSTRATOR
ESSENTIALS

Figure 11-20.   *The original filled type rectangle at the top and four type rectangles at the bottom*

Exercising Your "Typing" Skills

You can create the sign shown in Figure 11-21 by following these steps:

1. If the grid is hidden, choose View | Show Grid (CTRL-"/⌘-") to show it.

2. Using the Ellipse tool (L) and SHIFT, drag a circle with a red fill and a 1-point black stroke.

3. Select the circle, and create an offset inside the circle by choosing Object | Path | Offset Path, typing **–40pt** in the Offset text box, and clicking OK.

4. Open the Pathfinder palette by choosing Window | Pathfinder (SHIFT-F9).

5. After selecting both circles with the Selection tool (V), click the Exclude Overlapping Shape Areas button (the fourth button from the left in the top row of the Pathfinder). Illustrator removes the smaller inner circle. (Note the grid showing behind the location of the deleted circle.)

6. Activate the Rectangle tool (M) and draw a black-filled rectangle from one side of the circular path to the other side.

7. Activate the Free Transform tool (E) and drag the black rectangle to a diagonal position.

8. With the rectangle selected, choose Object | Arrange | Send to Back (CTRL-SHIFT-[/⌘-SHIFT-[).

9. Activate the Line Segment tool (\) and draw a diagonal line down the middle of the rectangle.

10. Change both the fill and stroke to white.

11. With the Path Type tool, enter a message on the path. (The type in the figure is Myriad Bold; the point size is 54 pt.)

12. If you need to center the message, use the Selection tool (V) to drag the insertion point.

Figure 11-21. *From left to right in each of the rows, the progression toward the completed sign; the grid demonstrates the true shape of circle*

The
Complete
Reference

Chapter 12

Editing Type

In Chapter 11 you learned how to add type to your artwork in various ways: extending from a point in the illustration window, within objects, and along paths. In this chapter you'll discover ways in which you can enhance type in your images—either as type or as type converted to graphical objects.

Before you format type, you must find and select it. In the first pages of the chapter you'll learn how to search for and optionally replace specific words and phrases, as well as particular fonts to be changed in one or more ways. When you looked through and tested various tasks in Chapter 11, you found out you can select type using the tools on the Type toolslot, the Selection tool, and the Direct Selection tool. In this chapter you'll discover other ways of selecting characters, phrases, and entire paragraphs and documents. Then, throughout the chapter you'll learn how to apply character and paragraph formats and enhancements using the Character, Paragraph, and Tab Ruler palettes; Type menu commands; and the Eyedropper and Paint Bucket tools.

Because working with type is just one subset of Illustrator's many features, sometimes it's worthwhile to convert type to graphic objects, to partake of more features and tools. In this chapter you'll find out how to convert type to graphical objects so that you can work on them even more.

Finding and Replacing Type

You can use Illustrator's find and replace features to make almost-simultaneous changes to words, phrases, and fonts throughout a document. For example, if one of your client companies changes its name or is acquired, you can open each document in which its name appears, search for the old name, and replace it with the new one. When you find and replace in Illustrator, your overall design does not change: The Find command only finds and optionally replaces; the command does not change the color, style, spacing, or other attributes of the type as it is currently laid out.

Learning About the Find/Change Dialog Box

The Find/Change dialog box (see Figure 12-1) enables you to find and optionally replace a word or phrase in the current Illustrator document. To open the dialog box, choose Type | Find/Change.

The options in the Find/Change dialog box are as follows:

- In the Find What text box, type one or more characters, a word, or a phrase that you want to find in the document.

- In the Change To text box, type one or more characters, a word, or a phrase with which you want to replace the contents of the Find What text box.

- Check the Whole Word check box to find an entire word or phrase only. If this check box is unchecked (the default), Illustrator looks for entire words and instances of the "find" characters and words within words and phrases.

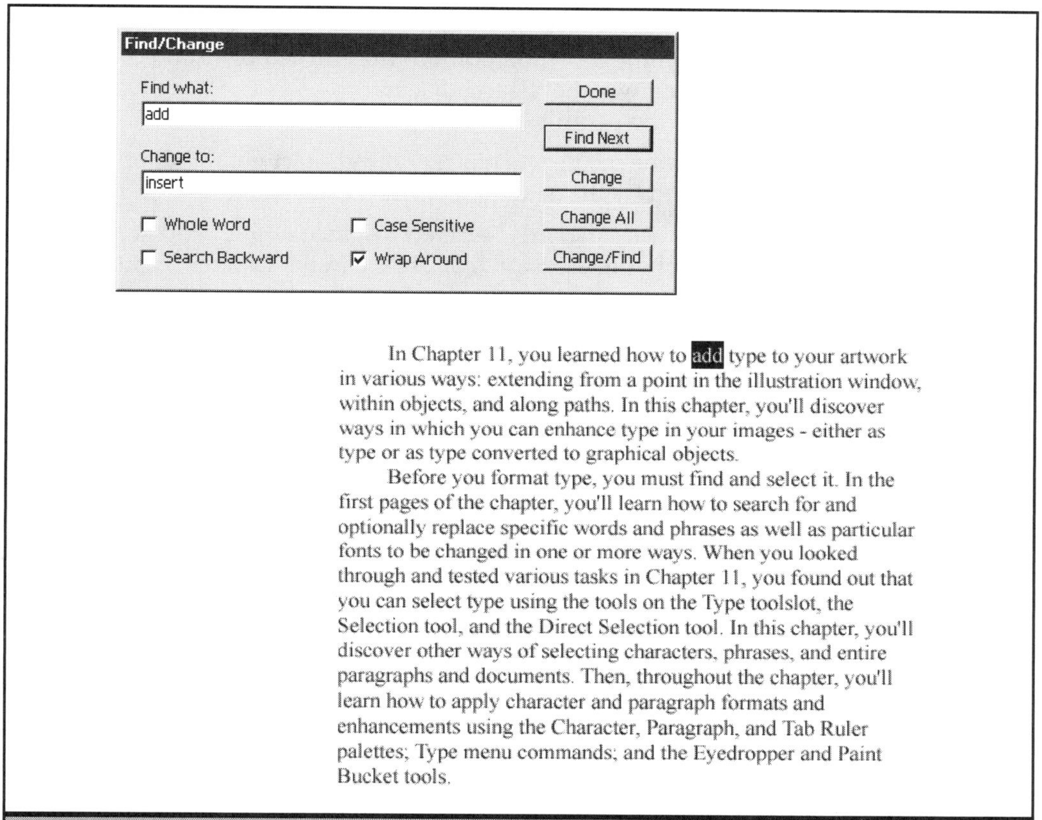

Find/Change

Find what:
add

Change to:
insert

☐ Whole Word   ☐ Case Sensitive

☐ Search Backward   ☑ Wrap Around

Done

Find Next

Change

Change All

Change/Find

In Chapter 11, you learned how to ▮add▮ type to your artwork in various ways: extending from a point in the illustration window, within objects, and along paths. In this chapter, you'll discover ways in which you can enhance type in your images - either as type or as type converted to graphical objects.

Before you format type, you must find and select it. In the first pages of the chapter, you'll learn how to search for and optionally replace specific words and phrases as well as particular fonts to be changed in one or more ways. When you looked through and tested various tasks in Chapter 11, you found out that you can select type using the tools on the Type toolslot, the Selection tool, and the Direct Selection tool. In this chapter, you'll discover other ways of selecting characters, phrases, and entire paragraphs and documents. Then, throughout the chapter, you'll learn how to apply character and paragraph formats and enhancements using the Character, Paragraph, and Tab Ruler palettes; Type menu commands; and the Eyedropper and Paint Bucket tools.

Figure 12-1.   *The Find/Change dialog box with one word in the Find What text box and another in the Change To text box*

- Check the Search Backward check box to search from the current position of the insertion point up to the top of the document. If this check box is unchecked (the default), Illustrator looks for the "find" character, word, or phrase from the insertion point down to the end of the document.

- Check the Case Sensitive check box to have Illustrator search for an exact match of the uppercase and lowercase characters entered in the Find What text box. (For example, if you type **OrAnGe** in the text box, Illustrator ignores occurrences of ORANGE or orange.) If this check box is unchecked (the default), Illustrator looks for the "find" word in both uppercase and lowercase.

- Check the Wrap Around check box to search through the entire document starting at the current location of the insertion point through the beginning or end of the document (depending on whether Search Backward is checked or unchecked) down or up to the insertion point. If this check box is unchecked, Illustrator searches from the insertion point to the end or beginning of the document (depending on whether Search Backward is checked or unchecked). A checked check box is the default.

- Click Find Next to find the next occurrence of the characters, word, or phrase in the direction indicated by the Search Backward check box.

- Click Change to change the currently selected instance of the "find" characters, word, or phrase to the characters, word, or phrase in the Change To text box.

- Click Change All to change all instances of the "find" characters, word, or phrase in the document to the characters, word, or phrase in the Change To text box.

- Click Change/Find to change the currently selected instance of the "find" characters, word, or phrase to the characters, word, or phrase in the Change To text box, and then search for the next occurrence of the contents of the Find What text box.

Finding Characters, Words, and Phrases

To find type in an Illustrator document, follow these steps:

1. Choose Type | Find/Change. Illustrator opens the Find/Change dialog box.

2. In the Find What text box, enter the characters, words, or phrases for which you want to search.

3. To limit the search, check or clear the four check boxes at the bottom of the dialog box.

4. Click Find Next to search for the next occurrence of the "find" characters, word, or phrase.

5. When you have completed the search, click Done.

Finding and Replacing Characters, Words, and Phrases

To find and replace type in an Illustrator document, follow these steps:

1. Choose Type | Find/Change. Illustrator opens the Find/Change dialog box.

2. In the Find What text box, enter the characters, words, or phrases for which you want to search.

3. In the Change To text box, enter the characters, words, or phrases with which you want to replace the contents of the Find What text box.

4. To limit the search, check or clear the four check boxes at the bottom of the dialog box.

5. To search for the first occurrence of the "find" characters, word, or phrase, click Find Next.

6. To replace the selected "find" text with the contents of the Change To text box, click Change.

7. To replace all instances of the "find" text with the contents of the Change To text box, click Change All.

8. To replace the currently selected "find" text with the contents of the Change To text box and then search for the next instance of the "find" text, click Change/Find.

9. When you have completed the search, click Done.

Finding and Replacing Fonts

You also can find and replace a particular font. For example, if your design team plans to work with a new set of fonts to apply a new look to your brochures or reports, Illustrator enables you to search for a specific font and replace it with another. When you use this feature, Illustrator opens a dialog box in which all the fonts in the current document are listed. Using the options in the dialog box, you can search for one or more classes of fonts. Then, you can replace the fonts with others in the document or from your computer system, replace one style with another, and save a list of the fonts in its own file. When you use the Font Find command, you can limit your fonts to those at your commercial printer. If you discover that you are using several fonts where one or two could do, you can find each superfluous font and replace it with another current font.

Learning About the Find Font Dialog Box

The Find Font dialog box (see Figure 12-2) contains a list of the fonts in the current document and options with which you can find and optionally replace one or more fonts in the active document. To open the dialog box, choose Type | Find Font.

The options in the Find Font dialog box are as follows:

- The Fonts in Document list box catalogs all the fonts used in the active document. The number on the right side above the list box is the number of fonts used in the document.

- The Replace Font From drop-down menu enables you to choose from Document, to show the fonts used in the active document, or System, to show all the fonts installed on your computer system. The number on the right side of the menu is the number of fonts available from your document, if you have chosen Document, or from your computer system, if you have selected System.

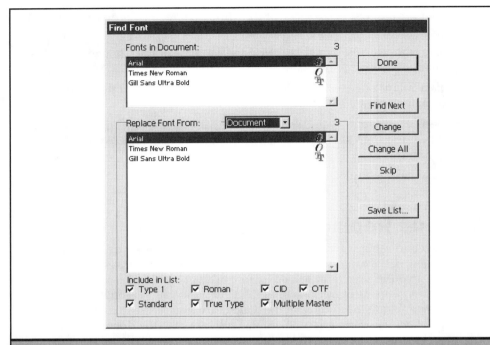

Figure 12-2. *The Find Font dialog box lists the fonts in the current document and enables you to replace a selected font with another—either from the document or from all the fonts installed on your computer system*

- The Replace Font From list box shows all the fonts from which you can choose in the active document or your computer system. On the right side of each entry on the list is an icon representing the font type.

- Check the Type 1 check box to find all Type 1 fonts.

- Check the Standard check box to find all Standard fonts, including versions of the following fonts: Chicago, Courier, Geneva, Helvetica, Hobo, Monaco, New York, Souvenir, Symbol, and Times.

- Check the Roman check box to find all Roman (that is, not boldface, not italicized) fonts.

- Check the True Type check box to find all TrueType fonts.

- Check the CID check box to find all Type 1 CID (character index description) fonts, which are Type 1 PostScript fonts developed by Adobe for use in formatting large character sets (such as Chinese, Japanese, and Korean (CJK) character sets).

- Check the Multiple Master check box to find all Multiple Master fonts. To find all Multiple Master fonts, you also must check Type 1.

- Check the OTF check box to find all OpenType fonts. OpenType is an international standard for PostScript font designs.

- Click Find Next to find the next occurrence of the selected font in the document.

- Click Change to change the currently selected font.

- Click Change All to change all occurrences of the selected font to the replacement font.

Finding a Font

To find a font in your file, follow these steps:

1. Choose Type | Find Font. Illustrator opens the Find Font dialog box, which lists the current fonts used in the document and highlights one of those fonts in the Fonts in Document list box. Illustrator also highlights the selected font in the document.

2. To highlight another font in the Fonts in Document list box, click that font. Illustrator highlights the font in your document.

3. Click Find Next to find the next instance of the font. Illustrator highlights the font in your document.

4. To save a list of all fonts found in the file, click Save List, type the name of the file in which the list will be placed, and click Save.

5. Click Done.

Finding and Replacing a Font

To find and replace fonts in your file:

1. Choose Type | Find Font. Illustrator opens the Find Font dialog box, which lists the current fonts used in the document, highlights one of those fonts in the Fonts in Document list box, and lists the replacement fonts from your document or computer system, depending on whether you have selected Document or System from the Replace Font From drop-down menu. Illustrator also highlights the selected font in the document.

2. To select a font to be replaced, click that font in the Fonts in Document list box. Illustrator highlights the font in your document.

3. To show a list of potential replacement fonts that appear in your document, choose Document from the Replace Font From drop-down menu.

ILLUSTRATOR
ESSENTIALS

4. To list the fonts installed on your computer system from which you can replace the currently selected font, choose System from the Replace Font From drop-down menu.

5. To narrow your choices of fonts, check or clear any combination of the Include in List check boxes.

6. Select a replacement font from the Replace Font From list box.

7. To change the selected instance of the found font to the replacement font, click Change. If the found font is no longer used in your document, Illustrator removes its name from the list in the Fonts in Document list box.

8. To find the next instance of the font to be replaced in your document, click Find Next. Illustrator highlights the entire block of text from that font.

9. To change all instances of the found font to the replacement font, click Change All. Illustrator removes the found font from the list in the Fonts in Document list box.

10. To change another font, repeat steps 2–9.

11. To save a list of all fonts found in the file, click Save List, type the name of the file in which the list will be placed, and click Save.

12. Click Done.

Selecting Type

Before you can edit a word, phrase, block of type, or type within a path, you must select it. In Chapter 11, you found out that you can use the Selection tool (V) or Direct Selection tool (A) to select type for certain actions and the tools on the Type toolslot to select type for other actions. You also can use the mouse, the keyboard, or both in combination with one of the type tools to select different sections of type. Table 12-1 summarizes your type selection possibilities with a type tool, the mouse, and the keyboard.

To Select	Take the Following Action
One word	Double-click the word.
One word and one or more words to the right	With a type tool activated, press and hold down CTRL-SHIFT-→/⌘-SHIFT-→.
One word and one or more words to the left	With a type tool activated, press and hold down CTRL-SHIFT-←/⌘-SHIFT-←.

Table 12-1. *Illustrator Selection Actions*

To Select	Take the Following Action
One or more characters, words, phrases, or more on a single line	With the mouse and a type tool activated, drag to the left or right. To reduce the selection, drag to the right or left, respectively.
One or more characters, words, phrases, or more to the right on a single line	With a type tool activated, press and hold down SHIFT, and repeatedly press →. To reduce the selection, press and hold down SHIFT, and repeatedly press ←.
One or more characters, words, phrases, or more to the left on a single line	With a type tool activated, press and hold down SHIFT, and repeatedly press ←. To reduce the selection, press and hold down SHIFT, and repeatedly press →.
One or more characters up to and including a block of text	With the mouse and a type tool activated, drag to the left, right, top, or bottom. To reduce the selection, press and hold down SHIFT, and drag in the opposite direction from the original drag.
One or more characters, words, phrases, or more from the current location to one or more lines toward the top of the document	With a type tool activated, press and hold down SHIFT, and repeatedly press ↑. To reduce the selection, press and hold down SHIFT, and repeatedly press ↓.
One or more characters, words, phrases, or more from the current location to one or more lines toward the bottom of the document	With a type tool activated, press and hold down SHIFT, and repeatedly press ↓. To reduce the selection, press and hold down SHIFT, and repeatedly press ↑.
One or more characters, words, phrases, or more from the current location to one or more lines to the top of the document	With a type tool activated, press SHIFT-HOME. To remove the selection, press SHIFT-END.

Table 12-1. *Illustrator Selection Actions* (continued)

ILLUSTRATOR ESSENTIALS

To Select	Take the Following Action
One or more characters, words, phrases, or more from the current location to one or more lines to the bottom of the document	With a type tool activated, press SHIFT-END. To remove the selection, press SHIFT-HOME.
One paragraph	With a type tool activated, move the mouse pointer within the paragraph and triple-click.
The current paragraph and, optionally, one or more previous paragraphs	With a type tool activated, press and hold down CTRL-SHIFT/⌘-SHIFT, and repeatedly press ↑. To reduce the selection, press and hold down CTRL-SHIFT/⌘-SHIFT, and repeatedly press ↓.
The current paragraph and, optionally, one or more following paragraphs	With a type tool activated, press and hold down CTRL-SHIFT/⌘-SHIFT, and repeatedly press ↓. To reduce the selection, press and hold down CTRL-SHIFT/⌘-SHIFT, and repeatedly press ↑.
All lines of text in the document	Click with the Selection tool (T) or Direct Selection tool (A).
All lines of text in the document	Choose Select | Object | Text Objects.
The entire document and its container	With a type tool activated, click the document. Then choose Select | All (CTRL-A/⌘-A). To deselect the entire document, choose Select | Inverse.

Table 12-1. *Illustrator Selection Actions* (continued)

For information about all the Illustrator shortcut keys, refer to Appendix F.

Modifying Character Attributes

As you know, the purpose of selecting type is to act on it in some way. With the Character palette and commands on the Type menu, you can control the look of individual characters, words, phrases, and more. Using these features, you can change the font and point size. Illustrator also enables you to shift characters, words, and lines of text closer to the lines above. You also can move type above and below the baseline and switch the orientation of type—either existing, selected type, or type that you will enter at the insertion point. In this section you'll learn all about these type management features.

Exploring the Character Palette

The Character palette (see Figure 12-3) enables you to change the characteristics of characters, words, and phrases. To toggle between showing and hiding the palette,

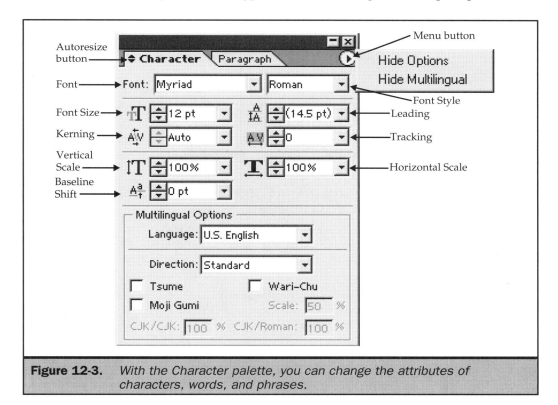

Figure 12-3. *With the Character palette, you can change the attributes of characters, words, and phrases.*

choose Window | Type | Character (CTRL-T/⌘-T). Another way of opening the palette is choosing Type | Size | Other.

The Character palette contains nine options:

- From the Font option box/text box/drop-down menu, select the font for the selected type.

- From the Font Size option box/text box/drop-down menu, select a point size for the selected type. Most fonts range from 6 points to 72 points in size. However, you can type another size.

- From the Kerning option box/text box/drop-down menu, select the *kerning* value, the space between two selected characters. (You also can track three or more characters using the Tracing option box/text box/drop-down menu.)

- From the Vertical Scale option box/text box/drop-down menu, select the vertical scale value to modify the relationship between the height and width of the type from the baseline. You can change the scaling, compression, and expansion of characters both in width and height. (You also can use the Horizontal Scale option box/text box/drop-down menu to scale selected type horizontally.)

- From the Baseline Shift option box/text box/drop-down menu, select the baseline-shift value, which raises selected type above the baseline (that is, superscript) or below the baseline (that is, subscript).

- From the Font Style option box/text box/drop-down menu, select an enhancement (normal, boldface, italics, bold italics, and so on) for the selected type.

- From the Leading option box/text box/drop-down menu, select the *leading* value, the measurement of space between baselines.

- From the Tracking option box/text box/drop-down menu, select the *tracking* value, the spacing between three or more selected characters. (You also can kern two selected characters using the Kerning option box/text box/ drop-down menu.)

- From the Horizontal Scale option box/text box/drop-down menu, select the horizontal scale value to modify the relationship between the height and width of the type from the baseline. You can change the scaling, compression, and expansion of characters both in width and height. (You also can use the Vertical Scale option box/text box/drop-down menu to scale selected type vertically.)

Click the Autoresize button to change the size of the palette in four ways: showing only the tab, only six options (Font, Font Style, Font Size, Kerning, Leading, and Tracking), only nine options (Font, Font Style, Font Size, Kerning, Vertical Scale, Baseline Shift, Leading, Tracking, and Horizontal Scale), or the nine options plus the Multilingual options.

To open the palette's menu, click the menu button.

- The Show Options command shows the palette with nine options (Font, Font Style, Font Size, Kerning, Vertical Scale, Baseline Shift, Leading, Tracking, and Horizontal Scale) but no Multilingual options; the Hide Options command shows six options (Font, Font Style, Font Size, Kerning, Leading, and Tracking) only.

- The Show Multilingual command opens a Multilingual Options section at the bottom of the palette; the Hide Multilingual command closes the Multilingual Options section. The Multilingual Options section enables you to choose a language, the direction in which type will run, and one of the following proportional spacing options: Tsume, Moji Gumi, and Wari-Chu.

Changing the Font and Font Style

In the "Finding and Replacing a Font" section earlier in this chapter, you learned one method of replacing fonts. You also can select fonts and, optionally, the font style from the Character palette or by choosing the Type | Font command and selecting a submenu command.

Changing the Font and Font Style Using the Character Palette

To replace a font and font style using the Character palette, follow these steps:

1. Select the target type path with the Selection tool (V) or the Direct Selection tool (A), or select a target block of type using any of the type tools.

2. To select a font by typing, start entering the font name in the Font text box. Illustrator narrows the available names and eventually fills in the correct font name.

3. To select a font from the drop-down menu, scroll through the fonts until you find the desired one. Once the Font drop-down menu is active, you also can press ALT-SHIFT-↑/OPTION-SHIFT-↑ repeatedly to scroll up the list of fonts or press ALT-SHIFT-↓/OPTION-SHIFT-↓ repeatedly to scroll down the list.

4. To select a font style by typing, start entering the style in the font style text box to the right of the Font text box. Illustrator responds to your typing by filling in the proper style name.

5. To select a font style from the drop-down menu, open the menu and select the appropriate style. Once the Font Style drop-down menu is active, you also can press ALT-SHIFT-↑/OPTION-SHIFT-↑ repeatedly to scroll up the list of fonts or press ALT-SHIFT-↓/OPTION-SHIFT-↓ repeatedly to scroll down the list.

6. If you need to apply the new font and/or style to the selected type, press ENTER/RETURN or TAB. (If Illustrator has already filled in the proper font and font style, you don't need to press the shortcut key.)

Changing the Font and Font Style Using the Type Menu

Choose Type | Font to open a series of submenus listing all the fonts installed on your computer system. If your computer system has more fonts than a single Font submenu can display, the More command heads the list of fonts. Choose More to display the next in the series of submenus. If a particular font name is followed by a right-pointing arrow, the font has a submenu displaying a set of styles from which you can choose.

To choose a font and font style from the Type menu, follow these steps:

1. Select the target type path with the Selection tool (V) or the Direct Selection tool (A), or select a target block of type to be modified using any of the type tools.

2. Choose Type | Font. Illustrator opens a submenu when you move the mouse pointer over the Font command. Note that a check mark precedes the current font of the type selection.

3. To find the replacement font, move the mouse pointer down the submenu. If the font name does not appear on the current Font submenu, choose More to open the next submenu.

4. Repeat step 3 until you have located the replacement font.

5. Move the mouse pointer to the replacement font to select it.

6. If the font name is followed by a right-pointing arrow, move the mouse pointer to open the style submenu.

7. Select a style. Illustrator replaces the current font and style with the newly selected font and style.

Selecting a Point Size

For Illustrator documents, the default point size is 12 points—just as it is for many word processors. Illustrator enables you to select a point size from the Character palette or by choosing the Type | Size command. You can choose from the following units of measure: points (the default); inches; millimeters; pixels; or Q, which is equal to 0.25 millimeters or about 0.71 point and which is popular in countries such as Japan and Germany. To learn how to change the unit of measure, refer to "Setting the Unit of Measure" in Chapter 6. You can find out how to set other preferences in Appendix B.

Setting the Point Size Using the Character Palette

To change the point size using the Character palette, follow these steps:

1. Select the target type path with the Selection tool (V) or the Direct Selection tool (A), or select a target block of type to be modified using any of the type tools.

2. To select a point size by typing, enter the number in the Font Size text box.

3. To choose a point size from the option box, click the up arrow on the right side of the box to display a higher number or click the down arrow on the

right side of the box to display a lower number. After the Font Size Font Size option box/text box/drop-down menu is active, you can press ↑ or ↓ to increase or decrease the point size slightlyt or press ALT-SHIFT-↑/OPITION-SHIFT-↓ to increase or decrease the point size by a greater amount. Illustrator *greeks* characters at a selected small-point-size level. Greeking shows indecipherable characters as gray bars. To learn how to set the greeking level of small characters, refer to Appendix B.

4. To select a point size from the menu, open the drop-down menu and choose a value—usually between 6 and 72. If you have chosen a point size smaller than 8 or larger than 72, the menu might list those values during the current Illustrator session only.

5. If you need to apply the new point size to the selected type, press ENTER/ RETURN or TAB. (If Illustrator has already filled in the proper point size, you don't need to press the shortcut key.)

Setting the Point Size Using the Type Menu

Choose Type | Size to open a submenu listing all the point sizes for the current font. An Other command heads the list of point sizes. If the Character palette is closed, selecting Other reveals the Character palette with the Font Size option box/text box/ drop-down menu active.

To choose a point size from the Type menu, follow these steps:

1. Select the target type path with the Selection tool (V) or the Direct Selection tool (A), or select a target block of type to be modified using any of the type tools.

2. Choose Type | Size. Illustrator opens a submenu when you move the mouse pointer over the Size command. Note that a check mark precedes the current point size of the type selection.

3. If the desired point size appears on the Size submenu, move the mouse pointer over that point size and release the mouse button. Illustrator changes the point size of the selection.

4. If the desired point size does not appear on the Size submenu, choose Other. Illustrator opens the Character palette with the Font Size option box/text box/drop-down menu active. Select a point size as you did in the previous set of steps.

Kerning Characters

As you learned in your travels around the Character palette, kerning expands or contracts the space between two selected characters. With Illustrator, you will normally kern using the Character palette. However, you also can turn on kerning that is part of the design of certain fonts. Illustrator enables you to display the measurement of the kerning between two selected characters using the Info palette. In addition, you can view the tracking for one or more words. Remember that tracking is the spacing between three or more selected characters, so kerning and tracking are closely related.

In Illustrator, each change in kerning is measured by one-thousandth of an em space, a very small size indeed. (Imagine the width of a typical *m* divided by 1,000.) The point size of the selected characters also plays a part in measuring kerning. So, if a character in a certain font is 10 points in size, one em space is 10 points wide, which means you can fit 100 kerning elements (that is, one-thousandth of one em space) into a single point.

Kerning works particularly well with larger point sizes; for example, for headings and headlines. In fact, the larger the characters, the farther apart they seem to be: They sometimes look like individual letters or numbers that happen to be on the same line. So kerning can move individual characters together so that—once again—they appear to be words. Figure 12-4 illustrates automatic kerning versus manual kerning. On the top is a headline that Illustrator has automatically kerned using built-in defaults. Note the variation of spaces between some pairs of characters. The lower headline shows tight kerning. For example, kerning between *G* and *O* is –50; the space between *A* and *W* is –100; between *W* and *A* is –90; and between *A* and *Y* is –150.

Viewing the Kerning Between Two Characters

To view the measurement of the kerning between two characters, follow these steps:

1. Select a type tool.

2. Move the insertion point mouse pointer between the two characters whose kerning you want to measure.

3. If the Info palette is not in the illustration window, choose Window | Info (F8). Illustrator displays the Info palette (see Figure 12-5) and two lines about the two characters.

In the figure, all three examples (with information shown in the Info palette) have the same first line (24 pt Myriad-Bold), which states the point size (24 points), the font (Myriad), and the font style (Bold). For the tightly kerned letters *AW* in the top example, the second line reads –100 = 0–100 / 1000 em. This indicates that the characters have –100/1000 (or –1/10) em spacing, a negative kerning value between the characters. Tracking is 0/1000, or no tracking measurement at all.

GO AWAY
GO AWAY

Figure 12-4.   *Examples of automatic kerning (above) and manual kerning (below)*

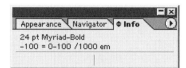

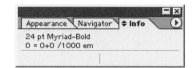

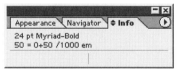

Figure 12-5. *Three examples of kerning—condensed, none, and expanded—and the values in the Info palette*

The second example shows no kerning (0 = 0+0 /1000) and no tracking, either. The third example shows expanded kerning between the two characters. The value 50 = 0+50 /1000 em says that the characters have 50/1000 (or 1/20) em kerning and the entire word has 0/1000 em tracking (once again, no tracking value).

Kerning Characters Manually Using the Character Palette

To change the kerning value manually using the Character palette, follow these steps:

1. Activate any of the type tools.

2. Move the insertion point mouse pointer between the two characters whose kerning you want to modify.

3. To expand the kerning by typing, enter a positive value in the Kerning text box.

4. To condense the kerning by typing, enter a negative value in the Kerning text box.

5. To choose a kerning value from the option box, click the up arrow on the right side of the box to display a higher number or click the down arrow on the right side of the box to display a lower number. After the Kerning option box/text box/drop-down menu is active, you can press ↑ or ↓ to expand or condense the kerning by a greater amount.

6. To select a kerning value from the menu, open the drop-down menu and choose a value, ranging from –100 to 200. (If you select Auto, Illustrator uses automatic kerning, the kerning value that is designed into the font, for the two selected characters.)

7. If you need to apply the new kerning value to the selected characters, press ENTER/RETURN or TAB. (If Illustrator has already changed the spacing between the two characters, you don't need to press the shortcut key.)

Kerning Characters Automatically with the Character Palette

Quite often, font designers build kerning between particular characters when they design a particular font. When you select Auto from the Kerning drop-down menu, you accept a font's built-in kerning information. For example, if you look at the top example in Figure 12-4, you'll see that the kerning between each pair of characters varies: The space between G and O at the beginning of the example is much less than that of A and Y at the other end. In contrast, the kerning between A and W and W and A is somewhat condensed.

You can apply automatic kerning to pairs of characters or all the characters in a document: Use the preceding steps to apply automatic kerning to two characters, and use the following steps to use automatic kerning for the entire document.

To employ automatic kerning for all the type in a document, follow these steps:

1. Choose Select | All (CTRL-A/⌘-A).

2. In the Character palette, either select Auto from the Kerning drop-down menu or type **Auto** in the Kerning text box.

To turn off automatic kerning, either select 0 from the Kerning drop-down menu or type **0** in the Kerning text box.

Tracking Type

Tracking and kerning behave in much the same way. The main difference is that kerning adjusts the spacing between two characters, and tracking adjusts the spacing between characters in a selected block of type. Another difference is the selection process: When you kern two characters, you move the insertion point mouse pointer between the characters. However, when you track you select a block of type. Like kerning, a positive tracking value expands spaces between characters and a negative tracking value condenses spacing. Also like kerning, tracking is measured in 1/1000 of em spaces.

To adjust the tracking for a block of type using the Character palette, follow these steps:

1. Activate one of the type tools.

2. Drag to select a block of type to be tracked.

3. To expand the tracking by typing, enter a positive value in the Tracking text box.

4. To condense the tracking by typing, enter a negative value in the Tracking text box.

5. To choose a tracking value from the option box, click the up arrow on the right side of the box to display a higher number or click the down arrow on the right side of the box to display a lower number. After the Tracking option box/text box/drop-down menu is active, you can press ↑ or ↓ to expand or condense the tracking slightly or press ALT-SHIFT-↑/OPTION-SHIFT-↑ or ALT-SHIFT-↓/OPTION-SHIFT-↓ to expand or condense the tracking by a greater amount.

6. To select a tracking value from the menu, open the drop-down menu and choose a value, ranging from –100 to 200.

7. If you need to apply the new tracking value to the selected characters, press ENTER/RETURN or TAB. (If Illustrator has already changed the tracking, you don't need to press the shortcut key.)

Figure 12-6 illustrates the difference between no tracking (the top example)—or at least the default tracking designed into the Arial Black font—and tracking set to –100 (the bottom example).

PLEASE GO AWAY RIGHT NOW!

PLEASE GO AWAY RIGHT NOW!

Figure 12-6. *Examples of large type before and after tracking*

Shifting from the Baseline

Illustrator enables you to move type above or below the baseline. Rather than calling this action "superscripting" or "subscripting," Illustrator chooses to name this baseline "shift." Shifting from the baseline is very useful in adjusting type you want in a particular place in an artwork. For example, you can place the numbers around a circular path for a clock design on, above, or below the path—just as you wish. So not only can you adjust a line of type at a specific location on a path (see "Moving Type on a Path" in Chapter 11), you can also move the line of type over or under the path, too.

A positive baseline shift value increases the distance of type above the baseline, and a negative value increases the distance of type below the baseline.

To shift type from the baseline using the Character palette, follow these steps:

1. Select the target type path with the Selection tool (V) or the Direct Selection tool (A), or select a target block of type using any of the type tools.

2. If you cannot see the Baseline Shift option box/text box/drop-down menu, either choose Show Options from the palette's menu or click the Autoresize button until the option is a visible part of the palette.

3. To move the selected type above the baseline, enter a positive value in the Baseline Shift text box. Valid values range from –1,296 to 1,296.

4. To move the selected type below the baseline, enter a negative value in the Baseline Shift text box.

5. To choose a baseline shift value from the option box, click the up arrow on the right side of the box to display a higher number or click the down arrow on the right side of the box to display a lower number. After the Baseline Shift option box/text box/drop-down menu is active, you can press ↑ or ↓ to shift up or down from the baseline slightly or press ALT-SHIFT-↑/OPTION-SHIFT-↑ or ALT-SHIFT-↓/OPTION-SHIFT-↓ to shift up or down from the baseline by a greater amount.

6. To select a baseline shift value from the menu, open the drop-down menu and choose a value. Values on the menu range from –12 to 12.

7. If you need to apply the new baseline shift value to the selected type, press ENTER/RETURN. (If Illustrator has already shifted the characters from the baseline, you don't need to press the shortcut key.)

Figure 12-7 shows three samples of baseline shift. From top to bottom, the type on top of the circular path is on the path (its original state), above the path, and below the type. All examples are selected so that you can see the path.

Scaling Type Horizontally and Vertically

Horizontal and vertical scaling control the width and height of type, respectively, using a percentage. The default horizontal and vertical scaling is 100%. You can scale type to

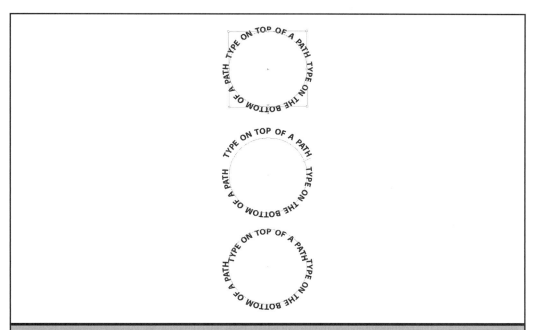

Figure 12-7. *Original type on a path, shifted above the path, and moved below the path*

fit it onto one line or into a type container whose dimensions you want to maintain. When you scale type, the leading, tracking, and baseline shift are also changed. The indention of a paragraph containing the scaled type also might be affected.

To scale type horizontally or vertically, follow these steps:

1. Select the target type path with the Selection tool (V) or the Direct Selection tool (A), or select a target block of type using any of the type tools.

2. If you cannot see the Horizontal option box/text box/drop-down menu or the Vertical option box/text box/drop-down menu, either choose Show Options from the palette's menu or click the Autoresize button until the option is a visible part of the palette.

3. To horizontally or vertically scale the selected type, enter a percentage in the Horizontal Scale text box or the Vertical Scale text box, respectively. Valid values range from 1% to 10,000%.

4. To choose a horizontal scale or vertical scale value from the option box, click the up arrow on the right side of the box to display a higher percentage or click the down arrow on the right side of the box to display a lower percentage. After an option box/text box/drop-down menu is active, you can press ↑ or ↓

to increase or decrease the scaling slightly, or press ALT-SHIFT-↑/OPTION-SHIFT-↑ or ALT-SHIFT-↓/OPTION-SHIFT-↓ to increase or decrease scaling by a greater amount.

5. To select a scaling value from the menu, open the drop-down menu and choose a value. Values on each of the menus range from 25% to 200%.

6. If you need to apply the new scaling value to the selected type, press ENTER/ RETURN. (If Illustrator has already changed the scaling, you don't need to press the shortcut key.)

7. To return to the original horizontal or vertical scaling, enter or select 100% in each of the option boxes/text boxes/drop-down menus.

Figure 12-8 demonstrates horizontal and vertical scaling. The example in the top- left corner shows the original type horizontally and vertically scaled at 100%. The example below that illustrates horizontal scaling at 130%, much larger than you usually would scale selected type. In the upper-right corner is a sample of 130% vertical scaling. The example in the lower-right corner shows an increase in scaling to 130% horizontally and vertically.

Selecting an Appropriate Font

One method of emphasizing a certain section of type is to change its font. You'll do this for headings, headlines, notes, tables of contents, and so on. For example, most headings, which are meant to draw your attention, are shown in a large, bold, sans serif font, and body text, which can go on for pages and should be easy to read, is usually formatted in a smaller serif font. You should limit the number of fonts per page to two. Otherwise, your document will begin to look like a ransom note.

Selecting an Appropriate Font

One method of emphasizing a certain section of type is to change its font. You'll do this for headings, headlines, notes, tables of contents, and so on. For example, most headings, which are meant to draw your attention, are shown in a large, bold, sans serif font, and body text, which can go on for pages and should be easy to read, is usually formatted in a smaller serif font. You should limit the number of fonts per page to two. Otherwise, your document will begin to look like a ransom note.

Selecting an Appropriate Font

One method of emphasizing a certain section of type is to change its font. You'll do this for headings, headlines, notes, tables of contents, and so on. For example, most headings, which are meant to draw your attention, are shown in a large, bold, sans serif font, and body text, which can go on for pages and should be easy to read, is usually formatted in a smaller serif font. You should limit the number of fonts per page to two. Otherwise, your document will begin to look like a ransom note.

Selecting an Appropriate Font

One method of emphasizing a certain section of type is to change its font. You'll do this for headings, headlines, notes, tables of contents, and so on. For example, most headings, which are meant to draw your attention, are shown in a large, bold, sans serif font, and body text, which can go on for pages and should be easy to read, is usually formatted in a smaller serif font. You should limit the number of fonts per page to two. Otherwise, your document will begin to look like a ransom note.

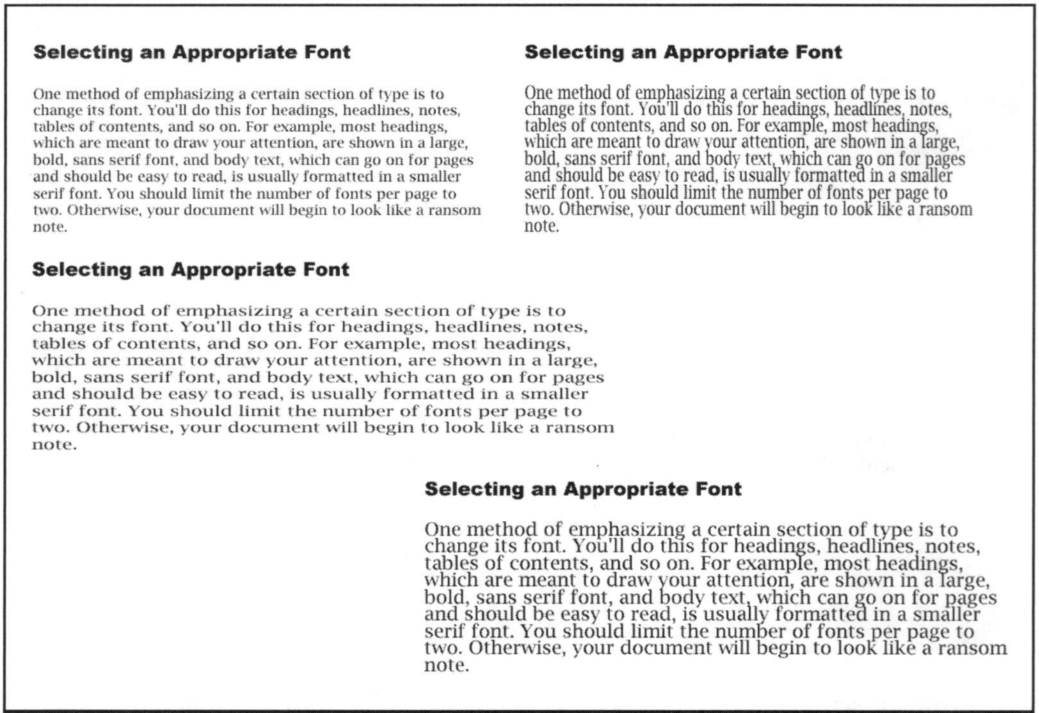

Figure 12-8.   *Four samples of horizontal and vertical scaling—the original 100% scaling (in the top left), increased horizontal scaling (below that), higher vertical scaling (in the top right), and expanded horizontal and vertical scaling (at the bottom right)*

Adjusting Leading

Fonts always have a certain amount of *leading,* which is the vertical spacing between baselines, built into their designs. Otherwise, lines of type would be scrunched onto the page with little or no white space between the lines or, in contrast, would appear to be floating on the page as individual lines rather than blocks of related type. The general proportion of leading to point size in most fonts is 120%; that is, if a point size is 10, the leading would be 12 points. That leaves two points of space between the tops of ascenders and the baseline immediately above.

Illustrator enables you to adjust leading using the Character palette or the Paragraph palette (see "Exploring the Paragraph Palette" later in this chapter). To learn how to adjust the amount of space between paragraphs, refer to "Spacing Before Paragraphs" later in this chapter.

To change the leading using the Character palette, follow these steps:

1. Select the target type path with the Selection tool (V) or the Direct Selection tool (A), or select a target block of type using any of the type tools.

2. To set the leading for the selected type, enter a value in the Leading text box.

3. To choose a leading value from the Leading option box, click the up arrow on the right side of the box to display a higher percentage or click the down arrow on the right side of the box to display a lower percentage. After an option box/text box/drop-down menu is active, you can press ↑ or ↓ to increase or decrease the leading slightly or press ALT-SHIFT-↑/OPTION-SHIFT-↑ to increase or decrease the leading by a greater amount.

4. To select a leading value from the Leading menu, open the drop-down menu and choose a value, between 6 and 72 for most fonts.

5. To select automatic leading (that is, 120% of the selection's point size) from the Leading menu, choose Auto.

6. To make the leading equal to the point size, double-click the leading icon, which precedes the Leading option box/text box/drop-down menu.

7. To reset leading to its default value, press CTRL/⌘ and click the leading icon.

8. If you need to apply the new leading value to the selected type, press ENTER/ RETURN. (If Illustrator has already changed the leading, you don't need to press the shortcut key.)

Fitting a Headline

You can use the Fit Headline command to fit type between the left and right margins of a type rectangle or type area. If the selected type uses a Multiple Master font, Illustrator adjusts both the boldness and tracking; for any other kind of font, Illustrator just changes the tracking.

To fit selected type, follow these steps:

1. Select type within a type container using a type tool.
2. Choose Type | Fit Headline.

Using Fit Headline for most fonts is similar to clicking the Justify All Lines button in the Paragraph palette. Refer to "Aligning and Justifying Paragraphs" later in this chapter to learn how to justify selected type.

Changing the Orientation of Type

In Chapter 11 you created horizontally and vertically aligned type of all sorts. If you decide to change all the type in a type area from horizontally aligned to vertically aligned or from vertically aligned to horizontally aligned, Illustrator has a command for you: Type Orientation.

To change the orientation of type in a type area, follow these steps:

1. Activate the Selection tool (V) or the Direct Selection tool (A).
2. Click the area whose type will be changed.
3. Choose Type | Type Orientation. Choose Horizontal to change the orientation of all the type to horizontally aligned. Choose Vertical to change the orientation of the type to vertically aligned. (If the type is already oriented in the chosen alignment, Illustrator ignores the command.)

Changing the Direction of Type

Using the Direction drop-down menu in the Character palette, you can change the direction in which vertical type runs. The difference between orientation and direction is that the Type Orientation command affects the horizontally aligned or vertically aligned type in a type area, but the options in the Direction menu control individual vertically aligned characters.

To change the direction of vertically aligned type, follow these steps:

1. With any type tool, select one or more characters.
2. If you cannot see the Multilingual Options section in the Character palette, either choose Show Multilingual from the palette's menu or click the Autoresize button until the section is a visible part of the palette.
3. To run the selected characters in the same way the page is oriented, select Standard from the Direction drop-down menu.
4. To rotate the selected characters 90° from their present orientations, select Rotate from the Direction menu. This option works only on Roman fonts and one-byte characters.
5. To rotate the selected characters opposite to the orientation of unselected characters, select Tate Chu Yoko from the menu.

Figure 12-9 shows a sample of vertically oriented type in different typefaces. Some characters have been rotated using the Rotate option.

Figure 12-9. *Some standard and some rotated characters*

Using the Eyedropper and Paint Bucket on Type

In Chapter 8 (see the "Using the Eyedropper and the Paint Bucket Tools" section), you learned how to use the Eyedropper tool (I) to "grab" many types of styling information, including color, and then used the Paint Bucket tool (K) to place the information on a selected object. You can also use the Eyedropper to obtain particular type characteristics, namely character, fill, stroke, and optionally paragraph attributes from a type selection—depending on the amount of type you have selected.

The type that contains the attributes can be in another Illustrator document or can be locked in the current document. You have to select at least one paragraph to get paragraph attributes. Then, you can use the Eyedropper or the Paint Bucket to apply those attributes to other type.

Remember you can use the Paintbucket/Eyedropper dialog box to choose attributes to be sampled and applied. Refer to "Setting Eyedropper and Paint Bucket Preferences" in Chapter 8 to refresh your memory on how to use the Paintbucket/Eyedropper dialog box.

Applying Attributes with the Eyedropper

To apply attributes to selected type using the Eyedropper, follow these steps:

1. Select the type path to be changed by the Eyedropper using the Selection tool (V) or the Direct Selection tool (A), or select one or more characters, words, blocks of text, or paragraphs using any of the type tools.

2. Activate the Eyedropper tool (I). Because you are using the Eyedropper on type, Illustrator adds a small *T* to the Eyedropper mouse pointer.

3. Click the type that contains the attributes to be applied. Illustrator changes the attributes of the selected type to match the source of those attributes. If you have grabbed attributes from a paragraph and are applying those to another paragraph, Illustrator employs character, paragraph, fill, and stroke attributes. If the selection is less than a paragraph, Illustrator applies character, fill, and stroke attributes. In either case, the target type remains selected in case you want to change its attributes again.

■ If you click the Eyedropper while pressing and holding down SHIFT, Illustrator picks up the color only from the object and applies those characteristics to selected objects. If clicking the Eyedropper doesn't gather information from a section of a particular object, try SHIFT-clicking to obtain the color from that section.

■ To toggle between the Eyedropper and the Paint Bucket, whichever is currently active, press ALT/OPTION.

Pasting Type Attributes with the Paint Bucket

Although you can copy and paste attributes onto selected type using the Eyedropper (I) by itself, you can use the Paint Bucket (K) to apply the contents of the Eyedropper; that is, the current fill and stroke, font, point size, and other characteristics set by using the Character palette and Type menu to all the type at a particular point in the illustration window or within a type container. If the target type is one or more paragraphs, the attributes in the Paragraph palette apply, too. So, you can customize the fill and stroke and other type characteristics and then apply those custom attributes by clicking the Paint Bucket.

Figure 12-10 illustrates changes made using the Eyedropper and the Paint Bucket. The first line shows the original type from which the Eyedropper grabs attributes, and the second line shows those results. The third line demonstrates the Paint Bucket in action; the entire line takes on the current fill, stroke, character attributes, and paragraph settings.

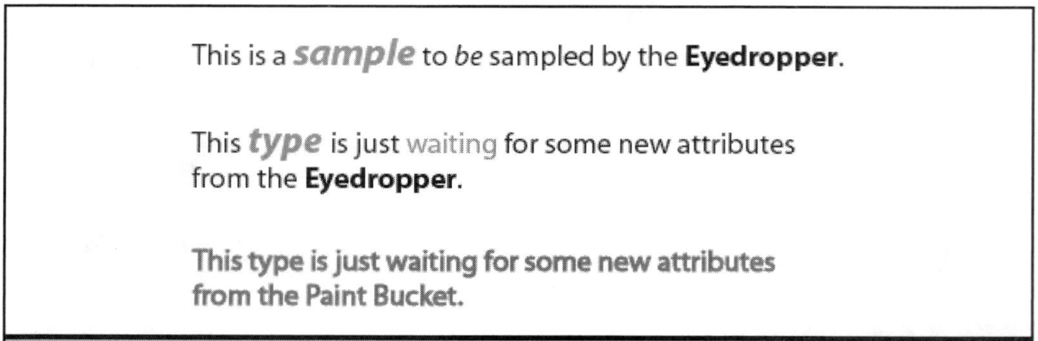

This is a *sample* to *be* sampled by the **Eyedropper**.

This *type* is just waiting for some new attributes from the **Eyedropper**.

This type is just waiting for some new attributes from the Paint Bucket.

Figure 12-10.   *A demonstration of the Eyedropper and Paint Bucket at work*

Tabbing Type

Illustrator's Tab Ruler palette is almost like any word processor's ruler: You can use the preset tabs set at regular intervals along the ruler, or you can set a variety of horizontally and vertically aligned tabs using the current unit of measure. With the Tab Ruler you can create as many as 15 tab stops that represent the locations with which type will align when you press TAB. For horizontally aligned type, you can set tab stops that work as follows:

■ With left-aligned tabs, the first character in a type string aligns with the tab stop and the remaining characters flow toward the right margin.

■ With right-aligned tabs, the first character in a type string aligns with the tab stop and the remaining characters flow toward the left margin.

■ With decimal-aligned tabs, any decimal point is aligned with the tab stop. Numbers to the left of the decimal point flow toward the left margin, and numbers to the right of the decimal point flow toward the right margin.

For vertically aligned type, you can set tab stops that work as follows:

■ With top-aligned tabs, the first character in a type string aligns with the tab stop and the remaining characters flow toward the bottom margin.

■ With bottom-aligned tabs, the first character in a type string aligns with the tab stop and the remaining characters flow toward the top margin.

For both horizontally and vertically aligned tabs, center-aligned tabs center type on the tab stop. The remaining characters flow equally toward the left and right margins or toward the top or left margin.

Exploring the Tab Ruler Palette

The single purpose of the Tab Ruler palette (see Figure 12-11), which does not resemble the typical palette, is to set or adjust user-defined tabs. To toggle between showing and hiding the Tab Ruler, choose Window | Type | Tab Ruler (CTRL-SHIFT-T/⌘-SHIFT-T).

If you open the Tab Ruler when you are creating or editing horizontal type, the Tab Ruler runs horizontally. If you display the Tab Ruler when you are producing or changing vertical type, the Tab Ruler runs vertically.

The Tab Ruler palette contains the following options, which you can use to set and adjust tabs and indentions:

■ To indent the first line of type within a type container, drag the first line indent marker to the left or right along the Tab Ruler.

■ To indent all but the first line of type within a type container, drag the remaining lines' indent markers to the left or right along the Tab Ruler.

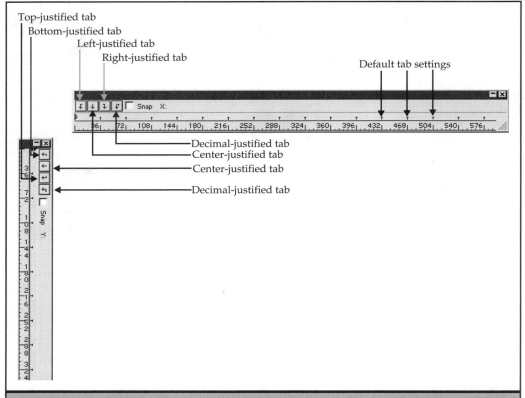

Top-justified tab
Bottom-justified tab
Left-justified tab
Right-justified tab
Default tab settings

Decimal-justified tab
Center-justified tab
Center-justified tab
Decimal-justified tab

Figure 12-11.   *With the Tab Ruler, you can set or adjust tabs for both horizontally and vertically aligned type*

- On the horizontal Tab Ruler, click the Left-Justified Tab button to align horizontally aligned type with the tab stop and flow the type to the right side of the illustration window.

- On the horizontal Tab Ruler, click the Center-Justified Tab button to center horizontally aligned type with the tab stop and flow the type to both the left and right sides of the illustration window.

- On the vertically aligned Tab, click the Center-Justified Tab button to center vertically aligned type with the tab stop and flow the type to both the top and bottom of the illustration window.

- On the horizontal Tab Ruler, click the Right-Justified Tab button to align horizontally aligned type with the tab stop and flow the type to the left side of the illustration window.

- On the horizontal Tab Ruler, click the Decimal-Justified Tab button to align horizontally aligned type with a decimal point and flow characters preceding the decimal point to the left side of the decimal point and characters following the decimal point to the right side of the decimal point.

■ On the vertical Tab Ruler, click the Decimal-Justified Tab button to align vertically aligned type with a decimal point and flow characters preceding the decimal point to the top of the decimal point and characters following the decimal point to the bottom of the decimal point.

■ Check the Snap check box to have tab stops snap to the tick marks on either version of the Tab Ruler.

■ The X: display on the horizontal ruler, or the Y: display on the vertical ruler shows the current position of the selected or dragged tab.

You can increase or decrease the size of both types of Tab Ruler palettes by dragging the lower-right corner. The Tab Ruler does not include a menu.

Setting Tabs with the Tab Ruler

By default, tabs are set every half-inch on the Tab Ruler. To set a tab on the horizontal Tab Ruler, click one of the four tabs: Left-Justified, Center-Justified, Right-Justified, or Decimal-Justified. To set a tab on the vertical Tab Ruler, click one of the four tabs: Top-Justified, Center-Justified, Bottom-Justified, or Decimal-Justified. Then click the Tab Ruler at the point at which you want the tab located. When you set a tab, Illustrator removes the default tab marks to the left of the new tab.

To set tabs with the Tab Ruler, follow these steps:

1. Select type or a type container in one of the following ways: Use the Selection tool (V) or the Direct Selection tool (A), click an insertion point within a line of type using any of the type tools, or drag across the type to select a block of type.

2. Choose Window | Type | Tab Ruler (CTRL-SHIFT-T/⌘-SHIFT-T). Illustrator opens the horizontal or vertical Tab Ruler palette, depending on whether the selected type is horizontally or vertically aligned.

3. To align the Tab Ruler with the left margin of horizontally aligned type or the top margin of vertically aligned type, click within the Tab Ruler to the right of the four tab buttons, the Snap box, and the X: display.

4. To be able to snap a tab stop to ruler ticks as you drag it to its desired location just as you would snap an object to the grid, check the Snap check box. To toggle between a checked and unchecked Snap check box, press and hold down CTRL/⌘ while you drag the tab.

5. To set a tab stop, click a tab alignment button. Then click the Tab Ruler to create a tab stop. Illustrator displays the position of the tab following the X, and removes the default tab icons preceding the new tab stop.

6. To apply a tab to the selected type, press TAB. To remove a tab setting from the selected type, press BACKSPACE/DELETE.

Adjusting a Tab Setting

To change the position of an existing user-defined tab stop, drag the tab stop icon along the Tab Ruler. As you drag, Illustrator moves a line within selected type and displays the current location of the tab in the X: area.

- If you drag toward the left (in the horizontal Tab Ruler) or toward the top (in the vertical Tab Ruler), Illustrator adds default tab stops on the right side of the drag (in the horizontal Tab Ruler) or the bottom side of the drag (in the vertical Tab Ruler).

- If you drag toward the right (in the horizontal Tab Ruler) or toward the bottom (in the vertical Tab Ruler), Illustrator removes all default tab stops on the left side of the drag (in the horizontal Tab Ruler) or the top side of the drag (in the vertical Tab Ruler).

- If you press and hold down SHIFT as you drag to the left or right, Illustrator moves all user-created tab stops along the Tab Ruler.

Realigning a Tab

To change the alignment of a particular tab stop, follow these steps:

1. Select the tab stop whose type you want to change. Illustrator highlights the tab and displays its position to the right of the X: label.

2. Click one of the four tab-type buttons on the Tab Ruler palette. Illustrator changes the look of the tab stop icon.

Removing a Tab Setting

To delete a user-defined tab stop from the Tab Ruler, drag it off the Ruler. (You cannot remove default tab stops from the Ruler.) As you drag the tab stop off the Ruler, Illustrator displays *delete* following the X: label.

Removing All Tab Settings

To simultaneously delete all user-defined tab stops from the Tab Ruler, select one tab stop, and drag it off the Ruler while pressing and holding down SHIFT. As you drag all the tab stops off the Ruler, Illustrator displays *delete* following the X: label.

Indenting with the Tab Ruler Palette

In Illustrator you can indent paragraphs in one of two ways: using the Paragraph palette and using the Tab Ruler palette. (To find out how to use the Paragraph palette to indent paragraphs, refer to "Indenting Paragraphs" later in this chapter.) The first line indent marker and remaining lines indent marker enable you to indent in three ways: hanging indents, first line indents, and block indents.

- A hanging indent shifts the first line in a paragraph less than the rest of the lines. To create a hanging indent, drag the first line left indent marker a little or no distance from the left margin. Then drag the left indent marker farther than the position of the first line indent marker. Typically, you'll use a hanging indent to format a numbered list or bulleted list.

- A first line indent shifts the first line in a paragraph farther than the rest of the lines. To create a first line indent, drag the first line left indent marker from the left margin. Then drag the left indent marker a little or no distance from the left margin.

- A block indent aligns all the lines in the paragraph the same distance from the left margin. To create a block indent, drag the first line left indent marker and the left indent marker the same distance from the left margin. In Illustrator, a block indent aligned with the left margin is the default.

Tip *The Character, Paragraph, and Tab Ruler palettes keep their settings during an Illustrator session, so if the type within a type container doesn't behave exactly the way you think it should, consider opening the Type palettes to check and possibly change their settings.*

Figure 12-12 shows examples of the three types of indention and the Tab Ruler settings for each type.

Wrapping Type Around an Object

Most full-featured word processors enable you to wrap type around graphical objects. Illustrator is no slouch in this area; the program provides a feature sometimes known as *graphical tabs*. The type to be wrapped should be in a container; that is, a closed path. If you want to use an open path, both its fill and stroke should be set to None.

Illustrator does not support type wrapping for point type or path type. To wrap type, the path should be in front of the type container. If you want to create a buffer zone between the type and the path, consider offsetting it and then making the offset invisible (that is, with its fill and stroke equal to None).

To wrap type around an object, follow these steps:

1. Create an object.

2. Within a type area, enter some type. Optionally, format the type using Character palette options. (You can do this before or after you wrap.)

3. With the Selection tool (V) or the Direct Selection tool (A), select the closed path and move it in front of the type container by choosing Object | Arrange | Bring to Front (CTRL-SHIFT-]/⌘-SHIFT-]).

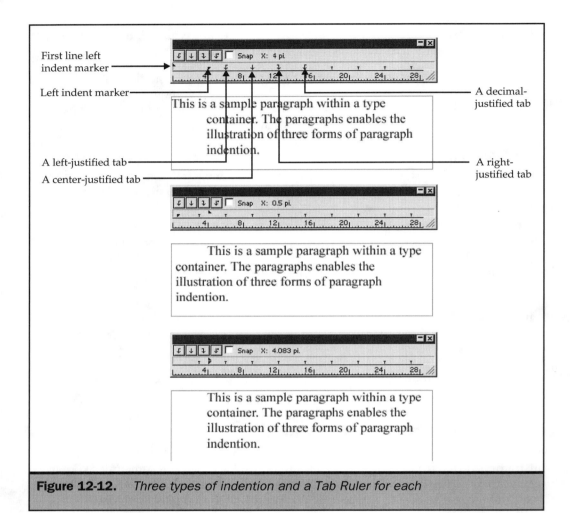

First line left
indent marker

Left indent marker

A left-justified tab

A center-justified tab

A decimal-
justified tab

A right-
justified tab

Figure 12-12. *Three types of indention and a Tab Ruler for each*

4. To create a buffer between the path and the type, select the path again, if it is no longer selected. Then choose Object | Path | Offset Path. In the Offset text box in the Offset Path dialog box, type a value such as 10 pt. Then click OK.

5. Select the path and the type container, and choose Type | Wrap | Make. Illustrator wraps the type around the path.

You can then change both type and object attributes to make the artwork more attractive. You also can drag the object around the type container to wrap the type in a more pleasing way. Figure 12-13 illustrates the process of wrapping type and modifying the end result.

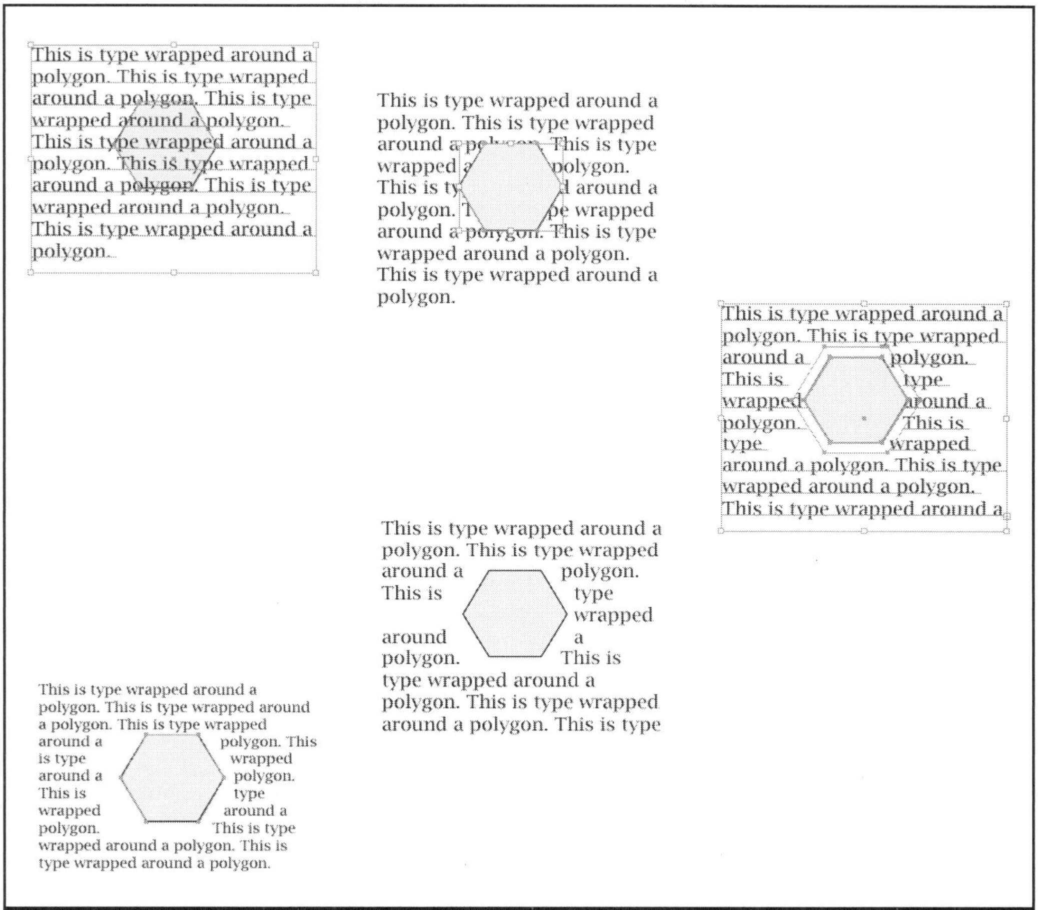

This is type wrapped around a polygon. This is type wrapped around a polygon. This is type wrapped around a polygon. This is type wrapped around a polygon. This is type wrapped around a polygon. This is type wrapped around a polygon. This is type wrapped around a polygon. This is type wrapped around a polygon.

This is type wrapped around a polygon. This is type wrapped around a polygon. This is type wrapped around a polygon. This is type wrapped around a polygon. This is type wrapped around a polygon. This is type wrapped around a polygon. This is type wrapped around a polygon.

This is type wrapped around a polygon. This is type wrapped around a polygon. This is type wrapped around a polygon. This is type wrapped around a polygon. This is type wrapped around a polygon. This is type wrapped around a polygon. This is type wrapped around a

This is type wrapped around a polygon. This is type wrapped around a polygon. This is type wrapped around a polygon. This is type wrapped around a polygon. This is type wrapped around a polygon. This is type wrapped around a polygon. This is type

This is type wrapped around a polygon. This is type wrapped around a polygon. This is type wrapped around a polygon. This is type wrapped around a polygon. This is type wrapped around a polygon. This is type wrapped around a polygon. This is type wrapped around a polygon.

Figure 12-13. *From the top to bottom, the steps toward wrapping type and enhancing its look*

To unwrap type, activate the Selection tool (V), click to select the type container and the object, and choose Type | Wrap | Release.

Linking Blocks of Type

You can use the Link command to cause type within a type area to flow from one type container to another or place type that has overflowed its original container in a different one. Illustrator uses the order in which the type containers were created to "flow" the type, but you can use the Object | Arrange commands to rearrange the order before or after you use the Link command.

Illustrator provides the Unlink command to unlink the linked type containers so that you can rearrange type containers and relink them. When you unlink linked containers, the type remains in the latest container in which it was placed. The only way to return type to its original container is to copy or cut and paste.

All linked type containers become one group, so when you use the Selection tool (V), all linked containers are selected simultaneously. To select an individual container in the group, activate the Direct Selection tool (A) instead.

 If you want to view the type containers and the enclosed type, choose View | Outline (CTRL-Y/⌘-Y).

Linking Type from One Type Area to Another

To link type from one type container to another, follow these steps:

1. Activate the Selection tool (V).

2. Draw a marquee large enough to enclose parts of all the type containers you have created.

3. Choose Type | Blocks | Link. Illustrator runs overflow type from its original type container into the new type containers until the type is complete or it runs out of containers.

You can use the Direct Selection tool (A) to select a particular type container so that you can resize it or drag it to a new location in the illustration window. To unlink linked type containers, draw a marquee around them using the Selection tool. Then choose Type | Blocks | Unlink. The type looks unchanged; it remains in the type containers.

Deleting Linked Type Containers

To delete a linked type container, follow these steps:

1. Choose View | Outline (CTRL-Y/⌘-Y) to switch to outline view so you can see the linked type containers.

2. Activate the Group Selection tool.

3. Carefully click the edge of the type container you want to select to choose the type container only. If the type within the container is selected, deselect and try selecting again.

4. Press DELETE. Illustrator removes the type container and runs the type into the previous type container in the order of containers. In fact, that type container probably will have a small plus sign icon indicating that the type is within.

Figure 12-14 illustrates the linking of three type containers and the flow of type from the first, through the second, and concluding in the third. Note that the first group of containers and type are shown in outline view.

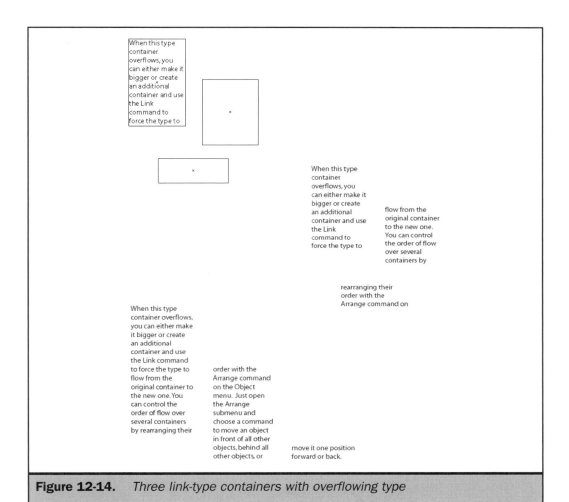

When this type
container
overflows, you
can either make it
bigger or create
an additional
container and use
the Link
command to
force the type to

When this type
container
overflows, you
can either make it
bigger or create
an additional
container and use
the Link
command to
force the type to

flow from the
original container
to the new one.
You can control
the order of flow
over several
containers by

rearranging their
order with the
Arrange command on

When this type
container overflows,
you can either make
it bigger or create
an additional
container and use
the Link command
to force the type to
flow from the
original container to
the new one. You
can control the
order of flow over
several containers
by rearranging their

order with the
Arrange command
on the Object
menu. Just open
the Arrange
submenu and
choose a command
to move an object
in front of all other
objects, behind all
other objects, or

move it one position
forward or back.

Figure 12-14.   *Three link-type containers with overflowing type*

Modifying Paragraph Attributes

Now that you have learned all there is to know about formatting characters, phrases, and words, we'll step up to a higher level: the paragraph. Illustrator enables you to format paragraphs in many ways: You can indent paragraphs and align type, in ways similar to and different from those you have already done using the Tab Ruler and other character-based features. In this section you also will find out how to adjust spacing between paragraphs and words. You'll learn about an entirely new type formatting topic: hyphenation.

Exploring the Paragraph Palette

The purpose of the Paragraph palette (see Figure 12-15) is to modify column and paragraph formats. To toggle between showing and hiding the palette, choose Window | Type | Paragraph (CTRL-M/⌘-M).

The Paragraph palette contains the following options:

■ Click the Align Left button to align paragraphs with the left margin and have ragged type at the right margin.

■ Click the Align Center button to center paragraphs between the left and right margins.

■ Click the Align Right button to align type with the right margin and have ragged type at the left margin.

■ Click the Justify Full Lines button to justify complete lines only in paragraphs between the left and right margins. Lines that do not reach all the way to the right margin are left aligned.

■ Click the Justify All Lines button to justify all the lines (full or shorter than that) in paragraphs between the left and right margins.

■ In the Left Indent option box/text box, select or type the distance between the left margin and the indention for the start of each line of each selected paragraph.

■ From the First Line Left Indent option box/text box, select or type the distance between the left margin and the indention for the first line of each selected paragraph.

■ From the Right Indent option box/text box, select or type the distance between the right margin and the indention from the end of each line of selected paragraphs.

■ From the Space Before Paragraph option box/text box, select or type the distance between the end of one paragraph and the beginning of another.

Click the Autoresize button to change the size of the palette in three ways: showing the tab only; nine options (Align Left, Align Center, Align Right, Justify Full Lines, Justify All Lines, Left Indent, First Line Left Indent, Right Indent, and Space Before Paragraph); or the prior nine options plus the Word Spacing section, the Letter Spacing section, and the Options section.

To open the palette's menu, click the menu button.

■ The Show Options command shows the complete palette with all its options and sections; the Hide Options command shows the Align Left, Align Center, Align Right, Justify Full Lines, Justify All Lines, Left Indent, First Line Left Indent, Right Indent, and Space Before Paragraph options.

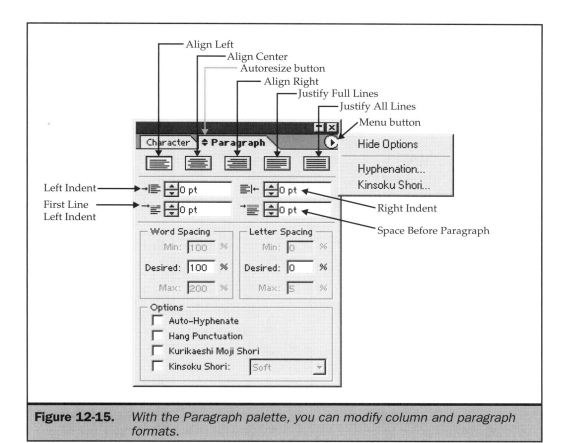

Figure 12-15. *With the Paragraph palette, you can modify column and paragraph formats.*

■ The Hyphenation command opens the Hyphenation Options dialog box with which you can set the number of letters from the beginning and the end of a word to be hyphenated and limit the number of line-ending hyphenations in a row.

■ The Kinsoku Shori command opens the Kinsoku Shori dialog box, which enables you to control link breaking for Kanji vertically aligned typefaces only.

Aligning and Justifying Paragraphs

When you read the "Fitting a Headline" and, to a lesser extent, "Indenting with the Tab Ruler Palette" sections, you got your first brief exposure to paragraph alignment. Alignment directs how paragraphs are formatted in relation to the left and right margins: aligned with the left or right margin or centered between the margins. Illustrator provides the following types of alignment:

- Left alignment aligns the lines of a paragraph along the left margin and wraps the right side of each line in a ragged way.

- Center alignment centers the lines of a paragraph between the left and right margins.

- Right alignment aligns the lines of a paragraph along the right margin and wraps the left side of each line in a ragged way.

- Full-Lines justification aligns all the complete lines of a paragraph along both the left and right margins, leaving spaces between individual words in each line. Last lines that do not reach all the way to the right margin are left aligned with ragged right sides.

- All-Lines justification aligns every line of a paragraph along both the left and right margins. Last lines, however short they are, are forced to be justified, too.

To set alignment using the Paragraph palette, follow these steps:

1. Select type or a type container using the Selection tool (V) or the Direct Selection tool (A), or click an insertion point in a paragraph using any of the type tools.

2. Click one of the five buttons along the top of the palette. Illustrator sets alignment for any paragraph within the selection.

3. To control whether single instances or double instances of punctuation symbols (that is, periods, commas, colons, semicolons, apostrophes, hyphens, single quotes, quotation marks, em dashes, or en dashes) falling at the ends of lines as paragraphs are aligned, use the Hang Punctuation check box. Check the check box to place punctuation symbols outside the margins; clear the check box to keep punctuation symbols within the margins. This option always applies to 1-byte type (type that is 1 byte long) and affects 2-byte type only if there is room at the end of the line.

Indenting Paragraphs

In "Indenting with the Tab Ruler Palette," earlier in the chapter, you found out how to create three forms of indention: hanging indents, first line indents, and block indents. These normally apply to short paragraphs such as bulleted and numbered lists. When you use the Tab Ruler palette to set indention, you don't have the opportunity to indent from the right margin. When you use the Paragraph palette, you can create hanging indents, first line indents, and block indents using both the left and right margins. You can enter or select positive or negative values.

To indent one or more selected paragraphs, follow these steps:

1. Select type or a type container using the Selection tool (V) or the Direct Selection tool (A), or click an insertion point in a paragraph using any of the type tools.

2. To indent all selected paragraphs from the left margin, enter a value in the Left Indent text box, click ↑ to display a higher level of indention, or click ↓ to display a lower level of indention.

3. To indent all selected first lines only from the left margin, enter a value in the First Line Left Indent text box, click ↑ to display a higher level of indention, or click ↓ to display a lower level of indention.

   ■ To create a hanging indent, the value in the Left Indent text box must be greater than the value in the First Line Left Indent text box.

   ■ To create a first line indent, the value in the First Line Left Indent text box must be greater than the value in the Left Indent text box.

   ■ To create a block indent, the values in the Left Indent text box and the First Line Left Indent text box must be identical.

4. To indent all selected paragraphs from the right margin, enter a value in the Right Indent text box, click ↑ to display a higher level of indention, or click ↓ to display a lower level of indention.

5. If you need to apply the new indention to the selected paragraph, press ENTER/RETURN or TAB. (If Illustrator has already applied the changes, you don't need to press the shortcut key.)

Once an indention option box/text box is active, you also can press ↑ (one point at a time) or ALT-SHIFT-↑/OPTION-SHIFT-↑ (six points at a time) repeatedly to scroll through higher values or press ↓ (one point at a time) or ALT-SHIFT-↓/OPTION-SHIFT-↓ (six points at a time) repeatedly to scroll through lower values.

Spacing Before Paragraphs

In the "Adjusting Leading" section, earlier in this chapter, you learned how to apply leading between selected lines. In this section you'll find out how to increase or decrease the space above selected paragraphs for area type only. Although Illustrator allows you to enter or select negative values, you won't want to do this often: Paragraphs overlap each other when you use negative values.

To set the amount of space before paragraphs, follow these steps:

1. Select all the paragraphs in an area using the Selection tool (V), select one paragraph by clicking within it using any type tool, or drag to select one or more paragraphs using any of the type tools.

2. To insert space before all selected paragraphs, enter a value in the Space Before Paragraph text box, click ↑ to display a higher level of indention, or click ↓ to display a lower level of indention. Once the option box/text box is active, you also can press ↑ (one point at a time) or ALT-SHIFT-↑/OPTION-SHIFT-↑ (six points at a time) repeatedly to scroll through higher values or press ↓ (one point at a time) or ALT-SHIFT-↓/OPTION-SHIFT-↓ (six points at a time) repeatedly to scroll through lower values.

3. If you need to apply the new indention to the selected paragraph, press ENTER/RETURN or TAB. (If Illustrator has already applied the changes, you don't need to press the shortcut key.)

Adjusting Space Between Words and Letters

When you justify paragraphs, you can fine-tune spacing between words and even some letters using options in the Paragraph palette. In fact, you can even adjust spacing for left-aligned, centered, and right-aligned paragraphs. Use the Word Spacing options to increase or decrease spacing between all the words in a selected paragraph and the Letter Spacing options to change spacing between letters in a selected paragraph. Remember you can adjust individual characters by kerning them (see "Kerning Characters" earlier in this chapter), and you can adjust words using tracking (see "Tracking Type" earlier in this chapter). Illustrator bases word spacing and letter spacing measurements on the width of a space in the current point size.

Changing Word Spacing in Paragraphs

To change word spacing in paragraphs, follow these steps:

1. Select all the paragraphs in an area using the Selection tool (V), select one paragraph by clicking within it using any type tool, or drag to select one or more paragraphs using any of the type tools.

2. If you cannot see the Word Spacing section, either choose Show Options from the palette's menu or click the Autoresize button until the option is a visible part of the palette. If the selected paragraph is justified, all three options in the Word Spacing section are available. If the paragraph is merely aligned, only the Desired text box is available.

3. To set minimum spacing between words, type a percentage value in the Min text box. Valid values range from 0 to 1,000; the default value is 100% (or no space added). The value that you enter should be equal to or less than the value in the Desired text box.

4. To set the desired spacing between words, type a percentage value in the Desired text box. Valid values range from 0 to 1,000; the default value is 100%.

5. To set maximum spacing between words, type a percentage value in the Max text box. Valid values range from 0 to 1,000; the default value is 200%. The value you enter should be equal to or greater than the value in the Desired text box.

6. If you need to apply the new word-spacing values to the selected paragraph, press ENTER/RETURN or TAB. (If Illustrator has already applied the changes, you don't need to press the shortcut key.)

Changing Letter Spacing in Paragraphs

To change letter spacing in paragraphs, follow these steps:

1. Select all the paragraphs in an area using the Selection tool (V), select one paragraph by clicking within it using any type tool, or drag to select one or more paragraphs using any of the type tools.

2. If you cannot see the Letter Spacing section, either choose Show Options from the palette's menu or click the Autoresize button until the option is a visible part of the palette. If the selected paragraph is justified, all three options in the Letter Spacing section are available. If the paragraph is merely aligned, only the Desired text box is available.

3. To set minimum spacing between letters, type a percentage value in the Min text box. Valid values range from –50 to 500; the default value is 0% (or no space added). The value you enter should be equal to or less than the value in the Desired text box.

4. To set the desired spacing between letters, type a percentage value in the Desired text box. Valid values range from –50 to 500; the default value is 0%.

5. To set maximum spacing between letters, type a percentage value in the Max text box. Valid values range from –50 to 500%; the default value is 5%. The value you enter should be equal to or greater than the value in the Desired text box.

6. If you need to apply the new word spacing values to the selected paragraph, press ENTER/RETURN or TAB. (If Illustrator has already applied the changes, you don't need to press the shortcut key.)

Using Hyphenation

You can have Illustrator automatically hyphenate words at the end of lines in the current document by merely checking the Auto-Hyphenate check box near the bottom of the Paragraph palette. You can either accept all Illustrator's hyphenation choices or select your own options. To set hyphenation options, use the Hyphenation Options dialog box, which is available from the Paragraph palette's menu. Once you set hyphenation for a document, it remains until you turn it off during the current or a future Illustrator session.

ILLUSTRATOR ESSENTIALS

Turning on Auto Hyphenation

To turn on the Auto-Hyphenate feature for the current document, open the Paragraph palette and check the Auto-Hyphenate box. If the Paragraph palette is not at its largest size, the Auto-Hyphenate check box is not part of the palette. To expand the palette, choose Show Options or click the Autoresize button once or twice.

Inserting a Hyphen Manually

You can enter hyphens manually to break words. Illustrator always honors user-entered hyphens (regardless of whether you have added the hyphen at a correct break point). In Illustrator circles, a manual hyphen is known as a *discretionary hyphen.* If you enter a hyphen by pressing -, that hyphen remains in the word regardless of its position on the line. For example, if you have added or deleted words to change the location of the word at the end of the line, the hyphen stays where you inserted it. In contrast, when you insert a discretionary hyphen, Illustrator removes the hyphen when the position of the word changes in the document.

To enter a discretionary hyphen, follow these steps:

1. Activate any type tool.
2. Click at the point at which you want to insert the hyphen.
3. Press CTRL-SHIFT--/⌘-SHIFT--.

Setting Hyphenation Options

You can set hyphenation options, regardless of whether you have activated automatic hyphenation. To select auto-hyphenate options, follow these steps:

1. Open the Paragraph palette menu and choose Hyphenation. Illustrator opens the Hyphenation Options dialog box (see Figure 12-16).
2. To limit the position of hyphens at the beginning of a word, type the number of letters with which each word must start before hyphenation is allowed in the Hyphenate Letters from Beginning text box. The default is 2.
3. To limit the position of hyphens at the end of a word, type the number of letters with which each word must end and which must not include any hyphen in the Hyphenate Letters from End text box. The default is 2.
4. To limit the number of consecutive lines ending in a hyphen, type a number in the Limit Consecutive Hyphens to text box. The default is 3.
5. Click OK to apply the options and close the dialog box.

 You also can set hyphenation preferences by choosing Edit | Preferences | Hyphenation for Windows computers or Illustrator | Preferences | Hyphenation for Macintosh computers. For more information, refer to Appendix B.

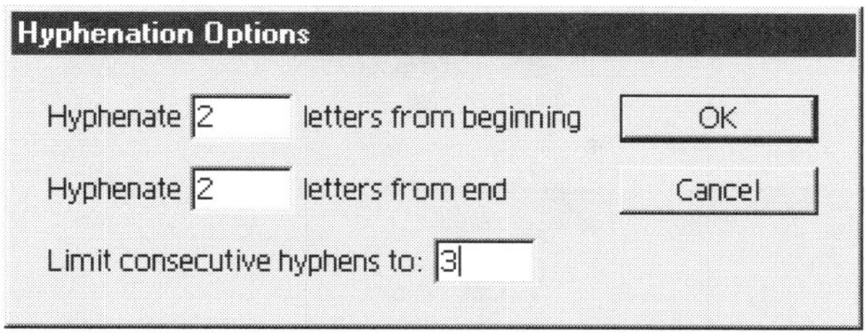

Figure 12-16. *The Hyphenation Options dialog box with its default settings*

Converting Type to a Graphical Object

When you work with type, you are somewhat limited in how you can modify it. For example, you can use the Character, Paragraph, and Tab Ruler palettes to format and enhance type—to a certain extent—but you can't apply some of the color and other enhancements you have explored in the chapters before Chapters 11 and 12.

So, Illustrator enables you to convert most forms of type (including Type 1 PostScript fonts and TrueType fonts, but not including bitmapped fonts and Type 3 PostScript fonts) to graphical objects (known as *editable paths* or *outlines* in Illustrator-speak). Illustrator converts point type, type within containers, and type on paths to editable paths. Once you have converted type to an editable path, you can fill it with color, patterns, or gradients and you can apply all sorts of effects and filters (see Chapter 16 for more information).

Converting type to editable paths is a very popular procedure in Illustrator. In fact, if you inventoried all the advertisements and marketing and sales materials you get in the mail or see in newspapers and periodicals, you'd probably find that most chunks of type in illustrations are actually editable paths.

To convert type to an object, follow these steps:

1. Activate any of the selection tools.

2. Select the type to be converted.

3. Choose Type | Create Outlines (CTRL-SHIFT-O/⌘-SHIFT-O). Illustrator changes the type to one or more compound paths with anchor points. As you have learned, compound paths are composed of two or more paths that intersect at some locations. Where compound paths overlap, Illustrator creates a transparent hole. So, in the case of converted type, you can see behind the holes in the body of letters such as *a, b, d, p,* and so on.

Figure 12-17 illustrates type as unconverted type (on the top) and as individual objects (on the bottom).

FANCY TYPE

FANCY TYPE

Figure 12-17.   *Before and after examples of type and editable paths*

 Note   *The only way to convert an editable path to type is to choose Edit | Undo (CTRL-Z/⌘-Z) immediately after you have changed it from type to an editable path.*

Enhancing an Editable Path

Once you have converted type to an editable path, you can go all out to decorate it. For example, you can change its fill color, its stroke color, or both; you also can apply a gradient or a pattern. In addition, you can distort the editable path with any number of Illustrator tools—those on the Transform toolslot, the Free Transform tool, and the Gradient tool, as well as features and tools that will be covered in future chapters. About the only thing you can't do is return the editable path to type so that you can put it on a curving path or change its font, point size, and other type attributes. Figure 12-18 shows our sample editable path with a variety of looks.

Following are some tips:

- To transform an entire line, activate the Selection tool (V) and click to select.

- To transform one character (that is, one path), activate the Direct Selection tool (A) and click to select.

- Most editable paths contain many anchor points. When you use the Direct Selection tool to distort a character, you might have to be more delicate than usual in selecting and dragging single points. Consider zooming in to get a clear view of a path.

- The Selection tool enables you to rotate, move, and size an entire line or a single character. To work on one character, select one character with the Direct Selection tool. Then click the Selection tool to modify the selected character.

- To place type on a circle, use the combination of the Direct Selection tool and the Selection tool to arrange each character in order. First, draw a circle and give it a stroke weight of about 2 points. Then place the characters around, making sure the bottom of each character conforms as closely as possible to the circle. When you have completed your work, select and delete the circle.

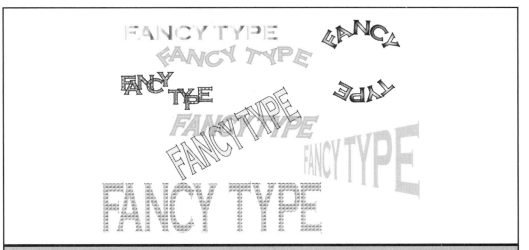

Figure 12-18.   *Several examples of editable path transformations*

Uniting Characters in an Editable Path

Up to now, you have modified one or more individual characters at a time. If you make a set of characters into a single entity, you can change the path in different ways. For example, rather than applying a gradient to individual characters, you can spread the gradient across the entire group. To unite characters in an editable path, follow these steps:

1. Activate the Direct Selection tool (A).

2. Drag each character to the left so that it partly covers the preceding character.

3. Repeat step 2 until all the characters slightly overlap.

4. Choose Window | Pathfinder (SHIFT-F9). Illustrator opens the Pathfinder palette.

5. Use the Selection tool (V) to select the entire group of overlapping characters.

6. In the Pathfinder palette, click the Merge button (the third button from the left in the bottom row). Illustrator unites the selected characters into one element and fills the inside of some of the characters.

7. If necessary, drag some of the fills away from the united path and then delete them.

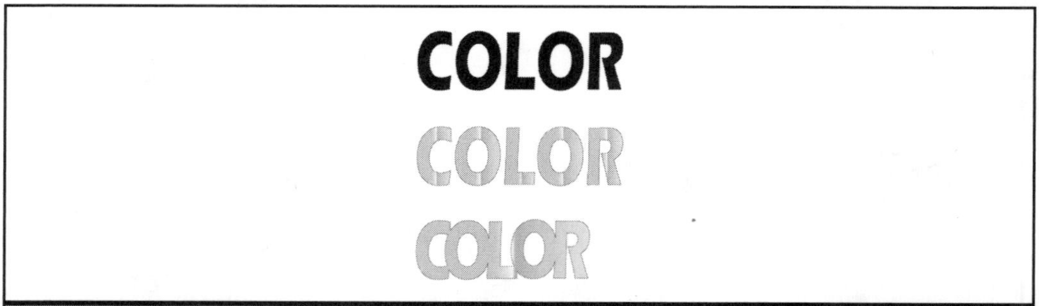

COLOR

COLOR

COLOR

Figure 12-19. *Type (at the top), a converted editable path with individual characters (in the middle), and (at the bottom) a united editable path*

Figure 12-19 illustrates the conversion of type into an editable path and then a united path. In the center of the figure is an editable path made up of individual characters. Notice that the gradient is applied to each character separately. At the bottom of the figure, however, is the united path. Now the gradient sweeps across the entire path.

Chapter 13

Painting Objects

P ainting in Illustrator is much like painting in other art programs, with one important difference: Normally when you use most painting programs, you create bitmap images; in Illustrator, you paint vector strokes. In this chapter you will learn all about painting strokes in Illustrator. First you'll get a background in Illustrator's painting features: the Paintbrush tool and the Brushes palette. You'll also learn that you don't have to use the Paintbrush to brush a path; you can use any of Illustrator's path creation tools. Next you'll discover how to use each of the four brushes. Finally, you'll find out how to create custom brushes and modify brushes in many ways.

Learning About the Paintbrush and the Brushes Palette

The Paintbrush tool (B) in the toolbox is the instrument of choice with which you apply brushstrokes to artwork, and the Brushes palette is the container from which you select particular brushes and set brush widths. If you want to change from the default 3-point round Calligraphic brush to another brush, you must select it from the Brushes palette before you can use the Paintbrush.

An Overview of Illustrator Brushes

Illustrator offers four types of brushes, each with its own behavior and attributes. You can use a brush from the Brushes palette or create one of your own. The four types of Illustrator brushes are Calligraphic, Scatter, Art, and Pattern.

- A Calligraphic brush reproduces the look of a calligraphic pen. You can use or create a completely round brush or a brush with an angle.

- A Scatter brush scatters copies of a graphical image on and near a selected path. While it is spraying images around, Illustrator transforms them in various ways, depending on the selected brush's attributes.

Note *Illustrator also enables you to place symbols around a document. Adding symbols is similar to scattering images using the Scatter brush. To learn about using the symbols feature, refer to "Using Symbols" in Chapter 18.*

- An Art brush extends a graphical image from a center point on a selected path.

- A Pattern brush repeats all or part of a graphical image, including its sides and corners, on a selected path. Note that Pattern brushes place the pattern precisely on the path; in contrast, Scatter brushes place the image near and sometimes on the path.

When you use the Paintbrush or another tool and a brush to create a brushed path, you can avail yourself of many brushstrokes designed by professionals or yourself, which enables you to be consistent among related artworks. Figure 13-1 illustrates four paths

Figure 13-1.   *Calligraphic, Scatter, Art, and Pattern*

resulting from painting with each type of brush. On the left is a path created with the 12-pt. Oval Calligraphic brush; following that is a path from the Banana-Leaf Scatter brush; the next to last path is the outcome of using the Dry Ink Art brush; and finally, the result of painting with the Polynesian Pattern brush.

Exploring the Brushes Palette

The Brushes palette (see Figure 13-2) is the Paintbrush tool's partner in art. From the palette you can view and select from the predefined brushes and, using the palette commands and buttons, you can create and modify brushes of all four types. To toggle between showing and hiding the palette, choose Window | Brushes (F5).

The Brushes palette contains a set of predefined brushes and buttons with which you can specify brush actions:

- Click the Remove Brush Stroke button to erase the selected brush stroke from its path. The counterpart command on the palette menu is Remove Brush Stroke.

- Click the Options of Selected Object button to modify the brush options of one or more selected objects without changing the options for unselected objects. The counterpart command on the palette menu is Options of Selected Object.

- Click the New Brush button and select a brush type to create a new brush. The counterpart command on the palette menu is New Brush.

- Click the Delete Brush button to delete one or more selected brushes. The counterpart command on the palette menu is Delete Brush.

To open the palette's menu, click the menu button. Commands on the menu are

- The New Brush command creates a new brush of a certain brush type. The counterpart button at the bottom of the palette is New Brush.

- The Duplicate Brush command duplicates one or more selected brushes.

- The Delete Brush command deletes one or more selected brushes The counterpart button at the bottom of the palette is Delete Brush.

ILLUSTRATOR
ESSENTIALS

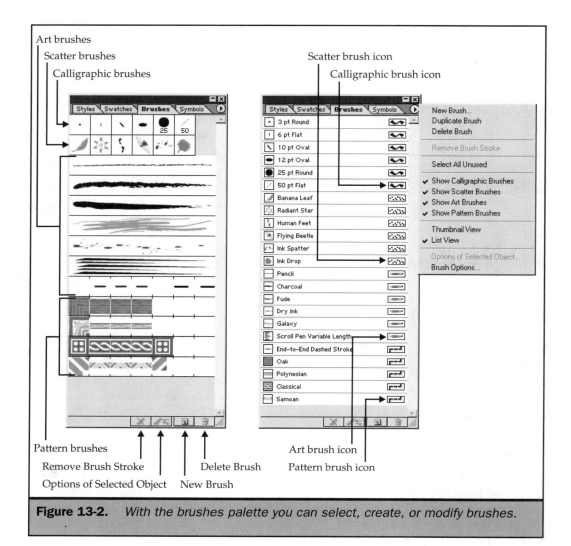

Figure 13-2. *With the brushes palette you can select, create, or modify brushes.*

- The Remove Brush Stroke command erases the selected brush stroke from its path. The counterpart button at the bottom of the palette is Remove Brush Stroke.

- The Select All Unused command selects all the brushes that you haven't used in the current document.

- The Show Calligraphic Brushes command displays or hides all the Calligraphic brushes in the palette. If a check mark precedes the command, the Calligraphic brushes are on display.

- The Show Scatter Brushes command displays or hides all the Scatter brushes in the palette. If a check mark precedes the command, the Scatter brushes are on display.

- The Show Art Brushes command displays or hides all the Art brushes in the palette. If a check mark precedes the command, the Art brushes are on display.

- The Show Pattern Brushes command displays or hides all the Pattern brushes in the palette. If a check mark precedes the command, the Pattern brushes are on display.

- The Thumbnail View command shows all brushes in the palette as a thumbnail image. If a check mark precedes the command, Thumbnail view is active and List view is inactive.

- The List View command lists the names of all brushes in the palette. Next to each entry is an icon representing the brush type. If a check mark precedes the command, List view is active and Thumbnail view is inactive.

- The Options of Selected Object command enables you to modify the brush options of one or more selected objects without changing the options for unselected objects. The counterpart button at the bottom of the palette is Options of Selected Object.

- The Brush Options command opens a dialog box for the selected brush.

If You Have Selected This Type of Brush	Illustrator Opens This
Calligraphic brush	Calligraphic Brush Options dialog box
Scatter brush	Scatter Brush Options dialog box
Art brush	Art Brush Options dialog box
Pattern brush	Pattern Brush Options dialog box

Caution *Whenever you finish using the Brushes palette, make sure that you select the default 3-pt. Round Calligraphic brush in the upper-left corner of the palette before closing the palette. If you forget this step and want to do more work during this Illustrator session, you might inadvertently apply the active brushstroke to any paths that you create or select. When you exit Illustrator, the Brushes palette automatically reverts to the 3-pt. Round Calligraphic brush.*

Brushing a Path Using Another Tool

Illustrator enables you to create a brushed path using any of the following tools: the Pen (P), Pencil (N), Line Segment (\), Arc, Spiral, Rectangular Grid, Polar Grid, Rectangle (M), Rounded Rectangle, Ellipse (L), Polygon, and Star. You can either select a brush to be applied to the path as you create it or apply the brush after creating the path.

Creating a brushed path in this way allows you to take advantage of specific tools. For example, why use the Paintbrush tool to create a star when you can use the Star tool to do so? After constructing the path, you can modify it using editing tools, palettes, and menu commands.

To create a brushed path using an Illustrator path creation tool, follow these steps:

1. Activate a path creation tool.
2. To brush the path as you draw it, choose Window | Brushes (F5). Click a brush in the Brushes palette.
3. Create the path.
4. To brush the path after you have drawn it, either select the path and select a brush from the Brushes palette or drag the brush onto the path.

 Illustrator enables you to apply a new brush to a path that has already been brushed before. To completely replace the preceding brush's attributes (such as color, size, spacing, rotation, and so on) with those of the new brush, select the path and click the replacement brush in the Brushes palette. To replace the prior brush with the new brush but maintain the prior brush's attributes, press ALT/OPTION and click the replacement brush in the Brushes palette.

Using the Paintbrush Tool

 With one exception, the Paintbrush tool works just about like any other path creation tool. Unlike other tools with which you construct paths, the Paintbrush must have an accompanying brush—either the default 3-pt. Round Calligraphic brush or a brush that you select from the Brushes palette. To use the Paintbrush, activate it, select a brush, and then drag a freeform path in the illustration window. Illustrator brushes the path with the selected brushstroke. Then edit the path either by using the multitude of path editing tools and features or by modifying the Paintbrush or brushstroke options or even designing a new brush. As this chapter continues, you'll learn about all these choices.

Drawing with the Paintbrush

Remember you can use several path creation tools to make open or closed brushed paths. For example, you can draw an open path with the Pen, Pencil, Line Segment, and Arc tools. Or you can construct a closed path using the Rectangle, Ellipse, and Star tools. The Paintbrush enables you to draw an open or closed brushed path. An open path is the default. You can use the Paintbrush to create a completely new path or work with a preexisting path.

Drawing an Open Brushed Path

To draw an open path using the Paintbrush tool, follow these steps:

1. Choose Window | Brushes (F5). Illustrator opens the Brushes palette.

2. Click a brush to activate it.

3. Activate the Paintbrush (B).

4. Move the mouse pointer to the illustration window. Illustrator changes the mouse pointer:

5. Drag a path. Illustrator smoothes the path, applies the brushstroke, and selects the path for further action.

Drawing a Closed Brushed Path

To draw a closed path using the Paintbrush tool, follow these steps:

1. Choose Window | Brushes (F5). Illustrator opens the Brushes palette.

2. Click a brush to activate it.

3. Activate the Paintbrush (B).

4. Move the mouse pointer to the illustration window.

5. As you start dragging a path, press and hold down ALT/OPTION. To indicate that you are drawing a closed path, Illustrator adds a small loop to the paintbrush mouse pointer:

6. When the path is complete, release the mouse button without releasing the shortcut keys. Illustrator closes the path.

7. Release ALT/OPTION.

Modifying Paintbrush Attributes

When you want to change attributes of many Illustrator tools, you can double-click a toolbox to open an options dialog box. The Paintbrush is no different: Just double-click to launch the Paintbrush Tool Preferences dialog box (see Figure 13-3). The Paintbrush Tool Preferences dialog box is virtually identical to the Pencil Tool Preferences dialog box (see "Setting Pencil Tool Preferences" in Chapter 6).

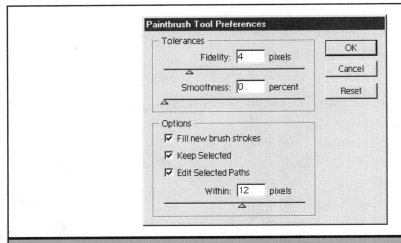

Figure 13-3. *The Paintbrush Tool Preferences dialog box with its default options*

The options in the dialog box are as follows:

■ The Fidelity text box/slider controls how faithful the brushed stroke is to the original path—if you are applying the brush to an existing path. Either enter or slide the distance, in pixels, from which the brushstroke can drift the path. Valid values range from 0.5 to 20 pixels. A low value means the stroke adheres closely to the path, regardless of whether you have moved the paintbrush mouse pointer smoothly. A high value forgives extra hand movement; Illustrator straightens out nicks and dents in the path. The default is 4.

■ The Smoothness text box/slider controls the smoothness of the path. Either enter or slide the percentage of smoothness. The higher the percentage, the more Illustrator smoothes the path. Valid values range from 0% (the default) to 100%.

■ Check the Fill New Brush Strokes check box (the default) to apply fill to paths drawn by the brush.

■ Check the Keep Selected box (the default) for Illustrator to keep the new path and the brush with which it was stroked selected when you have finished drawing the path.

■ Check the Edit Selected Paths box (the default) to enable the modification of selected paths. Slide the Within slider to define how close the mouse pointer has to be to the path to be able to edit it. Valid values range from 2 to 20 pixels. The default is 12 pixels.

If you would like to replace the standard Paintbrush mouse pointer with a cross-hairs mouse pointer with a small dot marking the location of the path that you are drawing, you can toggle between the two mouse pointers by repeatedly pressing the CAPS LOCK key. This technique also works for the following Illustrator tools: Add Anchor Point (+), Column Graph (J) and all the other graph tools, Delete Anchor Point (-), Lasso, Magic Wand (Y), Pen (P), Pencil (N), Slice (SHIFT-K), and Symbol Sprayer (SHIFT-S) and all the other symbols tools. Note that the cross-hairs mouse pointer is the only mouse pointer for the following tools: Arc, Auto Trace, Ellipse, Gradient (G), Line Segment (\), Measure, Page, Polar Grid, Polygon, Rectangle, Rectangular Grid, Reflect (O), Rotate (R), Rounded Rectangle, Scale (S), Scissors (C), Shear, Spiral, Star, and Twist.

Modifying Brushed Paths

Illustrator enables you to edit one or more brushed paths in a variety of ways: You can redraw it, convert it to an outlined path, remove the brush part of the path, or delete it altogether. You'll learn all these operations in this section. (Later in the chapter you'll learn how to create and modify brushes.)

Selecting Brushed Paths

As with almost any other Illustrator action, you must select a brushed path before you can modify it.

■ To select one brushed path, click it with a selection tool or press CTRL/⌘ when using another tool.

■ To select more than one path, click it with a selection tool or press CTRL/⌘ when using another tool. At the same time, press and hold down SHIFT, and repeatedly click paths you want to add to the selection.

■ To select all brushed paths in the active document, choose Select | Object | Brush Strokes.

Redrawing a Brushed Path

You can use the Paintbrush tool to redraw segments of a brushed open or closed path. To edit a brushed path using the Paintbrush, follow these steps:

1. Select the path to be edited.

2. Activate the Paintbrush (B).

3. Drag a new path over a segment of the brushed path. Whenever you release the mouse button, Illustrator redraws the new segment.

4. Repeat step 3 until you have corrected all the errors in the original brushed path.

If you draw from one end of an open brushed path to another or redraw an entire closed brushed path, Illustrator creates a second brushed path rather than redrawing the existing brushed path.

Converting a Brushed Path to an Outlined Path

You can convert a brushed path, regardless of the brush with which it was created, to an outlined path. If you used a Calligraphic or Art brush to make the brushed path, Illustrator outlines the brushed path with a new path containing anchor points. If you convert a brushed path created with a Scatter or a Pattern brush, Illustrator applies paths and points to all the images along the path and the path itself. Other than the changes to the path itself, all the attributes (that is, color, brush size, and so on) of the original brushed path remain.

To convert a brushed path to an outlined path, follow these steps:

1. Select the brushed path to convert.

2. Choose Object | Expand Appearance. Illustrator performs the conversion.

Removing a Brush from a Brushed Path

You can remove a brushstroke from a brushed path by using one of two Illustrator palettes or the toolbox. To remove a brushstroke from a brushed path, select the brushed path and take one of the following actions:

- Click the Remove Brush Strokes button at the bottom of the Brushes palette.

- Choose the Remove Brush Strokes command from the palette menu.

- In the toolbox, make sure the stroke is active by pressing X or clicking the stroke. Then remove the stroke by clicking the None button (/).

- Open the Color palette by choosing Window | Color (F6). Click the Stroke box.

- In the toolbox or the Color palette, click the Stroke box (X) and click the None section on the left side of the spectrum at the bottom of the palette.

Illustrator removes the brushstroke from the path, which remains in the illustration—selected and ready to be edited.

Setting Up a New Brush

Using a button or command in the Brushes palette, you can create any type of new brush. Illustrator does not allow you to make a brush with bitmap or raster images, blends, brushstrokes, gradients, graphs, masks, mesh objects, or placed files. In addition, you cannot construct an Art brush or Pattern brush with type. However, you can start with type, convert it to an editable path, and then use it for an Art brush or Pattern brush.

Getting Set to Create a New Brush

Before you create a new brush of any type, you have to take some preliminary steps.
First, either click the New Brush button at the bottom of the palette, or open the palette's
menu and select the New Brush command. In response, Illustrator opens the New Brush
dialog box (see Figure 13-4). Then, select a type for the new brush (note that a Calligraphic
brush is the default), and click OK.

After the New Brush dialog box closes, Illustrator opens one of four dialog boxes:
Calligraphic Brush Options, Scatter Brush Options, Art Brush Options, or Pattern
Brush Options. Just select the options and click OK to close the dialog box, create the
new brush, and add it to the appropriate section of the Brushes palette.

Inspecting the Calligraphic Brush Options Dialog Box

Use the Calligraphic Brush Options dialog box to define a Calligraphic brush. Figure 13-5
shows a line with a random angle between 10° and 75°, random roundness from 0% to
40%, and a random diameter from 0 points to 20 points set in the dialog box, and the
new brush in the Brushes palette.

Use the options in the dialog box as follows:

- In the Name text box, enter a brush name. Illustrator allows you to use as many
  as 30 characters for the name.

- The preview area contains two sections. Within the window on the left, you can
  change options; on the right you can view the effects of the selected options. If
  you want to ensure that you are viewing the latest selections in the preview area,
  click the mouse pointer in a different text box from that in which you typed the
  latest value.

- In the Angle text box, type the tilt angle at which the brushstroke is applied to
  the path. To rotate the angle within the preview area, drag the arrowhead outside
  the circle, the circle, or the area within the circle. Just make sure you don't drag
  one of the black disks on the circle, which affects the level of roundness and not
  the angle. Valid values range from –180° to 180°. The default is 0°.

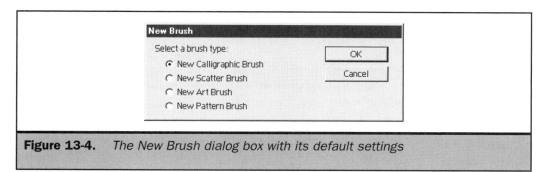

Figure 13-4.   *The New Brush dialog box with its default settings*

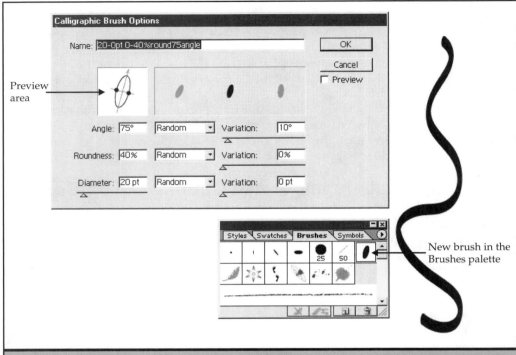

Figure 13-5. *The Calligraphic Brush Options dialog box showing the settings for the line on its right*

- In the Roundness text box, type the percentage of roundness of the brushstroke. To set the roundness in the preview area, drag one of the black disks toward the other black disk. Valid values range from 0% (completely flat) to 100% (completely round). The default is 100%.

- In the Diameter text box or slider, type or slide the diameter of the brushstroke. Valid values range from 0 (that is, barely visible) to 1,296 points. The default is 9 points.

- From the Angle, Roundness, and Diameter drop-down menus, select Fixed, Random, or Pressure. Please note:

    - If you choose Fixed for any of the options, Illustrator always uses the value shown in the text box.

    - If you choose Random for any of the options, Illustrator varies the value in the text box by the value that you type in the Variation text box or slide the Variation slider. So, if the Diameter value is 9 points and the Variation value is 4 points, the diameter can be 5, 6, 7, 8, 9, 10, 11, 12, 13, and 14 points (that is,

4 points on either side of 9) as you draw the path. For the Roundness option, Variation is not available for values of 0% or 100%. For the Diameter option, Variation is not available for values of 0 points or 1,296 points.

■ If you select Pressure for any of the options, Illustrator enables you to indicate the pressure of a stylus on a graphics tablet, which affects the look of the brushstroke as you draw the path. Pressure also factors in the brush attributes when determining the stroke's appearance. The Pressure option is available only if you have a graphics tablet installed on your computer system.

Inspecting the Scatter Brush Options Dialog Box

Before you create a Scatter brush, you must select the image the brush will scatter along its path. Otherwise, the New Scatter Brush radio button in the New Brush dialog box will not be available. Then, use the Scatter Brush Options dialog box (see Figure 13-6) to define the Scatter brush.

Use the options in the dialog box as follows:

■ In the Name text box, enter a brush name of as many as 30 characters.

■ In the Size text box/slider, type or slide to a percentage value for the size of the scattered objects. Valid percentages range from 1% to 10,000%. The default percentage is 100%.

■ In the Spacing text box/slider, type or slide to a percentage value of the space between the scattered objects. Valid percentages range from 1% to 10,000%. The default percentage is 100%.

■ In the Scatter text box/slider, type or slide to a percentage value for the distance of the scattered objects from the selected path. Valid percentages range from –10,000% (close to the path) to 10,000% (far away from the path). The default percentage is 0%.

■ In the Rotation text box/slider, type or slide to a percentage value for the angle of rotation of the scattered objects. Valid percentages range from 0° to 360%. The default is 0°.

■ From the Size, Spacing, Scatter, and Rotation drop-down menus, choose Fixed, Random, or Pressure.

■ If you choose Fixed for any of the options, Illustrator always uses the value shown in the active text box. Each slider bar contains one slider icon.

■ If you choose Random for any of the options, Illustrator varies the value in the text box or slider by the value that you type in the text box to the right of the Size, Spacing, Scatter, or Rotation text box or slide the Variation slider. The text box on the left holds the minimum value; the one on the right contains the maximum value. Each slider bar contains two slider icons—one each for minimum and maximum. The leftmost text box shows the minimum value, and the rightmost text box shows the maximum.

ILLUSTRATOR ESSENTIALS

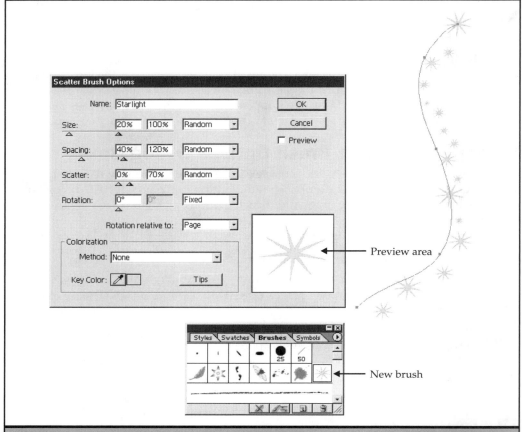

Figure 13-6.   *The Scatter Brush Options dialog box with the settings and image used to create the selected path to its right, and the Brushes palette showing the new brush*

■ If you choose Pressure for any of the options, Illustrator enables you to indicate the pressure of a stylus on a graphics tablet, which affects the look of the brushstroke as you draw the path. The leftmost text box shows the minimum pressure (which results in smaller objects), and the one on the right contains the maximum pressure (which results in larger objects). The Pressure option is available only if you have a graphics tablet installed on your computer system.

Note *When you slide the sliders under Size, Spacing, Scatter, or Rotation, you can determine both the minimum and maximum values at once. To increment or decrement both values by the same number (for example, changing 50% minimum and 75% maximum to 60% minimum and 85% maximum), slide while pressing and holding down* SHIFT. *To move the minimum and maximum values away from a center point (for example, changing minimum and maximum values from 100% each to 75% minimum and 125% maximum), slide while pressing and holding down* ALT/OPTION.

- From the Rotation Relative To drop-down menu, Page rotates the scattered objects in proportion to the top of the page and Path rotates the scattered objects in proportion to the path.

Exploring Colorization Options

The Scatter, Art, or Pattern Brush Options dialog boxes contain options with which you can adjust or change brush colors: the Method drop-down menu, the Key Color eyedropper and box, and the Tips button:

- From the Method drop-down menu, select the colorization method: None, Tints, Tints and Shades, or Hue Shift:

  - None (the default) displays the colors of the selected brush as they look in the Brushes palette. If you choose None, the brush color remains as it is.

  - Tints displays the colors of the selected brush in tints of the current stroke color. (A *tint* is the result of adding white from the hue.) Black parts of the brushstroke become the stroke color; white sections remain white; and nonblack, nonwhite parts become tints of the stroke color. Tints is the best choice for black and white or spot color brushes. (For more information about spot color, refer to "Working with Swatches" in Chapter 7.)

  - Tints and Shades displays the colors of the selected brush in tints and shades of the current stroke color. Black parts of the brushstroke remain black, white sections remain white, and shades between vary from black to gray to white and tints of the stroke color. Tints and Shades is the best choice for grayscale brushes.

  - Hue Shift uses the present or new key color (shown in the Key Color box) as the stroke. Black, white, and gray parts of the brushstroke remain those colors. Other colors become gradations of the stroke color. Choose Hue Shift for multicolored brushes.

Answering Questions about Colorization

When you have a question about which Method option to select or what the colorization effects would be on the brush that you are creating, Illustrator provides the Tips dialog box (see Figure 13-7), which displays information and examples of the four methods. To open the dialog box, click the Tips button between the Key Color box and the Preview box.

Changing the Key Color

You can change the *key color* (which is the main color in the selected artwork) of a brush to a color in the currently selected artwork. To do so, the Scatter Brush Options dialog box, Art Brush Options dialog box, or Pattern Brush Options dialog box must be open. Then follow these steps:

1. Click the Key Color eyedropper in the bottom-left corner of the dialog box.

2. Move the eyedropper to a color in the Preview box and click. Illustrator replaces the key color with the clicked color.

3. To deselect the eyedropper, click it.

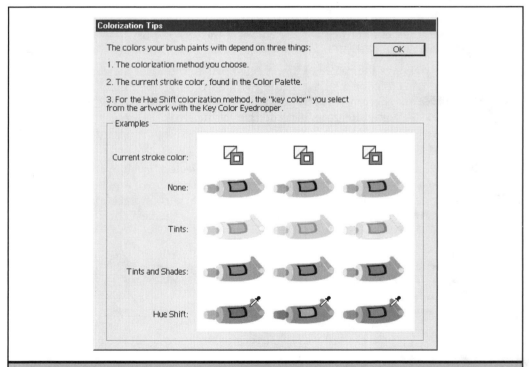

Figure 13-7. *The Tips dialog box, which never changes*

Inspecting the Art Brush Options Dialog Box

Before you create an Art brush, you must select the image with which the brush will paint.
Otherwise, the Art Brush radio button in the New Brush dialog box will not be available.
Then use the Art Brush Options dialog box (see Figure 13-8) to define the Art brush.

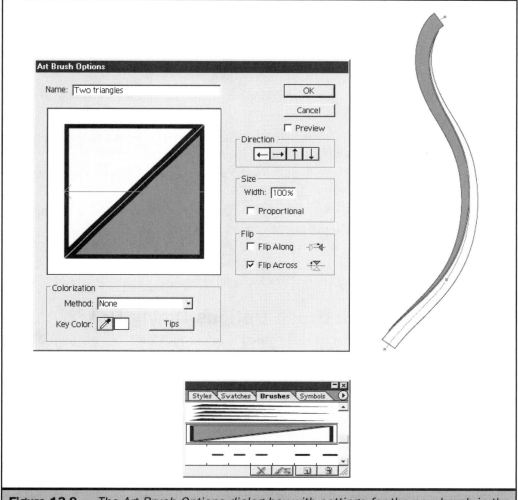

Figure 13-8.   *The Art Brush Options dialog box with settings for the new brush in the Brushes palette, and the resulting path to its right*

Use the options in the Art Brush Options dialog box as follows:

- In the Name text box enter a brush name of as many as 30 characters.
- The Direction buttons control the direction in which the selected image is drawn as you drag the brush. The arrowhead on each button shows the end of the stroke:
  - Click ← (the default) to end the stroke on the left side of the image.
  - Click → to end the stroke on the right side of the image.
  - Click ↑ to end the stroke on the top of the image.
  - Click ↓ to end the stroke on the bottom of the image.

When you click a button, Illustrator changes the direction of the blue arrow in the Preview box.

- In the Width text box, scale the width of the image by a percentage of its current size. Valid values range from 1% to 10,000%. The default is 100%.
- Check the Proportional check box to keep the image in proportion as Illustrator scales it.
- To reflect the art along the horizontal axis, check the Flip Along check box.
- To reflect the art from top to bottom, check the Flip Across check box.
- Choose Colorization options. For more information about colorization, refer to "Exploring Colorization Options," "Answering Questions about Colorization," and "Changing the Key Color," earlier in this chapter.

Inspecting the Pattern Brush Options Dialog Box

Pattern brushes bring to mind a custom-made tile or parquet floor, or a wooden floor with inlaid borders; so they lend themselves to closed paths in particular. Pattern brushes can be composed of start and end tiles, inner and outer corner tiles, and side tiles, but you can create a pattern using just a side tile. Before you create a Pattern brush, you must choose or create one to five images with which the brush will compose its pattern: You can create as many as five pattern swatches for the Swatches palette, choose existing swatches from the Swatches palette, or construct original artwork. Then use the Pattern Brush Options dialog box (see Figure 13-9) to define the patterns for the Pattern brush.

Use the options in the dialog box as follows:

- In the Name text box, enter a brush name of as many as 30 characters.
- Click one of the five tile buttons to define one of the tiles that makes up the pattern. You can choose from Side Tile, Outer Corner Tile, Inner Corner Tile, Start Tile, or End Tile.

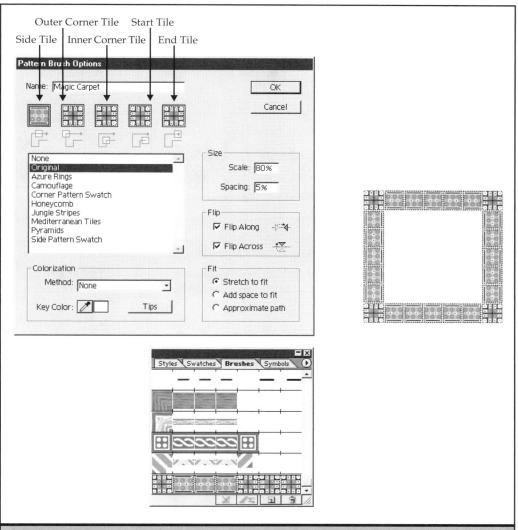

Figure 13-9. *The Pattern Brush Options dialog box with the settings used to create the pattern shown in the closed path to its right, and the new patterns in the Brushes palette*

■ The large list box in the dialog box catalogs the patterns in the Swatches palette, including those you have created and placed in the Swatches palette. If the pattern you want to apply to the chosen tile type appears in the list box, select its name. Illustrator changes the look of the tile button to the pattern you have chosen. Choose the top two entries in the list to edit an existing pattern. Select None to delete the selected button if you are modifying a pattern; choose Original to change a customized tile to its original version.

- In the Scale text box, type the percentage by which you want to scale the pattern. Valid values range from 1% to 10,000%. The default is 100%.

- In the Spacing text box, type the percentage of white space between the tiles. Valid values range from 1% to 10,000%. The default is 0%.

- To reflect the art along the horizontal axis, check the Flip Along check box.

- To reflect the art from top to bottom, check the Flip Across check box.

- In the Fit section, choose from the radio buttons:

  - Stretch to Fit (the default) expands or contracts the tiles to fit the path.

  - Add Space to Fit inserts or removes white space between the tiles to fit the path.

  - Approximate Path fits the tiles by not conforming strictly to the path. This option is available for rectangles and squares only.

- Choose Colorization options. For more information about colorization, refer to "Exploring Colorization Options," "Answering Questions about Colorization," and "Changing the Key Color," earlier in this chapter.

Creating Pattern Brushes

As you know, you can create pattern brushes in two ways: from the Swatches palette or from artwork in the illustration window. For both methods, make sure to open the Brushes palette. Consider the following:

- If you use the Swatches palette to create a pattern brush, you'll probably have to construct a pattern, drag it to the palette, and name it. (For more information about adding a pattern to the Swatches palette, refer to "Adding a Swatch to the Swatches Palette" in Chapter 7.) Then, you'll open the Pattern Brush Options dialog box to click a tile button, select the name of the desired pattern swatch in the list box, and repeat clicking buttons and selecting names until you have specified the necessary number of tiles. Then, you'll select options from the rest of the dialog box and click OK to add the tiles to the Brushes palette.

- If you use original artwork to create a pattern brush, display it in the illustration window. Drag the artwork for one tile to the Brushes palette. When Illustrator opens the New Brush dialog box, click New Pattern Brush and click OK. Illustrator opens the Pattern Brush Options dialog box with the dragged art in the Side Tile box. Fill in the rest of the dialog box and click OK to add the tile to the Brushes palette. To insert additional tiles in the pattern brush, drag them one at a time while pressing and holding down ALT/OPTION. Every time you add a tile, Illustrator opens the Pattern Brush Options dialog box for the pattern. Change your selections, if you wish, and click OK to add the tile to the pattern brush.

Manipulating Brushes

Illustrator enables you to manipulate brushes in several ways by duplicating them so that you can edit a copy and keep the original in its original condition. You also can use options dialog boxes to change certain attributes for each of the brushes. If you would like to apply most of the characteristics of a brush to a new brush, you can duplicate it and then edit the copy while keeping the original sacrosanct. You can even delete a brush if it is no longer useful.

Changing Options for a Brush

One way of modifying an existing brush is by using the Calligraphic Brush Options dialog box, Scatter Brush Options dialog box, Art Brush Options dialog box, or Pattern Brush Options dialog box. To open one of these dialog boxes, either double-click the brush you want to change or select the brush and then choose the Brush Options command from the Brushes palette menu. The dialog box that opens depends on the type of brush you have selected. These dialog boxes are exactly the same as those you learned about earlier in this chapter. For more information, refer to "Inspecting the Calligraphic Brush Options Dialog Box," "Inspecting the Scatter Brush Options Dialog Box," "Inspecting the Art Brush Options Dialog Box," and "Inspecting the Pattern Brush Options Dialog Box."

Modifying a Brush

Illustrator provides four other dialog boxes—this time for modifying brushstrokes in the current artwork. To open one of these dialog boxes, select the brushed path in the illustration window and either click the Options of Selected Object button at the bottom of the Brushes palette or choose the Options of Selected Object command from the palette's menu. Illustrator opens one of four dialog boxes (see Figure 13-10): Stroke Options (Calligraphic Brush), Stroke Options (Scatter Brush), Stroke Options (Art Brush), or Stroke Options (Pattern Brush).

When you change options using these dialog boxes, the current artwork might be affected. The original brush and its options might remain unchanged, depending on the answer you give to a message box Illustrator might display when you change options:

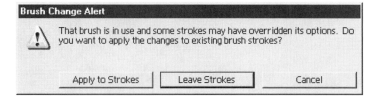

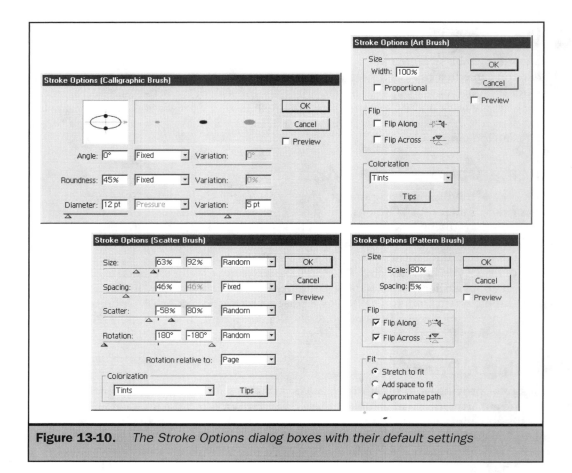

Figure 13-10. *The Stroke Options dialog boxes with their default settings*

To apply the changes to all the other brushstrokes you have applied with the brush that you have just modified, click Apply to Strokes. To keep all the other brushstrokes in their original conditions, click Leave Strokes.

Each of the dialog boxes contains the same options as those in these counterpart dialog boxes: Calligraphic Brush Options, Scatter Brush Options, Art Brush Options, and Pattern Brush Options.

Duplicating a Brush

You can have it both ways—keep an original brush and its settings and create a new brush based on those settings—by duplicating the brush and then editing the copy. You can select a single brush or a multitude.

To duplicate a brush, follow these steps:

1. Select a brush by clicking it. To select several brushes, click one brush; then press and hold down CTRL/⌘ while clicking each additional brush. To select a range of brushes, click a brush at one end of the range, press and hold down SHIFT, and click a brush at the other end of the range.

2. Either choose the Duplicate Brush command from the Brushes palette's menu or drag the brush to be duplicated to the New Brush button at the bottom of the palette. Illustrator adds the duplicate brush to the palette.

3. Double-click the new brush to rename it and optionally edit its settings.

Deleting a Brush

If you don't plan to use a particular brush again, you can delete it—but be very careful: Once a brush is gone, it's gone forever—or at least until you reinstall Illustrator. You can delete one brush at a time, several brushes, or a range of brushes.

To delete a brush from the Brushes palette, follow these steps:

1. Select a brush by clicking it. To select several brushes, click one brush; then press and hold down CTRL/⌘ while clicking each additional brush. To select a range of brushes, click a brush at one end of the range, press and hold down SHIFT, and click a brush at the other end of the range.

2. Click the Delete Brush button at the bottom of the Brushes palette, choose the Delete Brush command from the palette's menu, or drag the selected button or buttons to the Delete Brush button. If no brushstrokes formatted with the brush to be deleted are in the current artwork, Illustrator deletes the brush without asking you to confirm the deletion. If you have formatted any brushstrokes in the current artwork with the brush to be deleted, Illustrator displays a message box:

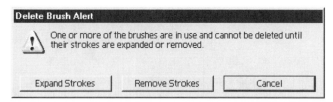

3. If you click the Expand Strokes button, Illustrator expands any strokes formatted with the brush to be deleted. If you click Remove Strokes, Illustrator removes the brushstroke from any strokes affected by the target brush.

Using Brushes Libraries

In "Selecting a Swatches Library" in Chapter 7, you learned how to use and create libraries of swatches. The Brushes libraries (see Figure 13-11) work in the same way as Swatches libraries. For example, when you use a brush from a Brushes library in your current artwork, the brush becomes part of the Brushes palette for the present document only. Additionally, you cannot edit a brush when it's in a Brushes library, but you can change it once it is part of the Brushes palette. You also can create one or more custom libraries with your selection of brushes.

You can work with Brushes libraries in several ways: Obviously, to use a library, you must be able to open it; then, you can select brushes and move them to the Brushes palette.

Opening a Brushes Library

To open a Brushes library, choose Window | Brush Libraries and then choose the library from the submenu. Note that the Default_CMYK and Default_RGB libraries contain the same brushes you will find in the standard Brushes palette.

Moving a Brush to the Brushes Palette

You can move a brush into the Brushes palette by selecting it (which usually automatically places it in the Brushes palette), using it in the current artwork, or by dragging the brush to the Brushes palette.

Creating a Brushes Library

To create a Brushes library, follow these steps:

1. Start a new Illustrator document.

2. Choose Window | Brushes (F5) to open the Brushes palette.

3. Add brushes to the Brushes palette by doing one of the following:
   - Create brushes, being sure to give them unique names.
   - Duplicate brushes and change some or all of their options.

4. Delete brushes that you don't want to have in the Brushes palette.

5. Save the document into the folder in which other Brushes libraries are located (for example, Brushes). Brushes library documents have Illustrator's .ai extension.

6. To open a custom Brushes library that you have created, choose Window | Brush Libraries | Other Library. From the Select a Library to Open dialog box, double-click the library name.

ILLUSTRATOR
ESSENTIALS

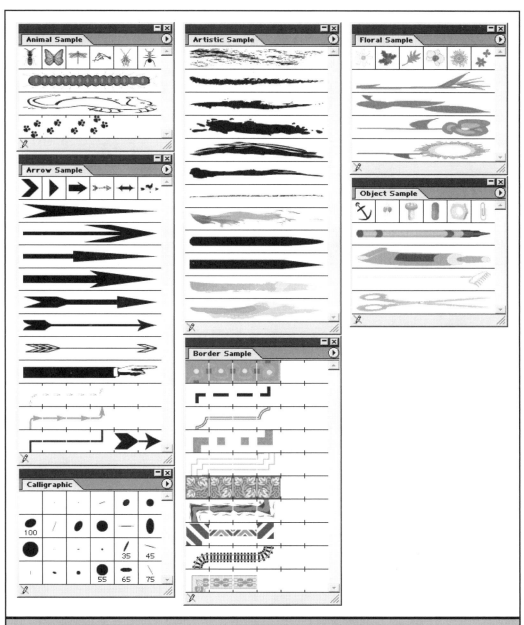

Figure 13-11.   *Sample custom Brushes libraries from Illustrator*

Figure 13-12 shows the Floral Sample library document in the illustration window.

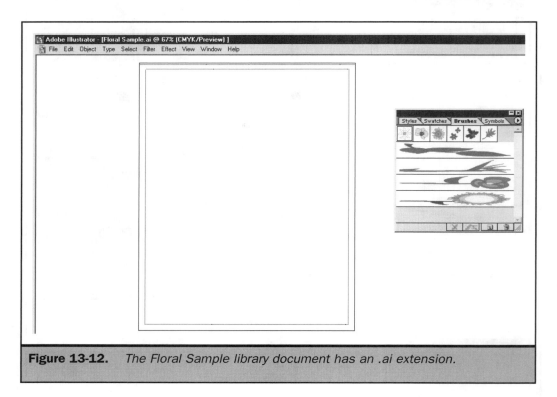

Figure 13-12. *The Floral Sample library document has an .ai extension.*

The
Complete
Reference

Chapter 14

Working with Layers

When you create complicated artworks that contain many objects and paths, you can either juggle them (possibly losing one or two along the way), or you can place them in layers. Layers are Illustrator's way of telling you to organize. By default, each Illustrator document contains one layer on which all artwork resides. The number of layers and *sublayers*—which are nested under layers—you can create for a document is limited only by your computer memory.

Think of a layer or sublayer as a transparent sheet that contains some kind of artwork. Whenever you change the position of a sheet in the stack of sheets, Illustrator changes the stacking order of the objects on all the layers and sublayers in the stack (that is, all the layers and sublayers in a document). So if you move a layer that contains a red triangle above a layer with a blue rectangle, the look of the document changes.

Each layer has its own attributes, so when you move an object from one layer to another, the object takes on the attributes of its new layer. A layer can contain objects such as paths, groups, compound paths, *envelopes* (objects with which you manipulate other objects), and *compound shapes* (two or more paths, other Illustrator components, including other compound shapes, all of which make up original objects that you can edit).

You use the Layers palette to create and manipulate layers and sublayers and move layers, sublayers, and objects on those layers and sublayers. With the Layers palette you can create template layers on which you can trace artwork and *clipping masks*, which crop artwork so that some sections are hidden and others appear at the location of the masks. You also can import Photoshop layers into Illustrator.

Exploring the Layers Palette

With the Layers palette (see Figure 14-1), you can create and modify layers and sublayers, and you can move objects from one layer or sublayer to another. The Layers palette is like a storyboard filled with individual pages of illustrations. The Layers palette lists all the layers in the current document in any order you wish. Illustrator records the content of each layer by labeling paths, groups, sublayers, envelopes, compound shapes, compound paths, and images. You can choose to view or hide layers and their contents, and you can control behavior of layers by using the palette's commands and buttons and by clicking or dragging with your mouse. To toggle between showing and hiding the palette, choose Window | Layers (F7).

The Layers palette contains many elements, each of which has a specific meaning and with which you can specify layer actions:

- The view/hide icon, which changes in appearance depending on its mode, serves three purposes: toggling between showing or hiding the selected layer (click the icon), viewing the layer in Preview or Outline mode (click the icon while pressing and holding down CTRL/⌘), and showing and hiding all layers

GIANT PANDA MOTHER & CUB

DraSan' Nitti
Silver Dragon Studio
www.silverdragonstudio.com

PEACEFUL LIVING

Valeri Darling
Missing Masterpiece Graphx
http://www.missingmasterpiece.com

VISIONS OF BEAUTY

Valeri Darling
Missing Masterpiece Graphx
http://www.missingmasterpiece.com

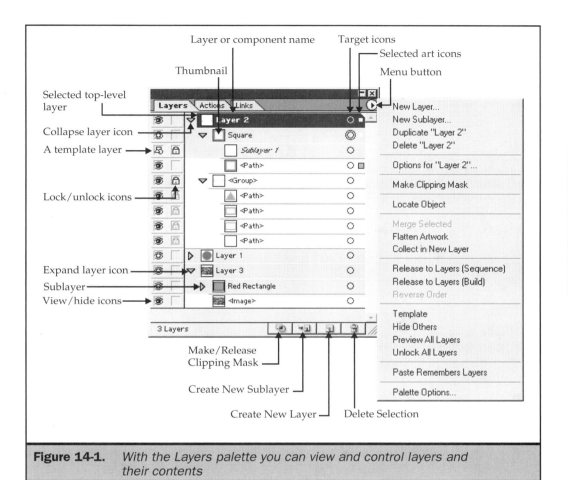

Figure 14-1. *With the Layers palette you can view and control layers and their contents*

other than the selected one (click the icon while pressing and holding down ALT/OPTION). The counterpart commands on the palette menu are Show All Layers/Hide Others and Preview All Layers/Outline Others.

■ Click a lock/unlock icon to toggle between locking and unlocking the selected layer or component. When you see a small picture of a lock, the layer or component is locked from editing. When the space does not contain a lock icon, you can edit the layer or component. The counterpart command on the palette menu is Unlock All Layers/Lock Others.

■ The thumbnail contains a small picture of the contents of a layer, sublayer, group, path, image, or other component of a layer.

■ Click an expand layer icon or collapse layer icon to show or hide all the sublayers and objects under a layer, respectively.

■ The large area in the center of the palette identifies layers (that is, the rows with a gray background) and components (that is, the white rows). The first layer listed is the top layer in the order of layers, and the last layer is the bottom in the order. The currently selected layer is the active layer to which Illustrator adds any new paths and images. You can change the order of layers by dragging up or down the list. As you drag a layer, Illustrator marks potential new locations with a bold horizontal line. To select one layer or object, click it; to select two or more noncontiguous layers or objects, click and then press and hold down CTRL/⌘ and continue clicking to add to the selection. To select two or more contiguous layers or objects, click one end of the range; then press and hold down SHIFT, and click the other end of the range.

■ The target icon is a radio button with which you can control the appearance of attributes for a selected layer or component or apply those attributes to another layer.

■ The selected art icon shows the color that you or Illustrator has given the layer or object and indicates that you have selected an object or its parent object. A triangle in the upper-right corner of the selected layer or object is another indication that the layer or object is selected and ready to edit.

■ Click the Make/Release Clipping Mask button to create a clipping mask from the selected object or release a clipping mask from the selected layer. The counterpart command on the palette menu is Make/Release Clipping Mask.

■ Click the Create New Sublayer button to insert a sublayer under the selected layer. The counterpart command on the palette menu is New Sublayer.

■ Click the Create New Layer button to create a new layer without naming it or setting options. To make a new layer, name it, specify options, and click Create New Layer while pressing and holding down ALT/OPTION. The counterpart command on the palette menu is New Layer.

To open the palette's menu, click the menu button. Commands on the menu are

■ The New Layer command opens the Layer Options dialog box so that you can create, name, and set options for a new layer. If you press and hold down ALT/OPTION before you open the menu, the command name becomes New Layer Above *"selected layer name"* or New Top Layer, depending on whether you have selected a layer or another object, respectively. The counterpart button at the bottom of the palette is Create New Layer.

■ The New Sublayer command opens the Layer Options dialog box so that you can create, name, and set options for a new sublayer under the currently selected layer. The counterpart button at the bottom of the palette is Create New Sublayer.

■ The Duplicate "*name*" command duplicates one or more selected layers or objects.

■ The Delete "*name*" command deletes one or more selected layers or objects. The counterpart button at the bottom of the palette is Delete Selection.

■ The Options for "*name*" command opens the Layer Options dialog box or an Options dialog box, depending on whether you have selected a layer or other object. Another way to open one of the two dialog boxes is to double-click the layer or object whose options you want to change.

■ The Make/Release Clipping Mask command creates a clipping mask from the selected object or releases a clipping mask from the selected layer. The counterpart button at the bottom of the palette is Make/Release Clipping Mask.

■ The Locate Object command locates the layer on which the selected object resides.

■ The Merge Selected command merges all the selected layers into one layer, combining all artwork from the selected layers and deleting empty layers in the selection.

■ The Flatten Artwork command combines all layers—regardless of whether you have selected them—into a single layer.

■ The Collect in New Layer command creates a new layer that converts the current layer, its sublayers, and other contents into a sublayer under the new layer.

■ The Release to Layers (Sequence) command converts each of the sublayers and objects under the selected layer into their own individual layers.

■ The Release to Layers (Build) command converts the sublayers and objects under the selected layer into layers, each of which contains an increasing number of the released sublayers and objects.

■ The Reverse Order command reverses the current hierarchy of two or more selected layers.

■ The Template command converts a layer into a template layer.

■ The Show All Layers command shows all the layers and their objects in the illustration window. The Hide All Layers command hides all the layers and their objects in the illustration window. The Show Others command shows all the layers and sublayers on the same level as the selected layer or sublayer. The Hide Others command hides all the layers on the same level as the selected layer or sublayer; sublayers of the selected layer remain visible. You also can toggle between the current two Hide and Show commands by clicking the view/hide icon while pressing and holding down ALT/OPTION.

- The Preview All Layers command shows all the layers and objects onscreen in Preview mode. The Outline All Layers command shows all the layers and objects onscreen in Outline mode. The Preview Others command shows all the layers and sublayers on the same level as the selected layer or sublayer in Preview mode. The Outline Others command shows all the layers and sublayers on the same level as the selected layer or sublayer in Outline mode. You also can toggle between the two commands by clicking the view/hide icon.

- The Lock All Layers command locks all the layers and objects onscreen. The Unlock All Layers command unlocks all the layers and objects onscreen. The Lock Others command locks all the layers and sublayers on the same level as the selected layer or sublayer. The Unlock Others command unlocks all the layers and sublayers on the same level as the selected layer or sublayer. You also can toggle between the two commands by clicking the lock/unlock icon.

- The Paste Remembers Layers command controls the location of pasted artwork. If you activate the command, Illustrator pastes copied or cut artwork into the layer from which it was copied or cut. If the command is inactive (the default), Illustrator pastes copied and cut artwork onto the active layer.

- The Palette Options command opens the Layers Palette Options dialog box with which you can set row size and turn on or off thumbnails.

Creating Layers and Sublayers

At the beginning of an Illustrator document's life, it has one layer. The document will stay that way until you explicitly add one or more layers and sublayers. In fact, you can add as many layers and sublayers as your computer's memory will allow. However, every time you add a layer, Illustrator slows down a bit and your job in working on the document gets a little more complicated. So, it's a good idea to limit the number of layers to only those you need to create your layered artwork.

Inspecting the Layer Options Dialog Box

You can create a layer or sublayer without using the Layer Options dialog box (see Figure 14-2), but you should consider using the dialog box when you make any layer or sublayer. Thus, you should learn about the options that the dialog box provides.

In addition to defining options for new layers and sublayers, you can use the Layer Options dialog box to modify options for existing layers and sublayers. To edit an existing layer or sublayer, double-click it or choose the Options for *"name"* command

Figure 14-2. *The Layer Options dialog box with the default settings for a new layer*

from the Layers palette. When Illustrator opens the dialog box, set the desired options, and click OK to apply the changed attributes and close the dialog box.

The options in the dialog box are as follows:

- The Name text box displays the current name, which by default is Layer *n*, where *n* represents the next number in the series of layers for the active document.

- The Color drop-down menu and the box to its right show the current color of the layer. Illustrator's layer color coding helps you recognize the sublayers and objects that compose the content of a particular layer. By default, Illustrator selects a color for you. However, you can choose a color by opening the drop-down menu and clicking a color.

- Check the Template check box to make the new layer a template layer. An unchecked box (that is, a standard layer) is the default.

- Check the Show check box to show all the objects in the layer in the illustration window. This is the default.

- Check the Preview check box to show all the objects in the layer in the illustration window in Preview mode. This is the default.

- Check the Lock check box to lock all the objects in the layer (that is, you cannot edit locked objects). An unchecked check box (that is, enabling editing) is the default.

- Check the Print check box to enable printing of all the objects in the layer. This is the default.

■ Check the Dim Images To check box and enter a percentage of dimming of bitmap objects in the text box. Valid values range from 0% to 100%; the default value is 50%.

Adding a Layer or Sublayer

Illustrator enables you to add a layer above the selected layer or above all layers in the order of layers. You also can insert a sublayer under the selected layer.

When you add a layer or sublayer, Illustrator displays it in a row in the Layers palette. If you accept the defaults, the layer or sublayer is visible and in Preview mode, so the view icon appears in the left column; the layer or sublayer is unlocked so you won't see the lock icon in the second column. The layer or sublayer—including all the objects that it holds—appears on a thumbnail, its name is Layer *n* (which represents the next available layer number), and it is selected.

Creating a Layer Above the Current Layer

You can create a layer immediately above the selected layer in two ways:

■ To create a layer using the Illustrator defaults (that is, a name and color assigned by Illustrator), click the Create New Layer button at the bottom of the Layers palette. Illustrator creates a layer without opening the Layer Options dialog box.

■ To create a layer using the Layer Options dialog box, either click the Create New Layer button while pressing and holding down ALT/OPTION or choose the New Layer command from the palette's menu. In the dialog box name the layer, assign a color, check or clear the check boxes, and click OK.

Creating a Layer in Front of All Layers

You can create a layer that is above all the other layers in the Layers palette. The new layer does not include the rest of the layers in the palette; it is on the same level as the top-level layers. Because the new layer appears at the top of the palette, its artwork is in front of all other layers (as it would be if you selected the artwork and chose Object | Arrange | Bring to Front (CTRL-SHIFT-]/⌘-SHIFT-])).

To create a new layer at the top of the layer list, click the New Layer button while pressing and holding down CTRL/⌘. An alternative method of creating the top layer is to select the top layer in the palette and perform one of the instructions in the "Creating a Layer Above the Current Layer" section.

Creating a Sublayer Within the Current Layer

The main difference between creating a layer above the current layer and making a sublayer is the location of the new sublayer and its place in the hierarchy in the Layers palette. A sublayer is below the selected layer in the list and subordinate to the selected layer. The actual creating of the sublayer is just about the same as creating a layer.

■ To create a sublayer using the Illustrator defaults (that is, a name and color assigned by Illustrator), click the Create New Sublayer button at the bottom of the Layers palette.

■ To create a layer using the Layer Options dialog box, either click the Create New Sublayer button while pressing and holding down ALT/OPTION or choose the New Sublayer command from the palette's menu. In the dialog box name the layer, assign a color, check or clear the check boxes, and click OK.

Adding an Object to a Layer

When you create a new path or place an object in the illustration window, Illustrator adds the object to the current layer and adds a row for that object under the layer in the Layers palette. If you accept the Illustrator layer defaults, the row has the view icon in the left column, an empty second column, a thumbnail, and the default name (such as <Path> or <Group>), and Illustrator selects the row.

You can change the default options by double-clicking the row or selecting the Options for "*name*" command from the Layers palette. Illustrator opens the Options dialog box (see Figure 14-3), a condensed version of the Layer Options dialog box.

In the Name text box, you can overtype the default name with a unique name. You can check (the default) or clear the Show check box to either show or hide the object in the Layers palette. Additionally, you can check or clear (the default) the Lock check box to lock the object to prevent editing, or unlock the object to make it editable.

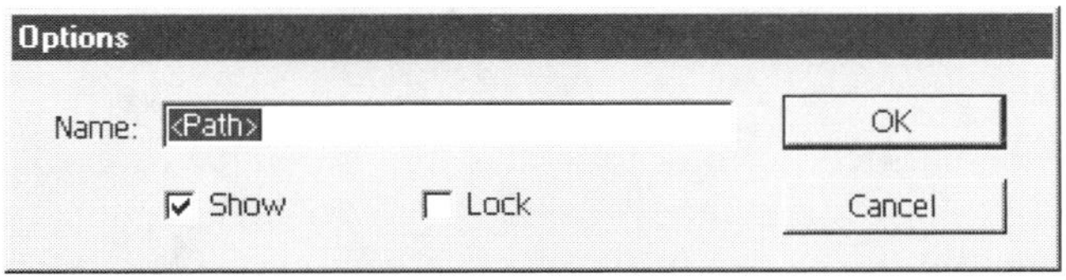

Figure 14-3. *The Options dialog box for a selected path*

Changing the Look of the Layers Palette

At this point you probably are thinking how complicated the Layers palette is. However, once you get to know it, you will discover that the palette is an easy way to control layers and sublayers—as well as the artwork that they contain. Using the palette, you can select, show or hide, lock or unlock, and rearrange layers and sublayers (as you will learn in the following sections). You also can streamline the look of the palette and temporarily make a complicated piece of art much less complex as you focus on creating and editing particular objects in the artwork.

Expanding and Collapsing Layers

You can show or hide all the sublayers and objects under a layer. To show (or *expand*) all the contents of a layer, click the expand layer icon—the right-pointing triangle to the left of the layer name or number. To hide all the contents of a layer (or *collapse*), click the collapse layer icon—the downward-pointing triangle to the left of the layer name or number. The layer remains on display in the Layers palette, but all the sublayers and objects under the layer disappear from view.

Setting Palette Display Options

Choose the Palette Options command, at the bottom of the Layers palette, to open the Palette Options dialog box (see Figure 14-4). Using the dialog box, you can set viewing options for the palette.

The options in the dialog box are as follows:

- Check the Show Layers Only box to show layers and sublayers only. Illustrator hides groups, paths, and other objects that are not layers or sublayers. The default is an unchecked box.

- Use the Row Size section to set row height. You can select Small, Medium (the default), or Large or enter a custom size in the Other text box. When you select Small, Illustrator dims the Thumbnails section, indicating that this small size does not enable the display of thumbnails. Valid values range from 12 to 100 pixels. The default is 20 pixels.

- In the Thumbnails section, you can set the objects that have associated thumbnails. You can show thumbnails for all layers, top-level layers only, groups, and objects. Note that the more thumbnails that are on display, the more slowly Illustrator runs—especially for documents with many layers and objects on those layers. The default displays thumbnails for layers, groups, and objects (that is, all elements that can be listed in the Layers palette).

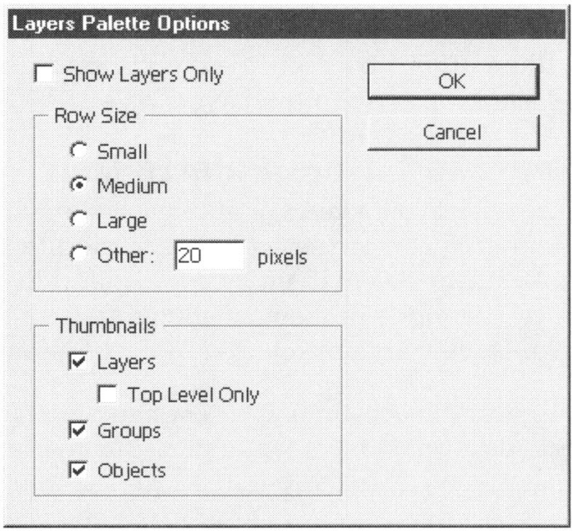

Figure 14-4. *The Layers Palette Options dialog box with its default settings*

Manipulating Layers and Their Contents

When you manipulate a layer, you also control the objects on that layer. For example, when you hide or lock a layer, you also hide or lock all the sublayers and objects on those layers and sublayers. Or when you switch from Preview mode to Outline mode for a layer, you'll actually view all the objects on that layer in either Preview or Outline mode. So, you can view some collections of objects on certain layers using one viewing mode and other sets of objects on other layers in the other viewing mode.

Selecting Layers and Objects on Layers

Selecting layers and particular objects on layers in the Layers palette requires different actions. When you select a layer, you select all the objects on that layer or its sublayers. However, when you select an object from the palette, only that object is selected. Note also that when you select an artwork in the illustration window, that object also is selected in the Layers palette.

Selecting a Layer or Sublayer

You can select one layer or sublayer on the Layers palette. When you select a layer or sublayer, only that row is selected; objects on that layer or sublayer are not selected.

To select one layer in the Layers palette without selecting its contents in the palette or the illustration window, click its row in the Layers palette. (If you click the right side of the layer or sublayer, Illustrator also selects the objects in the illustration window.) Figure 14-5 shows the selected top layer in the Layers palette.

Selecting Objects in the Layers Palette Only

You can select one or more objects on a layer or sublayer in much the same way you select other objects in Illustrator. You can select layers to modify them in some way. For example, you can duplicate or delete them, or even collect them to move to another layer. However, you cannot edit them as you would other objects in the illustrations—mainly because they are not selected in the illustration window.

- To select noncontiguous objects on one layer or sublayer, click one layer and then click to select additional layers while pressing and holding down CTRL/⌘.

- To select contiguous objects on one layer or sublayer, click an object at one end of the range, press and hold down SHIFT, and click the layer at the other end of the range.

Figure 14-6 illustrates three selected objects in a group gathered by clicking while pressing and holding down CTRL/⌘. The order of items selected is the top row; the bottom row; and then the middle row, which is active.

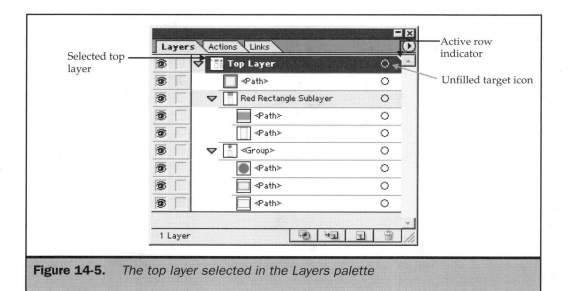

Figure 14-5.   *The top layer selected in the Layers palette*

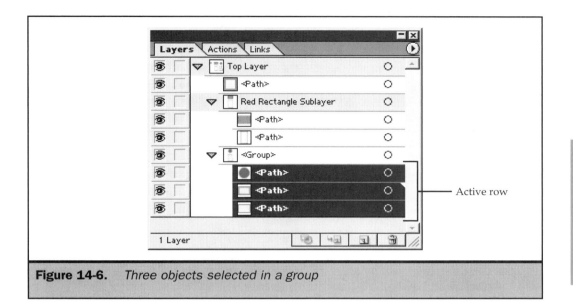

Active row

Figure 14-6. *Three objects selected in a group*

Selecting Objects in a Layer and the Illustration Window

When you make a selection on the Layers palette, the palette really lights up. To select an element in the Layers palette, click the right side of the palette or any part of a row and press and hold CTRL-ALT/⌘-OPTION.

- If you select a layer, sublayer, or group, Illustrator highlights the row and subordinate rows in the palette; fills in target radio buttons at the right side of the palette; displays selected art icons for the layer, sublayer, or group and its subordinate rows and parent layers above the object's layer or sublayer; and highlights the selected objects in the illustration window.

- If you select an object, Illustrator highlights the row in the palette; fills in target radio buttons at the right side of the palette; displays selected art icons for the object, its group (if it is associated with a group), and the layers and any sublayers above it; and highlights the object in the illustration window.

If you have clicked the right margin or pressed and held down CTRL-ALT/⌘-OPTION while clicking any part of a row to select objects, you can add to the selection. Just press and hold down SHIFT while repeatedly clicking.

Figure 14-7 shows the results of selecting the top layer (on the left) in the Layers palette and selecting a sublayer (on the right). In the example on the left, every object in the illustration window and every layer and object in the Layers palette is selected, and the top layer is active.

The example on the right illustrates that some objects in the illustration window are selected and others are not; in the palette, the top layer is selected, the sublayer is the active layer, and the sublayer's objects have selected art icons and filled-in target icons. Notice the difference in the size between the selected art icons in the examples. Because the Top Layer is the active row in the palette on the left, the selected art icon is large. However, in the example on the right, the small selected art icon indicates that the Top Layer is above the sublayer that is actually chosen.

Selecting All Objects in a Layer and the Illustration Window

You can select all the artwork in a particular layer by performing one of the following actions:

- Click a layer name or thumbnail while pressing and holding down ALT/OPTION.
- Click the right side of a row in the layer or press and hold down CTRL-ALT/⌘-OPTION while clicking any part of the row, and then choose Select | Object | All on Same Layers.
- Click the right side of a layer.

Note   *To deselect a selection, click the illustration window outside the Layers palette.*

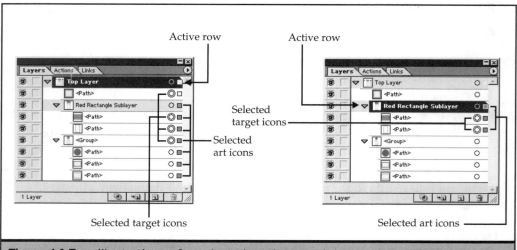

Figure 14-7.   *Illustrations of a selected top layer and the results on the left, and a selected sublayer and the consequences on the right*

Locating an Object in the Layers Palette

If you are working on a very complex artwork with many layers, sublayers, and objects, you can use a selection tool to choose that object in the illustration window. For example, you might have collapsed some layers to spend time working on other layers. Obviously, if a layer is collapsed, you can't see its contents. If you want to find that object in the Layers palette, you can get a little help by using the Locate Object command. Note that if you have hidden all the objects by choosing the Hide All Layers command from the palette's menu, the Locate Object command is dimmed and not available.

To locate an object, follow these steps:

1. Activate a selection tool.

2. Click one or more objects in the illustration window.

3. Choose Locate Object from the Layer palette's menu. Illustrator reveals the object and any layers above it on the palette. If you have chosen more than one object, Illustrator locates the topmost object in the stacking order.

Showing and Hiding Layers, Sublayers, and Objects

In the "Hiding and Showing Objects" section in Chapter 3, you learned how to hide and show objects without concerning yourself with layers. The Hide All Layers, Hide Others, Show All Layers, and Show Others commands in the Layers palette not only hide layers and sublayers, but as a side effect show and hide the objects on those layers.

If you want to concentrate on some of the objects in a particular set of layers and sublayers for a complicated artwork, you can hide some layers to clear parts of the illustration window. If you choose to hide the top layer, Illustrator hides all the objects in the document; so you are better off hiding sublayers and individual objects. If you hide a layer, Illustrator dims the eye icons for the objects on the layer. If you hide an object, Illustrator completely clears the eye icon from the palette.

Illustrator provides several methods for showing and hiding layers, sublayers, and objects:

■ To toggle between viewing and hiding a layer or object, click an eye icon.

■ To toggle between viewing and hiding a layer or sublayer, double-click the layer or sublayer name, or select a layer or sublayer and choose the Options for "*name*" command. In the Layer Options dialog box, clear the Show check box to hide the selected layer or sublayer or check Show to show the layer or sublayer. Then click OK to apply the change and close the dialog box.

■ To toggle between viewing and hiding an object, double-click the object name or select the object and choose the Options for "*name*" command. In the Options dialog box, clear the Show check box to hide the selected object or check Show to show the object. Then click OK to apply the change and close the dialog box.

- To toggle between viewing and hiding several layers, sublayers, and objects simultaneously, drag up or down the column that contains the eye icons.

- If all layers and sublayers are shown in the Layers palette, you can hide all layers and sublayers by selecting the top layer and choosing Hide All Layers from the palette's menu.

- If all layers and sublayers on the same level (but not the top level) as the selected layer or sublayer are shown, you can hide them by choosing Hide Others from the palette's menu.

- If all layers and sublayers are hidden in the Layers palette, you can show all layers and sublayers by selecting the top layer and choosing Show All Layers from the palette's menu.

- If all layers and sublayers on the same level (but not the top level) as the selected layer or sublayer are hidden, you can show them by choosing Show Others from the palette's menu.

Figure 14-8 illustrates two versions of the Layers palette—one with all layers and sublayers shown and the other with all layers and sublayers hidden. Notice the difference between the illustration window's contents.

| Note |

You can use the show and hide features of the Layers palette to control the layers or objects that are printed or exported. For example, if you want to fine-tune an object for printing, you can hide all other objects and concentrate on editing the target object. In the Layers palette, Illustrator provides two other ways of preventing the printing of layers and sublayers (and their contents), both involving the Layers Options dialog box. To open the dialog box, double-click the layer or sublayer, or select the layer or sublayer and choose the Options for "name" command from the palette's menu. In the dialog box, either remove the check mark from the Print check box or check the Template check box to convert the object to a template layer, which cannot print.

Switching Between Preview and Outline Modes

In the "Viewing in Preview and Outline Modes" section in Chapter 3, you learned how to view all objects in the illustration window in Preview mode or Outline mode. Using the Layers palette, you can view objects on some layers or sublayers in Preview mode and others in Outline mode. When a layer or sublayer is in Preview mode, the pupil of the eye icon in the leftmost column is filled and the objects on the layer appear as they will print; when a layer or sublayer is in Outline mode, the pupil is unfilled and its objects appear as outlines in the illustration window. Figure 14-9 shows the top layer in a document in Preview mode; one sublayer on the Layers palette is in Outline mode. In the illustration window, the two objects in the sublayer are in Outline mode, selected to enable them to be seen more clearly. All other objects are in Preview mode.

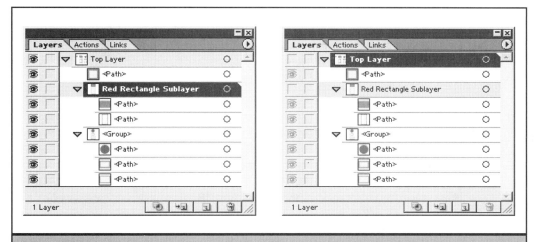

Figure 14-8. *Two illustrations of the Layers palette, one with all layers and sublayers shown and the other with all layers and sublayers hidden*

Illustrator provides several ways with which you can switch between Preview and Outline mode:

- To toggle between Preview and Outline mode, click an eye icon for a layer, sublayer, or object while pressing and holding down CTRL/⌘.

- To toggle from one mode to another, double-click a layer or sublayer name, or select the layer or sublayer and choose the Options for "*name*" command.

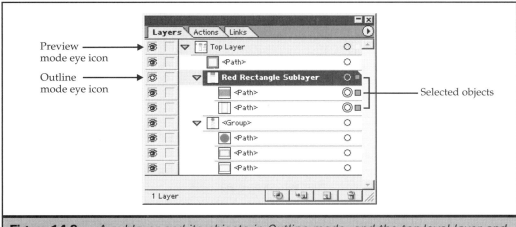

Figure 14-9. *A sublayer and its objects in Outline mode, and the top-level layer and its other contents in Preview mode*

In the Layer Options dialog box, clear the Preview check box to show the selected layer in Outline mode or check Preview to show the layer in Preview mode. Then click OK to apply the change and close the dialog box.

- To toggle a layer or sublayer in Outline mode to Preview mode, click an Outline mode eye icon while pressing and holding down CTRL-ALT/⌘-OPTION.

- If all layers and sublayers are shown in Preview mode, you can show all layers and sublayers in Outline mode by selecting the top layer and choosing the Outline All Layers command from the palette's menu.

- If all layers and sublayers on the same level (but not the top level) as the selected layer or sublayer are shown in Preview mode, you can change them to Outline mode by choosing Outline Others from the palette's menu. If there are no other layers or sublayers on the same level, Illustrator ignores the command.

- If all layers and sublayers are shown in Outline mode, you can show all layers and sublayers in Preview mode by selecting the top layer and choosing Outline Others from the palette's menu.

- If all layers and sublayers on the same level (but not the top level) as the selected layer or sublayer are shown in Outline mode, you can change them to Preview mode by choosing Preview Others from the palette's menu. If there are no other layers or sublayers on the same level, Illustrator ignores the command.

Locking and Unlocking Layers

In the "Locking and Unlocking Objects" section in Chapter 3, you learned about locking and unlocking objects without even knowing about the Layers palette. The Lock All Layers, Lock Others, Unlock All Layers, and Unlock Others commands in the Layers palette lock and unlock layers and sublayers and also lock and unlock the objects contained in the affected layers and sublayers.

When you lock an object in the Layers palette, you cannot select or change it in any way. If a layer or sublayer is locked, all its contents are also locked. When you attempt to select or edit a locked object using toolbox tools, Illustrator changes the mouse pointer to a pencil with a line drawn through it. This is another hint that you cannot select or edit the object.

Illustrator provides the following methods for locking and unlocking layers and sublayers:

- To toggle between locking and unlocking a layer, sublayer, or object, click the column to the right of the eye icon. A lock icon indicates that the layer, sublayer, or object is locked. An empty column shows that the layer, sublayer, or object is unlocked and ready for editing.

- To toggle between locking and unlocking a layer or sublayer, double-click the layer or sublayer name, or select a layer or sublayer and choose the Options for "*name*" command. In the Layer Options dialog box, clear the Lock check box to unlock the selected layer or sublayer or check Lock to lock the layer or sublayer. Then click OK to apply the change and close the dialog box.

■ To toggle between locking and unlocking an object, double-click the object name or select the object and choose the Options for "*name*" command. In the Options dialog box, clear the Lock check box to unlock the selected object or check Lock to lock the object. Then click OK to apply the change and close the dialog box.

■ If all layers and sublayers are unlocked in the Layers palette, you can lock all layers and sublayers by selecting the top layer and choosing Lock All Layers from the palette's menu.

■ If all layers and sublayers on the same level (but not the top level) as the selected layer or sublayer are unlocked, you can lock them by choosing Lock Others from the palette's menu.

■ If all layers and sublayers are locked in the Layers palette, you can unlock all layers and sublayers by selecting the top layer and choosing Unlock All Layers from the palette's menu.

■ If all layers and sublayers on the same level (but not the top level) as the selected layer or sublayer are locked, you can unlock them by choosing Unlock Others from the palette's menu.

Figure 14-10 shows the Layers palette with some locked and some unlocked rows.

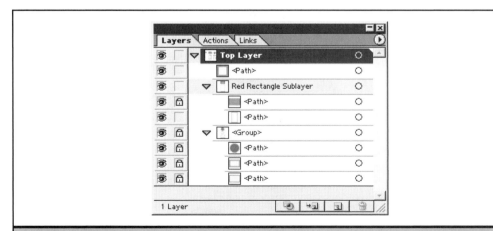

Figure 14-10.   *The Layers palette illustrating locked and unlocked elements of a document*

Arranging Layers, Sublayers, and Objects

When you initially create a layer or sublayer, Illustrator places it right above the currently active row at that row's level. For example, if you add a layer above the top-level layer, its thumbnail is aligned with the left margin of the Layers palette—just like the top-level layer's thumbnail. So, if you have selected the fifth row in the Layers palette, any new layer or sublayer pushes the contents of the fifth row down to the sixth position and puts itself in the fifth row at the same level as the current fifth row; the two thumbnails are the same distance from the left margin.

Illustrator enables you to arrange layers, sublayers, and objects by using the Arrange commands, by dragging and dropping in the Layers palette, and by reversing the order of elements by choosing a Layers palette command.

Arranging Layers by Using the Arrange Commands

In the "Arranging Objects and Groups" section in Chapter 3, you learned how to arrange (or *stack*) objects in the illustration window using the four commands on the Arrange submenu on the Object menu. To move a selected object to the front of all other objects, you chose Object | Arrange | Bring to Front (CTRL-SHIFT-]/⌘-SHIFT-]); to move the selection ahead of the next higher object, you chose Object | Arrange | Bring Forward (CTRL-]/⌘-]); to move the selection behind the object behind it, you chose Object | Arrange | Send Backward (CTRL-[/⌘-[); and to move the selection behind every object, you chose Object | Arrange | Send to Back (CTRL-SHIFT-]/⌘-SHIFT-]).

When you choose one of these commands for a selected object in the illustration window, Illustrator reorders the rows in the Layers palette, depending on the level of the selected layer, sublayer, or object. For example, only a layer can be in the top row and the top-level layer's objects will only move within the layer. If you select an object in the eighth row and choose Object | Arrange | Bring to Front (CTRL-SHIFT-]/⌘-SHIFT-]), Illustrator moves that object to the top row of its layer or sublayer.

Dragging and Dropping Elements Within the Layers Palette

Illustrator provides several ways of rearranging layers, sublayers, or objects in the Layers palette using the drag-and-drop feature.

- You can drag a layer or sublayer (but not the top layer) up or down the rows of the palette. When Illustrator displays a dark horizontal line with small arrows between rows, you can drop the dragged layer or sublayer in its new location. If the horizontal line does not appear, you know that you cannot drop the element in that position, probably because you are inadvertently attempting to change the level of the layer to one that is superior or subordinate to its current location under the top layer.

- You can drag an object up or down the rows of the palette. When Illustrator displays a dark horizontal line with small arrows between rows, you can drop the dragged object in its new location in its current layer or sublayer or in another layer or sublayer.

- You can select an object to drag by clicking the right edge of its row and dragging the object's selected art icon to its new position.

- You can drag an entire layer or sublayer and its contents by clicking the right edge of its row and dragging the layer's or sublayer's selected art icon to its new location.

Note *You also can cut and paste objects from one layer to another: Select an object in the illustration window and choose Edit | Copy (CTRL-C/⌘-C) to copy the object to the Clipboard, or Edit | Cut (CTRL-X/⌘-X) to cut the object to the Clipboard. Then move the mouse pointer to the location at which you want the object to be placed. Choose Edit | Paste (CTRL-V/⌘-V) to put the object in front of the selected row.*

Reversing Elements in the Layers Palette

The Layers palette's menu provides a command with which you can reverse the order of layers, sublayers, or objects in the Layers palette. Note that the selected elements must be at the same level; for example, under a particular layer or sublayer. To reverse the order of set of objects, follow these steps:

1. To select noncontiguous objects, click an object and then press and hold down CTRL/⌘. Click repeatedly to add each desired object to the selection.

2. To select contiguous objects, click an object at one end of the range, and then press and hold down SHIFT. Click an object at the other end of the range to select all the objects in the range.

3. Choose Reverse Order. Illustrator reverses the order of the selected objects within their layer or sublayer.

Sending an Object to the Current Layer

You can use an Illustrator command to move an object from one layer to another. To do so, follow these steps:

1. In the illustration window, select an object to be moved.

2. In the Layers palette, click the thumbnail or name of the target layer. (Do not click the right side of the row because when the selected art icon appears in the Layers palette, Illustrator ignores the command.)

3. Choose Object | Arrange | Send to Current Layer. Illustrator moves the selected object to its new layer.

Merging and Flattening Sublayers and Objects

When you choose the Merge Selected and Flatten Artwork commands from the Layers palette's menu, you unite sublayers, groups, and paths in a new layer or group. With the Merge Selected command, you have complete control over the selection of elements: You explicitly choose them one at a time. On the other hand, choosing Flatten Artwork automates the selection process: Illustrator selects all the components that are not hidden.

Merging Layers, Sublayers, and Groups

To merge layers, sublayers, and groups into one layer or group, follow these steps:

1. In the Layers palette, select one or more layers or groups. (If you select paths, the Merge Selected command is not available.)

2. Choose the Merge Selected command from the Layers palette's menu. Illustrator merges the selected elements.

Figure 14-11 shows before and after versions of the Layers palette. The palette on the left illustrates the before version with two selections (see the target icons): the Red Rectangle sublayer and an unnamed group. On the right is the after version with one sublayer, Red Rectangle.

Flattening Sublayers and Objects

To flatten all the visible elements—including layers and sublayers—in an artwork, follow these steps:

1. In the Layers palette, select a layer that will become the home of the visible objects. The layer must be visible and unlocked and must not be a template layer.

2. Choose the Flatten Artwork command from the Layers palette's menu.

3. If Illustrator prompts you to make any hidden artwork visible or delete it, respond to the prompt.

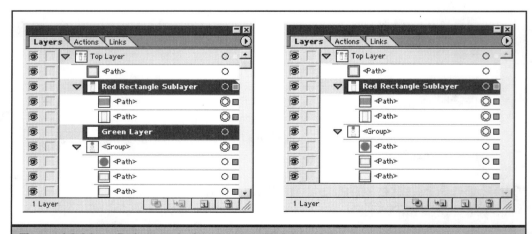

Figure 14-11.   *Before and after demonstrations of the merge process*

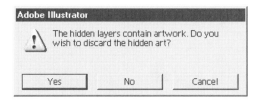

When Illustrator flattens an artwork (see Figure 14-12), you might not notice the difference at first; after all, the names, levels, and thumbnails are the same. However, remember that Illustrator displays layer and sublayer rows with a gray background. After flattening, all the rows under the selected layer now have a white background. Furthermore, if you double-click any name within the home layer, Illustrator reveals the Options dialog box rather than the Layer Options dialog box.

Releasing Elements to Separate Layers

By using the Release to Layers command in the palette's menu, you can allocate the contents of a selected layer or group to separate layers. This enables you to separate an artwork into individual layers for further work, such as adding new objects or moving some elements to other layers.

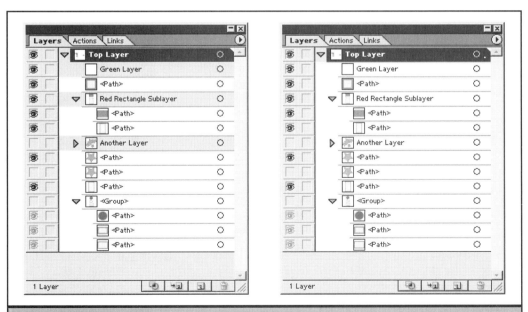

Figure 14-12.   *The Layers palette before and after using the flattening feature*

Illustrator provides two versions of the command: Release to Layers (Sequence) and Release to Layers (Build):

■ Choose Release to Layers (Sequence) to have Illustrator release each element in the selected layer to its own layer.

■ Choose Release to Layers (Build) to instruct Illustrator to release the elements into layers in which the elements are accumulated. For example, the first new layer includes all the contents of the layer, the second new layer contains all but one, the third layer holds all but two, and so on. Imagine what you can do with these layers when creating a Web animation.

To release elements to separate layers, follow these steps:

1. In the Layers palette, select a layer or group to be released.

2. From the palette's menu, choose one of the Release to Layers commands. Illustrator creates new layers.

Figure 14-13 illustrates the two versions of using the Release to Layers command. On the left is the original version of the Layers palette with one layer selected. The center palette shows the results of choosing the Release to Layers (Sequence) command. On the right side of the figure you can see the outcome of choosing Release to Layers (Build). Note that the rightmost version has large rows so that you can see the changing number of objects in new Layers 3, 4, 5, and 6. (Remember that you can set row size by choosing Palette Options from the bottom of the palette's menu and selecting Small, Medium, Large, or Other in the Row Size section of the Layers Palette Options dialog box.)

Collecting Objects in a New Layer

Using the Collect in New Layer command is almost the reverse of the Release to Layers commands. When you choose Collect in New Layer, Illustrator gathers the selected elements in the Layers palette into a new layer.

To collect objects in a new layer, follow these steps:

1. Select one or more items to be collected in a new layer.

2. Choose Collect in New Layer from the palette's menu. Illustrator creates a new layer and places the selected elements under it.

Figure 14-14 illustrates before and after versions of the Layers palette. Notice that two paths are selected in the before version (on the left). In the after version, the selected paths are contained in a new layer of their own.

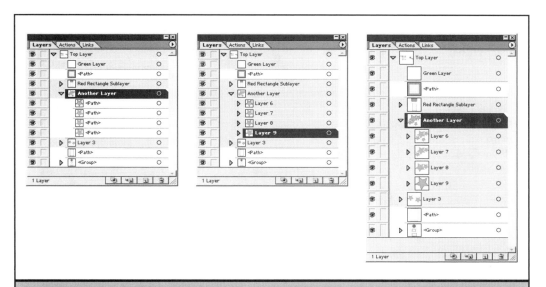

Figure 14-13. *On the left, the original Layers palette; in the center, the consequences of Release to Layers (Sequence); and on the right, the result of choosing Release to Layers (Build)*

ILLUSTRATOR
ESSENTIALS

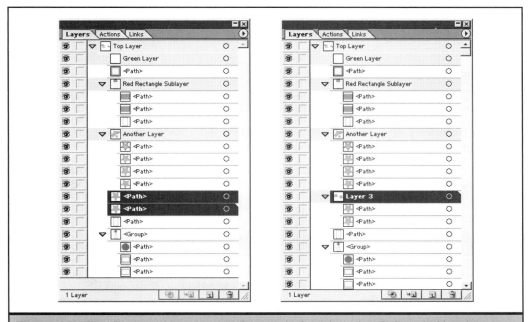

Figure 14-14. *The Layers palette before and after choosing Collect in New Layer*

Pasting Objects in Certain Layers

By choosing the Paste Remembers Layers command in the Layers palette menu, you can determine the layer on which Illustrator pastes one or more copied or cut objects. Normally, Illustrator pastes a copied or cut object on the active layer in the palette (which means that, the Paste Remembers Layers command is inactive by default). However, if you select Paste Remembers Layers, you can have Illustrator paste the object onto the layer from which you copied or cut it—either in the current document or from one document to another.

Paste Remembers Layers works very well when you are copying or cutting objects from one document to another. If the source document has a layer with a particular name, you can activate Paste Remembers Layers to paste objects in a layer with the same name in the target document. If the target document does not include a layer with the same name, Illustrator creates one for you.

Duplicating a Layer

By using the Duplicate *"name"* command in the Layers palette's menu, you can duplicate or copy any element listed in the Layers palette. For example, you can duplicate a path so that you can make subtle changes for an animation, you can duplicate a group of small paths to change their stroke or fill colors for a decorative border, or you can duplicate a sublayer or layer containing paths and groups composing an "congratulatory" certificate.

Illustrator changes the name of the Duplicate command depending on the elements that you select. For example, if you select several paths or a combination of layers and paths, the command is Duplicate Selection. Or, if you select a layer named "Green Layer," the command is named Duplicate "Green Layer."

To duplicate objects in the Layers palette, follow these steps:

1. Select one or more elements from the Layers palette.

2. To duplicate the selection and place it above the selection, choose the Duplicate command from the menu or drag the selection to the New Layer button at the bottom of the palette.

3. To duplicate the selection and put it in a location of your choosing, start dragging the selection to its new location in the palette, and press and hold down ALT/OPTION.

Deleting an Object, Group, Sublayer, or Layer

To delete any object or set of objects from the Layers palette, do one of the following:

- Select one or more items and click the Delete Selection button at the bottom right of the palette.

- Select one or more items and drag them to the Delete Selection button.

- Choose Delete Selection or Delete *"name"* from the palette's menu.

When you delete a layer or sublayer that contain objects, Illustrator deletes the layer or sublayer and all the contents without confirming the deletion. However, you can undo a deletion by choosing Edit | Undo (CTRL-Z/⌘-Z).

Dimming a Raster Image

As you know, you can use raster (that is, bitmap) images opened or placed in Illustrator documents. Table 14-1 lists the raster file types that Illustrator supports.

Illustrator provides a command in the Layers palette's menu to dim a raster image layer in the illustration window. (For more information on working with raster images, refer to Chapters 19 and 20.) When you dim a bitmap, you push it into the background of a picture and emphasize objects in the foreground. You might want to dim a raster image that you are using as a background for a work of art. You could create an artwork with a patterned or landscape rasterized background, and painted objects in the

File Type	File Extension(s)
Adobe Photoshop	.PSD, .PDD
Amiga IFF	.IFF (both raster and vector)
Bitmap	.BMP, .RLE
CompuServe GIF89A	.GIF
Computer Graphics Metafile	.CGM
Encapsulated PostScript	.EPS (both raster and vector)
Filmstrip	.FLM
JPEG	.JPG
Macintosh PICT	.PIC, .PCT
PCX	.PCX
Pixar	.PXR
Portable Document Format	.PDF (both raster and vector)
Portable Network Graphics (PNG-8 and PNG-24)	.PNG
Targa	.TGA, .VDA, .ICB, .VST
TIFF	.TIF

Table 14-1. *Raster Files Supported by Illustrator*

foreground. For example, you could scatter a bunch of scorpions on a dessert background or a few butterfly brushstrokes on a shrub background (see Figure 14-15).

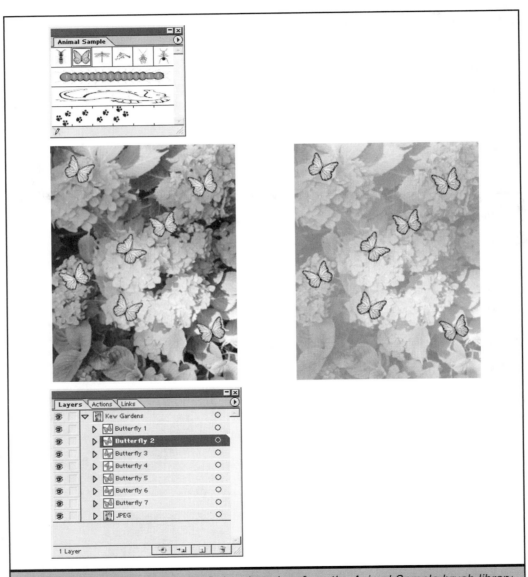

Figure 14-15. *Illustrator butterfly brushstrokes from the Animal Sample brush library and a photographic raster image in the background*

To dim a bitmap, follow these steps:

1. In the Layers palette, double-click the layer on which the raster image resides or select the layer and choose Options for "*name*" from the palette's menu. Illustrator opens the Layers Options dialog box.

2. Check the Dim Images check box. Illustrator undims the text box to the right of the check box.

3. In the Dim Images text box, type the percentage by which you want to dim the raster image. Valid values range from 0% to 100%; the default is 50%.

4. Click OK. Illustrator closes the dialog box and dims the raster image.

Using Template Layers

You use template layers in the Layers palette to create a template on which you can base an object. Templates are especially useful for using the Auto Trace tool (see the "Tracing Artwork" section later in this chapter).

Illustrator restricts template layers in the following ways:

- You cannot select, edit, print, or export a template layer or any of the objects in the layer.

- Illustrator locks all template layers, which means you cannot select or edit the contents of a template layer.

- You cannot toggle the layer between showing and viewing and Preview and Outline mode.

- You cannot create a sublayer for a template layer.

- When you create a template layer, Illustrator limits any existing objects on the layer to raster images. (To learn more about working with raster images, refer to Chapters 19 and 20.)

To create a template layer, do one of the following:

- If you want to convert an existing layer to a template layer, select the layer and choose Template from the Layers palette menu. Illustrator places a check mark in front of the Template command.

- If you want to create a new template layer, choose New Layer from the palette's menu. When Illustrator opens the Layer Options dialog box, check the Template check box, optionally select other options, and then click OK. Note that you can use this method when a template layer is selected in the Layers palette.

- If you want to create a new template layer, choose File | Place. From the Place dialog box, select an image file and check the Template check box; then click OK.

Note that you cannot use this method when a template layer is selected in the Layers palette: The Place command is not available.

When Illustrator creates a template layer, it replaces the view/hide icon with a bitmap icon in the first column of the Layers palette and places a lock icon in the second column.

Tracing Artwork

You can trace a drawing for Illustrator rather than starting from scratch with a blank illustration window. For example, you can open an old drawing or photograph whose copyright has run out or a document created in another program, trace it, and edit it to make it your own. Illustrator provides two ways to trace artwork: using the Auto Trace tool to automatically create a path or drawing over a raster image on a template layer using the Pen tool (N) or the Pencil tool (P).

Tracing with the Auto Trace Tool

The Auto Trace tool automates the tracing process. Just select the tool and then click the edge of a closed or open path to be traced. The end result is always an outline of the object; that is, a closed path. Use the Auto Trace tool to trace objects with very few twists and turns or color variations. The Auto Trace tool is programmed to sense the difference between colors in the target image.

To trace a path using the Auto Trace tool, follow these steps:

1. Open a raster image to be automatically traced.

2. Activate the Auto Trace tool.

3. To trace part of the image or the complete image, move the cross-hairs mouse pointer within 6 pixels of the edge of the image, and click.

4. To trace part of the image, drag the mouse pointer from the beginning to the end of the area to be traced within 2 pixels of the edge of the image.

5. If part of the image has not been traced, repeat steps 3 and 4.

To learn how to adjust the distance between gaps in tracing, refer to the "Type and Auto Tracing" section in Appendix B.

Figure 14-16 demonstrates the conversion of a raster image to an auto-traced one. The raster image was created in Adobe Photoshop, saved as a .BMP document, and opened in Illustrator. First, the Auto Trace tool traced the head and body followed by the partial wheel. Note that once you have saved a raster image as an Illustrator document, it is no longer a raster image; so you can no longer use the Auto Trace tool on it.

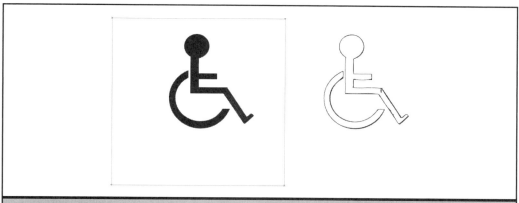

Figure 14-16. *A raster image converted to an auto-traced path in two clicks of the Auto Trace tool*

Tracing a Template Layer

You can use the Pencil tool (N) or Pen tool (P) to manually trace an object. If you draw outside the object's border, you can always adjust by using the Direct Selection tool (A) and moving specific anchor points. Figure 14-17 shows a digital photograph of a puppy before and after using the Pencil to trace around the body, eye, nose, ear, and so on. Before starting to trace, I zoomed the photograph to 200%, set the fill to None, and made sure the stroke was 1-point black. After tracing, I used the Direct Selection tool to move the stroke where it had strayed from the desired route. Finally, I deleted the photograph to view the paths by themselves.

Figure 14-17. *A JPG picture before and after manual tracing with the Pencil*

Using Clipping Masks

When you create a *clipping mask*, you are using an object or group to change the look of the underlying object or group: Part of the object or group shows through the mask, and the masked part is hidden from view. The entire set of layers composed of one or more clipping masks, and the objects that are masked, are known as a *clipping set*.

A Primer on Clipping Masks

When you use clipping masks, keep these rules in mind:

■ The layer at the top of the Layers palette cannot be a clipping mask, but it can contain a clipping mask.

■ An entire clipping set must be in the same layer, sublayer, or group in the Layers palette.

■ The first element in a layer, sublayer, or group is the clipping mask.

■ When you create a clipping mask from an object, both fill and stroke are set to None.

■ In the Layers palette, a clipping path is enclosed within a dotted border and, by default, is named <Clipping Path>.

Creating a Clipping Set

Before you create a clipping set, you should have a plan for the final shape of the object or objects to be covered by the mask. Create each object in the clipping set and then decide how to arrange or rearrange them in the Layers palette. Remember that nothing is final in a design: Illustrator always has the tools and features with which you can edit any artwork or object within that artwork.

To create a clipping set, follow these steps:

1. Decide on the layer, sublayer, or group in the Layers palette that will contain the elements of the future clipping set.

2. If necessary, move the object that will become the clipping mask to the top of the layer, sublayer, or group.

3. To convert the top object to a clipping mask, select its layer and click the Make/Release Clipping Mask button at the bottom of the Layers palette or choose Make Clipping Mask from the palette's menu.

Figure 14-18 shows the illustration and Layers palette before (on the top of the figure) and after (on the bottom) the creation of a clipping mask. The clipping mask path is a rounded rectangle whose sides were adjusted with the Direct Selection tool (A). Notice the clipping mask is surrounded by a dotted border in the after version.

Figure 14-19 shows the final artwork with the clipping mask and another layer containing a border around the clipped photograph and type converted to an outline with a 3-point black stroke. Before making the clipping mask, a top layer was added and the 8-point border in the figure was created by selecting the future clipping mask, making a copy, pasting the copy at the top of the illustration window, choosing Object | Path | Offset Path, setting an offset value of 15 points, and clicking OK.

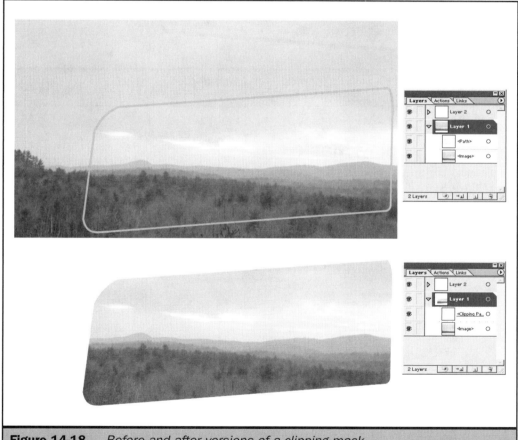

Figure 14-18.   *Before and after versions of a clipping mask*

ILLUSTRATOR
ESSENTIALS

Figure 14-19.   *The final illustration with an added border and type*

Releasing a Clipping Mask

To release a clipping mask (that is, convert the clipping mask to the original object), follow these steps:

1. Select the layer, sublayer, or group in the Layers palette that contains the clipping set.

2. Click the Make/Release Clipping Mask button at the bottom of the Layers palette or choose Release Clipping Mask from the palette's menu.

The Complete Reference

Adobe Illustrator 10

Part III

Illustrator FX

The
Complete
Reference

Chapter 15

Enhancing Art with Transparency

435

Illustrator enables you to adjust the levels of opacity or transparency of layers, sublayers, groups, and objects in your artwork with the Transparency palette. By default, all objects in Illustrator are 100% opaque (or 0% transparent): A completely opaque object blocks the view of parts of underlying objects. On the other hand, an object that is 100% transparent (that is, 0% opaque) is completely invisible: Any underlying objects are open to view.

You can use commands and check boxes on the Transparency palette to create opacity and transparency effects. For example, Illustrator provides 16 blending modes with which you can mix colors of a base object and a blending object. You also can check the Knockout Group check box to adjust the view of semitransparent objects in one layer with respect to objects in underlying layers. In addition, you can fine-tune a knockout effect for semitransparent gradient fills.

In this chapter you'll learn all about setting opacity and transparency levels and applying transparency and blending effects. Working with opacity and transparency can affect printing and other output. To learn more about printing documents with semitransparent layers, sublayers, groups, or objects, refer to the "Printing Documents with Transparent Artwork" section in Chapter 22.

Exploring the Transparency Palette

With the Transparency palette (see Figure 15-1), you can adjust the level of opacity from completely opaque, the Illustrator default, to totally transparent (which makes objects invisible) for one or more selected objects; create opacity masks (which are similar to the clipping masks you learned about in Chapter 14); or blend colors of two or more objects. To toggle between showing and hiding the palette, choose Window | Transparency (SHIFT-F10).

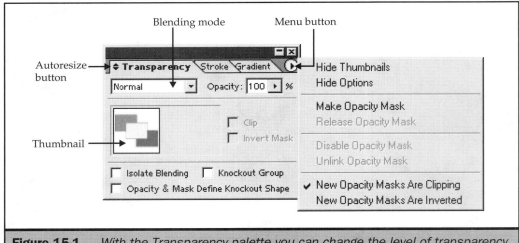

Figure 15-1. *With the Transparency palette you can change the level of transparency or opacity for one or more selected objects.*

The Transparency palette contains the following elements:

- The Blending Mode drop-down menu lists the available blending modes with which you can combine the color of the selected transparent object with the objects that are in the background of the artwork. Your choices are Normal (the default), Multiply, Screen, Overlay, Soft Light, Hard Light, Color Dodge, Color Burn, Darken, Lighten, Difference, Exclusion, Hue, Saturation, Color, and Luminosity.

- The Opacity text box/drop-down menu/slider enables you to select a level of opacity. You can type, select, or slide to choose from 100% opacity (the default) to 0% opacity and opacity/transparency percentages between.

- The thumbnail box contains a small picture of the selected objects in the illustration window. If you have created an opacity mask, the thumbnail box grows to show both the opacity mask and the current selection.

- Check the Clip check box to make a clipping mask from an opacity mask. If you check Clip and Invert Mask, Illustrator creates a clipping mask with inverted luminance.

- Check the Invert Mask check box to reverse the opacity mask. For example, if the original mask reveals artwork inside the mask and covers artwork outside the mask, Invert Mask shows the artwork outside the mask and hides the artwork inside the mask.

- Check the Isolate Blending check box to exclude certain blending modes from a target layer, sublayer, group, or object.

- Check the Knockout Group check box to remove all or part of an image from another image.

- Check the Opacity & Mask Define Knockout Shape to control the knockout effect, depending on the level of opacity or transparency.

To toggle through the palette's four resize settings, repeatedly click the Autoresize button.

To open the palette's menu, click the menu button. Commands on the menu are:

- The Show Thumbnails command increases the size of the palette so that you can view the thumbnail section. The Hide Thumbnails command decreases the size of the palette so that you no longer view the thumbnail section. Remember that you can automatically resize the palette by repeatedly clicking the Autoresize button.

- The Show Options command either shows the entire palette or the palette without the three check boxes at the bottom of the palette—depending on the current size of the palette. The Hide Options command hides the bottom three check boxes in the palette.

■ The Make Opacity Mask command creates an opacity mask.

■ The Release Opacity Mask command eliminates the active opacity mask. This command is available only if you have selected an opacity mask in the current document.

■ The Disable Opacity Mask command inactivates the active opacity mask but does not remove it. This command is available only if you have selected an opacity mask. The Enable Opacity Mask command restores an inactivated opacity mask.

■ The Unlink Opacity Mask command unlinks an opacity mask from its associated artwork. This command is available only if you have selected a linked opacity mask. The Link Opacity Mask command relinks an unlinked opacity mask and its artwork.

■ The New Opacity Masks Are Clipping command checks the Clip check box so that all new opacity masks are also clipping masks. A checked box is the default.

■ The New Opacity Masks Are Inverted command checks the Invert Mask check box so that all new opacity masks are inverted. A cleared check box is the default.

Setting Transparency

You can apply transparency for an entire layer, sublayer, group, or object; or set a level of transparency for the fill or stroke of an individual object. By default, Illustrator applies transparency to a layer, sublayer, group, or object. Note that when you move a sublayer, group, or object to another layer, it takes on the characteristics of that new layer.

Applying Transparency to an Element

To set transparency for a layer, sublayer, group, or object as a whole, follow these steps:

1. Select the element by using one of these techniques:

   ■ To select one object or group, activate the Selection tool (V) or the Direct Selection tool (A) and click the object or group.

   ■ To select more than one object or group, activate the Selection tool (V) or the Direct Selection tool (A). Then press and hold down SHIFT, and click the object or group, or draw a bounding box with either one of the selection tools.

   ■ To select a layer, sublayer, group, or object, choose Window | Layers (F7) to open the Layers palette. Then click the target icon in the row holding the target element.

2. Choose Window | Transparency (SHIFT-F10) to open the Transparency palette.

3. Either type a percentage from 0% (complete transparency and invisibility) to 100% (completely opaque) in the Opacity text box, or open the Opacity slider and slide to the desired level of opacity or transparency.

Figure 15-2 illustrates three rectangles set—from left to right—at 100% opacity (or 0% transparency), 10% opacity (or 90% transparency), and 50% opacity (or 50% transparency). Are you an optimist if you call an object half transparent or half opaque?

If you were able to see colors in Figure 15-2, you'd note that the overlapping areas for two transparent elements contain a combination of the two elements' colors. For example, the color in the overlap of a blue object and a yellow object is green. In the Layers palette, you'd also notice a change in the target icon's fill. When you change the opacity setting from 100%, Illustrator fills in the target button with a mix of graytones.

Applying Transparency to the Fill or Stroke

To set transparency for a selected object's fill or stroke, you should open both the Transparency palette (to set the transparency as in the previous set of steps) and the Appearance palette (to select the fill or the stroke). You'll learn more about the Appearance palette in the "Exploring the Appearance Palette" section and the following sections in Chapter 18.

To set transparency for an object's fill or stroke, follow these steps:

1. Activate the Selection tool (V) or the Direct Selection tool (A) and click the object, or open the Layers palette and click the target icon of the target object while pressing and holding down CTRL-ALT/⌘-OPTION. Illustrator shows the paths for the selected object.

2. Choose Window | Appearance (SHIFT-F6) to open the Appearance palette.

3. Select the fill or stroke of the object by clicking the Fill or Stroke in the Appearance palette.

4. In the Transparency palette, either type a percentage from 0% to 100% in the Opacity text box or open the Opacity slider and slide to the desired level of opacity or transparency.

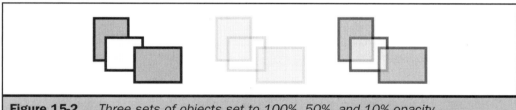

Figure 15-2.   *Three sets of objects set to 100%, 50%, and 10% opacity*

When you print a document with objects that are not completely 100% opaque, make sure you have settled on the final levels of opacity and transparency. During the processing that leads to printing, Illustrator flattens the artwork, which means individual layers are merged under a single layer with one opacity setting. In fact, Illustrator prompts you by displaying the message "This document contains artwork that requires flattening" at the bottom of the Print dialog box.

Using the Transparency Grid

The transparency grid enables you to adjust the whole illustration window so that you view the opaque, semi-opaque, and transparent objects therein. In this section you'll learn how to show and hide the transparency grid and set transparency grid options.

Showing and Hiding the Transparency Grid

To show the transparency grid, choose View | Show Transparency Grid (CTRL-SHIFT-D/⌘-SHIFT-D); to hide the grid, choose View | Hide Transparency Grid. Figure 15-3 illustrates three rectangles whose fills are at 50%, 100%, and 25% opacity. The stroke of all remains at the default 100% opacity. The Appearance palette shows that the leftmost rectangle is selected; the Transparency palette illustrates the 50% opacity level. The transparency grid demonstrates the various levels of transparency.

Setting Transparency Grid Options

In Chapter 5 you got your first exposure to the Document Setup dialog box for setting up the artboard. You also can use this dialog box to adjust the settings for the transparency grid and a few other transparency options. To open the Document Setup dialog box (see Figure 15-4) for transparency attributes, choose File | Document Setup and then select Transparency from the drop-down menu at the top of the dialog box.

 To learn more about using the Transparency section of the Document Setup dialog box to set attributes for printing documents with transparent objects, refer to the "Printing Documents with Transparent Artwork" section in Chapter 22.

Exploring the Transparency Section of the Document Setup Dialog Box

The transparency grid options in the Transparency section of the Document Setup dialog box are as follows:

- From the Grid Size drop-down menu, choose the size of the checkerboard grid: Small, Medium (the default), or Large. The large Preview box on the right side of the section shows the current size selection.

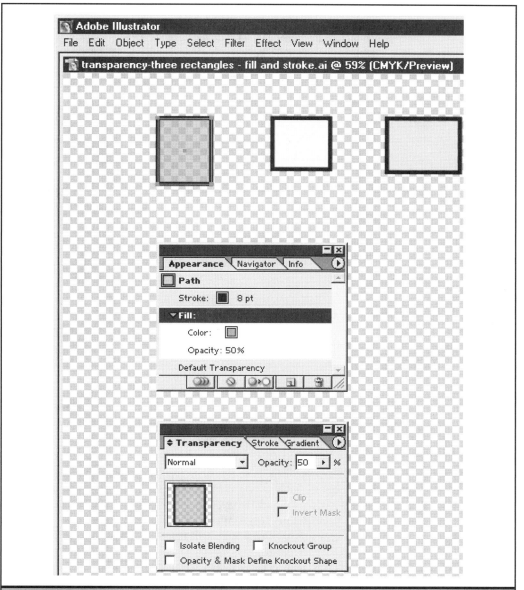

Figure 15-3. *Three rectangles with fills set at 50%, 100%, and 25% opacity; and strokes of 100% opacity*

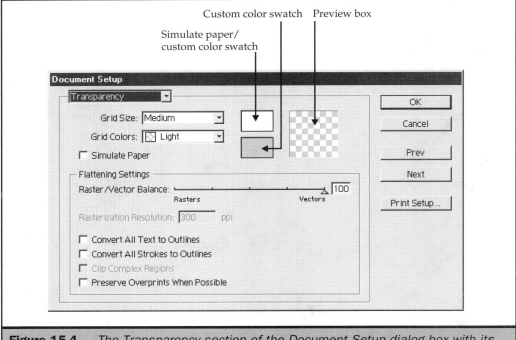

Figure 15-4.   *The Transparency section of the Document Setup dialog box with its default settings*

■ From the Grid Colors drop-down menu, choose from three lightness/darkness levels; the colors Red, Orange, Green, Blue, or Purple; or select Custom to mix a custom color from the Color Picker dialog box. The two small Preview boxes show the current light and dark colors.

■ Check the Simulate Paper check box to view the active document as it would look if printed on the color of the top swatch in the dialog box. This option is not available when you turn on the transparency grid. If you check this box for a CMYK document to be printed on white paper, Illustrator previews the document a little more accurately than it would if the check box were unchecked.

Selecting Custom Colors for the Transparency Grid

To select custom colors for the transparency grid checkerboard, follow these steps:

1. Click a swatch to the right of the Grid Size and Grid Colors drop-down menus.

2. When the Color Picker opens, choose a color and click OK. Illustrator changes the color of the swatch to the selected color.

3. Repeat steps 1 and 2 for the other swatch.

4. Click OK to close the Document Setup dialog box.

Refer to "Using the Color Picker" at the end of Chapter 7 to learn more about choosing colors from the Color Picker.

Using Blending Modes

When you use Illustrator's blending modes, which are listed in a drop-down menu in the Transparency palette, you can affect the way colors of overlapping objects appear in your documents. Before we continue, you should learn some blending terms:

- The active transparent or semitransparent object contributes the *blend color*.
- The object immediately under the active transparent or semitransparent object supplies the *base color*.
- The *resulting color* is the mix of the blend color and the base color.

Defining the Blending Modes

Illustrator supports 16 blending modes, briefly described and illustrated in this section. When you test blending modes, the chosen base and blend colors have a great deal to do with the resulting color.

The following illustrations contain the same set of objects. The overlying objects shown in the illustrations are set at 80% opacity, and the underlying rectangle is 100% opaque. The base color of the rectangle is 75% blue C=75 M=37.5 in the Swatches palette. The triangle on the left side of each illustration is 25% Orange M=12.5 Y=25. The diagonally aligned rectangle in the center is White, and the diagonally aligned rectangle on the right side is Black.

Normal

If you select Normal, the default blending mode, Illustrator keeps the base color and any blend colors separate, which means the colors remain original.

Multiply

The Multiply blending mode multiplies the base color by the blend color, which always produces a darker color. If Illustrator multiplies the base color by black, the result is black. If Illustrator multiplies the base color by white, the resulting color is the same as the base color.

Screen

The Screen blending mode multiplies the inverse of both the base and blend colors, which always produces a lighter color. If Illustrator multiplies the base color by black, the resulting color is the same as the blend color. If Illustrator multiplies the base color by white, the resulting color is white.

Overlay

The Overlay blending mode either multiplies or screens the colors. The resulting color is lighter or darker, depending on the base color, and also keeps the light and dark areas of the base color or pattern.

Soft Light

The Soft Light blending mode either lightens or darkens the colors, depending on the blend color. If the blend color is lighter than 50% gray, Illustrator produces a lighter resulting color. If the blend color is white, the resulting color is slightly darker than white but lighter than the base color. If the blend color is darker than 50% gray, the resulting color is darker than the blend color. If the blend color is black, the resulting color is somewhere between black and the base color.

Hard Light

Hard Light either multiplies or screens the colors, depending on the blend color. If the blend color is lighter than 50% gray, Illustrator screens the colors, producing a lighter resulting color. If the blend color is white, the resulting color is just about white. If the blend color is darker than 50% gray, Illustrator multiplies the colors, producing a darker resulting color. If the blend color is black, the resulting color is black.

Color Dodge

The Color Dodge blending mode adjusts the blend color to be a lighter version of the base color.

Color Burn

The Color Burn blending mode adjusts the blend color to be a darker version of the base color.

Darken

Darken selects the base color or blend color, depending on which color is darker. If the base color is darker than the blend color, Illustrator replaces the blend color with the base color or a slightly darker color. If the base color is lighter than the blend color, Illustrator replaces the base color with the blend color. If the blend color is white,

Illustrator changes the white areas of the artwork with the base color. If the blend color is black, Illustrator does not change the blend color.

Lighten

The Lighten blending mode selects the base color or blend color, depending on which is the lighter color. If the base color is lighter than the blend color, Illustrator replaces the blend color with the base color or a slightly lighter color. If the base color is lighter than the blend color, Illustrator replaces the base color with the blend color. If the blend color is white, Illustrator does not change the blend color. If the blend color is black, Illustrator changes the black areas of the artwork with the base color.

Difference

The Difference blending mode uses the level of brightness to determine whether to subtract the blend color from the base color or the base color from the blend color. Illustrator subtracts the brighter color from the other color. If the blend color is black, Illustrator usually produces a resulting color that is lighter than black. Note that Difference does not work with spot colors.

Exclusion

The Exclusion blending mode is very similar to Difference: Exclusion's resulting colors are slighter lighter. If the blend color is black, Illustrator usually produces a resulting color that is lighter than black. Note that Exclusion does not work with spot colors.

Hue

The Hue blending mode produces a resulting color that matches the luminosity and saturation of the base color and the hue of the blend color. If the blend color is black, Illustrator usually produces a resulting color that is lighter than black. Note that Hue does not work with spot colors.

Saturation

Saturation produces a resulting color that matches the luminosity and hue of the base color and the saturation of the blend color. If the blend color is black, Illustrator usually produces a resulting color that is lighter than black. Note that Saturation does not work with spot colors.

Color

Color produces a resulting color that matches the luminosity of the base color and the hue and saturation of the blend color. If the blend color is black, Illustrator usually produces a resulting color that is lighter than black. Note that Color does not work with spot colors. The Color blending mode is helpful when you apply color to monochrome objects and tint color objects.

Luminosity

The Luminosity blending mode produces a resulting color that matches the hue and saturation of the base color and the luminosity of the blend color. This is the inverse of the Color blending mode. If the blend color is black, Illustrator usually produces

ILLUSTRATOR FX

a resulting color that is lighter than black. Note that Luminosity does not work with spot colors.

Applying a Blending Mode

Illustrator enables you to apply blending modes to layers, sublayers, groups, and objects. To select a blending mode, follow these steps:

1. Activate the Selection tool (V) or the Direct Selection tool (A) and click the object, or open the Layers palette and click the target icon of the target object while pressing and holding down CTRL-ALT/⌘-OPTION. Illustrator shows the paths for the selected object.

2. Open the Blending Mode drop-down menu in the Transparency palette, and choose a blending mode. Illustrator applies the blending mode to the selection.

Excluding Blending Modes

Typically, Illustrator applies blending modes to all objects below the group in the stack. To exclude those objects from the newly selected blending modes (except for the default Normal), you can check the Isolate Blending check box on the Transparency palette. To exclude certain blending modes from a target layer, sublayer, group, or object, follow these steps:

1. Activate the Selection tool (V) or the Direct Selection tool (A), and click the object; or open the Layers palette, and click the target icon of the target object while pressing and holding down CTRL-ALT/⌘-OPTION. Illustrator shows the paths for the selected object.

2. Check the Isolate Blending check box.

Using Knockout Groups

A *knockout* is the removal of all or part of an image from another image. In print processing, knocking out enables an image to print in its true color rather than taking on the color of an overlapping image. In Illustrator, creating a knockout group prevents you from seeing through the transparent objects in a group but allows you to view objects in underlying groups. Use the Knockout Group check box in the Transparency palette to control knockouts.

Most check boxes have two conditions: on or active (that is, checked) and off or inactive (that is, unchecked). The Knockout Group check box has three states: checked, unchecked, and neutral (a gray background with a dimmed check mark). A checked check box creates a knockout group for selected objects; an unchecked check box (the default) does not enable a knockout group. The neutral state indicates that you want to create a group that does not automatically take on the knockout attributes of the layer, sublayer, or group of which the group is part. Note that you also can use the Knockout Group check box to control the behavior of fills and strokes set by using the Appearance palette. You can use Illustrator to create knockout groups for vector and raster images.

Creating a Knockout Group

When you create a knockout group, you select a target group or layer that will selectively block the view from the underlying layers. To create a knockout group, follow these steps:

1. Activate the Selection tool (V) or the Direct Selection tool (A), and click the target icon of the target group in the Layers palette.

2. If you can't see the Knockout Group check box in the Transparency palette, choose Show Options from the palette's menu or click the Autoresize button until the check box appears.

3. Check the Knockout Group check box.

Figure 15-5 illustrates the steps toward creating a knockout group. The topmost illustration in the figure shows a set of five objects—three in the top layer and two in the bottom layer. The three semitransparent objects in the top layer will be knocked out. The middle example shows the selected objects in the top layer and the current condition of the Layers and Transparency palettes. When you check the Knockout Group check box (at the bottom of the figure), you can no longer see the borders of the objects within the group that composes the top layer, but you can view the objects in the bottom layer.

Varying the Effect of a Knockout Group

When you check the Opacity & Mask Define Knockout Shape check box, Illustrator varies the effect of the knockout—depending on the level of opacity or transparency applied to the objects in the target group. If an object is almost entirely or completely opaque, the outcome of creating a knockout group is powerful; you might barely notice the effect in more transparent areas. This change in appearance works very well on objects filled with a gradient. To affect the appearance of a knockout group, select one or more appropriate objects in the group, and check Opacity & Mask Define Knockout Shape in the Transparency palette.

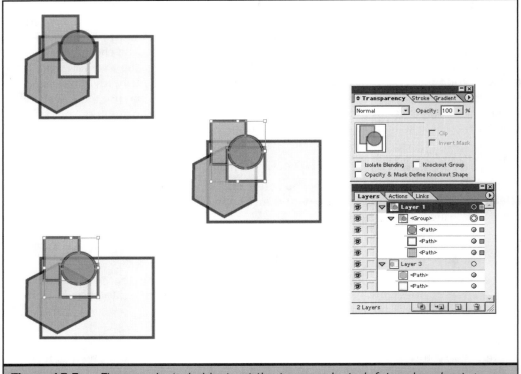

Figure 15-5.   *Five unselected objects at the top; a selected, future knockout group in the middle; and the objects after the creation of the knockout group at the bottom*

Turning Off a Knockout Group

To turn off a knockout group, follow these steps:

1. Activate the Selection tool (V) or the Direct Selection tool (A), and click the target icon of the knockout group.

2. If you can't see the Knockout Group check box in the Transparency palette, choose Show Options from the palette's menu or click the Autoresize button until the check box appears.

3. Click the Knockout Group check box until it is completely clear (that is, no check mark is within).

Using Opacity Masks

Opacity masks are close relatives of the clipping masks you learned about in the "Using Clipping Masks" section in Chapter 14. Remember clipping masks change the look of the underlying object or group: Part of the object or group shows through the mask, and the masked part is hidden from view. *Opacity masks* also show and hide parts of objects or groups below the mask in the stacking order. However, opacity masks mask semitransparent objects depending on the luminosity levels of the mask.

Creating an Opacity Mask

Remember you create a clipping mask from the topmost object in a layer or sublayer. The same is true for an opacity mask. However, once you have completed the steps to create an opacity mask, Illustrator places a thumbnail in the Transparency palette next to the masked object and shows the link between the mask and object with a link icon (see Figure 15-6). Illustrator enables you to create opacity masks from many different objects, including mesh objects, gradient fills, and patterned fills. You can create an

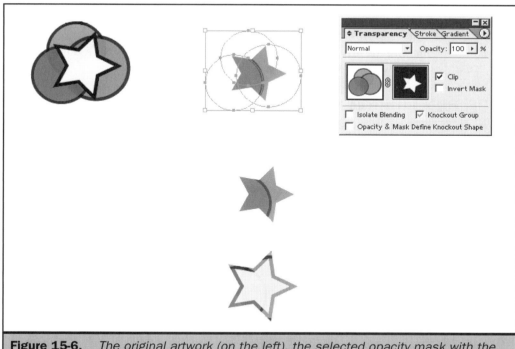

Figure 15-6. *The original artwork (on the left), the selected opacity mask with the Transparency palette (both on the right), and the unselected opacity mask and its inverted version (both below that)*

opacity mask by using an existing object or group as the mask, or you can start with an empty mask area and draw the mask.

To create an opacity mask, follow these steps:

1. Activate the Selection tool (V) or the Direct Selection tool (A), and click an object or group; or open the Layers palette and click the target icon of the target object.

2. Choose the Make Opacity Mask command from the Transparency palette's menu, or double-click the right side of the preview box in the palette.

3. To invert an opacity mask, check the Invert Mask box.

Figure 15-6 illustrates a document before (at the top) and after (in the center with the Transparency palette) the creation of an opacity mask (unselected below that) and its inversion (at the bottom).

Editing an Opacity Mask

You can edit an opacity mask even after creating it by enabling mask editing mode and then using any of Illustrator's tools or features. To enter mask editing mode, click the mask's thumbnail in the Transparency palette. To isolate an opacity mask by hiding the objects being masked and enter mask editing mode, click the mask's thumbnail while pressing and holding down ALT/OPTION. After modifying the mask, leave mask editing mode by either clicking the artwork's thumbnail or clicking the mask's thumbnail again while pressing and holding down ALT/OPTION.

Unlinking and Linking an Opacity Mask

You can unlink an opacity mask from its artwork. When the mask and the artwork are linked, you cannot move either element around the illustration window separately. When you unlink the mask and the artwork, you have control over each of the elements. To unlink a mask, select the artwork and either click the link icon between the thumbnails or choose the Unlink Opacity Mask command from the Transparency palette's menu. Illustrator removes the link icon, signaling that you have separated the mask from the artwork. To link the mask and artwork again, either click the place in which the link icon was located or choose Link Opacity Mask from the menu.

Disabling and Enabling an Opacity Mask

Disabling an opacity mask actually removes the mask from the current document. To disable an opacity mask, choose the Disable Opacity Mask command in the Transparency palette's menu. Illustrator draws a red X through the mask's thumbnail and removes the mask (see Figure 15-7). To enable the opacity mask, choose Enable Opacity Mask from the menu. Illustrator removes the X and restores the mask.

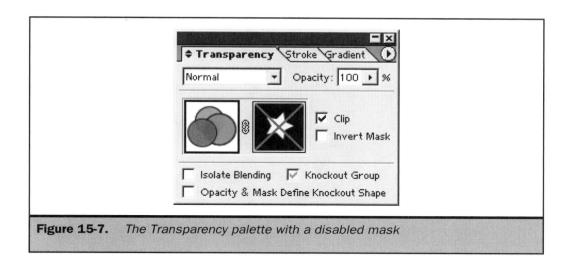

Figure 15-7.   *The Transparency palette with a disabled mask*

Releasing an Opacity Mask

Releasing an opacity mask keeps the mask onscreen but converts it to a standard object in the document. To release an opacity mask, choose the Release Opacity Mask command from the Transparency palette's menu. Illustrator removes the mask's thumbnail from the palette. To remake a released opacity mask, choose Make Opacity Mask from the menu. Illustrator inserts the mask's thumbnail and restores the link icon between the thumbnails.

ILLUSTRATOR FX

The
Complete
Reference

Adobe
Illustrator
10

Chapter 16

Using Filters
and Effects

Illustrator devotes two menus, Filter and Effect, and all or part of two toolbox toolslots to enable you to change the look or shape of vector and raster artwork. Some filters and effects work with vector objects only, and others apply to just raster objects. Some work with RGB and grayscale colors only; others work with RGB, grayscale, and CMYK colors.

A commonly used filter and effect, drop shadows give depth to objects. Other filters and effects enable you to make an artwork look as if it were painted by a pointillist or pastel painter. You can use some filters and effects to apply special brushstrokes and crosshatching. Using other filters and effects, you can change the appearance of the edges of objects; you also can cover an object with a chrome or plastic coating. Many commands on the Filter menu also appear on the Effect menu. In fact, both menus contain two Stylize commands with dedicated submenus: one version for vector artwork and the other for raster artwork. In addition, between the Filter and Effect menus are three Distort commands and one Distort & Transform command.

This chapter starts by reviewing the toolbox tools that are dedicated to reshaping objects. The remaining sections describe and illustrate each filter and effect command in the Illustrator repertoire and a couple of odds and ends.

Modifying Shapes with Toolbox Tools

Illustrator provides a set of seven reshaping tools on the Warp toolslot, which are known as the *liquify tools,* and one tool on the Rotate toolslot (see Figure 16-1). As you will discover, some of these tools are associated with certain commands on the Filter and Effect menus, and other tools are unique.

Using the Reshaping Tools

When you select all but the Twist tool, Illustrator draws a circle around the mouse pointer. As you move the mouse pointer, Illustrator modifies paths and adds anchor points to the edges within the circle. However, if you use one of these tools on a photograph, you can modify the inside as well as the outside. Illustrator treats the photograph as a mesh object. Note that you cannot use one of these tools on graphs, type, or objects that contain symbols.

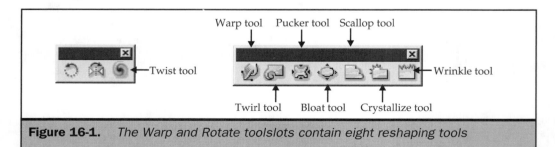

Figure 16-1.   *The Warp and Rotate toolslots contain eight reshaping tools*

Figure 16-2 shows the objects that Illustrator will act on throughout the chapter. Note that the leftmost object in the second row is a scaled-down photograph.

Warp Tool

You can use the Warp tool (SHIFT-R) to stretch selected objects or parts of objects. When you move the mouse pointer, any part of an object within the circle becomes elastic. Notice that the gradient and pattern fills do not stretch with the object but photographs do (see the top left of Figure 16-3). Illustrator provides a Warp submenu on the Effect menu. Refer to the "Warping Objects" section later in this chapter to learn more about the commands on the submenu.

Twirl Tool

The Twirl tool swirls the selected part of an object. When you click the mouse pointer, any part of the object within the circle swirls. The longer you hold the mouse button down, the more the object swirls. If you move the mouse pointer as you hold down the mouse

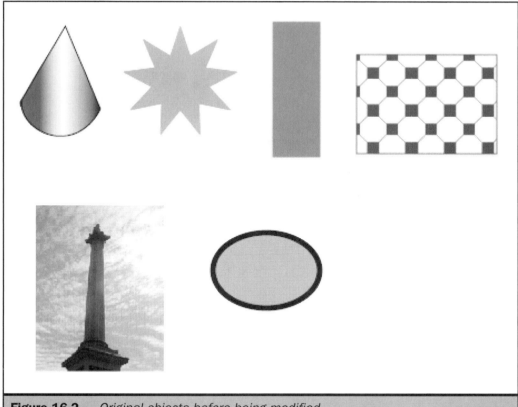

Figure 16-2.   *Original objects before being modified*

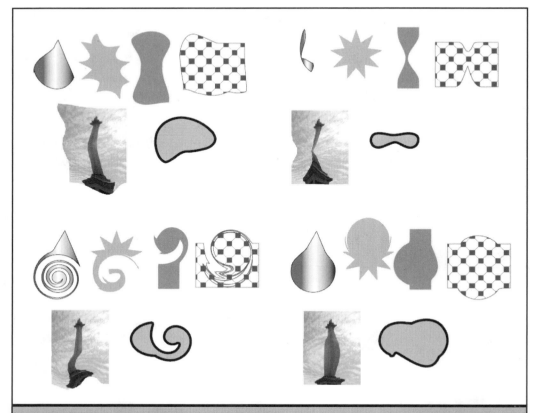

Figure 16-3.   *In the top-left corner, warped objects; at the bottom left, twirled objects; in the top right, puckered objects; on the bottom right, bloated objects*

pointer, you can move the area of the swirl (see the bottom left of Figure 16-3). There is no counterpart command on the Filter or Effect menu.

Pucker Tool

The Pucker tool moves the anchor points and paths within the circle toward the center of the circle, and the Bloat tool moves the anchor points and paths away from the center of the circle. The examples of puckering are at the top right of Figure 16-3; bloating examples appear at the bottom right. The more you click with either tool, the more you pucker or bloat an object. To apply a counterpart command, choose Filter | Distort | Pucker & Bloat or Effect | Distort & Transform | Pucker & Bloat. Refer to "Puckering and Bloating Objects" later in this chapter to learn more.

Scallop Tool

The Scallop tool adds sharp arcs to the edge of an object (see the top of Figure 16-4). Illustrator does not provide a counterpart command for scalloping.

Crystallize Tool

The Crystallize tool adds crystal-like formations to the edge of an object (see the bottom left of the figure). The more you click with either tool, the more arcs you add.

Wrinkle Tool

The Wrinkle tool wrinkles the edge of an object (see the top right of Figure 16-4). The more you click, the more wrinkles you add. Illustrator does not provide a counterpart command.

Figure 16-4.   *In the top-left corner, scalloped objects; on the bottom left, crystallized objects; in the top right, wrinkled objects; at the bottom right, the results of using the Twist tool*

Twist Tool

If you expect a reshaping tool that lives on a different toolslot to behave a little differently, you won't be disappointed by the Twist tool. Rather than the liquify tools, which act as soon as you select them and drag or click an object, you have to explicitly select an object before using the Twist tool. After activating the Twist tool, move the mouse pointer around the center of the selected object. Notice that the Twist tool has no effect on photographs. To apply a counterpart command, choose Filter | Distort | Twist or Effect | Distort & Transform | Twist. Refer to "Twisting an Object" later in this chapter to learn more. The bottom-right corner of Figure 16-4 illustrates the Twist tool in action.

Changing Liquify Tool Options

In prior chapters you learned that you can set tool options by double-clicking the tool and filling in a dialog box. By using this method, you can change characteristics for all the liquify tools. The Twist tool does not have an associated options dialog box.

Setting Global Brush Dimensions

To open any liquify tool options dialog box (see Figure 16-5), double-click the tool. The Global Brush Dimensions section takes the most space in every one of the dialog boxes.

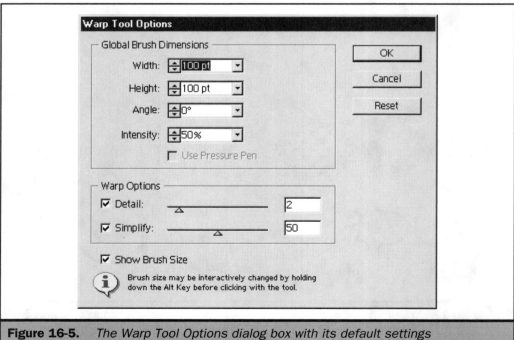

Figure 16-5. *The Warp Tool Options dialog box with its default settings*

The options in the Global Brush Dimensions section are as follows:

■ In the Width list box/text box/drop-down menu, type or select the width of the circle surrounding the mouse pointer. Valid values range from 1 point to 1,000 points. The default is 100 points.

■ In the Height list box/text box/drop-down menu, type or select the height of the circle surrounding the mouse pointer. Valid values range from 1 point to 1,000 points. The default is 100 points.

 You also can change the width and height of the circle for a tool by pressing and holding down ALT/OPTION *and then dragging the tool to resize it.*

■ In the Angle list box/text box/drop-down menu, type or select the degree to which the tool is slanted. Valid values range from 0° (the default) to 360°.

■ In the Intensity list box/text box/drop-down menu, type or select the intensity of the effect. Valid values range from 1% to 100%. The default is 50%.

■ Check the Use Pressure Pen check box, which is an option of Intensity, if you are using a pressure pen. Note that if a pressure pen is not installed on your computer system, the check box is unavailable.

■ Check the Show Brush Size check box to view the circle in the illustration window.

■ Click Reset to return to the default values.

Selecting Specific Tool Options

Each of the options dialog boxes for the liquify tool contains unique settings—for one or more tools. For each entry in this section, the tools to which certain options apply are enclosed within parentheses. The options are as follows:

■ Check the Detail check box (the default), and either slide the slider or type a value in the text box to restrict the spacing between pairs of anchor points within the circle. This option is related to the Complexity option. Valid values range from 1 to 10. The default is 2. (Warp, Twirl, Pucker, Bloat, Scallop, and Crystallize)

■ Check the Simplify check box (the default), and either slide the slider or type a value in the text box to prevent the addition of anchor points that will not involve the change of shape. Valid values range from 0.2 to 100. The default is 50. (Warp, Twirl, Pucker, and Bloat)

■ With the Twirl Rate slider and text box, you control the speed or slowness of the twirl. The higher the value, the faster the twirl. Valid values range from −180° to 180°. The default is 40°. (Twirl)

■ The Complexity list box/drop-down menu sets the complexity of a specific tool on the edge of the object. This option is related to the Detail option. (Scallop, Crystallize, and Wrinkle)

■ Check the Brush Affects Anchor Points check box for the brush to change anchor points of the object. (Crystallize and Wrinkle)

■ Check the Brush Affects In Tangent Handles for the brush to change the inside control handles on the object. (Scallop, Crystallize, and Wrinkle)

■ Check the Brush Affects Out Tangent Handles for the brush to change the outside control handles on the object. (Scallop, Crystallize, and Wrinkle)

■ In the Horizontal list box/text box/drop-down menu, type or select the horizontal percentage from one anchor point to another. Valid values range from 0% to 100%; the default is 0%. (Wrinkle)

■ In the Vertical list box/text box/drop-down menu, type or select the vertical percentage from one anchor point to another. Valid values range from 0% to 100%. The default is 100%. (Wrinkle)

Figure 16-6 shows the Wrinkle Tool Options dialog box with similar and different options.

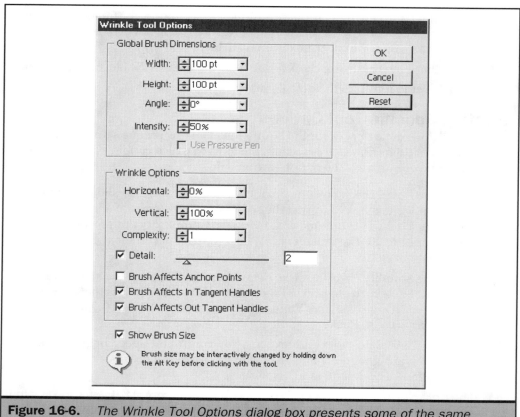

Figure 16-6.   *The Wrinkle Tool Options dialog box presents some of the same options for several tools and some unique to the Wrinkle tool.*

Introducing Filters

A filter (that is, a command on the Filter menu or one of its submenus) changes the structure of the selected object. Most filters work with unlinked raster objects. If you try to filter a linked raster object, Illustrator might apply the filter to an embedded copy of the object instead. You can use a filter to change the appearance of a single object. Select an object by using the Selection tool (V) or the Direct Selection tool (A), or target it on the Layers palette.

The following tables list the filters for vector objects, raster objects, and photographs in the CMYK and RGB color modes. Table 16-1 covers vector objects and photographs in the CMYK mode; Table 16-2 comprises vector objects and photographs in the RGB mode. Table 16-3 summarizes raster objects and photographs in both CMYK and RGB modes.

Menu | Command	Vector CMYK Objects	Vector CMYK Photos
Filter | Colors	All but Convert to RGB	Adjust Colors, Convert to CMYK, Convert to Grayscale, Invert Colors, Saturate
Filter | Create	Trim Marks only	All
Filter | Distort	All	None
Filter | Pen & Ink	All but Photo Crosshatch	All but Hatch Effects
Filter | Stylize	All	None
Filter | Artistic	None	None
Filter | Brush Strokes	None	None
Filter | Distort	None	None
Filter | Sketch	None	None
Filter | Stylize	None	None
Filter | Texture	None	None

Table 16-1. *Illustrator Filters for Vector CMYK Objects and Photographs*

Menu I Command	Vector RGB	Vector RGB Photos
Filter I Colors	All but Convert to CMYK	Adjust Colors, Convert to Grayscale, Convert to RGB, Invert Colors, Saturate
Filter I Create	Trim Marks only	All
Filter I Distort	All	None
Filter I Pen & Ink	All but Photo Crosshatch	All but Hatch Effects
Filter I Stylize	All	None
Filter I Artistic	None	All
Filter I Brush Strokes	None	All
Filter I Distort	None	All
Filter I Sketch	None	All
Filter I Stylize	None	All
Filter I Texture	None	All

Table 16-2.   *Illustrator Filters for Vector RGB Objects and Photographs*

Menu I Command	Raster CMYK Objects & Photos	Raster RGB Objects & Photos
Filter I Colors	Adjust Colors, Convert to CMYK, Convert to Grayscale, Invert Colors, Saturate only	Adjust Colors, Convert to Grayscale, Convert to RGB, Invert Colors, Saturate only
Filter I Create	All	All
Filter I Distort	None	None
Filter I Pen & Ink	All but Hatch Effects	All but Hatch Effects
Filter I Stylize	None	None
Filter I Artistic	None	All
Filter I Brush Strokes	None	All
Filter I Distort	None	All
Filter I Sketch	None	All
Filter I Stylize	None	All
Filter I Texture	None	All

Table 16-3.   *Illustrator Filters for Raster Objects and Photographs in CMYK and RGB*

Introducing Effects

An effect (that is, a command on the Effect menu or one of its submenus) changes the look of a selected object. The underlying structure of the object remains in its original form. Note the following:

■ Most effects work with either vector paths and blocks of type (but not individual characters within that type) or raster objects.

■ Illustrator developers have duplicated some effect commands on other menus particularly the Object menu.

■ Illustrator restricts many effects to RGB documents only. So if you apply effects to an RGB object and then convert that object to CMYK, Illustrator might remove most of the effects during the conversion.

■ Use an effect to change the appearance of a group, object, stroke, fill, or style. To select an object or group, use the Selection tool (V) or the Direct Selection tool (A). You also can target an object in the Layers palette. You can select a stroke or fill by using the Appearance palette. Note that you will learn about styles in Chapter 18.

Note
You also can use filters and effects from other Adobe programs, such as Photoshop, and from other software developers. These are known as plug-ins. *A plug-in is a small, single-purpose program that plugs into a larger program. Once you have installed a filter or effect plug-in, its commands appear on the Illustrator Filter menu, Effect menu, or both.*

For vector objects, raster objects, and photographs in the CMYK and RGB color modes, Illustrator supports the following commands on the Effect menu and submenus: Effect | Convert to Shape, Effect | Distort & Transform, Effect | Path, Effect | Pathfinder, Effect | Rasterize, Effect | Stylize, Effect | SVG Filters, and Effect | Warp.

Applying Filters and Effects

Changing your artwork using commands from the Filter and Effect menus follows a general set of steps: Select a stroke or fill, an object, or a group; then choose a command. If a dialog box opens, fill it in; watch for the results regardless of whether you have a dialog box. If you don't like what you see, choose Edit | Undo (CTRL-Z/⌘-Z) and try either another filter or effect, or the same filter or effect with different values specified in its dialog box.

ILLUSTRATOR FX

What If a Filter or Effect Is Unavailable?

If a filter or effect command is not available for a selected object, check the object. Does it use CMYK colors rather than RGB? Is it a vector object rather than raster? Chances are Illustrator has evaluated the object, and it doesn't fit the particular command. So, you might be able to solve the problem by reading the solutions in this section.

Changing from CMYK to RGB

If an artwork uses the CMYK color model (the default for Illustrator), certain filters and effects are unavailable. However, Illustrator filters and effects work on an RGB (or grayscale) artwork. If changing from CMYK to RGB will not affect your artwork when you print it or get it ready for process printing, go ahead. To do so, choose File | Document Color Mode | RGB Color. Then save the document.

The Filter menu has three color conversion commands on the Colors submenu:

- To convert a selected object to CMYK, choose Filter | Colors | Convert to CMYK. Illustrator will not convert a raster graphic in RGB mode to CMYK.

- To convert a selected object to grayscale, choose Filter | Colors | Convert to Grayscale. Illustrator will convert any vector and raster graphics to grayscale.

- To convert a selected object to RGB, choose Filter | Colors | Convert to RGB. Illustrator will not convert vector and raster graphics in the CMYK mode to RGB.

These commands are not available for vector graphics in the RGB mode.

 You also can convert from CMYK or RGB to grayscale by using the Adjust Colors filter. Refer to "Adjusting Colors" later in this chapter for more information.

Changing from Vector to Raster

When you create an Illustrator document, it is a vector graphic by default. To apply certain Illustrator filters and effects, a selected object must be a raster graphic. Illustrator provides permanent and temporary ways to rasterize an object—even if its document remains a vector document.

To permanently convert an object, choose Object | Rasterize. To temporarily convert an object, choose Effect | Rasterize. In both cases, fill in the Rasterize dialog box and click

OK. The object's appearance changes slightly, but you'll notice that additional Filter and Effect commands are now available. You can undo both types of rasterization by choosing Edit | Undo (CTRL-Z/⌘-Z). You'll learn much more about rasterizing objects and working with raster graphics starting with the "Rasterizing Graphics" section in Chapter 19.

Applying the Last Filter or Effect

When you first start Illustrator, the top two commands on the Filter menu are Filter | Apply Last Filter (CTRL-E/⌘-E) and Filter | Last Filter (CTRL-ALT-E/⌘-OPTION-E); the top commands at the top of the Effect menu are Effect | Apply Last Effect (CTRL-SHIFT-E/⌘-SHIFT-E) and Effect | Last Effect (CTRL-SHIFT-ALT-E/⌘-SHIFT-OPTION-E).

If you have just launched Illustrator, the commands are generic: Apply the last filter or effect and the name of the last filter or effect. However, once you select a filter or effect from the Filter or Effect menu, the commands at the top change: They incorporate the names of the last filter or effect you used. For example, if you choose Filter | Distort | Pucker & Bloat and apply the bloat filter to an object, the next time you open the Filter menu, you'll see Apply Pucker & Bloat (CTRL-E/⌘-E) and Pucker & Bloat (CTRL-SHIFT-ALT-E/⌘-SHIFT-OPTION-E).

So, if you want to continue bloating the same object or a different one, just select one of the top two commands on the Filter menu rather than searching through menus and submenus. Once you apply a different filter, Illustrator replaces the two commands with the name of that filter.

Note *Until this section in the book, you haven't had to really look at Illustrator menus. In most cases, the menus are similar to many other menus in other Windows or Macintosh programs. The Filter and Effect menus actually look like any other menu, too. However, as pointed out before, each menu has two Stylize commands. In addition, the Filter and Effect menus share three Distort commands and one Distort & Transform command. These duplications make the Filter and Effect menus unique among most programs because the commands in the group below the horizontal line under the Last Filter and Filter commands and above the lower horizontal line are primarily for vector filters and effects, and the commands below the lower horizontal line are for raster filters and effects—but not to black-and-white (known as 1-bit) images. Of course, there are exceptions to every rule, so as you learn about specific filters and effects in the following sections, you'll discover any limitations.*

Using Color Filters

You can modify the colors of objects in various ways by choosing Filter | Colors and selecting a command from the submenu. For example, you can modify the colors of objects in various ways within a particular color mode, change from one color mode to another for an entire document, blend color fills for three or more objects, invert colors for selected objects, and increase or decrease color values for selected objects.

Adjusting Colors

The Adjust Colors command enables you to modify the colors of the selected object within its color mode. Choose Filter | Colors | Adjust Colors to open the Adjust Colors dialog box (see Figure 16-7) for the color mode of the selected object or objects. Note that Illustrator will not adjust the colors of gradient fills and pattern fills.

The options in the dialog boxes are as follows:

- The purpose of choosing from the Color Mode drop-down menu is to convert from RGB or CMYK to grayscale. To do so, check the Convert check box and select Grayscale from the Color Mode. If you try to choose another mode without checking Convert, you will not be able to use the sliders and text boxes in the dialog box; they are not available.

- To adjust one color component (for example, cyan, magenta, yellow, or black for CMYK, or red, green, or blue for RGB), either slide a slider or type a percentage value in the text box. Valid values for all the color mode sliders/text boxes are −100% to 100%. The default value is 0%, which is the starting point for the current color component.

- Check the Fill or Stroke check boxes, or both to adjust options for the fill, stroke, or both.

- To preview the results of your color selections, check the Preview check box.

Tip *Whenever a filter or effect dialog box has a Preview check box, it's a good idea to check the check box; Illustrator takes a long time and a great deal of computer memory to apply some filters and effects—particularly for RGB objects.*

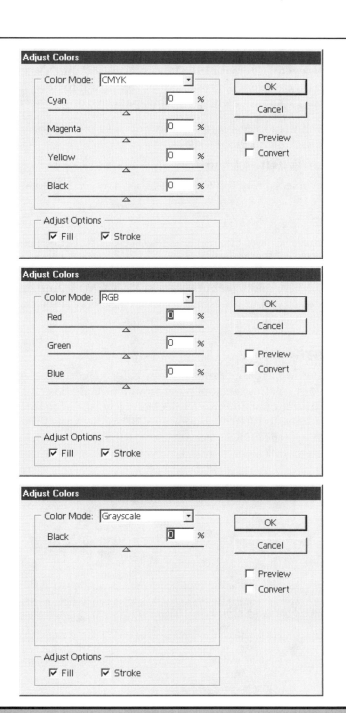

Figure 16-7. *The Adjust Colors dialog boxes for CMYK, RGB, and grayscale modes*

Blending Colors

Illustrator provides several filters for blending color fills within a selected group of at least three objects; you can blend a group's color from front to back, horizontally, or vertically. Note that you cannot blend gradients, patterns, or global colors.

- To blend from the top object to the bottom object in stacking order, choose Filter | Colors | Blend Front to Back.
- To blend the objects from left to right, choose Filter | Colors | Blend Horizontally.
- To blend the objects from top to bottom, choose Filter | Colors | Blend Vertically.

Inverting Colors

When you use the Invert Colors filter on a selected object, Illustrator changes the fill color of the object to its inverse. For example, if you select an object filled with red, Illustrator changes the fill to blue, green becomes magenta, yellow turns to blue, and so on. Although this filter works for vector and raster graphics in RGB, CMYK, and grayscale modes, it is more effective for RGB and grayscale objects. To invert colors, choose Filter | Colors | Invert Colors.

Saturating Colors

Use the Saturate filter to increase or decrease the color values for selected objects. Choose Filter | Colors | Saturate to open the Saturate dialog box (see Figure 16-8).

To change the saturation values for a selected object, slide the Intensity slider. Valid values range from –100% to 100%. The default is 10%. Check the Preview check box to see the effect before you click OK.

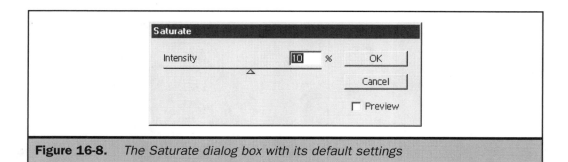

Figure 16-8. *The Saturate dialog box with its default settings*

Applying the Object Mosaic Filter

The Object Mosaic filter applies tiles to pixels in unlinked raster graphics, including photographs. If you select one object, Illustrator converts that object to a mosaic. If you select several objects, Illustrator converts them to one mosaic.

With the Object Mosaic dialog box (see Figure 16-9), you can set the size and number of tiles and the spacing between tiles. To use the filter on one or more selected objects, choose Filter | Create | Object Mosaic. The options in the dialog box are as follows:

- The Current Size section shows the current width and height of the selection in the default unit of measure.

- In the New Size section, type the desired width and height in the Width and Height text boxes, respectively. Valid values for each text box range from 0 point to 8,640 points. The default value in the text boxes is the current width and height.

- In the Tile Spacing section, type the distance between each tile. Valid values range from 0 point (the default) to 8 points for each text box.

- In the Number of Tiles section, type the number of tiles in each row (that is, the width) and column (that is, the height). Valid values for each text box range from 0 point to 8,640 points. The default width and height is 10.

- To constrain the width or height to the original width or height of the raster image, click the Width or Height radio button. If you constrain the width or height, Illustrator calculates a suitable number of tiles for the width or height. A filled-in Width radio button is the default.

- Choose to show the mosaic in color or in grayscale by clicking the Color or Gray radio button, respectively. A filled-in Color radio button is the default.

- To have Illustrator change the size of the mosaic using percentages rather than point sizes, check the Resize Using Percentages check box, and then type percentages in the Width and Height text boxes in the New Size section. An unchecked check box is the default.

- To delete the raster graphics on which the mosaic is based, check the Delete Raster check box. An unchecked check box is the default.

- Click the Use Ratio button to create square tiles using the values in the Number of Tiles section.

Figure 16-9 shows the Object Mosaic dialog box showing its default settings and illustrates the conversion of three objects to mosaics.

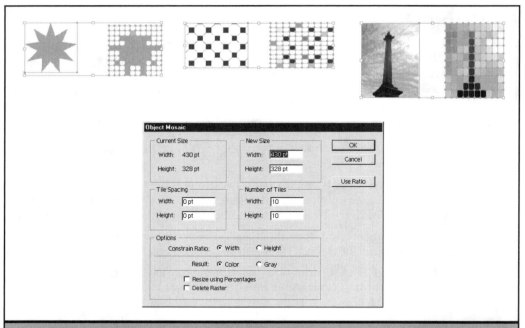

Figure 16-9.   *The Object Mosaic dialog box showing its default settings and the conversion of three objects to mosaics*

Distorting Vector Objects

As you know, Illustrator provides two Distort commands on the Filter menu. The Effect menu contains the Distort & Transform command as well as another Distort command. Some of these commands apply only to raster images, and others work with vector images. For example, on the Filter menu you use the top Distort command for filtering vector images; the bottom Distort command is devoted to changing RGB raster images. Note that you usually cannot distort a photograph pasted into a vector document.

Using the Free Distort Command

The Free Distort command, which is on both the Filter and Effect menus, enables you to reshape a selected object by dragging its corners. To use the Free Distort filter or effect on a selected object, follow these steps:

1. Choose Filter | Distort | Free Distort or Effect | Distort & Transform | Free Distort to open the Free Distort dialog box (see Figure 16-10).
2. To distort the selected object, drag one of the four handles.
3. Repeat step 2 for the other three handles, if you wish.

4. Check the Preview check box to see a preview of the distortions in the preview box in the dialog box. (If the box is unchecked, you'll view the four handles only.)

5. To return the selected object to its original shape, click the Reset button.

6. Click OK to close the dialog box and apply the changes.

Puckering and Bloating Objects

In the "Using the Reshaping Tools" section earlier in this section, you learned how to use the Pucker tool and the Bloat tool to manually change the shape of a selected object. The Pucker & Bloat commands on the Filter and Effect menus automate the puckering and bloating processes with the help of the Pucker & Bloat dialog box.

To open the dialog box and either pucker or bloat a selected object, follow these steps:

1. Choose Filter | Distort | Pucker & Bloat or Effect | Distort & Transform | Pucker & Bloat. Illustrator opens the Pucker & Bloat dialog box.

2. Check the Preview check box to see the change to the object in the illustration window.

3. To pucker the object, drag the slider toward the left side of the dialog box, or type a value from –200% to 0% in the text box.

4. To bloat the object, drag the slider toward the right side, or type a value from 0% to 200% in the text box.

5. When the object has the desired look, click OK to close the dialog box and apply the effect.

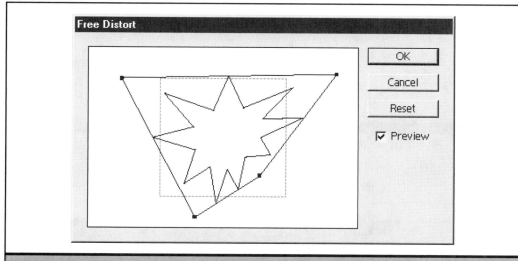

Figure 16-10.   *The Free Distort dialog box with the selected object in the preview box*

ILLUSTRATOR FX

Figure 16-11 illustrates two versions of the Pucker & Bloat dialog box with a star in a puckered condition (on the left) and the star in a bloated state (on the right).

Roughening Objects

To use the Roughen filter or effect, open the Roughen dialog box (see Figure 16-12), with which you add anchor points in a jagged pattern along the edges of an object. To roughen a selected object, choose Filter | Distort | Roughen or Effect | Distort & Transform | Roughen.

The options in the Roughen dialog box are as follows:

■ Slide the Size slider or type a value in its text box to specify the size of the distortion by percentage or a set value, depending on whether you fill the Relative or Absolute radio button. Valid values range from 0% to 100%, or 0 to 7,200 points. The default is 5%, or 5 points.

■ Click the Relative radio button (the default) to set a relative percentage of distortion, or click the Absolute radio button to specify a particular size.

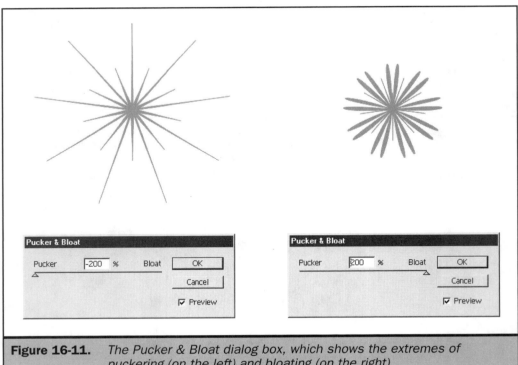

Figure 16-11. *The Pucker & Bloat dialog box, which shows the extremes of puckering (on the left) and bloating (on the right)*

- Determine the number of details per inch by sliding the Detail slider or typing a value in the text box. Valid values range from 0 to 100 per inch. The default is 10 per inch.
- Click the Smooth radio button to soften the rough edges with smooth corners, or click Corner (the default) to sharpen the edges with sharp corners.
- Check the Preview check box to see the change to the object in the illustration window.

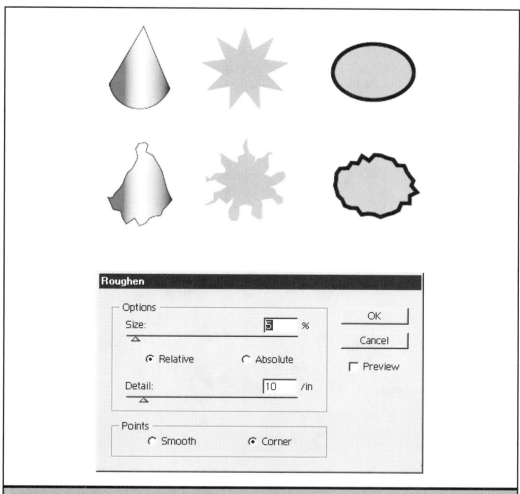

Figure 16-12.   *The Roughen dialog box and three objects, before and after roughening*

Scribbling and Tweaking Objects

The Scribble & Tweak command on both the Filter and Effect menus enables you to move anchor points away from a selected object within its selection bounding box. When you scribble an object, you enter a percentage value to move the anchor points; when you tweak an object, you enter an absolute value for the anchor points' movement. To open the Scribble & Tweak dialog box (see Figure 16-13), choose Filter | Distort | Scribble & Tweak or Effect | Distort & Transform | Scribble & Tweak.

The options in the Scribble & Tweak dialog box are as follows:

■ Slide the Horizontal slider or type a value in its text box to specify the amount or percentage of horizontal movement of the selected object's edges, depending on whether you fill the Relative or Absolute radio button. Valid values range from 0% to 100%, or 0 point to 7,200 points. The default is 30%, or 30 points.

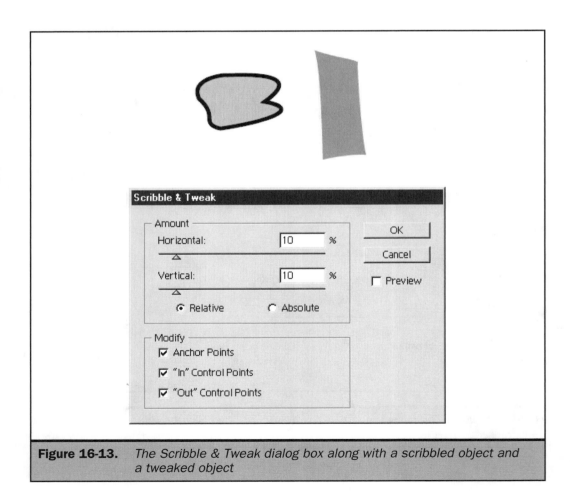

Figure 16-13. *The Scribble & Tweak dialog box along with a scribbled object and a tweaked object*

- Slide the Vertical slider or type a value in its text box to specify the amount or percentage of vertical movement of the selected object's edges, depending on whether you fill the Relative or Absolute radio button. Valid values range from 0% to 100%, or 0 point to 7,200 points. The default is 10%, or 10 points.

- Click the Relative radio button (the default) to set a relative percentage of distortion, or click the Absolute radio button to specify a particular size.

- Check the Anchor Points check box to allow anchor points to move. An unchecked check box freezes the anchor points in place. A checked box is the default.

- Check the "In" Control Points check box to move control points that are on the inside of the anchor points on the path. A checked box is the default.

- Check the "Out" Control Points check box to move control points that are on the outside of the anchor points on the path.

- Check the Preview check box to see the change to the object in the illustration window.

Using Transforming Effects

You can use the Transform command to modify a wide variety of objects. The Transform Effect dialog box (see Figure 16-14) is almost a twin of the Transform

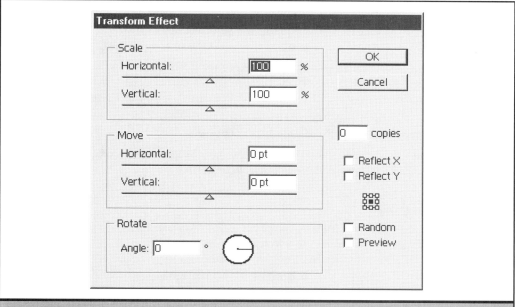

Figure 16-14. *The Transform Effect dialog box with its default settings*

Each dialog box (see Figure 10-4 in Chapter 10). Both dialog boxes work in the same way: They contain options with which you can scale, move, rotate, or reflect the selected object. To transform objects using the Transform Effect dialog box, choose Effect | Distort & Transform | Transform.

The options in the Transform Effect dialog box are as follows:

■ In the Scale section, slide the Horizontal or Vertical slider or type a value in the text box to scale the selected object horizontally or vertically, either lower or higher than its current size. Valid values for both options range from –4,000% to 4,000%. The default value for both options is 100% (that is, no scaling).

■ In the Move section, slide the Horizontal or Vertical slider, or type a value in the text box to move the selected object to the left or right or up or down in the illustration window. Valid values for both options range from –4,000 to 4,000 points, although the slider shows only –100 to 100 points. The default value for both options is 0 points, or no horizontal move.

■ In the Rotate section, either type the degree of rotation in the Angle text box or drag the line around the circle. Valid values range from 0° (the default) to 360°.

■ To make a certain number of copies of the selected object, type a number in the Copies text box. Illustrator copies the selected object at its new location, closes the dialog box, and keeps the original object in its pre-transformation condition and location. Valid values range from 0 (the default) to 360 copies.

■ Check the Reflect X check box to flip the selected object from one side to another along the horizontal plane toward the left side of the illustration window.

■ Check the Reflect Y check box to flip the selected object from the bottom to the top along the vertical plane toward the top edge of the illustration window.

■ Click one of the small squares in the reference point box to indicate the location of the origin point of the selected object from which the object is transformed. The squares represent parts of the object—just as they do in the Transform palette.

■ Check the Random check box to transform the selected object randomly using the changed options in the dialog box as a guide.

■ Check the Preview check box to see a preview of the transformations you have selected in the dialog box before they become final.

Twisting an Object

The Twist filter and effect are the counterparts to the Twist tool, which is on the Rotate toolslot. However, whereas the Twist tool enables you to twist an object manually, choosing the Twist command opens the Twist dialog box (see Figure 16-15) with which you can set the angle of the twist. To twist an object using the Twist dialog box, choose

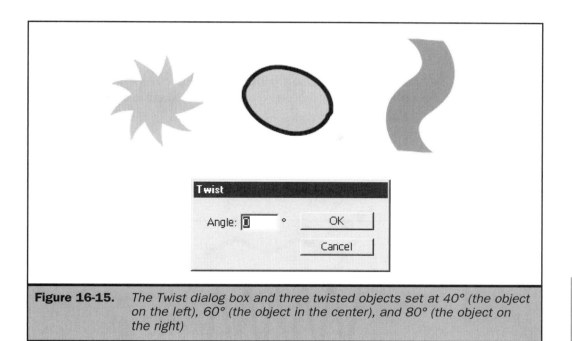

Figure 16-15.   *The Twist dialog box and three twisted objects set at 40° (the object on the left), 60° (the object in the center), and 80° (the object on the right)*

Filter | Distort | Twist or Effect | Distort & Transform | Twist. Valid values for the Angle text box range from –3,600° to 3,600°. The Twist filter is available for vector images in CMYK, RGB, and grayscale. The Twist effect works for raster and vector images in CMYK, RGB, and grayscale.

Creating Zig Zags

You can change straight paths to jagged paths by using the zig zag filter and effect. To open the Zig Zag dialog box, choose Filter | Distort | Zig Zag or Effect | Distort & Transform | Zig Zag.

The options in the Zig Zag dialog box are as follows:

- ■ Slide the Size slider or type a value in its text box to specify the size of the distortion by percentage or a set value, depending on whether you fill the Relative or Absolute radio button. Valid values range from 0% to 100%, or 0 point to 7,200 points. The default is 10%, or 10 points.

- ■ Click the Relative radio button to set a relative percentage of zig zag, or click the Absolute radio button (the default) to specify a particular size.

■ Determine the number of ridges per segment by sliding the slider or typing a value in the text box. Valid values range from 0 to 100 per segment. The default is 4 per segment.

■ Click the Smooth radio button to soften the rough edges with smooth corners, or click Corner (the default) to sharpen the edges with sharp corners.

■ Check the Preview check box to see the change to the object in the illustration window.

Figure 16-16 shows the Zig Zag dialog box and two zig zag lines. The top line uses the default values in the dialog box; the bottom line zig zags using a size of 100 points and 10 ridges per segment.

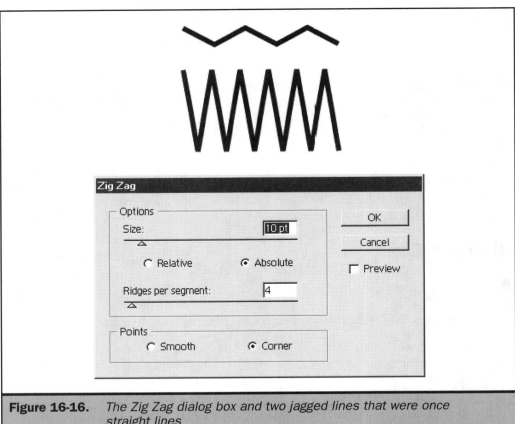

Figure 16-16. *The Zig Zag dialog box and two jagged lines that were once straight lines*

Distorting Raster Objects

Use the bottom-most Distort menus on the Filter and Effect menus to apply filters and effects to selected objects. Note that some of the Distort filters use a great deal of memory; processing might take more time than the application of other filters.

All three of the dialog boxes for these effects are similar. Each has a preview box you can manipulate. You can drag to move the image around the preview box, and you can zoom the image within the preview box. Click the + button below the preview box to zoom in the object in the preview box; click the - button to zoom out. Illustrator displays the current zoom level (by percentage) between the two buttons. If you see a flashing line below the preview box, you will have to wait until Illustrator has completed the new preview.

Applying a Diffuse Glow

Use the Diffuse Glow filter or effect to apply a glow and set graininess for the selected object. To create a diffuse glow for a selected object, choose Filter I Distort I Diffuse Glow or Effect I Distort I Diffuse Glow. Illustrator opens the Diffuse Glow dialog box. The options in the dialog box are as follows:

- To adjust the graininess of the object, slide the Graininess slider or type a value in the text box. Valid values range from 0 (no graininess) to 10 (a great deal of graininess). The default is 6.

- To adjust the amount of the glow of the object, slide the Glow Amount slider or type a value in the text box. Valid values range from 0 (no glow) to 20 (a great deal of glow). The default is 10.

- To adjust the amount of white over the object, slide the Clear Amount slider or type a value in the text box. Valid values range from 0 (all white) to 20 (no white). The default is 15.

Figure 16-17 illustrates a distorted photograph and the Diffuse Glow dialog box. For the photograph, the graininess is 6, the glow amount is 8, and the clear amount is 9.

Distorting Through Glass

When you apply the glass filter or effect, Illustrator places a glass-like surface over the object. To apply a glass filter or effect to the selected object, choose Filter I Distort I Glass or Effect I Distort I Glass. When the Glass dialog box appears, choose from the following options:

- To adjust the distortion of the glass, slide the Distortion slider or type a value in the text box. Valid values range from 0 (no distortion) to 20 (a great deal of distortion). The default is 5.

■ To adjust the smoothness of the glass, slide the Smoothness slider or type a value in the text box. Valid values range from 1 (not smooth) to 15 (no change in the original appearance). The default is 3.

■ From the Texture drop-down menu, choose the texture of the glass: Blocks, Canvas, Frosted (the default), or Tiny Lens. To load a custom texture, choose Load Texture, fill in the resulting dialog box, and click OK.

■ To adjust the scale of the glass by percent, slide the Scale slider or type a value in the text box. Valid values range from 50% (no scaling) to 200% (maximum scaling). The default is 100%.

■ To invert the glass on the object, check the Invert box.

The left side of Figure 16-18 illustrates the Glass dialog box with its default settings and an object whose distortion is 2, smoothness is 4, texture is frosted, and scaling is 100%.

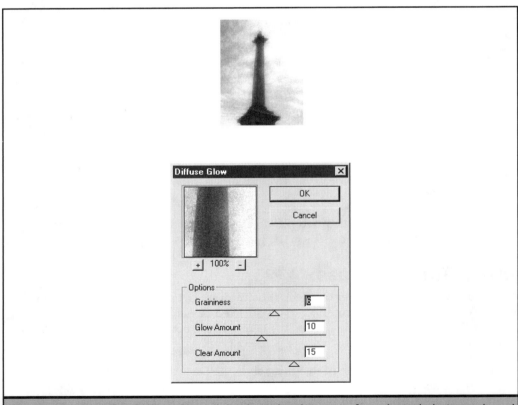

Figure 16-17.   *The Diffuse Glow dialog box showing part of a selected photograph and the default settings; above that, the diffused-glow photograph itself*

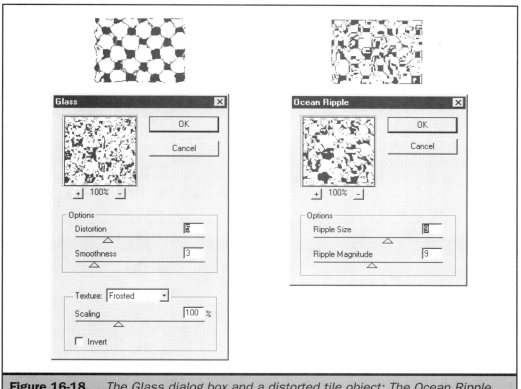

Figure 16-18.   *The Glass dialog box and a distorted tile object; The Ocean Ripple dialog box and an object with the Ocean Ripple effect applied*

Rippling an Object

The Ocean Ripple filter and effect is similar to the Glass filter and effect. When you apply Ocean Ripple, Illustrator covers the selected object with ripples. To apply Ocean Ripple, choose Filter | Distort | Ocean Ripple or Effect | Distort | Ocean Ripple. Illustrator opens the Ocean Ripple dialog box whose options are as follows:

■ To adjust the ripple size, slide the Ripple Size slider or type a value in the text box. Valid values range from 1 (many small ripples) to 15 (fewer large ripples). The default is 9.

■ To adjust the ripple magnitude, slide the Ripple Magnitude slider or type a value in the text box. Valid values range from 1 (no magnitude) to 20 (the greatest magnitude). The default is 9.

The right side of Figure 16-18 illustrates the Ocean Ripple dialog box with the default settings and a selected object with a ripple size of 15 and ripple magnitude of 12.

ILLUSTRATOR FX

Using Pen & Ink Filters

The Pen & Ink filters add cross-hatches to selected objects so that they are similar to pen-and-ink drawings. You can apply hatch effects and photo cross-hatches to a variety of objects. Illustrator provides hatch effects and libraries in which you can store hatches you design, and photo cross-hatches for photographs and other objects.

Applying the Hatch Effects Filter

Illustrator enables you to define many hatch effects, combining a variety of options from the Hatch Effects dialog box (see Figure 16-19). To apply or create a hatch effect filter for a selected object, choose Filter | Pen & Ink | Hatch Effects. When Illustrator opens

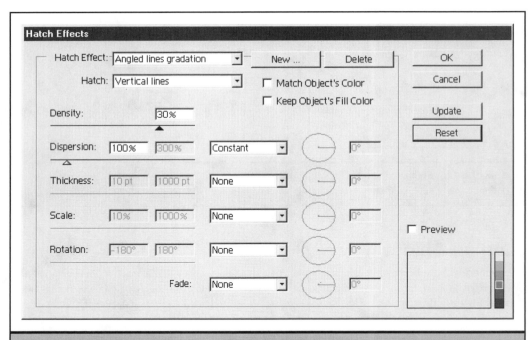

Figure 16-19.   *The Hatch Effects dialog box with its default settings*

the dialog box, select from the numerous options. Note that the default settings and the availability of some options vary depending on the selected hatch effect and hatch.

The options in the dialog box are as follows:

- From the Hatch Effect drop-down menu, choose from a multitude of hatch effects. The default is Angled Lines Gradation.
- From the Hatch drop-down menu, select from seven hatches.
- Slide the Density slider or type a density value in the text box. Valid values range from 1% to 100%.
- Slide the two Dispersion sliders or type values in the text boxes to space the individual elements in the hatch. Valid values range from 0% to 300%.
- Slide the two Thickness sliders or type values in the text boxes to adjust the weight of the strokes of the individual elements. Valid values range from 10 points to 1,000 points.
- Slide the two Scale sliders or type values in the text boxes to specify the size of the hatch elements. Valid values range from 10% to 1,000%.
- Slide the two Rotation sliders or type values in the text boxes to rotate the hatch elements to a particular angle. Valid values range from −180° to 180°.
- To the right of the Dispersion, Thickness, Scale, and Rotation text boxes is a drop-down menu from which you can choose the change in the hatch effect within its shape:
  - None does not influence the effect.
  - Constant does not vary the effect.
  - Linear increases the intensity of the effect linearly.
  - Reflect increases the intensity of the effect from the center toward the edges.
  - Symmetric keeps the effect in proportion throughout its container.
  - Random varies the effect in an unpredictable way.
  - For the Linear, Reflect, and Symmetric options, you can adjust the angle of the hatch elements by either dragging the line around the circle or typing a value in the text box to set the angle of the line.
- From the Fade drop-down menu, select a type of fade effect for the hatch: None (no fade, which is the default), To White (fade the hatch element to white), To Black (fade the hatch element to black), or Use Gradient (to maintain the gradient fill for the selected object).

■ Click New to open a dialog box in which you can save the current hatch effect settings in the dialog box under a unique name.

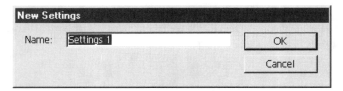

■ Click Delete to delete the hatch effect setting for the selected object. Illustrator prompts you to confirm the deletion.

■ Check the Match Object's Color check box for the hatch fill to match the fill of the selected object. The default is an unchecked check box.

■ Check the Keep Object's Fill Color check box to place the hatch above the selected object's fill without changing the color of the hatch. The default is an unchecked check box.

■ Click the Update button to update the hatch effect for the selected object. This button is unavailable if you have not changed the hatch effect options for the selected object.

■ Click the Reset button to return the dialog box to its starting values.

■ Check the Preview check box to see a preview of the hatch effect you have selected in the dialog box before it becomes final.

Figure 16-20 shows a variety of hatch effects (the type in the top row of the labels) and hatches (the second row of the label). For every chosen combination, the other options in the rest of the dialog box were unchanged. Imagine the variety of possible hatch effects if other options were modified.

Applying the Photo Crosshatch Filter

After you apply the Photo Crosshatch filter, the selected object looks like a pen-and-ink drawing, which is composed of a set of hatch layers that are arranged by levels of lightness and darkness.

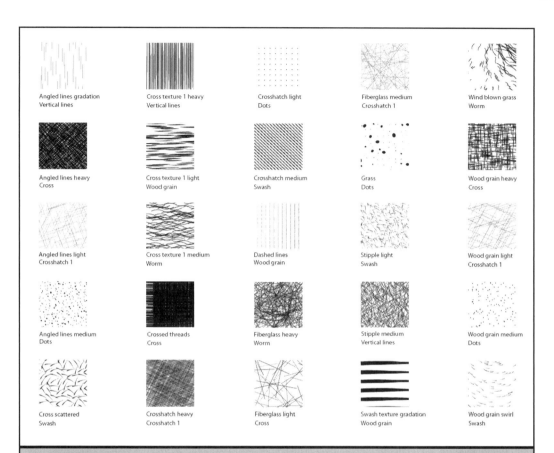

Figure 16-20. *All the hatch effects and hatches available from the Hatch Effects dialog box*

To create a photo cross-hatch, choose Filter | Pen & Ink | Photo Crosshatch. When Illustrator opens the Photo Crosshatch dialog box (see Figure 16-21), you have several options:

■ Slide the Density slider or type a value in the text box to set the density of hatch elements. Valid values range from 0.5 point to 10 points. The default is 1.2 points.

■ Slide the Dispersion Noise slider or type a value in the text box to set the space between hatch elements. Valid values range from 0% to 300%. The default is 0%.

■ Slide the Thickness slider or type a value in the text box to control the stroke weight of the hatch elements. Valid values range from 0.1 point to 10 points. The default is 0.2 points.

■ Slide the Max Line Length slider or type a value in the text box to set the maximum length of the hatch elements. Valid values range from 5 points to 999 points. The default is 24 points.

■ Slide the Rotation Noise slider or type a value in the text box to set the rotation of hatch elements randomly within their layers. Valid values range from −360° to 360°. The default is 0°.

■ Slide the Rotation Variance slider or type a value in the text box to set the change of rotation from layer to layer. Valid values range from 0% to 100%. The default is 100%.

■ Set the Top Angle, which controls the rotation in the top layer in the stack of layers, by dragging the line within the circle or typing a number of degrees in the text box. Valid values range from −360° to 360°. The default is 40°.

■ The histogram box indicates the number of pixels for each lightness value in a range from 0 to 255. You can slide the three sliders under the histogram as follows: Slide the slider on the left end to set the amount of darkness, slide the rightmost slider to set the amount of lightness, and slide the middle slider to slant the cross-hatch toward light or dark. You can see the lightness/darkness levels in the bar between the histogram and the sliders.

■ In the Hatch Layers option box/text box/drop-down menu, set the number of layers in the cross-hatch. For every layer, Illustrator adds a tick mark to the slider under the histogram. Each layer contains a lightness value ranging from 0 to 255; the range of values for each layer changes depending on the number of layers you select. You can choose from 1 (the default) to 8.

Figure 16-21 shows the Photo Crosshatch dialog box and the modified tower photograph.

Creating a Hatch Effect

Although the Hatch Effect dialog box has so many choices of hatch effects, Illustrator enables you to create and save new hatch effects. To create a hatch effect, follow these steps:

1. In the illustration window, create objects that will become a hatch.

2. Use the Selection tool (V) to select one object. To add more objects to the selection, press and hold down SHIFT as you click.

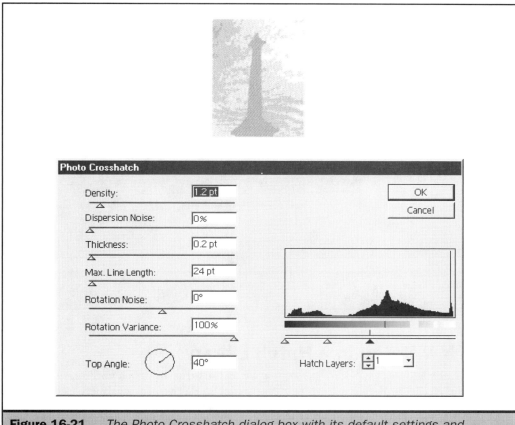

Figure 16-21.   *The Photo Crosshatch dialog box with its default settings and a photograph changed by applying the Photo Crosshatch filter*

3. Choose Filter | Pen & Ink | New Hatch. Illustrator opens the New Hatch dialog box.

4. Click New. In the small New Hatch dialog box, type the name of the new hatch and click OK.

5. Check the Preview box to see the new hatch.

6. To paste the hatch into the illustration window, click Paste.

7. To delete the hatch (or any other hatch in the Hatch drop-down menu), select it from the menu and click Delete. Illustrator prompts you to confirm the deletion.

8. Click OK to close the dialog box.

Figure 16-22 shows the objects created for the new hatch and the two versions of the New Hatch dialog box.

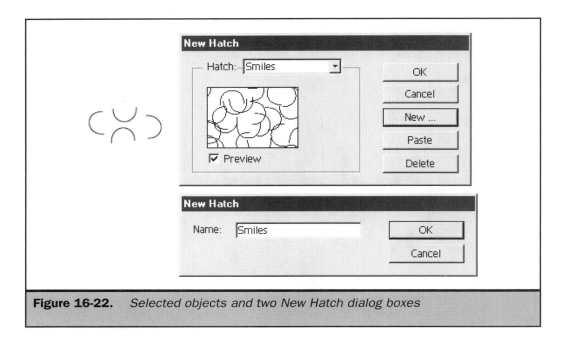

Figure 16-22. *Selected objects and two New Hatch dialog boxes*

Saving a New Hatch in a Hatch Library

The hatch libraries don't work in the same way as the other libraries you learned about earlier in the book (for example, in the "Selecting a Swatches Library" section in Chapter 7 and in the "Using Brushes Libraries" section in Chapter 13). Hatch effects are not Illustrator palettes like the members of the Swatches and Brushes libraries, stored in Illustrator documents; they are stored in the Pen and Ink subfolder of the Illustrator Filters folder.

After you have created a hatch, you can save it in a hatch library—either the default HatchSets or in a new one you can create as you save the hatch. To save a hatch, follow these steps:

1. Choose Filter | Pen & Ink | Library Save As.

2. In the Save the Library As text box, locate the Pen and Ink folder, give the library a unique name, and click OK.

Opening a Hatch Library

To open a hatch library, follow these steps:

1. Choose Filter | Pen & Ink | Library Open.

2. In the Select Library to Open dialog box, choose the library and click Open. Illustrator places the contents of the library into the Hatch Effects dialog box (see Figure 16-19, earlier in this chapter).

3. To select a filter, open the Hatch drop-down menu and click your choice.

Stylizing Objects

The Effect menu contains two Stylize commands, and the Filter menu includes one such command. You can use the Stylize filters and effects to accomplish a variety of modifications: You can apply drop shadows to objects and groups, fade out objects' edges, add a glow, change the shape of corners, and so on.

Note *The Stylize command on the Effect menu and the top Stylize command on the Filter menu enable you to add arrowheads to straight and arced paths. To learn how to use the Add Arrowheads commands, refer to "Adding Arrowheads to a Line" in Chapter 3.*

Applying Drop Shadows to Objects

Drop shadows perhaps are the most popular filter or effect Illustrator offers. Drop shadows make an object look as if it has depth, that it's floating over the page, not solidly planted. When you add a drop shadow to an object, Illustrator creates a transparent raster object on two sides of the selected object.

To apply a drop shadow, choose Filter | Stylize | Drop Shadow or Effect | Stylize | Drop Shadow. When the Drop Shadow dialog box opens, select from the following options:

- From the Mode drop-down menu, select a blending mode. The default is Multiply. For more information about blending modes, refer to "Using Blending Modes" in Chapter 15.

- In the Opacity drop-down slider or text box, set the level of transparency or opacity. Valid values range from 0% (completely transparent) to 100% (completely opaque). The default is 75%.

- Either select or type the size of the horizontal x-axis offset in the X Offset list box/text box. Valid values range from –1,000 points to 1,000 points. A negative value moves the shadow to the left of the object; a positive value moves the shadow to the right. The default is 7 points.

- Either select or type the size of the vertical y-axis offset in the Y Offset list box/text box. A negative value moves the shadow above the object; a positive value moves the shadow below. Valid values range from –1,000 points to 1,000 points. The default is 7 points.

- From the Blur drop-down slider or text box, select the number of points that the blur extends from the selected object. When Illustrator adds a blur to the shadow, it creates a transparent raster object. Valid values range from 0 point to 144 points. The default is 5 points.

- To select a color for the shadow, click the Color radio button. This opens the Color Picker from which you can choose. For more information about the Color Picker, refer to "Using the Color Picker" in Chapter 7.

- To select a level of black for the shadow, click Darkness (the default). Valid values range from –100% to 100%. The default value is 50%.

- If you are applying the drop shadow filter to a group of overlapping objects, check the Create Separate Shadows check box to apply separate shadows to each member of the group and clear the check box to apply one shadow to the entire group. This option is not available if you use the drop shadow effect.

Figure 16-23 shows the Drop Shadow dialog box for the drop shadow effect, three objects, and two groups given drop shadows.

Feathering an Object

Feathering fades out the edges of an object. If the object has a distinctive stroke, both the fill and stroke fade but you'll still be able to see both parts of the object.

To feather a selected object, follow these steps:

1. Choose Effect | Stylize | Feather. Illustrator opens the Feather Radius dialog box.

2. In the Feather Radius list box/text box, select or type the radius of the feathering. Valid values range from 0.2 point to 250 points. The default value is 5 points.

3. To see a preview of the feathered object before you close the dialog box, check the Preview check box.

4. Click OK when you have finished selecting the options.

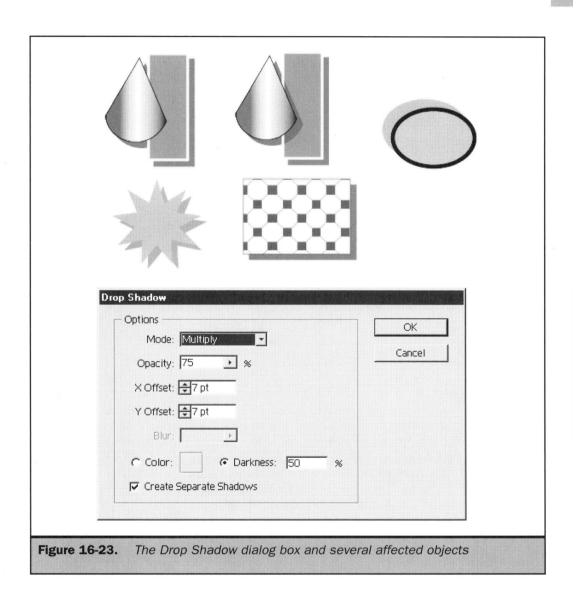

Figure 16-23.   *The Drop Shadow dialog box and several affected objects*

Figure 16-24 illustrates feathering for four objects; the third with a wide black stroke and the fourth a photograph.

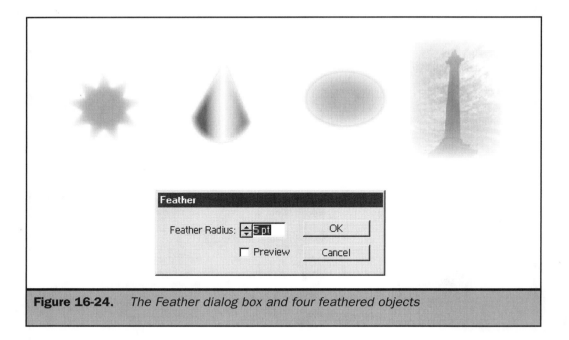

Figure 16-24.   *The Feather dialog box and four feathered objects*

Making Objects Glow

The Inner Glow and Outer Glow effects enable you to add radiance to the inside of an object or its edges. Illustrator creates an inner glow by creating a raster object inside an opacity mask. An outer glow is similar to a drop shadow: Illustrator creates a transparent raster object around the edges of the selected object.

To apply an inner glow, choose Effect | Stylize | Inner Glow. To apply an outer glow, choose Effect | Stylize | Outer Glow. When Illustrator opens the Inner Glow dialog box or Outer Glow dialog box, select from the following options:

- Open the Mode drop-down menu to select a blending mode. The default is Screen. For more information about blending modes, refer to "Using Blending Modes" in Chapter 15.

- If you want to change the color of the glow from the default pale yellow, click the box to the right of the Mode drop-down menu to open the Color Picker, in which you can choose a color.

- In the Opacity drop-down slider or text box, set the level of transparency or opacity. Valid values range from 0% (completely transparent) to 100% (completely opaque). Valid values range from 0% to 100%. The default is 75%.

- From the Blur drop-down slider or text box, select the number of points that the blur extends from the selected object. Valid values range from 0 point to 144 points. The default is 5 points.

■ Click the Center radio button to apply the glow from the center of the object; click Edge (the default) to apply the glow at the edges of the object. This option is available only in the Inner Glow dialog box.

■ To preview the results of the selected options before you close the dialog box, check the Preview check box.

Figure 16-25 shows the Inner Glow and Outer Glow dialog boxes and some objects with inner glows applied. The settings for the leftmost object are Screen blending mode, pale yellow color, 75% opacity, and Center. The center object is set to the Hard Light blending mode, white color, 40% opacity, and Edge. The settings for the rightmost object

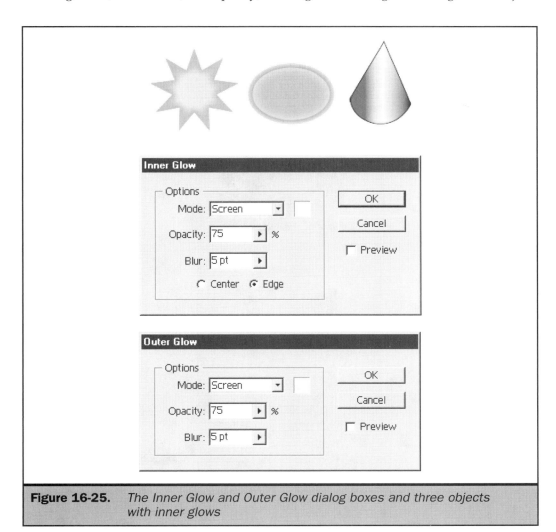

Figure 16-25. *The Inner Glow and Outer Glow dialog boxes and three objects with inner glows*

ILLUSTRATOR FX

are Multiply blending mode, light blue color, 65% opacity, and Center. All objects are set to 10-point blur.

Applying Glowing Edges

With the Glowing Edges filter, you can add a glow to the changes between one color and another in an artwork. To apply glowing edges, choose Filter | Stylize | Glowing Edges. In the Glowing Edges dialog box, choose from the following options:

- Edge Width sets the width of the glowing edges. Valid values range from 1 (the smallest width) to 14 (the largest). The default is 2.

- Edge Brightness specifies the brightness of the edges. Valid values range from 0 (no brightness) to 20 (the maximum brightness). The default is 6.

- Smoothness sets the smoothness of the edges. Valid values range from 1 (less smooth) to 15 (smoother). The default is 5.

Figure 16-26 shows the Glowing Edges dialog box and two objects that have been modified with the filter.

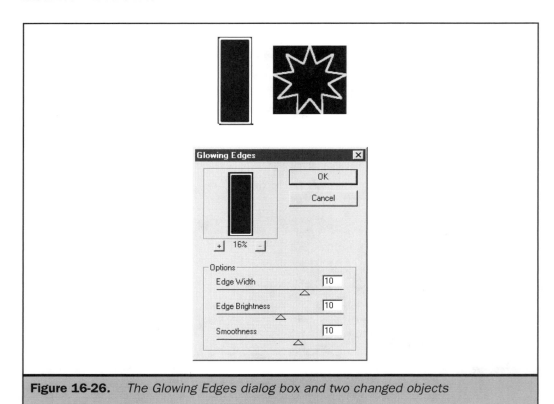

Figure 16-26. *The Glowing Edges dialog box and two changed objects*

Using the Flare Tool

With the Flare tool, which is on the Rectangle toolslot, you can place flare objects over an object. Flares consist of an intense light in the center, a halo around the light, and outer rings and rays from the center of the flare. In this section you'll learn how to create a flare and set flare options.

Creating a Flare with the Flare Tool

After clicking the Flare tool to activate it, press and hold down ALT/OPTION, and click the object to place the flare on top of it. (If you click the object without pressing down ALT/OPTION, Illustrator opens the Flare Tool Options dialog box.) Drag away from the center of the click to increase the size of the flare; drag toward the center to reduce the flare's size. Then release ALT/OPTION for Illustrator to draw the flare.

Before you release the mouse button to signal Illustrator to create the flare, you can use the following keys to change the flare's attributes:

- To force beams to stay at their current angles, press and hold down SHIFT while dragging the flare larger or smaller. If you don't press and hold down SHIFT, dragging rotates the flare and its beams.
- To add halos to the selected flare, repeatedly press ↑.
- To remove beams from the selected flare, repeatedly press ↓.
- To make the points grow longer while the center of the flare remains the same size, press CTRL/⌘ while dragging.
- To create flares with several halos, press and hold down ` (back tick or left single quote on the left side of the keyboard) while dragging.
- To move a flare as you create it, press SPACEBAR and drag the flare.

Figure 16-27 shows several flares created with the Flare tool. The first flare in the series emanates from the star object.

Creating a Flare Using a Dialog Box

As with the basic Illustrator shapes, you also can use the Flare tool to open the Flare Tool Options dialog box (see Figure 16-28) with which you can specify exact dimensions for the center, rays, halo, and rings. If you have used this installed version of Illustrator to create a flare before, either with the Flare tool or the Flare Tool Options dialog box, those values remain in the dialog box; otherwise, Illustrator's default values appear. To open the Flare Tool Options dialog box, either click the illustration window while the Flare tool is active or double-click the Flare tool in the toolbox.

Once the dialog box is open, you can reset the options to the default settings. To do so, press and hold down ALT/OPTION and click the Reset button, which replaces the Cancel button.

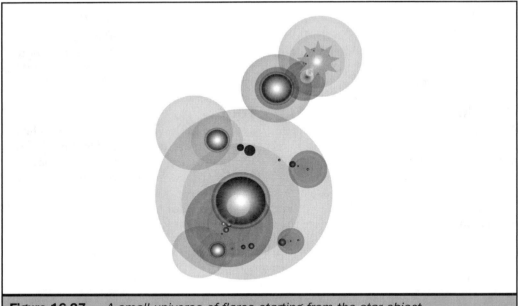

Figure 16-27. *A small universe of flares starting from the star object*

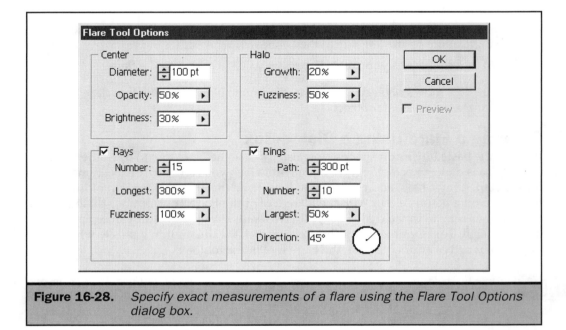

Figure 16-28. *Specify exact measurements of a flare using the Flare Tool Options dialog box.*

The options in the Flare Tool Options dialog box are as follows:

- With the Diameter list box/text box, select or type the diameter of the flare. Valid values range from 0 points to 1,000 points. The default value is 100 points.

- In the Opacity slider/text box, select or type the percentage of opacity. Valid values range from 0% to 100%. The default is 50%.

- Using the Brightness slider/text box, select or type the percentage of brightness. Valid values range from 0% to 100%. The default is 30%.

- If you want the flare to contain rays, check the Rays check box. A checked check box is the default.

- In the Number list box/text box, select or type the number of rays. Valid values range from 0 to 50. The default is 15.

- With the Longest slider/text box, select or type the length of the longest ray compared to the average ray as a percentage. Valid values range from 0% to 1,000%. The default is 300% larger than the average ray length.

- Using the two Fuzziness sliders/text boxes, select or type the fuzziness of the rays and halo. Valid values range from 0% (not fuzzy at all) to 100% (very fuzzy). The default row ray is 100%, and for the halo it is 50%.

- In the Growth slider/text box, select or type the increase in size of the halo as a percentage. Valid values range from 0% to 300%. The default value is 20% larger than the average halo.

- If you want the flare to contain rings, check the Rings check box. A checked check box is the default.

- With the Path list box/text box, select or type the length of the path from the center of the inner halo to the center of the ring that is farthest away from the center. Valid values range from 0 point to 1,000 points. The default is 300 points.

- In the Number list box/text box, select or type the number of rings in the flare. Valid values range from 0 to 50. The default is 10.

- Using the Largest slider/text box, select or type the increase in size of the largest ring by percentage. Valid values range from 0% to 250%. The default is 50% larger than the average ring.

- With the Direction text box or the line within the circle to its right, set the direction of the rings. Valid values range from 0° and 359°. The default is 45°.

Editing a Flare

To edit a flare after you create it, you can choose from one of the following actions:

- Activate the Flare tool, select the flare, and drag the paths to resize or move them.

- Select the flare and double-click the Flare tool to open the Flare Options dialog box to change options, which are described in the following section.

- Select the flare and choose Object | Expand. In the Expand dialog box, click OK; then edit the flare by dragging its paths.
- Use the Direct Selection tool (A) to select individual components of the flare. Then use other Illustrator tools and features to modify the flare.

Rounding Corners

In the "Rounding a Rectangle's Corners" section in Chapter 2, you learned how to round a rectangle's corners all the way from straight corners to a completely rounded ellipse. With the Round Corners filter and effect, you can round any object's corners. To round the corners of a selected object, choose Filter | Stylize | Round Corners or Effect | Stylize | Round Corners. The resulting Round Corners dialog box is virtually the same for both filter and effect. The only difference is the presence of the Preview check box for the effect. When Illustrator opens the dialog box, type the radius of the new curve, optionally click the Preview check box, and click OK. Figure 16-29 illustrates both dialog boxes and three objects with rounded corners.

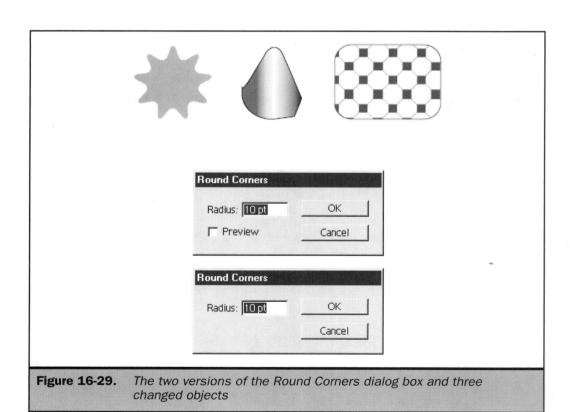

Figure 16-29. *The two versions of the Round Corners dialog box and three changed objects*

Warping Objects

The Warp command on the Effect menu has a submenu loaded with a variety of effects you can apply to objects. Note that these effects are related to the Warp tool, which was covered in "The Warp Tool," earlier in this chapter. To apply a warp effect, choose Effect | Warp and then select a subcommand: Arc, Arc Lower, Arc Upper, Arch, Bulge, Shell Lower, Shell Upper, Flag, Wave, Fish, Rise, Fisheye, Inflate, Squeeze, or Twist (which is a close relative of the Twist tool). Choosing any subcommand opens a dialog box (see Figure 16-30) containing the same options, except for the name of the subcommand at the top.

The options in the Warp Options dialog box are as follows:

- The Style drop-down menu displays the name of the effect you have chosen from the Warp submenu. You can open the menu and choose a different effect.
- The Horizontal radio button turns the object along the horizontal axis; the Vertical radio button twists the object on the vertical axis.
- Use the Bend slider/ text box to set the bend percentage. Valid values range from –100% to 100%. The default is 50%.
- With the Distortion sliders/text boxes, you can specify the percentage of distortion on the horizontal or vertical plane. Valid values range from –100% to 100%. The default for both is 0%.

Figure 16-31 shows each of the warp effects, with the default settings, applied to three objects. In the leftmost column, starting at the top, the effects are Arc, Arc Lower,

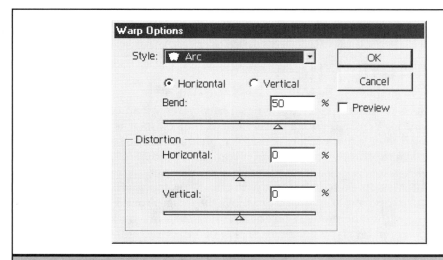

Figure 16-30. *The Warp Options dialog box is the same for each subcommand of the Warp command*

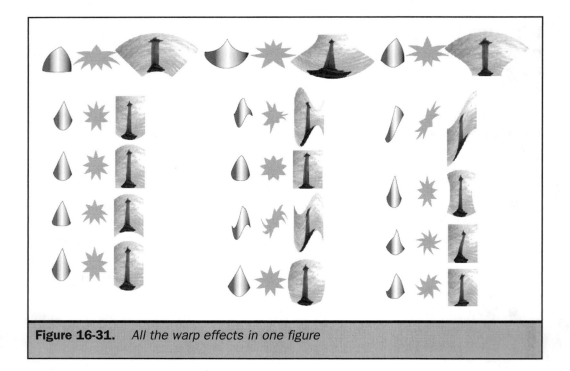

Figure 16-31. *All the warp effects in one figure*

Arc Upper, Arch, and Bulge. In the middle column, starting at the top, the effects are Shell Lower, Fish, Fisheye, Flag, and Inflate. In the rightmost column, starting at the top, the effects are Shell Upper, Rise, Squeeze, Twist, and Wave.

Applying Artistic Filters

All the Artistic filters enable you to make objects—especially multicolored ones such as photographs—look more like pencil drawings, pastels, frescos, and collages; and oil and water color paintings created with a variety of techniques, such as fresco, palette knife, and sponging. Other Artistic filters and effects change the surface of an object by adding grain, plastic wrap, and smudges. And if you haven't had enough of glows, an Artistic filter enables you to apply a neon glow filter to an object.

Each Artistic filter has its own dialog box with a large preview window in the left corner and a brief list of options. You can drag to move the image around the preview box and zoom the image within the preview box by pressing the + or – button. Illustrator displays the current zoom level (by percentage) between the two buttons. If you see a flashing line below the preview box, you will have to wait until Illustrator finishes drawing the new preview. Most of the dialog boxes contain three options with which you can adjust the look of the filter.

Coloring an Object with a Pencil

The Colored Pencil filter changes the selected object so that it looks as if you have drawn it with colored pencils on a plain background. To apply a colored pencil look to the selected object, choose Filter | Artistic | Colored Pencil. Illustrator opens the Colored Pencil dialog box, which contains the following options:

- In the Pencil Width slider/text box, select or type the width of the pencil used to draw the pencil lines on the object. Valid values range from 1 to 24. The default value is 4.

- With the Stroke Pressure slider/text box, indicate the pressure with which Illustrator draws the pencil lines. Valid values range from 0 to 15. The default value is 8.

- In the Paper Brightness slider/text box, determine the amount of black or white in the drawing. Valid values range from 0 to 50. The default value is 25.

Converting an Object to a Collage

The Cutout filter treats the selected object as a collage made up of colored paper. To apply the Cutout filter, choose Filter | Artistic | Cutout. Illustrator opens the Cutout dialog box, which contains the following options:

- In the No. of Levels slider/text box, select or type the number of levels of virtual paper cutouts. Valid values range from 2 to 8. The default is 4.

- In the Edge Simplicity slider/text box, select or type the complexity or simplicity of the cutout edges. Valid values range from 0 to 10. The default is 4.

- With the Edge Fidelity slider/text box, select or type the faithfulness to the location of the original edges. Valid values range from 1 to 3. The default is 2.

Using a Dry Brush on an Object

The Dry Brush filter uses a dry brush technique to paint the edge of the selected object. The end result is an object made up of fewer colors. To apply a dry brush look to the selected object, choose Filter | Artistic | Dry Brush. Illustrator opens the Dry Brush dialog box, which contains the following options:

- With the Brush Size slider/text box, select or type the width of the brush. Valid values range from 0 to 10. The default is 2.

- Using the Brush Detail slider/text box, select or type the amount of detail the brush applies. Valid values range from 0 (more detail) to 10 (less detail). The default is 8.

- With the Texture slider/text box, select or type the amount of texture to add to the selected object. Valid values range from 1 (less texture) to 3 (more texture). The default is 1.

Adding a Film Grain to an Object

The Film Grain filter applies a pattern to the dark and mid-tones of the selected object, saturates the light tones, and smooths the entire object so that it looks as if you have drawn it with colored pencils. To apply a film grain to the selected object, choose Filter | Artistic | Film Grain. Illustrator opens the Film Grain dialog box, which contains the following options:

- With the Grain slider/text box, select or type the level of graininess of the object. Valid values range from 0 (less graininess) to 20 (much graininess). The default is 4.

- In the Highlight Area slider/text box, select or type the amount of highlighting throughout the selected object. Valid values range from 0 (fewer highlights) to 20 (many highlights). The default is 0.

- Using the Intensity slider/text box, select or type the intensity of the color. Valid values range from 0 (little intensity) to 10 (much intensity). The default is 10.

Adding a Fresco Coating to an Object

The Fresco filter applies a fresco coating to the selected object. To apply a fresco look to the selected object, choose Filter | Artistic | Fresco. Illustrator opens the Fresco dialog box, which contains the following options:

- In the Brush Size slider/text box, select or type the size of the brush. Valid values range from 0 (smaller) to 10 (larger). The default is 2.

- With the Brush Detail slider/text box, select or type the detail applied to the surface. Valid values range from 0 (more detail) to 10 (less detail). The default is 8.

- With the Texture slider/text box, select or type the amount of texture to add to the selected object. Valid values range from 1 (less texture) to 3 (more texture). The default is 1.

Figure 16-32 illustrates the Colored Pencil, Cutout, Dry Brush, Film Grain, and Fresco dialog boxes. Next to each dialog box is an example of the filter applied to a photograph using the default options.

Applying a Neon Glow to an Object

The Neon Glow filter is the last glow effect discussed in this chapter. When you apply a neon glow to the selected object, Illustrator adds glows in different colors while it smoothes the look of the object. To apply a neon glow to the selected object, choose

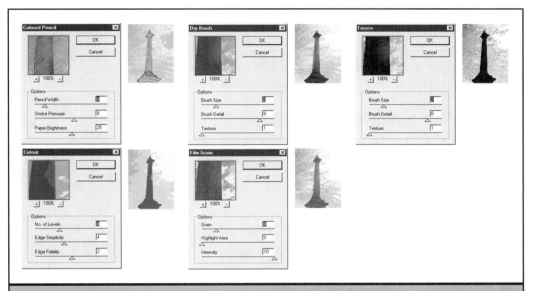

Figure 16-32.   *The Colored Pencil, Cutout, Dry Brush, Film Grain, and Fresco dialog boxes; and an example of each filter on the right side of its dialog box*

Filter | Artistic | Neon Glow. Illustrator opens the Neon Glow dialog box, which contains the following options:

- In the Glow Size slider/text box, select or type the placement of the glow. Valid values range from –24 (a glow on the dark sections of the object) to 24 (a large-size glow on the edges of the dark sections). The default is 5.

- With the Glow Brightness slider/text box, select or type the brightness of the glow. Valid values range from 0 (completely dark) to 50 (bright ranging to monochrome over the entire object). The default is 15.

- Click the Glow Color color box to open the Color Picker from which you can select a glow color. The default color is in the family of the main color in the object.

Daubing an Object with Paint

The Paint Daubs filter spreads paint on the selected object. By changing the brush type, you can change the look of the filter dramatically. To apply a paint daubs look to the selected object, choose Filter | Artistic | Paint Daubs. Illustrator opens the Paint Daubs dialog box, which contains the following options:

- With the Brush Size slider/text box, select or type the width of the brush. Valid values range from 1 (small) to 50 (large). The default is 8.

- Using the Sharpness slider/text box, select or type the level of sharpness between the colors. Valid values range from 0 (not sharp) to 40 (very sharp). The default is 7.

- From the Brush Type drop-down menu, select the brush type: Simple (the default), Light Rough, Dark Rough, Wide Sharp, Wide Blurry, or Sparkle.

Using a Palette Knife on an Object

The Palette Knife filter changes the selected object by diminishing its detail and showing any underlying surface. To use a palette knife on the selected object, choose Filter | Artistic | Palette Knife. Illustrator opens the Palette Knife dialog box, which contains the following options:

- Using the Stroke Size slider/text box, select or type the stroke size of the palette knife. Valid values range from 1 (small) to 50 (large). The default is 25.

- In the Stroke Detail slider/text box, select or type the amount of detail of the palette knife strokes. Valid values range from 1 (less detail) to 3 (more detail). The default is 3.

- With the Softness slider/text box, select or type how much softness is applied to the object. Valid values range from 0 (less soft) to 10 (softer). The default is 0.

Applying Plastic Wrap to an Object

The Plastic Wrap filter applies plastic wrap on the surface of the selected object. To apply plastic wrap to the selected object, choose Filter | Artistic | Plastic Wrap. Illustrator opens the Plastic Wrap dialog box, which contains the following options:

- In the Highlight Strength slider/text box, select or type the strength of the plastic wrap highlight applied to the object. Valid values range from 0 (no highlight) to 20 (strong highlight). The default is 15.

- In the Detail slider/text box, select or type the number of highlights added to the object's surface. Valid values range from 1 (fewer highlights) to 15 (many highlights). The default is 9.

- In the Smoothness slider/text box, select or type the level of smoothness. Valid values range from 1 (less smooth) to 15 (smoother). The default is 7.

Giving Poster Edges to an Object

The Poster Edges filter simplifies the selected object by shrinking the number of colors and emphasizes the edges of images by adding black lines. To apply poster edges to the selected object, choose Filter | Artistic | Poster Edges. Illustrator opens the Poster Edges dialog box, which contains the following options:

- Using the Edge Thickness slider/text box, select or type the thickness of the poster edges. Valid values range from 0 (less thick) to 10 (thicker). The default is 2.

- In the Edge Intensity slider/text box, select or type the strength of the dark colors added to the object. Valid values range from 0 (the least intensity) to 10 (the most intensity). The default is 1.

- With the Posterization slider/text box, select or type the brightness of contrast between the colors in the object. Valid values range from 0 (very bright) to 6 (less bright). The default is 2.

Figure 16-33 illustrates the Neon Glow, Paint Daubs, Palette Knife, Plastic Wrap, and Poster Edges dialog boxes. Next to each dialog box is an example of the filter applied to a photograph using the default options.

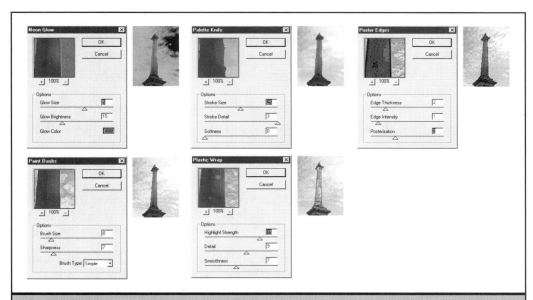

Figure 16-33.   *The Neon Glow, Paint Daubs, Palette Knife, Plastic Wrap, and Poster Edges dialog boxes; and an example of each filter on the right side of its dialog box*

Using Rough Pastels on an Object

The Rough Pastels filter overlays the selected object with pastel stroke marks and changes the texture of the background of the object. To apply a rough pastel look to the selected object, choose Filter | Artistic | Rough Pastels. Illustrator opens the Rough Pastels dialog box, which contains the following options:

- In the Stroke Length slider/text box, select or type the length of the stroke marks. Valid values range from 0 (short) to 40 (long). The default is 6.

- Using the Stroke Detail slider/text box, select or type the detail of the stroke marks. Valid values range from 1 (little detail) to 20 (great detail). The default is 4.

- From the Texture drop-down menu, select the texture of the background of the object. You can choose from Brick, Burlap, Canvas, or Sandstone or load a custom-defined texture. The default is Canvas. To load a custom texture, choose Load Texture, fill in the resulting dialog box, and click OK.

- With the Scaling slider/text box, select or type a value with which to enlarge or reduce the width of the stroke marks on the object and on the background. Valid values range from 50% to 200%. The default is 100%.

- In the Relief slider/text box, select or type the smoothness or harshness of the background. Valid values range from 0 (very smooth) to 50 (very harsh). The default is 20.

- From the Light Direction drop-down menu, select the direction from which light on the object appears. You can choose from Bottom, Bot. Left, Left, Top Left, Top, Top Right, Right, and Bot. Right. The default is Bottom.

- Check the Invert check box to reverse the stroke marks on the background. The effects can be very subtle. The default is an unchecked check box.

Smudging an Object

The Smudge Stick filter smudges the dark parts and lightens lighter areas of the selected object. To smudge the selected object, choose Filter | Artistic | Smudge Stick. Illustrator opens the Smudge Stick dialog box, which contains the following options:

- In the Stroke Length slider/text box, select or type the length of the stroke marks. Valid values range from 0 (short) to 10 (long). The default is 2.

- In the Highlight Area slider/text box, select or type the amount of highlighting throughout the selected object. Valid values range from 0 (less highlighting) to 20 (more highlighting). The default is 0.

- Using the Intensity slider/text box, select or type the intensity of the color. Valid values range from 0 (little intensity) to 10 (much intensity). The default is 10.

Sponging an Object

The Sponge filter adds texture and contrast to the selected object as if you had sponged the colors onto the object's surface. To apply a sponged look to the selected object, choose Filter | Artistic | Sponge. Illustrator opens the Sponge dialog box, which contains the following options:

- With the Brush Size slider/text box, select or type the width of the brush. Valid values range from 0 (narrow) to 10 (wide). The default is 2.

- From the Definition slider/text box, select or type the definition of the sponge marks. Valid values range from 0 (little definition) to 25 (great definition). The default is 12.

- In the Smoothness slider/text box, select or type the level of smoothness. Valid values range from 1 (less smooth) to 15 (smoother). The default is 5.

Underpainting an Object

The Underpainting filter adds texture to the background, copies the object onto the background, and places another copy in the foreground. To underpaint the selected object, choose Filter | Artistic | Underpainting. Illustrator opens the Underpainting dialog box, which contains the following options:

- With the Brush Size slider/text box, select or type the width of the brush. Valid values range from 0 (narrow) to 40 (wide). The default is 6.

- In the Texture Coverage slider/text box, select or type the amount of text applied to the object and the background. Valid values range from 0 (little texture coverage) to 40 (a great deal of texture). The default is 16.

- From the Texture drop-down menu, select the texture of the background of the object. You can choose from Brick, Burlap, Canvas, and Sandstone or load a custom-defined texture. The default is Canvas. To load a custom texture, choose Load Texture, fill in the resulting dialog box, and click OK.

- With the Scaling slider/text box, select or type a value with which to enlarge or reduce the width of the stroke marks on the object and on the background. Valid values range from 50% to 200%. The default is 100%.

- In the Relief slider/text box, select or type the smoothness or harshness of the background. Valid values range from 0 (very smooth) to 50 (very harsh). The default is 4.

- From the Light Direction drop-down menu, select the direction from which light on the object appears. You can choose from Bottom, Bot. Left, Left, Top Left, Top, Top Right, Right, and Bot. Right. The default is Top.

- Check the Invert check box to reverse the stroke marks on the background. The effects can be very subtle. The default is an unchecked box.

Painting with Watercolor

The Watercolor filter paints the selected object as a wet watercolor painting done with an intermediate-sized brush. To paint the selected object with watercolors, choose Filter | Artistic | Watercolor. Illustrator opens the Watercolor dialog box, which contains the following options:

- Using the Brush Detail slider/text box, select or type the amount of detail that the brush applies. Valid values range from 1 (more definition) to 14 (less definition). The default is 9.

- In the Shadow Intensity slider/text box, select or type the intensity of the shadow. Valid values range from 0 (less intensity) to 10 (great intensity). The default is 1.

- With the Texture slider/text box, select or type the amount of texture to add to the selected object. Valid values range from 1 (less texture) to 3 (more texture). The default is 1.

Figure 16-34 illustrates the Rough Pastels, Smudge Stick, Sponge, Underpainting, and Watercolors dialog boxes. Next to each dialog box is an example of the filter applied to a photograph using the default options.

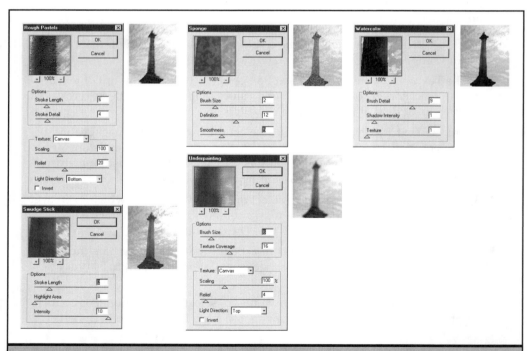

Figure 16-34. *The Rough Pastels, Smudge Stick, Sponge, Underpainting, and Watercolors dialog boxes; and an example of each filter on the right side of its dialog box*

Working with Brush Strokes

Brush Strokes filters work in much the same way as the Artistic filters you just explored. With Brush Strokes you can emphasize the edges of an object, apply various brush strokes over an object, and spatter or spray the object. As with Artistic filters, Brush Strokes work best on multicolored ones such as photographs.

Each of the Brush Strokes filters—just like the Artistic filters—has its own dialog box with a large preview window in the left corner and a short list of options. To move the image around the preview box, drag with the Hand tool (which automatically appears when you move the mouse pointer to the preview image). You also can zoom the preview image by pressing the + or - button. Illustrator displays the current zoom level (by percentage) between the two buttons. If you see a flashing line below the preview box, wait until Illustrator has finished drawing the new preview image.

Accenting the Edges of an Object

The Accented Edges filter emphasizes the edges of the selected object with a light chalk or dark ink look. To apply the Accented Edges filter to the selected object, choose Filter | Brush Strokes | Accented Edges. Illustrator opens the Accented Edges dialog box, which contains the following options:

- ■ In the Edge Width slider/text box, select or type the width of the edges. Valid values range from 1 (the smallest width) to 14 (the largest). The default is 2.

- ■ Using the Edge Brightness slider/text box, select or type the brightness of the edges. Valid values range from 0 (no brightness) to 50 (the maximum brightness). The default is 38.

- ■ With the Smoothness slider/text box, select or type the smoothness of the edges. Valid values range from 1 (less smooth) to 15 (smoother). The default is 5.

Angling Strokes on an Object

The Angled Strokes filter applies diagonal brushstrokes to the selected object. To apply the Angled Strokes filter to a selected object, choose Filter | Brush Strokes | Angled Strokes. Illustrator opens the Angled Strokes dialog box, which contains the following options:

- ■ With the Direction Balance slider/text box, select or type the angle of the brushstrokes. Valid values range from 0 (moving between the top-left corner and the bottom-right corner) to 100 (moving between the top-right corner and the bottom-left corner). The default is 50.

- ■ In the Stroke Length slider/text box, select or type the length of the brushstrokes. Valid values range from 3 (short) to 50 (long). The default is 15.

- ■ Using the Sharpness slider/text box, select or type the level of sharpness between the colors. Valid values range from 0 (not sharp) to 10 (very sharp). The default is 3.

Adding Crosshatching to an Object

The Crosshatch filter adds texture and coarsens the edges of the colored portions of the selected object. To apply the Crosshatch filter, choose Filter | Brush Strokes | Crosshatch. Illustrator opens the Crosshatch dialog box, which contains the following options:

- In the Stroke Length slider/text box, select or type the length of the stroke marks. Valid values range from 3 (short) to 50 (long). The default is 9.

- Using the Sharpness slider/text box, select or type the level of sharpness between the colors. Valid values range from 0 (not sharp) to 20 (very sharp). The default is 6.

- In the Strength slider/text box, select or type the strength of the crosshatching. Valid values range from 1 (the least intensity) to 3 (the most intensity). The default is 1.

Using Dark Strokes on an Object

The Dark Strokes filter blackens the dark areas with short strokes and lightens the light areas of the selected object with long strokes. To apply the Dark Strokes filter to the selected object, choose Filter | Brush Strokes | Dark Strokes. Illustrator opens the Dark Strokes dialog box, which contains the following options:

- In the Balance slider/text box, select or type the angle of the strokes. Valid values range from 0 (from the top-right corner to the bottom-left corner angle) to 10 (from the top-left corner to the bottom-right corner). The default is 5.

- With the Black Intensity slider/text box, select or type the intensity of black strokes. Valid values range from 0 (a little intensity) to 10 (much intensity). The default is 6.

- In the White Intensity slider/text box, select or type the intensity of white strokes. Valid values range from 0 (a little intensity) to 10 (much intensity). The default is 2.

Figure 16-35 illustrates the Accented Edges, Angled Strokes, Crosshatch, and Dark Strokes dialog boxes. Next to each dialog box is an example of the filter applied to a photograph using the default options.

Outlining an Object with Ink

The Ink Outlines filter draws pen-and-ink lines over the selected object. To apply the Ink Outlines filter, choose Filter | Brush Strokes | Ink Outlines. Illustrator opens the Ink Outlines dialog box, which contains the following options:

- In the Stroke Length slider/text box, select or type the length of the stroke marks. Valid values range from 1 (short) to 50 (long). The default is 4.

- With the Dark Intensity slider/text box, select or type the intensity of dark strokes. Valid values range from 0 (little intensity) to 50 (much intensity). The default is 20.

- In the Light Intensity slider/text box, select or type the intensity of light strokes. Valid values range from 0 (little intensity) to 50 (much intensity). The default is 10.

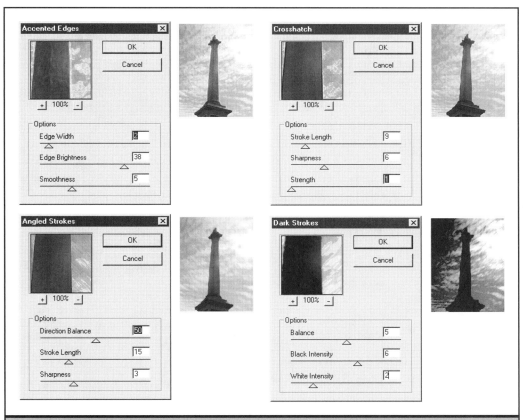

Figure 16-35. *The Accented Edges, Angled Strokes, Crosshatch, and Dark Strokes dialog boxes; and an example of each filter on the right side of its dialog box*

ILLUSTRATOR FX

Spattering an Object

The Spatter filter airbrushes the selected object. To apply the Spatter filter to the selected object, choose Filter | Brush Strokes | Spatter. Illustrator opens the Spatter dialog box, which contains the following options:

- Using the Spray Radius slider/text box, select or type the radius of the spray. Valid values range from 0 (small radius) to 25 (large radius). The default is 10.

- With the Smoothness slider/text box, select or type the smoothness of the edges. Valid values range from 1 (less smooth) to 15 (smoother). The default is 5.

Spraying Strokes on an Object

The Sprayed Strokes filter paints the selected object with sprayed and angled strokes, emphasizing its main colors. To apply the Sprayed Strokes filter to the selected object, choose Filter | Brush Strokes | Sprayed Strokes. Illustrator opens the Sprayed Strokes dialog box, which contains the following options:

- In the Stroke Length slider/text box, select or type the length of the stroke marks. Valid values range from 0 (short) to 20 (long). The default is 12.

- Using the Spray Radius slider/text box, select or type the radius of the spray. Valid values range from 0 (small radius) to 25 (large radius). The default is 7.

- From the Stroke Direction drop-down menu, select the direction of the stroke: Right Diag. (the default), Horizontal, Left Diag., or Vertical.

Using the Sumi-e Filter

The Sumi-e filter paints the selected object using a wet, black brush. To paint the selected object using the Sumi-e filter, choose Filter | Brush Strokes | Sumi-e. Illustrator opens the Sumi-e dialog box, which contains the following options:

- In the Stroke Width slider/text box, select or type the width of the brushstroke. Valid values range from 3 (narrow) to 15 (wide). The default value is 10.

- With the Stroke Pressure slider/text box, indicate the pressure with which Illustrator paints the strokes. Valid values range from 0 (light pressure) to 15 (heavy pressure). The default value is 2.

- In the Contrast slider/text box, determine the amount of black or white in the drawing. Valid values range from 0 (little contrast) to 40 (much contrast). The default value is 16.

Figure 16-36 illustrates the Ink Outlines, Spatter, Sprayed Strokes, and Sumi-e dialog boxes. Next to each dialog box is an example of the filter applied to a photograph using the default options.

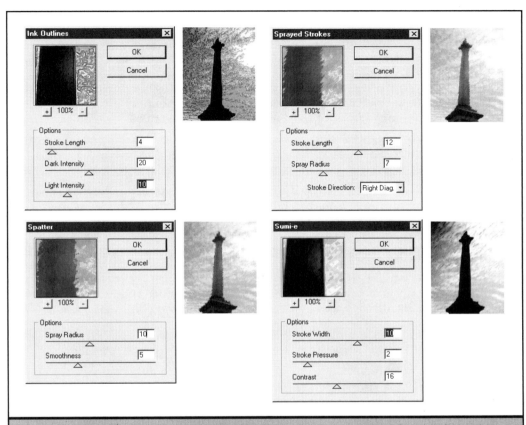

Figure 16-36. *The Ink Outlines, Spatter, Sprayed Strokes, and Sumi-e dialog boxes; and an example of each filter on the right side of its dialog box*

Sketching Objects

The 14 filters associated with the Sketch command apply texture or convert a selected object to a three-dimensional version. Some Sketch filters—just like the Artistic and Brush Strokes filters—enable you to change objects so they look more like pencil and crayon drawings.

Each of the Sketch filters has its own dialog box with a large preview window in the left corner and a brief list of options. You can move the image around the preview box by dragging and zoom the image within the preview box by pressing the + or – button. Illustrator displays the current zoom level (by percentage) between the two buttons. If you see a flashing line below the preview box, you must wait until Illustrator has completed drawing the new preview.

Applying Bas Relief

The Bas Relief filter sculpts the selected object into a shallow three-dimensional shape. To apply the Bas Relief filter to the selected object, choose Filter | Sketch | Bas Relief. Illustrator opens the Bas Relief dialog box, which contains the following options:

- With the Detail slider/text box, select or type the amount of detail in the glass. Valid values range from 1 (less detail) to 15 (more detail). The default is 13.

- To adjust the smoothness of the glass, slide the Smoothness slider or type a value in the text box. Valid values range from 1 (not smooth) to 15 (very smooth). The default is 3.

- From the Light Direction drop-down menu, select the direction from which light on the object appears. You can choose from Bottom (the default), Bot. Left, Left, Top Left, Top, Top Right, Right, and Bot. Right.

Using Chalk and Charcoal

The Chalk & Charcoal filter redraws the selected object using thick chalk, emphasizing shadows with black charcoal. To apply the Chalk & Charcoal filter, choose Filter | Sketch | Chalk & Charcoal. Illustrator opens the Chalk & Charcoal dialog box, which contains the following options:

- Using the Charcoal Area slider/text box. Valid values range from 0 to 20. The default is 6.

- Using the Chalk Area slider/text box. Valid values range from 0 to 20. The default is 6.

- With the Stroke Pressure slider/text box indicate the pressure with which Illustrator draws the pencil lines. Valid values range from 0 to 5. The default value is 1.

Drawing with Charcoal

The Charcoal filter redraws the selected object with lines of black charcoal. To apply the Charcoal filter, choose Filter | Sketch | Charcoal. Illustrator opens the Charcoal dialog box, which contains the following options:

- With the Charcoal Thickness slider/text box, select or type the size of the charcoal. Valid values range from 1 (thin) to 7 (thick). The default is 1.

- Using the Detail slider/text box, select or type the amount of detail that the brush applies. Valid values range from 0 (more detail) to 5 (less detail). The default is 5.

- In the Light/Dark Balance slider/text box, select or type the balance between light and dark values in the selected object. Valid values range from 0 to 100. The default is 50.

Applying a Chrome Surface to an Object

The Chrome filter overlays the selected object with a chrome surface. To apply the Chrome filter to the selected object, choose Filter | Sketch | Chrome. Illustrator opens the Chrome dialog box, which contains the following options:

- In the Detail slider/text box, select or type the number of highlights added to the object's surface. Valid values range from 0 (fewer highlights) to 10 (many highlights). The default is 4.

- In the Smoothness slider/text box, select or type the level of smoothness. Valid values range from 0 (less smooth) to 10 (smoother). The default is 7.

Crayoning an Object

The Conté Crayon filter emphasizes the dark and white sections of the selected object by simulating the appearance of dark and light Conté crayons. To apply the Conté Crayon filter to the selected object, choose Filter | Sketch | Conté Crayon. Illustrator opens the Conté Crayon dialog box, which contains the following options:

- With the Foreground Level slider/text box, select or type the lightness or darkness of the foreground. Valid values range from 1 (light) to 15 (dark). The default is 11.

- With the Background Level slider/text box, select or type the lightness or darkness of the background. Valid values range from 1 (light) to 15 (dark). The default is 7.

- From the Texture drop-down menu, select the texture of the background of the object. You can choose from Brick, Burlap, Canvas, or Sandstone or load a custom-defined texture. The default is Canvas. To load a custom texture, choose Load Texture, fill in the resulting dialog box, and click OK.

- With the Scaling slider/text box, select or type a value with which to enlarge or reduce the width of the stroke marks on the object and on the background. Valid values range from 50% to 200%. The default is 100%.

- In the Relief slider/text box, select or type the smoothness or harshness of the background. Valid values range from 0 (very smooth) to 50 (very harsh). The default is 4.

- From the Light Direction drop-down menu, select the direction from which light on the object appears. You can choose from Bottom, Bot. Left, Left, Top Left, Top, Top Right, Right, and Bot. Right. The default is Top.

- Check the Invert check box to reverse the stroke marks on the background. The effects can be very subtle. The default is an unchecked box.

Figure 16-37 illustrates the Bas Relief, Chalk & Charcoal, Charcoal, Chrome, and Conté Crayon dialog boxes. Next to each dialog box are two examples of the filter applied to an object and a photograph using the default options.

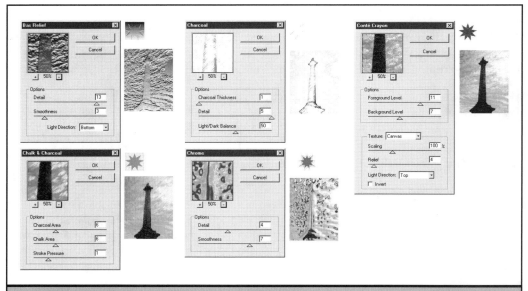

Figure 16-37. *The Bas Relief, Chalk & Charcoal, Charcoal, Chrome, and Conté Crayon dialog boxes; and two examples of each filter on the right side of its dialog box*

Using the Graphic Pen

The Graphic Pen filter applies contrasting lines to the foreground of the selected object with a fine pen and applies a paper appearance to the background. To apply the Graphic Pen filter to the selected object, choose Filter | Sketch | Graphic Pen. Illustrator opens the Graphic Pen dialog box, which contains the following options:

- In the Stroke Length slider/text box, select or type the length of the stroke marks. Valid values range from 1 (short) to 15 (long). The default is 15.

- In the Light/Dark Balance slider/text box, select or type the balance between light and dark values in the selected object. Valid values range from 0 (light) to 100 (dark). The default is 50.

- From the Stroke Direction drop-down menu, select the direction of the stroke: Right Diag. (the default), Horizontal, Left Diag., or Vertical.

Applying Halftone Patterns

The Halftone Pattern filter changes the appearance of the selected object to that of a halftone screen but keeps the current color tones. To apply the Halftone Pattern filter, choose Filter | Sketch | Halftone Pattern. Illustrator opens the Halftone Pattern dialog box, which contains the following options:

- In the Size slider/text box, select or type the size of the selected pattern. Valid values range from 1 (small) to 12 (large). The default is 1.

- Using the Contrast slider/text box, select or type the contrast between the light and dark parts of the pattern. Valid values range from 0 (very little contrast) and 50 (great contrast). The default is 5.

- From the Pattern Type drop-down menu, select the pattern: Circle, Dot (the default), or Line.

Using Note Paper

The Note Paper filter applies a layer of note paper to the selected object and lightly embosses it. To apply the Note Paper filter to the selected object, choose Filter | Sketch | Note Paper. Illustrator opens the Note Paper dialog box, which contains the following options:

- In the Image Balance slider/text box, select or type the balance between light and dark colors in the selected object. Valid values range from 0 (all light colors with no dark-color balance) to 50 (all medium colors with no light- or dark-color balance). The default is 25.

- With the Graininess slider/text box, select or type the amount of graininess in the note paper. Valid values range from 0 (no graininess) to 20 (the maximum graininess). The default is 10.

- In the Relief slider/text box, select or type the amount of relief or texture applied to the note paper. Valid values range from 0 (no relief) to 25 (the maximum relief). The default is 11.

Photocopying an Object

The Photocopy filter changes the look of the selected object to a photocopy with washed-out white areas and strongly applied dark areas. To apply the Photocopy filter to the selected object, choose Filter | Sketch | Photocopy. Illustrator opens the Photocopy dialog box, which contains the following options:

- With the Detail slider/text box, select or type the amount of detail in the selected object. Valid values range from 1 (little detail) to 24 (much detail). The default is 7.

- Using the Darkness slider/text box, select or type the amount of darkness applied to the selected object. Valid values range from 1 (not dark) to 50 (very dark). The default is 8.

Plastering an Object

The Plaster filter applies a three-dimensional plaster-like coat to the selected object using the main foreground and background colors. To plaster the selected object, choose Filter | Sketch | Plaster. Illustrator opens the Plaster dialog box, which contains the following options:

- In the Image Balance slider/text box, select or type the balance between light and dark in the selected object. Valid values range from 0 (all light) to 50 (all dark). The default is 20.

- With the Smoothness slider/text box, select or type the smoothness of the edges. Valid values range from 1 (smooth) to 15 (less smooth). The default is 2.

- From the Light Position drop-down menu, select the direction from which light on the object appears. You can choose from Bottom, Bot. Left, Left, Top Left, Top, Top Right, Right, and Bot. Right. The default is Top.

Figure 16-38 illustrates the Graphic Pen, Halftone Pattern, Note Paper, Photocopy, and Plaster dialog boxes. Next to each dialog box are two examples of the filter applied to an object and a photograph using the default options.

Applying Reticulation to an Object

The Reticulation filter adds a grainy surface to the selected object. To apply the Reticulation filter to the selected object, choose Filter | Sketch | Reticulation. Illustrator opens the Reticulation dialog box, which contains the following options:

- Using the Density slider/text box, select or type the amount of darkness or lightness of the filter. Valid values range from 0 (dark) to 50 (light). The default is 12.

- With the Black Level slider/text box, select or type the amount of black in the pattern. Valid values range from 0 (little black) to 50 (a great deal of black). The default is 40.

- With the White Level slider/text box, select or type the amount of white in the pattern. Valid values range from 0 (little white) to 50 (a great deal of white). The default is 5.

Stamping an Object

The Stamp filter stamps the selected object as if you were applying a rubber stamp. Note that Illustrator help states that this filter is best applied to black-and-white images. To stamp the selected object, choose Filter | Sketch | Stamp. Illustrator opens the Stamp dialog box, which contains the following options:

- In the Light/Dark Balance slider/text box, select or type the balance between light and dark values in the selected object. Valid values range from 0 (light) to 50 (dark). The default is 25.

- In the Smoothness slider/text box, select or type the level of smoothness. Valid values range from 1 (less smooth) to 50 (smoother). The default is 5.

ILLUSTRATOR FX

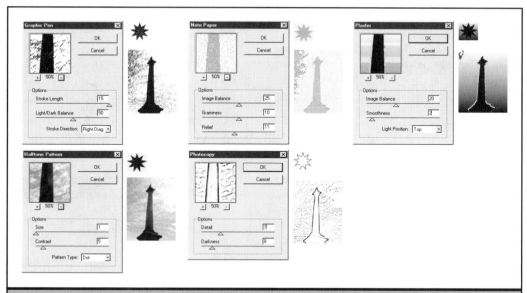

Figure 16-38. *The Graphic Pen, Halftone Pattern, Note Paper, Photocopy, and Plaster dialog boxes; and two examples of each filter on the right side of its dialog box*

Tearing Edges

The Torn Edges filter applies a tattered surface to the selected object and then applies the main colors to it. To apply the Torn Edges filter to the selected object, choose Filter | Sketch | Torn Edges. Illustrator opens the Torn Edges dialog box, which contains the following options:

- With the Image Balance slider/text box, select or type the balance of light and dark in the selected object. Valid values range from 0 (light) to 50 (dark). The default is 25.

- In the Smoothness slider/text box, select or type the level of smoothness. Valid values range from 1 (less smooth) to 15 (smoother). The default is 11.

- In the Contrast slider/text box, determine the amount of black or white in the drawing. Valid values range from 1 (little contrast) to 25 (much contrast). The default value is 17.

Using Water Paper

The Water Paper filter makes the selected object look as if it has been dampened and then painted with colors that bleed from their original locations. To apply the Water Paper filter to the selected object, choose Filter | Sketch | Water Paper. Illustrator opens the Water Paper dialog box, which contains the following options:

- In the Fiber Length slider/text box, select or type the length of the fibers covering the selected object. Valid values range from 3 (short) to 50 (long). The default is 15.

- Using the Brightness slider/text box, specify the brightness of the selected object. Valid values range from 0 (no brightness) to 100 (very bright). The default is 60.

- In the Contrast slider/text box, determine the amount of black or white in the drawing. Valid values range from 0 (no contrast) to 100 (much contrast). The default value is 80.

Figure 16-39 illustrates the Reticulation, Stamp, Torn Edges, and Water Paper dialog boxes. Next to each dialog box are two examples of the filter applied to an object and a photograph using the default options.

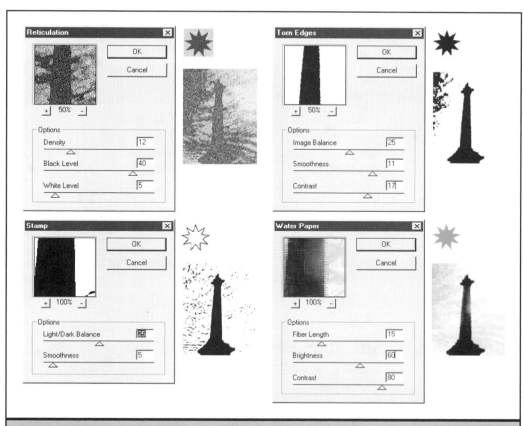

Figure 16-39.   *The Reticulation, Stamp, Torn Edges, and Water Paper dialog boxes; and two examples of each filter on the right side of its dialog box*

Applying Texture to Objects

The Texture filters apply texture or give a three-dimensional look to the surface of the selected object. Each of the dialog boxes associated with the Texture filters is similar to the dialog boxes for the Artistic, Brush Strokes, and Sketch filters; the typical dialog box includes a large preview window in the left corner and a brief list of options. You can move the image around the preview box by dragging and zoom the image within the preview box by pressing the + or – button. Illustrator displays the current zoom level (by percentage) between the two buttons. If you see a flashing line below the preview box, you will have to wait until Illustrator has completed drawing the new preview.

Cracking the Surface of an Object

The Craquelure filter assumes that the selected object has a bumpy, thick surface covered with small cracks. To apply the Craquelure filter to the selected object, choose Filter | Texture | Craquelure. Illustrator opens the Craquelure dialog box, which contains the following options:

- In the Crack Spacing slider/text box, specify the spaces between cracks. Valid values range from 2 (many spaces) to 100 (few spaces). The default is 15.
- With the Crack Depth slider/text box, specify the perceived depth of the cracks. Valid values range from 0 (no depth) to 10 (the maximum depth). The default is 6.
- Using the Crack Brightness slider/text box, specify the brightness of the selected object. Valid values range from 0 (dark) to 10 (bright). The default is 9.

Applying Grained Surfaces to an Object

The Grain filter applies one of a variety of grains to the selected objects. To apply the Grain filter to the selected object, choose Filter | Texture | Grain. Illustrator opens the Grain dialog box, which contains the following options:

- In the Intensity slider/text box, select or type the intensity of the grain. Valid values range from 0 (less intensity) to 100 (great intensity). The default is 40.
- In the Contrast slider/text box, select or type the amount of black or white in the drawing. Valid values range from 0 (no contrast) to 100 (much contrast). The default value is 50.
- From the Grain Type drop-down menu, select the grain type: Regular (the default), Soft, Sprinkles, Clumped, Contrasty, Enlarged, Stippled, Horizontal, Vertical, and Speckle.

Making a Mosaic of an Object

The Mosaic Tiles filter shows the selected object as it would look if it were broken into many mosaic tiles. To apply the Mosaic Tiles filter to the selected object, choose Filter | Texture | Mosaic Tiles. Illustrator opens the Mosaic Tiles dialog box, which contains the following options:

- In the Tile Size slider/text box, select or type the size of the tiles. Valid values range from 2 (very small) to 100 (very large). The default is 12.

- With the Grout Width slider/text box, select or type the width of the grout between the tiles. Valid values range from 1 (narrow) to 15 (very wide). The default is 3.

- From the Lighten Grout slider/text box, select or type the darkness or lightness of the grout. Valid values range from 0 (very dark) to 10 (so light that it is invisible). The default is 9.

Figure 16-40 illustrates the Craquelure, Grain, and Mosaic Tiles dialog boxes. Next to each dialog box are two examples of the filter applied to an object and a photograph using the default options.

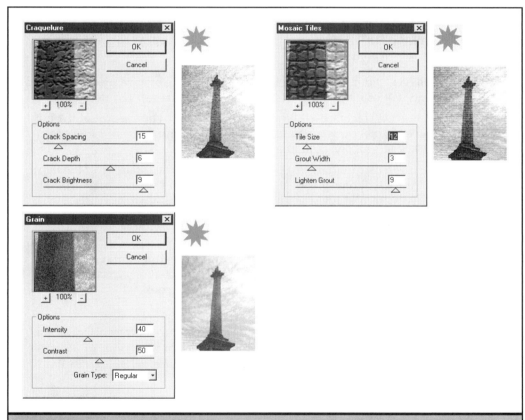

Figure 16-40.   *The Craquelure, Grain, and Mosaic Tiles dialog boxes; and two examples of each filter on the right side of its dialog box*

Making Patchwork of an Object

The Patchwork filter makes the selected object look as if it has been cut into squares or large tiles. To apply the Patchwork filter to the selected object, choose Filter | Texture | Patchwork. Illustrator opens the Patchwork dialog box, which contains the following options:

- In the Square Size slider/text box, select or type the size of the squares. Valid values range from 0 (very small size) to 10 (large squares). The default is 4.

- Using the Relief slider/text box, select or type the detail of the squares. Valid values range from 0 (little detail) to 25 (great detail). The default is 8.

Changing an Object to Stained Glass

The Stained Glass filter converts the selected object into joined, uneven stained glass pieces or mosaic tiles, each with one color. To apply the Stained Glass filter to the selected object, choose Filter | Texture | Stained Glass. Illustrator opens the Stained Glass dialog box, which contains the following options:

- In the Cell Size slider/text box, select or type the size of each piece of stained glass. Valid values range from 2 (small) to 50 (very large). The default is 10.

- From the Border Thickness slider/text box, select or type the size of the border separating each piece of stained glass. Valid values range from 1 (very thin) to 20 (extremely large). The default is 4.

- In the Light Intensity slider/text box, select or type the intensity of the light showing through lighter pieces of stained glass. Valid values range from 0 (little intensity) to 10 (higher intensity). The default is 3.

Texturizing an Object

The Texturizer filter applies a predefined or user-defined texture to the surface of the selected object. To apply the Texturizer filter to the selected object, choose Filter | Texture | Texturizer. Illustrator opens the Texturizer dialog box, which contains the following options:

- From the Texture drop-down menu, choose the texture of the surface of the selected object: Brick, Burlap, Canvas (the default), or Sandstone or a custom texture. To load a custom texture, choose Load Texture, fill in the resulting dialog box, and click OK.

- With the Scaling slider/text box, select or type a value with which to enlarge or reduce the width of the stroke marks on the object and on the background. Valid values range from 50% to 200%. The default is 100%.

■ In the Relief slider/text box, select or type the smoothness or harshness of the texture. Valid values range from 0 (very smooth) to 50 (very harsh). The default is 4.

■ From the Light Direction drop-down menu, select the direction from which light on the object appears. You can choose from Bottom, Bot. Left, Left, Top Left, Top, Top Right, Right, and Bot. Right. The default is Top.

■ Check the Invert check box to reverse the stroke marks on the background. The effects can be very subtle. The default is an unchecked check box.

Figure 16-41 illustrates the Patchwork, Stained Glass, and Texturizer dialog boxes. Next to each dialog box are two examples of the filter applied to an object and a photograph using the default options.

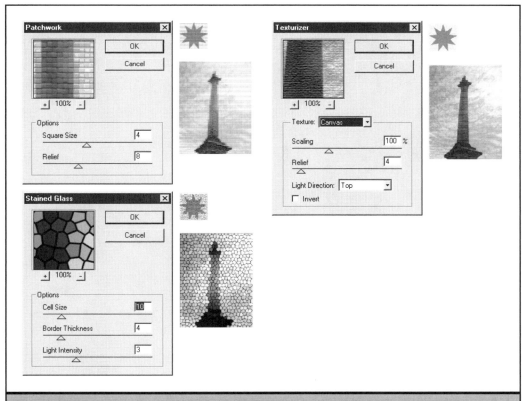

Figure 16-41. *The Patchwork, Stained Glass, and Texturizer dialog boxes; and two examples of each filter on the right side of its dialog box*

Chapter 17

Creating and Playing Actions

As you work in Illustrator, you have many chances to create innovative and fantastic works of art. However, more often you'll find yourself doing completely tedious work. For example, you might decide to export a set of files to Photoshop, rotate or scale an entire set of objects using the same values every time, or change a transparency setting for most of the paths in the illustration window. After spending mind-numbing days on work that is anything but creative, you might say to yourself, "I wish I could automate this process." In this chapter you'll learn to use actions to save yourself from all the tedium.

What Are Actions and Action Sets?

If you've spent some time working with computers, you have heard about *macros*, which are sets of commands, keystrokes, and mouse clicks you record, script, or both. Illustrator's term for the macro is *action*. When you create an action, you record a set of procedures from beginning to end—sometimes pausing to fill in a value. For a straightforward action, you might select an object, choose a command that opens a dialog box, and click OK to accept the defaults. A more complicated action might mean choosing a series of commands, entering different values in each dialog box that pops up, applying a filter or two, and saving the file for the Web or exporting it to another Adobe application. Then, when you play an action, you can have Illustrator run through the entire action or skip a command or two from time to time.

An *action set* is just what it says—a set of actions. Action sets enable you to unite a set of well-tested actions into a reliable yet complicated series of steps. Illustrator provides many default actions, which have been designed and tested by the Illustrator development team and others and which appear in the Actions palette. As you create your own actions, the list from which you can choose in the Actions palette will grow much longer and you'll be able to tackle day-to-day chores much more easily and efficiently.

Exploring the Actions Palette

With the Actions palette (see Figure 17-1), you can control every aspect of actions: You can play the default actions; plan, record, and play your own actions; modify them; and even delete them. To toggle between showing and hiding the palette, choose Window | Actions.

The Actions palette contains many elements, each of which has a specific meaning and with which you can control actions:

- Click the Toggle Item On/Off icons to toggle between activating and deactivating the selected action or command. If the action or command is selected (the default), the icon is a check mark within a box. If you have deselected the action, the box does not contain a check mark.

■ Click the Toggle Dialog On/Off icons to toggle between opening a dialog box or accepting the default values without opening the dialog box as you play an action. If an action does not include a command for opening a dialog box, Illustrator does not provide a box to contain the Toggle Dialog On/Off icon.

■ Click an expand icon or collapse icon to show or hide all the commands within an action, and actions and commands within an action set.

■ Click the menu button to open the Actions palette's menu.

■ Click the Stop Playing/Recording button to stop recording an action.

■ Click the Begin Recording button to start recording a named and selected action. The counterpart command on the Actions palette's menu is Start Recording.

■ Click the Play Current Selection button to play the current action. The counterpart command on the palette's menu is Play.

■ Click the Create New Set button to open the New Set dialog box so that you can name a new action set. The counterpart command on the Action palette's menu is New Set.

■ Click the Create New Action button to open the New Action dialog box so that you can create, name, and set other attributes for a new action. The counterpart command on the Action palette's menu is New Action.

■ Click the Delete Selection button to delete the selected action. The counterpart command on the palette's menu is Delete.

■ The large area in the center of the palette identifies commands within actions and the actions and commands within action sets. Action sets and actions are preceded by an expand icon or collapse icon. Action sets have a gray background, and actions have a white background. Note that the text *(selection)* next to an action name indicates that you must select an object before playing the action. You can change the order of actions or action sets by dragging up or down the list. As you drag an action, Illustrator marks potential new locations with a bold horizontal line. To select an action, click it; to select two or more noncontiguous action sets or actions, click; then press and hold down CTRL/⌘, and continue clicking to add to the selection. To select two or more contiguous action sets or actions, click at one end of the range; then press and hold down SHIFT, and click at the other end of the range.

To open the palette's menu, click the menu button. Commands on the menu are

■ The New Action command opens the New Action dialog box so that you can create, name, and set other attributes for a new action. The counterpart button at the bottom of the palette is Create New Action.

ILLUSTRATOR FX

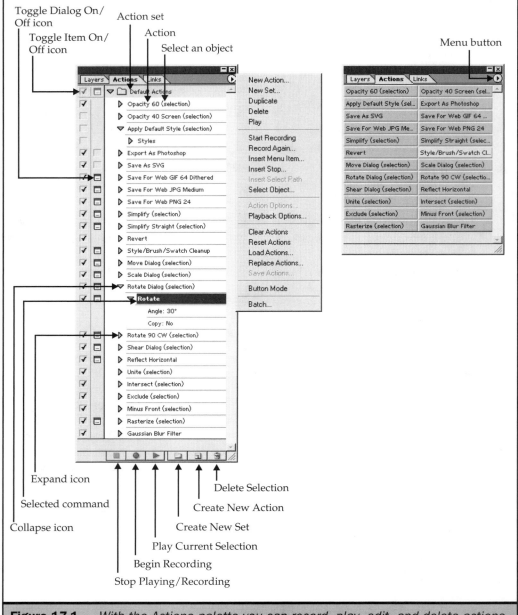

■ The New Set command opens the New Set dialog box so that you can name a new action set. The counterpart button at the bottom of the palette is Create New Set.

■ The Duplicate command duplicates one or more selected actions.

■ The Delete command deletes one or more selected actions. The counterpart button at the bottom of the palette is Delete Selection.

■ The Play command plays the selected action. The counterpart button at the bottom of the palette is Play Current Selection.

■ The Start Recording command starts recording an action. The counterpart button at the bottom of the palette is Begin Recording.

■ The Record Again command records the selected action again from the first command, opening dialog boxes every time one is available so you can change options.

■ The Insert Menu Item command inserts a command that cannot be recorded into an action.

■ The Insert Stop command enables you to insert a "temporarily stop playing" command into an action at a particular point during the playing of that action.

■ The Insert Select Path command enables you to select a path to be inserted into the action at a particular point during the playing of that action.

■ The Select Object command enables you to select an object at a particular point during the playing of that action.

■ The Action Options command opens the Action Options dialog box. You also can double-click an action to open the dialog box.

■ The Playback Options command opens the Playback Options dialog box in which you can set the speed of play.

■ The Clear Actions command deletes all the actions from the Actions palette.

■ The Reset Actions command returns the Actions palette to the default actions.

■ The Load Actions command loads a set of actions into the Actions palette.

■ The Replace Actions command replaces the current action set with one you have selected.s

■ The Save Actions command saves a newly recorded action.

■ The Button Mode command converts the list in the Actions palette to a set of buttons that enable you to play—but not record—an action.

■ The Batch command enables you to play an action on a folder or subfolder in which Illustrator documents are stored.

ILLUSTRATOR FX

Playing Actions

When you play certain selected actions, Illustrator executes each of the commands in those actions—from the top command to the bottom one without stopping. Illustrator gives you the latitude to play an action starting at any of its commands. You can even skip certain commands and continue to the others in order. Other actions include built-in pauses, which enable you to respond to dialog-box prompts by clicking, typing values, pressing a key, or combining mouse clicks and keystrokes.

You can play actions in two ways, depending on whether you have selected list mode (the default) or button mode for the Actions palette.

■ If you activate the Button Mode command in the palette's menu (that is, a check mark precedes the command), the Actions palette is in button mode, which displays a set of buttons—each containing the name of an action. If you are quite familiar with the contents of each action and you want to save space in the illustration window, you can keep the Actions palette in button mode.

■ When the Actions palette is in the default list mode (that is, a check mark does not precede the Button Mode command), you can view each action and its contents by clicking the expand icon to the left of the action name.

Playing an Action from Top to Bottom

It is easy to play a particular action without skipping commands or replying to Illustrator prompts—unless you have added stops. You select the row containing the name of the action and let 'er rip.

To play an action from top to bottom, follow these steps:

1. Open the file on which you will work.

2. If the Actions palette is not onscreen, choose Window | Actions to open it.

3. In the Actions palette, select the action that you wish to play.

4. If the action includes the text *(selection)* in its name, you must select an object or path before you start playing the action.

5. Click the Play Current Selection button at the bottom of the palette, or choose the Play command from the palette's menu. Illustrator processes each command until the action is complete.

Playing an Action Selectively

Illustrator provides you with several choices when you play an action: You can play an action starting at a command somewhere between the top and bottom, play individual commands, or skip over certain commands:

■ To play an action from a particular point, select the name of the action you want to play or the command from which you want to start. Then click the Play Current Selection button or choose the Play command.

- To play one command, press and hold down CTRL/⌘ and either click the Play Current Selection button at the bottom of the palette or double-click the command.

- To not play a particular command as you play the selected action, remove the check mark to the left of the action or command by clicking it.

Playing an Action at a Certain Speed

You can choose the speed at which you play actions. This is particularly useful when you want to test a lengthy or complex action that doesn't seem to work as you planned it. To set playback speed, choose the Playback Options command from the Action palette's menu. When Illustrator opens the Playback Options dialog box (see Figure 17-2), click one of the three radio buttons:

- Click the Accelerated radio button (the default) to run the actions at standard speed without any hesitation—except for built-in stops.

- Click the Step By Step radio button to run the action command by command. After Illustrator completes a command, it refreshes the objects in the illustration window. Use this option when you are testing an action or when you want to change or insert an object manually.

- Click the Pause For radio button to pause the action command by command for a certain number of seconds. Valid values range from 0 to 100 seconds.

Creating Actions

Illustrator enables you to create unique actions of your own by recording them. When you record an action, you click a button and then start using tools, menus, and palettes as you usually do. As Illustrator records, it commits almost every keystroke and mouse click to memory. On the surface, this seems quite simple; however, if you perform an action out of order or select the wrong value in a dialog box, Illustrator blindly follows

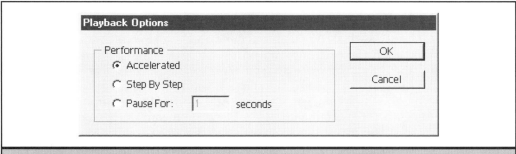

Figure 17-2.   *The Playback Options dialog box with its default setting*

ILLUSTRATOR FX

your instructions to the letter. In addition, Illustrator might ignore some of your requests if Illustrator thinks they are invalid. This means that before you create an action—particularly a complicated one—you should plan ahead, list the steps you want Illustrator to perform, and then follow those steps comprehensively.

Before recording, think of the following questions and comments:

- Do you want Illustrator to fill in any or all of the values for you? If you want to enter some values, plan to open one or more dialog boxes.

- Do you want to record an action that includes commands you might skip sometimes? Does it make sense to record one action that contains the command and another that does not contain the command?

- The behavior of an action depends on the current conditions of a document and the limits of recording an action. For example, if a rectangle's fill color is red and you record a command that changes a fill to red, you won't see a result. Or if you want to use an action to apply an effect to an object, you won't be able to because you cannot record any command on the Effect menu.

To Record or Not to Record

Illustrator refuses to record certain commands or use particular palettes and tools. For example, if you want to change your view of a document, you'll have to select commands from the View menu; you cannot record most commands from the View menu in an action. Or if you want to apply any effect, you'll have to do that manually; you cannot record any command from the Effect menu. However, many Effect menu commands have counterparts on the Filter menu, so consider applying filters rather than effects—after checking to see if Illustration supports the recording of those filters.

You can use the following commands on Illustrator menus in recorded actions:

- On the File menu you can record the New, Open, Revert, Close, Save As, Save a Copy, Save for Web, Place, Export, and Print commands.

- On the Edit menu you can record the Cut, Copy, Paste, Paste in Front, Paste in Back, and Clear commands.

- On the Object menu you can record the following commands from the Transform submenu: Transform Again, Move, Rotate, Reflect, Scale, Shear, and Transform Each. You can record all commands on the Arrange submenu. You also can record the Group and Ungroup commands; the three commands on the Lock submenu; the Unlock All command; the three commands on the Hide submenu; the Show All, Expand, Flatten Transparency, and Rasterize commands; the Outline Stroke, Offset Path, Simplify, and Add Anchor Points commands on the Path submenu; all the commands on the Blend submenu; all the commands on the Envelope Distort submenu; both commands on the Clipping Mask submenu; both commands on the Compound Path submenu; and both commands on the Crop Marks submenu.

- On the Type menu, you can record the Font and Size commands; both commands on the Blocks submenu; both commands on the Wrap submenu; the Fit Headline and Create Outlines commands; the Find/Change (if you click a button other than Done before clicking Done); the Find Font command (use the dialog box to record the command); and the Change Case, Rows & Columns, Show Hidden Characters, and Type Orientation commands.

- On the Select menu you can record the All, Deselect, Reselect, Inverse, Next Object Above, and Next Object Below commands. From the Same submenu you can record Blending Mode, Fill & Stroke, Fill Color, Opacity, Stroke Color, and Stroke Weight. From the Object submenu, you can record Brush Strokes, Clipping Mask, Stray Points, and Text Objects.

- On the Filter menu (depending on the vector or raster attributes and color mode of the selected objects) you can record all the commands from the Colors, Create, and Distort submenu, and the top Stylize submenu.

- You cannot record any command from the Effect menu.

- On the View menu you can record the commands on the Guides submenu.

- With commands on the Window menu you can record options by using the following palettes: Align, Attributes, Brushes, Color, Gradient, Layers, Pathfinder, Stroke, Swatches, Transform, and the Character, MM Design, Paragraph, and Tab Ruler commands on the Type submenu.

- Illustrator enables you to record the actions of the following toolbox tools: Arc, Ellipse (L), Line Segment (\), Slice (SHIFT-K), Polar Grid, Polygon, Rectangle (M), Rectangular Grid, Reflect (O), Rotate (R), Rounded Rectangle, Scale (S), Selection (V), Spiral, Star, and Twist.

Recording an Action

Before you record an action, you can let Illustrator name it and supply all the options without opening a dialog box, or you can create it by opening a dialog box, in which you can give it a name, specify the action set in which the action is stored, and set a color for its display in the Actions palette.

Creating and Recording an Action Using the Default Options

When you create an action without using a dialog box, Illustrator names the action, does not provide a function key, saves the completed action in the default action set folder, and does not color-code it when it is placed in the Actions palette.

To create and record a new action without opening a dialog box, follow these steps:

1. Press and hold down ALT/OPTION, and either click Create New Action or choose New Action. Illustrator adds the new action, which is named Untitled-*n* (where *n* represents a number), at the bottom of the other actions in the Actions

palette and starts recording. Note that when Illustrator starts recording an action, the Begin Recording button changes to red.

2. To construct the action, choose supported commands and toolbox tools and fill in dialog boxes that open.

3. To stop recording, either click the Begin Recording button or choose Stop Recording, which replaces Begin Recording as you record an action.

Creating and Recording an Action Using a Dialog Box

Creating an action with a dialog box enables you to give the action a memorable name (that should be related to the recorded commands), place the action in the default action set or in another set, assign a function key, and select a color for its display in the Actions palette.

To create and record a new action by filling in a dialog box, follow these steps:

1. Click Create New Action or choose New Action. Illustrator opens the New Action dialog box (see Figure 17-3).

2. To name the action, type a name in the Name text box.

3. To save the action in an action set, either choose Default Actions (which stores the action with the default action set) from the drop-down menu or select another set you have already saved. To learn about saving action sets, refer to "Creating an Action Set" and "Saving an Action Set" later in this chapter.

4. To create a shortcut for playing the action, select a key from the Function Key drop-down menu. Your choices range from F2 to F12. The default is None, which means no function key.

5. If your chosen function key is assigned, you can refine your choice by checking SHIFT, CTRL/⌘, or both. Note that when you choose a function key that is already associated with an Illustrator command, Illustrator assigns it to the action. For information about all the Illustrator shortcut keys, including the function keys, refer to Appendix F.

6. To choose a color code for the action's button when you display the Actions palette in button mode, open the Color drop-down list box and select from one of seven rainbow colors. The default is Gray.

7. Click the Begin Recording button at the bottom of the Actions palette, or choose the Start Recording command from the palette's menu. Illustrator changes the color of the Begin Recording button to red.

8. To create the action, choose supported commands and toolbox tools and fill in the dialog boxes that open.

9. To stop recording, either click the Begin Recording button or choose Stop Recording, which replaces Begin Recording as you record an action.

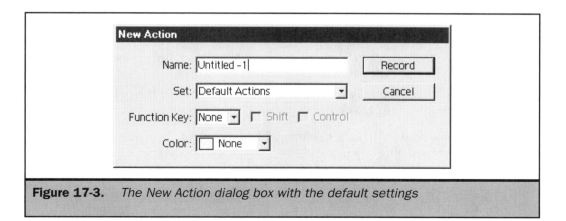

Figure 17-3.   *The New Action dialog box with the default settings*

Note   *If you are creating a complicated action, which might be prone to errors until you test it thoroughly, choose File | Save a Copy to save a copy of the document in which you are working. This preserves the original document until you have tested the action against the copy and edited the action until it is free of errors.*

Selecting Recording Options

As you record an action, you are not limited to working on objects in the illustration window: You can use commands from the Actions palette's menu to enhance the action and add commands.

Naming and Selecting an Object

When you plan to change an object during an action, you select it in the same way you would select any object to work on it in Illustrator. If you want to select an object as you record an action, you must name the object first by using the Attributes palette (see "Exploring the Attributes Palette" in Chapter 20). Then select the object by using the Select Object command from the Actions palette's menu.

To name and select an object as you are recording an action, follow these steps:

1. In the illustration window, select the object to be named.

2. If the Attributes palette is not open in the illustration window, choose Window | Attributes (F11).

3. From the Attributes palette's menu, choose Show Note. Illustrator adds a list box to the bottom of the Attributes palette.

4. In the list box type the name of the selected object.

5. To place the selected object at the end of the action, select the name of the action.

ILLUSTRATOR FX

6. To place the selected object after a specific command, select the name of the command.

7. From the Actions palette's menu, choose Select Object. Illustrator opens the Set Selection dialog box.

8. In the text box, type the exact name of the selected object; then click OK. Illustrator adds the *Set Selection* command to the action.

Figure 17-4 shows the Attributes palette with the name of the selected rectangle and the Set Selection dialog box in which the same name appears.

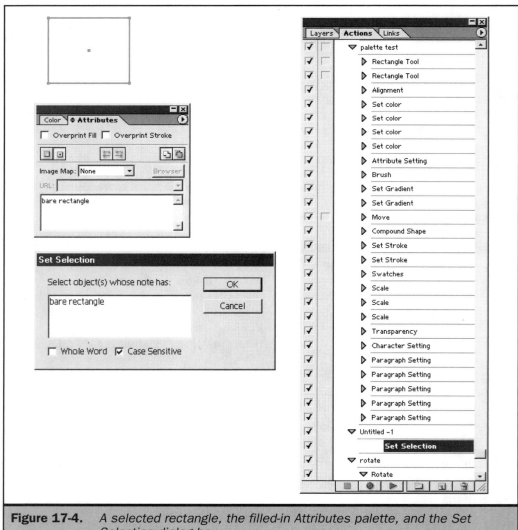

Figure 17-4. *A selected rectangle, the filled-in Attributes palette, and the Set Selection dialog box*

Recording a Path

You can choose the Insert Select Path command from the palette's menu to add a path to an action. For example, you might want to insert a path in an action to create a compound path with another path or even demonstrate an editing technique in an Illustrator tutorial.

To record a path, follow these steps:

1. Create and start recording an action.

2. To place the selected object at the end of the action, select the name of the action.

3. To place the selected object after a specific command, select the name of the command.

4. Select the path you want to add to the action.

5. From the Actions palette's menu, choose Insert Select Path. Illustrator adds the Set Work Path command to the action.

Inserting Commands You Cannot Record

In a preceding section, you learned that you cannot record every Illustrator command, tool, or palette action. However, Illustrator enables you to insert a command that you cannot record into an action. Then, when you play the action, the inserted command is executed in its turn.

To insert an unrecordable command into an action, follow these steps:

1. To place the command at the end of the action, select the name of the action.

2. To place the command after a specific command, select the name of the command.

3. From the Actions palette's menu, choose the Insert Menu Item command. Illustrator opens the Insert Menu Item dialog box (see Figure 17-5) with one text box.

4. To record a command in the text box, click the menu on which the command is located and then select the command. Illustrator inserts the menu and command.

5. To type a command in the text box, start typing the command. If you can't remember the complete name of the command, click the Find button. Illustrator completes the command with its choice.

6. When the appropriate command is in the text box, click OK. Illustrator inserts the command from the text box into the action.

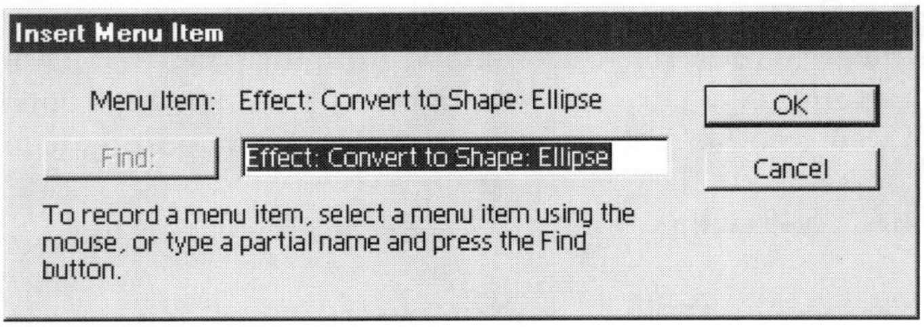

```
┌─────────────────────────────────────────────────────────────┐
│  Insert Menu Item                                             │
│                                                               │
│        Menu Item:   Effect: Convert to Shape: Ellipse    ┌────────┐  │
│                                                          │   OK   │  │
│         Find:       ┌─────────────────────────────────┐  └────────┘  │
│                     │ Effect: Convert to Shape: Ellipse│  ┌────────┐  │
│                     └─────────────────────────────────┘  │ Cancel │  │
│        To record a menu item, select a menu item using the └────────┘  │
│        mouse, or type a partial name and press the Find       │
│        button.                                                │
│                                                               │
└─────────────────────────────────────────────────────────────┘
```

Figure 17-5.   *The Insert Menu Item dialog box with a recorded menu, command, and subcommand separated by colons*

Inserting a Stop in an Action

When you want to pause an action before moving on to the end, you can use the Insert Stop command to display a message box so that you can stop or continue the action. For example, you might want to pause to do some nonrecordable or distinctive work in the illustration window or to alert yourself or another Illustrator user about the commands that end the action. You might even offer the choice of continuing or stopping.

To insert a stop in an action, follow these steps:

1. To place the command at the end of the action, select the name of the action.

2. To place the command after a specific command, select the name of the command.

3. From the Actions palette's menu, choose the Insert Stop command. Illustrator opens the Record Stop dialog box (see Figure 17-6).

4. Type a message in the text box.

5. To insert a Continue button in the message box in addition to the Stop button, check the Allow Continue check box. If the check box is unchecked, the only button in the dialog box is Stop.

Figure 17-6 illustrates the Record Stop dialog box and the message box, both with the same message.

Opening or Avoiding a Dialog Box

After you record an action that would open one or more dialog boxes or a single command that might reveal a dialog box, you can indicate whether Illustrator opens the dialog boxes as it plays the action. In fact, you can open the dialog box sometimes, and you can leave it closed and accept its current settings at other times. In Illustrator terminology, a pause that offers the opportunity to open a dialog box is a modal control. A *control* is a tool, such as a button, with which you signal an act. A *modal tool* entails

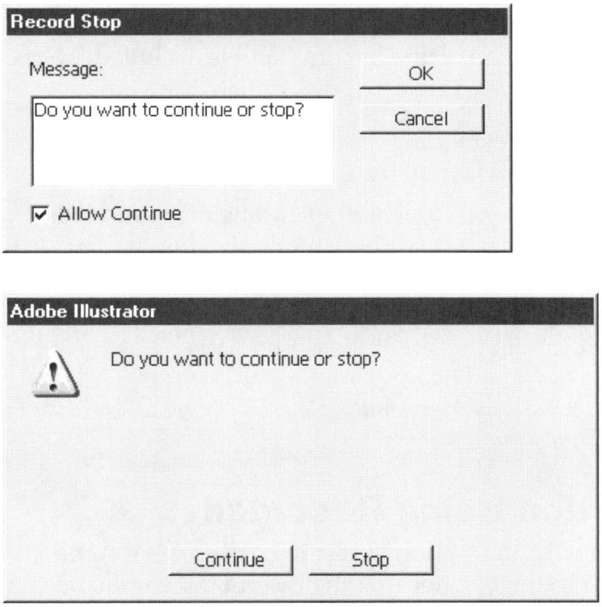

Figure 17-6.   *The Record Stop dialog box with a message and the message box itself*

your pressing ENTER/RETURN; a modal control is the ENTER/RETURN key. To set a modal control, the Actions palette must be in list mode.

You turn modal controls off and on in the column that contains the Toggle Dialog On/Off icons (refer to Figure 17-1). When the dialog box icon is in the column, the modal control is active (a dialog box will open if it is associated with the command); when the icon is absent, the modal control is inactive (a dialog box will not open and Illustrator will accept the current values in the dialog box).

- ▪ To toggle between opening and ignoring all dialog boxes for an action, click the Toggle Dialog On/Off icon to the left of the action name.

- ▪ To toggle between opening and ignoring the dialog box for a command, click the Toggle Dialog On/Off icon to the left of the command.

Excluding and Including Commands

Excluding and including commands from an action works in much the same way as turning off and on modal controls: Click a column to the left of the action or command name. Rather than clicking the Toggle Dialog On/Off icons, you click the Toggle Item

On/Off icons, which are in the leftmost column of the Actions palette. By default, all actions and commands are included; a check mark appears in a box to the left of the action or command. When an action or command is excluded, no check mark appears; the box is empty.

- To toggle between excluding and including an individual command, click the Toggle Item On/Off icon to the left of the command name.
- To toggle between excluding and including all commands but the selected one, press and hold down ALT/OPTION while clicking the Toggle Item On/Off icon to the left of the command name.
- To toggle between excluding and including a complete action, click the Toggle Item On/Off icon to the left of the action name.

If a dialog box opens as a command is played, clicking OK records the command and clicking Cancel does not.

Stopping an Action Being Recorded

Earlier in this chapter, in the section "Inserting a Stop in an Action," you learned how to insert an automatic stop by choosing the Insert Stop command from the Actions palette's menu. You also can manually stop an action as you are recording it and then start recording again. To stop recording an action, click the Stop Playing/Recording button at the bottom of the palette or choose Stop Recording from the palette's menu. To start recording again, click the Begin Recording button or choose Start Recording from the menu.

Organizing Actions

By default, Illustrator stores all actions in the Action sets subfolder under the Presets folder; you don't have to explicitly save them. However, you don't have to accept this location; you can save sets of actions in any folder on your computer system. For example, you might want to group related actions or organize actions created by different people in different folders and give them unique names or even rename them to conform to a company or department standard. Once you have saved action sets, you can either load them or use them to replace the current contents of the Actions palette. After using the actions in the saved action sets, you can revert to the default actions.

If you have spent a great deal of time creating complicated actions, consider always saving them in action sets and backing them up.

Creating an Action Set

You can create a new action set by clicking a button at the bottom of the Actions palette or choosing a command from the palette's menu. To make a new action set using the Actions palette, follow these steps:

1. Click the Create New Set button at the bottom of the palette, or choose the New Set command from the palette's menu. Illustrator opens the New Set dialog box (see Figure 17-7).

2. Type a unique and memorable name for the set, and click OK.

Renaming an Action Set

You are not stuck with the name Illustrator assigns or you originally give to an action set. Renaming an action set is just as easy as creating an action set. In fact—except for the dialog box names—the two dialog boxes used for naming and renaming are identical. To rename a set of actions using the Actions palette, follow these steps:

1. Either double-click the name of the action set, or select the action set and choose Set Options from the palette's menu. Illustrator opens the Set Options dialog box (see Figure 17-8).

2. Type a unique and memorable name for the set and click OK.

Saving an Action Set

When you save an action set, you have the choice of the location in which it is stored. To save an action set, follow these steps:

1. In the Actions palette, select an action set.

2. From the palette's menu, choose Save Actions. Illustrator opens the Save Set To dialog box (see Figure 17-9).

3. If you want to change the set's name, type the new name in the File Name text box.

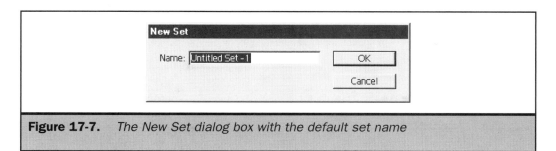

Figure 17-7. *The New Set dialog box with the default set name*

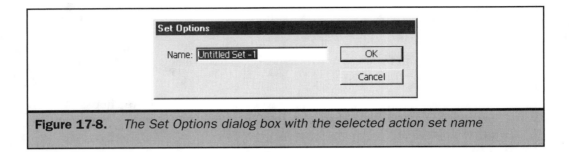

Figure 17-8.   *The Set Options dialog box with the selected action set name*

4. In the Save In drop-down menu, choose a folder in which you want to store the set. You can click the Create New Folder icon to create a new folder in which to store the set.

5. When you have completed typing and selecting options, click Save to save the set. Notice that the extension for an action set is .AIA.

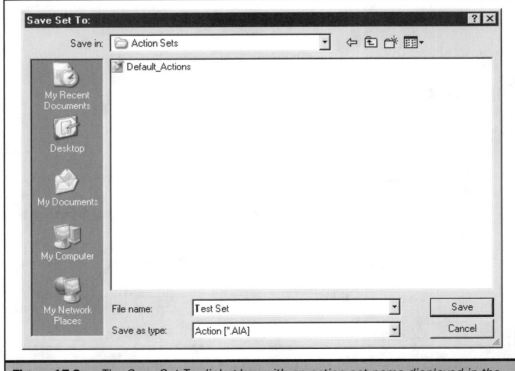

Figure 17-9.   *The Save Set To dialog box with an action set name displayed in the File Name text box and the selected location shown in the Save in drop-down menu*

Putting a New Action Set in the Actions Palette

Once you have saved several action sets, you can replace—temporarily or permanently—the default actions in the Actions palettes with one of the saved sets. Note that Illustrator enables you to place action sets only in the Actions palette; you cannot load individual actions.

When you decide to use actions other than the default actions, you can either load a new set into the Actions palette below the present action sets or replace the current contents of the palette. To load or replace, Illustrator provides two commands—Load Actions and Replace Actions—in the palette's menu.

Adding an Action Set

When you add an action set to the Actions palette, Illustrator places it below the current sets in the palette. To add an action set, follow these steps:

1. From the Actions palette's menu, choose Load Actions. Illustrator opens the Load Set From dialog box, which looks exactly like the Save Set To dialog box (refer to Figure 17-9).

2. Select the desired action set.

3. Click the Open button. Illustrator inserts the action set and its contents at the bottom of the list in the palette.

Replacing an Action Set

When you use the Replace Actions command, you replace the entire list of action sets and actions in the Actions palette.

 The Replace Actions command is a destructive command: If you haven't saved the current contents of the Actions palette, you could lose everything. To learn how to save an action set, refer to the preceding section, "Saving an Action Set."

To replace all actions in the Actions palette, follow these steps:

1. From the Actions palette's menu, choose Replace Actions. Illustrator opens the Load Set From dialog box, which is identical to the Save Set To dialog box (refer to Figure 17-9).

2. Select the desired action set.

3. Click the Open button. In the Actions palette, Illustrator replaces the current action set and its contents with the set you have selected.

ILLUSTRATOR FX

Moving Actions and Commands

You can move an action or command from one action set to another, move a copy of an action while keeping the original in its current set, and move an action or command within its current set. As you move an action or command, Illustrator sometimes shows a highlighted line, which indicates that you can drop the action or command.

- To move an action or command to a different action set, drag it from its current location to the name of its new action set.

- To copy an action or command to a different action set, press and hold down ALT/OPTION, and drag it from its current location to the name of its new action set.

- To move an action or command within its action set, drag it above its new location. Then drop the action or command.

- To copy an action or command within its action set, press and hold down ALT/OPTION, and drag it above its new location. Then drop the action or command.

To drag an action set to a new location in the Actions palette, you must place it above another action set. Illustrator does not allow you to move an action set to a location within another action set.

 Once you have moved actions or commands to a different action set, make sure you save the set.

Restoring the Default Actions

Once you have finished using a loaded or replacement action set, you can return to the Default Actions set. To reset the actions in the Actions palette to the defaults, follow these steps:

1. From the Actions palette's menu, choose Reset Actions. Illustrator displays a message box:

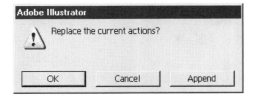

2. To add the Default Actions to the bottom of the Actions palette, click Append.

3. To replace the current actions with the Default Actions, click OK.

Duplicating an Action Set, Action, or Command

You can duplicate action sets, actions, and commands so that you can test a copy or create a closely related action set, action, or command that you can edit. Duplicating an action set, action, or command means you don't have to re-record it. Remember to rename the copy after the duplication process is over. To make a duplication, do one of the following:

- To duplicate one action set, action, or command, select it in the Actions palette and then choose Duplicate from the palette's menu.

- To duplicate an action or command, drag it to the Create New Action button at the bottom of the palette.

- To duplicate an action set, drag it to the Create New Set button at the bottom of the palette.

- To duplicate more than one noncontiguous action sets, actions, or commands, click the first item, press and hold down CTRL/⌘, and click additional items to add them to the selection. Then choose Duplicate from the palette's menu.

- To duplicate more than one contiguous action sets, actions, or commands, click the first item in the range, press and hold down SHIFT, and click the last item in the range. Then choose Duplicate from the palette's menu.

When you duplicate an action set, action, or command, Illustrator places the copy after the original.

Recording an Action Again

When you use the Record Again command from the Actions palette's menu, you play an action from top to bottom. As Illustrator executes each command, it opens a dialog box associated with the command if one is available. This gives you the opportunity to change options. To record an action again, follow these steps:

1. Select the action to be re-recorded.

2. Choose the Record Again command from the Actions palette's menu.

3. If Illustrator opens a dialog box, change options if you wish and then click OK, press ENTER/RETURN to set the changes, or click Cancel or press ESC to cancel the changes.

Recording a Command Again

In addition to recording an entire action again, you can re-record an individual command in an action. When you record a command originally or re-record it the twentieth time,

ILLUSTRATOR FX

you must select an object on which the command can work. For example, if you want to record or re-record a command that changes the attributes of type, you must select type.

To record a command again, follow these steps:

1. Select an appropriate object.
2. Double-click the command in the Actions palette.
   Illustrator opens a dialog box associated with the command.
3. In the dialog box, type or select values.
4. Click OK to save the new values.

Setting New Options for an Action

You can change an action's attributes by choosing the Action Options command from the Actions palette's menu. When Illustrator opens the Action Options dialog box (see Figure 17-10), type and select options in the same way you filled in the New Action dialog box (refer to Figure 17-3). For information about the New dialog box, refer to the "Creating and Recording an Action Using a Dialog Box" section, earlier in this chapter.

Deleting an Action or Command

Deleting an action or command is just like deleting many items in Illustrator palettes: Drag the action or command to the Delete Selection button in the bottom-right corner of the Actions palette (or press and hold down ALT/OPTION and click Delete Selection); or select the action or command, and choose the Delete command from the palette's menu.

You can delete an action set from the Actions palette by using the Delete Selection button or the Delete command. However, this action just deletes the set from the palette, but it does not remove the set from the folder in which it is stored.

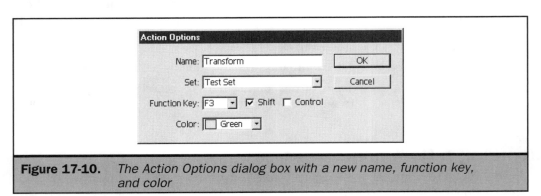

Figure 17-10. *The Action Options dialog box with a new name, function key, and color*

You can remove more than one command or action simultaneously. To select noncontiguous actions or commands, click the first item to be deleted, press and hold down CTRL/⌘, and continue to click selections. To select contiguous actions or commands to be deleted, click an item at one end of the range, press and hold down SHIFT, and click the item at the other end of the range.

When you drag the selection to the Delete Selection button, Illustrator does not prompt you to confirm the deletion. However, when you choose the Delete command, Illustrator opens a message box. To delete all the selected actions and commands, choose Clear Actions from the Actions palette menu. Click OK to delete all the selected actions and commands. You also can delete all the actions from the Actions palette by choosing Clear Actions from the palette's menu and responding to the prompt in the message box.

Chapter 18

Appearances, Styles, Blends, Symbols, and Envelopes

A*ppearance attributes* are characteristics such as effects and transformations that you apply to an object. Unlike filters, appearance attributes do not change the framework of the object; they overlay the object. For example, if you create a rectangle and then change its fill color, apply a brushstroke to the stroke, insert a glow, convert it to an ellipse, and roughen the edges, the rectangle is still a rectangle under all the changes. You use the Appearance palette to track all the changes you make to an object, pinpoint a fill or stroke for modifications, and even add extra fills and strokes.

Styles are saved and named sets of appearance attributes that you can apply to future objects. The Styles and Appearance palettes work hand in hand to control attributes and styles. Use the Styles palette to create, store, apply, and edit styles. Use blends to morph a starting object's shape, attributes, and colors into a final object's characteristics, while incorporating the shape, attributes, and colors of intermediate objects. You can create blends that are arranged in a particular order using a specific number of steps that are oriented to the page dimensions and placed along paths.

Symbols are small pieces of art that you can use in one or more documents. For example, if you want to show a flock of birds flying above a meadow, you can create one bird, define it as a symbol in the Symbols palette, and then add an entire flock of birds with one mouse click.

Envelopes enable you to enclose and distort paths and type. With envelopes, Illustrator provides another way to filter objects. You also can create an envelope mesh to transform and distort points on a grid. In this chapter you'll learn all about appearance attributes, styles, blends, symbols, and envelopes.

Using Appearance Attributes

When you use appearance attributes on an artwork, you are employing many of the Illustrator features you have learned about in prior chapters. However, using appearance attributes enables you to manage the attributes. For example, by viewing the contents of the Appearance palette, you can see whether you changed the shape of a rectangle before or after you roughened its stroke or applied a glow to its fill. You also can change the order in which attributes are applied to a selected object.

Exploring the Appearance Palette

You were introduced to the Appearance palette in the "Applying Transparency to the Fill or Stroke" section in Chapter 15. In this section you'll look at the palette and its workings in great detail.

Without the Appearance palette open in the illustration window, any effects or transformations you apply to an object change the entire object. With the Appearance palette onscreen, you can not only view the effects that have changed a variety of selected objects (including paths, groups, layers, images, mesh objects, type, and graphs), you also can modify the attributes of selected objects—or their strokes and fills—and even add extra strokes or fills with their own attributes to objects. The Appearance palette changes to reflect the attributes for your new selection when you select another object in the illustration window. The palette is an excellent tool for viewing the attributes you have applied to complicated artwork. To toggle between showing and hiding the palette, choose Window | Appearance (SHIFT-F6).

Figure 18-1 illustrates several versions of the Appearance palette with different components selected and various appearance attributes applied.

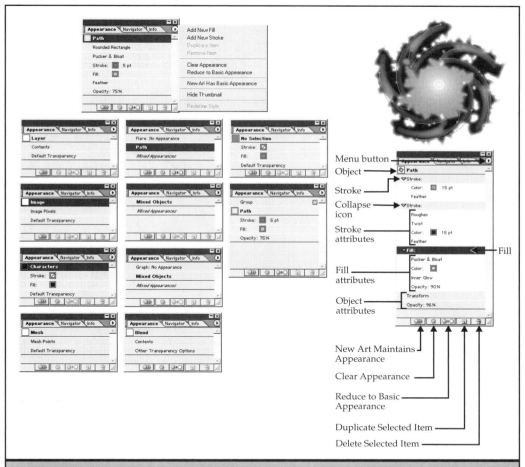

ILLUSTRATOR FX

Figure 18-1. *With the Appearance palette, you can change the appearance of any number of different objects and their strokes and fills*

The Appearance palette contains a number of elements, each of which has a specific meaning and with which you can control actions:

■ Click the Stroke row to activate the Stroke (X) in the toolbox and in the Color palette if it is in the illustration window. Double-click the Stroke row to open the Color palette.

■ Click the Fill row to select it to activate the Fill (X) in the toolbox and in the Color palette if it is in the illustration window. Double-click the Fill row to open the Color palette.

■ If the selected object is a group, double-click the Contents row to show the components of the group. To hide the components, click the tiny checkerboard box on the right side of the Group row.

■ If the selected object has an opacity setting, double-click the Opacity row to open the Transparency palette.

■ If you have applied one or more effects to the selected object, double-click the effect name row to open an options dialog box.

■ Click an expand icon or collapse icon to show or hide all the commands within an action and actions and commands within an actions set.

■ Click the menu button to open the Appearance palette's menu.

■ Click the New Art Maintains Appearance/New Art Has Basic Appearance button to set appearance attributes for future objects. Click New Art Maintains Appearance for objects to receive attributes from the selected object; click New Art Has Basic Appearance to start new objects with a fill and stroke only. The counterpart command on the palette's menu is New Art Has Basic Appearance.

■ Click the Clear Appearance button to clear all selected objects and their appearance attributes from the illustration window and the Appearance palette. The counterpart command on the palette's menu is Clear Appearance.

■ Click the Reduce to Basic Appearance button to delete all attributes and extra fills and strokes from the selected object. The counterpart command on the palette's menu is Reduce to Basic Appearance.

■ Click the Duplicate Selected Item button to duplicate one or more selected items in the Appearance palette. The counterpart command on the palette's menu is Duplicate Item.

■ Click the Delete Selected Item button to remove one or more selected items from the Appearance palette. The counterpart command on the palette's menu is Remove Item.

To open the palette's menu, click the menu button. Commands on the menu are

■ The Add New Fill command adds a new fill on top of the selected object. The new fill, which is the same color as the current fill, matches the dimensions of the current fill but does not have all its attributes.

- The Add New Stroke command adds a new stroke on top of the selected object. The new stroke, which is the same color as the current stroke, matches the dimensions of the current stroke but does not have all its attributes.

- The Duplicate Item command duplicates one or more selected items in the Appearance palette. The counterpart button at the bottom of the palette is Duplicate Selected Item.

- The Remove Item command deletes one or more selected items from the Appearance palette. The counterpart button at the bottom of the palette is Delete Selected Item.

- The Clear Appearance command clears all selected objects and their appearance attributes from the illustration window and the Appearance palette. The counterpart button at the bottom of the palette is Clear Appearance.

- The Reduce to Basic Appearance command deletes all attributes and extra fills and strokes from the selected object. The counterpart button at the bottom of the palette is Reduce to Basic Appearance.

- The New Art Has Basic Appearance command toggles between future objects having all the appearance attributes of the selected object or starting with a basic fill and stroke. The counterpart button at the bottom of the palette is New Art Maintains Appearance/New Art Has Basic Appearance.

- The Show/Hide Thumbnail command toggles between showing and hiding the thumbnails on the Appearance palette.

- The Redefine Style command enables you to select an object whose attributes you want to replace and then select or target an object whose attributes will replace the originals. To learn more about styles, refer to "Using Styles," later in this chapter.

Using the Appearance Palette

The Appearance palette serves several purposes:

- You can use the Appearance palette to apply appearance attributes to an entire object and its fills and strokes and to keep track of those changes.

- The Appearance palette shows the components of the selected object: At the top are the object and its type (path, group, layer, and so on). Under the object and indented from left side of the palette are the object's fills and strokes, each with its own attributes. At the bottom of the palette are any attributes that you have applied to the entire object. Notice that those attributes are aligned with the object.

- You can check the hierarchy of attributes and the order in which you applied them. Immediately under the object and each fill and stroke are the attributes at the top of the stacking order (those you added most recently). At the bottom of the list (and at the bottom of the stacking order) are attributes you applied first.

- The Appearance palette is the only Illustrator tool with which you can insert multiple fills and strokes to the objects that comprise your artwork. Insert fills and strokes so that you can add more depth and color to an artwork.

- Within the Appearance palette, you can drag appearance attributes from one part of an object to another, from one part of the stacking order to another, or to the Styles palette to create a new style.

Viewing Information in the Appearance Palette

The Appearance palette shows various information when you choose Window |
Appearance (SHIFT-F6). If an object is selected, the palette provides information about
that object. If an object is not selected, the palette shows the settings of the object you
most recently selected (even if you have deleted it in the meantime), but displays the
message "No Selection" at the top of the palette. If you have just opened a new, empty
document, the palette displays No Selection, plus Illustrator's default settings of a 1-point,
black stroke; a white fill; and 100% opacity.

The Appearance palette enables you to activate the Fill and Stroke boxes near the
bottom of the toolbox: Click Stroke in the palette to activate the Stroke box, and click
Fill in the palette to activate Fill in the toolbox.

You can double-click areas of the Appearance palette to open certain palettes and
dialog boxes. Double-click Stroke or Fill to open the Color palette; double-click Default
Transparency to reveal the Transparency palette. When you add attributes to the selected
object, a stroke, or a fill, double-click an attribute to show an options dialog box with
which you can adjust the options.

When you apply an attribute to a stroke or fill, the name Stroke or Fill in the
Appearance palette is preceded by an Expand or Collapse icon, depending on whether
the attributes are shown or hidden. Click the Expand icon to reveal all the attributes for
an object; click Collapse to hide the attributes.

If the selected object is a *container* (that is, the selection contains paths and other
objects) such as a group or layer, Illustrator displays Contents below the object type
in the Appearance palette. Double-click Contents to reveal the contents of the container.
If the contents share the same attributes, Illustrator shows them. Otherwise, Illustrator
displays the message "Mixed Appearances."

Moving Items and Attributes

As you know, the order in which objects are stacked affects the appearance of your
artwork. The stacking order of attributes affects a single object in the same way. For
example, an object that is bloated and then feathered looks completely different from the
same object that is feathered and then bloated.

Additionally, if you apply an attribute to an object without using the Appearance
palette to select the fill or stroke, Illustrator employs the attribute over the entire object.
For example, if you apply a 50% opacity to an object without selecting the fill or stroke
using the Appearance palette, every part of the object is 50% opaque. However, if you
open the Appearance palette, select the fill, and set 50% opacity, the stroke will remain
completely opaque—unless you have changed its opacity earlier in your Illustrator session.

Within the Appearance palette, you can drag a component such as a fill or stroke to change its position in the stacking order; you also can drag an appearance attribute to a different location in the stacking order, to a different component, or to a location in which it affects the entire object. As you drag an appearance attribute, watch for the horizontal line—the same line you see when you drag a path, group, or sublayer from one location to another. When the line appears, you can drop the appearance attribute in its new location.

Figure 18-2 illustrates movement of appearance attributes in the Appearance palette. In the top-left corner of the figure is the original object with its 15-point, black stroke, roughened, twisted, and feathered. The original's fill has an inner glow and is bloated. The object in the top-right corner shows the results of dragging the Roughen attribute from the Stroke section to the Fill section. The bottom-left corner contains a new version of the object, the consequence of dragging Twist to join Roughen in the Fill section. Finally,

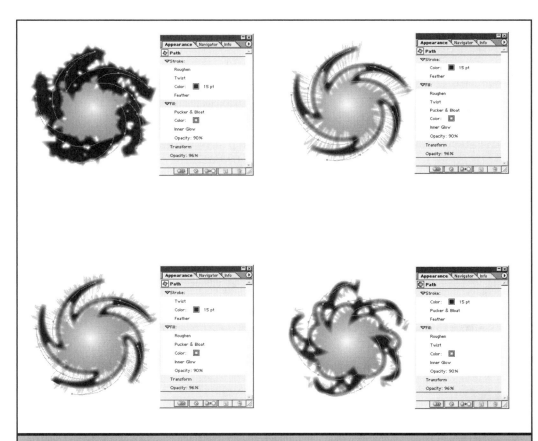

Figure 18-2.   *In the top-left corner, the original object; in the other corners, the results of dragging attributes between the Fill section and the Stroke section*

ILLUSTRATOR FX

the object in the bottom-right corner demonstrates moving Pucker & Bloat from the Fill to the Stroke. Note that if you drag an attribute to the bottom of the Appearance palette, Illustrator would apply the attribute to the entire object.

Inserting an Extra Stroke or Fill

Adding an extra stroke or fill to an object enables you to make an object look more complex. For example, you can place a stroke with a different color, weight, and roughness on top of the original stroke; you could enhance an object's sense of dimension by increasingly adding strokes that gradually become lighter in weight. Or you can coat the original fill with a semitransparent, light-colored fill covered with cross-hatches. Note that the top-most strokes and fills usually are those Illustrator shows in the toolbox.

When you add a new stroke or fill, Illustrator applies the stroke or fill to one or more objects. If the object is a path, Illustrator adds one stroke or fill. However, if the object is a layer or group, all "members" of the layer or group receive the stroke or fill.

To add a new stroke or fill to an object, follow these steps:

1. Select an object, or target the object in the Layers palette.

2. To add a new stroke, choose Add New Stroke from the Appearance palette's menu. Illustrator inserts a stroke that has the same attributes as the original.

3. To add a new fill, choose Add New Fill from the palette's menu. Illustrator inserts a fill that has the same attributes as the original.

Figure 18-3 illustrates an object with its original stroke and an additional stroke. The Appearance palette in the figure shows the attributes for each of the strokes. The Layers palette demonstrates that a complicated object does not always consist of multiple layers.

Editing Appearance Attributes

The Appearance palette contains several commands and shortcuts with which you can change appearance attributes. You can use the palette to copy all or some of the attributes of one object to another, duplicate selected attributes, and delete an attribute.

Copying an Appearance Attribute

The Appearance palette enables you to copy an appearance attribute from a selected object (the source) to another object (the target) in the illustration window. Before you copy an attribute, ensure that the thumbnail for the selected object is on display in the palette.

To copy attributes to an object, follow these steps:

1. Create a target object to which you will apply appearance attributes.

2. Select the source object that contains the attributes you want to copy.

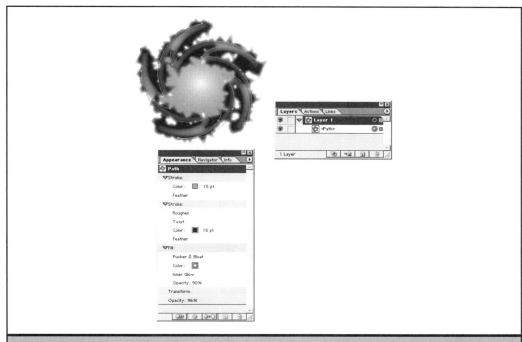

Figure 18-3.   *A selected object with its original stroke and an extra stroke in a different color*

3. If the Appearance palette does not display a thumbnail preceding the selected source object, choose Show Thumbnail from the palette's menu.

4. Drag the source object's thumbnail from the Appearance palette to the target object in the illustration window.

Duplicating an Appearance Attribute

You can duplicate the appearance attributes of one or more selected items in the Appearance palette. Note that Illustrator duplicates the attributes in the Appearance palette. You don't see any changes in the selected object unless you edit one or both sets of attributes.

To duplicate an appearance attribute, follow these steps:

1. In the illustration window, select the object with an attribute to be duplicated. The Appearance palette shows the selected object, its fills and strokes, and the appearance attributes for each.

2. To duplicate a fill or stroke and its attributes, select the fill or stroke in the palette;
then click the Duplicate Selected Item button at the bottom of the palette or choose
the Duplicate Item command from the palette's menu. Illustrator copies the fill
or stroke and places it above the original in the palette.

3. To duplicate one appearance attribute under a fill or stroke, select the attribute
in the palette. Then click the Duplicate Selected Item button or choose the Duplicate
Item command from the menu. Illustrator copies the attribute and places it above
the original in the palette.

Figure 18-4 shows the Appearance palette with a duplicated fill and a duplicated
attribute. To create this figure, the first item duplicated was the fill, followed by the
Pucker & Bloat attribute.

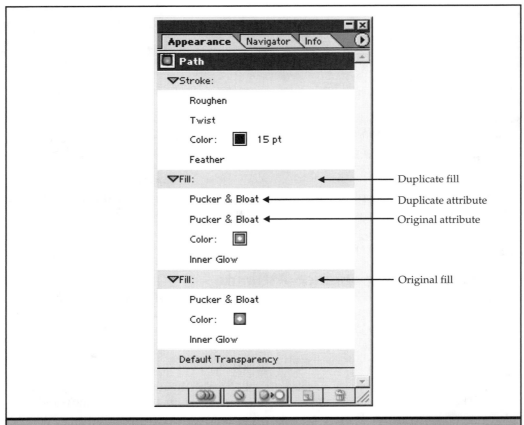

Figure 18-4.   *The Appearance palette with a duplicated fill and duplicated attribute*

Deleting Items from the Appearance Palette

You can delete fills, strokes, and appearance attributes from the Appearance palette. To delete an item you can click a button, drag the item to the button, or choose a command from the palette's menu. When Illustrator deletes an item, it undoes the action you used to create the item; so expect a short wait while Illustrator works. As Illustrator removes the item, you'll probably be able to see its progress in a message box.

To delete a selected fill, stroke, or attribute from the Appearance palette, do one of the following:

- Click the Delete Selected Item button in the lower-right corner of the Appearance palette.
- Drag the selection to the Delete Selected Item button.
- Choose Remove Item from the palette's menu.

Illustrator also enables you to delete all appearance attributes from the Appearance palette by clicking a button or choosing a command.

- You can delete all fills, strokes, and appearance attributes by selecting an object and either clicking the Clear Appearance button at the bottom of the palette or choosing the Clear Appearance command from the palette's menu. The result is an empty Appearance palette with both fill and stroke equal to None (see the left side of Figure 18-5).
- You can delete all attributes and extra fills and strokes by selecting an object and either clicking the Reduce to Basic Appearance button at the bottom of the palette or choosing the Reduce to Basic Appearance command from the palette's menu. Illustrator removes all the attributes and extra fills and strokes from the selected object (see the right side of Figure 18-5). The result is the original fill and stroke with their most recent colors, patterns, or gradients (for the fill only).

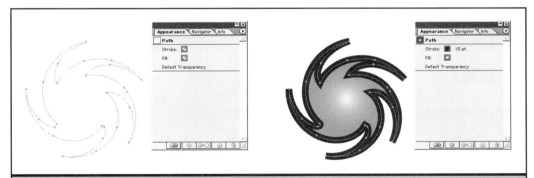

Figure 18-5.   *The Appearance palette after clearing appearances from an object (on the left) and reducing the object to its basic appearance (on the right)*

ILLUSTRATOR FX

Setting Attributes for Future Objects

Illustrator enables you to affect the appearance of objects you haven't created yet. You can make new objects that receive all the appearance attributes from a selected object or produce barebones objects that have the basic attributes of the selected object—a fill and stroke with the current fill and stroke colors. Use a button/command combination in the Appearance palette to affect the appearance of future objects.

To set the look of new objects, follow these steps:

1. Select or target an object whose attributes will affect future objects.

2. For future objects to inherit all the attributes from the selected object, click the New Art Maintains Appearance button at the bottom of the Appearance palette or choose the New Art Has Basic Appearance command from the palette's menu. Illustrator changes the appearance of the button so it looks pressed down and places a check mark in front of the command.

3. For future objects to inherit the fill and stroke colors from the selected object but none of the other attributes, click the New Art Maintains Appearance button or choose the New Art Has Basic Appearance command. The New Art Maintains Appearance button does not look pressed down, and Illustrator removes the check mark before the command.

Figure 18-6 illustrates the difference between an object that has just received the fill and stroke of the selected object and one that has all the attributes of the object. At the top of the figure is the original object and the Appearance palette for the object with the

---

Using the Layers Palette to Change Attributes

You can modify the appearance of objects by using the Layers palette. For example, you can select a layer or sublayer and apply effects and other appearance attributes, which affects every element under that layer. If you give appearance attributes to a single element (such as a path or group) within a layer or sublayer, Illustrator changes the appearance of that path or the group and its paths only. Note that if you change the appearance attributes for an entire layer and then move a path out of that layer to a different layer, the moved path does not keep the layer-wide appearance attributes; it assumes any attributes applied to its new home layer.

When you target an element in the Layers palette, the target icons tell you whether the element has appearance attributes.

 This icon specifies that you have not targeted the element, and it does not have appearance attributes.

 This icon specifies that you have not targeted the element, and it has appearance attributes.

This icon specifies that you have targeted the element, but it does not have appearance attributes.

 This icon specifies that you have targeted the element, and it has appearance attributes.

You can use the Layers palette to move, copy, and delete appearance attributes.

- ■ To move appearance attributes from one element to another, drag the target icon of the source element to the target element.
- ■ To copy appearance attributes from one element to another, press and hold down ALT/OPTION and drag the target icon of the source element to the target element.
- ■ To delete appearance attributes from an element, drag the target icon of the element to the Delete Selection at the bottom of the Layers palette. Illustrator removes the appearance attributes except the original fill and stroke.

fill and stroke only. At the bottom of the figure is the object with the fill and stroke (on the left) and the full inheritor (on the right).

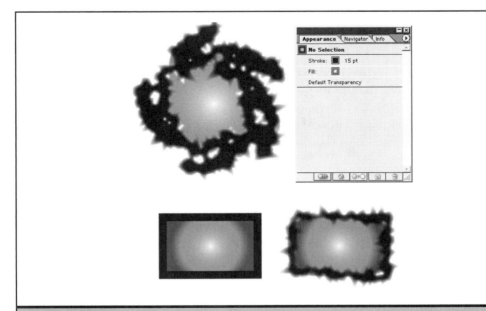

Figure 18-6.   *On the left, an object that has not received every attribute; on the right, an object that has inherited everything*

Using Styles

When you create a group of appearance attributes that you would like to use on future objects, you can save and name them. As you know, a set of saved appearance attributes is known as a style. Use the Styles palette to create, apply, and modify styles. Once you apply a style to an object and edit that style, Illustrator automatically changes the object to reflect the change in the style.

 The Styles palette is unique for the current document. So, if you create custom styles or delete styles from the palette, these changes apply only to the palette for the active document.

Exploring the Styles Palette

With the Styles palette (see Figure 18-7), you can control every aspect of styles: You can create and name styles, modify styles, apply styles to objects, and even delete styles. To toggle between showing and hiding the palette, choose Window | Styles (SHIFT-F5).

The Styles palette contains several elements, each of which has a specific meaning and with which you can control styles:

- Click the menu button to open the Styles palette's menu.

- Click the Break Link to Style button to explicitly break the link between an object and its style. The counterpart command on the palette's menu is Break Link to Style.

- Click the New Style button to create a new style and add its thumbnail or entry to the palette, depending on the view of the palette. The command on the Styles palette's menu that is nearly a counterpart is New Style. When you create a style by clicking New Style, Illustrator assigns a name to the style.

- Click the Delete Style button to delete the selected style. The counterpart command on the palette's menu is Delete Style.

- The center of the palette displays thumbnails or lists entries (depending on the view that you have chosen) of styles. The first nine styles in the palette are defined by Illustrator. The first of those styles is the standard white fill and black stroke that Illustrator applies to any object by default.

To open the palette's menu, click the menu button. Commands on the menu are as follows:

- The New Style command opens the Style Options dialog box so that you can name the new style. The counterpart button at the bottom of the palette is New Style. When you create a style by choosing New Style, you can name the style.

- The Duplicate Style command duplicates one or more selected styles.

- The Merge Styles command enables you to merge two or more selected styles into a single style.

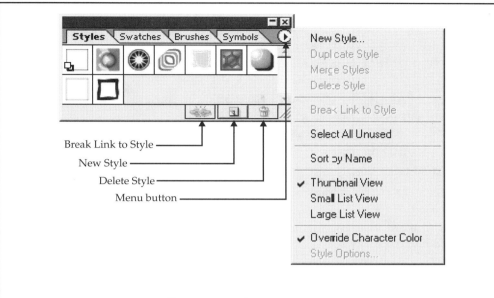

Break Link to Style ──
New Style ──
Delete Style ──
Menu button ──

ILLUSTRATOR FX

Figure 18-7. *Three views of the Styles palette, with which you can create, name, modify, apply, and delete styles*

- The Delete Style command deletes one or more selected styles. The counterpart button at the bottom of the palette is Delete Style.

- The Break Link to Style command explicitly breaks the link between an object and its style. The counterpart button at the bottom of the palette is Break Link to Style.

- The Select All Unused command selects all styles that are not used in the current document.

- The Sort by Name command sorts all styles currently in the Styles palette by name, in alphabetical order.

- The Thumbnail View command (the default) displays small images of the styles.

- The Small List View command shows the name of each style preceded by a small thumbnail of the style.

- The Large List View command shows the name of each style preceded by a larger thumbnail of the style.

- The Override Character Color command affects selected type only. If Override Character Color is active (that is, it is preceded by a check mark), Illustrator applies the fill color, stroke color, and transparency attributes from the style to the type. If the command is not active (that is, there is no check mark), Illustrator keeps the current fill color, stroke color, and transparency settings.

- If you selected a type object, select Override Character Color from the Styles palette menu to apply the style's fill.

- The Style Options command opens the Style Options dialog box with which you can name or rename the selected style.

Using the Styles Palette

You can use the Styles palette to accomplish several goals—creating and naming a style, and duplicating and deleting selected styles. You also can use the Appearance and Styles palettes in tandem: Drag appearance attributes you have constructed from the Appearance palette to the Styles palette, and then name and save them as a new style. And—just like the Brushes and Swatches palettes—the Styles palette is associated with a set of libraries.

Viewing the Styles Palette

Illustrator provides three ways to view the styles in the Styles palette. You can view thumbnails for each style by choosing Thumbnail View from the Styles palette's menu. You can view lists of styles by choosing Small List View or Large List View. As you might imagine, Small List View lists styles, each preceded by a small thumbnail, and

Large List View lists styles, each preceded by a larger thumbnail. Figure 18-7 illustrates each view.

Creating a Style

A style can be composed of any combination of appearance attributes: one or more fills, one or more strokes, colors, gradients, patterns, transparency and opacity settings, transformations, and effects from the Effects menu—in other words, any attributes you could possibly see in the Appearance palette. To make a style, either construct a new object in the illustration window and populate it with appearance attributes or find an object that already has the desired attributes. Then you move the attributes to the Styles palette in a variety of ways, which are detailed in this section.

Dragging a Style from the Appearance Palette   To create a style from the Appearance palette, follow these steps:

1. Select or target the object that will be the source of the appearance attributes.

2. Choose Window | Appearance (SHIFT-F6) to open the Appearance palette if it isn't open.

3. Select the source object in the Appearance palette and drag it to a location in the thumbnail or list section of the Styles palette or to the New Style button at the bottom of the palette.

Dragging a Style from the Illustration Window   To create a style from a selected object, follow these steps:

1. Select or target the object that will be the source of the appearance attributes.

2. Drag the source object to a location in the thumbnail or list section of the Styles palette or to the New Style button at the bottom of the palette.

Creating and Naming a Style from an Object   To create a style from a selected object, follow these steps:

1. Select or target the object that will be the source of the appearance attributes.

2. To create a style without a name, click the New Style button at the bottom of the Styles palette.

3. To create a named style, choose the New Style command from the palette's menu. Illustrator opens the Style Options dialog box (see Figure 18-8) and places a thumbnail for the style in the Styles palette.

4. Type the name of the style in the Style Name text box, and click OK.

ILLUSTRATOR FX

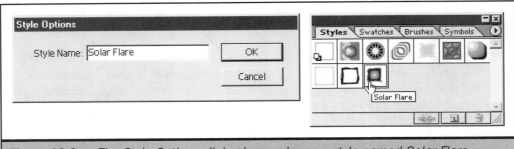

Figure 18-8. *The Style Options dialog box and a new style named Solar Flare*

Replacing a Style

You can replace a style in the Styles palette with a new and improved version, or an altogether different style. To replace a style, you can use a shortcut and drag a style or object to the Styles palette. To replace one style with another, use one of the following methods:

■ While pressing and holding down ALT/OPTION, drag the style onto the style to be replaced in the Styles palette.

■ Select or target an object with the desired style. Then, while pressing and holding down ALT/OPTION, drag the object onto the style to be replaced in the Styles palette.

 If you don't use the ALT/OPTION shortcut in conjunction with dragging, Illustrator will create a new style instead of replacing an old one.

Redefining a Style

When you redefine a style, you use the Appearance and Styles palettes. To redefine a style, follow these steps:

1. In the Styles palette, select the style to be replaced.

2. Select artwork (or target an item in the Layers palette) that has the attributes you want to use. Note that if you select the artwork before you select the style in the Styles palette, Illustrator automatically applies the style to the selected artwork.

3. Choose Redefine Style "*Style name*" from the Appearance palette menu. Illustrator replaces the selected style with the attributes of the selected artwork.

Applying a Style to an Object

To apply a style to an object, either select the object and click the style in the Styles palette, or drag the style from the palette to the object. Note that when an applied style doesn't seem to include all the attributes you expected, one or more attributes might have been applied to the entire object rather than a fill or stroke. To repair this condition, open the Appearance palette and drag the attribute from the bottom of the palette to a location under a fill or stroke. Then drag the edited style to the Styles palette and give the style a unique name.

Near the end of Chapter 8 you learned that you can use the Eyedropper (I) and the Paint Bucket (K) tools in tandem to obtain many types of styling information and then place the information on a selected object. This means you can click an object with the Eyedropper to "pick up" all its styles and attributes and apply those styles and attributes to another object with the Eyedropper or the Paint Bucket. For more information about using the Eyedropper and Paint Bucket, refer to the "Using the Eyedropper and the Paint Bucket Tools" section in Chapter 8.

Duplicating a Style

You can duplicate a style to start with a set of attributes you like. Then you can add more attributes to give the duplicate style a look of its own.

To duplicate a style, follow these steps:

1. In the Styles palette, click the style to be duplicated.

Caution   *If an object is selected in the illustration window, Illustrator will apply the style you have just clicked.*

2. From the palette's menu, choose the Duplicate Style command. Illustrator adds a new thumbnail that duplicates the look of the selected style.

3. To rename the style, choose Style Options from the palette's menu or double-click the thumbnail. Illustrator opens the Style Options dialog box with a suggested name in the Style Name text box (for example, for the Ice Burst style the suggested name is Ice Burst 1). Click OK.

Merging Styles

What if you like the look of two styles? For example, one style might have a stroke with a rough look, which you might not be able to reproduce easily; the other style might have a fill that contains an outstanding color and bright glow. Illustrator enables you to merge two or more styles. After you merge styles, you can remove superfluous attributes and unnecessary fills and strokes by using the techniques you learned in "Editing Appearance Attributes," earlier in the chapter.

To merge Illustrator styles, follow these steps:

1. To select two or more noncontiguous styles, click; then press and hold down CTRL/⌘, and continue clicking to add to the selection.

2. To select two or more contiguous styles, click one end of the range; then press and hold down SHIFT, and click the other end of the range.

3. Choose Merge Styles from the palette's menu. Illustrator merges all the styles into a new style, which it places at the end of the existing styles. Additionally, Illustrator creates a new thumbnail that illustrates the characteristics of the merged styles and opens the Style Options dialog box.

4. Type the name of the style in the Style Name text box and click OK.

Breaking the Link Between an Object and Its Style

When you edit an object with an applied style, Illustrator automatically breaks the link between the object and the style, thereby forcing you to create and name a new style. You can explicitly break the link between an object and its style by selecting the object and either clicking the Break Link to Style button at the bottom of the Styles palette or choosing the Break Link to Style command from the palette's menu.

Once you have completed your editing changes, you can create a new style based on the new attributes. Refer to "Creating a Style," earlier in this chapter to learn how to create a style.

Deleting a Style

When you know that you will never use a particular style again (for example, you might have developed a more sophisticated set of appearance attributes), you can delete it from the Styles palette. You can click a button, drag the style to that button, or choose a command from the palette's menu to delete a style. To delete a style, select the style and do one of the following:

- Drag the selection to the Delete Style button in the lower-right corner of the Styles palette. Illustrator deletes the style and its thumbnail without prompting you to confirm the deletion.

- Click the Delete Style button. Illustrator displays a message box to prompt you to confirm the deletion.

- Choose the Delete Style command from the palette's menu. Illustrator prompts you to confirm the deletion.

Selecting All Unused Styles

The main reason you select all unused styles is to delete them and keep track of all the remaining (that is, used) styles. To select all styles whose attributes are not being used in the current document, choose the Select All Unused command from the Styles palette's menu. Illustrator highlights the unused styles except the default style. To delete the selected styles, drag the group of highlighted styles to the Delete Style button, click the Delete Style button, or choose the Delete Style command.

Using Style Libraries

In Chapter 7 you learned about swatches libraries, and you found out about brushes libraries in Chapter 13. As you might expect, style libraries are similar yet different from swatches and brushes libraries: Apply predefined styles to your artwork, or create your own styles and store them in a library.

When you use a style from a style library in your current artwork, the style becomes part of the Styles palette for the present document only. Additionally, you cannot edit a style when it's in a style library, but you can change it once it is part of the Styles palette. You also can create one or more custom libraries with your selection of styles. Figure 18-9 shows all the predefined, populated style libraries.

You can work with style libraries in several ways: Obviously, to use a library, you must be able to open it; then you can select styles and move them to the Styles palette.

Opening a Style Library

To open a style library, choose Window | Style Libraries and then choose the library from the submenu. Note that some libraries might take a few seconds to load. A style library looks very much like the Styles palette; however, if you look closely, you'll find some differences. For example, because you cannot edit a style library, the buttons along the bottom of the palette are missing. In addition, a style library's menu contains a few different commands from the Styles palette's menu:

- ■ Choose the Add to Styles command to add the selected style from a library palette to the Styles palette. You also can drag the style from the library palette to the Styles palette.

- ■ Choose the Persistent command for Illustrator to automatically keep the library in the illustration window until you deactivate the Persistent command.

Moving a Style to the Styles Palette

You can move a style into the Styles palette by selecting it (which usually automatically places it in the Styles palette), using it in the current artwork, or dragging the style to the Styles palette.

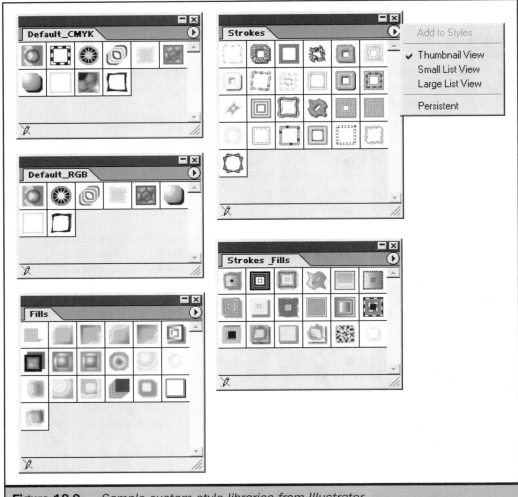

Figure 18-9.   *Sample custom style libraries from Illustrator*

Creating a Style Library

To create a style library, follow these steps:

1. Start a new Illustrator document.

2. Choose Window | Styles (SHIFT-F5) to open the Styles palette.

3. Add styles to the Styles palette by doing one of the following:
   - Create styles, making sure to give them unique names.
   - Duplicate styles and change some or all their options.
4. Delete styles you don't want to have in the Styles palette.
5. Save the document as you would save any Illustrator document into the folder in which other style libraries are located (for example, Styles). Note that style library documents have Illustrator's .ai extension.
6. To open a custom style library that you have created, choose Window | Style Libraries | Other Library. From the Select a Library to Open dialog box, double-click the library name.

Figure 18-10 shows the Default_CMYK library document in the illustration window.

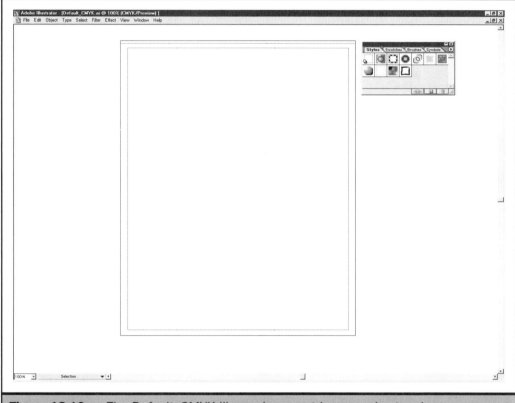

Figure 18-10. *The Default_CMYK library document has an .ai extension.*

ILLUSTRATOR FX

Blending Objects

In Chapter 16 you learned how to blend color fills within a selected group of at least three objects, from front to back, horizontally, or vertically. You can enhance your blending abilities by using the Blend tool (W) and the Blend submenu on the Object menu.

With the Blend tool and the Blend commands, you can change the shape and color of two or more objects by selecting one object, possibly dragging through one or more other objects, or clicking sequential or nonsequential objects and selecting the final object in the blend. Once you have selected objects to blend and chosen a Blend command or used the Blend tool, Illustrator morphs the first object into the last object, using the intermediate objects along the way.

Illustrator enables you to create blends using open and closed paths (but not mesh objects) that have various shapes, colors, gradients, attributes, and levels of transparency. Note that you can only partially blend objects with pattern fills: Illustrator ignores the pattern and uses the fill color of the topmost object in the blend. Note also that when you blend objects that already have blends applied, only the topmost object's blend survives.

If you are not satisfied with the look of a blend, you can change its appearance by using the Blend Options dialog box, commands on the Blend submenu, transformation tools, other commands, and palettes.

How Illustrator Computes a Blend

To create a blend, Illustrator calculates the number of steps from the first to last object in a blend. Illustrator evaluates the color of the objects it will blend and uses process or spot colors as follows:

- If you blend one object filled or stroked with a spot color and another with a process color, Illustrator blends using a process color.

- If the first and last objects in a blend are filled or stroked with spot colors, Illustrator blends intermediate parts using process colors.

- If the objects are filled or stroked with different tints of one spot color, Illustrator blends using the same spot color.

- When Illustrator creates a blend that is composed of objects with many complicated attributes, it tries to incorporate every attribute (but is not always successful).

- An Illustrator blend is a knockout transparency group. If you blend transparent objects, the blend's transparency levels might conflict with the transparency levels of individual objects. You can adjust a blend's transparency by removing the check mark from the Knockout Group check box.

Creating a Blend

Illustrator provides two methods for creating a blend: You can use the Blend tool (W) or choose Object | Blend | Make (CTRL-ALT-B/⌘-OPTION-B). Regardless of whether you use the tool or the command, you must start with two or more objects; preferably with different shapes and colors.

Blending with a Command

When you make a blend with a command, you select the objects to be blended and choose the command.

To blend several objects using a command, follow these steps:

1. With a selection tool, select all the objects that will be part of the blend.

2. Choose Object | Blend | Make (CTRL-ALT-B/⌘-OPTION-B). Illustrator joins the objects and blends their colors.

Figure 18-11 illustrates two before-and-after blend looks. At the top-left corner of the figure there is a rectangle with a light blue fill and stroke, an ellipse with a yellow fill and stroke, and a triangle with a light green fill and stroke. The selected, blended

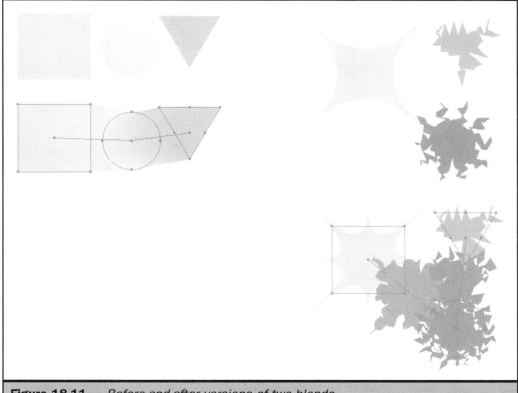

Figure 18-11.   *Before-and-after versions of two blends*

object below the original objects looks like a pastel gradient fill on a long, irregular object. The rectangle, ellipse, and triangle in the top-right corner have had several effects applied to them. The resulting blend below the original objects actually creates two new objects, which are blends of the first and second and the second and third original objects.

Blending with the Blend Tool

It's usually an unwritten rule in Illustrator that using a command to complete a task almost always enables you to do more than using a toolbox tool. Illustrator breaks the rule when you blend objects: The Blend tool (W) enables you to accomplish more than the Make command. With the Blend tool you can determine the order of the blend, add an object to the blend more than once, and select anchor points that start or end a blend.

To blend several objects using the Blend tool, follow these steps:

1. Activate the Blend tool (W).

2. Click each object to be added to the blend in the order in which you want it blended. After you click the second object, Illustrator creates a blend between the first and second objects. As you continue to click, Illustrator adds to the blend.

The top-left corner of Figure 18-12 shows the original light blue rectangle, yellow ellipse, and light green triangle. Those objects are clicked with the Blend tool in the following order: ellipse, rectangle, triangle, and ellipse. The results are shown below the original objects. In the top-right corner of the figure are the distorted rectangle, ellipse, and triangle. Those objects are clicked with the Blend tool in the same order as the first blend.

Changing a Blend

Once you have created a blend, you can change it in a variety of ways: You can adjust the number of steps from the beginning to the end of the blend, align the blend to the page or the path, change the order of a blend or its underlying objects, and release a blend. Keep in mind that you also can edit a blend using transformation and color tools.

Using Illustrator Tools and Palettes to Edit a Blend

You can use selection tools, editing tools and palettes, and other Illustrator features to modify a blend. Figure 18-13 illustrates changing the original rectangle-ellipse-triangle blend shown in Figures 18-11 and 18-12 by using the Direct Selection tool (A) to drag anchor points of the rectangle (to form a triangle) and triangle (to reshape the triangle into a freeform object), the Selection tool (V) to drag the blend and its three objects and,

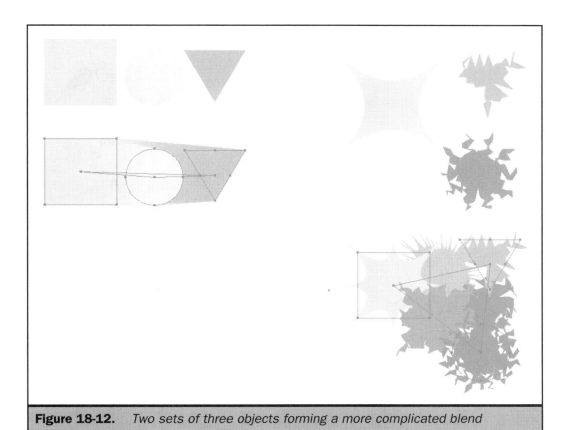

Figure 18-12.   *Two sets of three objects forming a more complicated blend*

the Swatches palette to change the fill and stroke colors of the rectangle to white and the triangle to medium blue. Figure 18-13 shows the new blend, selected to show the shape of the blended objects and unselected to show the blend itself.

Using the Blend Options Dialog Box to Edit a Blend

You can adjust blend attributes by using the Blend Options dialog box (see Figure 18-14). To open the dialog box, either double-click the Blend tool (W) or choose Object | Blend | Blend Options.

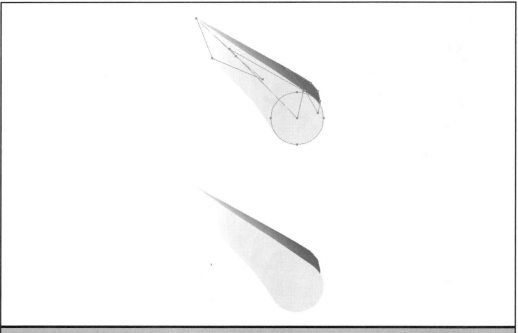

Figure 18-13.   *A comet-like blend made from the original rectangle, ellipse, and triangle shown in the preceding two figures*

The options in the Blend Options dialog box are as follows:

■ From the Spacing drop-down menu, select an option:

■ Smooth Color (the default) enables Illustrator to compute the number of steps in a blend based on the number of colors or the distance between the first and last objects. If the blend is composed of many objects with many colors, Illustrator probably will compute more steps than it would for a blend composed of a few objects with a few colors. If a future blend contains objects with the same colors, gradients, or patterns, Illustrator uses the distance between the first and last objects to compute the number of steps.

■ The Specified Steps option enables you to override Illustrator's calculations to set the number of the steps from the beginning to the end of the blend. Valid values range from 1 to 1,000. The default is 8.

■ Specified Distance enables you to override Illustrator's calculations to set a distance from the beginning to the end of the blend. Valid values range from 0.1 point and 1,000 points. The default is 4 points.

■ Click an Orientation button to change the orientation of the path. Click Align to Page to align the blend with the x-axis of the page on which the blend is located; click Align to Path to align the blend with the path on which it sits.

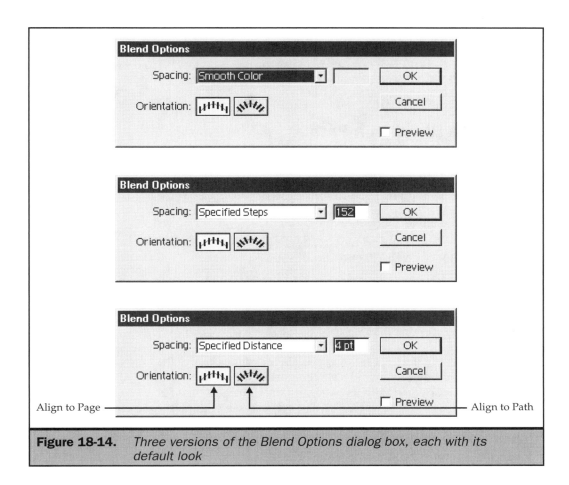

Figure 18-14.   *Three versions of the Blend Options dialog box, each with its default look*

Placing a Blend on a Path

You can create a blend and then set it on a path so that you can control its appearance in an artwork. For example, you can enclose another object within the blended path, or you can wind a blended path containing a corporate logo around a corner of a page.

The command with which you put a blend on a path is Replace Spine, where Spine refers to the spine (or backbone) of the blend—as its original objects were originally aligned or along its new path. When you choose Replace Spine, you are actually replacing the spine of the blend.

To place a blend on a path, follow these steps:

1. Draw a curved or straight path.
2. Create a blend.

3. Select the path and entire blend by activating a selection tool, clicking the path or blend, pressing and holding down SHIFT, and clicking the blend or path to add it to the selection. You also can use the Selection tool (V) to draw a bounding box around the path and blend.

4. Choose Object | Blend | Replace Spine. Illustrator moves the blend onto the path.

Orienting a Blend on a Path

Before or after you place a blend on a path, you can determine the blend's orientation: with the x-axis of the page or with the path. To do so, choose a command, which opens a dialog box; then click one of two buttons.

To orient a blend on its path, follow these steps:

1. Select the blend that you want to orient.

2. Double-click the Blend tool (W) or choose Object | Blend | Blend Options. Illustrator opens the Blend Options dialog box.

3. To align the blend with the x-axis of the page on which the blend is located, click the Align to Page button.

4. To align the blend with the path on which it sits, click the Align to Path button.

5. Click OK to close the dialog box and apply the orientation setting.

Figure 18-15 illustrates a set of grayscale rectangles before they are changed into a blend, the resulting blend, and two versions of the blends on a curved path. The leftmost blend is oriented with its page, and the rightmost blend is oriented to its path. All items in the figure are selected so that you can see both paths and every object.

Reversing a Blend

It takes one command to transpose the order of a blend on or off a path from one side to the other. To reverse the direction of a blend, follow these steps:

1. Select the blend (and optionally its path if it is on a path) by activating a selection tool and clicking. You also can also use the Selection tool (V) to draw a bounding box around the blend.

2. Choose Object | Blend | Reverse Spine. Illustrator reverses the direction of the blend.

Reversing the Path Order

Reversing the path order rearranges the stacking order of the blended objects on the path. This works particularly well when the blended objects overlap each other. To reverse the stacking order, select the blend and then choose Object | Blend | Reverse Front to Back.

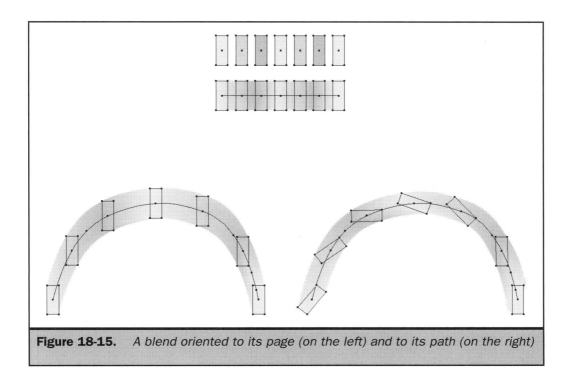

Figure 18-15.   *A blend oriented to its page (on the left) and to its path (on the right)*

Figure 18-16 illustrates the switch of a blend that is composed of a series of grayscale circles. The circles were drawn from left to right, so the rightmost circle is at the top of the stacking order. The blend of the circles is in the second row of the figure. After choosing Reverse Front to Back, the stacking order is reversed (as shown in the third row): The leftmost circle is now at the top of the order; the rightmost circle is at the bottom. The bottom row shows the circles after releasing the blend.

Expanding a Blend

As you learned in the "Expanding Selected Shape Areas" section in Chapter 6, expanding a path combines all (that is, flattens) the paths within a compound shape into a single path. You also can expand a blend by selecting it and then choosing Object | Blend | Expand. Illustrator converts the blend to one path. If the blend was composed of multicolored objects (which usually is the case), the resulting path looks very much like a gradient. To reverse the Expand command, press CTRL-Z/⌘-Z or choose Edit | Undo.

Releasing a Blend

Releasing a blend reverses the blend: Illustrator returns the original objects on which the blend was based. To release a blend, choose Object | Blend | Release. Note that the bottom row of Figure 18-16 shows a released blend.

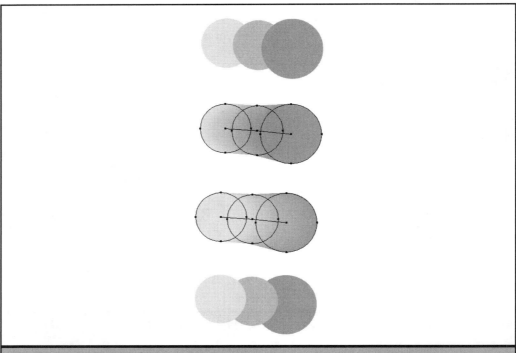

Figure 18-16.   *A demonstration of reversing a blend from front to back*

Using Symbols

Symbols are small artworks you save and use inone or more documents. Symbols can range from art you can duplicate (for example, one fish can become a school of fish; one tree can become a forest) and icons that almost everyone understands (such as stop signs and arrows). Illustrator enables you to duplicate, edit, delete, and create new symbols. Illustrator also provides an entire toolslot filled with eight tools for working with symbols. The tools on this toolslot are nicknamed the Symbolism tools.

Exploring the Symbols Palette

With the Symbols palette (see Figure 18-17), you can control every aspect of styles: You can create and name styles, modify styles, apply styles to objects, and even delete styles. To toggle between showing and hiding the palette, choose Window | Symbols (SHIFT-F11).

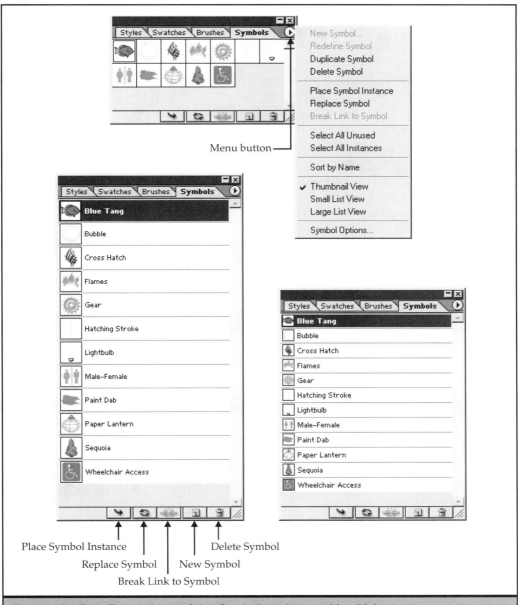

Menu button ——

Place Symbol Instance

Replace Symbol   New Symbol

Break Link to Symbol

Delete Symbol

Figure 18-17.   *Three views of the Symbols palette, with which you can create, duplicate, modify, apply, and delete symbols*

The Symbols palette contains several elements, each of which has a specific meaning and with which you can control symbols:

■ Click the menu button to open the Symbols palette's menu.

■ Click the Place Symbol Instance button to insert a symbol instance in a document. The counterpart command on the palette's menu is Place Symbol Instance.

■ Click the Replace Symbol button to replace one symbol with another in the Symbols palette. The counterpart command on the palette's menu is Replace Symbol.

■ Click the Break Link to Symbol button to explicitly break the link between a symbol and its document, converting the symbol to an object. The counterpart command on the palette's menu is Break Link to Symbol.

■ Click the New Symbol button to create a new symbol and add its thumbnail or entry to the palette, depending on the view of the palette. New Symbol is the command on the Symbols palette's menu that is nearly a counterpart. When you create a symbol by clicking New Symbol, Illustrator assigns a name to the style.

■ Click the Delete Symbol button to delete the selected symbol. The counterpart command on the palette's menu is Delete Symbol.

■ The center of the palette displays thumbnails or lists entries (depending on the view that you have chosen) of symbols. The first 12 styles in the palette are defined by Illustrator.

To open the palette's menu, click the menu button. Commands on the menu are as follows:

■ The New Symbol command opens the Symbol Options dialog box so that you can name a symbol. The counterpart button at the bottom of the palette is New Symbol. When you create a symbol by choosing New Symbol, you can name the symbol.

■ The Redefine Symbol command enables you to redefine a symbol and automatically replace the symbols you have inserted in the current document.

■ The Duplicate Symbol command duplicates one or more selected symbols.

■ The Delete Symbol command deletes one or more selected styles. The counterpart button at the bottom of the palette is Delete Symbol.

■ The Place Symbol Instance command inserts a symbol instance in a document. The counterpart button at the bottom of the palette is Place Symbol Instance.

■ The Replace Symbol command replaces one symbol with another in the Symbols palette. The counterpart button at the bottom of the palette is Replace Symbol.

- The Break Link to Symbol command explicitly breaks the link between a symbol and its document, converting the symbol to an object. The counterpart button at the bottom of the palette is Break Link to Symbol.

- The Select All Unused command selects all symbols that are not used in the current document.

- The Select All Instances command selects all instances of the selected symbol in the document.

- The Sort by Name command sorts all symbols currently in the Symbols palette by alphabetically ordered name.

- The Thumbnail View command (the default) displays small images of the symbols.

- The Small List View command shows the name of each symbol preceded by a small thumbnail of the symbol.

- The Large List View command shows the name of each symbol preceded by a larger thumbnail of the symbol.

- The Symbol Options command opens the Symbol Options dialog box with which you can name or rename a symbol.

Learning about the Symbolism Tools

In the toolbox, Illustrator provides eight tools (see Figure 18-18) with which you can create and edit the symbol instances in a document. Use the Symbolism tools to apply symbols and edit symbols and sets of symbols. As you read the rest of this chapter, you'll learn how all these tools work.

- The Symbol Sprayer tool (SHIFT-S) inserts sets of symbol instances into a document.

- The Symbol Shifter tool moves sets of symbol instances around the illustration window.

- The Symbol Scruncher tool moves individual symbols away from or closer to other symbols in the set.

- The Symbol Sizer tool scales symbol instances within sets.

- The Symbol Spinner tool moves symbol instances in the direction in which you drag the mouse pointer.

- The Symbol Stainer tool changes the hue of symbol instances.

- The Symbol Screener tool adjusts transparency of sets of symbol instances.

- The Symbol Styler tool applies a style to a symbol instance.

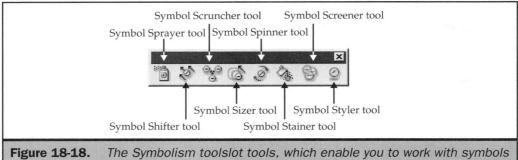

Figure 18-18. *The Symbolism toolslot tools, which enable you to work with symbols*

Using the Symbols Palette

You can use the Symbols palette to achieve several objectives such as creating and naming a symbol and duplicating and deleting selected symbols. And—just like the Brushes, Swatches, and Styles palettes—the Symbols palette is associated with a set of libraries.

Viewing the Symbols Palette

Illustrator provides three ways of viewing the symbols in the Symbols palette. You can view thumbnails for each symbol by choosing Thumbnail View from the Symbols palette's menu. You can view lists of symbols by choosing Small List View or Large List View. As you might imagine, Small List View lists symbols, each preceded by a small thumbnail; Large List View lists symbols preceded by a larger thumbnail. Figure 18-17 illustrates each view.

Creating a Symbol

A symbol can be composed of one or more objects: blends, brushstrokes, compound paths, effects, groups, mesh objects, paths, raster and vector images, symbols, and type. However, you cannot make a symbol from graphs or placed art. To make a symbol, construct an object in the illustration window, select it, and then move it to the Symbols palette in a variety of ways, which are detailed in this section. Depending on the method of creation, you can give the symbol a name or let Illustrator do it.

You can create an object of any size to use as a symbol. When you create a symbol from an object, Illustrator will resize it to fit the Symbols palette. However, when you use the symbol in an artwork, it resumes its original size.

Dragging a Symbol from the Illustration Window   To create a symbol from a selected object, follow these steps:

1. Select or target the object that will become the symbol.

2. Drag the source object to a location in the thumbnail or list section of the Symbols palette or to the New Symbol button at the bottom of the palette. If necessary, Illustrator resizes the object to fit the palette. Additionally, Illustrator names the new symbol.

Creating a Symbol from an Object   To create a symbol using a selected object, follow these steps:

1. Select or target the object that will become the symbol.

2. Click the New Symbol button at the bottom of the Symbols palette. Illustrator names the new symbol.

3. To create a named symbol, choose the New Symbol command from the palette's menu. Illustrator opens the Symbol Options dialog box (see Figure 18-19) and places a thumbnail for the style in the Styles palette.

4. Type the name of the style in the Style Name text box, and click OK.

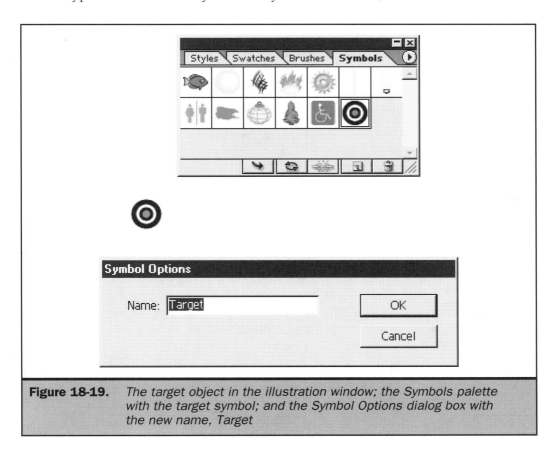

Figure 18-19.   *The target object in the illustration window; the Symbols palette with the target symbol; and the Symbol Options dialog box with the new name, Target*

Inserting a Symbol Instance in a Document

You can insert one or more symbols in the illustration window by using a command or tool. First, you'll select a symbol from the Symbols palette. Then do one of the following:

- To insert the selected symbol in the center of the artboard, click the Place Symbol Instance button from the bottom of the palette or choose the Place Symbol Instance command from the palette's menu.

- To insert the selected symbol anywhere in the illustration window, drag it from the palette to the desired location.

- To insert a set of symbols, activate the Symbol Sprayer tool (SHIFT-S). When you move the mouse pointer to the illustration window, Illustrator encloses the mouse pointer within a circle, which indicates the area in which you will be able to spray symbols. If you click rapidly, Illustrator inserts one or two symbols. However, the longer you hold down the mouse button, the more symbols Illustrator adds to the illustration window.

Replacing a Symbol

You can replace a symbol in the Symbols palette with another symbol or an object. To replace a symbol, you can use a shortcut and drag a future symbol to the palette. To replace one symbol with another, use one of the following methods:

- While pressing and holding down ALT/OPTION, drag the symbol onto the symbol to be replaced in the Symbols palette.

- Select or target an object that will become a symbol. Then, while pressing and holding down ALT/OPTION, drag the object onto the symbol to be replaced in the Symbols palette.

If you don't use the ALT/OPTION shortcut in conjunction with dragging, Illustrator will create a new symbol instead of replacing an old one.

Redefining a Symbol

When you redefine a symbol, you not only replace the symbol in the Symbols palette, but you also replace the symbols used in the current document with the replacement version, which you have edited in one or more ways. As you can see, redefining a symbol is similar to replacing a symbol. However, whereas replacing a symbol works in the Symbols palette only, redefining a symbol affects symbols already added to the document.

To redefine a symbol, follow these steps:

1. Select a symbol instance in the illustration window.
2. Click the Break Link to Symbol button at the bottom of the palette, or choose Break Link to Symbol from the palette's menu.
3. Modify the symbol.
4. If the symbol you just edited is not selected in the Symbols palette, select it.
5. Choose Redefine Symbol from the palette's menu, or press and hold down ALT/OPTION and drag the edited symbol to the thumbnail of the original symbol in the palette.

Duplicating a Symbol

You can duplicate a symbol to start with a symbol you like; then modify the symbol until it is unique. To duplicate a symbol, follow these steps:

1. In the Symbols palette, click the symbol to be duplicated.
2. From the palette's menu, choose the Duplicate Symbol command. Illustrator adds a new thumbnail that duplicates the look of the selected symbol.
3. To rename the style, choose Symbol Options from the palette's menu or double-click the thumbnail. Illustrator opens the Symbol Options dialog box with a suggested name in the Name text box (for example, for a duplicate of the Bubble symbol, the suggested name is Bubble 1). Click OK.

Breaking the Link of a Symbol

When you edit a symbol instance in the illustration window, Illustrator automatically breaks the link between the document and the symbol instance: The symbol is just another object in the illustration window; it's no longer a symbol. You also can explicitly break the link by selecting the symbol and either clicking the Break Link to Symbol button at the bottom of the Styles palette or choosing the Break Link to Symbol command from the palette's menu.

Deleting a Symbol

When you know you will never use a particular symbol again (for example, your manager has said she never wants to see that stupid rabbit again), you can delete it from the Symbols palette. You can click a button, drag the symbol to that button, or choose a command from the palette's menu to delete a symbol. To delete a symbol, select the symbol and do one of the following:

- Drag the selection to the Delete Symbol button in the lower-right corner of the Symbols palette. Illustrator deletes the symbol and its thumbnail without prompting you to confirm the deletion.

- Click the Delete Symbol button. Illustrator displays a message box to prompt you to confirm the deletion.

- Choose the Delete Symbol command from the palette's menu. Illustrator prompts you to confirm the deletion.

Selecting All Unused Symbols

The main reason you select all unused symbols is to delete them and keep track of all the remaining symbols—those you have used in the current document. To select all symbols whose attributes are not being used, choose the Select All Unused command from the Symbols palette's menu. Illustrator highlights the unused symbols. To delete the selected symbols, drag the group of highlighted styles to the Delete Symbol button, click the Delete Symbol button, or choose the Delete Symbol command.

Selecting a Set of Symbol Instances in a Document

When you want to find all the same symbols in a document, select that symbol in the Symbols palette, and then choose the Select All Instances command from the palette's menu. Illustrator selects each instance of the symbol.

Using Symbol Libraries

In Chapters 7 and 13, you learned about swatches and brushes libraries, respectively. And in the "Using Style Libraries" section earlier in this chapter, you found out about style libraries. Symbols libraries work in much the same way as the other libraries: Use additional sets of symbols in your documents, and create your own symbols and store them in a library.

When you use a symbol from a symbol library in your current artwork, the symbol becomes part of the Symbols palette for the present document only. Additionally, you cannot edit a symbol when it's in a symbol library, but you can change it once it is part of the Styles palette. You also can create one or more custom libraries with your selection of symbols. Figure 18-20 illustrates all the predefined symbol libraries.

Opening a Symbol Library

You can work with symbol libraries in several ways: You can open it, select one or more symbols, and move them to the Symbols palette. To open a symbol library, choose Window | Symbol Libraries and then choose the library from the submenu. It looks

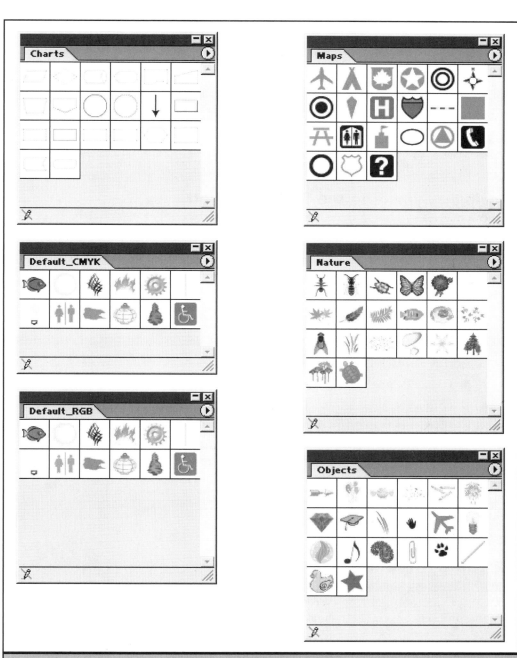

Figure 18-20.   *Sample custom symbol libraries from Illustrator*

ILLUSTRATOR FX

very much like the Symbols palette, but you'll see some differences. For example, because you cannot edit a symbol library, the buttons along the bottom of the palette are missing. In addition, a symbol library's menu contains fewer and different commands than those on the Symbols palette's menu:

- Choose the Add to Symbols command to add the selected symbol from a library palette to the Symbols palette. You also can drag the symbol from the library palette to the Symbols palette.

- Choose the Persistent command to have Illustrator automatically keep the library in the illustration window until you deactivate the Persistent command.

Moving a Symbol to the Symbols Palette

You can move a symbol into the Symbols palette by selecting it (which usually automatically places it in the Symbols palette), using it in the current artwork, or dragging the symbol to the Symbols palette.

Creating a Symbol Library

To create a symbol library, follow these steps:

1. Start a new Illustrator document.
2. Choose Window | Symbols (SHIFT-F11) to open the Symbols palette.
3. Add symbols to the Symbols palette by doing one of the following:
   - Create symbols, making sure to give them unique names.
   - Duplicate symbols and change some or all of their options.
4. Delete symbols that you don't want to have in the Symbols palette.
5. Save the document as you would save any Illustrator document into the folder in which other symbol libraries are located (for example, Symbols). Note that symbol library documents have Illustrator's .ai extension.
6. To open a custom symbol library you have created, choose Window | Symbol Libraries | Other Library. From the Select a Library to Open dialog box, double-click the library name.

Using the Symbolism Tools

In the "Inserting a Symbol Instance in a Document" section, you learned how to use the Symbol Sprayer tool (SHIFT-S). The remaining symbolism tools enable you to edit individual symbols and sets of symbol instances in a document.

Shifting Sets of Symbol Instances

When you use the Symbol Shifter tool, you can move all or part of a set of symbol instances to a new location in the illustration window. As you drag symbols, those within the circle can change position; the symbols outside the circle stay in their original locations. To move a set of symbol instances, follow these steps:

1. Select the set of symbol instances.

2. Activate the Symbol Shifter tool. When you move the mouse pointer to the illustration window, Illustrator encloses the mouse pointer within a circle.

3. Drag all or part of the set to its new location.

4. If you move the mouse pointer in a circle, Illustrator moves individual symbols within the set.

5. To move one symbol instance above others that it overlaps, press and hold down SHIFT and double-click the symbol instance. The change might be difficult to see.

6. To move one symbol instance below others that it overlaps, press and hold down ALT/OPTION, and double-click the symbol instance. The change might be difficult to see.

Scrunching Symbol Instances

The Symbol Scruncher tool works in two ways: It moves individual symbols toward the center of the set or away from the center—both very rapidly. If you move symbols toward the center of the set, sooner or later all symbols are far away from the artboard. To move symbols toward the center, follow these steps:

1. Select the set of symbol instances.

2. Activate the Symbol Scruncher tool. When you move the mouse pointer to the illustration window, Illustrator encloses the mouse pointer within a circle.

3. To move symbols toward the center of the set, move the mouse pointer so that the symbol instances are within the circle and click. If you click repeatedly or hold down the mouse button, Illustrator continues to move the symbols closer to the center.

4. To move symbols away from the center of the set, press and hold down ALT/ OPTION while moving the mouse pointer so that the symbols are within the circle. Click quickly to move the symbols a short distance. If you click repeatedly or hold down the mouse button, Illustrator continues to move the symbols farther apart.

Scaling Symbol Instances

The Symbol Sizer tool scales symbol instances larger or smaller within their sets, adding depth to the symbol instance set. To scale symbol instances up or down, follow these steps:

1. Select the set of symbol instances.

2. Activate the Symbol Sizer tool. When you move the mouse pointer to the illustration window, Illustrator encloses the mouse pointer within a circle.

3. To scale symbols larger than their current sizes, move the mouse pointer so that the symbol instances you want to change are within the circle and click. If you click repeatedly or hold down the mouse button, Illustrator continues to scale the symbols.

4. To scale symbols smaller than their current sizes, move the mouse pointer so that the symbol instances you want to change are within the circle, press and hold down ALT/OPTION, and click. If you click repeatedly or hold down the mouse button, Illustrator continues to scale the symbols.

Moving Symbol Instances

The Symbol Spinner tool moves selected symbol instances in the direction in which you drag the mouse pointer. If you enclose all the symbols within the mouse pointer circle, you can turn the symbols in the same direction. If you enclose part of the symbols, the turning results are mixed. To spin symbol instances, follow these steps:

1. Select the set of symbol instances.

2. Activate the Symbol Spinner tool. When you move the mouse pointer to the illustration window, Illustrator encloses the mouse pointer within a circle.

3. Drag the mouse pointer in a circular movement. Illustrator turns all or some of the symbols.

Colorizing Symbol Instances

With the Symbol Stainer tool, you can change the hue of selected symbol instances by using a solid fill color, not a gradient or pattern. If you don't choose a fill color, the Symbol Stainer tool removes the color from the selected symbols. When you use shortcuts with the tool, you can increase or decrease the color.

To colorize symbol instances, follow these steps:

1. Select the set of symbol instances.

2. If the Color or Swatches palette is not open in the illustration window, choose Window | Color (F6) or Window | Swatches. The Color or Swatches palette appears.

3. If the Fill box is not active in the toolbox, click it or press X.

4. Select a solid fill color.

5. Activate the Symbol Stainer tool. When you move the mouse pointer to the illustration window, Illustrator encloses the mouse pointer within a circle.

6. To stain the selected symbols with the new fill color, move the circle mouse pointer to the symbols to be changed and click or drag.

7. To remove some of the stain from the selected symbols, move the mouse pointer to the symbols to be changed, press and hold down ALT/OPTION, and click or drag.

8. To keep the amount of the stain steady but stain with the new fill color, press and hold down SHIFT and click or drag.

Adjusting the Transparency of Sets of Symbol Instances

To adjust the transparency of symbol instances, use the Symbol Screener tool. You can increase or decrease the transparency levels of the selected symbols.

To change transparency levels up or down, follow these steps:

1. Select the set of symbol instances.

2. Activate the Symbol Screener tool. When you move the mouse pointer to the illustration window, Illustrator encloses the mouse pointer within a circle.

3. To make selected symbols more transparent, move the mouse pointer so that the symbol instances you want to change are within the circle and click. If you click repeatedly or hold down the mouse button, Illustrator continues to increase the transparency level.

4. To make selected symbols less transparent, move the mouse pointer so that the symbol instances you want to change are within the circle, press and hold down ALT/OPTION, and click. If you click repeatedly or hold down the mouse button, Illustrator continues to decrease the transparency.

Styling Symbol Instances

With the Symbol Styler tool and the Styles palette, you can apply a style to a symbol instance. This tool works best when you have used the Symbol Scruncher tool to move the symbols apart.

To style one or more symbol instances, follow these steps:

1. Activate the Symbol Styler tool. When you move the mouse pointer to the illustration window, Illustrator encloses the mouse pointer within a circle.

2. Select the set of symbol instances.

3. If the Styles palette is not open in the illustration window, choose Window | Styles (SHIFT-F5). The Styles palette appears.

4. Select a style to apply to the selected symbols.

5. To apply the style to the selected symbols, move the circle mouse pointer to the symbols to be changed and click. If you release the mouse button quickly, Illustrator lightly applies the style. If you hold down the mouse button, Illustrator continues to apply the style.

6. To remove some of the style from the selected symbols, move the mouse pointer to the symbols to be changed, press and hold down ALT/OPTION, and click or drag.

7. To keep the level of style the same but stain with the new fill color, press and hold down SHIFT and click or drag to change the current style of the symbol to the new style.

Figure 18-21 demonstrates the results of using the symbolism tools. In the top row, the leftmost symbol instance set is the original sprayed by the Symbol Sprayer tool. The next illustration shows the work of the Symbol Shifter tool. The final two sets in the top

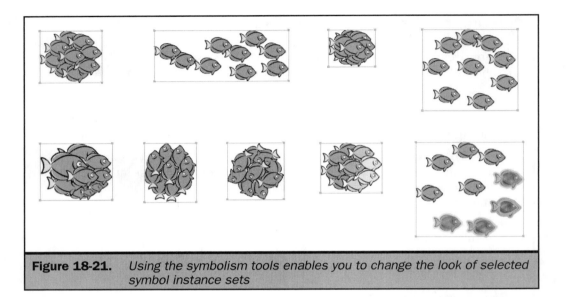

Figure 18-21.   *Using the symbolism tools enables you to change the look of selected symbol instance sets*

row are the outcome of scrunching in and out with the Symbol Scruncher tool. The first set in the bottom row demonstrates the use of the Symbol Size tool to increase or decrease the size of symbols. The second and third illustrations in the bottom row show how the Symbol Spinner tool spins all or part of a symbol instance set. The fourth set in the row demonstrates the colorization techniques of the Symbol Stainer tool. The final set in the row illustrates how the Symbol Styler tool replaces the style of the symbol with a new style; in this case, Honeycomb Silk.

Modifying Symbolism Tools

You can change options for the Symbolism tools by double-clicking a tool and clicking a button in the resulting Symbolism Tools Options dialog box (see Figure 18-22).

The options for all the symbolism tools are described as follows:

■ In the Diameter text box/slider, type or select the diameter of the circle surrounding the mouse pointer. Valid values range from 1 point to 999 points; the default is 200 points. (This option applies to all tools.)

■ From the Intensity text box/slider, type or select the intensity with which the tool changes the symbol. Valid values range from 1 (less intense) to 10 (very intense). The default is 8. (This applies to all tools.)

■ If you are using a pressure pen, you can replace the Intensity setting by checking the Use Pressure Pen check box. (All tools)

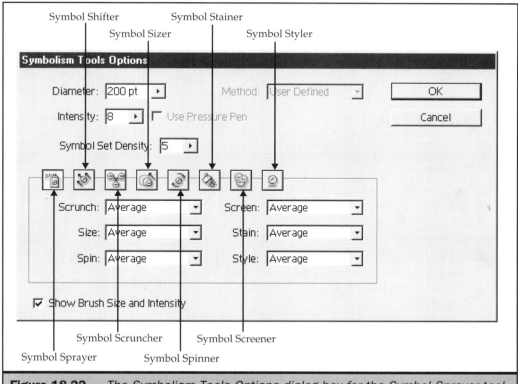

Figure 18-22.   *The Symbolism Tools Options dialog box for the Symbol Sprayer tool*

- From the Symbol Set Density text box/slider to set the density with which a symbol instance set is placed or compressed in the illustration window. This setting affects all sets in the current document. Valid values range from 1 (less compressed) to 10 (more compressed). The default is 5. (All tools)

- From the Method drop-down menu, choose a method that varies depending on the selected tool. For each tool you can choose Average, User Defined, or Random. In general, Average smooths as it modifies a set and Random modifies randomly. User Defined works differently for each tool. (Symbol Scruncher, Symbol Sizer, Symbol Spinner, Symbol Stainer, Symbol Screener, and Symbol Styler)

  - For the Symbol Scruncher tool, User Defined scrunches selected symbols slowly away or toward the cursor.

  - For the Symbol Sizer tool, User Defined scales selected symbols slowly.

- For the Symbol Spinner tool, User Defined aligns selected symbols with the direction of the drag.

- For the Symbol Stainer tool, User Defined slowly colorizes and tints selected symbols.

- For the Symbol Screener tool, User Defined slowly increases or decreases the transparency level of the selected symbols.

- For the Symbol Styler tool, User Defined slowly replaces the current style with the new style.

- To change the dialog box to that for another tool, click one of the symbolism tool buttons.

- From the Scrunch drop-down menu, choose Average to spray a new symbol instance using the average values of prior symbol instances in the current document. Choose User Defined to spray sets in a density that depends on the size of the original symbol. (Symbol Sprayer)

- From the Size drop-down menu, choose Average to spray a new symbol instance using the average values of prior symbol instances in the current document. Choose User Defined to spray sets using the size of the original symbol. (Symbol Sprayer)

- From the Spin drop-down menu, choose Average to spray a new symbol instance using the average values of prior symbol instances in the current document. Choose User Defined to spray sets using the direction of the drag or in the symbol's original orientation if you click. (Symbol Sprayer)

- From the Screen drop-down menu, choose Average to spray a new symbol instance using the average values of prior symbol instances in the current document. Choose User Defined to spray symbols with 100% opacity. (Symbol Sprayer)

- From the Stain drop-down menu, choose Average to spray a new symbol instance using the average values of prior symbol instances in the current document. Choose User Defined to spray symbols with the current fill color and total tint. (Symbol Sprayer)

- From the Style drop-down menu, choose Average to spray a new symbol instance using the average values of prior symbol instances in the current document. Choose User Defined to spray symbols that use the original style of those symbols. (Symbol Sprayer)

- Check the Show Brush Size and Intensity check box (the default) to show the circle enclosing the mouse pointer. Remove the check to hide the circle. (All tools)

- Check the Proportional Resizing check box (the default) to scale symbols in proportion with the original symbol. (Symbol Sizer)

- Check the Resizing Affects Density check box (the default) to adjust the distance between symbols as you scale them. (Symbol Sizer)

Using Envelopes

In the "Entering Type in a Rectangle" section in Chapter 11, you learned how to enter type within a rectangular area and then distort that area. With envelopes, you can move a step further: You can create an envelope of any shape and then enclose, transform, and distort the paths and type within. For more detailed results, you can create envelope meshes, which are like mesh objects, to transform and alter points on or within a grid.

The objects within an envelope can be any object or group in the illustration window except a graph or guide. Linked images are restricted to GIF, JPEG, and TIFF files.

Creating an Envelope

Illustrator enables you to create an envelope using three methods: You can make an envelope with a path or group that you have produced, a predefined warp shape, or a mesh.

Creating an Envelope with an Object or Group

When you create an envelope with an object or group, you must have created the object or group to be used as an envelope and the objects or groups that will appear within the envelope. The object or group that will become the envelope must be at the top of the stacking order. Regardless of whether you are sure about the object's or group's position, select the object or group and then choose Object | Arrange | Bring to Front (CTRL-SHIFT-]/⌘-SHIFT-]).

To create an envelope with an object or group, follow these steps:

1. Select the object or group to be converted into an envelope and the object or group that will be placed inside the envelope.

2. Choose Object | Envelope Distort | Make with Top Object (CTRL-ALT-C/⌘-OPTION-C). Illustrator removes the fill and stroke colors of the topmost object and converts it to an envelope. Additionally, Illustrator moves the underlying objects or groups within the envelope.

Figure 18-23 shows two objects, an ellipse that will become the envelope and type that will be within the envelope (at the top of the figure), and the envelope and its contents (at the bottom).

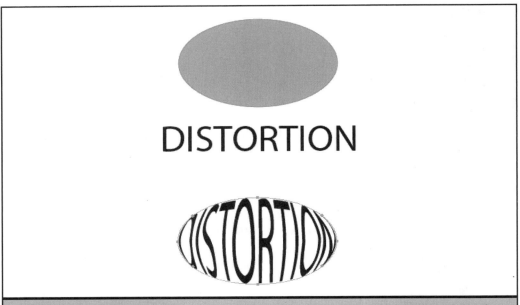

Figure 18-23.   *An ellipse that will become an envelope, type that will be within the envelope, and the new envelope with its contents*

Creating an Envelope with a Predefined Warp Shape

When you create an envelope with a warp shape, you must have created the artwork or type that will appear within the envelope.

To create an envelope with a predefined warp shape, follow these steps:

1. Select the artwork or type that Illustrator will place inside the envelope.

2. Choose Object | Envelope Distort | Make with Warp (CTRL-ALT-W/⌘-OPTION-W). Illustrator opens the Warp Options dialog box.

3. Select options from the dialog box and click OK. Illustrator places the artwork or type within the warp-shaped envelope.

Note   *To refresh your memory about using the Warp Options dialog box, refer to "Warping Objects" in Chapter 16.*

Figure 18-24 illustrates the artwork, the Warp Options dialog box, and the artwork within the warp-shaped envelope.

Creating an Envelope with a Mesh

Making an envelope with a mesh works best if you use a rectangular or square shape because the mesh lines are vertical and horizontal. (However, Illustrator does not

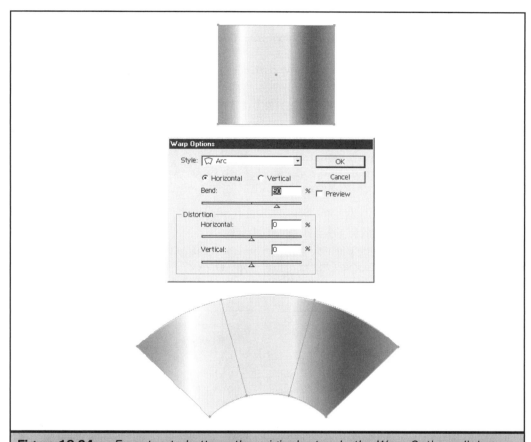

Figure 18-24.   *From top to bottom, the original artwork, the Warp Options dialog box, and the new envelope*

restrict the shape of an envelope in any way.) Then if you wish to change the shape of the envelope, do so after the conversion. To learn more about working with mesh objects, refer to "Using Mesh Objects" and "Modifying a Mesh Object" in Chapter 9.

To create an envelope with a mesh, follow these steps:

1. Select the artwork or type that Illustrator will convert to the envelope.

2. Choose Object | Envelope Distort | Make with Mesh (CTRL-ALT-M/⌘-OPTION-M). Illustrator opens the Envelope Mesh dialog box.

3. Select Rows and Columns options from the dialog box, and click OK. Illustrator converts the selected artwork or type and applies mesh lines and mesh points to the envelope.

Figure 18-25 shows the creation of an envelope mesh object with a photograph in the JPEG file format. The original photograph is in the upper-left corner of the figure; below that is the Envelope Mesh dialog box. In the upper-right corner of the figure is the new mesh envelope; below that is the distorted mesh envelope.

Changing Envelopes and Their Contents

Regardless of the method by which you create an envelope, Illustrator follows the same procedure: It forms a group of the envelope and the artwork within it. You can edit both the envelope and its artwork, each separately. On the Envelope Distort submenu, Illustrator provides two commands with which you can toggle between editing the contents of an envelope and the envelope itself: Edit Contents (the default) and Edit Envelope.

Editing the Contents of an Envelope

Illustrator provides only one path by which you can modify the contents of an envelope: Select the envelope and choose Object | Envelope Distort | Edit Contents. When you select the command, Illustrator selects the contents (see Figure 18-26). Make changes

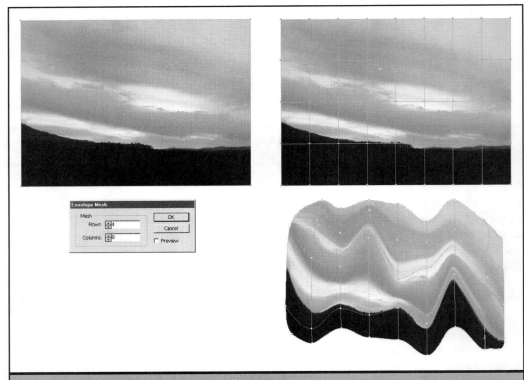

Figure 18-25. *A photograph before and after being changed to an envelope*

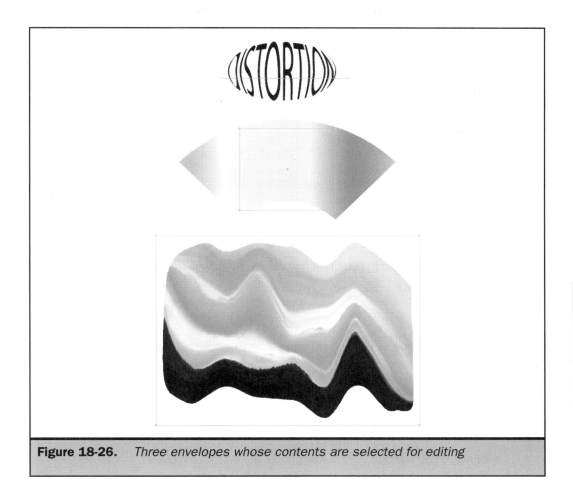

Figure 18-26.   *Three envelopes whose contents are selected for editing*

using the tools and features with which you would edit any Illustrator object. To end the editing session, choose Object | Envelope Distort | Edit Envelope (CTRL-SHIFT-V/⌘-SHIFT-V).

Editing an Envelope

You can edit an envelope in several ways. You can choose Object | Envelope Distort | Edit Envelope (CTRL-SHIFT-V/⌘-SHIFT-V) if you have just finished editing the contents of the envelope; otherwise, you can go ahead and edit without choosing the command—being able to edit the envelope is the default condition. Remember that you cannot edit an envelope if you are editing its contents.

Illustrator provides other ways to edit selected envelopes:

■   You can activate the Direct Selection tool (A), select one or more anchor points in any type envelope, and drag to change the shape of the envelope just as you would another Illustrator path.

- You can use the Mesh tool (U) to edit a mesh object envelope in the same way you would edit any mesh object.

- You can choose Object I Envelope Distort I Reset with Warp (CTRL-ALT-W/ ⌘-OPTION-W) to convert a mesh envelope to a warp envelope or to change the type of warp in a warp envelope.

- You can choose Object I Envelope Distort I Reset with Mesh (CTRL-ALT-M/ ⌘-OPTION-M) to convert a warp envelope to a mesh envelope or to change the mesh lines in a mesh envelope. When you choose Reset with Mesh, Illustrator opens the Reset with Mesh dialog box (see Figure 18-27), which is almost identical to the Envelope Mesh dialog box. The only difference is the Maintain Envelope Shape check box in the Reset with Mesh dialog box. Check that check box (the default) to keep the current envelope shape and edit only the interior mesh lines and mesh points.

Selecting Envelope Options

With the Envelope Options dialog box (see Figure 18-28), you can set the appearance of a raster envelope, a method by which an envelope's shape is preserved, the accuracy with which an artwork fits the envelope, and three types of envelope distortion. To open the Envelope Options dialog box, choose Object I Envelope Distort I Envelope Options. The options in the Envelope Options dialog box are as follows:

- Check the Anti-Alias check box (the default) to smooth pixels as much as possible when the shape of the envelope produces a jagged look.

- From the Preserve Shape Using radio buttons, specify the method Illustrator will use to preserve the shape of a raster graphic. Either click Clipping Mask (the default) to create a clipping mask, or click Transparency to set an *alpha channel* (which is a set of bits that controls the color or masking of the other bits in a pixel).

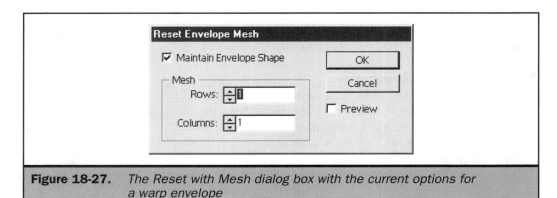

Figure 18-27. *The Reset with Mesh dialog box with the current options for a warp envelope*

- With the Fidelity slider or text box, slide it or type a value with which Illustrator adjusts the artwork to the borders of the envelope. Valid values range from 0 (a relatively loose fit) to 100 (a tight fit); the default is 50. If you choose high fidelity, Illustrator might take a longer time to redraw the envelope and its contents when you edit one or the other.

- Check the Distort Appearance check box (the default) to distort the appearance of the artwork within the envelope as well as its structure.

- Check the Distort Linear Gradients check box to distort an artwork's linear gradient fill as well as its structure.

- Check the Distort Pattern Fills check box to distort an artwork's patterned fill as well as its structure.

- Check the Preview check box to preview the changes to the selected envelope and contents before you make a permanent change by clicking OK.

Reverting an Envelope

When you revert an envelope, you return it to its original state or convert it to an object with the envelope's shape. Choose the Release command to reverse the envelope; choose the Expand command to remove the envelope but keep the object's new shape.

If you choose Object | Envelope Distort | Release, you release the envelope and its contents. The envelope and artwork return to their conditions before the envelope was

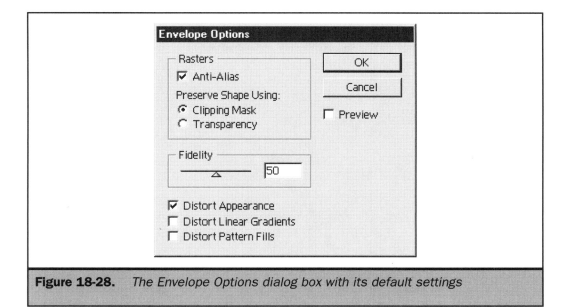

Figure 18-28.   *The Envelope Options dialog box with its default settings*

created. If you release an envelope that you created from an object or a warp, the result is the two original objects; the object that became the envelope is above the artwork in stacking order. If you release a mesh envelope, the result is the original object and the mesh; the mesh is on top of the artwork.

If you choose Object | Envelope Distort | Expand, Illustrator removes the envelope and expands the artwork, keeping it in its newly distorted shape.

Remember that you can undo the most recent action by choosing Edit | Undo (CTRL-Z/⌘-Z).

The Complete Reference

Adobe Illustrator 10

Part IV

Outside Illustrator

Chapter 19

Optimizing and Saving Illustrator Images for the Web

Graphics for the Web open several doors that we haven't completely explored in prior chapters. As you know, most images created for the Web are raster graphics, which are composed of pixels. You already know that Illustrator images are vector graphics by default. You already have compared vector and raster graphics in "Vector Graphics Versus Raster Graphics" in Chapter 2, learned how to push a raster image into the background in "Dimming a Raster Image" in Chapter 14, and converted vector images to raster images in "Changing from Vector to Raster" in Chapter 16.

Illustrator provides several features that produce effective, attractive web graphics and lay out eye-catching web pages. Perhaps the most important is the Save for Web dialog box, which is the largest and probably most complex dialog box Illustrator offers. With the Save for Web dialog box, you can optimize your Web graphics, use a special palettes that are "glued" to the dialog box, and save your Illustrator-based vector and raster artworks using several file types that work well for raster images to be posted on the Web. For a complete list of raster file formats supported by Illustrator, refer to Table 14-1, "Raster Files Supported by Illustrator," in Chapter 14.

In this chapter you'll learn how to use Illustrator to save your artwork as raster illustrations for use on the Web. You'll also find out about the ins and outs of the complex Save for Web dialog box and discover the differences and similarities of files types used for web-based graphics.

What Can Illustrator Do for Web Graphics?

When you create artwork for process printing, you start with attractive images and work from there; you'll have to plan for print production. For example, you'll have to decide on the best combination of process and spot colors, select from a variety of papers, determine the print process, and so on.

When you create artwork for the Web, you'll have to answer a new set of questions: What are the best colors to use? How can I speed up loading time? What file format is best for the planned image? As you will learn, these three questions do not stand alone: The answer to each question usually has an effect on your answers to the other two.

Selecting Colors

In the "Introducing Illustrator Color Models" section in Chapter 2, you learned about the color systems (CMYK, RGB, Web-Safe RGB, HSB, and Grayscale) Illustrator supports; by default, Illustrator supports CMYK. However, when you create images for web pages, your only color choices are RGB or Web-Safe RGB. Remember that Web-safe RGB is a version of RGB created to recognize the lack of unified RGB standards in the three main operating systems: Windows, Macintosh, and UNIX. For example, GIF, a common web graphical file type, supports 256 RGB colors; but the Windows, Macintosh, and UNIX operating systems support 216 RGB colors in common.

If you are using a relatively new computer, you might not even have to stick with the 216 Web-safe colors, which are the best choice for 8-bit color graphics. Now that most computer systems support 24-bit and 32-bit color graphics, RGB probably is the best selection.

To set the color mode for a document to Web-Safe RGB, follow these steps:

1. Choose File | Document Color Mode | RGB Color.
2. If the Color palette is not already in the illustration window, choose Window | Color (F6).
3. From the palette's menu, choose the Web Safe RGB command.

  The swatches libraries discussed in the "Selecting a Swatches Library" section in Chapter 7 include a library of Web safe color swatches. To open that library, choose Window | Swatch Libraries | Web.

Loading Images Quickly

The first few seconds of a user's visit to a web site affects his or her positive or negative feelings about that site. For example, if a site's graphics take a long time to load, some users will give up and move on to another site. Therefore, loading speed is an important factor in building attractive and efficient web sites. Some factors that contribute to speedy or slow loading speeds are file size and file type. Later in this chapter, you'll learn how to use the Save for Web dialog box to optimize files you have created for the Web.

  When you decrease the number of colors in an image, you reduce the file size and the time it takes for the image to load on a user's computer screen.

Choosing a File Type

Illustrator's Save for Web dialog box enables you to save images in several file types: GIF, JPEG, PNG-8, PNG-24, SWF, and SVG. The file type that you choose determines the look of an image, the size of the file, and the time that a user has to wait for an image to appear onscreen.

In the early days of the Web, most graphics were in the raster formats: GIF (Graphics Interchange Format) and JPEG (developed by the Joint Photographic Experts Group). Now many browsers support additional file types: PNG, which is a raster format, and SWF and SVG, which are vector types.

GIF

One of the most popular file formats for the Web, GIF is an 8-bit raster file format created by CompuServe, the online service. Because GIF files use few colors (256 and fewer), they are small and load quickly. The GIF format enables you to specify one color that will become transparent; so if you use the transparent color at or near the border of an image, the result is an irregularly shaped object. You can load a GIF image in stages (that is, *interlace* a file), so that visitors to your web site don't have to stare at a blank space onscreen while they wait for a complete image to load at once. Use GIF for line art and drawn illustrations.

 GIF files use the Lempel-Zif-Welch (LZW), a lossless (that is, data is not lost when a file is saved) data compression method. Unisys, which owns the patent for LZW, sometimes charges a license fee for its use.

JPEG

The other popular file format for the Web, JPEG is a 24-bit raster file format that is excellent for photographs and other continuous tone images. The JPEG format enables you to use as many as 16,777,216 different colors in an image. JPEG files compress effectively without losing much image quality—if you save from the original each time you edit the file. However, whenever you save a JPEG file, the saving process adds *artifacts* (superfluous dots, patterns, and bands), which reduce the quality of the image.

PNG-8 and PNG-24

According to the World Wide Web Consortium (W3C), "PNG (Portable Network Graphics) is an extensible file format for the lossless, portable, well-compressed storage of raster images. PNG provides a patent-free replacement for GIF and can also replace many common uses of TIFF. Indexed color, grayscale, and Truecolor images are supported, plus an optional alpha channel. Sample depths range from 1 to 16 bits."

Note *In GIF89a files, transparency for a particular pixel is either on or off, a state known as binary transparency. For more advanced files, you can set variable transparency: A pixel can vary from totally opaque to completely transparent. Variable transparency uses the alpha channel to determine the remaining channels in an image. According to the Microsoft Press Computer Dictionary, Third Edition, an alpha channel is "the high-order 8 bits of a 32-bit graphics pixel used to manipulate the remaining 24 bits for purposes of coloring or masking."*

PNG-8 is an 8-bit raster file format, so it supports up to 256 colors—just like GIF. PNG-8 also supports transparency. Unlike GIF, PNG supports Truecolor and grayscale images.

PNG-24 is similar to JPEG in that it is a 24-bit raster file format used primarily for photographs. However, PNG-24 supports transparency—unlike JPEG. Note that GIF and JPEG are still supported by more Web browsers than the PNG formats.

SVG and SWF

SVG and SWF are both vector formats: They describe an image by using mathematical calculations to determine the location, span, and course of straight or curved paths. SVG uses the XML markup language to define shapes, and SWF supports some XML features. You can use both file types to create effects, interact with users, produce animations, and add sound to Web pages. Scalable Vector Graphics (SVG) is an official standard of the World Wide Web Consortium (W3C); Shockwave Flash (SWF) has been developed by Macromedia, Inc. SVG and SWF files are usually smaller than GIF, JPEG, and PNG files.

When you use symbols in an Illustrator document that is saved as an SWF file, Illustrator saves one symbol instance, thereby reducing the size of the file. To learn more about using symbols, refer to "Using Symbols" in Chapter 18.

Figure 19-1 shows versions of a photograph in the file formats supported by Illustrator. In the top row, from left to right, are GIF, JPEG, and SVG versions. In the bottom row, from left to right, are PNG-8, PNG-24, and SWF images.

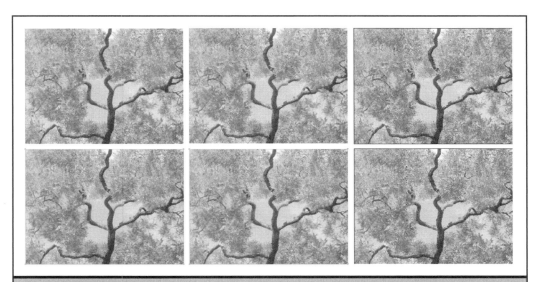

Figure 19-1.   *Six versions of a photograph in each of the Illustrator-supported web file types*

OUTSIDE ILLUSTRATOR

Touring the Save for Web Dialog Box

The gigantic and complex Save for Web dialog box (see Figure 19-2) enables you to perform a variety of actions on artwork that you will use on web pages. With the dialog box, you can *optimize* (that is, make web images both quick to load and high in quality) the artwork for the Web and preview it on a single page, two side-by-side pages, or four pages. To open the dialog box, choose File | Save for Web (CTRL-ALT-SHIFT-S/⌘-OPTION-SHIFT-S).

The options in the dialog box are as follows:

- Click the Hand tool (H) (or press SPACEBAR) to move the image around the preview window.

- Click the Slice Select tool (K), the default, to select a slice on a web page. When you *slice* components of a web page, you can control the behavior of individual components. You'll learn more about slicing images in the "Using Slices" section in Chapter 20.

- Click the Zoom tool (Z) to zoom the image in the preview window. You also can choose a zoom level from the pop-up menu in the lower-left corner of the dialog box.

- Click the Eyedropper tool (I) to select a color from the image in the preview window. When you click the Eyedropper, Illustrator selects the color in the Color Table palette.

- Click the Original tab to view the image as it looked originally.

- Click the Optimized tab (the default) to view the image as it will appear optimized with the default optimization settings for the chosen file type.

- Click the 2-Up tab to view two versions of the image on two side-by-side pages (for example, to compare the images with different optimization settings).

- Click the 4-Up tab to view four versions of the image on two sets of two side-by-side pages.

- Illustrator calls the bottom of the dialog box the *annotation area*. If you click the Original tab to view the original version of the image, the annotation area shows the filename and file size. If you click the Optimized tab, the annotation area reveals different information—depending on the selected file type. For more information about the annotation area, refer to the "Viewing the Annotation Area," later in this chapter.

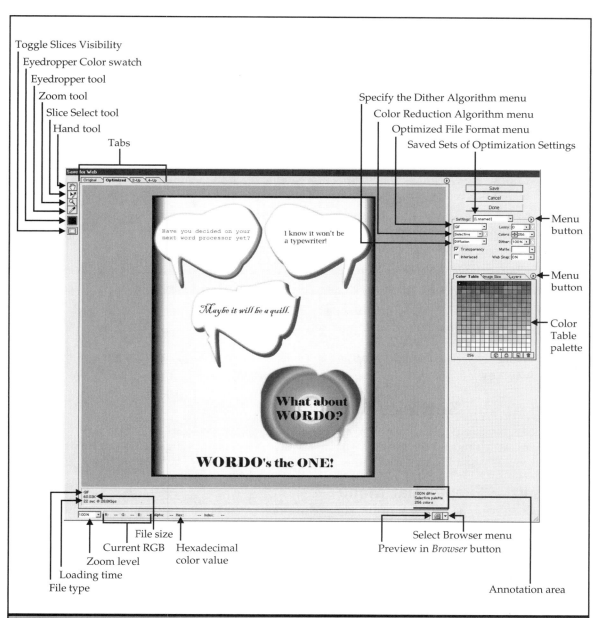

Figure 19-2. *The Save for Web dialog box with its default settings*

Summarizing the Settings Menu

The Save for Web dialog box includes a menu with which you can optimize, edit, delete, and customize output settings. To open the Settings menu, click the menu button. The commands on the menu are as follows:

- Choose the Save Settings command to save the optimization settings that you have selected in the Settings section of the Save for Web dialog box.
- Choose the Delete Settings command to delete the selected named or predefined optimization settings.
- Choose the Optimize to File Size command to open the Optimize to File Size dialog box to apply optimization settings and create a file of a desired size.
- Choose the Repopulate Views command to refresh the views in 4-Up mode to show the current optimization settings.
- Choose the Link Slices command to link selected slices.
- Choose the Unlink Slice command to remove the link between two or more slices.
- Choose the Unlink All Slices command to unlink all linked slices.
- Choose Edit Output Settings to open the Output Settings dialog box with which you can modify the current output settings.

 For more information about slices and how to use them, refer to "Using Slices" in Chapter 20.

Looking at the Settings Section

The Settings section of the Save for Web dialog box enables you to select or specify optimization settings for the file that you are about to save. The Settings section includes some options for all file types and other options that are unique to certain file types.

Optimized File Format Menu

To choose a file type and, as a result, change the look of the Settings section, select a file type from the Optimized File Format drop-down menu. As you know, you can choose from the following file types: GIF, JPEG, PNG-8, PNG-24, SWF, and SVG.

Saved Sets of Optimization Settings Menu

For every web file format that Illustrator supports, the Save for Web dialog box includes the Saved Sets of Optimization Settings drop-down menu with which you can select from named optimization settings for the web file type to which you will save the image. Listed are the following named, predefined settings: GIF 128 Dithered, GIF 128 No Dither, GIF 32 Dithered, GIF 32 No Dither, GIF 64 Dithered, GIF 64 No Dither, GIF iMODE 1-bit,

GIF iMODE 256, GIF Web Palette, JPEG High, JPEG Low, JPEG Medium, PNG-24, and PNG-8 128 Dithered.

Following is an explanation of some of the terms used in the named settings:

■ In the named settings the numbers 128, 32, and 64 represent the number of colors in the Color Table palette.

■ Dithered and No Dither refer to *dithering*, a method by which a graphics application blends adjacent pixels of different colors to correct the appearance of jagged borders. Dithered indicates that Illustrator has dithered the image; No Dither specifies that Illustrator has not dithered the image.

■ iMODE is a form of GIF for handheld devices. iMODE uses c-HTML, which is a compact version of HTML.

The [Unnamed] setting is the default. Before you select a named optimization setting or when you manually change optimization options for a particular image, Illustrator automatically chooses [Unnamed].

GIF and PNG-8 Optimization Settings

When you choose GIF or PNG-8 settings from the Optimized File Format drop-down menu, you can choose from the following options in the Settings section:

■ With the Lossy text box/slider (for GIF images only), you set a value for lossy compression, a method by which a file is compressed (thereby reducing the size of the file) and loses some data (thereby reducing quality) as you save it. When you successfully apply lossy compression, you have balanced compression against the reduction in quality. Valid values range from 0% (the default) to 100%. According to the Illustrator User Guide, "You can often apply a Lossy value of 5 to 10, and sometimes up to 50, without degrading the image. File size can often be reduced 5% to 40% using the Lossy option." Note that the Lossy text box/slider is not available when you check the Interlaced check box or select a Noise or Pattern from the Specify the Dither algorithm drop-down list box.

■ From the Color Reduction Algorithm drop-down menu, select the way with which Illustrator sets the number of colors in the color table. You can choose from the following default methods:

  ■ Perceptual, which is programmed to select colors that are most pleasing to the eye and closest to those in the original image.

  ■ Selective (the default), which combines Perceptual colors and many other colors, including Web-safe colors.

  ■ Adaptive, which reviews the colors in the original image and chooses the most common colors.

- Web, which uses the 216-color Web palette and which is the safest selection for viewing with any browser. The primary advantage of using this color table is greater control over automatic dithering by a browser application. The main disadvantage is the possibility of a larger color palette, resulting in increased file size. If you choose Web, Illustrator changes the default in the Colors list box/text box to Auto.

- Custom, which freezes the current Perceptual, Select, or Adaptive color table. As you edit the image, Illustrator does not increase or decrease the number of colors in the color table.

- Black & White, which converts the colors in the image and the color table to two—black and white.

- Grayscale, which converts the colors in the image and the color table to grayscale and the color table to varying shades of gray.

- Mac OS, which converts the colors in the image to those compatible with the Macintosh color palette.

- Windows, which converts the colors in the image to those compatible with the Macintosh color palette.

After you have chosen from the Color Reduction menu, you can select the maximum number of colors in the Colors list box/text box.

- If the image is associated with an alpha channel, click the Channel button to set a quality range based on the alpha channel.

- Colors list box/text box/drop-down menu works in tandem with the Color Reduction Algorithm drop-down menu. Once you have selected a color reduction method from the menu, you can type or select the maximum number of colors in the image from the Colors list box/text box/drop-down menu. Note that if you reduce the number of colors in an image, you also reduce the size of the file. If you have chosen the Web color reduction method, you can select Auto, which enables Illustrator to choose the number of colors. Note that the color table can contain only the number of colors in the current version of the image, so if you have selected a greater number of colors from the Colors list box/text box/drop-down menu, Illustrator disregards your choice.

- The Specify the Dither Algorithm drop-down menu enables you to select a method by which Illustrator instructs a browser to dither the image onscreen. You can choose from the following dithering methods:

  - No Dither results in no dithering.

  - Diffusion (the default) spreads dithering across contiguous pixels using a subtle pattern.

  - Pattern dithers pixels by applying a rectangular pattern.

  - Noise diffuses dithering without using a subtle pattern.

- The Dither text box/slider works in tandem with the Dither algorithm drop-down menu. After you have chosen a dither method, set the percentage of dithering with the Dither text box/slider. The Dither text box/slider is available only if you choose Diffusion from the Dither algorithm drop-down menu. To reduce file size, set a small percentage of dithering. If an image is composed of very few colors, you might not need to set any dithering. On the other hand, a photograph or other continuous-tone color might require dithering to ensure that the colors of the saved image blend. Valid values range from 0% (no dithering) to 100% (a great deal of dithering). The default is 100%.

- Check the Transparency check box in conjunction with the Matte color swatch/ drop-down menu to set the level of variable transparency for completely or partially transparent pixels. A checked check box is the default. Illustrator provides the following choices for blending or filling transparent pixels using the Transparency check box and the Matte color swatch/drop-down menu:

  - To keep completely transparent pixels transparent and blend partially transparent pixels with a matte color, check the Transparency check box and select a matte color from the Matte color swatch/drop-down menu.

  - To convert all pixels that are set to 51% or greater transparency to completely transparent and convert all pixels that are set to 50% or less transparency to completely opaque, check the Transparency check box and choose None from the Matte drop-down menu.

  - To fill completely transparent pixels and blend partially transparent pixels with a matte color, remove the check mark from the Transparency check box and select a matte color from the Matte color swatch/drop-down menu.

- The Matte color swatch/drop-down menu works in tandem with the Transparency check box to select a matte color to blend with variable transparent pixels (that is, the Transparency check box is checked) or a matte color to fill variable transparent pixels (that is, the Transparency check box is unchecked). You can use two methods to choose a matte color: Click the color swatch to open the Color Picker from which you can select a matte color, or open the drop-down menu to choose a command.

  - Choose None to indicate that you wish to keep the current levels of transparency and not select a matte color.

  - Choose Eyedropper Color to use the current Eyedropper color, which is displayed in the Eyedropper Color swatch in the upper-left corner of the Save for Web dialog box.

  - Choose White (the default) to set the matte color to white.

  - Choose Black to set the matte color to black.

  - Choose Other to open the Color Picker from which you can select a matte color.

- Check the Interlaced check box to produce a version of the image for interlacing, loading a low-resolution version of the image in stages. Note that an interlaced file is larger than one that is not interlaced. An unchecked check box is the default.

- With the Web Snap text box/slider, you specify the number of colors in the current image that are shifted to Web-safe colors. Valid values range from 0% (no colors shifted) to 100% (all colors shifted). The default is 0%.

Note   *To learn about using the Color Picker, refer to the "Using the Color Picker" section in Chapter 7.*

JPEG Optimization Settings

When you choose JPEG settings (see Figure 19-3) from the Optimized File Format drop-down menu, Illustrator offers several options for optimizing files that will be saved using the JPEG file type.

You can choose from the following options in the JPEG Settings section:

- Check the Optimized check box to optimize the look of a JPEG image and reduce the file size, too. Note that some browsers do not support Optimized JPEGs.

- From the Compression Quality drop-down menu, choose the level of compression: Low, Medium, High (the default), or Maximum. If you choose High or Maximum, Illustrator preserves the quality of the image, but the size of the file increases. Choosing Low or Medium reduces the quality level but reduces the size of the file.

- The Quality text box/slider and the Compression Quality drop-down menu work in tandem. You can set a compression quality percentage value by using the Quality text box/slider. Valid values range from 0% (Low) to 100% (Maximum). Note that Low Quality ranges from 0% to 29%, Medium ranges from 30% to 59%, High ranges from 60% (the default) to 79%, and Maximum ranges from 80% to 100%.

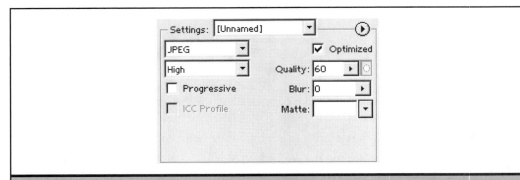

Figure 19-3.   *The Settings section for JPEG optimization with the default settings*

- If the image is associated with an alpha channel, click the Channel button to set a quality range based on the alpha channel.

- When you check the Progressive check box, a JPEG image loads in stages at a low resolution. When loading is complete, users can see the image at its normal high resolution. Progressive loading works only for images in the Optimized JPEG format and normally requires more RAM. Note that some browsers do not support Progressive JPEGs.

- With the Blur text box/slider, set the level of blur (which is analogous to the application of a Gaussian Blur filter). When you blur an image, you also apply additional compression, thereby reducing the file size. Valid values range from 0 (the default) to 2. Adobe recommends a value of 0.1 to 0.5.

- Check the ICC Profile check box to ensure that Illustrator applies the ICC profile to the image—if you have already saved the image in Illustrator with an ICC profile. The International Color Consortium (ICC) is an industry group that standardizes color management profiles.

- From the Matte color swatch/drop-down menu, select a matte color to fill completely transparent pixels or blend variable semitransparent pixels. You can use two methods to choose a matte color: Click the color swatch to open the Color Picker from which you can select a matte color, or open the drop-down menu to choose a command.

  - Choose None to indicate that you wish to keep the current levels of transparency and not select a matte color.

  - Choose Eyedropper Color to use the current Eyedropper color, which is displayed in the Eyedropper Color swatch in the upper-left corner of the Save for Web dialog box.

  - Choose White (the default) to set the matte color to white.

  - Choose Black to set the matte color to black.

  - Choose Other to open the Color Picker from which you can select a matte color.

To learn about using the Color Picker, refer to the "Using the Color Picker" section in Chapter 7.

PNG-24 Optimization Settings

When you choose PNG-24 settings (see Figure 19-4) from the Optimized File Format drop-down menu, Illustrator offers three options for optimizing files that will be saved using the PNG-24 file type.

OUTSIDE ILLUSTRATOR

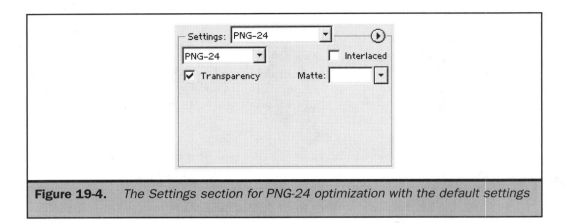

Figure 19-4. *The Settings section for PNG-24 optimization with the default settings*

You can choose from the following options in the PNG-24 Settings section:

■ Check the Interlaced check box to produce a version of the image for interlacing, loading a low-resolution version of the image in stages. Note that an interlaced file is larger than one that is not interlaced. An unchecked check box is the default.

■ Check the Transparency check box in conjunction with the Matte color swatch/drop-down menu to set the level of variable transparency for completely or partially transparent pixels. A checked check box is the default. Illustrator provides the following choices for blending or filling transparent pixels using the Transparency check box and the Matte color swatch/drop-down menu:

■ To keep completely transparent pixels transparent and blend partially transparent pixels with a matte color, check the Transparency check box and select a matte color from the Matte color swatch/drop-down menu.

■ To convert all pixels that are set to 51% or greater transparency to completely transparent and convert all pixels that are set to 50% or less transparency to completely opaque, check the Transparency check box and choose None from the Matte drop-down menu.

■ To fill completely transparent pixels and blend partially transparent pixels with a matte color, remove the check mark from the Transparency check box and select a matte color from the Matte color swatch/drop-down menu.

■ The Matte color swatch/drop-down menu works in tandem with the Transparency check box to select a matte color to blend with variable transparent pixels (that is, the Transparency check box is checked) or a matte color to fill variable transparent pixels (that is, the Transparency check box is unchecked). You can use two methods to choose a matte color: Click the color swatch to open the Color Picker from which you can select a matte color, or open the drop-down menu to choose a command.

- Choose None to save as many as 256 levels of transparency for the image and not select a matte color.

- Choose Eyedropper Color to use the current Eyedropper color, which is displayed in the Eyedropper Color swatch in the upper-left corner of the Save for Web dialog box.

- Choose White (the default) to set the matte color to white.

- Choose Black to set the matte color to black.

- Choose Other to open the Color Picker from which you can select a matte color.

SWF Optimization Settings

When you choose SWF settings (see Figure 19-5) from the Optimized File Format drop-down menu, Illustrator offers several options for optimizing files that will be saved using the SWF file type.

You can choose from the following options in the SWF Settings section:

- Check the Read Only check box to save the SWF image as a read-only file, which prevents users from editing the file.

- From the Type of Export drop-down menu, choose the method by which Illustrator exports the file:

  - Choose AI File to SWF File (the default) to export the entire image to a single SWF frame and preserve all the clipping masks in the image.

  - Choose Layers to SWF Frames to export each layer to a separate SWF frame. Select this option if you plan to create an animation from the file.

- With the Curve Quality text box/slider, set the quality of Bézier curves in the image. Valid values range from 0 (the lowest curve quality and a smaller file size) to 10 (the highest curve size and a larger file size). The default setting is 7.

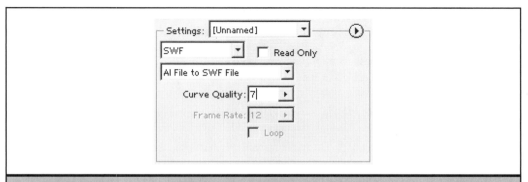

Figure 19-5.   *The Settings section for SWF optimization with the default settings*

■ With the Frame Rate text box/slider, set the rate at which the Macromedia Flash viewer plays this file as an animation. This option is available only if you choose Layers to SWF Frames from the Type of Export drop-down menu.

■ Check the Loop check box to have the Macromedia Flash viewer play the animation without end. If you remove the check mark from the check box, the Macromedia Flash viewer plays the animation once. This option is available only if you choose Layers to SWF Frames from the Type of Export drop-down menu.

SVG Optimization Settings

When you choose SVG settings (see Figure 19-6) from the Optimized File Format drop-down menu, Illustrator offers several options for optimizing files that will be saved using the SVG file type.

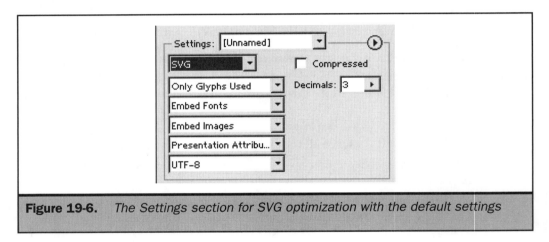

Figure 19-6. *The Settings section for SVG optimization with the default settings*

You can choose from the following options in the SWF Settings section:
In the Settings section for SVG files, you can choose from the following options:

■ Check the Compressed check box to save the file as a Compressed SVG (SVGZ) file. Note that not all browsers support SVGZ files.

- From the Font Subsetting drop-down menu, specify the fonts that are embedded or linked in the SVG file. Note that a *glyph* is the picture of an individual letter, digit, or symbol in a character set or font.
    - Choose None (Use System Fonts) to use the fonts that are installed on the users' computer systems.
    - Choose Only Glyphs Used (the default) to limit the glyphs to those embedded in the current image.
    - Choose Common English to be able to use all English-language characters.
    - Choose Common English & Glyphs Used to be able to use all English-language characters and the glyphs in the current image.
    - Choose Command Roman to use all Roman characters (that is, the characters used in all Romantic languages).
    - Choose Common Roman & Glyphs Used to use all Roman glyphs and the glyphs in the current image.
    - Choose All Glyphs to use all the available glyphs.
- From the Font Location drop-down menu, specify the location of fonts that are embedded or linked in the file. If you choose Embed Fonts (the default), the fonts are always available, regardless of their current location. If you choose Link Fonts, the fonts might not always be available, but you could reduce file size—if several SVG files use the same fonts.

- From the Image Location drop-down menu, specify the location of images that are embedded or linked in the file. If you choose Embed Images (the default), the images are always available, regardless of their current location. If you choose Link Images, they might not always be available, but you could reduce file size.
- From the CSS Properties drop-down menu, choose the method with which Illustrator saves Cascading Style Sheet (CSS) attributes in the XML code that describes the SVG file. Note that the differences are subtle. Figure 19-7 illustrates the SVG resulting from saving a small rectangle with a red fill and black stroke using the four CSS Properties options.

```
<?xml version="1.0" encoding="utf-8"?>
<!-- Generator: Adobe Illustrator 10.0, SVG Export Plug-In . SVG
Version: 3.0.0 Build 76)  -->
<!DOCTYPE svg PUBLIC "-//W3C//DTD SVG 1.0//EN"
"http://www.w3.org/TR/2001/REC-SVG-20010904/DTD/svg10.dtd" [
        <!ENTITY ns_flows "http://ns.adobe.com/Flows/1.0/">
        <!ENTITY ns_extend "http://ns.adobe.com/Extensibility/1.0/">
        <!ENTITY ns_ai "http://ns.adobe.com/AdobeIllustrator/10.0/">
        <!ENTITY ns_svg "http://www.w3.org/2000/svg">
        <!ENTITY ns_xlink "http://www.w3.org/1999/xlink">
]>
<svg  xmlns:x="&ns_extend;" xmlns:i="&ns_ai;"
xmlns:graph="&ns_graphs;"
        xmlns="&ns_svg;" xmlns:xlink="&ns_xlink;"
xmlns:a="http://ns.adobe.com/AdobeSVGViewerExtensions/3.0/"
width="148" height="98"
        viewBox="0.5 -0.5 148 98" overflow="visible" enable-
background="new 0.5 -0.5 148 98" xml:space="preserve">
        <g id="Layer_1_3_">
            <path fill="#FF3300" stroke="#000000"
d="M147.5,97.5H0.5v-97h147V97.5z"/>
        </g>
</svg>
```

Figure 19-7. *An SVG document written in XML for a small rectangle*

■ Choose Presentation Attributes (the default) to have Illustrator place attributes within a <path> tag. For example, when saving a small red rectangle with a black stroke, the line in the XML document contains fill, stroke, their colors, and other attributes. The code looks something like this:

```
<path fill="#FF3300" stroke="#000000"
    d="M147.5,97.5H0.5v-97h147V97.5z"/>
```

■ Choose Style Attributes for Illustrator to insert the CSS code as attributes within a <style> start tag immediately after the path element. According to the Illustrator User Guide, you should "choose this method if the SVG code will be used in transformations; for example, transformations using Extensible Stylesheet Language Transformation (XSLT)." For our sample rectangle, the <path> tag includes a style tag for the fill and stroke and a d attribute. The code looks something like this:

```
<path style="fill:#FF3300;stroke:#000000;"
    d="M147.5,97.5H0.5v-97h147V97.5z"/>
```

■ Choose Entity References for Illustrator to use entity references to set a style. The sample rectangle includes a <path> tag that encloses a style tag with an entity reference. The code looks something like this:

```
<path style="&st0;"
   d="M147.5,97.5H0.5v-97h147V97.5z"/>
```

■ Choose Style Element for Illustrator to use a style element that encloses a nested Cascading Style Sheet. The code looks something like this:

```
<path class="st0"
   d="M147.5,97.5H0.5v-97h147V97.5z"/>
```

■ From the Encoding Specifies the Format for Writing Characters drop-down menu, choose the encoding (that is, character set) for the SVG document. You can choose ISO 8859-1 (ASCII), which is the ISO Latin-1 numeric encoding; UTF-8, the Unicode Transformation Format, which is the 8-bit default character set for XML; or UTF-16, which is the alternate 16-bit character set. Note that the only choice that preserves file metadata is UTF-8.

■ With the Decimals text box/slider, set the decimal places for the vector data. If you choose a high number of decimal places, the SVG file will be larger than one with a low number of decimal places. Valid values range from one to seven decimal places. The default is three decimal places.

Viewing the Annotation Area

The annotation area in the bottom of the Save for Web dialog box displays optimization attributes of the image to be optimized and saved. On the left side of the annotation area are three lines that display the selected file type, the file size, and the estimated loading time. The file type, which varies depending on the file type selection in the Settings section of the dialog box, can be GIF (the default), JPEG, PNG-8, PNG-24, SWF, and SVG.

By default, the estimated time for file loading for an Internet connection (such as a modem) is 28.8 kilobits per second. If you right-click anywhere within the annotation area, Illustrator opens a menu from which you can select a loading rate and zoom level. The loading rates range from 9.6 kilobits per second to 2 megabits per second; the default is 28.8 kilobits per second. The zoom level ranges from 12.5% to 1,600%. You also can choose Fit on Screen. (Note that the normal zoom levels for Illustrator range from 1.3% to 6,400% and Fit on Screen.)

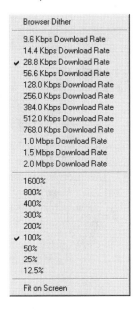

The content of the bottom-right corner varies depending on the selected file type and the values in the Settings section of the dialog box:

- For GIF and PNG-8 files are three lines that display the dithering percentage from the Dither text box/slider, the current color table palette from the Color Reduction Algorithm drop-down menu, and the number of colors for the file type from the Color Table palette.

- For JPEG files, the display is one line, the current value displayed in the Quality text box/slider.

- Illustrator does not display any information about PNG-24 files.

- For SWF files, the display is one line (the value in the Curve Quality text box/slider).

- For SVG files, the display is one line (the number of decimal places shown in the Decimals text box/slider).

Viewing Images in the Save for Web Dialog Box

The Save for Web dialog box enables you to view the file you are about to save in four ways: its original version, an optimized version, 2-Up (the original image and an optimized version of the image), and 4-Up (the original image in the upper-left corner and three other versions that you can optimize). If you view the file in 2-Up or 4-Up, you can compare the different versions for file type, file size, and loading time. Click an image to optimize a particular version in 2-Up or 4-Up (see Figure 19-8). Illustrator places a bold border around the selected image.

Viewing Graphics with a Browser

Before you save an optimized image, you can view the image in a window from your default browser. To do so, just click the Preview in *Browser* button at the bottom of the Save for Web dialog box. Illustrator shows the image at the top of the browser window and its HTML code at the bottom of the window.

When you test images for the Web, it's a good idea to view them using as many browser applications as you can. To the right of the Preview in *Browser* button is the

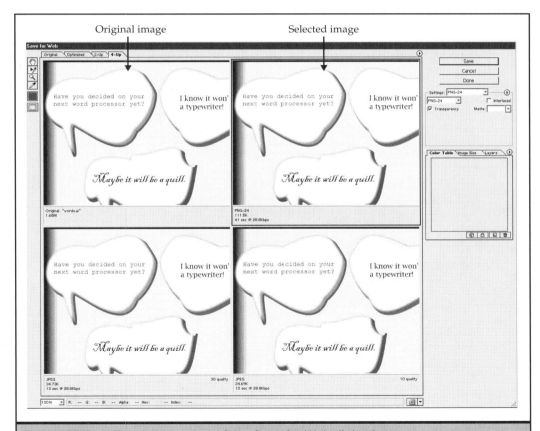

Figure 19-8.   *The 4-Up version of the Save for Web dialog box*

OUTSIDE ILLUSTRATOR

Select Browser Menu button. To select another browser, click the Select Browser Menu button. When you choose Other, Illustrator opens the Preview in Other Browser dialog box with which you can find another browser application that is already installed on your computer system.

Exploring the Color Table Palette

With the Color Table palette (see Figure 19-9), which is the default palette in the Save for Web dialog box, you can control colors for GIF and PNG-8 files. For example, you can ensure that colors are safe for use on the Web, add a color, select or deselect colors, sort the colors in three ways, load another color table, save the current color table, lock a color so that it can't be deleted, or delete an unlocked color.

The Color Table palette contains many elements, each of which has a specific meaning and with which you can control the use of color in a file:

- Click the Web Shift button to set one or more selected colors to the closest Web-safe colors. The counterpart command on the palette's menu is Web Shift/Unshift Selected Colors.

- Click the Lock Selected Colors button to block the selected color from being deleted or dithered. The counterpart command on the palette's menu is Lock/Unlock Selected Colors.

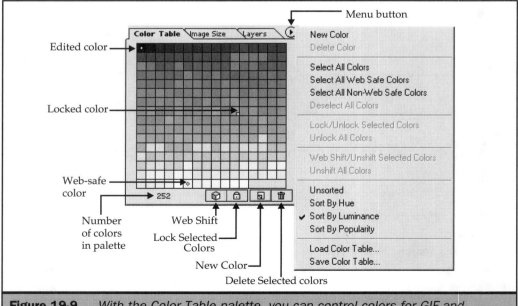

Figure 19-9. *With the Color Table palette, you can control colors for GIF and PNG-8 images.*

- Click the Color button to add the color from the Eyedropper Color swatch to the palette. The counterpart command on the palette's menu is New Color.

- Click the Deletes Selected Colors button to remove one or more selected colors from the palette. The counterpart command on the palette's menu is Delete Color.

- Click the menu button to open the Color Table palette's menu.

- The large area in the center of the palette displays all the colors in the file to be saved for use on the Web.

To open the palette's menu, click the menu button. Commands on the menu are as follows:

- The New Color command adds the color from the Eyedropper box to the palette. The counterpart button at the bottom of the palette is New Color.

- The Delete Color command removes one or more selected colors from the palette. The counterpart button at the bottom of the palette is Deletes Selected Colors.

- The Select All Colors command selects every color in the palette.

- The Select All Web Safe Colors command selects all the Web-safe colors in the palette. If the palette does not contain any Web-safe colors, the command is not available.

- The Select All Non–Web Safe command selects all the colors that are not safe for the Web. If the palette contains only Web-safe colors, the command is not available.

- The Deselect All Colors command deselects all selected colors.

- The Lock/Unlock Selected Colors command blocks the selected color from being deleted or dithered. The counterpart button at the bottom of the palette is Lock Selected Colors.

- The Unlock All Colors command unlocks all locked colors.

- The Web Shift/Unshift Selected Colors command sets one or more selected colors to the closest Web-safe colors. The counterpart button at the bottom of the palette is Web Shift.

- The Unshift All Colors command undoes Web shifting from any colors that have been shifted.

- The Unsorted command removes any sort from the color table.

- The Sort by Hue command sorts the colors in the color table by hue.

- The Sort by Luminance command sorts the colors in the color table by luminance. This is the default sorting command.

- The Sort by Popularity command sorts the colors in the color table by their popularity.

- The Load Color Table command loads a saved color table. When you load a different table, Illustrator adjusts the colors in the current image to fit the new color table.

- The Save Color Table command saves a color table that you have defined.

Selecting and Deselecting Colors

You can select colors in the image in the Save for Web dialog box and the Color Table palette by using a familiar tool, clicking in the Color Table palette, and choosing a command.

- To select a color in the image, activate the Eyedropper tool (I)—not the one in the toolbox—but the duplicate in the upper-left corner of the Save for Web dialog box. Illustrator changes the color in the Eyedropper box below the Eyedropper tool in the dialog box and encloses the color in the Color Table with a white border.

- To select a color in the Color Table palette, click the color swatch. This action does not highlight the color in the image or change the color in the Eyedropper box.

- To select a contiguous range of colors in the Color Table palette, click a swatch at one end of the range, press and hold down SHIFT, and click the swatch at the other end of the range. Illustrator highlights the selected color swatches.

- To select two or more noncontiguous colors in the Color Table palette, click a swatch, press and hold down CTRL/⌘, and click each color you want to select. As you select each color, Illustrator highlights it.

- To select all Web-safe colors in the Color Table palette, choose the Select All Web Safe Colors command from the palette's menu. If the palette does not contain any Web-safe colors, the command is not available. Note that Illustrator marks all Web-safe colors—regardless of whether they are selected—by placing a white diamond in the center of their swatches.

- To select all but Web-safe colors in the Color Table palette, choose the Select All Non–Web-Safe Colors command from the palette's menu. If the palette contains only Web-safe colors, the command is not available.

- To deselect all selected colors in the Color Table palette, choose the Deselect All Colors command from the palette's menu.

Shifting and Unshifting Colors

As you have learned, the best colors for the Web are Web-safe colors. When you want to save an image that you created with a different color palette, you can shift colors to the Web by using the Color Table palette. The swatch of a Web-safe color contains a small white diamond in its center.

To get ready for shifting colors, you can use the Web Snap text box/slider to change the number of colors that Illustrator can shift. If you choose a high value, Illustrator can change more colors to Web-safe colors. Setting a lower value instructs Illustrator to change fewer colors.

To shift colors to the Web, select one or more colors to be shifted and either click the Web Shift button at the bottom of the Color Table palette or choose the Web Shift/Unshift Selected Colors command from the palette's menu.

To restore the Web-safe colors to their original conditions, click the Web Shift button again, choose the Web Shift/Unshift Selected Colors command from the palette's menu, or choose Unshift All Colors from the menu.

Locking and Unlocking Colors

When you lock a color, you prevent Illustrator from removing it from the Color Table palette and from dithering it. The swatch of a locked color contains a small white square in its lower-right corner.

To lock colors, select one or more colors to be locked and either click the Lock Selected Colors button at the bottom of the Color Table palette or choose the Lock/ Unlock Selected Colors command from the palette's menu.

To unlock locked colors, click the Locks Selected Colors button, choose the Lock/ Unlock Selected Colors command from the palette's menu, or choose the Unlock All Colors command from the menu.

Adding a Color to the Palette

The Color Table palette can contain a maximum 256 colors, including one optional swatch for transparency. If the palette contains fewer than 256 colors, you can add new colors until the palette reaches the 256 maximum. Illustrator enables you to add a new color in one of two ways: You can add a color from the preview image or open the Color Picker and select a color.

Adding a Color from the Preview Image

To add a color from the preview image, follow these steps:

1. Activate the Eyedropper tool (I) in the upper-left corner of the Save for Web dialog box.

2. Click a color in the image preview. Illustrator changes the color of the Eyedropper Color swatch below the Eyedropper tool button.

3. Click the New Color button at the bottom of the palette, or choose the New Color command from the palette's menu. Illustrator adds a locked color swatch to the palette.

Adding a Color from the Color Picker

To add a color from the Color Picker, follow these steps:

1. Click the Eyedropper Color swatch in the upper-left corner of the Save for Web dialog box.

2. From the Color Picker, choose a color. To learn how to use the Color Picker, refer to the "Using the Color Picker" section in Chapter 7.

3. Click the New Color button at the bottom of the palette, or choose the New Color command from the palette's menu. Illustrator adds a locked color swatch to the palette.

Modifying a Color

When you add a color swatch to the Color Table palette, you can modify it by clicking the Eyedropper Color swatch to open the Color Picker and selecting a new color. If you change a color, Illustrator inserts a plus sign (+) in the center of its swatch and locks the swatch.

Sorting and Unsorting Colors

You can sort the colors in the Color Table palette by hue, luminance, or popularity to customize your view of the palette and sometimes enable you to organize colors for editing. Additionally, you can remove any sorting order completely.

- To sort the colors by hue, choose the Sort by Hue command from the palette's menu. Illustrator sorts the colors with blacks, grays, and whites first and then in red, orange, yellow, green, blue, indigo, and violet rainbow order.

- To sort the colors by luminance, choose the Sort by Luminance command (the default sorting order) from the palette's menu. Illustrator sorts the colors in the color table by brightness—from dark to light.

- To sort the colors by popularity, choose the Sort by Popularity command from the palette's menu.

- To remove the sorting order from the palette, choose the Unsorted command from the palette's menu.

Deleting a Color

Deleting a color is just about the same as deleting anything else in Illustrator. When you delete a color, Illustrator removes its swatch from the Color Table palette and the image. In the image, Illustrator replaces the deleted color with a closely related color from the palette. Illustrator also changes the name in the Color Reduction Algorithm drop-down menu to Custom, thereby eliminating the possibility of using the original color table without explicitly choosing it from the Settings section. Deleting colors reduces the size of the image file, thereby reducing the loading time on the Web page.

To delete a selected color, do one of the following:

■ Click the Deletes Selected Colors button at the bottom of the palette.

■ Drag the swatch to the Deletes Selected Colors button.

■ Choose the Delete Color command from the palette's menu.

Saving a Color Table

After you have customized the colors in the Color Table palette, you can save the new palette, enabling you to use it on other images for the Web. To save a unique color table, choose Save Color Table from the palette's menu. Illustrator opens the Save Color Table dialog box (see Figure 19-10). Type a unique filename in the File Name text box and click the Save button. Illustrator saves the table in the Color Tables folder with an .ACT (Adobe Color Table) extension.

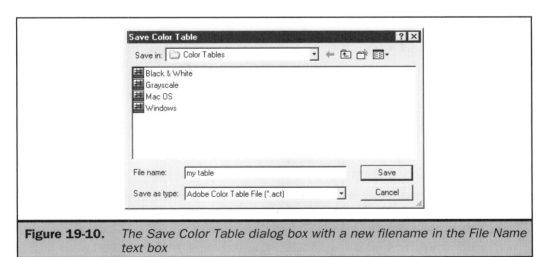

Figure 19-10.   *The Save Color Table dialog box with a new filename in the File Name text box*

Loading a Color Table

You can load a variety of color tables into the Color Table palette to use with images you plan to optimize and save for the Web. You can choose from several color-table formats: Photoshop Color Table File (*.act), Photoshop Swatch File (*.aco), Microsoft Palette File (*.pal), Compuserve GIF (*.gif), All Readable Formats (the default), and All Files (*.*).

To load a color table into the Color Table palette, follow these steps:

1. Choose the Load Color Table command from the palette's menu.

2. When Illustrator opens the Load Color Table dialog box (see Figure 19-11), select a color table and click Open. Illustrator loads the color table into the palette and changes the preview image to match the colors in the new table.

 If you open a GIF file in Illustrator and then open the Save for Web dialog box, Illustrator automatically loads the file's associated color table into the Color Table palette. You can save the custom color table by following the steps in the prior section. You can use the saved color table for other images in the future.

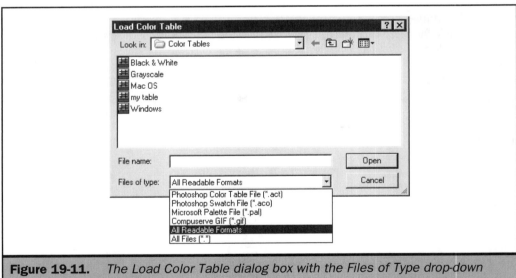

Figure 19-11. *The Load Color Table dialog box with the Files of Type drop-down menu open*

Exploring the Image Size Palette

With the Image Size palette (see Figure 19-12), you can resize the image you will save for the Web. You can change the dimensions of the image by absolute width and height (using the Web standard pixels as the unit of measure), in or out of proportion, or by percentage.

The Image Size palette looks very much like a small dialog box rather than a palette. Rather than containing the usual buttons and menu, the palette displays the current size of the image and contains three text boxes, three check boxes, and one command button:

- In the Width text box, type the new width, in pixels, of the image.

- In the Height text box, type the new height, in pixels, of the image.

- In the Percent text box, type the percentage by which you want to resize the image up or down. Valid values range from 0.01% to 789.47%. The default percent is 100.

- Check the Constrain Proportions check box to keep the image's width and height in proportion. Remove the check from the check box to resize the image without constraint. If you remove the check, Illustrator removes the link icon to the right of the Width and Height text boxes. The default is a checked check box.

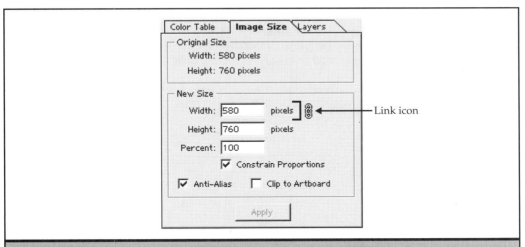

Figure 19-12. *With the Image Size palette, you can resize an image for the Web*

- Check the Anti-Alias check box to remove jagged edges from the resized image. The default is a checked check box.

- Check the Clip to Artboard check box to clip the image to fit its current Illustrator artboard dimensions, which removes all sections outside the borders of the artboard. The default is an unchecked check box.

- Click the Apply button to apply the changes to the image.

Exploring the Layers Palette

With Illustrator's second Layers palette (see Figure 19-13), you can create Cascading Style Sheet layers in the HTML file for the image shown in the Save for Web dialog box. With the options in the Layers palette, you can pinpoint individual layers and create interesting special effects for them.

Like the Image Size palette, the Layers palette looks very much like a small dialog box. Instead of the usual elements, the palette contains two check boxes, a drop-down menu, and a set of radio buttons:

- Check the Export As CSS Layers check box to prepare for exporting the image as Cascading Style Sheet layers. Illustrator makes available all the options in the palette. An unchecked check box is the default.

- From the Layer drop-down menu, select the layer with which you will set export options. The options in the menu depend on the number of layers in the image. So, if an image is composed of six layers, you'll be able to choose from all six.

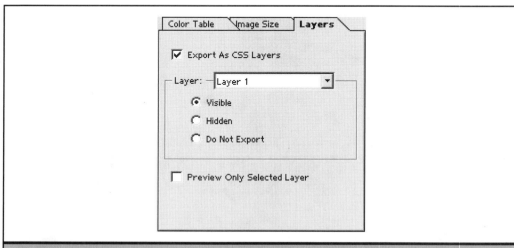

Figure 19-13. *With the Layers palette in the Save for Web dialog box, you can create Cascading Style Sheet layers in the image's HTML file*

- Click a radio button to specify options for the selected layer. Your choices are Visible (which shows the layer on the web page), Hidden (which hides the layer), and Do Not Export (which does not export the layer). The default is Visible.

- Check the Preview Only Selected Layer box to display the selected layer only in the preview area of the Save for Web dialog box. An unchecked check box, which shows all the layers for the image, is the default.

Optimizing Web Graphics

Now that you have completed your exploration of the Save for Web dialog box, it's time to learn how to use the dialog box: To apply the optimization settings from beginning to end, read the settings in the annotation area, view images using your default browser, and use the commands in the dialog box's menu.

 Note   *You'll learn about slices in Chapter 20. The Save for Web dialog box includes three commands (Link Slices, Unlink Slice, and Unlink All Slices) related to slices. You'll learn about these commands in the following chapter.*

Applying Optimization Settings

Although you have learned about the options for each of the file types that Illustrator supports for the Web, it's a good idea to show how to go through the process from start to finish.

To apply optimization settings, follow these steps:

1. In Illustrator, open the document that you want to optimize.
2. Choose File | Save for Web (CTRL-ALT-SHIFT-S/⌘-OPTION-SHIFT-S). Illustrator opens the Save for Web dialog box and loads the document into the preview window in Optimized view.
3. To change the view, click the Original, 2-Up, or 4-Up tab.
4. To change the current file type, choose a new file type from the Optimized File Format drop-down menu.
5. To apply a named optimization setting on the file, choose an applicable setting from the Saved Sets of Optimization Settings drop-down menu.
6. Select additional optimization options for the desired file type.
7. If you are using 2-Up or 4-Up view, select an image to save.
8. Click Save to save the optimization settings for the file. When Illustrator opens the Save Optimized As dialog box (see Figure 19-14), type the filename and select a location in which the file will be stored.

OUTSIDE ILLUSTRATOR

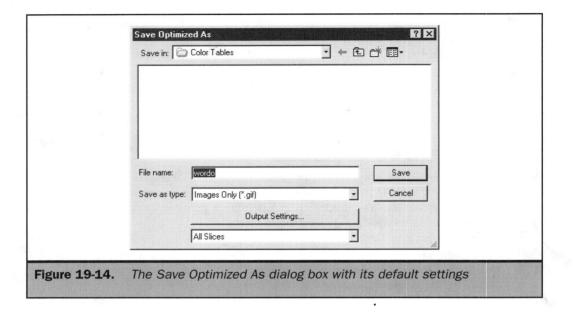

Figure 19-14.   *The Save Optimized As dialog box with its default settings*

9. From the Save As Type drop-down menu, choose from one of the following:

■ HTML and Images creates a web page coded in HTML and saves the image using the selected file type and the optimization settings. (In the following chapter, you'll learn how to save slices individually.)

■ Images Only saves the image using the optimization settings you have selected.

■ HTML Only creates a web page coded in HTML and does not save the image.

10. Click Save.

Optimizing to a Set File Size

You can instruct Illustrator to limit an optimized image file to a certain size. Just choose the Optimize to File Size command in the Save for Web dialog box's menu to open the Optimize to File Size dialog box (see Figure 19-15) in which you can specify options.

The options in the dialog box are as follows:

■ In the Desired File Size text box, type the optimum file size in kilobytes. The default value is 32K.

■ In the Start With section, click the Current Settings radio button to start with the current optimization settings or Auto Select GIF/JPEG to create a GIF or JPEG file—depending on Illustrator's evaluation of the colors in the image.

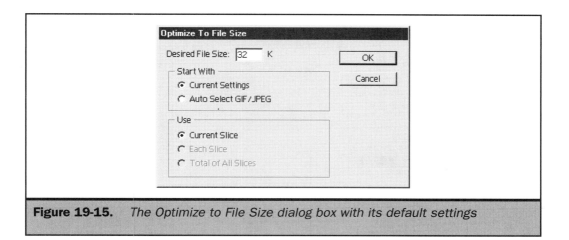

Figure 19-15.   *The Optimize to File Size dialog box with its default settings*

■ In the Use section, click a radio button to set a file size for the Current Slice, Each Slice, or Total of All Slices. Each Slice and Total of All Slices are not available unless you have created slices. For more information about slices, refer to the "Using Slices" section in Chapter 20.

Repopulating Optimization Settings

When you have changed optimization settings for any of the views in 4-Up mode, you can *refresh* (update the contents of the preview boxes to show the latest modifications) the views by choosing the Repopulate Views command from the Save for Web dialog box's menu. Note that Illustrator does not change the look of the original view and the view that is currently selected.

Saving Optimization Settings

Illustrator automatically saves your current optimization settings without you explicitly saving them—even if you close the Save for Web dialog box and open it again. However, Illustrator does not provide a new name for the settings and does not retain those settings after you edit them. So, the best way to retain settings you might use again is to save them as a named set. When you save and name a set, Illustrator adds the set to the Saved Sets of Optimization Settings menu.

To save and name the current optimization settings, follow these steps:

1. Choose the Save Settings command from the dialog box's menu. Illustrator opens the Save Optimization Settings dialog box (see Figure 19-16).

2. In the File Name text box, type a unique and descriptive name for the optimization settings.

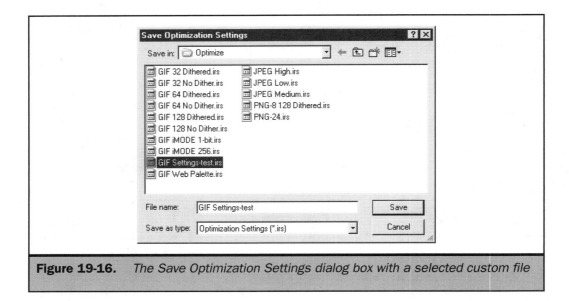

Figure 19-16. *The Save Optimization Settings dialog box with a selected custom file*

3. Click Save. Illustrator saves the optimization settings in the Optimize folder using the .IRS file extension and lists the new settings in the Settings menu.

4. To close the dialog box after saving, click Done.

5. To keep the dialog box open, press and hold down ALT/OPTION. When Illustrator changes the Done button to Remember, click Remember.

Editing Optimization Settings

You can edit optimization settings by selecting options from the Save for Web dialog box. When you make the first change to a named set of optimization settings, Illustrator changes the name of the settings file in the Saved Sets of Optimization Settings menu to [Unnamed]. To save the changed set, repeat the prior steps, either using the original name or providing a new name.

Restoring Optimization Settings

At times, you might decide that the optimization settings you have chosen for a document have gone beyond the proper level. If you can correct the current settings, go ahead. However, if you'd feel more comfortable starting all over again, Illustrator enables you to return to the settings that you saved most recently. To reset optimization settings to the last saved version, press and hold down ALT/OPTION. When Illustrator changes the Cancel button to Reset, click Reset.

Deleting Optimization Settings

When you decide to delete a named set of optimization settings, be very careful: Illustrator does not prompt you to confirm the deletion, and you can delete any set, including the predefined ones. To delete the selected optimization settings, choose the Delete Settings command from the Save for Web dialog box's menu.

Chapter 20

Illustrator's Web Graphics Features

You have probably noticed an evolution in the look of web sites from the early days of the Web until now. In the beginning, all web pages had gray backgrounds with the same black or blue type. Most illustrations were large, jagged, very slow to load, and usually unattractive. Today, you can see the magic touch of graphic artists in the layout of many web pages, variety in fonts, quality of artwork, and special effects—including animation, dynamic behavior, and interaction.

Until recently, web graphics were raster graphics of the GIF and JPEG file types. But now you can use vector programs such as Illustrator to create web graphics: You can not only create, export, and optimize raster graphics using the GIF, JPEG, and PNG file types, but you can also produce vector graphics such as SVG and SWF for the Web.

In the preceding chapter, you learned about optimizing and saving any type of Illustrator image (for example, a vector graphic or a rasterized vector graphic) for use on web pages. In this chapter, you'll find out how to use special features built into Illustrator to create images specifically for the Web.

Working with Raster Graphics in Illustrator

Writers know that documents are dynamic: it's rare for an original document to remain untouched; documents are made to be edited and improved. Graphic artists and web page designers are also prepared for constant changes to their work. If you save a graphic for the Web, you should be prepared to modify and edit it immediately or some time in the future.

In earlier chapters, you've learned how to edit Illustrator vector graphics. For example, you learned how to change the course of a path, the color of a fill, the width of a stroke, and how to perform other editing techniques. Illustrator also provides two commands dedicated to helping you edit raster graphics: Pixel Preview and Snap to Pixel.

Viewing with Pixel Preview

As a rule, when you save a vector graphic as a GIF, JPEG, or PNG file, the resulting artwork is set to 72 pixels per inch (ppi). Before you save and convert the graphic, you can view it as a raster graphic with the Pixel Preview feature. If you don't like the looks of a future raster graphic you can edit it (or, preferably, a copy of it) while it is a vector graphic, by using Illustrator tools and features. Then you can view the improved vector graphic in Pixel Preview. You can edit the graphic until you are satisfied and then optimize and save it using the Save for Web dialog box.

To preview a vector graphic as a raster graphic, choose View | Pixel Preview (CTRL-ALT-Y/⌘-OPTION-Y). When you activate Pixel Preview, Illustrator places a check mark before the Pixel Preview command. To turn off pixel preview, choose View | Pixel Preview (CTRL-ALT-Y/⌘-OPTION-Y) again. Illustrator removes the check mark preceding the command.

Figure 20-1. *From top to bottom, a zoomed vector graphic, a preview of it as a raster graphic, and a preview of it with a different font*

Figure 20-1 shows the subtle differences between a vector graphic (on the top) and the preview as a raster graphic (in the middle)—both zoomed in to 200% to show the differences. Based on the pixel preview, I decided to change to a different font, which is previewed again at 200% (at the bottom of the figure).

Enabling the Snap-to-Pixel Feature

Remember that as you create Illustrator objects, you can align those objects to the grid, which you can show or hide. You can also have objects snap to the grid for better alignment with other objects. For raster graphics, Illustrator provides another grid— always invisible—to which individual pixels snap as you edit or move an object around the illustration window. The grid divides the illustration window into cells that are 1 point by 1 point. By default, the Snap-to-Pixel feature is turned on.

To toggle the Snap-to-Pixel feature, choose View | Snap to Pixel (CTRL-SHIFT-"/⌘-SHIFT-"). When the command is active, Illustrator places a check mark in front of the command.

Using Image Maps

Image maps are graphics that contain one or more areas (known as *hot spots*) on which you can click to jump to another part of the current web page, a different page at the web site you are visiting, or a page on another site. Using Illustrator's Attributes palette, you can create image maps and perform other tasks unrelated to image maps.

OUTSIDE ILLUSTRATOR

Exploring the Attributes Palette

The Attributes palette (see Figure 20-2) serves three main purposes: defining image maps, modifying compound paths, and preventing knockout in colors that overlap. To toggle between showing and hiding the palette, choose Window | Attributes (F11).

 Illustrator provides slicing, a method you can use for creating objects to use as image maps or to behave in a certain way depending on an event being triggered. For more information, refer to the "Using Slices" section later in the chapter.

The Attributes palette contains several elements, each of which has a specific meaning and can be used to work with image maps, compound paths, and overlapping colors:

- Click the Menu button to open the Attributes palette's menu.
- Click the Don't Show Center button to hide the center point of the selected object.
- Click the Show Center button to show the center point of the selected object.
- Click the Reverse Path Direction Off button to have Illustrator calculate the areas in a non-zero winding compound path that are filled or that are holes.
- Click the Reverse Path Direction On button to have Illustrator calculate the areas in a non-zero winding compound path that are filled or that are holes.
- Click the Use Non-Zero Winding Fill Rule button to specify that Illustrator will use the non-zero winding fill rule, which calculates the relationship of a point to its shape to modify a compound path.
- Click the Use Even-Odd Fill Rule button to use the even-odd rule, which calculates the relationship of a point to its shape to modify a compound path.
- To open the palette's menu, click the Menu button. Commands on the menu are:

  - Overprint Only resizes the palette so that you see the Overprint check boxes only. Show All, the other command in that space on the menu, shows all sections of the palette.
  - Hide Note hides the large text box at the bottom of the palette. Note, the other command in that space on the menu, reveals the text box.
  - Palette Options opens a dialog box in which you can enter the maximum number of URL entries in the URL drop-down menu in the Attributes palette.

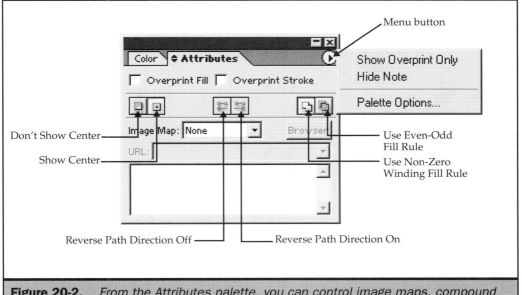

Figure 20-2.   *From the Attributes palette, you can control image maps, compound paths, and overlapping colors.*

Using Compound Paths

As you know, a compound path is composed of two or more open or closed, overlapping paths. Wherever compound paths overlap, Illustrator creates a transparent hole. For example, in the case of converted type, you can see behind the holes in the body of letters such as *a, b, d, p,* and so on. Illustrator treats compound paths as groups.

To make a compound path, you select each of the paths that will comprise the compound path and choose Object | Compound Path | Make (CTRL-8/⌘-8).

Use the Attributes palette to determine whether the overlapping areas of a compound path are filled or holes through which you can see underlying objects. Illustrator enables you to choose between two rules that calculate whether a point is inside or outside an object: non-zero winding fill and even-odd fill.

The *non-zero winding fill rule* (Illustrator's default) mathematically draws a line from a particular point in an object to infinity and then counts the number of times that part of the object crosses the line. If the segment never crosses the line, the result is zero and the point is inside the object (it is filled); otherwise, the point is outside (that is, a hole).

The *even-odd fill rule* mathematically draws a line from a point in any direction and then counts the number of times that part of the object crosses the line. If the count is odd, the point is inside the object; if the count is even, the point is outside the object.

You can toggle the non-zero winding fill rule and even-odd fill rule by clicking the Use Non-Zero Winding Fill Rule or the Use Even-Odd Fill Rule button on the right side of the Attributes palette.

If the intersections in a compound path are filled, you can change them to holes by clicking one of the reverse direction buttons in the center of the Attributes palette.

To revert a compound path to its original paths, choose Object | Compound Path | Release (CTRL-ALT-8/⌘-OPTION-8).

Creating an Image Map

Any time you have linked to a city or region from a map on a web page, you have used an image map. Image maps hide one or more links under a web page graphic. Your only hint that there's more to a graphic than its appearance is that your mouse pointer changes its appearance as you move it over the underlying hidden link.

You can use Illustrator to build various polygonal or rectangular hot spots into a GIF graphic—these can then be used to link to another page. For example, as a web page developer, you can create a link under the word *Home* or a small image of a house; when a user clicks the word or icon, the home page appears. Image maps are single files that include the graphic and the coordinates of each hot spot.

To test a newly created image map and its hot spots thoroughly, you should first create the web pages to which each hot spot will link. Then check the links using as many browsers as possible. At the least, always test every web page you create with the Internet Explorer and Netscape Navigator browsers.

An Illustrator image map graphic can be saved as a GIF or JPEG file. Otherwise, the hot spots are not viable.

To create an image map, follow these steps:

1. Create a graphic that you will use as an image map.

2. Choose Window | Attributes if the Attributes palette is not already in the illustration window.

3. Select a future hot spot area of the image-map graphic.

4. From the Image Map drop-down menu, select the shape of the hot spot:

   ■ None (the default) indicates that you will not create a hot spot.

■ Rectangle creates a rectangular hot spot the same size as the bounding box that Illustrator draws around the object when you select it.

■ Polygon creates a polygonal hot spot that outlines the object.

5. If you are using the link to the hot spot for the first time, type the URL of the target web page link in the URL text box/drop-down menu. You can enter a relative link (that is, a partial address, such as *home.html*) or an absolute link (that is, a complete address, such as *http://www.example.com/home.html*).

6. If you are reusing a link that you have already entered, choose it from the list in the URL drop-down menu.

7. To keep notes about the hot spot or link, enter text in the text box at the bottom of the palette.

8. If you wish to verify the link from the Attributes palette, click the Browser button. Illustrator launches your default browser, which searches for the URL.

9. Choose File | Save for Web, optimize the graphic, and save it as a GIF file with the file type of HTML and Images (*.html).

Figure 20-3 illustrates the image map in a browser window. Note the URL of the selected hot spot in the status bar.

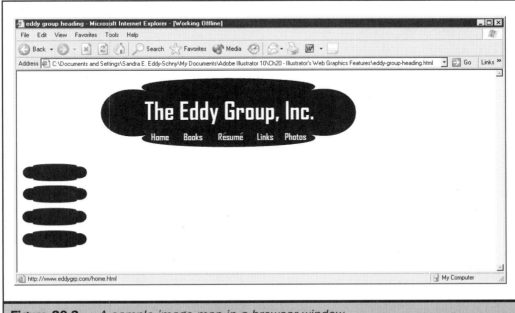

Figure 20-3. *A sample image map in a browser window*

Interpreting the HTML

The HTML code for the web page follows:

```
<HTML>
<HEAD>
<TITLE>eddy group heading</TITLE>
<META HTTP-EQUIV="Content-Type" CONTENT="text/html; charset=iso-8859-1">
</HEAD>
<BODY BGCOLOR=#FFFFFF>
<!-- ImageReady Slices (eddy group heading.ai) -->
<IMG SRC="eddy-group-heading.gif" WIDTH=649 HEIGHT=339 BORDER=0 ALT=""
USEMAP="#eddy_group_heading_Map">
<MAP NAME="eddy_group_heading_Map">
<AREA SHAPE="rect" ALT="" COORDS="251,106,285,128"
HREF="http://www.eddygrp.com/home.html">
<AREA SHAPE="rect" ALT="" COORDS="381,106,429,128"
HREF="http://www.eddygrp.com/resume.html">
<AREA SHAPE="rect" ALT="" COORDS="510,106,552,128"
HREF="http://www.eddygrp.com/photos.html">
<AREA SHAPE="rect" ALT="" COORDS="456,106,488,128"
HREF="http://www.eddygrp.com/links.html">
<AREA SHAPE="rect" ALT="" COORDS="314,106,350,128"
HREF="http://www.eddygrp.com/books.html">
</MAP>
<!-- End ImageReady Slices -->
</BODY>
</HTML>\
```

Note the following:

- The HTML code for the sample image map appears within the <MAP> and </MAP> tags. Note that *tags* are HTML (or XHTML or XML) commands within less-than and greater-than symbols.
- The <AREA> tag defines a hot spot.
- The SHAPE attribute states that the hot spot is rectangular.
- The COORDS attribute specifies two pairs of coordinates for each rectangle.
- The ALT attribute represents text that should appear if a browser cannot load the image map onto the web page or text that will appear when a user moves the mouse pointer over the image map area. To insert a comment, type it within the quotation marks in an HTML editor.

Setting Numbers of URLs in the URL Drop-Down Menu

You can specify a particular number of URLs shown in the URL drop-down menu by following these steps:

1. Choose Palette Options from the Attribute palette's menu. Illustrator opens the Palette Options dialog box.

2. Type a value from 1 to 30 (the default) in the text box.

3. Click OK.

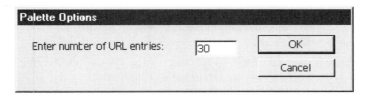

Removing a Hot Spot

To remove a hot spot from an image map, open the Attributes palette and select None from the Image Map drop-down menu.

Using Slices

Slices are the central feature for laying out web graphics and pages in Illustrator. When you *slice* a web page into individual rectangular-shaped components, you can control the behavior of each component. For example, you can convert several slices within an image to hot spots or assign an effect to a single slice (such as a button-shaped image).

In the preceding section, you discovered that an image map is a single file: When you define hot spots, they remain with the graphic and its web page. However, when you use slices to cut up an object that will work as an image map, each slice becomes an individual file. Additionally, in Illustrator you can create a rectangular or polygonal hot spot (and you can edit the SHAPE attribute in the HTML file to create elliptical hot spots). In contrast, a slice is rectangular only.

As the Web matures, it seems as though web pages become more complicated to explore—from a user's viewpoint—or to code—from a designer's perspective. A single web page can contain graphics, animation, special effects, interaction, and image maps, each behaving in its own individual way. Each page element has its own requirements, which can clash. If you slice a page into individual components, you can concentrate on each aspect and avoid conflicts between unlike elements.

Don't create hot spots in image maps or slices that already contain links to web pages. This multitude of URLs may confuse some browsers, which may completely ignore the link or jump to the wrong link.

Creating Slices

You can create a slice from one or more selected objects using a variety of methods:

- Choose Object | Slice | Make to create a slice whose dimensions are the same as those of the selected object. When you resize or move the object, the affected slice also changes and Illustrator may adjust other slices in the illustration window. The Make command is the only slice-creation tool that enables you to make a slice with HTML text.

- Activate the Slice tool (SHIFT-K) to drag a slice. By using the Slice tool with shortcut keys, you can control the tool's behavior.

- Choose Object | Slice | Create from Selection to create a slice from one or more selected objects.

- Choose Object | Slice | Create from Guides to create a slice from guides.

Except for the slices that you create with the Make command, the slices you create are separate from the selected objects. When slices and objects are independent of each other, you can work on a slice without affecting its associated object or edit an object without changing its slice. Additionally, separate slices and objects result in Illustrator adding manually created slices to the Layer palette.

When you make a slice, Illustrator follows your directions: It constructs a slice with certain dimensions, an identification number, and a slice symbol. For the remaining parts of the artwork, Illustrator creates automatic slices: *auto slices* for the areas of the artwork for which you didn't create slices and *subslices* for the areas in which slices overlap.

You cannot select individual subslices. Whenever you rearrange the order of slices in the illustration window, Illustrator refreshes the entire artwork and changes the dimensions of the subslices to fit the changed stacking order.

Illustrator gives all slices—including those you create and automatic slices—an identification number and symbol. Illustrator's slice numbering system starts with the topmost slice on the left side of the illustration window and flows from left to right from the top to the bottom of the window. If you move or add slices, Illustrator automatically renumbers the slices using its numbering system.

When you save your sliced artwork as a web page, Illustrator produces an HTML table made from the individual slices in the artwork.

Making a Slice

The Make command creates a slice with the same dimensions of one or more selected objects; the newly created slice contains the formatting attributes of the selected type.

To make a slice, follow these steps:

1. Using one of the selection tools, select one or more objects that will become a slice.
2. Choose Object | Slice | Make. Illustrator creates the requested slice and automatically makes other slices that cover the entire artwork.

Figure 20-4 shows a graphic with 17 slices that were created by selecting five pieces of type. The slices created manually (that is, 03, 05, 07, 09, and 11) are bolder than those that Illustrator made automatically. Remember that when you resize or move an object, Illustrator adjusts any slices that are affected by the transformation.

Slicing with the Slice Tool

The Slice tool (SHIFT-K), which shares a Toolslot with the Slice Selection tool, enables you to drag over an area to create a slice. Using this method, you can specify your own dimensions rather than having Illustrator set them for you.

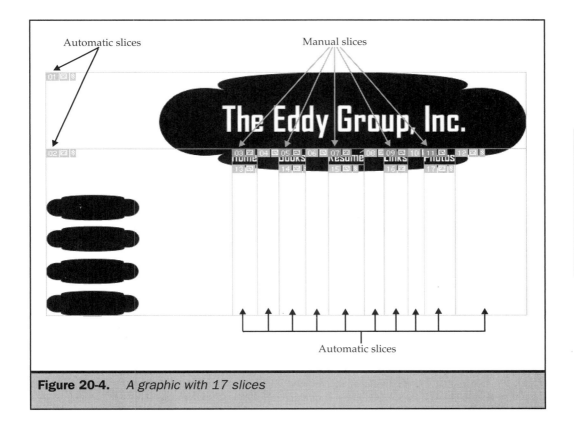

Figure 20-4.   *A graphic with 17 slices*

To create a slice with the Slice tool, follow these steps:

1. Activate the Slice tool (SHIFT-K).

2. From one corner of the future slice (for example, the upper-left corner), drag a bounding box toward the opposite corner (for example, the lower-right corner) over the area where you want to create a slice. Illustrator creates the requested slice and automatically makes other slices that cover the entire artwork.

Using shortcut keys can give you additional control of the slice:

■ To constrain the slice to a square shape, press and hold down SHIFT as you drag.

■ To create a slice outward and an even distance from the center of its rectangle, press and hold down ALT/OPTION as you drag.

Figure 20-5 illustrates a slice created with the Slice tool and automatic slices created by Illustrator. Notice that the Layers palette contains an item labeled <Slice>.

Creating a Slice from a Selection

The Create from Selection command is similar to the Make command: After you select one or more objects that will become a slice, you can issue the command. However,

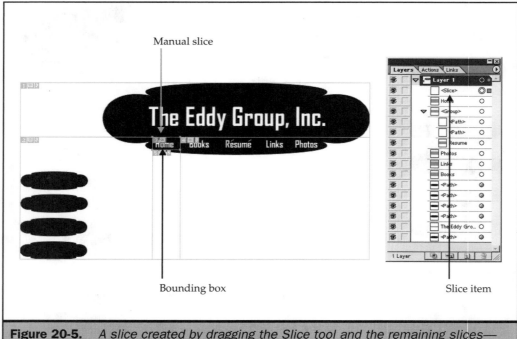

Figure 20-5. *A slice created by dragging the Slice tool and the remaining slices—all automatically created*

when you create a slice with the Create from Selection command, the slice and object are separate components of the page.

To create a slice from a selection, select one or more objects in the illustration window using one of the selection tools, and choose Object | Slice | Create from Selection. Illustrator slices all the artwork in the illustration window.

Figure 20-6 shows two manually created slices. The slice that encloses the heading could become a hot spot for a link to a page about the history of The Eddy Group, Inc.

Creating a Slice from Guides

You can create a slice using ruler guides and guide objects. You cannot use Smart Guides to create a slice. For more information about guides, refer to "Using Guides to Set Up Your Art" in Chapter 5.

When you use ruler guides to create a slice, you must enclose the future slice area on all four sides with four ruler guides (see Figure 20-7).

When you use a guide object to create a slice, make sure that you move the object that will become the guide object to the desired location of the slice and then convert it to a guide object. Note that regardless of the shape of the guide, the resulting slice is rectangular. Figure 20-8 illustrates the steps from creating and moving an object, converting it to a guide object, and enclosing it within a slice.

To create a slice from ruler guides or a guide object, choose Object | Slice | Create from Guides.

Figure 20-6. *Two manual slices, their entries in the Layers palette, and automatic slices in the illustration window*

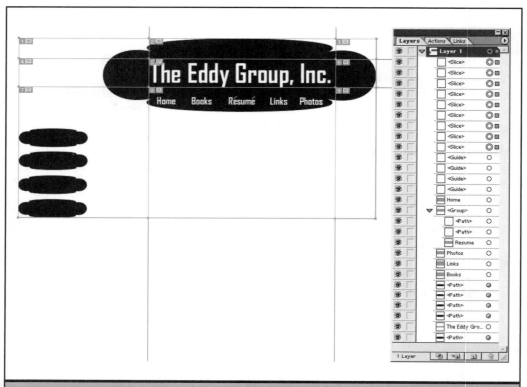

Figure 20-7.   *A slice created by the surrounding ruler guides and other slices in the illustration window*

 If Illustrator prevents you from creating a slice, make sure that slices aren't locked. If the Lock Slices command on the View menu is preceded by a check mark, slides are locked.

Selecting a Slice

Selecting a manually created slice is just about the same as selecting other objects in Illustrator. For example, you can use a selection tool to click a slice border as you would click the stroke of an object or to drag a bounding box around the slice as you would an object. Additionally, in the Layers palette, you can target a slice created with the Slice tool or the Create from Selection or Create from Guides command. Note that you cannot select an automatic slice.

To select a slice that you created with the Make command, select the artwork within the slice.

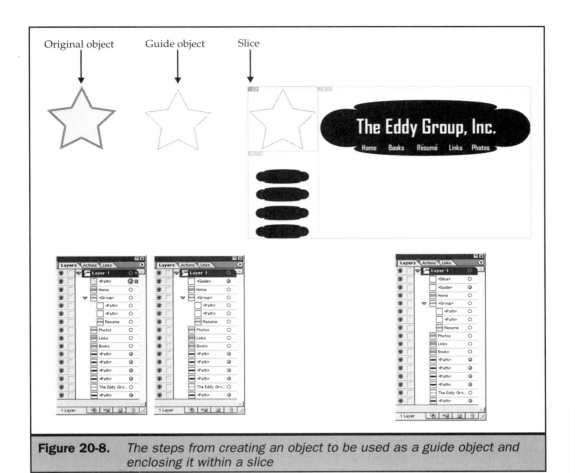

Figure 20-8. *The steps from creating an object to be used as a guide object and enclosing it within a slice*

 Use the Slice Selection tool to select any slices that you have created. To use the Slice Selection tool, activate it and click the border of a slice with the small arrow at the upper left of the mouse pointer. To add other manually created slices to the selection, press and hold down SHIFT and continue to click.

Specifying Slice Options

You can use the Slice Options dialog box (see Figure 20-9) to change the attributes of a selected slice. To open the dialog box, select or target a slice and choose Object | Slice | Slice Options.

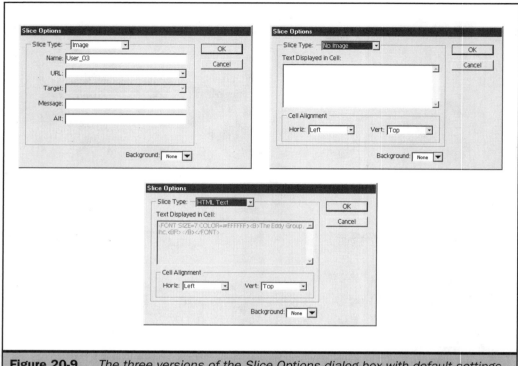

Figure 20-9. *The three versions of the Slice Options dialog box with default settings*

Note *You also can open the Slice Options dialog box from within the Save for Web dialog box to set options for one or more slices. To reveal the Slice Options dialog box for a single slice, double-click a slice in the preview window. To open the dialog box for a selection of several slices, double-click the slice that you most recently added to the selection.*

The options in the dialog box shown at the upper left of Figure 20-9 are as follows:

- From the Slice Type drop-down menu, select the type of content that will appear on the resulting web page:

  - Choose Image (the default) to have Illustrator make the image within the slice a linked image.

  - Choose No Image if the area enclosed by the slice will contain text or a solid color. To preview the page, use a web browser; Illustrator does not enable a preview.

- Choose HTML Text to maintain the formatting of the text object within the slice. Note that you cannot edit the HTML text on the web page; you must do so in Illustrator.

- In the Name text box, type the slice name that becomes the filename referred to in the web page.

- In the URL text box/drop-down menu, type or select the absolute or relative URL of the target name of the linked hot spot within the slice. If you have not used this URL in the document, type it in the text box. Otherwise, select the URL from the menu. This text box/drop-down menu is analogous to the URL text box in the Attributes palette that you use to create an image map.

- In the Target text box/drop-down menu, type or select the frame within the target page specified in the URL text box/drop-down menu.

- In the Message text box, type a short message that the browser displays in its status bar when a user moves the mouse pointer over the image within the slice.

- In the Alt text box, type a few words of alternative text that will display or sound if the browser cannot download the image within the slice or if the user moves the mouse pointer over the slice.

- From the Background drop-down menu, which is available in all three sections of the dialog box, select the background color of the slice area as it appears in the web page. Note that you will not see the background color in Illustrator. (Note that if you click the swatch box to the right of Background, Illustrator opens the Color dialog box from which you can choose a background color.) You can choose one of the following options:

    - None indicates that you do not wish to select a background color. If you click the swatch box to the right of Background, Illustrator sets the background color to black.

    - Matte sets the background color to the current fill color.

    - Eyedropper Color uses the current Eyedropper color.

    - White (the default) sets the background color to white.

    - Black sets the background color to black.

    - Other opens the Color dialog box from which you can select a color.

The options in the No Image section of the dialog box, shown in the upper-right of the figure are as follows:

- In the Text Displayed in Cell text box, enter or edit text in the selected slice as it will appear in the resulting web page. The text in the text box should not be larger than will fit in the slice area in the web page.

- From the Horiz drop-down menu, select a horizontal alignment option for the text within the slice. Options include Left (the default for slices), Center, Right, or Default (Illustrator's standard horizontal type alignment).

- From the Vert drop-down menu, Select a vertical alignment option for the text within the slice. Options include Top (the default for slices), Baseline, Middle, Bottom, and Default (Illustrator's standard vertical type alignment).

The options in the HTML Text section of the dialog box at the bottom of the figure are almost the same as those for No Image, the dialog box in the upper right of the figure. However, the Text Displayed in Cell text box is unavailable. To edit the text, change the Slice Type to No Image. When you do this, Illustrator "unlinks" the text in the dialog box from the text within the slice in the illustration window.

To have Illustrator disregard formatting of the text within the slice, precede text with the word <unformatted>.

Viewing and Hiding Slices

Illustrator enables you to show and hide slices in the illustration window. To view slices, choose View | Show Slices; to hide slices and just view the artwork, choose View | Hide Slices. Note that you can also view and hide slices in the Save for Web dialog box; click the Toggle Slices Visibility button (Q).

Moving a Slice

You can move a slice with or without its artwork—depending on the way in which you created it—to another location in the illustration window. To move a slice, select it with a selection tool and drag it to its new position. If you created the slice using the Make command, the slice and its associated artwork move together. If you used any other method to create the slice, the slice moves and its artwork stays behind in its original location.

Moving a slice with the Slice Selection tool gives you a little more control over the final position of the slice: Activate the Slice Selection tool and start dragging the slice by its border. To constrain the slice's movement to 45, 90, 135, 180, 225, 270, 315, or 360 degrees, press and hold down SHIFT as you drag.

Resizing a Slice

Illustrator provides two ways for you to change the size of a slice created with the Slice tool (SHIFT-K), the Create from Selection command, or the Create from Guides command: the Selection tool or the Transform palette.

To use the Selection tool (V), activate it and drag a slice by a handle or side. To change the dimensions of the two sides "attached" to a slice's corner, drag the corner handle. To change the width or height of the slice, drag a side in or out, up or down.

To use the Transform palette, choose Window | Transform (SHIFT-F8) to open the palette, and then type the coordinates in the X, Y, W, and H text boxes. To refresh your memory about using the Transform palette, refer to "Exploring the Transform Palette" in Chapter 10.

Restacking Slices

When you change the stacking order of slices, you can affect the appearance of the web page on which they are located. For example, let's say that you have created a square button with two overlapping strokes, each stroke with separate effects and within its own slice. If you switch the positions of the two slices, one set of effects overwhelm that of the other set.

Illustrator provides two methods of restacking slices—the first for slices created with the Slice tool, the Create from Selection command, and the Create from Guides command, and the second to restack slices created with all slice-creation features of Illustrator, including the Make command.

To change the stacking order of slices, use one of the following techniques:

- For slices created with anything but the Make command, target the slice in the Layers palette and then drag the slice item to a new location in the Layers palette.

- For slices created with all commands and the Slice tool, select the slice and choose one of the following, depending on the desired location of the selected slice:

  - Object | Arrange | Bring to Front (CTRL-SHIFT-]/⌘-SHIFT-])
  - Object | Arrange | Bring Forward (CTRL-]/⌘-])
  - Object | Arrange | Send Backward (CTRL-[/⌘-[)
  - Object | Arrange | Send to Back (CTRL-SHIFT-]/⌘-SHIFT-])

 Note   *To learn how these commands work, refer to "Arranging Objects and Groups" in Chapter 3.*

Aligning and Distributing Slices

Changing the alignment or distribution of slices works in the same way as aligning and distributing selected objects: If slices and their objects are aligned in a slightly uneven way, a web page doesn't look professional. Additionally, if you align or distribute slices, Illustrator may be able to remove some automatic slices, which can result in a smaller HTML document.

To align or distribute a set of slices, follow these steps:

1. Select the slices to be aligned or distributed.

2. If the Align palette is not onscreen, choose Window | Align (SHIFT-F7) to open the palette.

3. Click the appropriate button to realign or redistribute the selection. Illustrator moves all or some of the selected slices. If you created the slices with the Make command, the objects associated with the slices move as well.

    To refresh your memory about the Align palette, refer to "Aligning and Distributing Objects" in Chapter 3.

Duplicating a Slice

Duplicating a slice can ensure that two objects that *should* be the same size *are* exactly the same size. Illustrator provides two methods for duplicating slices—one new and one familiar:

■ Select the slice to be duplicated and choose Object | Slice | Duplicate Slice. Illustrator creates a new slice, which becomes the last slice in the illustration window.

■ Select the slice to be duplicated and choose Edit | Copy (CTRL-C/⌘-C). To paste the selection in the current document or in another document, choose Edit | Paste (CTRL-V/⌘-V).

Dividing a Slice

Illustrator enables you to divide a slice horizontally (that is, by adding one or more horizontal lines across the slice) or vertically (that is, by adding one or more vertical lines from the top to the bottom of the slice); horizontally and vertically; or evenly or not. For example, if you are redesigning a web site to include additional links, you might decide to place one or two extra hot spots within a graphic heading.

    You cannot divide a slice that you created with the Make command.

When you divide a slice evenly, Illustrator uses the number of new slices you want to create to calculate the width or height of the new slices. However, when you divide a slice unevenly according to a number of pixels per slice, Illustrator calculates the division and creates a new slice if pixels are left over.

To divide a slice, follow these steps:

1. Select a slice with a selection tool or the Slice Selection tool, or target the slice in the Layers palette.

2. Choose Object | Slice | Divide Slices. Illustrator opens the Divide Slice dialog box (see Figure 20-10).

3. To divide the slice horizontally, place a check mark in the Divide Horizontally Into check box. A checked box is the default.

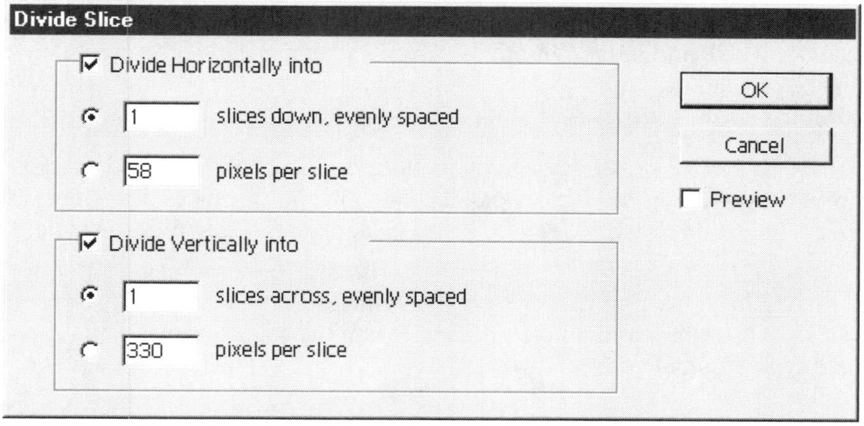

Divide Slice

☑ Divide Horizontally into

　⊙ [1] slices down, evenly spaced

　○ [58] pixels per slice

☑ Divide Vertically into

　⊙ [1] slices across, evenly spaced

　○ [330] pixels per slice

OK

Cancel

☐ Preview

Figure 20-10. *The Divide Slice dialog box with its default settings*

4. To divide the slice horizontally and evenly by the number of slices, which is the default, click the Slices Down, Evenly Spaced radio button and type the number of slices desired in the text box. The default number of slices is 1.

5. To divide the slice horizontally and unevenly by a number of pixels per slice, click the Pixels per Slice radio button and type the number of pixels per slice in the text box. The default number of pixels is the current height of the slice.

6. To divide the slice vertically, place a check mark in the Divide Vertically Into check box. A checked box is the default.

7. To divide the slice vertically and evenly by the number of slices, which is the default, click the Slices Across, Evenly Spaced radio button and type the number of slices desired in the text box. The default number of slices is 1.

8. To divide the slice vertically and unevenly by a number of pixels per slice, click the Pixels per Slice radio button and type the number of pixels per slice in the text box. The default number of pixels is the current width of the slice.

9. Click OK; Illustrator divides the slice as instructed and inserts a number in the new slice.

Merging Slices

Merging slices is the direct opposite of dividing slices. If you are redesigning a web page—perhaps creating an image map to handle half of your links rather than squeezing them into a single image map—you might want to distribute some of the old links into the second image map. In this situation, making some of the slices larger can accommodate the changes. Note that you cannot merge slices that you created with the Make command, and slices remain rectangular, regardless of the positions of the selected slices.

To combine slices, follow these steps:

1. Select two or more slices with a selection tool or the Slice Selection tool, or target the slices in the Layers palette. To select all the slices beyond the first, press and hold down SHIFT while you click to add slices to the selection.

2. Choose Object | Slice | Combine Slices. Illustrator combines contiguous slices into one large slice. When you choose noncontiguous slices, Illustrator merges the selected slices and all the slices between the selected ones. This could result in overlapping slices.

Locking and Unlocking Slices

When you lock slices, you cannot select them, which means that you cannot change their sizes or move them.

Note	*You cannot lock a slice that you created with the Make command.*

To lock slices, follow these steps:

1. Select two or more slices with a selection tool or the Slice Selection tool, or target the slices in the Layers palette. To select all the slices beyond the first, press and hold down SHIFT while you click to add slices to the selection.

2. Choose View | Lock Slices or click in the Toggles Lock column in the Layers palette. Illustrator locks the selected slices, places a check mark in front of the Lock Slices command, and displays the lock icon in the Layers palette.

To unlock locked slices, choose View | Lock Slices or click in the Toggles Lock column in the Layers palette. Illustrator removes the check mark preceding the Lock Slices command and the lock icons in the Layers palette.

Using the Save for Web Dialog Box for Slices

In Chapter 19, you learned almost everything there is to know about the Save for Web dialog box. In fact, there was a missing piece, slice handling, which is covered in this section.

Optimizing Slices

You can optimize one or more slices using the Save for Web dialog box. Remember that Illustrator saves each slice as an individual file; so if you wish to optimize, you'll have to do so to every slice.

To optimize slices, follow these steps:

1. Choose File | Save for Web (CTRL-SHIFT-ALT-S/⌘-SHIFT-OPTION-S). Illustrator opens the Save for Web dialog box (see Figure 20-11).

2. If you are in 4-Up view, select a version to be optimized.

3. With the dialog box's Slice Select tool (K), click a slice to be optimized. To add to the selection, press and hold down SHIFT and either continue clicking or drag across additional slices. Illustrator places a yellow border around your selection.

4. If needed, choose a file format from the Optimized File Format drop-down menu.

5. Optionally, select a named optimization setting from the Saved Sets of Optimization Settings drop-down menu.

6. From the Settings section for the selected file type, select other options.

7. Click Save. Illustrator saves the slice.

8. Repeat steps 1 through 7 for every slice in the current file.

Showing and Hiding Slices in the Save for Web Dialog Box

You can hide slices in the Save for Web dialog box so that you can work on the artwork rather than the slices. However, when you are ready to optimize individual slices, you can reveal the slices. To show or hide slices in the Save for Web dialog box, click the Toggle Slices Visibility button (Q).

Linking and Unlinking Slices

When you link slices using the Save for Web dialog box, you can apply the same optimization settings to them all, including colors and dithering. Linking ensures a seamless web page because all the linked slices have identical settings.

To link slices using the Save for Web dialog box, follow these steps:

1. With the dialog box's Slice Select tool (K), click a slice to be optimized. To add to the selection, press and hold down SHIFT and either continue clicking or drag across additional slices. Illustrator places a yellow border around your selection.

2. Choose the Link Slices command from the dialog box's menu (not the Color Table palette's menu) to link the selected slices. Illustrator highlights all the linked slices (see Figure 20-12).

3. Select optimization settings, and click Save to save the slices.

To remove the link from a selected slice, choose the Unlink Slice command from the dialog box's menu. To remove the links from all slices, choose Unlink All Slices from the menu.

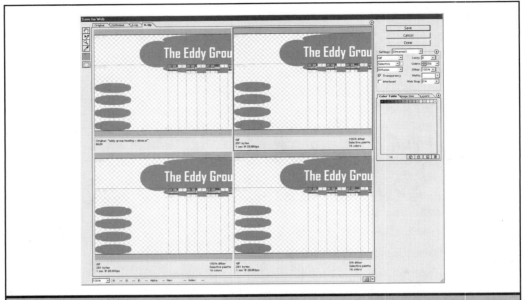

Figure 20-11. *The Save for Web dialog box in 4-Up view showing a file and its slices to be optimized*

Releasing and Deleting Slices

When you no longer need a slice or slices or want to move the artwork around the illustration and then start over with a different pattern of slices, you can either release or delete the slices. If you release a slice, you can avoid deleting the artwork within the slice.

Releasing a Slice

To release a slice, select the slice and choose Object | Slice | Release.

Deleting One or More Slices

Illustrator provides several ways to remove one or more slices from a document: a keystroke, a button click or menu command in the Layers palette, and a command in the Object menu:

■ To delete a slice created with the Slice tool, the Object | Slice | Create from Selection command, or the Object | Slice | Create from Guides command, select the slice and press DELETE. Illustrator deletes the slice but not the associated artwork.

■ To delete a slice created with the Object | Slice | Make command, select the slice and press DELETE. Illustrator deletes the slice and the associated artwork. In fact, the only way to remove a slice created with the Make command without removing the artwork is to release it.

Figure 20-12. *Highlighted, linked slices in the Save for Web dialog box*

■ To delete a slice created with the Slice tool, the Object | Slice | Create from Selection command, or the Object | Slice | Create from Guides command, target the slice in the Layers palette and drag the item to the Delete Selection button, click the Delete Selection button, or choose the Delete Selection command from the palette's menu. Illustrator deletes the slice but not the associated artwork.

■ To delete all slices from the document, choose Object | Slice | Delete All. Illustrator deletes all the slices, regardless of the commands you used to create them.

Creating Animations with Illustrator Layers

Animations are series of individual frames that contain slowly changing images. Each frame in an animation shows motion or another type of change, such as a different color or pattern, a larger or smaller stroke, or even the application of an effect.

In recent years, the most popular means of animation was known as GIF animation. After creating a series of GIF files, you could use a GIF-animation application to contain, test, and run the animation.

Now applications such as Macromedia Flash enable web page developers to create world-class animations. You can create files in programs such as Illustrator and export them to the SWF file format or produce animations in Flash. Flash animations are composed of individual frames within one file rather than individual files. With Flash, you can enhance animations with sound and interactivity.

Planning an Animation Graphic

When you design an animation in Illustrator, consider the following important notes:

- It's obvious that movement is important in an animation. If motion is not smooth, too many changes may be occurring from one frame to another. To correct this situation, insert intermediate frames between the existing ones. In the new frames, find a halfway point between the preceding and following frames.

- Unless you want to change an object's shape, color, or another attribute from frame to frame, make sure that you carefully maintain every characteristic of the object from frame to frame. If an animation flickers, it may contain inadvertent attribute changes from one frame to the next.

Illustrator layers are made for web animations. In one file, you can create an animation—with each change going on a layer. Then, export the file and all its layers so that each layer goes into a separate frame in SWF or SVG.

Creating an Animation in Illustrator

You can create simple animations in Illustrator by using basic shapes, such as rectangles, ellipses, stars, spirals, and so on. Then, transform the object in stages to change its look. If you transform the objects with a transformation dialog box, you can control the degrees of changes much better than using a toolbox tool.

To create a typical animation, follow these steps:

1. Choose View | Show Grid (CTRL-"/⌘-") to turn on the grid so that you can see the changes to your work.

2. If you want to change colors, select Web-Safe colors from the Color palette.

3. Activate the Ellipse tool (L) and make a circle with any fill color.

4. Select the circle and choose Edit | Copy (CTRL-C/⌘-C) to copy the circle.

5. Choose Edit | Paste (CTRL-V/⌘-V) to paste the circle into the illustration window.

6. Move the copy next to or below the original.

7. With the copy still selected, choose Object | Transform | Scale.

8. In the Scale dialog box, reduce the Horizontal percentage (for this example, by 10 percent for each object), and click OK.

9. Repeat steps 4 through 8, each time selecting the most recent copy first. You can repeat steps until the object has reached the desired size, shape, or color.

10. To return to the appearance of the original object, you can copy and paste some of the objects that you created earlier.

Figure 20-13 shows a set of circles and ellipses that will become an animation and the Layers palette on which they appear. When you look at the contents of the Layers palette, you can almost visualize the animation as it changes colors and appears to rotate.

Releasing to Layers

When you complete the "first draft" of an animation, each object is a separate item on one layer in the Layers palette. After you have created the objects that comprise an animation, you need to release the objects to separate layers by choosing Choose Release to Layers (Sequence). Illustrator places each object on a sublayer of the current layer (see Figure 20-14). To refresh your memory about releasing to layers, refer to "Releasing Elements to Separate Layers" in Chapter 14.

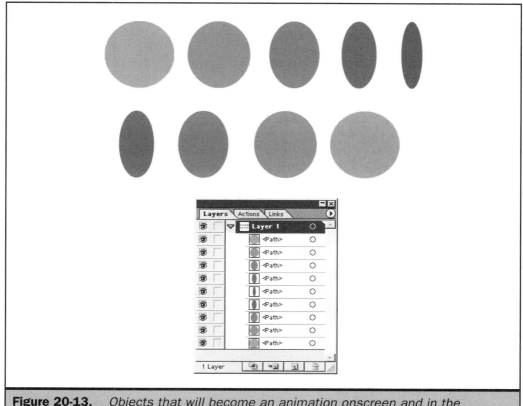

Figure 20-13.   *Objects that will become an animation onscreen and in the Layers palette*

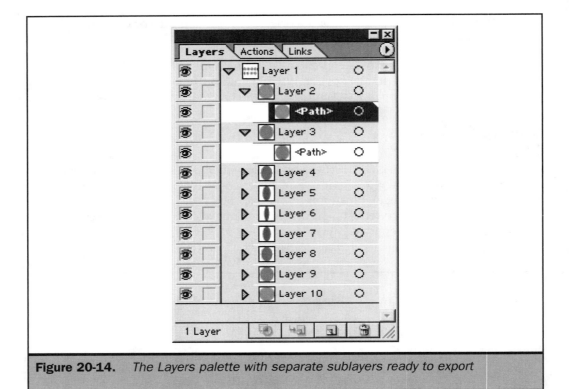

Figure 20-14. *The Layers palette with separate sublayers ready to export*

Getting Ready to Export SWF Files

In Chapter 19, you learned how to save a variety of files for the Web by using the Save for Web dialog box. Illustrator also enables you to export SWF files with the Export command. Once you have created an SWF file, you can enhance it in Macromedia Flash or another application that recognizes SWF files.

Preparing a File for SWF

When you create an Illustrator document that will ultimately become an SWF file, realize that no two applications are 100 percent compatible. So, when you work on a future SWF artwork, reflect on the following notes:

- SWF supports strokes with rounded caps and joins only and does not support square or beveled caps and joins.

- SWF does not support certain transparency effects. To export as many transparency attributes as possible to SWF, choose File | Document Setup

(CTRL-ALT-P/⌘-OPTION-P), choose Transparency from the drop-down menu at the top of the dialog box, and select options from the Flattening section. For more information about setting transparency preferences, refer to Appendix B. You also can flatten a transparency by choosing Object | Flatten Transparency, which opens the Flatten Transparency dialog box, whose options reflect those in the Document Setup dialog box.

- ■ SWF rasterizes all mesh objects and gradients with more than eight stops. To learn more about gradients and mesh objects, refer to Chapter 9.

- ■ SWF rasterizes patterns and converts them into tiled images; this action probably will change the patterns' appearances. Additionally, SWF converts pattern-filled type and strokes filled with patterns to pattern-filled paths.

- ■ When you use the Symbol Stainer and Symbol Styler tools, the resulting file may be larger than expected.

- ■ Macromedia Flash does not retain certain type attributes. For example, kerning, leading, and tracking characteristics disappear. Flash imitates these attributes by breaking type into separate records. One way of getting around this is to convert type to outlines by selecting the type and choosing Type | Create Outlines (CTRL-SHIFT-O/⌘-SHIFT-O). For more information, refer to "Converting Type to a Graphical Object" in Chapter 12.

- ■ To create an animation that you will export as an SWF file, put each animation frame on a layer. When you export the file, choose the AI Layers to SWF Frames option in the Export As drop-down menu in the Macromedia Flash (SWF) Format Options dialog box. To learn how to use this dialog box, refer to "Exploring the Macromedia Flash (SWF) Format Options Dialog Box," which follows this section.

Note   *You can play Flash animations with the Macromedia Flash Player. To download the player, go to the Macromedia Flash Player Download Center (http:// www.macromedia.com/ shockwave/download/index.cgi?P1_Prod_Version=ShockwaveFlash). This Web page contains links to information that can help you learn more about Flash. Note that Macromedia's home page is at http://www.macromedia.com.*

Exploring the Macromedia Flash (SWF) Format Options Dialog Box

As you export an SWF file, Illustrator displays the Macromedia Flash (SWF) Format Options dialog box (see Figure 20-15) with which you'll select export and image options. Note that you have seen some of these options before in the Save for Web dialog box for SWF. To open the dialog box, choose File | Export. Then fill in the dialog box fields and click OK.

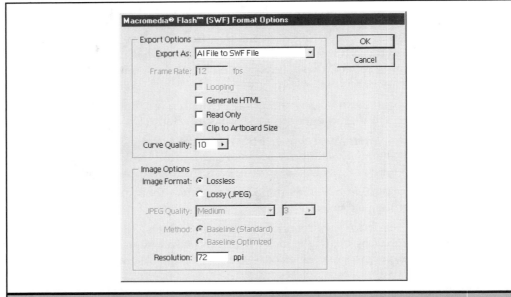

Figure 20-15.   *The Macromedia Flash (SWF) Format Options dialog box with its default settings*

The options in the dialog box are as follows:

- From the Export As drop-down menu, choose an export method:
  - AI File to SWF File (the default), which exports the file to a single SWF file. This choice maintains clipping masks.
  - AI Layers to SWF Frames, which exports each layer in the file to a single SWF frame.
  - AI Layers to SWF Files, which exports each layer in the file to a single SWF file.

- In the Frame Rate text box, set the rate, in frames per seconds, at which the Flash Player plays the animation. This text box is available only if you select the AI Layers to SWF Frames export option.

- Check the Looping check box to have the Macromedia Flash Player play the animation without end. If you remove the check mark from the check box, which is unchecked by default, the Macromedia Flash viewer plays the animation once. This check box is available only if you select the AI Layers to SWF Frames export option.

■ Check the Generate HTML check box to code a separate HTML file if you want to include the SWF file on a web page. Illustrator exports the SWF and HTML files in the same location. The default is an unchecked box.

■ Check the Read Only check box to prevent anyone from editing the SWF file. The default is an unchecked box.

■ Check the Clip to Artboard Size check box to clip the image to fit its current Illustrator Artboard dimensions, which removes all sections outside the borders of the Artboard. The default is an unchecked box.

■ With the Curve Quality text box/slider, set the quality of Bézier curves in the image. Valid values range from 0 (the lowest curve quality and a smaller file size) to 10 (the highest curve size and a larger file size). The default setting is 10.

■ Click one of the Image Format radio buttons to set the compression of the file: Click the Lossless radio button (the default) to save data without losing data; click Lossy (JPEG) to set the quality of the file based on the amount of data that is lost as the file is saved.

■ From the JPEG Quality drop-down menu, choose the level of compression: Low, Medium (the default), High, or Maximum. If you choose High or Maximum, Illustrator preserves the quality of the image, but the size of the file increases. Choosing Low or Medium reduces the quality level but reduces the size of the file. This option is available only if you select the Lossy (JPEG) radio button.

■ With the JPEG Quality text box/slider, set a compression quality percentage value. Valid values range from 0 (Low) to 10 (Maximum). Note that Low Quality ranges from 0 to 2, Medium ranges from 3 to 5, High ranges from 6 to 7, and Maximum ranges from 8 to 10. The default is 3. This option is available only if you select the Lossy (JPEG) radio button.

■ Click a Method radio button to select the type of JPEG compression. Click Baseline (Standard) to use a standard baseline compression, or click Baseline Optimized to use an optimized baseline compression. The default is Baseline (Standard). This option is available only if you select the Lossy (JPEG) radio button.

■ With the Resolution text box, set the screen resolution for raster images saved to SWF. Valid values range from 72 (the default) to 2,400 pixels per inch.

Exporting an SWF File

After you have created artwork for Macromedia Flash in Illustrator, you can export it as an SWF file. To export a file, you'll go through two dialog boxes.

To export a file to the SWF format, follow these steps:

1. Choose File | Export. Illustrator opens the Export dialog box, which looks like a typical Save dialog box.

2. In the File Name text box, type the filename or accept the current filename.

3. From the Save As Type drop-down menu, select Macromedia Flash (*.SWF).

4. Click Save. Illustrator opens the Macromedia Flash (SWF) Format Options dialog box.

5. Select options from the dialog box, and click OK. Illustrator exports the file.

Preparing an Illustrator Document for SVG

As you discovered in Chapter 19, you can save SVG files for the Web. You also can choose File | Save (CTRL-S/⌘-S) or File | Export to save or export Illustrator files as SVG files. Because an SVG file is written in XML, you can edit it as an XML file.

| Note | *Illustrator also enables you to choose File | Save (CTRL-S/⌘-S) to save a compressed SVG (SVGZ) file. Note that not all browsers support SVGZ files.* |

When you create an Illustrator document for use as an SVG file, plan your artwork carefully and experiment with the resulting SVG file to check for differences between Illustrator artwork and the artwork as coded in XML. When you work on a future SVG file, reflect on the following:

■ SVG supports transparency effects better than SWF. However, when you want objects to have a level of transparency, apply transparency to the objects themselves rather than the layers within which they reside.

■ In SVG files, layers become group elements with <g> tags as defined within the SVG specification. Sublayers are nested under the <g> tags, and layers that you have hidden are coded with the display:none property.

■ SVG does not support the scaling of raster objects. Like SWF, SVG rasterizes all mesh objects. Additionally, SVG rasterizes objects with certain styles and many filters. To ensure that SVG does not rasterize an object, apply an SVG effect rather than a standard Illustrator effect.

■ SVG supports symbols and simplified paths. To refresh your memory about using the Simply command, refer to "Simplifying Paths" in Chapter 6.

■ Brushes with rough brushstrokes may result in larger SVG files because of the XML code required to define the variations in the brushstrokes.

■ To insert links in SVG files, you can use image maps and slices.

- Like any other XML file, SVG supports scripting languages. You can write scripts that insert links and react to events such as mouse clicks, keystrokes, and mouse movement.

- SVG supports the Document Object Model (DOM). For more information about DOM, go to the World Wide Web Consortium DOM home page (http://www.w3.org/DOM/).

Exploring the SVG Interactivity Palette

With the SVG Interactivity palette (see Figure 20-16), you can write and organize JavaScript scripts that are triggered by certain events, such as keystrokes, mouse clicks, and mouse movements, when you save or export an Illustrator document to the Web. To toggle between showing and hiding the palette, choose Window | SVG Interactivity.

The SVG Interactivity palette contains the following elements:

- From the Event drop-down menu, select the event with which the JavaScript script is associated.

- In the JavaScript text box, write a JavaScript statement that is triggered when the event in the Event drop-down menu occurs.

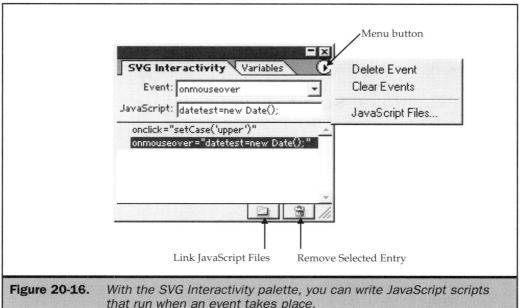

Figure 20-16. *With the SVG Interactivity palette, you can write JavaScript scripts that run when an event takes place.*

OUTSIDE ILLUSTRATOR

- The list box in the lower part of the palette contains the complete JavaScript statement, which includes the event and the contents of the JavaScript text box.

- Click the menu button to open the SVG Interactivity palette's menu.

- Click the Link JavaScript Files button to open the JavaScript Files dialog box, in which you can link a JavaScript file to the current document or unlink one or all JavaScript files linked to the current document.

- Click the Remove Selected Entry button to delete the selected JavaScript script from the list box in the palette. The counterpart command on the palette's menu is Delete Event.

To open the palette's menu, click the menu button. Commands on the menu are

- The Delete Event command deletes the selected JavaScript script from the list box in the palette. The counterpart button at the bottom of the palette is Remove Selected Entry.

- The Clear Events command removes all JavaScript scripts from the list box in the palette.

- The JavaScript Files command opens a dialog box with which you can apply, add, and edit JavaScript scripts or delete JavaScript scripts linked to the current document.

What Is an Event?

The JavaScript scripts that you write in the SVG Interactivity palette respond to certain events occurring. Table 20-1 lists and briefly describes the events listed in the Event drop-down menu of the palette.

Adding an Event and Script to an Object

It's easy to associate an event and a JavaScript script with an object in the current Illustrator document: Just select the object, and then use the SVG Interactivity palette as your coding location. For example, you can change the color of a button when a user moves the mouse over the button, display an error message when a browser is unable to finish loading an image, or highlight a scroll bar when a user starts to move the scroll box in a scroll bar.

To associate an event and a JavaScript script with an object, follow these steps:

1. With a selection tool or with the Layers palette, select or target an object.

2. If the SVG Interactivity palette is not in the illustration window, choose Window | SVG Interactivity. Illustrator opens the SVG Interactivity palette.

3. From the Event drop-down menu, choose an event.

4. In the JavaScript text box, type a JavaScript statement to be associated with the selected event.

5. Press ENTER/RETURN. Illustrator adds the JavaScript statement to the list box.

Event	Action
onfocusin	The user moves to the border of a target object.
onfocusout	The user moves away from the current object.
ongainselection	The user starts making a selection.
onloseselection	The user ends a selection.
onactivate	The user activates an object.
onmousedown	The user presses and holds down a mouse button over the current object.
onmouseup	The user releases the mouse button while over the current object.
onclick	The user clicks the current object.
ondblclick	The user double-clicks the current object.
onmouseover	The user moves the mouse over an object for the first time.
onmousemove	The user moves his or her mouse over an object.
onmouseout	The user moves the mouse away from the current object.
onkeydown	The user presses and holds down a keyboard key over the current object.
onkeypress	The user presses and releases a keyboard key over the current object.
onkeyup	The user releases the keyboard key while over the current object.
onload	The browser loads an object.
onerror	The browser prematurely stops loading an object when an error occurs.
onabort	The user stops an object from loading before completion.
onunload	The user leaves the current document.
onzoom	The user starts to zoom the current document.
onresize	The user starts to resize the current object.
onscroll	The user starts to move the scroll box in a scroll bar.

Table 20-1.   *The Common Events Listed in the SVG Interactivity Palette*

OUTSIDE ILLUSTRATOR

Organizing JavaScript Files

You have just learned how to write JavaScript statements for the current document. Illustrator enables you to link and unlink separate JavaScript files from the JavaScript Files dialog box (see Figure 20-17). To open the dialog box, click the Link JavaScript Files button at the bottom of the SVG Interactivity palette or choose the JavaScript Files command from the palette's menu.

 The Illustrator Extras folder on the Illustrator CD-ROM contains scripting resources, including documentation and sample scripts in both JavaScript and Visual Basic.

Using the Script Commands

Illustrator provides predefined scripts for you to apply to a document or type. To access the scripts, choose File | Scripts, and then choose a command from the submenu:

- The Add Watermark command adds a large, diagonal, editable text watermark to the document. For example, you can overlay a document with the watermark text *DRAFT* to indicate that you have not completed your work or *CONFIDENTIAL* to state that recipients should not distribute the document without your permission.

- The ApplyStyleToTextSelection command applies a rounded drop shadow and a blue gradient fill to selected type and changes the type size to 48 points.

- The ChangeSizesOfTextSelection command randomly changes the size of certain characters in a type selection.

- The ExportDocsAsFlash command opens the Export dialog box so you can export the current document as an SWF file.

- The SaveDocsAsPDF command opens the Save As dialog box so you can save the current document as a PDF file.

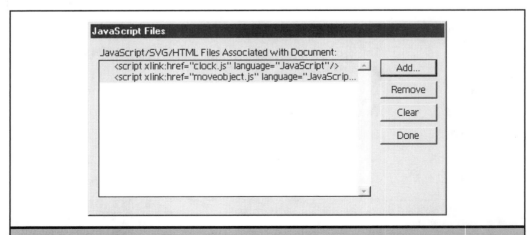

Figure 20-17.   *The JavaScript Files dialog box with two scripts listed*

Linking a JavaScript File

Linking a JavaScript file with the current Illustrator document lists it so that you have ready access to it. To link a JavaScript file with the current document, follow these steps:

1. Click the Link JavaScript Files button at the bottom of the SVG Interactivity palette, or choose the JavaScript Files command from the palette's menu. Illustrator opens the JavaScript Files dialog box.

2. Click the Add button. Illustrator opens the Add JavaScript File dialog box, as shown here:

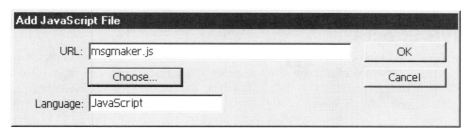

3. If you don't know the URL of the file, click the Choose button. Illustrator opens the Please Select a JavaScript dialog box, which looks like an Open dialog box.

4. Locate the JavaScript file, select it, and click Open. The dialog box closes, and you return to the Add JavaScript File dialog box.

5. Click OK. Illustrator returns to the JavaScript Files dialog box and adds the new script.

6. Click Done to close the dialog box, or continue working in the dialog box.

Unlinking a JavaScript File

When you unlink a JavaScript file, you do not delete it from your computer; you remove it from the list of linked files for the current document. If you change your mind about unlinking a file, just link it using the prior steps.

To unlink a JavaScript file, follow these steps:

1. Click the Link JavaScript Files button at the bottom of the palette, or choose the JavaScript Files command from the menu. Illustrator opens the JavaScript Files dialog box.

2. Select the script to be unlinked.

3. Click Remove. Illustrator removes the selected script from the dialog box without prompting you to confirm the deletion.

Clearing JavaScript Files

Clearing is a massive unlinking operation. To clear files, open the JavaScript Files dialog box and click the Clear button.

Deleting a Script from the SVG Interactivity Palette

When a JavaScript script has lost its usefulness in the current document, you can easily remove it from the SVG Interactivity palette. To delete a script from the palette, follow these steps:

1. In the SVG Interactivity palette, click a JavaScript event to highlight it.
2. Click the Remove Selected Entry button, or choose Delete Event from the palette's menu. Illustrator removes the script without prompting you to confirm the deletion.

Using SVG Effects

You can apply SVG effects to objects that will be saved or exported as SVG files. On the surface, SVG effects look about the same as other Illustrator effects. The main differences between the two types of effects is that SVG effects are coded XML elements and properties, so you can edit effects easily and use JavaScript scripts for special effects.

 If you apply filters to an object, choose any SVG filters after applying non-SVG filters. If you don't follow this rule, Illustrator converts the selected object to a raster object.

Choosing SVG Effects from the Effect Menu

To use an SVG effect on an object, select the object, choose Effect | SVG Filters, and then choose an effect from the submenu—as if you were applying any other Illustrator effect.

Figure 20-18 illustrates all 18 predefined SVG effects. In the top-left corner of the figure is the original object, a blue ellipse with a red, 6-point stroke. From top to bottom in the left column are ellipses with the AI_Alpha_1, AI_Alpha_4, AI_BevelShadow_1, AI_CoolBreeze, AI_Dilate_3, and AI_Dilate_6 effects. In the middle column, from the top, are the following effects: AI_Erode_3, AI_Erode_6, AI_GaussianBlur_4, AI_GaussianBlur_7, AI_PixelPlay_1, and AI_PixelPlay_2. From top to bottom, the right column shows the AI_Shadow_1, AI_Shadow_2, AI_Static, AI_Turbulence_3, AI_Turbulence_5, and AI_Woodgrain effects.

 Use the Adobe SVG Viewer, which is built into Illustrator and uses your default browser as a viewer, to display SVG files, including animated ones. One way of opening an SVG file is to find it on your computer and double-click the filename.

Using the Apply SVG Filter Command

With the Apply SVG Filter dialog box (see Figure 20-19), you can not only apply an SVG effect for one or more objects, but also edit an effect or create a new one.

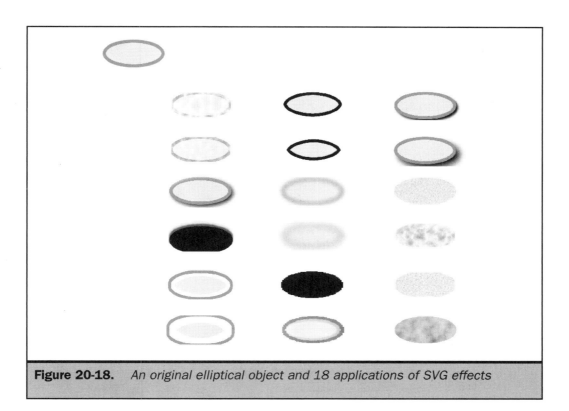

Figure 20-18.   *An original elliptical object and 18 applications of SVG effects*

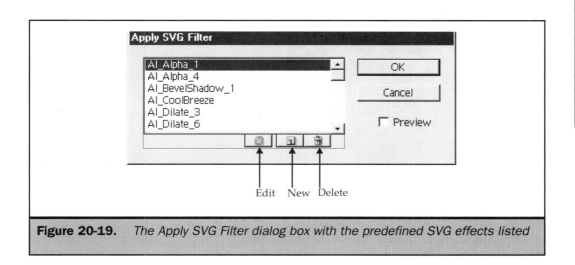

Figure 20-19.   *The Apply SVG Filter dialog box with the predefined SVG effects listed*

Applying a Filter   You can apply an SVG filter using the standard method as described in the preceding section, or you can use a dialog box, as described in this section.

To apply a filter, follow these steps:

1. Select or target an object.

2. Choose Effect | SVG Filters | Apply SVG Filter. Illustrator opens the Apply SVG Filter dialog box.

3. Select the name of a filter in the list box.

4. To preview the object with the filter applied before you close the dialog box, check the Preview check box.

5. Click OK.

Editing an SVG Effect   One benefit of using effects written in XML is you can edit the effects starting with the Apply SVG Filter dialog box and moving on to the Edit SVG Filter dialog box (see Figure 20-20).

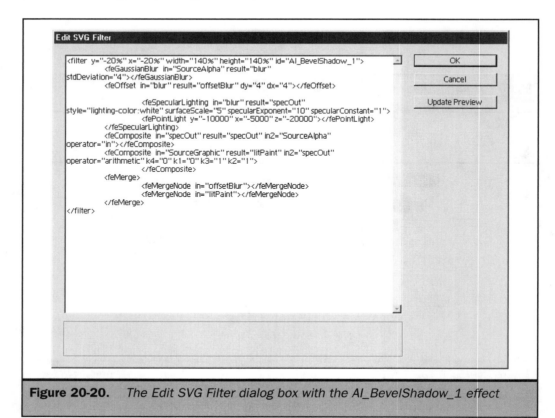

Figure 20-20.   *The Edit SVG Filter dialog box with the AI_BevelShadow_1 effect*

To edit an SVG effect, follow these steps:

1. Select or target an object.
2. Choose Effect | SVG Filters | Apply SVG Filter. Illustrator opens the Apply SVG Filter dialog box.
3. Select the name of a filter in the list box.
4. Click the Edit SVG Filter button. The Edit SVG Filter dialog box appears.
5. Edit the XML code in the large text box and click Update Preview. Illustrator applies the edited effect to the selected object.
6. Repeat step 5 until you are satisfied with the changes.
7. Click OK to accept your changes.

Note

If you cannot edit a particular filter using the Edit SVG Filter dialog box, an alternative plan is to edit the XML code with a text editor such as Windows Notepad. For example, if Illustrator displays a message that states, "The SVG filter you have specified cannot be previewed correctly in Illustrator," and closes the Edit SVG Filter dialog box, you have no other choice. The SVG effects are located in a single file, Adobe SVG Filters.svg, which is located in the Plug-Ins folder.

Creating an SVG Effect   You also can create an SVG effect starting at the Apply SVG Filter dialog box. Note that the new effect applies only to the current document. To create an SVG effect, follow these steps:

1. Choose Effect | SVG Filters | Apply SVG Filter. Illustrator opens the Apply SVG Filter dialog box.
2. Click the New SVG Filter button. The Edit SVG Filter dialog box sometimes appears with a one-line statement, which includes the <filter> start tag, an ID attribute in which you can type the name of the new filter, and the </filter> end tag; other times, the dialog box is empty.
3. Enter SVG code in the list box and click Update Preview. Illustrator applies the new effect to the selected object.
4. If you need to edit your code, repeat step 3 until the effect behaves in the desired way.
5. Click OK to add the new filter to the Adobe SVG Filters.svg file and to the list in the Apply SVG Filter dialog box.
6. Save the document.

Editing an Existing Effect into a New One

A good method for coding a new effect is to copy an existing effect into the Edit SVG Filter dialog box and edit the code until it is unique. When you create a new effect based on an old one, start simple. For example, modify something easy like a color or replace a number with a higher or lower number.

To create a new effect from an existing one, follow these steps:

1. Select or target an object.
2. Click the Edit SVG Filter button. Illustrator opens the Edit SVG Filter dialog box.
3. In the text box, select the code, and press CTRL-C/⌘-C to copy the filter.
4. Click Cancel to close the dialog box.
5. When you return to the Apply SVG Filter dialog box, click the New SVG Filter button to reopen the Edit SVG Filter dialog box.
6. Click in the text box, and press CTRL-V/⌘-V to paste the copied filter.
7. Start editing.
8. Click Update Preview to check the changes you have made.
9. Repeat steps 7 and 8 until the filter is one of a kind.
10. Click OK to save the new filter.

Deleting an SVG Effect from a Document   Deleting an SVG effect is almost the same as deleting an object, a swatch, a style, a symbol, and so on. To delete an SVG effect from the current document, select a filter in the Apply SVG Filters dialog box, and either click the Delete SVG button or drag the effect onto the button.

Importing SVG Filters into a Document

You can obtain SVG effects from an external SVG file. The procedure is similar to opening a file. To import SVG effects, choose Effect | SVG Filter | Import SVG Filter. When Illustrator opens the Select an SVG File dialog box, locate the file and click Open.

Exploring the Variables Palette

The Variables palette (see Figure 20-21) enables you to create and work with variables, dynamic objects and type, and data sets (which are not covered in this book). Illustrator permits you to work with four types of variables: graph data, linked files, text strings, and the state of visibility or invisibility. To toggle between showing and hiding the palette, choose Window | Variables.

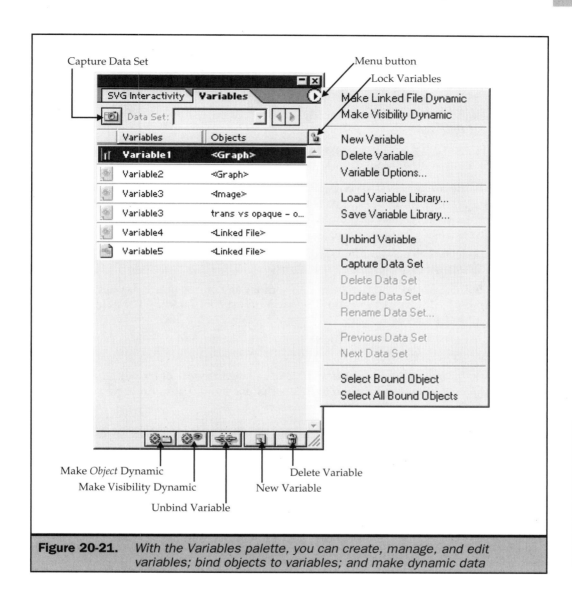

Figure 20-21. *With the Variables palette, you can create, manage, and edit variables; bind objects to variables; and make dynamic data*

The Variables palette contains several elements, each of which has a specific purpose:

- Click the menu button to open the Variables palette's menu.
- Click the Capture Data Set button to make a copy of a selected data set containing dynamic data. Note that at least one data set must be a bound

variable. (*Binding* attaches an object to a variable and makes the object dynamic.) The counterpart command on the palette's menu is Capture Data Set.

- Click the Variables button to sort the contents of the list box alphabetically by variable name. This is the default.

- Click the Objects button to sort the contents of the list box alphabetically by object type.

- Click the Lock Variables button to lock or unlock all the variables in the palette. When you lock variables, you cannot edit or delete them.

- Click the Make *Object* Dynamic button to define the selected type or object as dynamic and bind the type or object to the selected variable. The counterpart command on the palette's menu is Make *Object* Dynamic.

- Click the Make Visibility Dynamic button to make the visibility (or invisibility) of a selected object dynamic. The counterpart command on the palette's menu is Make Visibility Dynamic.

- Click the Unbind Variable button to remove the bonds between the selected variable and its object or type. The counterpart command on the palette's menu is Unbind Variable.

- Click the New Variable button to make a new unbound variable. The counterpart command on the palette's menu is New Variable.

- Click the Delete Variable button to delete all occurrences of the selected variable. Drag a variable to the button to delete that variable. The counterpart command on the palette's menu is Delete Variable.

To open the palette's menu, click the menu button. Commands on the menu are as follows:

- Make *Object* Dynamic defines the selected type or object as dynamic and binds the type or object to the selected variable. The counterpart button at the bottom of the palette is Make *Object* Dynamic.

- Make Visibility Dynamic makes the visibility (or invisibility) of a selected object dynamic. The counterpart button at the bottom of the palette is Make Visibility Dynamic.

- New Variable makes a new unbound variable. The counterpart button at the bottom of the palette is New Variable.

- Delete Variable deletes all occurrences of the selected variable. The counterpart button at the bottom of the palette is Delete Variable.

■ Variable Options opens the Variable Options dialog box in which you can name a variable or change its type (no type, Graph Data, Linked File, Text String, or Visibility).

■ Load Variable Library opens a dialog box in which you can type the name of an XML file, which contains variables, to be imported.

■ Save Variable Library opens a dialog box in which you can type the name of an XML file, which contains variables, to be exported as an SVG template.

■ Unbind Variable removes the bonds between the selected variable and its object or type. The counterpart button at the bottom of the palette is Unbind Variable.

■ Capture Data Set makes a copy of a selected data set containing dynamic data and variables. Note that at least one data set must be a bound variable. The counterpart button near the top of the palette is Capture Data Set.

■ Delete Data Set deletes the selected data set.

■ Update Data Set updates the current data set with the data in the illustration window. (If the name of the data set is italicized in the Data Set text box/ drop-down menu, Illustrator is telling you to update it.)

■ Rename Data Set opens the Rename Data Set dialog box so that you can rename the selected data set.

■ Previous Data Set selects the previous data set in the list box.

■ Next Data Set selects the following data set in the list box.

■ Select Bound Object enables you to select for editing an object bound to the selected variable in the Variables palette. An alternative way to start editing an object bound to a selected variable is to click the variable in the palette while pressing ALT/OPTION.

■ Select All Bound Objects selects all the bound objects in the Variables palette.

OUTSIDE ILLUSTRATOR

The
Complete
Reference

Chapter 21

Illustrator and Other Applications

693

Thanks to advancing technologies and some forethought, computer applications increasingly interact to help us work more efficiently. For example, you can import documents or objects from an application that specializes in creating a certain type of document or object into an application that focuses on a completely different technology. There you can edit those documents and objects using features that might not be part of the parent application or embed or link them within other documents. Then, you can export the enhanced documents to other applications for additional fine-tuning.

Illustrator has its share of collaborative applications. For example, the color insert in the middle of the book shows several artworks that were created in Illustrator and refined in Adobe Photoshop, were started in Photoshop and improved in Illustrator, or used the best features of both applications. Other Adobe applications with which Illustrator is compatible include Adobe Acrobat, Adobe InDesign, Adobe GoLive, Adobe AlterCast, and Adobe LiveMotion.

As you learned in Chapter 20, you can create Illustrator images and export them to use in Macromedia Flash and to the SVG file format. Illustrator also works with fellow vector-graphic applications such as Corel Draw. You also know that you can rasterize artworks that start as Illustrator vector graphics so you can use them on web pages— and the list goes on and on.

In this chapter you will learn about opening and placing documents from *foreign* (that is, non-Illustrator) applications and how Illustrator handles a document as you place it. You'll also find out how Illustrator saves and exports its own documents for use in foreign applications.

Acquiring Documents and Objects

To some people, *acquiring* always means scanning images into applications using an Acquire command; however, these days, the term "acquire" has generalized into any method by which you can get documents from a foreign application. Because a TWAIN-compliant scanner scans an image digitally, the result is a raster graphic. For that reason, you cannot scan images into Illustrator. However, you can scan an image into an application with which Illustrator is compatible and then open, copy and paste, drag and drop, or place it in Illustrator.

Opening Foreign Documents in Illustrator

Opening a document created in a non-Illustrator application is very much the same as opening an Illustrator document: Choose File | Open (CTRL-O/⌘-O). However, when a file opens, you might have to do some extra work. For example, when you open an Acrobat (PDF) file, the first object in the illustration window is the Acrobat PDF plug-in dialog box (see Figure 21-1) with or without thumbnails of the opening page of the document.

If the Acrobat file had thumbnails associated with it, you can click the buttons at the bottom of the dialog box to navigate the document. However, if there are no thumbnails, you won't be able to view each page. So you can move on, click OK to close the dialog box, and open one page in Illustrator. (To open a particular page, click the Go to page

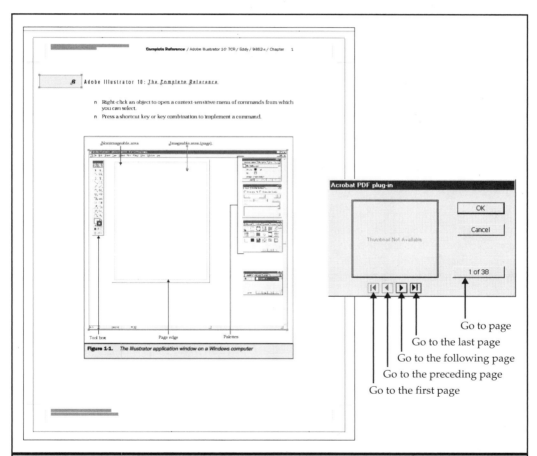

Figure 21-1.   *The Acrobat PDF plug-in dialog box for a document without thumbnails, and the opened document page in the background*

button in the Acrobat PDF Plug-In dialog box.) If Illustrator detects any compatibilities, it might display a message such as the following:

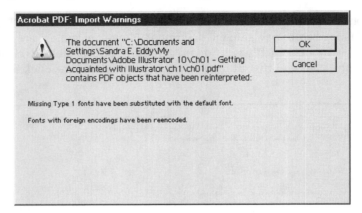

Click OK again to open one page of the document in the artboard.

 Table 2-1 in the "Illustrator-Supported File Types" section in Chapter 2 lists the types of files you can open or place in Illustrator.

When you open or import a foreign file in Illustrator, it becomes an Illustrator document. If the document is composed of vector graphics, Illustrator converts those graphics into Illustrator paths. Raster graphics imported into Illustrator behave like objects rasterized in Illustrator: You can use Illustrator transformation features and tools on them and apply filters that work for graphics rasterized in Illustrator.

Copying and Pasting from One Application to Another

As with most applications running under the Windows or Macintosh operating systems, you can copy a selected object from a source application into the Clipboard and paste the object from the Clipboard into a target application. In the source application, select the object to be copied and choose the Edit | Copy (CTRL-C/⌘-C) command. Activate the target application and paste the object by choosing Edit | Paste (CTRL-V/⌘-V).

Illustrator usually copies the object using the PICT file type. Depending on your copying preferences, you can set the Clipboard file type as PDF or AICB. To learn about setting copying preferences, refer to "Indicating Files & Clipboard Preferences" in Appendix B.

Dragging and Dropping from One Application to Another

Dragging and dropping enables you to copy and move objects from one application to another without issuing commands. In Windows, the applications must support OLE (*object linking and embedding*); on the Macintosh, the applications must support the Macintosh Drag Manager.

To drag and drop from Illustrator to an appropriate application (such as Photoshop), select the object, drag it into the application's workspace using an Illustrator selection tool, and drop it.

 If you press and hold down CTRL/⌘ *as you drag an object into Photoshop, the object becomes a Photoshop path.*

To drag and drop from an application into Illustrator, select the object using a suitable selection tool.

Placing an Object

In the "Opening Files and Placing Images" section in Chapter 2, you learned how to place objects in the Illustrator window. Now we'll go into more depth about placing and its byproduct processes: embedding and linking. You can place most raster graphics and type into Illustrator. For a complete list of file types that Illustrator supports for placing, refer to Table 2-1 in the "Illustrator-Supported File Types" section in Chapter 2.

Although you can place many file formats into Illustrator, evaluate the file format first. For example, many raster file types—especially those that produce large files—result in large Illustrator files that might strain your Illustrator processing times as well as your computer system's RAM.

Some objects do not travel well as they are placed. For example, the *Adobe Illustrator 10 User Guide* states, "Do not place an EPS file containing mesh objects or transparency objects if it was created in an application other than Illustrator. Instead open the EPS file, copy all objects, and then paste in Illustrator."

Illustrator enables you to place an object by linking (the default) or embedding.

- ■ If you embed an image, the actual image inhabits the illustration window— just as if you were pasting or dropping it. Because of its size, working on the Illustrator file might slow down Illustrator or your entire computer system.

- ■ If you link a placed image, you put a representation of the image in the illustration window—not the actual image. Linking helps you drastically reduce the size of the Illustrator file. When you want to edit a linked image, you return to the application in which it was created; you will edit an embedded image in Illustrator. Use Illustrator's Links palette to manage linked objects. For more information about modifying and updating linked, placed objects refer to the following section, "Working with Links."

To place a file into the illustration window, follow these steps:

1. Choose File | Place. Illustrator opens the Place dialog box, which looks like almost any Open dialog box.

2. Select the file to be placed in the illustration window. Illustrator makes the Link check box available.

3. To embed the file, make sure the Link check box does not contain a check mark.

4. To link the file, check the Link check box.

5. Click the Save button. Illustrator places the file in the illustration window.

Figure 21-2 shows three linked objects in the illustration window. In the top left is a raster graphic, below that is a file from Photoshop, and to the right is a page from a PDF document.

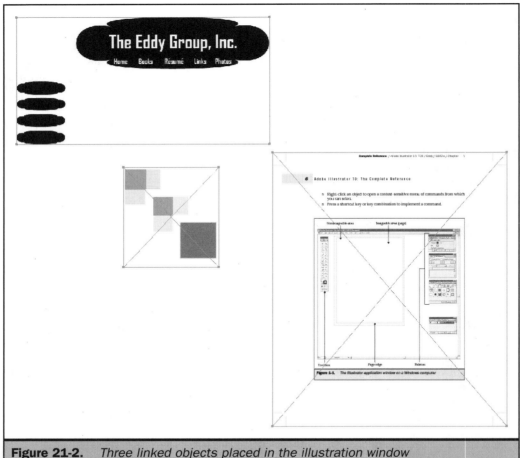

Figure 21-2.   *Three linked objects placed in the illustration window*

Displaying a Placed Image in Outline View

As you learned in the "Viewing in Preview and Outline Modes" section in Chapter 3, Illustrator provides two modes (Preview and Outline views) with which you can view objects in the illustration window. Figure 21-2 shows you three linked, placed objects in Preview view, and Figure 21-3 illustrates the same objects in Outline view. Note that Outline view can display certain placed objects in black and white.

To switch to Outline view, choose View | Outline (CTRL-Y/⌘-Y); to change to Preview view, choose View | Outline (CTRL-Y/⌘-Y).

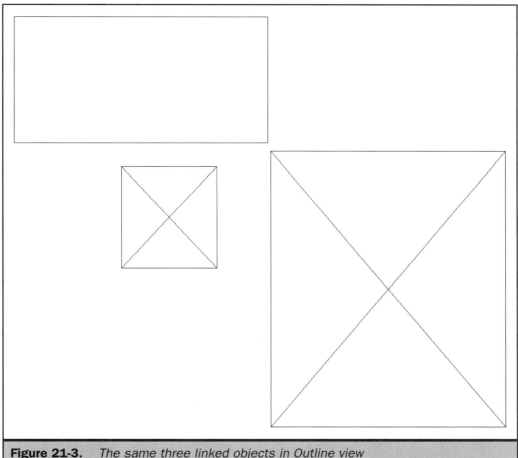

Figure 21-3.   *The same three linked objects in Outline view*

If you created an object in a foreign application and didn't save it with a preview image (many applications do this automatically), Illustrator cannot display the object in Illustrator. Instead, the image appears as a box containing two diagonal lines.

Editing Placed Objects in Illustrator

Illustrator enables you to transform and apply certain filters and effects to a placed object—depending on Illustrator's evaluation of the object. For example, if you place a raster graphic, it remains a raster graphic with the following characteristic:

- You can transform the raster graphic using any transformation feature or tool.
- If you scale up the raster graphic, the quality of the object tends to decline because of the fixed number of pixels in the graphic.
- If you scale down the raster graphic, the quality of the object tends to improve for the same reason.
- For placed raster graphics, Illustrator allows you to use only those filters and effects that it supports for raster graphics.
- You can use the Auto Trace tool on placed raster graphics but not on placed EPS files.

If you embed a vector graphic, Illustrator converts it to paths, so you can use almost any tool or feature for editing.

Note *Use the Direct Selection tool (A) to select individual placed images.*

Working with Links

The Links palette is the centerpiece of linked and embedded objects. With the buttons and commands in the palette, you can perform a variety of tasks. In this section you'll take a detailed tour of the palette and then learn how to use each feature on the palette.

Exploring the Links Palette

The Links palette (see Figure 21-4) enables you to organize, manage, select, and replace objects that have been linked or embedded in Illustrator. You also can use the palette to check for broken or missing links and open home applications for linked objects that are ready to be updated. To toggle between showing and hiding the palette, choose Window | Links.

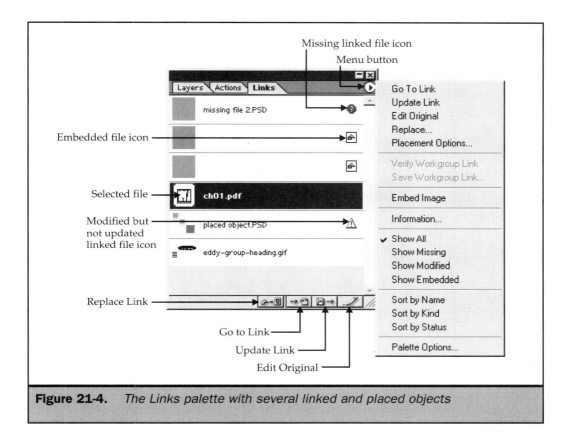

Figure 21-4.   *The Links palette with several linked and placed objects*

The Links palette contains several elements, each of which has a specific meaning and with which you can control linked and embedded objects in Illustrator:

- Click the menu button to open the Links palette's menu.

- Click the Replace Link button to replace one linked object with another in the illustration window. The counterpart command on the palette's menu is Replace.

- Click the Go to Link button to go to a link, select it, and center it in the illustration window. The counterpart command on the palette's menu is Go to Link.

- Click the Update Link button to update the appearance of one or more selected, linked objects that have been edited in their home applications. The counterpart command on the palette's menu is Update Link.

- Click the Edit Original button to open the selected, linked object in its home application workspace. The counterpart command on the palette's menu is Edit Original.

- The center of the palette displays all the linked and embedded objects in the current Illustrator document. Additionally, Illustrator displays icons for objects whose files might be missing, those you should update, and embedded objects.

To open the palette's menu, click the menu button. Commands on the menu are as follows:

- The Go to Link command goes to a link, selects it, and centers it in the illustration window. The counterpart button at the bottom of the palette is Go to Link.

- The Update Link command updates the appearance of one or more selected, linked objects that have been edited in their home applications. The counterpart button at the bottom of the palette is Update Link.

- The Edit Original command opens the selected, linked object in its home application workspace. The counterpart button at the bottom of the palette is Edit Original.

- The Replace command replaces one linked object with another in the illustration window. The counterpart button at the bottom of the palette is Replace Link.

- The Placement Options command opens the Transforms version of the Placement Options dialog box, which controls resizing, scaling, and placement of a linked object.

- The Verify Workgroup Link command compares the link on your computer with the same link on the WebDAV server to verify whether the links match each other or the link exists on the local computer.

- The Save Workgroup Link command saves managed links to their WebDAV (Web Distributed Authoring and Versioning) workgroup server. To learn more about managing documents with the WebDAV server, refer to the *Adobe Illustrator 10 User Guide* or go to http://www.webdav.org.

- The Embed Image command converts a linked object to an embedded object.

- The Information command opens the Link Information dialog box, which displays much information about the selected linked object or just transformation information about the selected embedded object.

- The Show All command (the default) shows all the linked and embedded objects in the current document.

- The Show Missing command shows only the linked objects in the current document whose original files are missing.

- The Show Modified command shows only the linked objects that have been edited in their home applications but have not yet been updated in Illustrator.

- The Show Embedded command shows only the embedded objects in the current document.

- The Sort by Name command sorts the objects in the palette alphabetically by name.

- The Sort by Kind command sorts the objects in the palette alphabetically by type.

- The Sort by Status command sorts the objects in the palette in the order of their statuses.

- The Palette Options command opens the Palette Options dialog box, in which you can set the size of the palette thumbnails and compare transparent and opaque objects.

Using the Links Palette

The combination of buttons at the bottom of the Links palette and the commands on the palette's menu enable you to perform a variety of tasks: You can evaluate the objects shown in the palette, change your view of the palette, select one or more embedded or linked objects, make one object the center of attention, update or replace links, change the status or placement of an object, and display information about an object.

Viewing the Palette

Not only does the Links palette automatically display all the embedded and linked objects in the current document; it also enables you to view the status of each object shown in the palette. You can tell quickly whether you have inadvertently deleted a file or forgotten to update a file that you have modified in its home application.

A small stop-sign icon indicates that the original file from which a linked object originates is no longer in the folder in which you stored it. This could mean that you have deleted the file or just moved it. If the file returns to its starting location, and you click the Update Link button or choose the Update Link command from the palette's menu, Illustrator removes the icon.

A small triangular icon that contains an exclamation point indicates that someone (maybe you) has modified the linked file in its home location but didn't click the Update Link button or choose the Update Link command.

An icon containing a rectangle and triangle indicates that its object is embedded rather than linked.

Changing the Look of the Links Palette

You can change the appearance of the Links palette or its contents in various ways: You can show some or all entries in the palette, sort the entries in three ways, and set palette options.

Showing and Hiding Items in the Palette   Use the Show commands from the Links palette's menu to show or hide items in the palette. For example, you might limit the display to those objects whose files are missing to search for those files so that you can open the document cleanly. You also can restrict the display to linked objects you have modified in their home programs so you can update the entire list one by one without wasting your efforts on those you have already updated. Normally, unless the current document is overflowing with linked and embedded objects, you should display all the linked and embedded objects in the palette.

- Choose the Show All command (the default) to display all the linked and embedded objects in the current document.

- Choose the Show Missing command to display all the linked objects whose original files are missing.

- Choose the Show Modified command to display all the linked objects that have been edited in their home applications but have not yet been updated in Illustrator.

- Choose the Show Embedded command to display only the objects that have been embedded in the current document.

Sorting Items in the Palette   Sorting entries serves a similar purpose to showing and hiding entries: better organization of the linked and embedded objects in the current document.

- Choose the Sort by Name command to sort the objects in the palette alphabetically by name. All the unnamed (that is, embedded) objects are first in the sorting order; followed by named, linked objects.

- Choose the Sort by Kind command to sort the objects in the palette alphabetically by type. All the embedded objects, which have no file types, are first in the sorting order; followed by linked objects sorted by their file extensions (for example, .GIF, .PDF, and PSD).

- Choose the Sort by Status command to sort the objects in the palette in the order of their status: Linked files whose original files are missing are first, followed by linked files that have not been updated, embedded objects, and all linked objects not in the file-missing or need-updating categories.

Setting Palette Options   When you choose the Palette Options command, which is located at the bottom of the palette's menu, you open a dialog box (see Figure 21-5) with which you can change the size of the palette thumbnails and compare transparent and opaque objects.

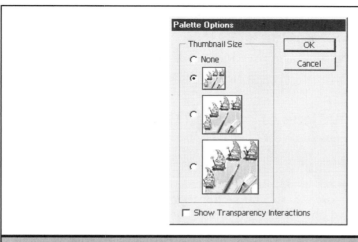

Figure 21-5.   *The Palette Options dialog box with its default settings*

The options in the dialog box are as follows:

- In the Thumbnail Size section, click the None radio button to hide the thumbnails in the palette or another button to choose one of three thumbnail sizes. The default is the smallest thumbnail.

- Check the Show Transparency Interactions check box to see how transparent linked objects relate with opaque ones. An unchecked check box is the default.

Selecting Objects in the Links Palette

Selecting one or more objects in the Links palette is the same as selecting other objects in Illustrator:

- To select a single object, click it.

- To select two or more noncontiguous objects, click the first; then press and hold down CTRL/⌘, and continuing clicking objects to add to the selection.

- To select two or more contiguous objects, click the object at one end of the range, press and hold down SHIFT, and click the object at the other end of the range.

Going to and Selecting an Object

Sometimes it's easier to find an object by using the Links palette rather than searching for it in the illustration window. With a button or command, Illustrator enables you to not only locate an object but also to select it and center it in the illustration window.

To go to a particular linked or embedded object, follow these steps:

1. Select the object in the Links palette.

2. Click the Go to Link button at the bottom of the palette, or choose the Go to Link command on the palette's menu. Illustrator selects the object and adjusts the illustration window so that the object is centered in the window.

Controlling Transformations of a Linked Object in Illustrator

You don't have to return to a linked object's home application to transform it. To set the limits of fitting and aligning a selected object inside its bounding box, choose the Placement Options command, which opens the Placement Options dialog box (see Figure 21-6). The dialog box is composed of five sections with which you can control future transformations. To choose a particular section, open the Preserve drop-down menu. When you have selected options in that section, click OK to apply the options and close the dialog box.

The options in the Placement Options dialog box are as follows:

- If you choose the Preserve Transforms section, you see the default placement settings, which fit the linked object to its bounding box. If you replace the object, Illustrator maintains any transformations performed in Illustrator but not the object's original boundaries.

- The Preserve Proportions (Fit) section fits the linked object inside its bounding box and maintains the object's proportions. To set the corner or side from which the fit takes place, click a box in the reference point box.

- The Preserve Proportions (Fill) section fills the bounding box with the object and maintains the object's proportions in the following ways:

  - To set the corner or side from which the fill takes place, click a box in the reference point box. Note that the edges may overlap on one side or corner.

  - To remove all sections of the object outside the borders of the bounding box, check the Clip to Bounding Box check box. The default is an unchecked box.

- The Preserve File Dimensions section preserves the linked object's original dimensions, regardless of the current size of the bounding box and transformations applied in Illustrator.

  - To set the corner or side from which the object is placed, click a box in the reference point box.

  - To remove all sections of the object outside the borders of the bounding box, check the Clip to Bounding Box check box. The default is an unchecked check box.

- The Preserve Bounds section fits the linked object to its bounding box, which maintains its original size. As a result, Illustrator might have to resize or rescale the linked object, regardless of its new proportions.

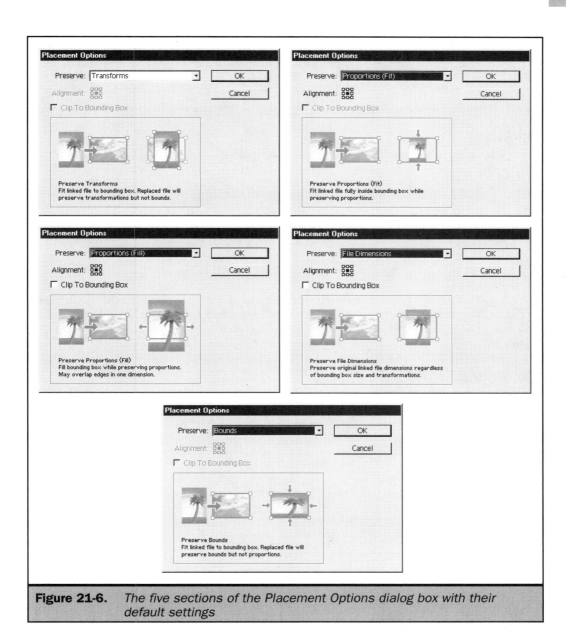

Figure 21-6. The five sections of the Placement Options dialog box with their default settings

Editing a Linked Object in Its Home Application

As you remember, one of the purposes of linking an object is to save space in the Illustrator document: Rather than embedding the object, a linked object is a representation of the object. Another advantage of linking is that you can edit linked objects in the applications in which they were created and developed. In most cases, the home application is the best location for editing those objects.

To edit a linked object in its home application, click the Edit Original button or choose the Edit Original command from the palette's menu. Then modify the object as you wish. When you return to Illustrator, it will prompt you to update the link.

Updating Links

Once you have edited an object in its home application, Illustrator prompts you to update it:

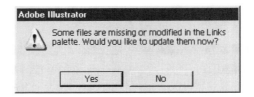

To update a linked object in Illustrator, click the Update Link button at the bottom of the Links palette or choose the Update Link command from the palette's menu. If you don't want to update immediately, remember that Illustrator places an icon on the right side of the object's entry in the palette.

Replacing Links

Using the Links palette, you can replace one linked object with another in the illustration window. For example, you might have changed your company logo to a new and improved version. By clicking Replace Link button at the bottom of the palette or choosing the Replace Link command from the palette's menu, you can quickly perform your replacement magic. To replace a linked object with a different one, follow these steps:

1. Select the object to be replaced in the illustration window, target it in the Layers palette, or select it in the Links palette.

2. Click the Replace Link button or choose the Replace Link command from the palette's menu. Illustrator opens the Place dialog box with the Links check box checked.

3. Choose the file to replace the selected object and click Place. Illustrator replaces the selected object with the selected file.

The replacement will not disrupt the current page layout because the replacement object automatically conforms to the size, placement, and transformations of the object that it is replacing.

Changing a Linked Object to an Embedded Object

You can easily convert a linked object to an embedded object. Just choose the Embed Image command from the Links palette and select options when prompted by a dialog box or two (see Figure 21-7).

Getting Information about an Object

You can get a few facts about embedded objects and much more information about linked objects from the Link Information dialog box (see Figure 21-8). To open the dialog box, select an object and choose the Information command from the Links palette's menu.

Opening Documents That Contain Linked Objects

When you open a document with linked files, Illustrator attempts to load linked objects one by one. When Illustrator has problems in loading, it prompts you in various ways. For example, if a file is missing and you didn't correct that situation in a prior Illustrator session, Illustrator asks you whether you want to replace the missing file

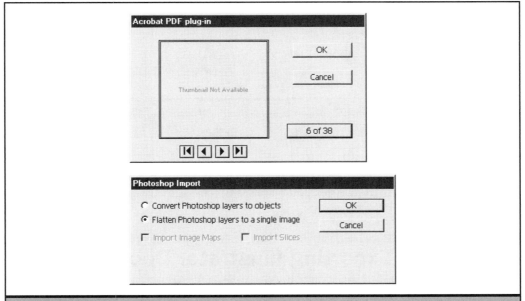

Figure 21-7.   *Two of the dialog boxes that might appear when you embed an object*

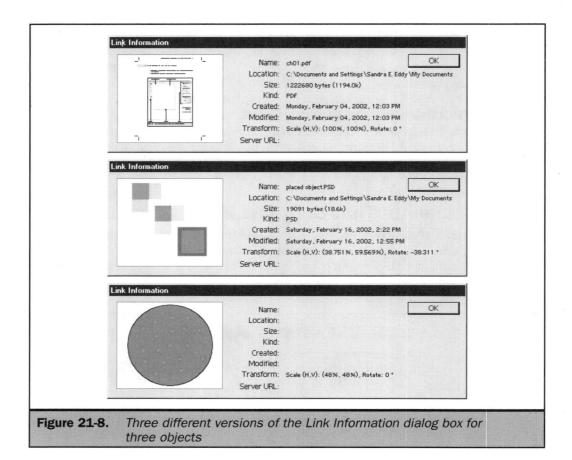

Figure 21-8.   *Three different versions of the Link Information dialog box for three objects*

with another. If you have linked a PDF file, you'll have to respond to the dialog box shown earlier in Figure 21-1. After you respond to message boxes of various kinds, Illustrator will open the document.

Saving and Exporting Illustrator Documents

You can save Illustrator to several formats: Adobe PDF, Adobe Illustrator, Adobe Illustrator EPS (you get the drift), as well as SVG and SVG Compressed (which were covered in Chapters 19 and 20). Illustrator also enables you to export to many popular file formats—some vector and some raster—and in most cases, helps the export process with a dialog box or two. In this section you'll learn how to save and export Illustrator documents to other file formats.

Table 2-1 in the "Illustrator-Supported File Types" section in Chapter 2, lists the types of files you can save or export in Illustrator.

Saving Down Illustrator Documents

If you behave like I do, you ignore the Illustrator Native Format Options dialog box (see Figure 21-9) when you save an Illustrator file. I click OK to save the file and move on to the next task. However, this dialog box is instrumental when you want to *save down* to an earlier release of Illustrator. The main reason for saving down is to create artwork files for colleagues with earlier versions of Illustrator.

 If you save a document to an earlier version of Illustrator, the resulting file might change because of improvements to Illustrator since the target release.

To save a document to an earlier Illustrator version, follow these steps:

1. In Illustrator, create or open a document to be saved to an earlier release.

2. If you haven't saved the document before, choose File | Save (CTRL-S/⌘-S).

3. If you have already saved and named the document, choose File | Save As (CTRL-SHIFT-S/⌘-SHIFT-S).

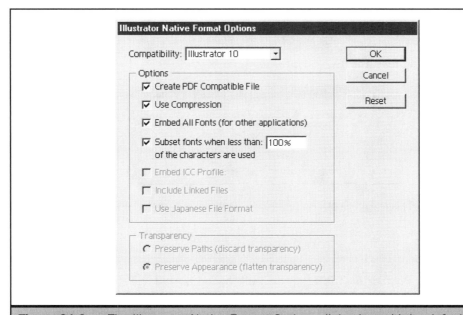

Figure 21-9. *The Illustrator Native Format Options dialog box with its default settings*

OUTSIDE ILLUSTRATOR

4. In the Save As dialog box, choose options and click the Save button once or twice. Illustrator opens the Illustrator Native Format Options dialog box.

5. From the Compatibility drop-down menu, choose the appropriate version:

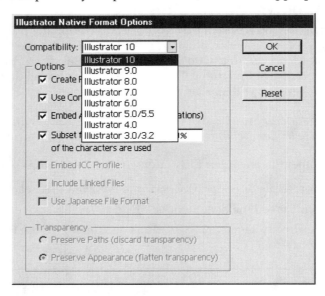

6. Click OK. Illustrator opens a message box that reminds you that you might lose some editing features if you continue.

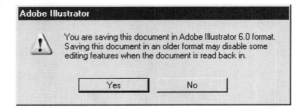

7. Click Yes to continue saving; click No to stop saving. Illustrator finishes saving the document.

Saving to EPS

The Encapsulated PostScript (EPS) file format is based on the widely supported PostScript language. After you choose File | Save (CTRL-S/⌘-S) or File | Save As (CTRL-SHIFT-S/⌘-SHIFT-S), choose Illustrator EPS (*.EPS) from the Save As Type drop-down menu in the Save As dialog box, and click the Save button, Illustrator opens the EPS Format Options dialog box (see Figure 21-10). Here you select the

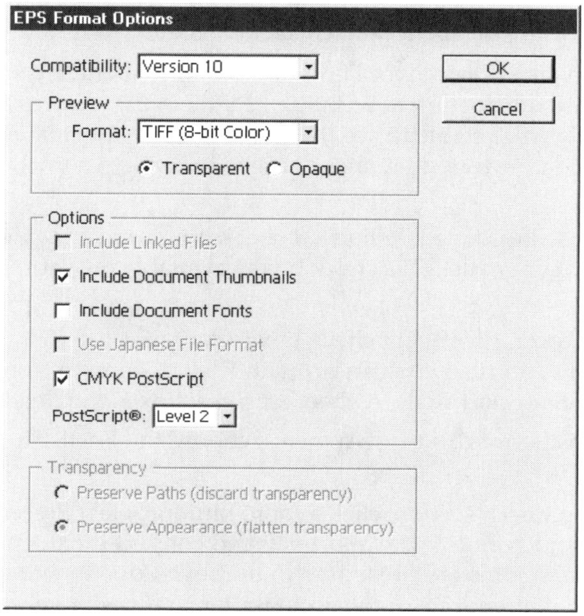

Figure 21-10. *EPS Format Options dialog box with its default settings*

document's compatibility as you did in the Illustrator Native Format Options dialog box. You'll also create a preview format and select other options.

The options in the EPS Format Options dialog box are as follows:

- From the Compatibility drop-down menu, choose the appropriate Illustrator EPS version: Versions 10 (the default), 9.0, 8.0, 7.0, 6.0, 5.0/5.5, 4.0, or 3.0/3.2.

- From the Format drop-down menu, choose a raster preview format or no format. To create a preview that will appear in foreign application workspaces, select TIFF (8-bit Color) or TIFF (Black & White). Note that a preview is not a thumbnail; it's available for foreign applications that cannot display the actual EPS file. The default is TIFF (8-bit Color). To create a placeholder with an X in it (that is, no preview), select None.

- If you have selected TIFF (8-bit Color), click the Transparent radio button (the default) to include a transparent background in the preview; click Opaque to include an opaque background.

- Check the Include Linked Files check box to embed all the documents that are linked with the document being exported.

- Check the Include Document Thumbnails check box to create a thumbnail for the saved document. A checked check box is the default.

- Check the Include Document Fonts check box to include the fonts that were used to create the document with the EPS file. This ensures that anyone who views the file will be able to see the document as you created it. Note that you cannot include protected Japanese-language fonts. An unchecked check box is the default.

- Check the Use Japanese File Format check box to save the document as a Japanese-language file. This check box is available only for Illustrator versions from 3.0 to 5.0.

- Check the CMYK PostScript check box to safeguard RGB-based documents in foreign applications so you can print an RGB document from an application that does not support RGB. A checked check box is the default.

- From the PostScript drop-down menu, choose the PostScript Level: 1, 2 (the default), or 3.

- In the Transparency section, click a radio button. Select Preserve Paths (discard transparency) to remove transparency and convert the document to 100% opacity so that paths are preserved in the saved document; select Preserve Appearance (flatten transparency) to flatten and preserve transparency in the document. The default is Preserve Paths (discard transparency). This option applies to documents saved down to Version 9 or earlier.

Saving to PDF

When you save an Illustrator document to the Adobe PDF format, the document becomes a single page without layers, path type, or patterned and gradient fills. Start the save process by choosing File | Save (CTRL-S/⌘-S) or File | Save As (CTRL-SHIFT-S/⌘-SHIFT-S). In the Save As dialog box, choose Adobe PDF (*.PDF) from the Save As Type drop-down menu and click the Save button. In turn, Illustrator opens the Adobe PDF Format Options dialog box (see Figure 21-11), which shows the General options for the Default options set.

The dialog box provides three options sets: Default (which is the default), Screen Optimized, and Custom. Select Default to start with the best set of options for printing the document; select Screen Optimized to optimize the document for use on Web pages in RGB mode; select Custom to select options unique to your particular situation. If you choose Default or Screen Optimized and modify an option, Illustrator changes the options set to Custom.

The other options in the General options section are as follows:

- In the File Compatibility section, click the radio button for the Acrobat version with which the saved document will be most compatible. Acrobat 5.0 (the default) is a relatively new version of the program, which preserves transparency, spot color, and type; Acrobat 4.0 is an earlier version, which might have a larger audience.

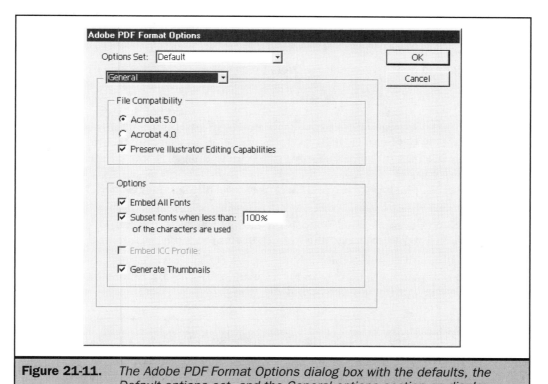

Figure 21-11.   *The Adobe PDF Format Options dialog box with the defaults, the Default options set, and the General options section on display*

- Check the Preserve Illustrator Editing Capabilities check box to be able to edit the document in Illustrator. A checked check box is the default.

- Check the Embed All Fonts check box to include the fonts that were used to create the document with the EPS file. This ensures that anyone who views the file will be able to see the document as you created it. A checked check box is the default.

- Check the Subset Fonts check box and set a percentage of a particular font's characters that must appear in the document before its font can be embedded. Valid values range from 0% to 100% (the default). A checked check box is the default.

- Check the Embed ICC Profile to create a color-managed document with an ICC profile.

- Check the Generate Thumbnails check box to produce a thumbnail for the saved document. A checked check box is the default.

Select Compression from the drop-down menu to open the Compression section (see Figure 21-12), which enables you to select compression options when you save the document to the PDF format.

The options in the Compression section are as follows:

- For color and grayscale bitmap images, check the Average Downsampling At check box to *down-sample* (that is, reduce the resolution of the document by decreasing the number of pixels as set in the ppi text box). All three check boxes are unchecked by default. In the Default options set section, the number of pixels per inch for color and grayscale bitmap images is 300; for monochrome bitmap images, it's 1,200. In the Screen Optimized options set section, the number of pixels is 72 for color and grayscale bitmap images, and 300 for monochrome.

- For color, grayscale, and monochrome bitmap images, check the Compression check box to indicate that Illustrator will compress the document as it saves it.

- For color and grayscale bitmap images, select the type of compression from the drop-down menu. Your choices for color and grayscale are Automatic (the default for Screen Optimized), JPEG, and ZIP (the default for Default). Automatic lets

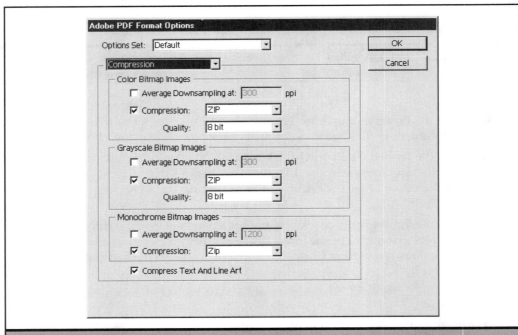

Figure 21-12. *The Compression section of the Adobe PDF Format Options dialog box and the default options for the Default options set*

Illustrator choose the best type and quality of compression for the document. ZIP compression works best for black-and-white documents or those with few colors, and for both types of documents with repeating patterns. JPEG compression is best for grayscale and color images, but loses data each time a document is saved.

■ For monochrome bitmap images, you can select ZIP (the default for Default), CCITT Group 3, CCITT Group 4 (the default for Screen Optimized), and Run Length compression. Note that CCITT (Consultative Committee on International Telegraphy and Telephony) Group 3 is the standard for many fax machines.

■ For color and grayscale bitmap images, the Quality drop-down menu contains options that are related to the selected type of compression. If you have selected Automatic, Illustrator chooses the level of quality. For ZIP compression, the Quality menu contains two entries: 8 bit (for the ZIP default for Default) and 4 bit, which should match the bits in the document for the best results. If you have selected JPEG, the Quality menu lists the following: Minimum, Low, Medium (for the Automatic default for Screen Optimized), High, and Maximum. If you choose High or Maximum, Illustrator preserves the quality of the image, but the size of the file increases. Choosing Minimum, Low, or Medium reduces the quality level but reduces the size of the file.

■ Check the Compress Text and Line Art check box to use ZIP compression on all line art and type in the document.

Exporting to Photoshop

It seems Illustrator and Photoshop are fraternal twins. They don't look alike, but they are together a good part of the time for many graphic artists. However, Illustrator's vector graphics must undergo some changes when they are exported to the Photoshop raster file format.

Start exporting by choosing File | Export. In the Export dialog box, choose Photoshop (*.PSD) from the Save As Type drop-down menu and click the Save button. Illustrator then opens the Photoshop Options dialog box (see Figure 21-13), from which you can select options.

The options in the dialog box are as follows:

■ From the Color Model drop-down menu, choose a color model: RGB, CMYK, or Grayscale. The starting value in the menu is the current color mode in Illustrator. It's probably a good idea to export the document using its current color mode. When the document arrives in Photoshop, you can change it.

■ In the Resolution section, select a resolution: Screen (72 ppi), Medium (150 ppi), High (300 ppi), or Other. The default is Medium. If you select Other, you can set the resolution in the text box.

■ Check the Anti-alias check box to turn on anti-aliasing, which smooths jagged edges from objects. The default is a checked check box.

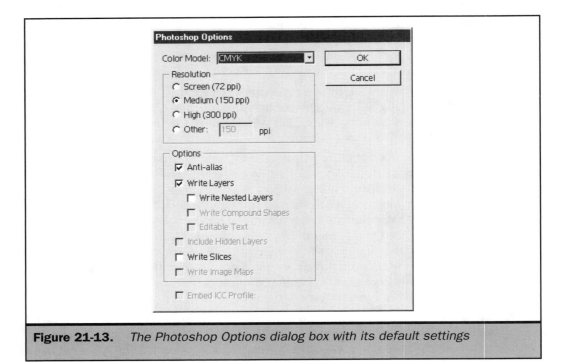

Figure 21-13.   *The Photoshop Options dialog box with its default settings*

■ Check Write Layers to export each top-level layer as an individual Photoshop layer. Both Write Layers and Write Nested Layers must be checked for top-level layers and sublayers to be exported. If you remove check marks from Write Layers and Write Nested Layers, Illustrator flattens the layers to one layer. A checked check box is the default.

■ Check Write Nested Layers to export each top-level sublayer as an individual Photoshop layer. An unchecked check box is the default.

Note   *Illustrator might not be able to export layers that contain objects with blending modes; however, if you apply a blending mode to a layer itself, the export might work.*

■ Check Write Compound Shapes to export compound shapes as separate layers. Note that Illustrator does not export compound shapes that contain styles, brushstrokes, or dashed strokes. The default is an unchecked check box. This check box is not available if a document does not contain compound shapes.

■ Check Editable Text to export horizontal and vertical point type (not area or path type) in a top-level layer as Photoshop editable text (if this does not change the look of the document in Photoshop). The default is an unchecked check box.

- Check the Include Hidden Layers check box to export hidden layers as hidden Photoshop layers. The default is an unchecked check box.

- Check the Write Slices check box to export slices as Photoshop slices (if this does not change the look of the document in Photoshop).

- Check the Write Image Maps check box to export image maps as Photoshop image maps (if this does not change the look of the document in Photoshop).

- Check the Embed ICC Profile check box to create a color-managed document with an ICC profile.

Exporting to TIFF

Tagged Image File Format (TIFF) is a standard raster file format. In fact, TIFF is so popular and effective that most images in most computer books—such as this one—are captured as TIFF files. So, it's important for Illustrator to support export to TIFF.

To export an Illustrator document to TIFF, choose File | Export. In the Export dialog box, choose TIFF (*.TIF) from the Save As Type drop-down menu and click the Save button. Illustrator opens the TIFF Options dialog box (see Figure 21-14), from which you can select options.

The options in the dialog box are as follows:

- In the Resolution section, select a resolution: Screen, Medium, High (the default), or Other. If you select Other, you can overwrite the 300 dpi resolution setting in the text box.

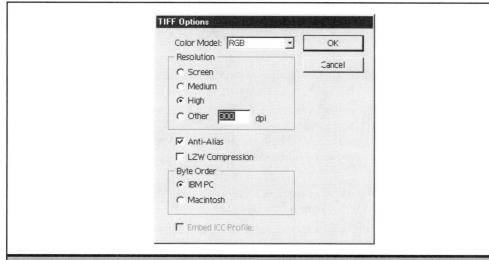

Figure 21-14.   *The TIFF Options dialog box with its default settings*

- Check the Anti-alias check box to turn on anti-aliasing, which smooths jagged edges from objects. The default is a checked box.

- Check the LZW Compression check box to compress the document with the lossless Lempel-Zif-Welch (LZW) method.

- In the Byte Order section, click a radio button: IBM PC to use the IBM byte order; Macintosh to use the Macintosh byte order.

- Check the Embed ICC Profile check box to create a color-managed document with an ICC profile.

Exporting to JPEG

As you learned in the "Choosing a File Type" section in Chapter 19, JPEG is a 24-bit raster file format, which is excellent for photographs and other continuous tone images. You also learned in Chapter 19 how to optimize and save Illustrator documents to use on web pages.

When you export a document to the JPEG file format, you follow the same routine as for other exports: Choose File | Export. However, in the Export dialog box, choose JPEG (*.JPG) from the Save As Type drop-down menu and click Save. Illustrator opens the JPEG Options dialog box (see Figure 21-15), from which you can select options.

The options in the dialog box are as follows:

- The Quality text box and drop-down menu work in tandem: Set a compression quality value with either option. Valid values range from 0 (Low) to 10 (Maximum). Note that Low Quality ranges from 0 to 2, Medium (the default) ranges from 3 to 5, High ranges from 6 to 7, and Maximum ranges from 8 to 10. If you choose High or Maximum, Illustrator preserves the quality of the image, but the size of the file increases. Choosing Low or Medium reduces the quality level but reduces the size of the file.

- The Image slider also sets the compression quality. As you slide the slider, Illustrator changes the values in the Quality text box and menu.

- With the Method drop-down menu, specify a JPEG Lossy compression method: Baseline (Standard) is a standard method; Baseline Optimized compresses using the standard method and optimizes the file; Progressive compresses a JPEG image in a number of scans starting at a low resolution and ending at a high resolution.

- From the Scans drop-down menu, select the number of scans for a Progressive compression. Valid values are 3 (the default), 4, or 5.

- With the Depth drop-down menu, select the number of colors for resolution: Screen (the default), Medium, High, or Custom. A higher number of colors results in a larger, high-quality file.

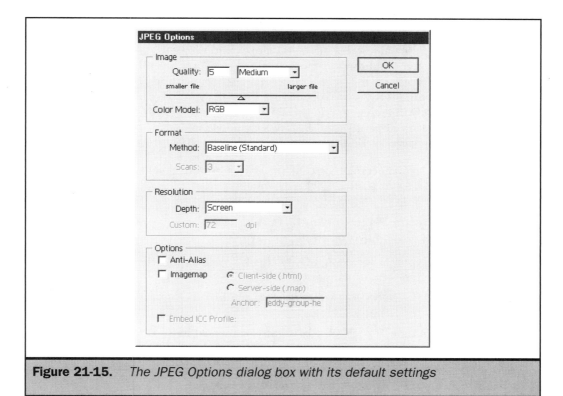

Figure 21-15.   *The JPEG Options dialog box with its default settings*

■ In the Custom text box, type the dots per inch (dpi) for the resolution. The default is 72 dpi for Screen, 150 dpi for Medium, and 300 dpi for High.

■ Check the Anti-alias check box to turn on anti-aliasing, which smooths jagged edges from objects. The default is an unchecked box.

■ Check the Imagemap check box to indicate that the document is an image map. Then click a radio button to indicate whether the image map is *client-side* (stored and runs on the user's computer system) or *server-side* (stored and runs on the server's computer system).

■ The name in the Anchor text box contains the name of the exported document, which is also the anchor of the image map by default. An *anchor* is the link from which a user can jump to a target link on the current Web page or on a page at another Web site. You can type the name of a different anchor in the text box.

■ Check the Embed ICC Profile check box to create a color-managed document with an ICC profile.

Exporting to AutoCAD

AutoCAD is a computer-aided design (CAD) application for engineers, architects, and drafters who create two- and three-dimensional model drawings. Illustrator supports two AutoCAD file types: DXF (Drawing Interchange Format) and DWG.

To export a document to AutoCAD, choose File | Export, select AutoCAD Drawing (*.DWG) or AutoCAD Interchange File (*.DXF) from the Save As Type drop-down menu and click Save. Illustrator opens the DXF/DWG Options dialog box (see Figure 21-16), from which you can select options for both formats.

- Select an AutoCAD version by clicking a radio button. You can select R13/LT95, R14/LT98/LT97, or 2000/LT2000 (the default).

- From the Number of Colors section, click a radio button to indicate the number of colors: 8, 16, or 256 (the default).

- Select a file format: BMP (the default) or JPEG.

- Check the Export Selected Art Only check box to export the selected objects rather than the entire document.

- Check the Alter Paths for Appearance check box to convert the appearance of the paths for easier viewing.

- Check the Outline Text check box to convert the text in the document to outlines.

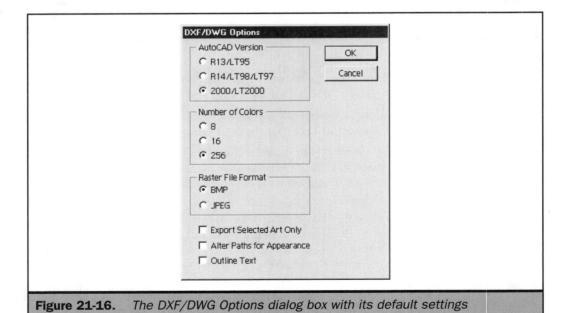

Figure 21-16. *The DXF/DWG Options dialog box with its default settings*

Exporting to Targa

According to the *Adobe Illustrator 10 User Guide*, "The TGA format is designed for use on systems that use the Truevision video board." When you export a document to the Targa format, you choose File | Export, select Targa (*.TGA) from the Save As Type drop-down menu and click Save. Illustrator opens the Rasterize Options dialog box (see Figure 21-17), from which you can select options for the Targa format.

The Rasterize Options dialog box pops up for several other file formats: BMP (another dialog box follows), PCX, and Pixar.

The options in the Rasterize Options dialog box are as follows:

- From the Color Model drop-down menu, choose a color model: RGB, Grayscale, or Bitmap. The starting value in the menu is the current color mode in Illustrator.

- In the Resolution section, select a resolution: Screen (72 ppi), Medium (150 ppi), High (300 ppi), or Other. The default is Screen. If you select Other, you can set the resolution in the text box.

- Check the Anti-alias check box to turn on anti-aliasing, which smooths jagged edges from objects. The default is a checked check box.

After you click OK to close the Rasterize Options dialog box, Illustrator opens the Targa Options dialog box (see Figure 21-18). In the Resolution section, click a radio button for the resolution. You can select 16, 24, or 32 bits per pixel.

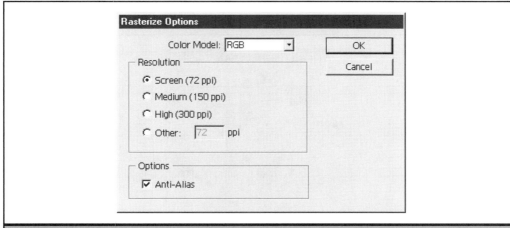

Figure 21-17.   *The Rasterize Options dialog box with its default settings*

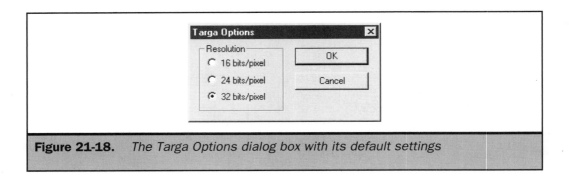

Figure 21-18. *The Targa Options dialog box with its default settings*

Exporting to BMP

Windows Bitmap format (BMP) is a popular and long-lasting file format for Windows computers. When you choose File | Export, select BMP (*.BMP) from the Save As Type drop-down menu and click Save. Illustrator opens the Rasterize Options dialog box (see Figure 21-17), from which you can select options.

When you click the OK button, Illustrator opens the BMP Options dialog box (see Figure 21-19) with which you can specify an operating system for the file format and, under some circumstances, select the RLE (Run Length Encoding) lossless compression method.

You can export to the CGM, EMF, Macintosh PICT, Text Format, and Windows Metafile file formats without using a separate options dialog box. To do so, choose File | Export, select the file type in the Save As Type drop-down menu, and click Save.

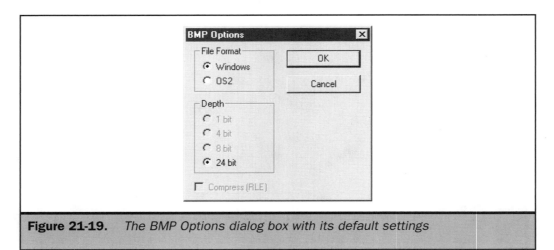

Figure 21-19. *The BMP Options dialog box with its default settings*

The
Complete
Reference

Chapter 22

Illustrator Output

In this chapter you will learn to print your artwork or prepare it to be printed commercially. In either case, you'll want to print draft copies occasionally as you move toward completion of an artwork.

What happens when your artwork refuses to print? In this chapter you'll learn about various techniques that might help you solve printing problems. Regardless of whether you print a proof as you create and modify an artwork, print the finished version, or get ready to print commercially, you should have your printers tuned and ready to go.

Learning about Printing Processes and Terms

Before digital printing, when you created artwork to be printed by a commercial printer, you'd follow these steps:

1. Artist: Design the artwork and get approvals.

2. Artist: Send printing specifications to printers to obtain bids.

3. Artist: Correct the artwork for the last time, and perform *typesetting* (set type using a typesetting machine).

4. Artist: Paste up the *mechanicals* (lay out by pasting type and illustrations on a board).

5. Artist: Proofread and correct the mechanicals.

6. Artist: Send work to the printer for *camera work* (photographing the mechanicals to create negatives) and *stripping* (assembling negatives on sheets).

7. Printer: Prepare *bluelines* (proofs made from negatives; printing areas show in blue).

8. Artist: Proofread bluelines.

9. Printer: Create the *plates* (a piece of metal or other hard material on which an image or type is photographically developed, drawn, or engraved).

10. Printer: Print the artwork.

When you print a document from within Illustrator or use Illustrator to prepare your artwork for commercial printing on a digital printing press or for film and plates, you follow an easier routine, which you'll find out about in the remaining pages of this chapter.

Printing on an Office or Home Printer

With business or home printers (that is, the machines on which we print all types of documents, ranging from letters and reports to colorful posters and photographs), you can do a great deal of production. Obviously, you can print proofs on your way to a finished artwork. You also can print your final on your own printer.

Preparing to Print

Before you print your artwork (or, for that matter, any other document), you should set up your printer to operate at the highest level of efficiency. Getting your printer ready to print not only involves cleaning the parts that will touch the paper but also matching the printer settings to the artwork or document.

In Illustrator, you can fine-tune your printer with the Document Setup dialog box, Print Setup dialog box (for Windows), Page Setup dialog box (for the Macintosh), and the Print dialog box.

Touring the Printing & Export Section of the Document Setup Dialog Box

When you print an Illustrator document using your own printer, it is important to fit the artwork—particularly one that contains complicated paths, gradients, and mesh objects—to your specific printer, its output resolution, and the desired quality. Use the Printing & Export section of the Document Setup dialog box to get the best results from your printer.

The Document Setup dialog box (see Figure 22-1) has three sections. You learned about the options in the Artboard section in "Setting Up the Artboard" in Chapter 5 and the top options of the Transparency section in "Exploring the Transparency Section of the Document Setup Dialog Box" in Chapter 15. On the following pages you'll learn

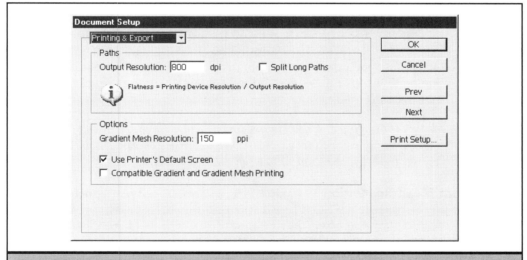

Figure 22-1.   *The Printing & Export section of the Document Setup dialog box with its default settings*

how to work with the Printing & Export section and the Flattening options in the Transparency section of the dialog box. To open the Printing & Export section of the Document Setup dialog box, choose File | Document Setup (CTRL-ALT-P/⌘-OPTION-P) and select Printing & Export from the drop-down menu at the top of the dialog box. The options in the Printing & Export section are described in the following sections.

The Output Resolution Text Box   In the Output Resolution text box, type the desired resolution of the curved paths in the artwork in the printed or exported output. If you plan to print at 300 dots per inch (dpi), Adobe recommends values between 100 and 300 dpi. If your printer supports printing at 2,400 dpi, Adobe recommends values between 800 and 2,400. Valid values range from 100 dpi (a flatter curve) and 9,600 dpi (a relatively accurate curve). The default is 800 dpi.

If you plan to print on a PostScript printer, the printer driver interprets the PostScript instructions by breaking curved paths into small, straight-line segments. This process makes the curves more accurate but also complex. If the number of line segments exceeds the limits of the printer memory, the printer might refuse to print, issuing a message instead.

When you set the output resolution, you are walking a fine line between a flatter curve and an almost precise curve. A higher resolution causes an accurate curve, but the printer driver might balk at sending the artwork to the printer. A lower resolution results in flatter curves; although the artwork might print, you might not like its appearance. One solution is to slightly adjust the output resolution up or down and try to print again. With a little trial and error, you'll be able to calculate output resolution for the current artwork, less complicated images, and more complex artworks.

The Split Long Paths Check Box   You might be able to choose a combination of higher output resolution and successful printing by checking the Split Long Paths check box, which splits long or complicated paths into two or more separate paths, thereby avoiding possible error messages and refusal to print. For more information, refer to the "Splitting Paths and Other Objects" section later in this chapter.

When you decide to split paths, you are treading a dangerous path that you might not be able to leave. Splitting paths is not easily undone; before you check the Split Long Paths check box, save the original document in a safe folder and work on a copy.

The Gradient Mesh Resolution Text Box   Some printers convert a document with gradients or mesh objects to a JPEG image before printing. In that case, the value in the Gradient Mesh Resolution text box is the resolution of the document. Valid values range from 1 pixel per inch (ppi) to 9,600 ppi; the default is 150.

Use Printer's Default Screen   The term *line screen*, which is also known as screen frequency and screen ruling, refers to halftone images composed of ink dots of varying sizes. (A *halftone* is a continuous-tone image (such as a photograph) that has been converted to black dots of varying sizes that simulate grayscale tones.) A fine line screen produces a pattern of small dots, which results in detailed images. A coarse line screen makes for large dots and a coarser image. Before laser and inkjet printers, commercial printers printed magazines with a line screen that ranged from 125 to 150 lines per inch (lpi), which is the equivalent of 225 to 300 dots per inch.

When you check the Use Printer's Default Screen check box, you use your printer's default line screen. An unchecked check box instructs Illustrator to use a line screen called Adobe screens. If you plan to print artworks with gradients and mesh objects to a low-resolution printer, you might get better quality artwork by using Adobe screens.

Note *If you plan to use an EPSF Riders plug-in to override separation setup settings, keep the Use Printer's Default Screen check box checked. To learn more about the EPSF Riders plug-in, refer to "Overriding Printer Settings" later in this chapter.*

Compatible Gradient and Gradient Mesh Printing   If your older PostScript printer or non-PostScript printer produces gradients and mesh objects with banding and other problems, consider placing a check mark in the Compatible Gradient and Gradient Mesh Printing check box. If you keep the check box checked, your printer might slow significantly. So in most situations, you should try other solutions (for example, removing gradients and mesh objects from objects, updating your printer driver, and so on) before checking the check box.

When a printer driver gets ready to print a document with at least one gradient or mesh object, the driver is programmed to keep the document in vector format or convert the document to JPEG so that printing can take place. Many non-PostScript printers and Level 2 PostScript printers prepare for printing by producing both vector and JPEG objects. However, PostScript Level 3 printers simply convert to vector objects unless the artwork is too complicated.

Printing Documents with Transparent Artwork

In the "Exploring the Transparency Section of the Document Setup Dialog Box" section in Chapter 15, you learned how to modify the transparency grid in the Document Setup dialog box's Transparency section (see Figure 22-2). At the bottom of the same section are some options for flattening artwork. To open the dialog box, choose File | Document Setup (CTRL-ALT-P/⌘-OPTION-P).

As Illustrator *flattens* an artwork, it evaluates the transparent parts of an artwork—especially areas in which they overlap nontransparent portions. Illustrator then divides the completely transparent and overlapping areas into components that can be kept in their original vector forms, and others that must be rasterized.

Use the flattening options as follows:

- Slide the Raster/Vector Balance slider to set the balance between raster and vector in the artwork. Valid values range from 0 (all raster) to 100 (almost all vector). The default is 100. When you slide to a value less than 100, Illustrator activates the Rasterization Resolution text box.

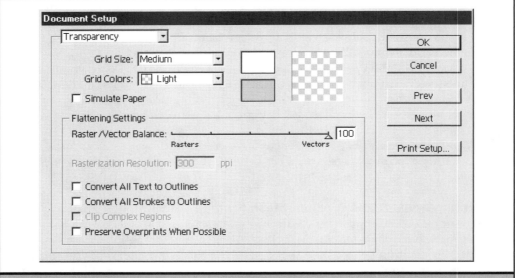

Figure 22-2. *The Transparency section of the Document Setup dialog box with the default settings*

- You can type a specific vector value in the Vectors text box rather than using the Raster/vector balance slider.

- You can type a particular raster value in the Rasterization Resolution text box rather than using the slider. The default value is 300 ppi, the recommended value. Note that mesh objects are not affected by this setting.

Note *The Raster/Vector balance controls the availability of the check boxes at the bottom of the Transparency section. If the Vectors text box for an artwork is set at 100, the Convert All Text to Outlines, Convert All Strokes to Outlines, and Preserve Overprints When Possible check boxes are available. If the Vectors setting is between 1 and 99, all four check boxes are available; if Vectors is set to 0, all the check boxes are dimmed.*

- Check the Convert All Text to Outlines to freeze the width of type at its current size but thicken smaller characters. The default is an unchecked check box.

- Check the Convert All Strokes to Outlines check box to freeze the width of strokes at their current sizes but thicken strokes with low widths. The default is an unchecked box.

- Check the Clip Complex Regions check box to place the borders between vector parts and rasterized sections on paths, ensuring that the borders are as seamless as possible. Some of the resulting paths might become much more complicated, thereby possibly affecting the capability to print. The default is an unchecked box.

■ Check the Preserve Overprints When Possible check box when the document, which should become a separation, includes objects that are overprinted. (*Overprinting* is a printing technique for printing colors on overlapping sections of an artwork.) According to the *Adobe Illustrator 10 User Guide*, "Selecting this option generally preserves overprint for objects that are not involved in transparency and therefore improves performance." The default is an unchecked check box.

Printing Documents with Color Blends, Gradients, and Mesh Objects

In the "Preparing to Print" section, you learned that Illustrator pays special attention to gradients and mesh objects when getting ready to print artwork that contains those objects. Because of the number of colors that are spread over a relatively short distance, Illustrator has to make many adjustments when it processes (opens, redraws, saves, prints, and so on) artwork with gradients and mesh objects. All the preceding also is true for color blends.

When you create artwork that you plan to print at some point, note the following:

■ Reduce the size of an object with a gradient or color blend, or decrease the size of a mesh object. Adobe recommends keeping blends shorter than 7.5 inches.

■ If you are using several process colors in a gradient, blend, or mesh object, the starting and ending color values should be at least 50% different from each other.

■ Lighten the colors in a blend to reduce the likelihood of banding between some colors.

■ Adobe recommends that you choose a line screen that retains 256 levels of gray.

Note *Page 364 of the* Adobe Illustrator 10 User Guide *contains a table that lists the maximum line screen to use for each printer resolution setting. Additionally, on page 365, you'll find out how to calculate the maximum blend length based on the change in color. Also, page 365 contains a chart that lists a series of maximum blend length measurements and the number of steps Illustrator recommends.*

Splitting Paths and Other Objects

Sometimes you can print an artwork only if you adjust the artwork to make it less memory intensive. As you learned in the "Preparing to Print" section earlier in this chapter, you can decrease the output resolution or split long paths, complicated paths, or both. In this section you'll explore the procedures for splitting paths, compound paths, and clipping masks, and for reconnecting split paths.

Before You Split a Path

Splitting a path is a destructive process: Save the original artwork and split paths using the copy; if things go wrong, you can always return to the original, make another copy, and continue working on the copy.

Additionally, note the following:

- When you check the Split Long Paths check box, you instruct Illustrator to examine each path in the document after you choose File | Save (CTRL-S/⌘-S) or File | Print (CTRL-P/⌘-P).

- Once Illustrator saves artwork with one or more split paths, you cannot undo the split.

- You can see split paths in Outline view (choose View | Outline (CTRL-Y/⌘-Y)) but not in Preview view (choose View | Preview (CTRL-Y/⌘-Y)) or on the printed page.

- After Illustrator splits a path, each segment is a separate path with attributes of its own; therefore, you must edit these paths individually or reconnect them. In other words, complete all editing before you allow Illustrator to split the paths right before it saves or prints.

- Checking the Split Long Paths check box controls the way in which Illustrator treats long paths—not compound paths. As you read on, you'll learn how to split compound paths and clipping masks.

Splitting All the Long Paths in a Document

To have Illustrator split paths in a document being saved or printed, follow these steps:

1. Choose File | Document Setup (CTRL-ALT-P/⌘-OPTION-P).

2. Select Printing & Export from the drop-down menu at the top of the Document Setup dialog box.

3. Check the Split Long Paths check box.

4. Select other options; then click OK.

Reconnecting a Split Path

You can reconnect split paths—often with great difficulty. Just imagine trying to reattach all the strands in a ball of twine that you have just hacked apart with a rusty ax and then trying to smooth out all the new connections.

To rejoin a split path, follow these steps:

1. Select all the split paths used to compose the original path.

2. Choose Window | Pathfinder (SHIFT-F9) if the Pathfinder palette is not in the illustration window.

3. In the palette, click the Add to Shape Area button (the leftmost button in the top row). Illustrator rejoins the paths and places one anchor point at each intersection.

4. Remove additional lines by selecting them and pressing DELETE, or clean up the entire document by choosing Object | Path | Clean Up, selecting options in the Clean Up dialog box, and clicking OK.

Splitting a Stroked Path

Illustrator does not split stroked paths when the Split Long Paths check box is checked and as it saves or prints a document. Therefore, you must split stroked paths manually. To split a stroked path, select the path and activate the Scissors tool (C). To split an open path, click anywhere on the path or an anchor point. To split a closed path, click one part of the path or an anchor point, and click another location on the path or an anchor point to finish the split. For more information, refer to "Splitting Paths with the Scissors Tool" in Chapter 6.

Splitting a Compound Path

When you choose Object | Compound Path | Make to create one object from two or more overlapping paths, the result is a compound path. When the Split Long Paths check box is checked, Illustrator does not evaluate and possibly split compound paths when it saves or prints. So split a compound path by choosing a command, cutting with the Scissors tool, and re-creating the compound path.

To split a compound path, follow these steps:

1. Select the compound path.

2. Release the compound path by choosing Object | Compound Path | Release (CTRL-ALT-8/⌘-OPTION-8).

3. Activate the Scissors tool (C).

4. Cut the path as described in the prior section.

5. Re-create the compound path by selecting its components and choosing Object | Compound Path | Make (CTRL-8/⌘-8).

For more information about compound paths, refer to the "Using Compound Paths" sidebar in Chapter 20.

Splitting a Clipping Mask

In the "Using Clipping Masks" section in Chapter 14 you learned how to create clipping masks, which hide parts of underlying artwork; the artwork shows through the clipping masks and all other sections are hidden. Splitting a clipping mask echoes the steps for splitting a compound path: Split a clipping mask by choosing a command, cutting with the Scissors tool, and re-creating the mask. To split a clipping mask, follow these steps:

1. Select the clipping mask.

2. Release the mask by choosing Object | Clipping Mask | Release (CTRL-ALT-7/⌘-OPTION-7).

3. Activate the Scissors tool (C).

4. Click one part of the path or an anchor point, and click another location on the path or an anchor point to finish the split.

5. Re-create the clipping mask by selecting its components and choosing Object | Compound Path | Make (CTRL-7/⌘-7).

OUTSIDE ILLUSTRATOR

Adding Marks to a Page

Crop marks and trim marks enable you to demonstrate the exact location at which you want pages trimmed after they are printed. For example, the pages for many books are originally printed on paper that is 8.5 inches by 11 inches and trimmed down to 6×9, 7.5×8.5, 7×9, and so on. Trimming enables commercial printers to fit pages to a standard size or to bleed images to the edge of the page. Illustrator provides three types of marks: crop marks, Japanese crop marks, and trim marks.

Note   *Japanese crop marks are a version of standard crop marks. To make Japanese crop marks rather than standard crop marks for a document, change your Illustrator general preferences. For more information, refer to Appendix B.*

Creating Crop Marks

You can create crop marks in two ways—by setting the crop marks on the outer edges of a rectangle or by changing the dimensions of the Artboard and then issuing a command.

Setting Crop Marks with a Rectangle   Creating crop marks with a rectangle is a short process: Display the rulers, draw a rectangle, and then choose a command. To create crop marks with a rectangle, follow these steps:

1. Turn on the rulers by choosing View | Show Rulers (CTRL-R/⌘-R).
2. Activate the Rectangle tool (M).
3. Draw a rectangle whose corners will mark the location of the crop marks. (Because Illustrator replaces the rectangle with the crop marks, you don't have to set the fill and stroke colors.)
4. Select the rectangle.
5. Choose Object | Crop Marks | Make. Illustrator replaces the rectangle with the crop marks.

Figure 22-3 shows the stages of rectangle-based crop marks: the type in the Artboard, the rectangle that forms the corners at which Illustrator places the crop marks, and the crop marks in place.

Setting Crop Marks with the Artboard   Creating crop marks at the edges of the Artboard is a shorter process than creating them with a rectangle: Displaying the rulers is less important, and you don't have to draw a rectangle. To create crop marks aligned with the Artboard (see Figure 22-4), choose Object | Crop Marks | Make.

Releasing Crop Marks   You cannot select, move, or edit crop marks in any way. You can change them only by releasing or undoing them. To release crop marks,

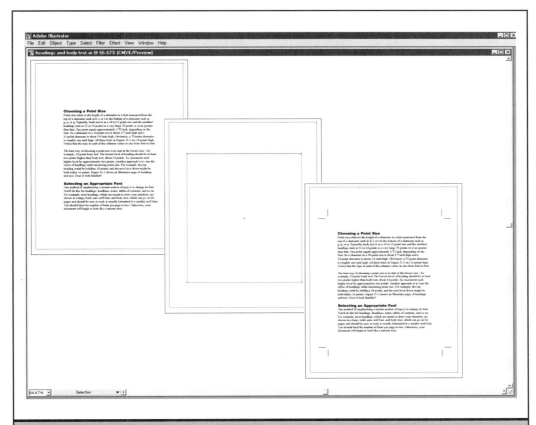

Figure 22-3. *Rectangle-based crop marks in the making, from the first step (at the top) to the last (at the bottom)*

choose Object | Crop Marks | Release. To undo crop marks—if you have just created them—choose Edit | Undo (CTRL-Z/⌘-Z).

Creating Trim Marks

Use the Trim Marks filter to draw trim marks along the edges of an artwork. Although you can use trim marks to show the edges of a page, they also can mark the edges of one or more objects within a page. For example, if your company announces an annual event by sending postcards to certain customers, you can mark the edges of several cards laid out on card stock.

Figure 22-4.   *Crop marks aligned with the artboard*

To create trim marks, select an object and choose Filter | Create | Trim Marks. Illustrator places trim marks at the selected points (see Figure 22-5). Note that Illustrator does not remove any crop marks that you have placed on the page.

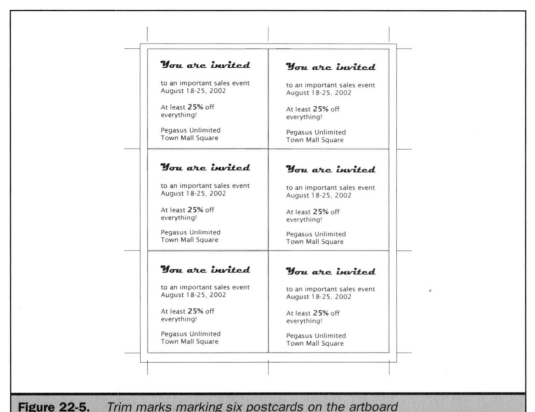

Figure 22-5.   *Trim marks marking six postcards on the artboard*

Setting Printer Options and Properties

If you have printed any document using any modern application, you have seen versions of the Print Setup dialog box (for Windows) or Page Setup dialog box (for the Mac) for the default printer. For Illustrator documents, these familiar dialog boxes appear and behave as they do when you print a report, spreadsheet, or graphic created in any other application. To open the Print Setup dialog box (see Figure 22-6) or Page Setup dialog box, perform one of the following actions:

- Choose File | Print Setup (CTRL-SHIFT-P) for Windows computers.
- Choose File | Page Setup (⌘-SHIFT-P) for Macintosh computers.
- Choose File | Document Setup (CTRL-ALT-P/⌘-OPTION-P), and click the Print Setup button (Windows) or Page Setup (Macintosh).

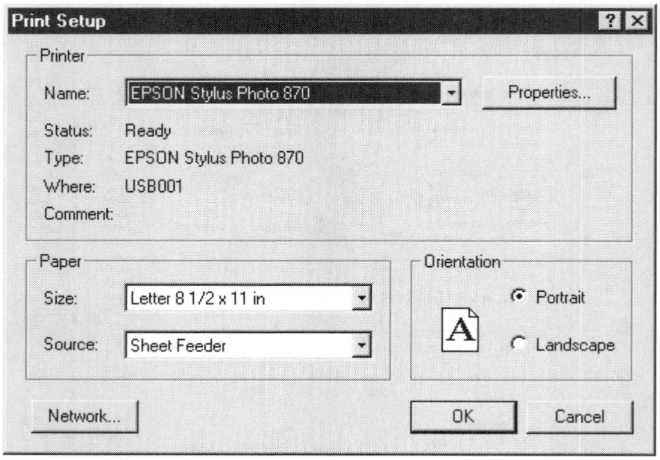

Figure 22-6. *The Print Setup dialog box with its default settings*

The top part of the Print Setup or Page Setup dialog box provides information about the current printer. Other options are as follows:

- From the Name drop-down menu, select the printer on which you want to print.

- From the Size drop-down list box, which might appear depending on your default printer or PPD file, select the size of the paper on which the document is printed. If you choose User Defined from the bottom of the menu, you can define your own paper size.

- From the Source drop-down menu, which might appear depending on your default printer or PPD file, select the source of the paper: Sheet Feeder, Roll Paper, or Roll Paper—No Margins.

- Set the orientation by clicking a radio button: Portrait for portrait orientation or Landscape for landscape orientation.

- Click Properties (for Windows computers) or Page Attributes or PostScript Options (for Macintosh computers) to open a dialog box for your particular printer. The Properties dialog box varies widely from printer to printer. Figure 22-7 shows the Main section of the Epson Stylus Photo 870 Properties dialog box.

When you're ready to print a standard artwork, choose File | Print (CTRL-P/⌘-P). When Illustrator opens the Print dialog box, select options and click OK. To learn about the options in the Print dialog box, refer to the "Printing Artwork and Color Separations" section later in this chapter.

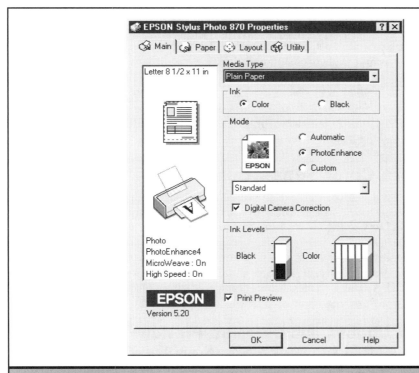

Figure 22-7. *One section of the Epson Stylus Photo 870 Properties dialog box*

Printing with a Commercial Printer

If you are a graphic artist or someone who is responsible for producing brochures, annual reports, posters, books, and the like, eventually you will work with a commercial printer. For example, if you plan to distribute hundreds or thousands of printed material, you probably won't get the desired look by using a small laser or inkjet printer: Commercial presses work faster, have more memory, and can often produce more professional-looking results.

When you use a commercial printer, you'll be asked to create *color separations,* in which you split your *composite* (the entire artwork with all its components on one page) into the four basic CMYK colors: cyan, magenta, yellow, and black (that is, Illustrator's default process color model). From the color separations, the printer makes photographic *negatives* (the reversal of colors on film so that the former white areas are now black and the prior black areas are now white) or *positives* (film prints that keep the original colors: The current white areas remain white and the blacks remain black), which in turn are made into master plates—one for each of the CMYK colors.

If you have used spot colors in your artwork, the printer produces separate plates—one for each spot color. In fact, sometimes you'll use spot colors rather than the CMYK colors. In this case, the printer will create one plate per spot color. (To renew your knowledge of spot colors and their uses, refer to "Working with Swatches" in Chapter 7.)

The first time you produce color separations, be sure to get plenty of advice from your commercial printer. He or she probably has unique procedures for you to follow. In addition, be sure to consult the Adobe Illustrator 10 User Guide, *which has pages of detailed information on making color separations with Illustrator.*

Before You Create Color Separations

Before you get started with color separating, you should calibrate your monitor so that the printed colors are as close to the colors you see on your monitor as possible. Refer to *Adobe Illustrator 10 User Guide* to learn how to calibrate your monitor with the Adobe Gamma utility.

When Illustrator creates color separations, it sometimes treats gradients in a special way. When a gradient contains process colors (that is, CMYK colors), those colors are separated onto the C, M, Y, and K plates. However, if a gradient also contains spot colors, Illustrator places tints of the same color on a single spot plate.

Using Overprint Options and Overprint Preview

When opaque colors overlap in an artwork, the top color in the stacking order knocks out (or overprints) the underlying colors. When you separate colors, you might want to preserve the colors under the top color by opening the Attributes palette (choose Window | Attributes (F11) and checking the Overprint Fill check box or Overprint Stroke check box.

Switch to Overprint Preview by choosing View | Overprint Preview (CTRL-SHIFT-ALT-Y/ ⌘-SHIFT-OPTION-Y) to check the results of your selecting overprint options. Figure 22-8 illustrates a graphic made up of objects colored in cyan, magenta, yellow, and black. At the top of the figure is the graphic shown in Preview view without the Overprint options selected. Below that is the graphic with the yellow body sent to the back of the stacking order. On the bottom left is the graphic in Outline Preview with the Overprint Fill check box checked; on the bottom right is the graphic in Outline Preview with Overprint Stroke checked. Notice that when you check Overprint Stroke, Illustrator reveals the hidden portion of the strokes only.

You can choose Filter | Colors | Overprint Black to set or remove black fill or stroke overprinting options.

Trapping to Correct Alignment Problems

If plates are not properly aligned during printing, the separation colors may not be joined border to border. Sometimes there are gaps between the colors; other times, the colors

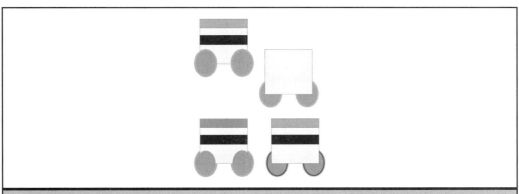

Figure 22-8. *Four versions of a graphic: the original at the top, the restacked version below that, Overprint Fill checked (on the bottom left), and Overprint Stroke checked (on the bottom right)*

overlap. Gaps between dissimilar colors stand out, so you need to correct them by a process called *trapping*, which adds color or tints to the gaps and joins the mismatched borders. Illustrator supports the correction of two types of traps: a *spread*, which corrects a gap by overlapping a dark-colored background with a light-colored image, and a *choke*, which corrects a gap by overlapping a light-colored background with a dark-colored image.

Note *When you trap type, it must remain sharp and readable. Trapping type without extra care results in thicker characters with a blurry look. According to the* Adobe Illustrator 10 User Guide, *"To trap type, you can add the stroke below the fill in the Appearance palette, and set the stroke to overprint (or set it to Multiply blending mode)."*

Making and Overprinting a Spread   You can select or add a stroke and then overprint it to form a spread for overlapping objects. To do this, you'll open and use several palettes.

To make and overprint a spread, follow these steps:

1. From two overlapping objects, select the one that is above the other in stacking order.

2. Using the Color or Swatches palette, make the stroke color of the selected object identical to its fill color. The color match creates the illusion that the object is larger than it is.

3. In the Width list box/text box/drop-down menu of the Stroke palette, type or select a stroke width that is twice the width of the future stroke. Adobe recommends a width between 0.6 (that is, a trap of 0.3 point) and 2.0 points (a trap of 1.0 point).

4. In the Attributes palette, check the Overprint Stroke check box.

Making and Overprinting a Choke   Overprinting a choke works in much the same way as overprinting a spread: You'll change the attributes of the stroke and then finish as you did with the spread. However, you will work on a stroke in a slightly different way than you do when you make a spread.

To make and overprint a choke, follow these steps:

1. From two overlapping objects, select the one that is above the other in stacking order.

2. Using the Color or Swatches palette, make the stroke color of the selected object identical to its background color. The color match creates the illusion that the object is smaller than it is.

3. In the Width list box/text box/drop-down menu of the Stroke palette, type or select a stroke width that is twice the width of the future stroke. Adobe recommends a width between 0.6 and 2.0 points.

4. In the Attributes palette, check the Overprint Stroke check box.

Making and Overprinting a Straight or Curved Trap   You can use a straight or curved line to create a trap. To make the trap, follow these steps:

1. Using the Line Segment tool (\), the Arc tool, the Pencil (N), or the Pen (P) create a line that follows the edge of the object for which you want to make a trap.

2. Select the line, stroke it with white, and set its width in the Stroke palette.

3. With the line still selected, choose Edit | Copy (CTRL-C/⌘-C) to copy the line and choose Edit | Paste in Front (CTRL-F/⌘-F) to paste it in front of the object.

4. If needed, adjust the width of the line in its location on top of the object.

5. Change the color of the new trap to create a spread or choke. (See the preceding two sections.)

6. In the Attributes palette, check the Overprint Stroke check box.

   You can follow a similar procedure to create a more complex trap that follows the border of a complicated object. With the Direct Selection tool (A), select the part you want to trap; then follow steps 3–6.

Using the Pathfinder Palette's Trap Command   You learned about the Pathfinder palette's editing buttons in the "Editing Paths with the Pathfinder Palette" section in Chapter 6. To open the Pathfinder palette, choose Window | Pathfinder (SHIFT-F9). On the palette's menu, you'll find the Trap command, which opens the Pathfinder Trap dialog box (see Figure 22-9) with which you can set trapping options.

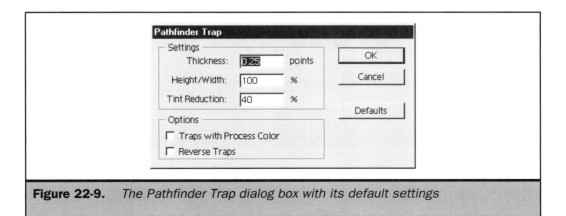

Figure 22-9. *The Pathfinder Trap dialog box with its default settings*

The options in the dialog box are as follows:

■ In the Thickness text box, type the width of the stroke. Valid values range from 0.01 to 5000 points. The default stroke width is 0.25 points.

■ In the Height/Width text box, type the proportion of the trap on horizontal lines to that of vertical lines as a percentage. Valid values range from 25% to 400%; the default is 100%. Values from 25% to 100% decrease the horizontal trap thicknesses without changing the vertical trap; values from 100% to 400% increase the horizontal trap thicknesses without changing the vertical trap.

■ In the Tint Reduction text box, type the percentage by which Illustrator changes the tint of the lighter-colored trap. Valid values range from 0 to 100%; the default is 40%. The dark-colored trap remains at 100%.

■ Check the Traps with Process Color check box to have Illustrator convert spot color traps to process color traps by creating an object from the lighter-colored trap and then overprinting it. The default is an unchecked box.

■ Check the Reverse Traps check box to create light-colored traps from darker colors, except for black that contains extra cyan, magenta, or yellow ink. The default is an unchecked box.

■ Click the Defaults button to return to the default values originally shown in the dialog box.

Setting the Boundaries and Adding Marks

Once you have set up your artwork for separation, you should specify the page dimensions by using the artboard or dragging a bounding box. You might remember reading about setting page dimensions earlier in the chapter: You learned about setting page dimensions before you applied crop marks and trim marks in the "Adding Marks to a Page" section. Illustrator enables you to set page dimensions as you did for crop marks and trim marks before you start the formal color separation process or by using the Separation Setup dialog box; you will learn about this next.

If you are creating a color separation and want to specify the exact location of crop marks, make the crop marks before starting the separation. Otherwise, Illustrator places them at the edges of the bounding box that you place around all the objects in the separation.

Learning About the Separation Setup Dialog Box

After you have prepared a file for color separation, the rest of your work takes place in the Separation Setup dialog box (see Figure 22-10). Opening the dialog box is either straightforward or convoluted. If your default printer is a PostScript printer, you can choose either File | Separation Setup or File | Print (CTRL-P/⌘-P), and then click the Separation Setup button to open the dialog box.

If your default printer is not a PostScript printer, the Separation Setup command is not available; so choose File | Print (CTRL-P/⌘-P). From the Name drop-down menu in the Print dialog box, select a PostScript printer driver and the Separation Setup button should become available.

If the Name menu in the Print dialog box does not contain PostScript printer, refer to the "PostScript Printer Drivers" section in Appendix C for information about drivers available for downloading from the Web.

When you open the Separation Setup dialog box, your problems might not be over. If your PostScript printer driver does not have PostScript Printer Description (PPD) information associated with it, the options are unavailable and no picture appears in the preview window. To resolve this situation, click the Open PPD button in the top-right corner of the dialog box. When the Open PPD dialog box opens, browse for a PPD file, which you'll find in the Utilities subfolder—some levels under the Adobe program files folder. Select a PPD file and click Open.

To ensure that your PPD file fits your printer's PostScript driver, test it; or better yet, contact your printer's manufacturer or go to the manufacturer's Web site.

How you use the Separation Setup dialog box depends on how your commercial printer separates and prints artworks, so be sure you consult with him or her before setting values in the dialog box.

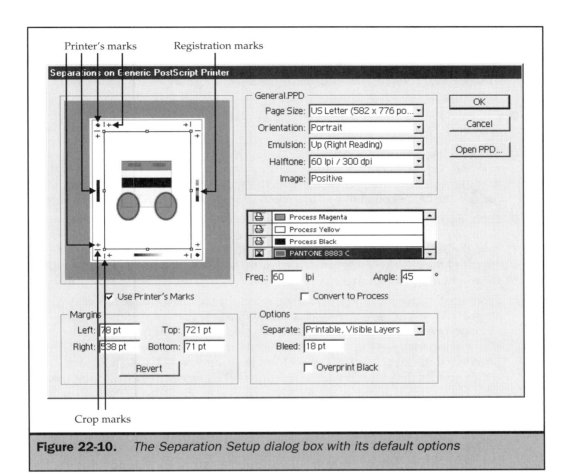

Printer's marks   Registration marks

Figure 22-10.   *The Separation Setup dialog box with its default options*

Crop marks

The options in the Separation Setup dialog box are as follows:

- Check the Use Printer's Marks check box to have Illustrator insert printer's marks: registration marks and star marks, both of which are used to align separation pages; labels, which include the filename, the line screen setting, and the *screen angle* (the angle at which the pattern of dots in a halftone screen appear on a printed page); and the color of each plate used to print the artwork. The default is a checked box.

- The preview window contains a copy of the artwork and shows the current options selected in the dialog box. You can drag the lines indicating the top, left, right, and bottom edges of the page to set new margins.

- In the Margins section, set specific page margins by typing in the Left, Top, Right, and Bottom text boxes. The default values are those of a bounding box around the artwork or the bounding box that you have dragged around the artwork to set crop marks. Illustrator measures the margins from the left side and bottom of the page.

- Click the Revert button to revert the page margins to their original settings when you first opened the dialog box.

- From the Page Size drop-down menu, choose a page size from the list. The selected page size controls the size of the image in the preview window. Note that the page sizes vary, depending on the active PPD file. Some PPD files include the Other command, which enables you to set custom page dimensions.

- From the Orientation drop-down menu, select Portrait or Landscape. Portrait prints the page in portrait mode in which the width of the page is narrower than the length. Landscape prints the page in landscape mode in which the length of the page is shorter than the width. Match the orientation mode with the orientation of the artwork.

- From the Emulsion drop-down menu, select the side of the page to which a *stripper* (an employee who works with the film and plates) would apply the *emulsion* (a chemical coating applied to one side of the film from which the plates are made). For digital printing, emulsion refers to the location of the photosensitive layer. You can select from the following: Up (Right Reading), which applies the emulsion to the top side of the page as it goes through the printer, and Down (Right Reading), which applies the emulsion to the underside of the page.

- From the Halftone drop-down menu, select lines per inch and dots per inch settings. Remember that lines per inch are the line screen resolution, and dots per inch refers to the actual dots.

- From the Image drop-down menu, select whether the printer will produce positives or negatives. For more information, refer to "Printing with a Commercial Printer," earlier in this chapter.

- The Colors list box shows all the colors in the current artwork: Process Cyan, Process Magenta, Process Yellow, and Process Black followed by any spot colors you have included in the artwork. The printer icon preceding each of the colors indicates that the color is set to print as a separation, the default. Click the icon to skip printing the separation for a particular color.

- In the Freq. text box, set a custom lines per inch value for the halftone. Valid values range from 0.0001 to 1,000. The default is 60. This check box is available only if you have selected a color from the Colors list box.

- In the Angle text box, set a custom screen angle for the halftone. Valid values range from 0 to 360 degrees. The default is 15 degrees. This check box is available only if you have selected a color from the Colors list box.

- Check the Convert to Process check box to convert all the spot colors to process colors before creating the separations. To convert a single spot color, remove a check mark from the Convert to Process check box, select the color, and click the Printer icon. After you respond to a warning that converting spot colors to process colors might cause problems with transparency or overprinting, Illustrator converts the color, and replaces the Printer icon with a four-color process icon.

- From the Separate drop-down menu, select one of three options for layers in the artwork:

  - Printable, Visible Layers produces separations for layers that you can print and are not hidden.

  - Visible Layers produces separations for layers that are not hidden.

  - All Layers produces separations for all layers, regardless of their printing and hidden statuses.

- In the Bleed text box, type the size of the area that extends beyond the crop marks on all sides to ensure that the artwork bleeds beyond the edge of the page. Valid values range from 0 to 72 points. The default is 18 points.

- Check the Overprint Black check box to overprint black in objects that have had the CMYK black applied.

Printing Artwork and Color Separations

Regardless of whether you want to print composite artwork or color separations, you open the Print dialog box but select some of the same options and some different ones. If you have created color separations, you have already selected some of the options in the Separation Setup dialog box.

 According to the Adobe Illustrator 10 User Guide, *"Adobe does not support PDF Writer format; if you attempt to print to PDF Writer, you may experience delays or errors in printing."*

To open the Print dialog box (see Figure 22-11), choose File | Print (CTRL-P/⌘-P). The options in the Print dialog box are as follows:

- From the Name drop-down list box, select the printer on which you want to print the current document.

- Status shows the current status of the selected printer. If you see the word Ready, the printer is ready for work.

- Type shows the name of the selected printer.

- Where shows the port to which the selected printer is attached.

- Comment sometimes shows additional information about the selected printer.

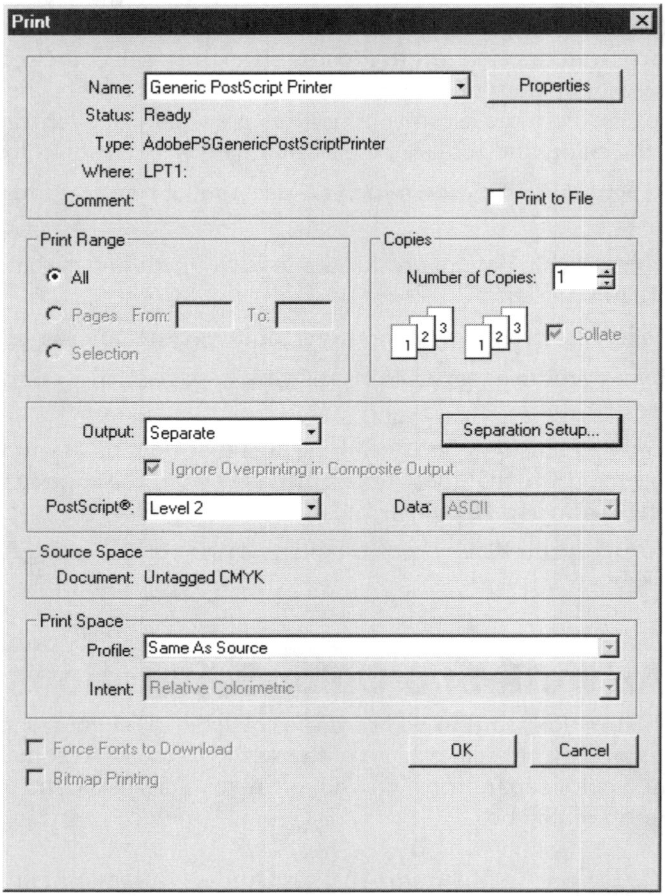

Figure 22-11. *Illustrator's Print dialog box with its default settings for a PostScript printer*

- Click the Properties button to open the Properties dialog box for the selected printer.
- Check the Print check box to save the document to a named file that maintains the current formats and print options. Then you can print the saved file at your convenience.
- Click a Print Range radio button to print a selected number of pages. All (the default) prints all the pages in a document. Click the Pages radio button to print

a range of pages: Type a starting page in the From text box and an ending page in the To text box. Click the Selection radio button to print the selected objects in the illustration window. If the Pages and Selection radio buttons are unavailable, the document consists of one page.

■ In the Number of Copies text box/list box, type the number of copies you want to print. Valid values range from 1 to 9,999 pages.

■ Check the Collate check box to print all the pages of a document in sequence. An unchecked check box prints all the requested copies of the first page, all the requested copies of the second page, and so on. The check box is not available if you are requesting one copy.

■ Select the type of output:

■ From the Output drop-down menu (Windows), choose Separate to print separations or Composite to print the composite artwork.

■ From the Options drop-down menu (Macintosh), choose Adobe Illustrator 10, and choose Separate or Composite from the Output drop-down menu.

Note *The Separate option is not available unless you define separation characteristics in the Separation Setup dialog box.*

■ Click the Separation Setup button to open the Separation Setup dialog box.

■ If you are printing a composite of the artwork, the Ignore Overprinting in Composite Output check box is available. Check the check box to instruct Illustrator to ignore the presence of overprinting options set in the Attributes palette.

■ From the PostScript drop-down menu, match the level of PostScript with your PostScript printer: Choose Level 2 or Level 3.

■ From the Data drop-down menu (Macintosh raster images only), select ASCII to make data in the document available to printers that support ASCII, or select Binary to reduce the data and increase printing speed.

■ From the Profile drop-down menu, choose a color profile, which describes a particular color management system.

■ From the Intent drop-down menu, choose a rendering intent, which translates colors to a different device's color management system.

■ Check the Force Fonts to Download check box to download fonts to the printer while it prints the document.

■ Check the Bitmap Printing check box to print a complex document as a bitmap image on a low-resolution, non-PostScript printer on a Windows computer. If the check box is unchecked, you might be unsuccessful in printing. Note that you might have better results if you install the fonts on the printer.

Overriding Printer Settings

Illustrator provides the EPSF Riders file, which is coded in the PostScript language, to set some of the options—namely, line screen and screen angle—in the Separation Setup dialog box and other options, including comments and error handling for all Illustrator documents. Options you specify in the EPSF Riders file override those in the Separation Setup dialog box.

Installing the EPSF Riders File

To use the EPSF Riders file, you must move the Riders plug-in from the Riders subfolder, which is under the Utilities folder, to the Plug-ins folder. Then let Illustrator recognize that the plug-in is in place. When Illustrator discovers the EPSF Riders plug-in, it adds an Other command to the Filter menu (unless you have added another plug-in in another Illustrator session). The Other command includes two subcommands: Delete Riders and Make Riders.

To install the EPSF Riders plug-in, follow these steps:

1. Open the Riders folder and the Plug-ins folder on your desktop.

2. Select the Riders plug-in, and drag it to the Plug-ins folder.

3. Open the Plug-ins folder, and drag the Riders plug-in to the folder.

4. Exit Illustrator and start it again. When you start Illustrator, it notices the presence of the Riders plug-in and adds it to the Other command on the Filter menu.

You can use these steps to install any Illustator plug-in.

Creating the EPSF Riders File

The newly installed Make Riders command creates one EPSF Riders file for all Illustrator documents that you will save or print in Illustrator. Note that Illustrator limits you to making one file. Note also that you should not change the name of the file; without the proper name, Illustrator does not understand the purpose of the file.

To create the EPSF Riders file, choose Filter | Other | Make Riders. When Illustrator opens the Make Riders dialog box (see Figure 22-12), select from the following options:

■ From the Screen Frequency drop-down menu, select the value for the line screen. You can choose None, 10 lpi, 30 lpi, 53 lpi (the default), 60 lpi, 85 lpi, 100 lpi, 133 lpi, 150 lpi, and 175 lpi, or choose Other to open the Riders dialog box in which you can type a frequency value ranging from 1 to 999.

■ From the Screen Angle drop-down menu, select the screen angle. You can choose None, 0 degree, 15°, 30°, 45° (the default), 90°, 105°, or 120°, or choose Other to open another version of the Riders dialog box in which you can type an angle from 0° to 360°.

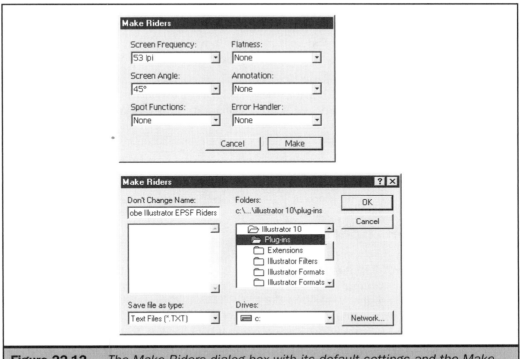

Figure 22-12.   *The Make Riders dialog box with its default settings and the Make Riders dialog box with which you save the file*

■ From the Spot Functions drop-down menu, choose the shape of the dot in the halftone. You can choose None (the default), Simple Round, Inverted Round, Euclidean Composite, Rhomboid, Line, Diamond, or Inverted Elliptical, or you can choose Import to open the Select Spot Function to Import so that you can import a file.

Caution   *A spot function must meet certain criteria: It must be written in the PostScript language and must be properly formatted. To learn more, refer to the Spot Function Template in the Riders folder.*

■ From the Flatness drop-down menu, choose a flatness setting with which you will adjust complex curves. You can choose None, 1, 3, 10, 100, or 200 or choose Other to open another version of the Riders dialog box in which you can type a flatness level. Valid values range from 0.2 to 200. Adobe recommends that you select None, the default, because the flatness setting replaces the output resolution setting.

OUTSIDE ILLUSTRATOR

- From the Annotation drop-down menu, choose an annotation for the printed page. You can choose None (the default), Include, or Setup. If you select Setup, Illustrator opens another Riders dialog box in which you can type an annotation with a maximum of 254 characters and select its font and point size.

- From the Error Handler drop-down menu, select None (the default) or Include to include an error handling routine, which prints any error information on the page with the artwork. For the Adobe PSPrinter and LaserWriter 8.0 (or greater) printer drivers, Adobe recommends that you use the printer's error handler instead. Check your printer's manual to see the manufacturer's recommendations.

After you have selected all the desired options from the dialog box, click Make to open the Make Riders dialog box in which you save the file, making sure you save the file in the Plug-ins folder—the place in which Illustrator expects the file to be located.

Moving the EPSF Riders File

Occasionally, you might want to use the Separation Settings dialog box rather than the settings saved in the EPSF Riders file. If you don't want to delete the file—only to reinstall it at a later time—you can move the file to another folder temporarily. To move the file, you'll repeat the steps in the "Installing the EPSF Riders File" section, except the names of the folders are different. Just drag the file from its current location in the Plug-ins folder to any other folder, from which you can drag it back to Plug-ins at your convenience.

Once you move the file to another folder, exit Illustrator and launch Illustrator again. If you examine the Filter menu, you won't find the commands related to the EPSF Riders file and you might not find the Other command either. The last step—a new one—is to resave all the files to which you have applied the EPSF Riders file settings. This replaces those settings with the default settings.

Deleting the EPSF Riders File

If you want to remove the EPSF Riders file permanently, use the Delete Riders command and then resave all the files to which you have applied the EPSF Riders file settings.

To delete the EPSF Riders file, follow these steps:

1. Choose Filter | Other | Delete Rider. Illustrator opens the Select "Adobe Illustrator EPSF Riders" to Delete dialog box (see Figure 22-13).
2. Choose Riders.aip, and click Delete.

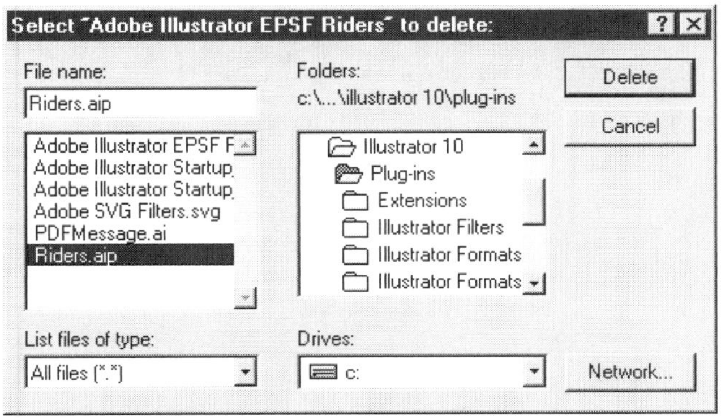

Figure 22-13. *The Select "Adobe Illustrator EPSF Riders" to Delete dialog box with the Riders file selected*

Exploring the Document Info Palette

With the Document Info palette (see Figure 22-14), you can view lists of information about many aspects of the current document: the document name and location; the objects from which the document is composed; the styles, brushes, spot colors, patterns, gradients, and fonts; and the linked and embedded images in the file. You can save the document information for those, such as a commercial printer, who will modify or use the file in some way. To toggle between showing and hiding the palette, choose Window | Document Info.

The Document Info palette contains a window in which appears information about the current document. Click the menu button to reveal the palette's most important element, its menu:

■ The Selection Only command enables you to see the information about one or more selected objects within the document.

■ The Document command (the default) shows information about the document: its name and location.

■ The Objects command lists the objects in the selection or document: the paths (and points), compound paths, compound shapes, and clipping masks.

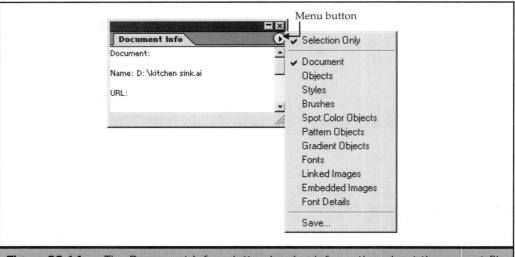

Figure 22-14.   *The Document Info palette showing information about the current file*

- The Styles command shows the number of styles and their names.
- The Brushes command displays the number of styles (and their names) applied to the fill and the stroke in the selection or document.
- The Spot Color Objects command shows the names of the spot colors for the selection or document.
- The Pattern Objects command lists the patterned objects in the selection or document.
- The Gradient Objects command shows the objects with gradient fills in the selection or document.
- The Fonts command lists the fonts and font types in the selection or document.
- The Linked Images command displays the linked images in the selection or document.
- The Embedded Images command displays the embedded images in the selection or document.

- The Font Details command provides operating system or PostScript information about the fonts in the selection or document.

- The Save command opens the Save Select Info As dialog box, with which you can save the information in an Info text file and document the settings in the document; you can distribute these to those who need the information.

Note   *You also can keep information about a document in the Attributes palette. Choose Window | Attributes (F11), select an object or the entire document, and type as many as 240 characters in the text box at the bottom of the palette.*

The Complete Reference

Part V

Appendixes

Appendix A

Installing Illustrator

This appendix provides information about the minimum requirements for installing Adobe Illustrator on computers running under the Windows or Macintosh operating systems. Before you install Illustrator, you should have installed your computer operating system and peripherals, including a mouse, printer, and modem or other connection to the World Wide Web.

If you have installed any application on your computer recently, you already know how to install Illustrator. The installation process is straightforward and very much the same as other installation procedures.

To ensure that you can reinstall Illustrator if you need to, make sure that you put the Illustrator CD in a safe place after you have completed the installation process.

Installing on a Windows PC

This section includes minimum system requirements for successfully using Illustrator on a Windows PC and installation instructions.

PC System Requirements

Adobe recommends certain minimum system requirements for installing and using Illustrator on a Windows PC. Of these, the processor, RAM, and operating system are the most important.

The minimum system requirements for Illustrator on a Windows PC are

- Intel Pentium II, III, or 4 (or greater) processor
- Windows 98, Windows 98 Special Edition, Windows Millennium Edition, Windows 2000 with Service Pack 2, or Windows XP (or greater)
- A CD-ROM or DVD drive
- 128MB of RAM installed; the more RAM on your computer, the better Illustrator will run
- 180MB of free hard-disk space for installation
- A video card supporting a minimum resolution of 800x600
- If you are using an Adobe PostScript printer: either Adobe PostScript Level 2 or Adobe PostScript 3

Installing Illustrator on a PC

Installing Illustrator is easy. Just follow the prompts as each dialog box opens and you'll complete the installation without any problems.

To install Illustrator, follow these steps:

1. Insert the Adobe Illustrator CD-ROM in your CD-ROM or DVD drive. Illustrator probably uses the Autoplay feature to display a Welcome screen; click Next.

Note   *If Autoplay does not open the screen, click the Start button, select Run, and type* **d:\AutoPlay.exe** *(where* d *represents the letter of your CD-ROM drive); then click OK.*

2. Click the Installation button.

3. In the Select Language dialog box, select the language; then click Next.

4. Read the software agreement. If you accept, click Yes to continue the installation.

5. Choose the Destination folder. If you accept the prompt, the program is placed in the Program Files folder; click Next.

6. Select the type of installation: Typical, Compact, or Custom Install; then click Next.

   ■ The Typical installation installs the typical file.

   ■ The Compact installation is the best for computers with limited processing power and hard drive space.

   ■ The Custom installation enables you to choose from a list of components. This is for expert users.

7. Continue responding to prompts until the installation is complete. You can see the status of the installation in a small box. When installation is finished, Illustrator displays a small message box.

8. After installation, you can register online.

Installing on a Macintosh

This section includes minimum system requirements for successfully using Illustrator on a Macintosh computer and installation instructions.

Mac System Requirements

Adobe recommends certain minimum system requirements for installing and using Illustrator on a Macintosh computer. Of these, the processor and RAM are the most important.

The minimum system requirements for Illustrator on a Macintosh computer are

■ A PowerPC processor: G3, G4, or G4 dual (or greater)

■ Mac OS version 9.1, version 9.2, or Mac OS X version 10.1 (or greater)

■ A CD-ROM or DVD drive

■ 128MB of RAM installed; the more RAM on your computer, the better Illustrator will run

■ 180MB of free hard-disk space for installation

■ A video card supporting a minimum resolution of 800x600

■ If you are using an Adobe PostScript printer: either Adobe PostScript Level 2 or Adobe PostScript 3

Installing Illustrator on a Mac

Installing Illustrator is as easy on a Mac as it is on a PC. Just follow the prompts as each dialog box opens and you'll complete the installation without any problems.

To install Illustrator, follow these steps:

1. Insert the Adobe Illustrator CD-ROM in your CD-ROM or DVD drive.

2. Double-click the Install Adobe Illustrator icon. When the Welcome screen appears, click Continue.

3. Select the language; click Next.

4. Read the software agreement. If you accept, click Yes to continue the installation.

5. Select the type of installation: Easy Install or Custom Install; then click Next.

   ■ The Easy Install installation installs the typical file.

   ■ The Custom installation enables you to choose from a list of components. This is for expert users.

6. If you wish, choose the folder in which the program files will be located.

7. Continue responding to prompts until the installation is complete. You can see the status of the installation in a small box. When the installation is finished, Illustrator displays a small message box.

8. After the installation, you can register online.

The Complete Reference

Adobe Illustrator 10

Appendix B

Setting Illustrator Preferences

This appendix provides information about making your copy of Illustrator your own by customizing your working environment.

Setting Illustrator Preferences in the Preferences Dialog Box

In Illustrator, the primary customization command is Preferences. Choose Edit | Preferences (CTRL-K/⌘-K) to open the General section of the Preferences dialog box. Then you can navigate the dialog box in one of two ways: Either choose the desired section from the drop-down menu at the top of the dialog box or click the Previous or Next button to cycle forward or backward through the sections. You can also go directly to a particular section by choosing Edit | Preferences and then choosing the section name from the submenu.

Specifying General Preferences

The options in the General Preferences section control some of the wide-ranging behavior of Illustrator. The options in the General section are as follows:

- You can move a selected object slightly by pressing an arrow key. In the Keyboard Increment text box, you can adjust the amount by which an arrow key moves the object by typing a value. Valid values range from 0 to 18 inches. The default is 1 point.

- In the Constrain Angle text box, type the angle at which you want to constrain objects during alignment. The default is 0 degree. When you set the Constrain Angle, you actually rotate the grid—whether it is hidden or displayed in the illustration window. (You learned how to rotate the grid, and therefore, set the constrain angle, in the "Rotating the Grid" section in Chapter 5.)

- In the Corner Radius text box, set the default shape of rounded rectangles. Valid values range from 0 to 1,296 points. The default is 12 points.

- Check the Use Area Select check box to be able to select an object by clicking its fill, in addition to being able to select by clicking a path or anchor point. The default is a checked check box.

- Use the Precise Cursors check box to set a cross-hatch mouse pointer rather than the standard mouse pointer for the Add Anchor Point (+), Column Graph (J) and all the other graph tools, Delete Anchor Point (-), Lasso, Magic Wand (Y), Pen (P), Pencil (N), Slice (SHIFT-K), and Symbol Sprayer (SHIFT-S) and other symbols tools. Note that the cross-hatch mouse pointer is the only mouse pointer for the following tools: Arc, Auto Trace, Ellipse (L), Gradient (G), Line Segment (\), Measure, Page, Polar Grid, Polygon, Rectangle (M), Rectangular Grid,

Reflect (O), Rotate (R), Rounded Rectangle, Scale (S), Scissors (C), Shear, Spiral, Star, and Twist. The default is an unchecked box.

- Check the Disable Warnings check box to prevent the display of certain warning messages. If you are an experienced Illustrator user, consider checking this check box. The default is an unchecked box.

- Check the Show Tool Tips check box to turn on tooltips. The default is a checked box.

- Check the Anti-aliased Artwork check box to turn on anti-aliasing to correct jagged edges in raster images. The default is a checked box.

- Check the Select Same Tint Percentage check box to have Illustrator select objects that have similar stroke or fill colors based on their tint percentages. The default is an unchecked box.

- Check the Disable Auto Add/Delete check box to halt the Pen tool's capability to add (that is, automatically switch to the Add Anchor tool) and delete (that is, automatically switch to the Delete Anchor tool) anchor points by clicking them. The default is an unchecked box.

- Check the Japanese Crop Marks check box to change the standard crop marks to Japanese crop marks. The default is an unchecked box.

- Check the Transform Pattern Tiles check box to place a check mark in a transformation dialog box so that Illustrator changes both an object and its patterned fill when you transform the object. Note that you can remove the check from the dialog box before you click OK. The default is an unchecked box.

- Check the Scale Strokes & Effects check box to scale an object's strokes and effects when you scale the object. The default is an unchecked box.

- Check the Use Preview Bounds check box to maintain the original dimensions of an object when you change the stroke width of the object or snap the object to the grid. The default is an unchecked box.

- Click the Reset All Warning Dialog button to return to the display of all warning messages that you have disabled.

Stipulating Type & Auto Tracing Preferences

The options in the Type & Auto Tracing section of the Preferences dialog box control some of the behavior of type and two attributes of the Auto Trace tool. The options are as follows:

- In the Size/Leading text box, type the measurement by which type size and leading are incremented by pressing the CTRL-SHIFT->/⌘-SHIFT->, CTRL-SHIFT-</⌘-SHIFT-<, ALT-↑/OPTION-↑, or ALT-↓/OPTION-↓ shortcuts. Valid values range from 0.1 point to 72 points. The default is 2 points.

- In the Baseline Shift text box, type the measurement by which you want to move selected type above or below the baseline by pressing the ALT-SHIFT↑/OPTION-SHIFT-↑ or ALT-SHIFT-↓/OPTION-SHIFT-↓ shortcut. Valid values range from 0.1 point to 72 points. The default is 2 points.

- In the Tracking text box, type the measurement by which you want to track or kern (insert space between selected characters) by pressing CTRL-→/⌘-→ or CTRL-←/⌘-← or inserting five spaces by pressing CTRL-ALT-→/⌘-OPTION-→ or CTRL-ALT-←/⌘-OPTION-←. Valid values range from –1,000 to 10,000. The default is 20.

- In the Greeking text box, set the font size below which Illustrator greeks type. Valid values range from 1 point to 1,296 points. The default is 6 points.

- Check the Type Area Select check box to be able to select type by clicking in its area in addition to clicking the path on which it sits. The default is a checked box.

- Check the Show Font Names in English check box to display font names in English rather than in symbols. The default is an unchecked box.

- In the Auto Trace Tolerance text box, type the accuracy with which Illustrator redraws auto-traced objects. Valid values range from 0 to 10 points. The default is 2 points.

- In the Tracing Gap text box, type the value by which Illustrator ignores gaps between auto-traced paths. Valid values range from 0 (the default) to 2 points.

Setting Units & Undo Preferences

The Units & Undo section of the Preferences dialog box controls the units of measure, the level of undos, and object names.

In the "Setting the Unit of Measure" section in Chapter 5, you learned how to select a unit of measure for the current document and all future documents. Valid units of measure are points (the default), picas, inches, millimeters, centimeters, and pixels.

Other options in the Units & Undo section of the Preferences dialog box are as follows:

- Check the Numbers Without Units Are Points check box to enable you to enter values without having to insert the pt (point) label. The default is an unchecked box.

- In the Minimum Undo Levels text box, enter the minimum number of actions that Illustrator "remembers" so that you can undo them. Note that the more undos that Illustrator has to remember, the more memory Illustrator has to use. Valid values range from 0 to 200. The default is 5.

■ In the Names section, click the Identify Objects By radio button to have Illustrator identify objects by their names (the default), or click the XML ID radio button to have Illustrator identify objects by their XML IDs. If, as a rule, you are creating objects for use in XML documents, click the XML ID radio button.

Setting Guides & Grid Preferences

The options in the Guides & Grid section of the Preferences dialog box control the color and style of guides and the grid. The options are as follows:

■ In the Guides section, choose the color of guide lines or dots from the Color drop-down menu. Either click a color or choose Other (the default) to open the Color dialog box. The color swatch shows the current color.

■ In the Guides section, choose the style of guides (Lines or Dots) from the Style drop-down menu. The default is Lines.

■ In the Grid section, choose the color of grid lines or dots from the Color drop-down menu. Either click a color or choose Other (the default) to open the Color dialog box. The color swatch shows the current color.

■ In the Grid section, choose the style of the grid (Lines or Dots) from the Style drop-down menu. The default is Lines.

■ In the Gridline Every text box, type the spacing between major lines in the grid. Valid values range from 0.01 point to 1,000 points. The default is 72 points.

■ In the Subdivisions text box, type the number of divisions within the major gridlines. Valid values range from 1 to 1,000. The default is 8.

■ Check the Grids in Back check box to place the grid behind the objects in the illustration window. An unchecked box places the gridlines in front of the objects.

Denoting Smart Guides & Slices Preferences

The options in the Smart Guides & Slices section of the Preferences dialog box control the look and placement of Smart Guides and the appearance of slices.

You learned about setting preferences for Smart Guides in the "Introducing Smart Guides" section in Chapter 5.

The other options are as follows:

■ Check the Show Slice Numbers check box to display slice numbers. The default is a checked box.

■ From the Line Color drop-down menu, choose the color of slice lines. If you choose Other (the default), you can select a color from the Color dialog box.

APPENDIXES

Specifying Hyphenation Preferences

The options in the Hyphenation section of the Preferences dialog box control hyphenation and list words that are exceptions to hyphenation rules. The options are as follows:

■ From the Default Language drop-down menu, select the default language you will use in Illustrator. The default language for those buying Illustrator in the United States is U.S. English.

■ The Exceptions list box lists words that you have instructed Illustrator never to hyphenate.

■ To add a word to the Exceptions list, type it in the New Entry text box; then click Add.

■ To delete a word from the Exceptions list, select it; then click Delete.

Setting Preferences for Plug-ins & Scratch Disks

The options in the Plug-ins & Scratch Disks section of the Preferences dialog box control the location of plug-ins and scratch disks. The options are as follows:

■ In the Plug-ins Folder section, Illustrator lists the folder in which plug-ins are stored by default. To change the plug-ins folder, click the Choose button and click OK.

■ From the Primary drop-down menu, choose the location of the scratch disk in which Illustrator stores processed information when it runs out of RAM. The default is Startup.

■ From the Secondary drop-down menu, choose the location of a secondary scratch disk. The default is None.

Indicating Files & Clipboard Preferences

The options in the Files & Clipboard section of the Preferences dialog box control the updating of linked images and how Illustrator copies objects to the Clipboard. The options are as follows:

■ From the Update Links drop-down menu, select how links are updated. Choose Ask When Modified (the default) to have Illustrator prompt you to update in Illustrator when you have updated a link in its home application; choose Automatically to have Illustrator automatically update the link, and choose Manually to enable you to update the link on your own.

■ Check the Use Low Resolution Proxy for Linked EPS check box to view raster versions of linked EPS images rather than high-resolution versions. The default is a checked box.

■ Check the Copy As PDF check box to copy Illustrator artworks in Portable Document Format when you are copying to an application that supports PDF. The default is a checked box.

■ Check the Copy As AICB check box to copy Illustrator artworks in the Adobe Illustrator Clipboard format. The default is an unchecked check box. Then, select either the Preserve Paths or Preserve Appearance (the default) radio button to preserve paths or appearance. Note that AICB does not support transparency.

Setting Workgroup Preferences

The options in the Workgroup section of the Preferences dialog box support the editing of Illustrator artworks by members of a workgroup. The options are as follows:

■ The Enable Workgroup Functionality check box activates working as a workgroup. The default is a checked check box.

■ From the Check Out from Server drop-down menu, select the way in which members of the work group check out files:

   ■ Choose Ask (the default) to open a dialog box that prompts you to check out a file that is not currently checked out from the workgroup server.

   ■ Choose Never to open a local copy of the file without displaying a dialog box and without formally checking out the file from the workgroup server.

   ■ Choose Always to check out the file automatically every time you request it from the workgroup server.

■ From the Update from Server drop-down menu, select the way in which you check out the latest update of updated files:

   ■ Choose Ask to open a dialog box that prompts you to check out the latest version from the workgroup server.

   ■ Choose Never to open a local copy of the file without displaying a dialog box and without obtaining the latest update from the workgroup server.

   ■ Choose Always (the default) to obtain the file automatically from the workgroup server.

■ From the Update Links from Server drop-down menu, select whether Illustrator updates links when you obtain a file with links:

   ■ Choose Ask to open a dialog box that prompts you to obtain the most recent versions of the linked files from the workgroup server.

   ■ Choose Never to open a local copy of the file without displaying a dialog box and without updating links to the desired file from the workgroup server.

- Choose Always to update the links automatically and obtain the file from the workgroup server.

- Choose Verify Only (the default) to verify whether links are broken and display icons for any broken links in the Links palette after obtaining the file from the workgroup server.

- From the Update Links from Server drop-down menu in the When Placing Managed Links section, select whether Illustrator updates links when you obtain a placed file with links:

  - Choose Ask to open a dialog box that prompts you to obtain the most recent versions of the linked files from the workgroup server.

  - Choose Never (the default) to open a local copy of the file without displaying a dialog box and without updating links to the desired file from the workgroup server.

  - Choose Always to update the links automatically and obtain the file from the workgroup server.

Specifying Adobe Online Preferences

Illustrator provides the Adobe Online service with which you can check for updates to the application and download them so that you always have the most current version of Illustrator.

To change your Adobe Online preferences, choose Edit | Preferences | Online Settings. When Illustrator opens the Online Settings dialog box, choose from among the following options:

- From the Check for Updates drop-down menu, choose the time at which Illustrator automatically checks for updates: Never, Once a Day, Once a Week (the default), or Once a Month.

- Check the Automatically Launch Installer When Download Is Complete check box to install the updates automatically. A checked check box is the default.

- Check the Show Download Progress to display a status box in which you can see how much of the update has completed.

- Click the About Adobe Online button to display a splash screen that shows the current version of Adobe Online and those who worked on the version.

- Click the Updates button to open the update status box.

Creating a Startup File

Illustrator provides two default startup files, Adobe Illustrator Startup_CMYK and Adobe Illustrator Startup_RGB, with which you can start a new document. Illustrator stores both files in the Plug-ins folder. A startup file is an Illustrator document that displays the current swatches in the Swatches palette, the styles in the Styles palette, and the symbols in the Symbols palette. The file also includes set Artboard and page dimensions, a starting zoom level, and a default viewing mode.

You can create custom startup files that specify different (or the same) swatches, styles, symbols, Artboard and page dimensions, zoom level, and viewing mode.

To create a custom startup file, follow these steps:

1. Make copies of the original startup files, and move them from the Plug-ins folder to a different folder. This ensures that you don't inadvertently edit the startup files.

2. Open one of the original startup files from the Plug-ins folder.

3. Edit the file by opening the Swatches, Styles, and Symbols palettes and adding, deleting, or modifying their contents. Whenever you change a palette, also change the associated object in illustration window.

4. Open Swatches or Styles libraries and add selected content to the illustration window. Make sure that Illustrator reflects the new content in the appropriate palettes.

5. You also can insert graph designs in the illustration window.

6. Select the desired zoom level, viewing mode, and Artboard and page dimensions.

7. Save the file in the Plug-ins folder using the proper name: Adobe Illustrator Startup_CMYK or Adobe Illustrator Startup_RGB.

8. To use the new startup file, exit Illustrator and start it again.

The Complete Reference

Appendix C

Online Resources

The Web contains a myriad of Illustrator resources, many of which can provide help, free tryouts and utilities, and examples of Illustrator usage. This appendix contains many of those links.

Resources at Adobe

Peruse the resources in the section from Illustrator's developer.

- The Adobe home page (http://www.adobe.com/)
- The Adobe Illustrator home page (http://www.adobe.com/products/illustrator/main.html)
- Acrobat Reader download page (http://www.adobe.com/products/acrobat/readstep.html)
- Adobe SVG Viewer download page (http://www.adobe.com/svg/viewer/install/main.html)
- The Adobe SVG Zone (http://www.adobe.com/svg/main.html)
- Illustrator FAQ page (http://www.adobe.com/products/illustrator/pdfs/ai10_faq.pdf)
- Adobe Illustrator Support home page (http://www.adobe.com/support/products/illustrator.html)
- Adobe CustomerFirst Support—Downloads (http://www.adobe.com/support/downloads/)
- Recent Illustrator tutorials (http://www.adobe.com/products/tips/illustrator.html)
- The Adobe Studio (http://eportfolio.studio.adobe.com/wa/login.asp)
- The Adobe Training home page (http://www.adobe.com/misc/training.html)
- The Adobe Illustrator Plug-in Software Development Kit from the download page (http://partners.adobe.com/asn/developer/gapsdk/IllustratorSDK.html)
- Adobe's Third-Party Plug-ins page (http://www.adobe.com/store/plugins/illustrator/main.html)
- Adobe Technical Announcements (http://www.adobe.com/support/emaillist.html)
- Adobe User to User Forums (http://www.adobe.com/support/forums/main.html)
- Adobe Recent Print Tutorials (http://www.adobe.com/print/tips/)
- Adobe Open Source Project - Python Plug-in for Adobe Illustrator (http://opensource.adobe.com/project2/project.shtml)

- Adobe Illustrator Expert Center
  (http://studio.adobe.com/expertcenter/illustrator/main.html)
- Encapsulated PostScript File Format Specification
  (http://partners.adobe.com/asn/developer/pdfs/tn/5002.EPSF_Spec.pdf)
- Illustrator Technical Guides
  (http://www.adobe.com/support/techguides/illustrator/main.html)
- Color Management Systems—Technical Guides (http://www.adobe.com/
  support/techguides/color/colormanagement/main.html)
- The Magic of Multiple Master Typefaces
  (http://www.adobe.com/type/topics/magicmm.html)
- Adobe Solution Network: Archived Technical Journal and Newsletters
  (http://partners.adobe.com/asn/developer/techjournal/main.html)
- Adobe Solutions Network: Type Technology
  (http://partners.adobe.com/asn/developer/type.html)
- Adobe Solutions Network: Technical Notes
  (http://partners.adobe.com/asn/developer/technotes/main.html)
- Font Formats (http://www.adobe.com/type/topics/info9.html)

Directories of Links

The pages listed in this section provide links to many Web sites—for Illustrator and your other art requirements.

- Hunt for Free Graphics (http://www.huntfor.com/design/freegraphics.htm)
- Gifpile (http://www.geocities.com/SoHo/Gallery/2681/main.html)
- Adobe Illustrator Resources (http://graphicssoft.about.com/cs/illustrator/)

Tutorials and Tips

In this section, you can find sources of tutorials and tips for Illustrator and other applications. Note that many of these sites have not updated to Illustrator 10 at the time of this writing.

- Adobe Illustrator—Intro (http://thetechnozone.com/bbyc/Illustrator.htm)
- Adobe Illustrator Tutorials—Basics and Setup
  (http://graphicssoft.about.com/cs/illustratorbasics/)
- Adobe Illustrator Tutorials (http://graphicssoft.about.com/cs/illustratortuts/)
- EyeWire: Tips (http://www.eyewire.com/tips/apps/)

- Fine Art and Graphic Design—Adobe Illustrator Tutorials (http://www.huntfor.com/design/tutorials/illustrator.htm)
- Creative Tools in Illustrator 9 (http://www.iboost.com/build/software/illustrator9/vector_artistry/10022.htm)
- Computer Arts Online (http://www.computerarts.co.uk/)
- Adobe Illustrator Tips and Techniques (http://www.desktoppublishing.com/tipsillustr.html)
- Kitty Corner: Illustrator Tips and Tricks (http://www.harperhouse.com/tricks/Illustratortrick.html)
- BARCO Graphics & Design for Color (http://www.illustrator-resources.com/links/)
- Lycos Help & How-To—Adobe Illustrator 8.0 (http://howto.lycos.com/lycos/topic/0,,10+55+140,00.html)
- JEDSITE (http://www.lvcm.com/jedart/)
- Illustrator Tutorials (http://www.sketchpad.net/illustrator.htm)
- Illustrator Tutorials (http://www.thinkdan.com/tutorials/illustrator.html)
- Illustrator Tips & Tutorials Index (http://www.rdrop.com/~half/Creations/Art/IllustratorTips/index.html)
- Adobe Illustrator Tutorials (http://www.nelsonsfreelance.com/tutorial/)
- Inside Adobe Illustrator (http://online.caup.washington.edu/courses/larcwi01/larc440/illust_Inside.htm)
- Adobe Tutorials (http://www.tutorialfind.com/tutorials/adobe/)
- Designs By Mark | Illustrator Tutorials (http://www.designsbymark.com/ai_tips/index.shtml)
- The Resource Center for Digital Illustrators (http://www.illustrator-resources.com/links/Adobe_Illustrator/Tutorials/)

Design Hints and Help

At this site, you can get general design information.

- The Internet Design & Publishing Center (http://www.graphic-design.com/)

Galleries

The gallery pages listed in this section include images created in Illustrator, other applications, and other media.

- Valeri Darling, Missing Masterpiece Graphx (http://www.missingmasterpiece.com)
- DraSan' Nitti, Silver Dragon Studio (http://www.silverdragonstudio.com)
- Brenda Bennett Design, Creative Design Solutions (http://www.BrendaGraphics.com)
- Janet McLeod (http://www.portfolios.com/illust/mcleod.janet)
- Liz Sanders Agency (http://www.lizsanders.com/)
- Andreas Seidel—Illustration Portfolio (http://www.grundsatz.de/aseidel/illustration.shtml)
- Lars Pruds Logotype Design Gallery (http://www.pryds.com/LP/logotype.html)
- LASF/Gallery/9-12 Lobby (http://www.lasf.org/gallery/9_12/lobby.html)
- Media Spin Presents Hank Grebe's Digital Art Gallery (http://www.mediaspin.com/hank/digihank.html)
- Suzanne Tornquist (http://tornquist-art.com/)
- John Pritchett (http://www.pritchettcartoons.com/illustration2.htm)
- Leslie Quagraine (http://mindartdesign.com/)

Online Newsletters, Magazines, and News

To get information from the experts and up-to-date Illustrator news, read the newsletters, magazines, and news in this section.

- EyeWire: Magazine (http://www.eyewire.com/magazine/)
- Design Tools Monthly (http://www.design-tools.com/)
- The Plugin Newsletter (http://thepluginsite.com/news/index.htm)
- Valeri Darling, Missing Masterpiece Graphx (http://www.missingmasterpiece.com)
- Illustrator News (http://www.creativepro.com/software/news/32.html)

Forums

You can ask your fellow artists Illustrator questions in the forum listed in this section. Additionally, visit the Adobe Web site to sign up for its forums.

- Tek-Tips—Adobe: Illustrator Technical Help Forum (http://www.tek-tips.com/gthreadminder.cfm/lev2/4/lev3/31/pid/226)

APPENDIXES

Plug-ins and Extensions

In this section, you'll find plug-ins and extensions with which you might be able to enhance Illustrator. Note that these plug-ins and extensions have not been tested during the writing of this book.

- Graffix plugins for Adobe Illustrator (http://personalpages.tds.net/~graffix/software/plugins.html)
- Stephen Vincent's Plug-in Page (http://www.kagi.com/svincent/default.html)
- Illustrator-Related Products (http://www.creativepro.com/software/relatedproducts/32.html)
- BARCO Graphics & Design for Color (http://www.finaleye.com/boostx.htm)
- Web JPEG Plug-in 3.0 (http://vimas.com/ve_plugin.htm)
- CADtools 2.1, Perspective, and MultiPage (http://www.hotdoor.com/)
- Vertigo, Vertigo 3D Words (http://www.vertigo3d.com/products)
- MAPublisher for Adobe Illustrator (http://www.directionsmag.com/products.asp?a=details&prodid=42)
- Artlandia Symmetry Works (http://www.artlandia.com/products/SymmetryWorks/)

Fonts and PostScript

This section provides a variety of information about fonts. Additionally, Adobe provides a selection of PostScript printer drivers. You also can check for PostScript drivers that are compatible with your printer at your printer manufacturer's Web site.

- PostScript Type 1 Fonts (http://www.math.utah.edu/~beebe/fonts/postscript-type-1-fonts.html)
- Printer Drivers for Windows (http://www.adobe.com/support/downloads/product.jsp?product=44&platform=Windows)
- Printer Drivers for Macintosh (http://www.adobe.com/support/downloads/product.jsp?product=44&platform=Macintosh)
- Adobe Printer Drivers: Windows PPD Files by Printer Manufacturers (http://www.adobe.com/products/printerdrivers/winppd.html)
- Frequently Asked Questions About Fonts (http://nwalsh.com/comp.fonts/FAQ/)

Bézier Curves

To learn more about Bézier curves, the foundation of Illustrator, visit the pages listed in this section.

- The Bézier Curve (http://id.mind.net/~zona/mmts/curveFitting/bezierCurves/bezierCurve.html)
- Using Bézier Curves (http://www.1960pcug.org/~imagery/bezier_curves.htm)
- Bézier Curves (http://www.webreference.com/dlab/9902/bezier.html)
- What's a Bézier Curve? (http://www.moshplant.com/direct-or/bezier/)
- Bézier Curves (http://electric-words.com/dict/b/beziercurves.html)

SWF and SVG

In this section are pages for Macromedia Flash, an application that can animate SWF documents created in Illustrator, and SVG.

- Macromedia—Flash—Trial Download (http://www.macromedia.com/software/flash/trial)
- Macromedia Flash Writer for Adobe Illustrator (http://www.macromedia.com/software/flash/download/flashwriter/)
- Smart Curves (http://www.illustratortraining.com/resources/99smtsdb.pdf)
- Serving Up Web-Friendly Animations: In a Flash (http://www.webreference.com/dev/flash/)
- Flash Kit Tutorials (http://www.flashkit.com/tutorials/index.shtml)
- FlashPlanet.com Resource Links (http://flashplanet.com/body_links.html)
- Semantics of Macromedia's Flash (SWF) Format and Its Relationship to SVG (http://www.ep.cs.nott.ac.uk/projects/SVG/flash2svg/swfformat.html)
- A Concise Guide to the SWF File Format (http://www.brandtkurowski.com/projects/flashmap/fileformat/SWF%20Spec/SWFfileformat.html)
- Open-Standard Upstart SVG Takes on Macromedia's SWF (http://www.creativepro.com/story/feature/8057.html)
- Comparing .SWF (Shockwave Flash) and .SVG (Scalable Vector Graphics) File Format Specifications (http://www.carto.net/papers/svg/comparison_flash_svg.html)

Glossaries and Terms

This section contains a list of glossaries and other words from which you can learn about color, printing production, graphics, and units of measurement.

- Color Glossary (http://www.balmar.com/col_gloa.html)
- Color Glossary (http://www.pmel.org/Color-Glossary.htm)
- Glossary of Color Management Terms (http://www.adobe.com/support/techguides/color/cms_glossary/main.html)
- Printing Terms (http://cmsmailserv.ucsc.edu/printing/custerms/custermsab99.html)
- Printing Terms Glossary (http://www.balmar.com/gloss_a.html)
- Postcard Glossary (http://www.modernpostcard.com/text/glossary.shtml)
- DPI's Glossary of Terms (http://www.dpia.org/glossary/a.html)
- An Artist's Real-Time 3D Glossary (http://www.mondomed.com/mlabs/glossary.html)
- Printing Terms (http://www.clackesd.k12.or.us/mediamain/printing/terminology.htm)
- A Dictionary of Units of Measure (http://www.unc.edu/~rowlett/units/)

Miscellaneous Resources

This section contains random resources that may help you understand certain Illustrator topics.

- What Is...every file format in the world (http://www.ace.net.nz/tech/TechFileFormat.html)
- Explaining PostScript (http://amath.colorado.edu/documentation/postscript/WhatIs.html)
- Resolution (http://www.medicalart.net/pages/resolu.html)
- The Graphics File Format Page (2D Specs) (http://www.dcs.ed.ac.uk/home/mxr/gfx/2d-hi.html)
- Compression FAQ (http://www.faqs.org/faqs/compression-faq/)
- 3Dcompression.com (http://www.3dcompression.com/)
- JPEG—Webopedia.com (http://www.webopedia.com/TERM/J/JPEG.html)
- International Color Consortium (http://www.color.org/)
- Portable Network Graphics (http://www.w3.org/Graphics/PNG/)

- PNG—The Other Web Graphics Format
  (http://www.webdevelopersjournal.com/articles/png_graphics_format.html)
- The Ultimate Truth about Resolution, DPI, and PPI
  (http://nilbs.com/techbabl/dpi_ultim.htm)
- Anti-aliasing and Transparency
  (http://www.w3.org/Conferences/WWW4/Papers/53/gq-trans.html)

Appendix D

The Adobe Certified Expert Progam

Adobe's Certified Expert Program

The Adobe Certified Expert (ACE) program is for graphic designers, Web designers, systems integrators, value-added resellers, developers, and business professionals seeking official recognition of their expertise on Adobe products.

What Is an ACE?

An *Adobe Certified Expert* is an individual who has passed an Adobe Product Proficiency Exam for a specific Adobe software product. Adobe Certified Experts are eligible to promote themselves to clients or employers as highly skilled, expert-level users of Adobe software. ACE certification is a recognized worldwide standard for excellence in Adobe software knowledge.

ACE Benefits

When you become an ACE for a particular Adobe product, you enjoy these special benefits:

- Professional recognition
- An ACE program certificate
- Use of the Adobe Certified Expert program logo on your website and promotional materials

  For more information on the ACE program, see http://partners.adobe.com/asn/training/faq.html.

How to Become an Adobe Certified Expert (ACE)

To become an Adobe Certified Expert, you must pass an Adobe Product Proficiency Exam for the product for which you want to be certified. The following chart shows what exams are available.

Exam Number	Exam Name	Language
9AO-023	Adobe Acrobat® 5.0	English, French, German, Japanese
9A0-010	Adobe After Effects® 4.1	English
9A0-017	Adobe FrameMaker® 6.0	English, French, German, Japanese
9A0-012	Adobe FrameMaker® 5.5 + SGML 5.5 Authoring	English, Japanese
9A0-013	Adobe FrameMaker® 5.5 + SGML 5.5 Developer	English, Japanese

Exam Number	Exam Name	Language
9A0-022	Adobe GoLive® 5.0	English, French, German, Japanese
9A0-018	Adobe Illustrator® 9.0	English, French, German, Japanese
9A0-115	Adobe InDesign™ 1.5	English, French, German
9A0-019	Adobe Photoshop® 6.0	English, French, German, Japanese
9AO-021	Adobe Premiere 6.0	English
9A0-020	Adobe LiveMotion™ 1.0	English
9A0-024	Adobe PageMaker™ 7.0	English, French, German

Certification exams for the ACE program are now available worldwide in English. Also, several of the exams are available in many languages around the world.

How Do I Get Certified?

Adobe has created easy-to-follow steps and offers a variety of resources to help you prepare for the ACE exams.

How to Prepare for the Exam

1. Download a copy of the Exam Bulletin for the exam you want to take.

2. Review the bulletin to become familiar with the exam topic areas and objectives.

3. Identify the topic areas and objectives you need to study.

4. Determine the study materials you need to improve your skills. These options are available for you:

   ■ Attend an instructor-led training class.

   ■ Review the product *User Guide*.

   ■ Practice using the product.

Study for the exam using the Adobe Product Proficiency Exam Bulletins available on Adobe's site at **http://partners.adobe.com/asn/training/acehowto.html#164209**.

Once you feel you have mastered a specific Adobe product and you're ready for the ACE exam, follow these five steps and you'll be on your way toward meeting the Adobe Product Proficiency Exam requirement.

1. Study for the exam. Become familiar with the topic areas and objectives in the Exam Bulletin for the exam you plan to take. For additional study recommendations, see "How to Prepare for the Exam" located online at http://partners.adobe.com/asn/training/acehowto.html#anchor13658.

2. Review the Adobe Certified Expert Program Agreement. The ACE agreement is available online in PDF form for your review.

   You will be required to accept the ACE agreement when you take the Adobe Product Proficiency Exam at a Sylvan Prometric Testing Center.

3. Register for the Adobe Product Proficiency Exam. In the U.S. and Canada, call 1-800-356-3926 to find a test center and times for exams.

   For registration numbers outside the U.S./Canada, visit the Prometric Web site at http://www.2test.com/index.jsp. When contacting Prometric, provide them with the name and number of the exam you want to take.

4. Pass the Adobe Product Proficiency Exam. Once you've signed up to take the exam, the next step is to take and pass the test.

5. Once you've passed the test, you'll receive your welcome kit from Adobe four to six weeks after the exam date. Then, you can begin using your benefits.

About the Adobe Product Proficiency Exams

The Adobe Product Proficiency Exams are computer-delivered, closed-book tests consisting of 60 to 90 multiple-choice questions. Each exam is approximately one to two hours long. The exams are currently available worldwide in English only, and in other languages as the preceding table shows. The tests are administered by Prometric, an independent worldwise testing center. Exam results will be given to you at the testing center immediately after you complete the test. Diagnostic information is included in your exam report.

Test Dates and Locations

Testing is offered at more than a thousand Prometric Authorized Testing Centers located in many countries. To obtain the location of your nearest testing center in North America, you may call the Prometric Regional Service Center at 1-800-356-3926. For information on testing outside the U.S. and Canada, visit the Prometric Web site.

- **Fees**   The fee for the Adobe Product Proficiency Exam is $150 (U.S.).

- **Recertification**   Recertification is required of each ACE within 90 days of a designated Adobe Product Proficiency Exam release date.To get recertified, call Prometric at 1-800-356-3926. You will need to verify your previous certification for that product. If you are getting recertified, you are entitled to a 25 percent discount. In order to receive this discount, give the code "RETEST." For information about registration outside the U.S., visit the Prometric Web site.

- **Retesting**   There are no restrictions on the number of times you may take the exam within a given period.

Appendix E

How the Color Insert Images Were Created

T his appendix provides information about how the artists created the images in the color pages in the center of the book. The artists used a variety of methods to create their works: Some images were made entirely in Illustrator; other works started with pen or pencil on paper and were completed in Illustrator; others resulted from using features from Illustrator and Photoshop.

Note   *To learn about the artists, refer to "About the Artists" in the frontmatter of this book.*

Mouse Maze: Planning Your Web Advertising Strategy

Artist: Janet McLeod, www.portfolios.com/illust/mcleod.janet
This artwork is composed of four layers.
Janet McLeod says, "The background was created using the Fude brush stroke. This created a graffiti look to convey the modern hype surrounding many of the issues of the Web."

A Shot of Grace: Healing for a Sick Child

Artist: Janet McLeod, www.portfolios.com/illust/mcleod.janet
This artwork is composed of six layers.
Janet McLeod says, "Combining vector shapes in the foreground with line shapes in the background creates visual interest. The negative or lighter value lines on the godly hand helps convey its supernatural nature."

Litesout: When the Company IT Plan Fails

Artist: Janet McLeod, www.portfolios.com/illust/mcleod.janet
This artwork is composed of two layers.
Janet McLeod says, "Extensive use of Pathfinder cutting tools helps to create the shattered shapes that comprise this technology meltdown scenario. The ominous blacks of the computer screens are made richer by adding 40% cyan and 40% magenta to the 100% black."

Deco Titanic

Artist: Valeri Darling, Missing Masterpiece Graphx, http://www.missingmasterpiece.com
This artwork is composed of 20 layers.

Valeri Darling says, "The ship and sea were drawn freehand with the Pen tools. Gradients were used for the water, ship, and sky. The sun is an ellipse with an Outer Glow. I used transparency on the sun for softness. Clouds were created using filters and transparency. The birds were drawn with a calligraphy brush. The sea is colored with linear gradients, and I added a drop shadow for depth. The ship is filled with a linear gradient; the black filled smoke stacks were duplicated and filled in with a linear gradient."

The deconstructed version on the facing page illustrates some of the elements that make up the artwork.

Lady of Grace—Roses and Woman

Artist: Valeri Darling, Missing Masterpiece Graphx, http://www.missingmasterpiece.com

This artwork is composed of 16 layers.

Valeri Darling says, "I used the Pen tool to draw freehand and added a stock gradient background. I created the sky with the Ellipse tool and colored it with a linear gradient. I used a gradient mesh for the dress, skin, and roses. The petals and leaves of the roses were colored with a gradient mesh. I made the star with a gradient, and then Pucker and Bloat for distortion; and copied and rotated it three times for fullness. For the hair, I colored with a linear gradient and gradient mesh. Then I used the Shear and Twirl tools to make curves and waves."

The deconstructed version on the facing page illustrates some of the elements that make up the artwork.

Logos: Wildcats, Free Bird, and Peaceful Living—TP

Artist: Valeri Darling, Missing Masterpiece Graphx, http://www.missingmasterpiece.com

This artwork is composed of three layers—one for each logo.

Valeri Darling says, "I used the Pen tool to draw all three logos. For the Wildcats logo, I used a black fill and white outline to create lines and dimension. Text was created on a path to flow with the body.

"For the Free Bird logo, I used some alignment tools for the wings. I used red and blue fill with no outline. Text was created on a path to flow with the body.

"I used a stock gradient background color for Peaceful Living—TP. The teepee uses a gradient mesh for colors. The feather is distorted with some Pucker and Bloat. The white part of the feather is set to 75% transparency for softness over the black background. I created shadows with the Copy, Paste, and Distort tools and softened the clouds with the Transparency palette. For the ground, I laid a rectangle of light brown for the foundation color. I created a second piece with a swirl of pinks and browns, and twirled, transformed, and stretched it. I applied 50% transparency to blend into the brown layer."

The deconstructed version on the facing page illustrates some of the elements that make up the artwork.

Corporate Logos: dMedia and GildedIvy

Artist: Brenda Bennett, Brenda Bennett Design, http://www.brendagraphics.com
Each logo on this page is composed of 1 layer.

About dMedia, Brenda Bennett says, "I typeset *dMedia*, then copied the word *Media*, pasted in back, and stroked. I enlarged the letter *d* to line up with the edges of the stroke. Then I started with one circle, copied, pasted in back, and enlarged an even percentage. I repeated this for the other two circles underneath that one. The last circle has a gradient to give the illusion of motion and spinning. I finished the logo by adding a tagline and adding the initials *dM* inside the circle."

About GildedIvy, she says, "I started with a hand drawing of the ivy, and then I retraced the image using the Pen tool. I duplicated sections and rotated them as needed to curve around the oval. I used the Gradient tool inside the ivy leaves to give highlights. The barn was originally a photo, which I scanned, streamlined, and brought into Illustrator for fine-tuning (for example, cleaning up the edges, deleting unnecessary points along the paths, and so on). The company name and tagline were typeset in Illustrator."

The deconstructed version on the facing page illustrates some of the elements that make up the artwork.

Dancing Feet

Artist: Brenda Bennett, Brenda Bennett Design, http://www.brendagraphics.com
This artwork is composed of 16 layers.

Brenda Bennett says, "Starting with a pencil sketch that was scanned and placed into the Illustrator document as a template, I traced over the image. I drew each component of the image using the Pen tool on a separate layer in the document. To keep organized, I labeled the layers accordingly and hid them while I traced the next component. The entire image (see Figure E-1) was then imported into Photoshop as a layered file. I placed a new layer underneath each layer and applied color. Sometimes where an outlined layer overlapped, it needed to be erased.

The final effect: The outline of the image is solid black color from Illustrator with painterly effects created in Photoshop. An alternative would be to create this image completely in Illustrator using sections of flat colors and gradients underneath each

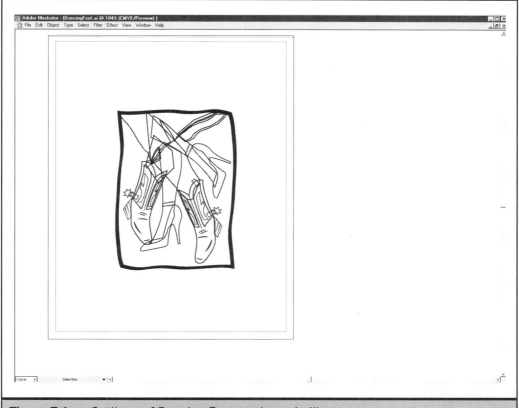

Figure E-1. *Outlines of Dancing Feet as drawn in Illustrator*

of the outlined layers. The advantage to this alternative is the image can then be scaled to any size without losing clarity because it is completely vector."

Rose

Artist: Brenda Bennett, Brenda Bennett Design, http://www.brendagraphics.com
This artwork is composed of one layer.

Brenda Bennett says, "I started with a pencil sketch and placed the graphic in the file as a template. I traced around the graphic using the Pen tool. I added strokes and gradients to give the illusion of depth."

APPENDIXES

Visions of Beauty

Artist: Valeri Darling, Missing Masterpiece Graphx, http://www.missingmasterpiece.com

This artwork is composed of 37 layers.

Valeri Darling says, "The whole drawing was made freehand with the Pen tools. I filled the kimono with a repeated flower print and then masked out to fill the robe with the floral print. Then I used gradient coloring to complete the silk effect. Gradient mesh was used in her skin, some of the flowers, and the ground to create the three-dimensional and shading effects. I used transparency on the clouds, mountain, and ground for depth and softening. I used calligraphy brushes for the tree limbs to give the effect of thin and thick branches, and on the folds in her robe to help the folds look more lifelike. I used transformation tools to create the flower blossoms to give them small and large combinations. I put drop shadows on the leaves to make them more realistic. The layers are kept in order of importance and always labeled for convenience."

Giant Panda Mother and Cub

Artist: DraSan' Nitti, Silver Dragon Studio, http://www.silverdragonstudio.com
This artwork is composed of six layers.

DraSan' Nitti says, "A rough black and white ink sketch (see Figure E-2) of the pandas was scanned in at a high resolution as a color photograph to pick up as much detail as possible, saved as a TIFF file, and then brought down to 72 ppi (pixels per inch) resolution before it was opened in Illustrator in Template mode. A tracing was created on its own layer with the Pencil tool, which is sensitive as a brush to the subtle movements of the cursor giving a brush-like edge.

A red line was used to trace the pandas so I could clearly see the drawing that was being created. The lines were then selected and changed to black. Value pattern transitions were defined and the values adjusted using the sliding value scale in the Color Palette. The shapes were selected and slightly softened by choosing Effect | Stylize | Feather set at 0.05.

The entire drawing was selected, copied, and pasted as pixels into Photoshop and onto a background. A motion blur was added to selected areas, giving a fur-like effect. The file was saved, placed into Illustrator, and then selected and locked. A new layer was created, and the eye was redrawn using the Ellipse tool with white line and black fill and then feathered too. Smaller ellipses were added in white for the highlights of the eyes. A drawing of the calligraphy and seal were files from a scan using the Pen tool, copied, and pasted onto the Panda artwork, then using the scale tool to bring them up to the needed size and positioned to finish the composition."

Figure E-2.   *The original ink sketch of the pandas*

Silver Dragon

Artist: DraSan' Nitti, Silver Dragon Studio, http://www.silverdragonstudio.com
This artwork is composed of one layer.

DraSan' Nitti says, "I created the dragon about five years ago exclusively for use on the Web. I scanned a rough sketch from my sketchbook (see Figure E-3) and then opened it in Illustrator. I used the Pen tool with no fill to bring the drawing to a finish and continued sketching with the Pen tool. I selected these still rough shapes and

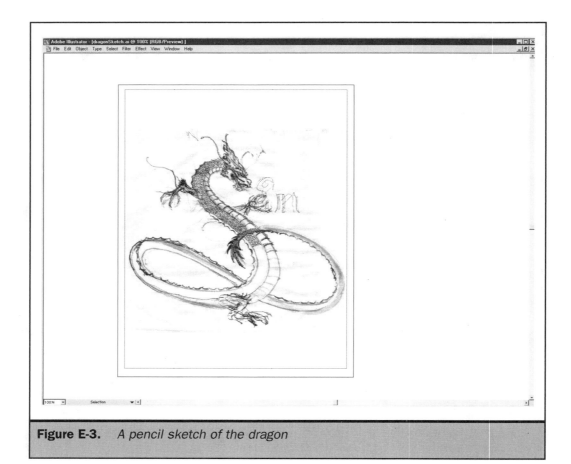

Figure E-3.   *A pencil sketch of the dragon*

moved them into guides. I drew the tightened drawing (see Figure E-4) from these guides. The main shapes were filled with gray fill of varying values to separate them. The type was moved into place, selected, and then converted into outlines. The dot above the *I* was deleted and a circle drawn with a gradated fill.

The entire drawing and type was selected and pasted into Photoshop, where I applied the Craquelure filter and Extensis PhotoBevel for the silvery effects. An Eye Candy smoke filter was applied to the *Studio.com* type and fire to the dot of the *i*. The dragon was placed back into Illustrator onto a background that was created in Painter. I used the Pen tool to redefine and sharpen the drawing, and to give the drawing and type snap."

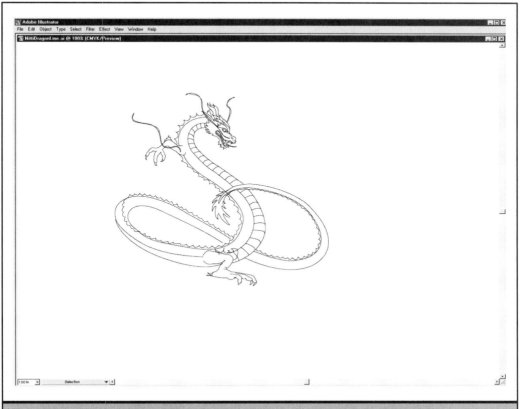

Figure E-4.   *A drawing of the dragon done with the Pen tool in Illustrator*

The Complete Reference

Adobe Illustrator

Appendix F

Illustrator Shortcut Keys

Illustrator provides many shortcut keys and key combinations that can help you streamline your work. You can use shortcuts with tools, commands, and other features. In the first part of this appendix, you'll learn how to define your own sets of shortcut keys. The second part of the appendix covers shortcuts for Illustrator menu commands, tools, and palettes.

Defining Shortcut Keys

Illustrator enables you to define and edit your own set of shortcut keys. If you use an Illustrator tool or feature regularly, you can access it more quickly with shortcut keys than you can by opening a menu, selecting a command, and selecting some options.

In the Keyboard Shortcuts dialog box (see Figures F-1 and F-2), you can view the default keys and their shortcuts, create and save custom shortcuts, and export the list as a text file. To open the dialog box, choose Edit | Keyboard Shortcuts (CTRL-SHIFT-ALT-K/ ⌘-SHIFT-OPTION-K).

Viewing Shortcut Keys

To view a set of shortcut keys, choose Tools or Menu Commands from the drop-down menu in the Keyboard Shortcuts dialog box and scroll through the list. At the end of both lists, shortcuts appear for the Illustrator palettes.

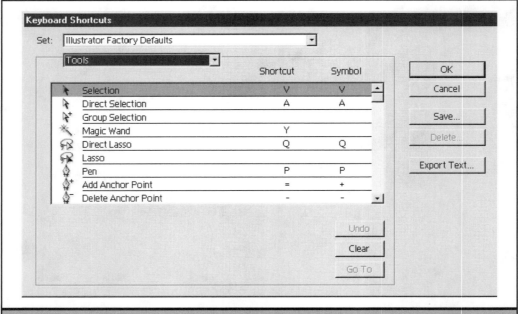

Figure F-1.   *The Keyboard Shortcuts dialog box with Tools shortcuts displayed*

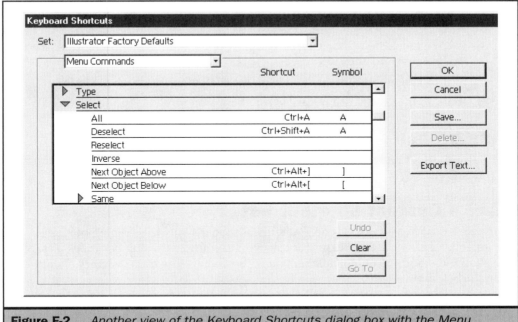

Figure F-2.   *Another view of the Keyboard Shortcuts dialog box with the Menu Commands shortcuts listed*

In the Menu Commands section of the dialog box, click a right-pointing arrow to expand the list under a particular command, or click a downward-pointing arrow to collapse the list. When a tool or command has an associated shortcut, Illustrator displays it under Shortcut or Symbol in the list box.

Defining and Saving a Custom Set of Shortcut Keys

If you use a tool or menu command often, you will probably want to define a shortcut. Or you might decide to change a commonly used but long shortcut combination to a more concise, easier-to-use shortcut. To define a shortcut key in the Keyboard Shortcuts dialog box, follow these steps:

1. From the Set shortcut menu, choose a set of shortcut keys. If you have not defined a custom set before, Illustrator does not allow you to choose [Custom].

2. From the drop-down menu immediately below the Set menu, choose Tools or Menu Commands—depending on the type of shortcut you want to define.

3. In the list box, select the tool or command for which you will define a shortcut. Illustrator lets you edit the Shortcut area of the selection.

4. Press the keys for the new shortcut. If you have pressed a shortcut that is already in use, Illustrator warns you that the shortcut is assigned. Also, note that all menu shortcuts must be preceded by CTRL/⌘.

5. In the Symbol column, enter a symbol if you want to replace the symbol that Illustrator suggests.

6. To save the custom shortcut set, click OK or Save. In the resulting dialog box, type a name and click OK.

7. To undo the new shortcuts and keep the dialog box open, click Undo.

8. To undo the new shortcuts and close the dialog box, click Cancel.

Clearing a Shortcut

To clear a shortcut, open the Keyboard Shortcuts dialog box, select a tool or command, and click Clear.

Deleting a Custom Shortcut Set

To delete a custom set of shortcuts, open the Keyboard Shortcuts dialog box, select the set, and click Delete. When Illustrator asks you to confirm the deletion, click Yes. Note that the Delete button is not available when you choose Illustrator Factory Defaults from the Set menu.

Creating a Text File of Shortcut Keys

To create a shortcut-keys text file—particularly for a custom set of shortcut keys—click the Export Text button. In the Save Key Set File As dialog box, type the filename in the File Name text box, followed by the .TXT extension, and then click Save. Illustrator saves the file and returns to the dialog box.

Shortcut Keys by Features and Tools

The remaining pages in the appendix contain tables of shortcut keys and key combinations.

General Shortcut Keys and Key Combinations

The following table contains keys and key combinations that are common to many Windows and Macintosh applications.

Windows/Mac Shortcut	Description
ALT/OPTION	Activates the menu bar
BACKSPACE/DELETE	Removes a tab setting from the selected type

Windows/Mac Shortcut	Description
ENTER/RETURN	Enters a label or data in a cell or a value in a palette's text box
TAB	Inserts a tab character; aligns type with the following tab stop

Menu Shortcuts

This section contains tables that show the shortcut keys and key combinations for Illustrator menus.

 In these tables, a single shortcut in the Windows/Mac Shortcut column means that the same key or key combination applies to both Windows and Macintosh computers.

File Menu Shortcuts

Menu Command	Windows/Mac Shortcut	Description
File | New	CTRL-N/⌘-N	Starts a new Illustrator document
File | Open	CTRL-O/⌘-O	Opens an Illustrator document
File | Revert	F12	Undoes all actions you have done since you last saved the file
File | Close	CTRL-W/⌘-W	Closes the active document
File | Save	CTRL-S/⌘-S	Saves the active document
File | Save As	CTRL-SHIFT-S/⌘-SHIFT-S	Saves the active document under an optional new name and/or in a new location
File | Save a Copy	CTRL-ALT-S/⌘-OPTION-S	Saves a copy of the file
File | Save for Web	CTRL-SHIFT-ALT-S/⌘-SHIFT-OPTION-S	Saves the active document for use on the Web
File | Document Setup	CTRL-ALT-P/⌘-OPTION-P	Sets up a new document

File Menu Shortcuts

Menu Command	Windows/Mac Shortcut	Description
File | Print Setup File | Page Setup	CTRL-SHIFT-P/⌘-SHIFT-P	Prepares a document for printing
File | Print	CTRL-P/⌘-P	Prints the current document
File | Exit	CTRL-Q or ALT+F4/⌘-Q	Exits Illustrator

Edit Menu Shortcuts

Menu Command	Windows/Mac Shortcut	Description
Edit | Undo	CTRL-Z/⌘-Z	Undoes the previous action
Edit | Redo	CTRL-SHIFT-Z/⌘-SHIFT-Z	Undoes the previous Undo
Edit | Cut	CTRL-X/⌘-X	Cuts the selection to the Clipboard
Edit | Copy	CTRL-C/⌘-C	Copies the selection to the Clipboard
Edit | Paste	CTRL-V/⌘-V	Pastes the contents of the Clipboard to the illustration window
Edit | Paste in Front	CTRL-F/⌘-F	Pastes the contents of the Clipboard in front of any other objects in the illustration window
Edit | Paste in Back	CTRL-B/⌘-B	Pastes the contents of the Clipboard in back of any other objects in the illustration window
Edit | Keyboard Shortcuts	CTRL-SHIFT-ALT-K/ ⌘-SHIFT-OPTION-K	Opens a dialog box that lists all keyboard shortcuts
Edit | Preferences | General	CTRL-K/⌘-K	Opens a dialog box that enables Illustrator customization

Object Menu Shortcuts

Menu Command	Windows/Mac Shortcut	Description
Object | Transform | Transform Again	CTRL-D/⌘-D	Repeats the previous transform
Object | Transform | Move	CTRL-SHIFT-M/ ⌘-SHIFT-M	Moves the selected object
Object | Transform | Transform Each	CTRL-SHIFT-ALT-D/ ⌘-SHIFT-OPTION-D	Scales, moves, rotates, and/or reflects the selected object
Object | Arrange | Bring to Front	CTRL-SHIFT-]/ ⌘-SHIFT-]	Moves the selected object to the front of all objects
Object | Arrange | Bring Forward	CTRL-]/⌘-]	Moves the selected object in front of the next higher object in the stack
Object | Arrange | Send Backward	CTRL-[/⌘-[	Moves the selected object in back of the next lower object in the stack
Object | Arrange | Send to Back	CTRL-SHIFT-[/ ⌘-SHIFT-[	Moves the selected object behind all objects
Object | Group	CTRL-G/⌘-G	Places all the selected objects in one group
Object | Ungroup	CTRL-SHIFT-G/ ⌘-SHIFT-G	Ungroups one or more selected groups
Object | Lock | Selection	CTRL-2/⌘-2	Locks a selection
Object | Unlock All	CTRL-ALT-2/ ⌘-OPTION-2	Unlocks all locked objects
Object | Hide | Selection	CTRL-3/⌘-3	Completely hides a selected object
Object | Show All	CTRL-ALT-3/ ⌘-OPTION-3	"Unhides" all hidden objects and selects them
Object | Path | Join	CTRL-J/⌘-J	Joins end points
Object | Path | Average	CTRL-ALT-J/ ⌘-ALT-J	Averages and realigns points
Object | Blend | Make	CTRL-ALT-B/ ⌘-OPTION-B	Creates a blend

Object Menu Shortcuts

Menu Command	Windows/Mac Shortcut	Description
Object | Blend | Release	CTRL-SHIFT-ALT-B/ ⌘-SHIFT-ALT-B	Releases a blend
Object | Envelope Distort | Make with Warp	CTRL-ALT-W/ ⌘-OPTION-W	Creates an envelope with a predefined warp shape
Object | Envelope Distort | Make with Mesh	CTRL-ALT-M/ ⌘-OPTION-M	Creates an envelope with a mesh
Object | Envelope Distort | Make with Top Object	CTRL-ALT-C/ ⌘-OPTION-C	Creates an envelope with the top object in the stack
Object | Envelope Distort | Edit Contents	CTRL-SHIFT-V/ ⌘-SHIFT-V	Edits the contents of an envelope
Object | Clipping Mask | Make	CTRL-7/⌘-7	Makes a clipping mask
Object | Clipping Mask | Release	CTRL-ALT-7/ ⌘-OPTION-7	Releases a clipping mask
Object | Compound Path | Make	CTRL-8/⌘-8	Makes a compound path
Object | Compound Path | Release	CTRL-ALT-8/ ⌘-OPTION-8	Releases a compound path

Type Menu Shortcut

Menu Command	Windows/Mac Shortcut	Description
Type | Create Outlines	CTRL-SHIFT-O/ ⌘-SHIFT-O	Converts type to an editable object

Select Menu Shortcuts

Menu Command	Windows/Mac Shortcut	Description
Select | All	CTRL-A/⌘-A	Selects all objects in the illustration window
Select | Deselect	CTRL-SHIFT-A/ ⌘-SHIFT-A	Reverses all current selections

Select Menu Shortcuts

Menu Command	Windows/Mac Shortcut	Description
Select	Reselect	CTRL-6/⌘-6	Reverts to the most recent selection
Select	Next Object Above	CTRL-ALT-]/⌘-OPTION-]	Selects the next higher object in the total order of objects
Select	Next Object Below	CTRL-ALT-[/⌘-OPTION-[	Selects the next lower object in the total order of objects

Filter Menu Shortcuts

Menu Command	Windows/Mac Shortcut	Description
Filter	Apply Last Filter	CTRL-E/⌘-E	Automatically applies the last filter without changing any options
Filter	Last Filter	CTRL-ALT-E/⌘-OPTION-E	Opens a dialog box (if one is available) to select options for the last filter to be applied, or issues a command

Effect Menu Shortcuts

Menu Command	Windows/Mac Shortcut	Description
Effect	Apply Last Effect	CTRL-SHIFT-E/⌘-SHIFT-E	Automatically applies the last effect without changing any options
Effect	Last Effect	CTRL-SHIFT-ALT-E/ ⌘-SHIFT-OPTION-E	Opens a dialog box (if one is available) to select options for the last effect to be applied, or issues a command

View Menu Shortcuts

Menu Command	Windows/Mac Shortcut	Description
View ǀ Outline/Preview	CTRL-Y/⌘-Y	Toggles between Outline and Preview modes
View ǀ Overprint Preview	CTRL-SHIFT-ALT-Y/ ⌘-SHIFT-OPTION-Y	Checks the results of your selecting overprint options
View ǀ Pixel Preview	CTRL-ALT-Y/ ⌘-OPTION-Y	Shows a vector graphic as a raster graphic
View ǀ Zoom In	CTRL-+/⌘-+	Zooms in the contents of the illustration window
View ǀ Zoom Out	CTRL--/⌘--	Zooms out the contents of the illustration window
View ǀ Fit in Window	CTRL-0/⌘-0	Zooms the artwork to fit in the illustration window
View ǀ Actual Size	CTRL-1/⌘-1	Zooms the artwork to 100 percent of its size
View ǀ Hide/Show Edges	CTRL-H/⌘-H	Hides or shows the edges of paths
View ǀ Hide/Show Template	CTRL-SHIFT-W/ ⌘-SHIFT-W	Hides or shows the template, if one is present
View ǀ Show/Hide Rulers	CTRL-R/⌘-R	Shows or hides the rulers
View ǀ Hide/Show Bounding Box	CTRL-SHIFT-B/ ⌘-SHIFT-B	Shows or hides bounding boxes
View ǀ Show/Hide Transparency Grid	CTRL-SHIFT-D/ ⌘-SHIFT-D	Shows or hides the transparency grid
View ǀ Guides ǀ Hide/Show Guides	CTRL-;/⌘-;	Shows or hides all guides
View ǀ Guides ǀ Lock Guides	CTRL-ALT-;/⌘-OPTION-;	Locks guides in place
View ǀ Guides ǀ Make Guides	CTRL-5/⌘-5	Makes a guide
View ǀ Guides ǀ Release Guides	CTRL-ALT-5/⌘-OPTION-5	Releases all guides

View Menu Shortcuts

Menu Command	Windows/Mac Shortcut	Description
View | Smart Guides	CTRL-U/⌘-U	Shows or hides Smart Guides
View | Show/Hide Grid	CTRL-"/⌘-OPTION-"	Shows or hides the grid
View | Snap to Grid	CTRL-SHIFT-"/⌘-SHIFT-"	Activates or deactivates the snap-to-grid feature
View | Snap to Point	CTRL-ALT-"/⌘-OPTION-"	Snaps one anchor point to another

Window Menu Shortcuts

Menu Command	Windows/Mac Shortcut	Description
Window | Align	SHIFT-F7	Displays or hides Align palette
Window | Appearance	SHIFT-F6	Displays or hides Appearance palette
Window | Attributes	F11	Displays or hides Attributes palette
Window | Brushes	F5	Displays or hides Brushes palette
Window | Color	F6	Displays or hides Color palette
Window | Gradient	F9	Displays or hides Gradient palette
Window | Info	F8	Displays or hides Info palette
Window | Layers	F7	Displays or hides Layers palette
Window | Pathfinder	SHIFT-F9	Displays or hides Pathfinder palette

APPENDIXES

Window Menu Shortcuts

Menu Command	Windows/Mac Shortcut	Description
Window | Stroke	F10	Displays or hides Stroke palette
Window | Styles	SHIFT-F5	Displays or hides Styles palette
Window | Symbols	SHIFT-F11	Displays or hides Symbols palette
Window | Tools	TAB	Displays or hides the toolbox and palettes
Window | Transform	SHIFT-F8	Displays or hides Transform palette
Window | Transparency	SHIFT-F10	Displays or hides Transparency palette
Window | Type | Character	CTRL-T/⌘-T	Displays or hides Character palette
Window | Type | Paragraph	CTRL-M/⌘-M	Displays or hides Paragraph palette
Window | Type | Tab Ruler	CTRL-SHIFT-T/ ⌘-SHIFT-T	Displays or hides Tab Ruler palette

Help Menu Shortcut

Menu Command	Windows/Mac Shortcut	Description
Help | Illustrator Help	F1	Opens the Illustrator help system

Toolbox Shortcuts

This section contains several tables that cover the Illustrator toolbox. The first table lists all the tools that you can activate by pressing a shortcut key or key combination. The remaining tables list shortcuts related to using individual tools.

Activation Shortcuts for Toolbox Tools

This table lists the shortcut keys and key combinations used to activate toolbox tools. Tools are arranged alphabetically. If a tool is not listed, Illustrator has not provided a shortcut.

Tool	Shortcut
Add Anchor Point	=
Blend	W
Color	< (at the bottom of the toolbox)
Column Graph	J
Convert Anchor Point	SHIFT-C
Default Fill and Stroke	D
Delete Anchor Point	-
Direct Lasso	Q
Direct Selection	A
Ellipse	L
Eyedropper	I
Fill/Stroke	X
Free Transform	E
Gradient	G (the tool)
Gradient	> (at the bottom of the toolbox, the button that switches to the last gradient)
Hand	H
Line Segment	\
Magic Wand	Y
Mesh	U
None	/ (at the bottom of the toolbox)
Paint Bucket	K
Paintbrush	B
Pen	P
Pencil	N
Rectangle	M
Reflect	O

Tool	Shortcut
Rotate	R
Scale	S
Scissors	C
Screen Modes	F
Selection	V
Slice	SHIFT-K
Swap Fill and Stroke	SHIFT-X
Symbol Sprayer	SHIFT-S
Type	T
Warp	SHIFT-R
Zoom	Z

Shortcuts for Many or All Toolbox Tools

Windows/Mac Shortcut	Description
CAPS LOCK	Toggles between a tool's mouse pointer and a cross-hatch mouse pointer for Add Anchor Point (+), Column Graph (J) and all the other graph tools, Delete Anchor Point (-), Lasso, Magic Wand (Y), Pen (P), Pencil (N), Slice (SHIFT-K), and Symbol Sprayer (SHIFT-S) and other symbols tools
CTRL-ALT/⌘-OPTION	Cycles through Toolslot tools
CTRL-SPACEBAR/ ⌘-SPACEBAR	Zooms in
CTRL/⌘	Temporarily selects the selection tool (Selection, Direct Selection, or Group Selection only) that you used most recently when you are using any tool but a selection tool
CTRL-ALT-SPACEBAR/ ⌘-OPTION-SPACEBAR	Zooms out
ALT/OPTION	Resizes the width and height of the circle surrounding some tools

Selection Tool Shortcuts

Windows/Mac Shortcut	Description
V	Activates the tool
ALT/OPTION	Creates a copy of an object while dragging; scales from the middle of the object while dragging a handle
CTRL-TAB/⌘-TAB	Toggles between the Selection tool and the Direct Selection tool or the Group Selection tool (depending on which of the tools is on the toolbox)
DEL	Deletes a selected object
SHIFT	Adds one path to or removes one selected path from a selection; constrains an object being scaled or reflected to its original proportions; constrains a shear to angles of 45, 90, 135, 180, 225, 270, 315, or 360 degrees; resizes a type rectangle while keeping its proportions

Pen Tool Shortcuts

Windows/Mac Shortcut	Description
P	Activates the tool
ALT	Changes the direction of a curve
SHIFT	Constrains a dragged line to 0, 45, 90, 135, 180, 225, 270, or 315 degrees

Add Anchor Point Tool Shortcuts

Windows/Mac Shortcut	Description
=	Activates the tool
ALT	Toggles between the Add Anchor Point tool and the Delete Anchor Point tool

Delete Anchor Point Tool Shortcuts

Windows/Mac Shortcut	Description
-	Activates the tool
ALT	Toggles between the Add Anchor Point tool and the Delete Anchor Point tool

Line Segment Tool Shortcuts

Windows/Mac Shortcut	Description
\	Activates the tool
SHIFT	Constrains the line segment to a vertical line, horizontal, or diagonal line

Spiral Tool Shortcuts

Windows/Mac Shortcut	Description
'	Creates multiple copies of a spiral
ALT/OPTION	Adds or deletes the number of turns in a spiral
CTRL/⌘	Winds the spiral tighter or looser
SHIFT	Creates a spiral whose trailing line is aligned to a 0-, 45-, 90-, or 135-degree angle
SPACEBAR	Moves a spiral as you are creating it

Rectangular Grid Tool Shortcuts

Windows/Mac Shortcut	Description
↑	Adds horizontal lines to a rectangular grid being created
↓	Removes horizontal lines from a rectangular grid being created

Rectangular Grid Tool Shortcuts

Windows/Mac Shortcut	Description
→	Adds vertical lines to a rectangular grid being created
←	Removes vertical lines from a rectangular grid being created
´	Creates several grids simultaneously
ALT/OPTION	Creates a rectangular grid that expands from all sides of the origin point
C	Increases the skew value for horizontal lines by 10 percent
DOUBLE-CLICK	Opens the Rectangular Grid Tool Options dialog box
F	Increases the skew value for vertical lines by 10 percent
SHIFT	Draws a square grid down from an origin point
SHIFT-ALT/ SHIFT-OPTION	Draws a square grid from a central origin point
SPACEBAR	Moves a rectangular grid as you are creating it
V	Decreases the skew value for horizontal lines by 10 percent
X	Decreases the skew value for vertical lines by 10 percent

Polar Grid Tool Shortcuts

Windows/Mac Shortcut	Description
↑	Adds concentric lines to a polar grid being created
↓	Removes concentric lines from a polar grid being created
→	Adds radiating lines to a polar grid being created
←	Removes radiating lines from a polar grid being created
´	Creates several grids simultaneously
ALT/OPTION	Creates a polar grid that expands from all sides of the origin point
C	Increases the skew value for concentric lines by 10 percent
DOUBLE-CLICK	Opens the Polar Grid Tool Options dialog box
F	Changes the skew value counterclockwise for radiating lines by 10 percent

APPENDIXES

Polar Grid Tool Shortcuts

Windows/Mac Shortcut	Description
SHIFT	Draws a circular grid down from an origin point
SHIFT-ALT/ SHIFT-OPTION	Draws a circular grid from a central origin point
SPACEBAR	Moves a polar grid as you are creating it
V	Changes the skew value clockwise for radiating lines by 10 percent
X	Decreases the skew value for concentric lines by 10 percent

Paintbrush Tool Shortcuts

Windows/Mac Shortcut	Description
B	Activates the tool
ALT/OPTION	Draws a closed path

Rotate Tool Shortcuts

Windows/Mac Shortcut	Description
R	Activates the tool
ALT	Rotates a copy of the object
SHIFT	Constrains the rotation to 45, 90, 135, 180, 225, 270, 315, or 360 degrees

Reflect Tool Shortcuts

Windows/Mac Shortcut	Description
O	Activates the tool
ALT	Flips a copy of the object
SHIFT	Constrains any new axis to 90, 180, 270, or 360 degrees

Symbol Shifter Tool Shortcuts

Windows/Mac Shortcut	Description
SHIFT and double-click	Moves one symbol instance above others that it overlaps
ALT/OPTION and double-click	Moves one symbol instance below others that it overlaps

Symbol Scruncher Tool Shortcut

Windows/Mac Shortcut	Description
ALT/OPTION	Moves symbols away from the center of the set

Symbol Sizer Tool Shortcut

Windows/Mac Shortcut	Description
ALT/OPTION	Scales symbols smaller than their current sizes

Symbol Stainer Tool Shortcuts

Windows/Mac Shortcut	Description
ALT/OPTION	Removes some of the stain from the selected symbols
SHIFT	Keeps the amount of the stain steady but stains with the new fill color

Symbol Screener Tool Shortcut

Windows/Mac Shortcut	Description
ALT/OPTION	Makes selected symbols less transparent

Symbol Styler Tool Shortcuts

Windows/Mac Shortcut	Description
ALT/OPTION	Removes some of the style from the selected symbols
SHIFT	Keeps the level of style the same but stains with the new fill color

Mesh Tool Shortcuts

Windows/Mac Shortcut	Description
U	Activates the tool
ALT/OPTION	Deletes a mesh point and the mesh lines that are associated with it when you click
SHIFT	Adds new mesh points and mesh lines as you create a mesh object but does not apply the current fill color; limits a mesh line to its original dimension and size in an existing mesh object so that the mesh line does not bend to adjust to the drag

Eyedropper Tool Shortcuts

Windows/Mac Shortcut	Description
ALT/OPTION	Toggles between the Eyedropper and the Paint Bucket
I	Activates the tool
SHIFT	Picks up the color only from the object and applies those characteristics to selected objects
SHIFT-ALT/ SHIFT-OPTION	Copies the object and its attributes

Paint Bucket Tool Shortcuts

Windows/Mac Shortcut	Description
K	Activates the tool
ALT/OPTION	Toggles between the Eyedropper and the Paint Bucket

Slice Tool Shortcuts

Windows/Mac Shortcut	Description
SHIFT-K	Activates the tool
SHIFT	Constrains a slice to a square shape
ALT/OPTION	Creates a slice from the center of its rectangle

Slice Selection Tool Shortcut

Windows/Mac Shortcut	Description
SHIFT	Constrains a slice's movement to 45, 90, 135, 180, 225, 270, 315, or 360 degrees

Hand Tool Shortcuts

Windows/Mac Shortcut	Description
H	Activates the tool
SPACEBAR	Moves the Artboard around the illustration window

Direct Selection Tool Shortcuts

Windows/Mac Shortcut	Description
A	Activates the tool
ALT	Creates a copy of an object while dragging
CTRL-TAB/⌘-TAB	Toggles between the Selection tool and the Direct Selection tool (if the Direct Selection tool is on the toolbox)
DEL	Deletes a selected object
SHIFT	Adds one path or anchor point to or removes one selected path or anchor point from a selection
SHIFT	Limits a mesh line to its original dimension and size in an existing mesh object so that the mesh line does not bend to adjust to the drag; resizes the type rectangle while constraining its proportions

Group Selection Tool Shortcuts

Windows/Mac Shortcut	Description
ALT	Creates a copy of an object while dragging
CTRL-TAB/⌘-TAB	Toggles between the Selection tool and the Group Selection tool (if the Group Selection tool is on the toolbox)
DEL	Deletes a selected object
SHIFT	Adds one path to or removes one selected path from a selection

Direct Select Lasso Tool Shortcuts

Windows/Mac Shortcut	Description
Q	Activates the tool
ALT	Deletes one selected path or point from a selection
CTRL-ALT/⌘-OPTION	Cycles between the Direct Select Lasso tool and the Lasso tool
DEL	Deletes the paths running from a selected point to unselected points
SHIFT	Adds one path or point to a selection

Lasso Tool Shortcuts

Windows/Mac Shortcut	Description
CTRL-ALT/⌘-OPTION	Cycles between the Direct Select Lasso tool and the Lasso tool
DEL	Deletes a selected object
SHIFT	Adds one path to or removes one selected path from a selection

Type Tool Shortcuts

Windows/Mac Shortcut	Description
T	Activates the tool
ALT/OPTION	Changes to the Area Type tool when over an open path; changes to the Path Type tool when over a closed path
ENTER/RETURN	Starts a new line in point type; starts a new paragraph in a type rectangle
SHIFT	Toggles between the Type tool and the Vertical Type tool; creates a type square while dragging diagonally

Area Type Tool Shortcuts

Windows/Mac Shortcut	Description
ALT/OPTION	Conzverts the tool to the Path Type tool
ENTER/RETURN	Starts a new paragraph in a type rectangle
SHIFT	Toggles between the Area Type tool and the Vertical Area Type tool

Path Type Tool Shortcuts

Windows/Mac Shortcut	Description
ALT/OPTION	Converts the tool to the Area Type tool; creates a copy of type in a new location on the path
ENTER/RETURN	Inserts a space at the insertion point as you enter type

Vertical Type Tool Shortcuts

Windows/Mac Shortcut	Description
ALT/OPTION	Changes to the Vertical Area Type tool when over an open path; changes to the Vertical Path Type tool when over a closed path

APPENDIXES

Vertical Type Tool Shortcuts

Windows/Mac Shortcut	Description
ENTER/RETURN	Starts a new line in point type; starts a new paragraph in a type rectangle
SHIFT	Toggles between the Type tool and the Vertical Type tool

Vertical Area Type Tool Shortcuts

Windows/Mac Shortcut	Description
ALT/OPTION	Converts the tool to the Vertical Path Type tool
ENTER/RETURN	Starts a new paragraph in a type rectangle
SHIFT	Toggles between the Area Type tool and the Vertical Area Type tool

Vertical Path Type Tool Shortcut

Windows/Mac Shortcut	Description
ALT/OPTION	Converts the tool to the Vertical Area Type tool

Rectangle Tool Shortcuts

Windows/Mac Shortcut	Description
M	Activates the tool
SHIFT	Forces the creation of a square

Ellipse Tool Shortcuts

Windows/Mac Shortcut	Description
L	Activates the tool
SHIFT	Compels the creation of a circle

Polygon Tool Shortcuts

Windows/Mac Shortcut	Description
´	Creates many copies of a polygon simultaneously
↑	Adds sides to a polygon
↓	Removes sides from a polygon
SHIFT	Creates a polygon whose bottom points rest on an invisible horizontal line
SPACEBAR	Moves a completed polygon

Star Tool Shortcuts

Windows/Mac Shortcut	Description
´	Creates several stars simultaneously
↑	Adds points to a star being created
↓	Removes points from a star being created
ALT/OPTION	Creates a star whose points and body are in proportion
CTRL/⌘	Makes points grow longer while the body remains the same size
SHIFT	Creates a star whose bottom points rest on an invisible horizontal line
SPACEBAR	Moves a star as you are creating it

Flare Tool Shortcuts

Windows/Mac Shortcut	Description
ALT/OPTION	Places a flare on top of an object
SHIFT	Forces beams to stay at their current angles
↑	Adds halos to the selected flare
↓	Removes beams from the selected flare
CTRL/⌘	Makes the points grow longer while the center of the flare remains the same size
'	Creates a flare with several halos
SPACEBAR	Moves a flare as you are creating it
ALT/OPTION and click the Reset button	Changes the Cancel button in the Flare Tool Options dialog box to Reset so that you can return to the default options

Pencil Tool Shortcuts

Windows/Mac Shortcut	Description
N	Activates the tool
ALT/OPTION	Changes the Pencil tool to the Smooth tool

Scale Tool Shortcuts

Windows/Mac Shortcut	Description
S	Activates the tool
ALT	Scales a copy of an object
SHIFT	Scales an object proportionally; scales an object vertically while constraining horizontal movement; scales an object horizontally while constraining vertical movement

Shear Tool Shortcuts

Windows/Mac Shortcut	Description
ALT	Shears a copy of an object
SHIFT	Constrains the shear to angles of 45, 90, 135, 180, 225, 270, 315, or 360 degrees

Free Transform Tool Shortcuts

Windows/Mac Shortcut	Description
E	Activates the tool
ALT/OPTION	Scales from the center of an object after you start dragging
CTRL/⌘	Changes one side or corner of an object after you start dragging
CTRL-ALT/⌘-OPTION	Shears an object after you start dragging
CTRL-ALT-SHIFT/ ⌘-OPTION-SHIFT	Moves opposite corners of an object after you start dragging
SHIFT	Forces an object to remain in proportion after you start dragging

Column Graph Tool Shortcuts

Windows/Mac Shortcut	Description
J	Activates the tool
ALT/OPTION	Draws the graph with the center point in the middle of the graph

APPENDIXES

All Graph Tools Shortcut

Windows/Mac Shortcut	Description
ALT/OPTION	Draws the graph with the center point in the middle of the graph

Gradient Tool Shortcuts

Windows/Mac Shortcut	Description
G	Activates the tool
SHIFT	Constrains the direction of the drag at 45, 90, 135, 180, 225, 270, or 315 degrees

Scissors Tool Shortcuts

Windows/Mac Shortcut	Description
C	Activates the tool
ALT/OPTION	Cuts a straight line only

Zoom Tool Shortcuts

Windows/Mac Shortcut	Description
Z	Activates the tool
ALT/OPTION	Changes the mouse pointer to zoom out

Illustrator Palette Shortcuts

Windows/Mac Shortcut	Description	Palette
SHIFT-TAB	Toggles between displaying and hiding all open palettes	All
SHIFT-ENTER/ SHIFT-RETURN	Re-highlights the text box into which you just typed a value	All
ENTER/RETURN or TAB	Applies a new value in a text box	All
ALT/OPTION	Toggles between excluding and including all commands but the selected one while you click the Toggle Item On/Off icon; creates and records a new action without opening a dialog box when you click Create New Action or choose New Action; copies an action or a command to a different action set; deletes an action or a command while clicking Delete Selection	Actions
CTRL/⌘	Plays one command when you click the Play Current Selection button or double-click the command	Actions
ALT/OPTION	Copies appearance attributes from one element to another	Appearance
ALT/OPTION	Replaces the prior brush with a new brush but maintains the prior brush's attributes	Brushes
↑	Moves up the list of fonts or font styles; increases the font size, kerning size, tracking size, baseline shift, scaling, and leading	Character
↓	Moves down the list of fonts or font styles; decreases the font size, kerning size, tracking size, baseline shift, scaling, and leading	Character
ALT-SHIFT-↑/ OPTION-SHIFT-↑	Scrolls up the list of fonts, font styles, font size, kerning size, tracking size, baseline shift, scaling, and leading	Character

Windows/Mac Shortcut	Description	Palette
ALT-SHIFT-↓/ OPTION-SHIFT-↓	Scrolls down the list of fonts, font styles, font size, kerning size, tracking size, baseline shift, scaling, and leading	Character
CTRL/⌘	Resets leading to its default value when you click the leading icon	Character
CTRL-SHIFT-ALT-F/ ⌘-SHIFT-OPTION-F	Opens the palette and highlights the Font text box/drop-down menu for the primary font	Character
CTRL-SHIFT-ALT-M/ ⌘-SHIFT-OPTION-M	Opens the palette and highlights the Font text box/drop-down menu for the secondary font (if one exists)	Character
SHIFT	Cycles through the Grayscale, RGB, HSB, CMYK, and Web Safe RGB palettes in conjunction with clicking in the spectrum bar	Color
SHIFT	Slides all the sliders in proportion in the CMYK, RGB, or Web Safe RGB version of the palette	Color
CTRL/⌘	Toggles a layer between Preview and Outline modes; creates a new layer at the top of the layer list (in conjunction with clicking the New Layer button) or a sublayer (in conjunction with clicking the Create New Sublayer button or choosing the New Sublayer command)	Layers
ALT/OPTION	Toggles between showing and hiding all layers but the selected one; makes, names, and specifies options for a new layer (in conjunction with clicking Create New Layer or choosing the New Layer command); makes, names, and specifies options for a new sublayer (in conjunction with clicking Create New Sublayer or choosing the New Subayer command); selects all the artwork in a particular layer	Layers

Windows/Mac Shortcut	Description	Palette
CTRL-ALT/ ⌘-OPTION	Selects an element	Layers
CTRL/⌘	Changes the dimensions of the rectangle to zoom and move the artwork at the same time	Navigation
ALT/OPTION	Expands the selected shape	Pathfinder
↑	Increases indention or space before a paragraph by 1 point	Paragraph
↓	Decreases indention or space before a paragraph by 1 point	Paragraph
ALT-SHIFT-↑/ OPTION-SHIFT-↑	Increases indention or space before a paragraph by 6 points	Paragraph
ALT-SHIFT-↓/ OPTION-SHIFT-↓	Decreases indention or space before a paragraph by 6 points	Paragraph
CTRL-ALT-O/ ⌘-OPTION-O	Opens palette and highlights the Desired text box	Paragraph
ALT/OPTION	Replaces one style with another	Styles
CTRL-ALT/ ⌘-OPTION	Finds a swatch by its name without opening the find field	Swatches
ALT/OPTION	Opens the New Swatch dialog box while clicking the New Swatch button; replaces a swatch with a new one from the Color or Gradient palette	Swatches
CTRL/⌘	Creates a new spot-color swatch while clicking the New Swatch button; deselects a selected swatch	Swatches
ALT/OPTION	Replaces one symbol with another or redefines a symbol	Symbols
CTRL/⌘	Toggles between a checked and unchecked Snap box	Tab Ruler
SHIFT	Moves all user-created tab stops; deletes all user-defined tab stops when you drag one off the ruler	Tab Ruler

Type Shortcuts

Windows/Mac Shortcut	Description
CTRL-SHIFT--/⌘-SHIFT--	Inserts a hyphen
CTRL-SHIFT-./⌘-SHIFT-.	Increases point size by a small amount
CTRL-SHIFT-,/⌘-SHIFT-,	Decreases point size by a small amount
CTRL-ALT-SHIFT-./ ⌘-OPTION-SHIFT-.	Increases point size by a large amount
CTRL-ALT-SHIFT-,/ ⌘-OPTION-SHIFT-,	Decreases point size by a large amount
CTRL-SHIFT-]/⌘-SHIFT-]	Increases the amount of kerning
CTRL-SHIFT-[/⌘-SHIFT-[	Decreases the amount of kerning
CTRL-ALT-K/⌘-OPTION-K	Increases the amount of tracking
CTRL-ALT-Q/⌘-OPTION-Q	Clears tracking
CTRL-SHIFT-X/⌘-SHIFT-X	Clears scaling
CTRL-SHIFT-L/⌘-SHIFT-L	Left-aligns type
CTRL-SHIFT-R/⌘-SHIFT-R	Right-aligns type
CTRL-SHIFT-C/⌘-SHIFT-C	Centers type
CTRL-SHIFT-J/⌘-SHIFT-J	Justifies complete lines of type
CTRL-SHIFT-F/⌘-SHIFT-F	Justifies all lines of type

Glossary

A

acquiring (1) Scanning images into applications using an Acquire command. (2) Any method by which you can obtain documents from a foreign application.

action A set of recorded commands, similar to macros, used to automate commonly used events. See **action set**, **control**, and **modal tool**.

action set A set of actions. Using action sets, you can unite a set of well-tested actions into a reliable yet complicated series of steps. See **action**.

additive primary colors The red, green, and blue primary colors that are produced by emitting (that is, adding) light. See **RGB**, **subtractive primary colors**, and **Web-safe RGB**.

AI The default Adobe Illustrator file type.

alignment The position of paragraphs in relation to the left and right margins.

alpha channel A set of bits that control the level of transparency, color, or masking of the other bits in a pixel. See **variable transparency**.

anchor The code that links a particular element on a Web page to an element on the current Web page or on a page at another Web site. The user can jump from the anchor to a target link by performing some action, such as a mouse click.

anchor point A rectangular control handle that marks a curve or corner in a path, the location at which two line segments join, and the ends of open paths. See **closed path**, **corner point**, **direction lines**, **direction point**, **end point**, **open path**, **path**, and **smooth point**.

angle See **screen angle**.

anti-aliasing The smoothing of jagged parts of an image, particularly in raster graphics. See **raster graphics**.

appearance attributes Characteristics, such as effects and transformations, that you apply to an object. See **style**.

Artboard A virtual board upon which the page that holds your printable artwork is located. See **scratch area**.

artifacts   Superfluous dots, patterns, and bands added to a JPEG file when it is compressed as it is saved. See **lossy compression**. See also **lossless compression**.

ascender   The part of a character that rises above the x-height. Characters with ascenders are **b**, **d**, **f**, **h**, **k**, and **l**. See **baseline**, **descender**, **font**, **font height**, **letter height**, and **x-height**.

axis   See **x-axis** and **y-axis**.

B

banding   An undesired horizontal, vertical, or diagonal pattern on a graphic. See **artifacts**.

bas relief   A raised relief in which an object extends slightly above the surface or above other objects. See **also embossed**.

base color   The color of the object immediately under the active transparent or semi-transparent object. See **blend color**, **blending mode**, and **resulting color**.

baseline   The imaginary horizontal or vertical line or curving path upon which type sits. See **ascender**, **baseline**, **descender**, **font**, **font height**, **leading**, **letter height**, and **x-height**.

bevel join   A squared turn of a corner. See **join**, **miter join**, and **round join**. See also **cap**.

Bézier curve   A curved path that is described by mathematical formulas and is the foundation of the curved paths used in Illustrator and other vector graphics programs. A Bézier curve has end points, other points that represent changes in direction, and direction points. When you move the handles on the direction points, you can change the shape of the curve or path. Pierre Bézier designed the Bézier curve. See **direction point**, **end point**, **path**, and **vector graphics**.

bit depth   The number of bits that denote one pixel in a raster graphic.

bleed   An area of an artwork that extends to the edge of the page or past the page margins.

blend   A gradual transition from one color and shape of an initial object through intermediate changes to a color and shape of a final object. In other applications, blending is known as **morphing**. See **also blending mode** and **gradient**.

blend color   The color of the active transparent or semi-transparent object. See **base color**, **blending mode**, and **resulting color**.

blending mode   The mix of the color of an original object and the color of the final object in a blend. See **base color**, **blend color**, and **resulting color**.

blueline   A blue-colored proof page produced by the printer that enables you to check for correctness and the appearance of the layout before a printer makes the final plates.

bounding box   Marquee; a dotted line that you draw to enclose a selection.

brightness   (1) Value; luminance, luminosity; the intensity of light reflected by a mixed color. (2) The brightness of a sheet of paper. See **HSB**, **hue**, and **saturation**.

brushes   Sets of defined brushstrokes with which you "paint" stroked paths in the illustration window using the Paintbrush tool (B).

butt cap   A square-shaped, non-projecting end of a stroke. See **cap**, **projecting cap**, and **round cap**. See also **join**.

C

camera work   Photographing the mechanicals to create negatives. See **camera-ready**, **mechanical**, and **negative**.

camera-ready   Copy that has been proofed and corrected and is ready to be photographed. See **camera work**, **mechanical**, and **negative**.

cap   The shape of the end of a stroke. Illustrator provides for butt, round, and projecting caps. See **butt cap**, **projecting cap**, and **round cap**. See also **join**.

category axis   See x-axis.

centimeters   Standard units of measure for the metric system. A centimeter is one hundredth of a meter and .3937 inch. See **inches**, **millimeters**, **picas**, **pixels**, **points**.

choke   A method of trapping that corrects a gap by overlapping a light-colored background with a dark-colored image. See **spread** and **trapping**.

client-side   A program or script that is stored and runs on the user's computer system. See **server-side**.

clipboard An area into which copied or cut information is held until it is replaced with other copied or cut information.

clipping mask Clipping path; an object that crops artwork so that some sections are hidden and others appear at the location of the mask. See **clipping set**, **mask**, and **opacity mask**.

clipping path See **clipping mask**.

clipping set The entire set of layers composed of one or more clipping masks, and the objects that are masked. See **clipping mask**.

closed path A continuous path that does not end. A closed path has anchor points but no end points. See **anchor point**, **end point**, **open path**, and **path**.

CMY A close relative of CMYK; an acronym that represents cyan-magenta-yellow, which produces all colors, including black. See **CMYK**.

CMYK An acronym that represents cyan-magenta-yellow-black, the process colors (subtractive primary colors) used for printing four-color separations. See **CMY**, **color model**, **process colors**, and **subtractive primary colors**.

collapse To hide all the contents—including sublayers, groups, and objects—of the selected layer or sublayer. See **expand**.

color model A system for designating colors for process printing, graphic arts, and computer graphics. See **CMYK**, **grayscale**, **HSB**, **RGB**, and **Web-safe RGB**.

color ramp See **spectrum bar**.

color separation The process of separating color images from the composite into their primary colors. For example, CMYK images are separated into four pages that contain one color (cyan, magenta, yellow, and black) only. See **composite**.

column gutter See **gutter**.

complementary color The color that is opposite a primary color on a color wheel. For example, yellow is the complementary color of blue (and blue opposes yellow), red opposes yellow, and black opposes white.

composite An entire artwork with all its components on one page. See **color separation**.

compound path   Two or more open or closed, overlapping paths made into one object by choosing Object | Compound Path | Make. See also **compound shapes**.

compound shapes   Two or more paths, which act as grouped objects, that you can join, separate, and cut using the Pathfinder palette buttons. See also **compound paths**.

compression   The act of reducing the size of a file as you save it. When a file is compressed, the compression routine removes duplicate patterns of bits and inserts code that documents it. See **Lempel-Ziv-Welch**, **lossless compression**, and **lossy compression**.

constrain   Force, control; in computing, controlling values or displays within certain levels. For example, when you press and hold down SHIFT while dragging a rectangle or ellipse, Illustrator is constrained to create a square or circle.

container   An object that contains paths and other objects.

continuous-tone image   An image, such as a photograph, that is made up of gradients of colors or shades of gray rather than clumps of colors. See **halftone**.

control   An object in the illustration window with which you can perform an action. You can operate a typical control by clicking a mouse button or pressing ENTER/RETURN. See **action**, and **modal tool**.

control handles   See **handles**.

corner point   A sharp and definite anchor point that shows a change of direction in a path. See **anchor point**, **direction lines**, **direction point**, **path**, and **smooth point**.

crop marks   Printer's marks at or near the corners of a page, lines that mark the points at which a page will be trimmed to its final printed dimensions. See **Japanese crop marks** and **trim marks**.

D

descender   The part of a character that rises below the body of a character such as a lowercase **x**. Letters with descenders are **g, j, p, q,** and **y**. See **ascender**, **baseline**, **font**, **font height**, **letter height**, and **x-height**.

direction lines Lines that extend from anchor point and show the direction in which the curve is heading at an anchor point. See **anchor point**, **corner point**, **direction point**, **path**, and **smooth point**.

direction point A point at the end of a direction line; a circular handle by which you can drag a direction line to a new course to change the shape of a path. See **anchor point**, **corner point**, **direction lines**, **path**, and **smooth point**.

disretionary hyphen A manual hyphen entered by the user.

distributing Placing objects equally distant from one another.

dithering A method by which a graphics application blends adjacent pixels of different colors to correct the appearance of jagged borders.

docking Attaching one palette to another.

dot One of the tiny components of varying sizes and shapes that make up a halftone. See **halftone**.

dots per inch dpi; the number of the dots per inch in a halftone. See **halftone**.

drag-and-drop The act of using a mouse to drag a selection from one location and drop that object at another location within one application or window or from one application or window to another.

E

editable path See **outline**.

effects Enhancements that change an object's appearance but maintain the object's original shape. See **filters**.

em dash A dash (—) between characters that is as wide as a lowercase letter m. See **en dash**.

em space A space between characters that is as wide as a lowercase letter m. See **en space**.

embedded image An actual image pasted or dragged onto the illustration window, sometimes resulting in a large increase to the size of the document. See **linked image**.

embossed A stamped relief in which an object extends slightly below the surface or other objects. See also **bas relief**.

emulsion A chemical coating applied to one side of the film from which plates are made by a commercial printer.

en dash A dash (–) between characters that is as wide as a lowercase letter n. See **em dash**.

en space A space between characters that is as wide as a lowercase letter n. See **em space**.

encapsulated PostScript EPS; a PostScript file that describes a file that is encapsulated (enclosed) within another PostScript page description. See also **PostScript**.

end point An anchor point that marks each end of an open path. See **anchor point**, **closed path**, **open path**, and **path**.

envelopes Objects with which you enclose and distort other objects in Illustrator.

expand To show all the contents—including sublayers, groups, and objects—of the selected layer or sublayer. See **collapse**.

F

fill A color, pattern, or gradient enclosed within a closed path or between the end points of a curving open path. See **gradient** and **stroke**.

filters Enhancements that change an object permanently. See **effects**.

flipping See **reflecting**.

font A typeface; a set of letters, numerals, and symbols based on one design. See **ascender**, **baseline**, **descender**, **font height**, **letter height**, and **x-height**.

font height The elevation from baseline to baseline of a particular typeface. See **ascender**, **baseline**, **descender**, **font**, **letter height**, and **x-height**.

four-color printing Printing, particularly by commercial printers, in the four primary CMYK colors, cyan, magenta, yellow, and black. See **CMYK**.

freeform Painting or drawing freely without giving structure to the work.

G

gamut The range of colors within the RGB or HSB color models. See **out-of-gamut**.

ghosting An image from a print that is superimposed on the light areas of a later print due to errors in the printing process, or an image that shows through the front of a page from the back of the page.

GIF Graphics Interchange Format; a popular 8-bit (up to 256 colors) raster file type created by CompuServe. Use GIF for Web page illustrations.

glyph The picture of an individual letter, digit, or symbol in a character set or font.

gradient A gradual transition from one color or shade of a color through intermediate colors to a final color or shade from one side of an image's fill to another or from the center of an object to its edge. See **fill**, **linear gradient**, and **radial gradient**. **See also blend**.

gradient mesh See **mesh object**.

graph A pictorial representation of related data. See **graph designs**, **legend**, **plot**, and **tick mark**.

graph designs Illustrator objects that represent data in columns and bars, and data markers in line and scatter graphs. See **graph**.

graphical tabs Tab positions that enable you to wrap type around graphical objects. In Illustrator, type to be wrapped should be in a closed path.

grayscale (1) Monochrome; a range of color values from white to black and all the grays between. White is at 0%; black is at 100%. (2) During the printing process, grayscale is a strip on the side of the page that serves as a printing reference. See **CMYK**, **color model**, **HSB**, **RGB**, and **Web-safe RGB**.

greeking The display of indecipherable characters as gray bars or nonsense words. Illustrator greeks type characters at a selected small point-size level.

grid Horizontal and vertical lines in the illustration window. The grid enables you to align multiple objects by eye or by snapping. See **snapping**. See also **transparency grid**.

group A set of objects that becomes a single object for future selecting and editing.

guide A path that is used to align objects in the illustration window. Illustrator provides three types of guides: guide objects, ruler guides, and Smart Guides. See **guide object**, **ruler guide**, and **Smart Guides**.

guide object An object (such as a line, rectangle, ellipse, or group) that starts as an open or closed path and is converted to a guide that is used to align objects in the illustration window. See **guide**, **ruler guide**, and **Smart Guides**.

gutter Space between columns on a page with two or more columns. Sometimes known as a column gutter.

H

halftone A continuous-tone image composed of different sized black dots or lines to simulate grayscale tones. See **continuous-tone image**, **dot**, **dots per inch**, and **screen angle**.

handles The tiny squares or diamonds that you drag to resize, scale, or perform other transformations on a selected object.

hot spot In an image map, an area on which you can click to jump to another area in the current page, another page, or a different Web site. See **image map**.

HSB An acronym that represents hue-saturation-brightness. See **CMYK**, **CMY**, **color model**, **grayscale**, **RGB**, and **Web-safe RGB**.

HTML Hypertext Markup Language; a subset of SGML and a close relative of XML and XHTML, HTML's successor. HTML is the language with which most Web site developers mark up documents with hypertext links and Web graphics.

hue The dominant color in a mixed color. See **brightness**, **HSB**, and **saturation**.

ICC The International Color Consortium; an industry group that standardizes color management profiles.

illustration window Illustrator's document window in which you create or open artwork. The Artboard is part of the illustration window. See **Artboard**.

image map   A graphical object that contain hotspots on which you can click to jump to another area in the current page, another page, or a different Web site. See **hot spot**.

imageable area   The image area; the part of the page—typically within the Artboard—that can be printed. See **Artboard**, **nonimageable area**, **page**, and **printable area**.

inches   Standard units of measure for those not using the metric system. An inch is 2.54 centimeters. See **centimeters**, **millimeters**, **picas**, **pixels**, **points**.

interlacing   Loading an image in stages rather than as a complete image.

J

Japanese crop marks   Special kinds of crop marks set as an Illustrator preference. See **crop marks** and **trim marks**.

JavaScript   A scripting language developed by Netscape Communications and Sun Microsystems. With JavaScript, you can write instructions so that a Web page is dynamic or interactive.

join   The shape of the turn of a corner. Illustrator provides for miter, round, and bevel joins. See **bevel join**, **miter join**, and **round join**. See also **cap**.

JPEG   A popular 24-bit (up to 16,777,216 colors) raster file type created by the Joint Photographic Experts Group. Use JPEG for Web page graphics, particularly photographs.

justification   The alignment of type and objects at both the left and right margins. When a program justifies type, it adds spaces between words.

K

kerning   The increase or decrease of space between two selected characters. See **tracking**.

key color   The main color in a selected artwork.

knockout   The removal of all or part of an image from another image. In print processing, knocking out enables an image to print in its true color rather than taking on the color of an overlapping image.

L

landscape orientation The orientation of a page in which its width is greater than its height. Spreadsheets are often formatted in landscape orientation. See **portrait orientation**.

lasso A selection tool with which you can draw an irregular border around one or more objects to be selected.

layer A single level of an artwork. Every piece of Illustrator art starts on one layer. However, you can add more layers as your artwork becomes more complex.

leading The measurement of space between baselines. See **baseline**.

legend The key to a graph; usually a small box that shows each data series and its associated color or pattern. See **graph**, **plot**, and **tick mark**.

Lempel-Ziv-Welch LZW; a lossy data compression method. Unisys, which owns the patent for LZW, sometimes charges a license fee for its use. See **lossless compression** and **lossy compression**.

letter height The elevation of a character, including the x-height, ascender, and descender. See **ascender**, **baseline**, **descender**, **font**, **font height**, and **x-height**.

libraries In Illustrator, collections of brushes, styles, swatches, and symbols—some predefined and others to be created by Illustrator users.

ligature Two or more individual characters (such as ae or oe) that are combined into a single character (such as the æ used in some forms of the word æsthetics or the œ used in amœba).

line screen Screen frequency and screen ruling; the varying size of halftone ink dots. See **dot**.

line segment A straight path with two end points. See **path**.

linear gradient A gradient that progresses from one edge of an object to the edge on the opposite side. See **gradient** and **radial gradient**.

linked image A representation of an image in the illustration window—not an actual copy, thereby avoid a large increase in the size of the document. See **embedded image**.

lossless compression   A compression method by which no data is lost when a file is saved; the quality of the saved file remains the same as the original. See **Lempel-Ziv-Welch** and **lossy compression**.

lossy compression   A compression method by which some data is lost when a file is saved; the quality of the file is reduced every time it is saved. See **Lempel-Ziv-Welch** and **lossless compression**.

luminance   See **brightness**.

luminosity   See **brightness**.

LZW   See **Lempel-Ziv-Welch**.

M

macro   See **action**.

marquee   See **bounding box**.

mask   (1) In printing, the process of blocking light from certain portions of a printing plate. (2) In Illustrator and other art-creation programs, an object that covers other objects so that some parts are hidden and others appear under the mask. See **clipping mask** and **opacity mask**.

mechanical   Paste-up; a board on which type and illustrations are pasted before camera work and plates. See **camera work**.

mesh lines   Horizontal and vertical lines that look like paths and with which you can change the shape of a mesh object. See **mesh object** and **mesh point**.

mesh object   A special filled path that contains one or more colors that act like spray-painted gradients with the object's original fill as a background mirroring. Also known as a gradient mesh. See **mesh lines** and **mesh point**. See also **gradient**.

mesh patch   In a mesh object, a section inside four mesh points within which you can apply color. See **mesh lines**, **mesh object**, and **mesh point**.

mesh point   A special kind of anchor point to which you can apply color. See **anchor point**, **mesh lines**, and **mesh point**.

metadata Data about the data in XML documents. Note that SVG documents are coded in XML. See **XML**.

millimeters Standard units of measure for the metric system. A millimeter is one thousandth of a meter and 0.03937 inch. See **centimeters**, **inches**, **picas**, **pixels**, and **points**.

miter join A sharply pointed turn of a corner. See **bevel join**, **join**, and **round join**. See also **cap**.

modal tool A tool, particularly part of an Illustrator action, that works only when you press ENTER/RETURN. See **action** and **control**.

monospace font A nonproportional font; a font in which characters are always the same width. See **font** and **proportional font**.

morph See **blend**.

N

negative The reversal of colors on a film print so that the former white areas are now black and the prior black areas are now white. See **positive**.

nonimageable area At or outside the margins of the page; you cannot print from this area. The nonimageable area is outside the Artboard and outside the page margins that a printer is capable of printing. See **imageable area**, **page**, and **printable area**.

O

object In Illustrator, a path; in other applications, an element on the computer screen.

offset (1) In Illustrator, creating a new path inside or outside the current path. (2) In printing, placing ink from a source location such as a roller to paper, cloth, or other material.

opacity (1) A lack of transparency; underlying objects cannot be seen through objects above in the stacking order. (2) In printing, the amount of image that can be seen through an unsubstantial sheet of paper. See **transparency**.

opacity mask   An object that covers semi-transparent objects depending on the luminosity levels of the mask. See also **clipping mask** and **mask**.

open path   A path that is made up of one or more line or arc segments and two or more anchor points, including two end points. See **anchor point**, **closed path**, **end point**, and **path**.

optimize   To make Web images both quick to load and of high quality.

orientation   The direction in which content appears on a page, with the page width greater or less than its height. See **landscape orientation** and **portrait orientation**.

out-of-gamut   A warning icon that indicates that the swatch color does not fall within the colors in the RGB or HSB color model. See **gamut** and **out-of-Web**.

out-of-Web   A warning icon that indicates that the swatch color does not fall within Web-safe colors. See **out-of-gamut**.

outline   Editable path; type converted to a graphical object. Once you have converted type to an outline, you can no longer correct the original spelling or punctuation, but you can apply effects and filters as you can with other objects.

overprinting   A technique for printing colors on overlapping sections of an artwork. See **trapping**.

P

page   The only area of the illustration window that contains the artwork you can print—although you can create artwork almost anywhere on the window. See **imageable area** and **nonimageable area**.

page description language   A language that describes the type and graphics on a page so that the page can be laid out properly for printing with a printer or displaying on a monitor. PostScript is a page description language. See **encapsulated PostScript** and **PostScript**.

palette   In Illustrator, a small window in which you can set options for a particular tool, feature, or category of artwork.

Pantone Color Matching System   PMS; a standard for spot colors. Illustrator provides swatches that match colors from the Pantone Color Matching System.

paste-up   See **mechanical**.

path   A set of straight and curved lines that form the outline of an object in a vector-based artwork. See **anchor point, closed path, corner point, direction lines, direction point, end point, open path, smooth point**, and **vector graphics**.

pattern tile   An image on a rectangle. Several pattern tiles make up a pattern. See **patterns**.

patterns   Small images that are repeated throughout a fill or stroke, in much the same way that wallpaper decorates the Windows Desktop. See **fill, pattern tile**, and **stroke**.

picas   Standard units of measure for typographers. A pica is equal to 12 points or about 1/6 inch. See **centimeters, inches, millimeters, pixels**, and **points**.

pixels   (1) Picture elements or pels; the smallest components of an image; a set of rectangular dots that make up the grid that composes raster-graphic images. (2) Standard units of measure for computer graphics, the smallest measurable units of a bitmap. The size of a pixel depends on the graphic resolution of the image or computer monitor. See **centimeters, inches, millimeters, picas, points**, and **raster graphics**.

placed image   A representation of an image created in another program. A placed image is not an actual image, thereby saving storage space in an Illustrator document.

plate   A sheet of metal or other solid material on which a commercial printer prints pages. See **camera work, camera-ready**, and **mechanical**.

plot   The core of a graph; the columns, bars, lines, areas, or slices of pie that present the data. See **graph, legend**, and **tick mark**.

plug-in   A small, single-purpose program that enhances one or more functions of a larger application in some way.

point size   The height of a character in a font measured from the top of a character with an ascender to the bottom of a character with a descender. See **ascender, descender, font**, and **points**.

point type   A block of type that starts at any place in the illustration window and does not wrap unless you press ENTER/RETURN.

points   Standard units of measure in the printing industry. A point is approximately 1/72 inch. See **centimeters, inches, millimeters, picas,** and **pixels**

portrait orientation   The orientation of a page where the height is greater than its width. Examples of portrait orientation are a letter, proposal, or report, and most books—including this one. The default position of the Artboard is in portrait orientation. See **landscape orientation**.

positive   A film print that keeps the original colors of the image: the current white areas remain white and the blacks remain black. See **negative**.

PostScript   Perhaps the best-known page description language, which was and continues to be developed by Adobe Systems Inc. See also **encapsulated PostScript**.

PPD file   PostScript Printer Description; information associated with a PostScript printer driver.

preferences   User-defined attributes; for example, the use of inches as a unit of measure rather than points, Illustrator's default unit.

printable area   See **imageable area**.

printer's marks   Lines and symbols on a page that help a printer align and trim printed pages. See **crop marks, Japanese crop marks,** and **trim marks**.

process color separation   See **color separation**.

process colors   Three or four primary colors on separate sheets that are combined into a color print on one sheet. Process colors can be the primary colors, cyan, magenta, and yellow along with the spot color black (that is, CMYK); or red, blue, and green (that is, RGB). See **CMYK, RGB, spot colors,** and **subtractive primary colors**.

projecting cap   A square-shaped stroke end that protrudes beyond the actual end of the line. See **butt cap, cap,** and **round cap**. See also **join**.

proportional font   A font in which characters have different widths. See **font** and **monospace font**.

PSD   Photoshop Document; the default Adobe Photoshop file type.

R

radial gradient   A gradient that radiates from the center of an object to the edges. See **gradient** and **linear gradient**.

raster graphics   Sets of pixels arranged in grids of rows and columns. See **pixels** and **vector graphics**.

rasterizing   Converting a vector object to a raster object.

reflecting   Flipping an object from one side of an axis to another, horizontally or vertically. See **transforming**.

refresh   Updating the contents of a list or a graphics display to show the latest modifications.

register marks   The color dots printed on color separations that enable alignment of the finished pages. See **registration**.

registration   The matching of color dots printed on color separations so that all the images are aligned and all colors print as planned, without gaps or overprinting. See **register marks**.

releasing   In Illustrator, removing an object from the illustration window.

resulting color   The mix of the blend color and the base color. See **base color**, **blend color**, and **blending mode**.

RGB   An acronym that represents red-green-blue (the additive primary colors). RGB is the primary color model for Web graphics—especially those viewed on a monitor. See **additive primary colors**.

round cap   A rounded shape of the end of a stroke. See **butt cap**, **cap**, and **projecting cap**. See also **join**.

round join   A curving turn of a corner. See **bevel join, join**, and **miter join**. See also **cap**.

ruler guide Horizontal and vertical guidelines that extend from one edge of the illustration window to the other. You create ruler guides by dragging from the horizontal or vertical ruler. See **guide**, **guide object**, and **Smart Guides**.

ruler origins The 0 point on both the horizontal and vertical rulers.

S

sans serif font A font without (that is, *sans*) serifs on its strokes. See **font**, **serif font**, **serifs**, and **stroke**.

saturation The amount of hue in a mixed color. The closer the gray value of a color is to white, the greater the saturation; the closer the gray value of a color is to black, the less the saturation. See **brightness**, **HSB**, and **hue**.

scaling Making an object larger or smaller—in proportion or not. See **reflecting**, **shearing**, and **transforming**.

scratch area Every part of the illustration window outside the Artboard. See **Artboard**.

screen angle The angle at which the pattern of dots in a halftone screen appear on a printed page. See **halftone**.

separation See **color separation**.

serif font A font that includes serifs. See **font**, **sans serif font**, and **serifs**.

serifs Small decorations at the ends of many of the strokes that make up a character. See **font**, **sans serif font**, **serif font**, and **stroke**.

server-side A program or script that is stored and runs on the server's computer system. See **client-side**.

shearing Slanting or skewing an object from one side to another. See **reflecting**, **scaling**, and **transforming**.

shortcut keys Single keys or key combinations that are implemented by pressing two or three keys at the same time.

skewing See **shearing**.

slicing Creating separate sections on a Web page so that you can control the dynamic behavior of individual components.

Smart Guides Temporary guidelines that flash onscreen when you create or transform an object. When you move an object or drag part of the object, and if an anchor point on that object is in alignment in some way with a nearby object in the illustration window, Illustrator shows a Smart Guide—if Smart Guides are turned on. See **guide**, **guide object**, **ruler guide**, and **transforming**.

smooth point A curved and smooth anchor point that indicates some sort of turn in a curved path. See **anchor point**, **corner point**, **direction lines**, **direction point**, and **path**.

smoothing The process of removing anchor points from a path to even out the lines of the path.

snapping Automatic movement of the selected object to the closest horizontal or vertical grid line. See **grid**.

spectrum bar At the bottom of the Colors and Gradient palette, a slider containing all the colors or grays that make up a color model. You can click within the color ramp to select a particular color.

spine The backbone of a blend—as its original objects were originally aligned or as it follows its new path.

spot colors Colors in an artwork that are printed with particular inks. Think of spot colors as individual tubes of paint, which can stand alone or be mixed to produce other colors. See **process colors**.

spread A method of trapping that corrects a gap by overlapping a dark-colored background with a light-colored image. See **choke** and **trapping**.

stack An arrangement of objects—from front to back or top to bottom—in a pile in the illustration window.

stripping Assembling negatives on sheets at a commercial printer.

stroke (1) A color or pattern that always uses a path as a center point. (2) One of the lines that makes up a character. See **fill**, **font**, **sans serif font**, **serif font**, and **serifs**.

style A set of saved appearance attributes. See **appearance attributes**.

subtractive primary colors The cyan, magenta, yellow, and black primary colors that are produced by absorbing (that is, subtracting) light. See **additive primary colors**, **CMYK**, and **process colors**.

SVG Scalable Vector Graphics; an official vector graphics standard of the World Wide Web Consortium (W3C). SVG uses XML to define shapes by using mathematical calculations to determine the location, span, and course of straight or curved paths. See **XML**.

swatches Samples of colors, patterns, and gradients in the Swatches palette.

SWF Shockwave Flash; a vector graphics file type that has been developed by Macromedia, Inc. SWF describes an image by using mathematical calculations to determine the location, span, and course of straight or curved paths.

symbol A small artwork that you can insert as one or more objects in Illustrator documents. You can "spray" and then edit several symbols simultaneously in the illustration window.

T

template layer An Illustrator layer on which you can trace artwork.

text rectangle See **type rectangle**.

thumbnail A small image of an object, group, type, swatch, or symbol.

tick mark A little horizontal or vertical line that identifies a value on one of the axes. See **graph**, **legend**, **plot**, **x-axis**, and **y-axis**.

TIFF Tagged Image File Format; a standard raster file format.

tiling The alignment of multiple pages or pattern brushes on all four sides within the Artboard or an artwork. See **Artboard**.

tint A shade of a color, especially one created by mixing the color with various quantities of white.

tooltip A rectangular box that contains the name of a tool or icon.

toolslot A hidden set of related tools on the Illustrator toolbox.

tracking The increase or decrease of space between three or more selected characters. See **kerning**.

transforming Moving, rotating, reflecting (that is, flipping), scaling, or shearing (skewing or slanting) an object. See **reflecting**, **scaling**, and **shearing**.

transparency (1) A lack of opacity; underlying objects can be seen through objects above in the stacking order. (2) In photography, a positive (that is, not a negative). See **opacity**.

transparency grid A checkerboard of light and dark colors in the illustration window. The transparency grid presents an ideal background for semi-transparent objects. See also **grid**.

trapping Adjusting for colors that are not properly aligned with adjacent or overlapping colors by overprinting a color, adding color or tints to the gaps. See **choke**, **overprinting**, and **spread**.

trim marks Printer's marks that show the edges of a page or mark the edges of one or more objects, such as business cards or post cards, within a page. See **crop marks** and **Japanese crop marks**.

type container A closed path that holds type.

type path An object that is converted so that it can hold type. See **type rectangle**.

type rectangle A text rectangle; a container in which you enter type. See **type path**.

typeface See **font**.

typesetting Setting type by typesetting machine.

U

unit of measure A standard by which you calculate the dimensions of an object. Illustrator supports the following units of measure: points (the default), picas, inches, millimeters, centimeters, and pixels.

V

value axis   See **y-axis**.

variable transparency   Using the alpha channel to set a pixel from totally opaque to completely transparent. See **alpha channel**.

vector graphics   Artworks that are created by using mathematical calculations to determine the location, span, and course of straight or curved lines (that is, paths). See **path** and **raster graphics**.

W

Web-safe colors   A set of 216 colors that you can safely use on Web pages. See **Web-safe RGB**.

Web-safe RGB   A version of RGB created to recognize the lack of unified RGB standards in the three main operating systems: Windows, Macintosh, and UNIX. See **additive primary colors**, **RGB**, and **Web-safe colors**.

wrapping   Moving type from the end of one line to another within the top, left, right, and bottom margins of the page.

X

x-axis   The horizontal axis, usually used for time or area data. In Illustrator, the x-axis is generally called the category axis. See **y-axis**.

x-height   The height of the body of a character, which in the past was the lowercase x. See **ascender**, **baseline**, **descender**, **font**, **font height**, and **letter height**.

XML   Extensible Markup Language; a subset of SGML and a close relative of HTML and XHTML, HTML's successor. Under XML, you can create custom languages for industries, technologies, and interest groups. See **HTML**.

Y

y-axis The vertical axis, usually used for units of measure (for example, years, weights, and currency). In Illustrator, the y-axis is usually known as the value axis. See **x-axis**.

 Z

zooming Increasing or decreasing the magnification level of the illustration window and any artwork therein.

Index

INTERNATIONAL CONTACT INFORMATION

AUSTRALIA
McGraw-Hill Book Company Australia Pty. Ltd.
TEL +61-2-9417-9899
FAX +61-2-9417-5687
http://www.mcgraw-hill.com.au
books-it_sydney@mcgraw-hill.com

CANADA
McGraw-Hill Ryerson Ltd.
TEL +905-430-5000
FAX +905-430-5020
http://www.mcgrawhill.ca

GREECE, MIDDLE EAST,
NORTHERN AFRICA
McGraw-Hill Hellas
TEL +30-1-656-0990-3-4
FAX +30-1-654-5525

MEXICO (Also serving Latin America)
McGraw-Hill Interamericana Editores S.A. de C.V.
TEL +525-117-1583
FAX +525-117-1589
http://www.mcgraw-hill.com.mx
fernando_castellanos@mcgraw-hill.com

SINGAPORE (Serving Asia)
McGraw-Hill Book Company
TEL +65-863-1580
FAX +65-862-3354
http://www.mcgraw-hill.com.sg
mghasia@mcgraw-hill.com

SOUTH AFRICA
McGraw-Hill South Africa
TEL +27-11-622-7512
FAX +27-11-622-9045
robyn_swanepoel@mcgraw-hill.com

UNITED KINGDOM & EUROPE
(Excluding Southern Europe)
McGraw-Hill Education Europe
TEL +44-1-628-502500
FAX +44-1-628-770224
http://www.mcgraw-hill.co.uk
computing_neurope@mcgraw-hill.com

ALL OTHER INQUIRIES Contact:
Osborne/McGraw-Hill
TEL +1-510-549-6600
FAX +1-510-883-7600
http://www.osborne.com
omg_international@mcgraw-hill.com